UNDERSTANDING HUMAN DEVELOPMENT

A multidimensional approach

Second Edition

LOUISE HARMS

OXFORD
UNIVERSITY PRESS
AUSTRALIA & NEW ZEALAND

OXFORD
UNIVERSITY PRESS

Oxford University Press is a department of the University of Oxford.
It furthers the University's objective of excellence in research,
scholarship, and education by publishing worldwide. Oxford is a registered
trademark of Oxford University Press in the UK and in certain other
countries.

Published in Australia by
Oxford University Press
253 Normanby Road, South Melbourne, Victoria 3205, Australia

First edition published 2005
Second edition published 2010
Reprinted 2011, 2012

National Library of Australia Cataloguing-in-Publication data

Harms, Louise
Understanding human development / Louise Harms.
2nd edn.

ISBN 978 0 19 555155 6 (pbk)

Includes index.
Bibliography.

Developmental psychology.
Life cycle, Human.
Resilience (Personality trait).

155.25

Reproduction and communication for educational purposes
The Australian *Copyright Act 1968* (the Act) allows a maximum of one chapter
or 10% of the pages of this work, whichever is the greater, to be reproduced
and/or communicated by any educational institution for its educational purposes
provided that the educational institution (or the body that administers it) has
given a remuneration notice to Copyright Agency Limited (CAL) under the Act.

For details of the CAL licence for educational institutions contact:

Copyright Agency Limited
Level 15, 233 Castlereagh Street
Sydney NSW 2000
Telephone: (02) 9394 7600
Facsimile: (02) 9394 7601
Email: info@copyright.com.au

Edited by Kirstie Innes-Will
Cover design by Design by Committee Pty. Ltd.
Text design by Norma van Rees
Typeset by Norma van Rees
Proofread by Valina and Anthony Rainer
Indexed by Karen Gillen
Printed and bound in Australia by Ligare Book Printers, Pty Ltd

Contents

List of Figures

List of Tables

Contributors

Anna Benton is a Master of Social Work student at the University of Melbourne. She has a keen interest in youth issues especially those pertaining to homelessness. Currently she works as a youth housing support worker at the South Port Community Housing Group in South Melbourne.

Kate Chester has completed a Bachelor of Social Work and Graduate Diploma of Cultural Studies at the University of Melbourne. She has also completed a Bachelor Arts at La Trobe University and is a nurse, with a Graduate Certificate in Renal, Transplant and Dialysis Nursing. Her work experience has been focused in areas of chronic illness, inter-country adoption at the Department of Human Services, child abuse and neglect and most recently local adoption and permanent care at Connections.

Samantha Clavant is a social worker who has worked in health settings since 1996. For the past eight years Sam has worked as a counsellor/advocate at CASA House (the Centre Against Sexual Assault) which is part of the Royal Womens Hospital. The counsellor/advocate role includes on-call, crisis and ongoing support to victim/survivors, group work, the provision of secondary consults and training along with public advocacy around the issue of sexual assault. Sam recently completed a research Master of Social Work degree.

Dr Julie Clark is an experienced social worker who has worked in statutory and non-statutory child protection and advocacy roles; as a hospital and community health social worker and in complaints management roles. She is Lecturer in the School of Human Services and Social Work at Griffith University.

Lisa Congdon is a social worker who has over the past 13 years worked in various roles that include direct service, training, program and policy development, and management within the fields of military social work, health and corrections. Lisa is currently working in child welfare in the United States. Lisa is also completing a Masters of Advanced Social Work (Clinical) Degree at the University of Melbourne.

Pip Cook studied and worked for several years as a classical pianist. Since completing a Master of Social Work from the University of Melbourne in 2009 she has worked as a women's support worker in a domestic violence shelter in Alice Springs, and is currently a community support worker in a Mental Health Rehabilitation Programme in Melbourne.

Dr Louise Harms is a social worker, who worked for nine years in hospital and educational settings, before moving into social work teaching and research. She has worked at the Department of Social Work, the University of Melbourne, since 2001 in a full time capacity, where she is now Associate Professor, Deputy Head and coordinator of the entry-to-practice MSW program.

Lee Kofman is a social worker, educator and writer. During her professional practice in mental health she developed a framework for working with people with mental illnesses based on creative writing techniques. She presented this framework at various mental health conferences, such as *TheMhs*, *Vicserv* and *An International Narrative Therapy Festive Conference*, and taught to health professionals. Currently she is a PhD candidate at the RMIT's Health Institute, investigating appearance-related effects of non-facial scars on women's well-being. She also teaches social work, social sciences and creative writing at the University of Melbourne, RMIT, Victoria University and other educational settings.

Christine Fejo-King is an Aboriginal woman from the Northern Territory. Christine has been involved in social work from grass roots, state and territory and national levels and is committed to moving social work practice from one that is culturally sensitive and aware to one that is culturally congruent and safe for Aboriginal people.

Susie Leech graduated from the University of Melbourne in 2009 with a Bachelor of Social Work and a Bachelor of Arts (Gender Studies). She is currently working as a social worker at The Alfred Hospital, where she covers the Cardiothoracic Unit and The Alfred Centre elective surgical hospital. Susie is interested in the areas of Trauma and Counselling, and hopes to pursue a career in these fields.

Dr John McCormack has worked professionally and academically in ageing and aged care. He has been a discharge planner in acute and sub-acute health care, as well as senior lecturer in health and gerontological social work. He is the Australian representative on the International Database on Longevity (IDL), and has an ongoing quality of life project called The Australian Centenarian Study underway. He maintains a progressive list of the oldest Australians, and is a frequent commentator in the media on this topic.

Fiona McDonald is a social welfare worker who has worked in both the community and government sectors for twenty years. Her main interest is infant and parent welfare and she has worked as both a Specialist Infant Practitioner and High Risk Infant Program Manager for the Victorian Department of Human Services for seven years. She currently works within the community sector and in private practice with infants and their families.

Lenice Murray is an accredited mental health social worker. She has worked for seven years in women specific services and mental health settings across metropolitan and remote areas of Australia. Currently she is undertaking a Masters of Public Health and is employed as a case manager on an intensive outreach team at Orygen Youth Health, a clinical mental health service for young people living with a mental illness.

Kirsten O'Brien completed her Master of Social Work degree in 2009 at The University of Melbourne. During this time, she undertook her final field education placement in a family service organisation.

Jill Parris is a psychologist who worked for twelve years in management of counselling and welfare services, before moving back to counselling with the Ecumenical Migration Centre to focus on supporting refugees settle in Australia in 2007. Her work centres on issues of relationship, child and family within the specific field of settlement into Australia.

Dr Melissa Petrakis has worked in public mental health service provision, management and research over the last decade, in substance use and mental illness treatment, suicide prevention, psychiatric disability rehabilitation and support services, crisis telephone counselling and referral, and adult inpatient acute psychiatry. Melissa's Master of Social Work research was in the area of applied solution-focused brief therapy (SFBT) for telephone counselling and referral. Her PhD was on suicide relapse prevention at the emergency department and community interface. Melissa has coordinated subjects, guest lectured and tutored in the undergraduate and Masters programs at University of Melbourne School of Social Work over the past nine years.

Dr David Rose is a social worker with over eighteen years experience in direct practice and management roles within the alcohol and drug treatment, offender support and forensic mental health areas. He is currently a lecturer at the University of Melbourne School of Social Work. His PhD examined the impact of drug use on siblings.

Jane Sullivan was a senior social worker for many years at a paediatric hospital. Before working at hospital, she was a social worker at Kew Cottages and for a regional intellectual disability service. Her areas of practice included chronic illness, disability, palliative and bereavement care, and student education. Jane holds degrees in adolescent and child psychology and theology and has a Master of Social

Work (by research). She is currently a full-time doctoral student. Her topic explores an aspect of ethics and the experience of parental bereavement. Jane believes that human development is a never ending process.

Menka Tsantefski is a lecturer in social work at the University of Melbourne, School of Social Work, where she specialises in child and family related subjects. She provided home-based services to children and families for over fifteen years. Menka has also conducted her doctoral research on parental substance-use and the impact of childhood chronic illness on families.

Karen White is a social worker with experience in the child and family, child protection and mental health fields. She has worked in these fields for over twenty-five years and has also been involved in social work teaching and research at the University of Melbourne. Karen has a particular interest in enabling children and young people to have a voice in policy and the wider community. She is currently working with Headspace, a National Youth Mental Health initiative, while completing a PhD on promoting the views of boys aged nine to twelve from vulnerable families.

Preface

Each person is uniquely shaped throughout their life by many significant dimensions: the historic era into which they are born; their family, neighbourhood and wider cultural context; their class, ethnicity, gender and race; religion, sexual preference, physical and intellectual abilities, personality and age; and unique life experiences, both positive and negative.

Social workers and other human service professionals need ways of understanding these many dimensions and how they interact to influence human adaptation and coping across the lifespan. An understanding of these individual, contextual and time dimensions is essential for the development of optimal practices, programs and policies. In the multicultural and diverse context of Australian life, this is a challenging task.

The aim of this book

This book is intended to introduce you to some of the core theoretical understandings of human behaviour, drawing from the vast body of developmental research and literature, as well as from the research and literature from more adversity-focused areas of trauma, grief and stress. Rather than working within one particular theoretical framework, this book advocates a multidimensional approach to understanding the complexities of human behaviour and development across the lifespan. The seven core themes of such an approach are:

1 An individual's inner world is multidimensional.
2 An individual's outer world is multidimensional.
3 Time is multidimensional.
4 Human experience is multidimensional.
5 Adaptation and coping are multidimensional.
6 Attempts to theorise human development and adaptation should be multidimensional.
7 Human services responses must be multidimensional.

The plan of this book

Part 1: A conceptual overview

In Part 1, Chapter 1 presents a detailed overview of the seven core themes of of a multidimensional approach, outlined above. Each of the critical dimensions of person, context, time and experience is explored. The concepts of human adaptation and resilience are introduced, emerging from an understanding of risk and protective factors. The chapter concludes with consideration of how personal values and experiences influence our understandings of human behaviour.

Part 2: The critical contexts of human development

The focus of Part 2 is the outer-world dimensions that influence human experience, recognising that these contextual dimensions are critical determinants of human experience. Chapter 2 looks at how we might understand the relational and social dimensions of well-being. Chapter 3 explores the structural and cultural dimensions of experience. Each chapter explores the ways in which these dimensions expose us to different risk and/or protective experiences and the way they potentially determine the resources available to us in a wide range of adversities.

Part 3: Adaptation following specific life events and experiences

Part 3 explores the ways in which different adversities are understood, incorporating both a developmental, or normative, perspective and an event-based, or adversity-focused, perspective. Chapters 4 to 6 each examine a specific type of adversity—stress, trauma or grief. While there are many points of overlap in the understandings of these experiences, distinctive fields of research, theory and practice have evolved for each. Risk and protective factors, and adaptation in the aftermath of each of these types of experiences, are considered.

Part 4: Development and adaptation across the lifespan

In Part 4, the focus is on how the various life stages can be understood. In this new edition, these chapters have been significantly expanded, with each lifespan stage now having a chapter of its own. Drawing on both socio-demographic data and theories of psychosocial development, the major understandings of human development in a Western context are outlined. The research literature relating to the various developmental stages and the controversies and difficulties of looking at human experience with a normative lens are examined. Chapters 7 to 13 each explore a phase of biopsychosocial-spiritual transition across the lifespan, from infancy through to late adulthood.

Part 5: Drawing the themes together

In the final part of this book, the major themes are revisited. The strengths and limitations of thinking about the different dimensions of individual experience, and about development and adaptation, are explored. The implications for theory and practice within social work are then considered.

In this second edition, I have updated and revised the content significantly. New additions include 'Practice in context' and 'Theory in context' boxes, in which practitioners and students reflect on their work and on how theory helps inform it. Each chapter begins with a list of aims and concludes with questions for personal reflection and an opportunity to directly apply a multidimensional approach to a real-life situation. In each chapter, I have also included a list of the websites and references that I have found useful as sources of research or sources of practice and policy materials.

No one book can encompass all aspects of a multidimensional approach in detail within the confines of several hundred pages. However, each chapter of this work gives an introduction to the ideas and research that might inform our practice across the lifespan by introducing you to some of the key debates, controversies and implications for practice. Each chapter could be a book in and of itself. What I hope this book will do is foster your thinking and your interest in a broad range of issues that have the potential to profoundly influence human behaviour and development.

My experience as a social worker in hospital, counselling and education settings, as a researcher, and as a teacher of social work students over many years, as well as my own personal and family experiences, have led me to think deeply about the traumas of life and the many ways in which individuals adapt. My hope is that this book will stimulate you to think about these issues for yourself and for your practice, and about what it is that promotes human resilience across the lifespan.

Lou Harms

June 2010

Acknowledgments

Many people have contributed to this book, in different and important ways.

I would like to thank the social work practitioners who have provided vignettes from their professional experience: Julie Clark, Samantha Clavant, Lisa Congdon, Christine Fejo-King, Lee Kofman, John McCormack, Lenice Murray, Jill Parris, Melissa Petrakis, David Rose, Jane Sullivan, Menka Tsantefski and Karen White.

I would also like to thank the social work students who generously shared their learning through providing the 'Theory in context' sections from their placements and work experiences: Anna Benton, Kate Chester, Phillipa Cook, Susie Leech, Fiona McDonald and Kirsten O'Brien. Thank you also to the many other students in the social work course at The University of Melbourne, whose exploration and critical reflections of these ideas keep me learning and shaping my ideas and my writing.

Throughout the writing process, invaluable direction was provided by several reviewers—I would like to thank you for anchoring the direction of this book at just the right time.

Similarly, the Oxford University Press team have been a vital anchor throughout this project—Debra James, as always and in particular; and Rachel Saffer, a new and also much appreciated support. For your expertise, insights and constancy, thank you both. I thank Kirstie Innes-Will also, who has been a great editor—providing excellent advice and insights.

This book has taken time, resources and focus. For that, I thank the Department of Social Work at The University of Melbourne for enabling that to be possible, particularly through the sabbatical in 2007 at Columbia University, New York.

My own family is a constant source of support, encouragement and love. I thank them all, my parents, Glenys and Peter, in particular.

For supporting unquestionably this project, and for always being there in the best possible ways, I thank Jane Sullivan.

PART 1

A Conceptual Overview

CHAPTER 1

A Multidimensional Approach

AIMS OF THIS CHAPTER

This chapter examines the core aspects of a multidimensional approach. It considers the following questions:

» What are the major dimensions within a multidimensional approach?
» How does a multidimensional approach help in understanding the individual, their contexts, time, experiences and adaptive capacities?
» What are risk, protective and resilience factors?
» What are the theory and practice implications of a multidimensional approach for workers in the human services?
» How do we engage in reflective and reflexive practice?

Stress, trauma and grief are common experiences for people all around the world. Threats and acts of terrorism and war occur, affecting the lives of millions of people. Millions of others live without adequate nutrition, medical care, housing or employment. Communities are threatened by natural disasters such as floods, fires and droughts. In the privacy of homes, family violence and the maltreatment of children continue to occur. Relationships end as a result of disagreement, disappearance or death. Illnesses, accidents and injuries leave many with physical and emotional wounds. Unemployment and poverty lead to daily stress and worry. As individuals, families, groups and communities, we inevitably experience a wide variety of events and conditions across the course of our life. These events and conditions are experienced in the context of our unique developmental trajectories. We adapt to these experiences in many different ways.

Social workers, along with educators, welfare workers, psychologists and other health professionals are concerned ultimately with influencing environments, relationships and inner experiences so that they are supportive of human growth, health and satisfaction (Germain & Gitterman 1995 p. 5). Human services exist in recognition of the fact that there are devastating consequences for individuals, families and communities if certain conditions and experiences are encountered and if adequate resources and supports are not in place. To this end, social workers need a framework for understanding human development and well-being, and the impact of adversity, in context. This includes finding ways of bringing together a wide range of knowledge about what it is to be human and what are the various impacts of key experiences, conditions and resources.

Over time, many forces have shaped understandings of human development. While understandings shift, often quite significantly, as a result of political, economic, religious, psychological, biological, legal or cultural forces, it is important that the search continues for deeper and more accurate understandings of what it is to experience and cope with adversity in different contexts. In highlighting the diversity and uniqueness of individual experience, postmodernism has left us thinking that we cannot assume any experiences are common to all individuals. The 'truths' of previous eras have been thoroughly questioned (Trainor 2002). While the uniqueness of individual experience must be acknowledged, such deconstructed perspectives have the potential to leave us with few grounds for understanding risk and resilience or for acting in the interests of vulnerable and marginalised groups—for example, children who have been abused or neglected. This book explores the many understandings we have of individual responses to adversity and brings them together through a **multidimensional approach** to understanding human development across the **life course**. Social workers in the Australian context have traditionally used Western theoretical perspectives to understand well-being, often privileging concepts of the individual and their independence. Recognising the limitations of these perspectives, a multidimensional approach offers a way of integrating culturally diverse ways of viewing well-being.

A multidimensional approach

For many years, ecological or ecosystemic theories informed much of the theoretical basis of social work. They gave the **biopsychosocial dimensions** prominence in proposing that individual and environmental influences were inseparable from each other, forming a system of interaction. More recently, a multidimensional approach has emerged as an overarching perspective of human behaviour and development (Hutchison 2003), which offers a holistic approach to understanding well-being but is not as tightly aligned with systems theory. In Chapter 14 (p. 402) we look at some of the reasons why a multidimensional approach, rather than ecological theory, is used in this book.

Within a multidimensional approach, each person is recognised as having unique biopsychosocial and spiritual dimensions (Germain & Bloom 1999; Hutchison 2003) as well as structural and **cultural dimensions**. The term **biopsychosocial-spiritual dimensions** is used to reflect the idea that an individual occupies more than any one dimension at any time—experience is continuously and simultaneously influenced by individual (biological, psychological, and spiritual) and environmental (social, including structural and cultural) factors. The interdependence of these dimensions is considered so fundamental in determining our lived experience that ecological theorists, such as Germain (1991), use the term, **person:environment configuration** or person:situation configuration.

Another way of thinking about these dimensions is to think of the **inner world** we occupy. This typically refers to our biological, psychological and spiritual experiences—which both influence and are influenced by the **outer world** we occupy—the relational, social, structural and cultural contexts. By referring to them as inner and outer worlds, the intention is not to see them as two different dimensions. Rather, they are interrelated and fluid in their reciprocal interactions, as this chapter will describe. Dividing aspects into inner and outer dimensions, or into personal and environmental dimensions, can therefore be inherently problematic, as any dimensions is necessarily *both* an inner and an outer world dimension. However, for the purposes of discussion, the contrived separation of these dimensions needs to be maintained at first to enable the exploration of the significance and interrelationship of each to the other, before bringing them together to fully understand a multidimensional approach.

An individual's inner world is multidimensional

Each of us has a unique sense of our own **inner world**. No one else can ever experience what goes on in another person's thoughts and emotions, or know what it is like to live in someone else's body or to experience their sense of spirituality. This is the **subjective experience**, sometimes referred to as the lived experience. Three dimensions are central to the inner world—the biological, psychological and spiritual dimensions. Each one of us has unique biological, psychological and spiritual experiences, as shown in Figure 1.1.

Biological dimensions
Biological processes determine our human existence. From its beginning in conception and birth through to its end in death, the body profoundly affects much

FIGURE **1.1** Inner-world dimensions

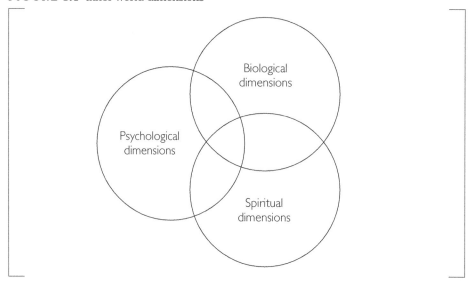

of human experience. **Biological dimensions** can be thought of as including 'all those processes necessary for the physical functioning' of the human body (Newman & Newman 2003 p. 6). These include the genetic, skeletal, sensory, motor, respiratory, endocrine, circulatory, waste elimination, sexual-reproductive, digestive and nervous systems (Newman & Newman 2003 p. 6). These systems change as a human matures throughout their life. They change also as a result of influences in the outer world, such as the impact of the physical environment, diet, social interactions and exposure to stress, to name a few.

The theory of lifespan development proposes that 'normal' milestones mark transitions across the life trajectory, particularly biological transitions such as those that occur in early childhood, adolescence, mid-life and late adulthood. Although important, the notion is controversial, as it can be seen to be prescribing normal behaviour and labelling anything outside of prescribed ranges as abnormal or deviant. Critics of a lifespan approach argue that human experience is too diverse to be adequately described using culture- and history-bound notions of what it is to be a particular age. Proponents of a lifespan approach argue that there are certain tasks and transitions associated with ages across the lifespan that are typically predictable and **normative**. In addition, social inequalities can be identified and addressed when there are key indicators of risk or lost opportunity—such as recognising the social and health inequalities that lead to the seventeen-year gap in longevity between Indigenous and non-Indigenous Australians.

The genetic basis of the human experience has been researched extensively in recent years, with the completion of the human genome project in 2003. Although concern has been expressed about the potential discrimination that may arise from genetic screening and intervention (Australian Academy of Science 2004), the project has enabled a far wider understanding of the genetic bases for human behaviour and many diseases such as cancer and neurological disorders. Similarly, neurobiological understandings have profoundly influenced understandings of development in infancy and early childhood, in particular, and the lifelong impact of adversities such as traumatic events on the developing brain of the child and adult.

The biological dimension is inextricably connected with other dimensions of experience. Our emotional well-being and cultural context have a strong impact on our biological experience and vice versa. For example, Vaillant, in his study of resilience in later life has found that 'objectively good physical health was less important to successful ageing than subjective good health. By this I mean that it is alright to be ill as long as you do not feel sick.' (2002 p. 13) Similarly, we do not think of our sexuality as a purely biological phenomenon. In conjunction with our biology, sexuality is a complex interplay of social and psychological influences.

While this book is focused primarily on the psychosocial aspects of human experience as the sites for social work intervention, it is critical to keep in mind the influences of the biological dimension or the role of the body in human experience and well-being (Cameron & McDermott 2007). This means taking into account the realities of the physical experiences people have—of pain, illness, limited mobility and/or disability (Barnes, Mercer & Shakespeare 1999).

Psychological dimensions

In addition to our bodily experiences, how we think and how we feel emotionally influences every aspect of our daily experience—our **psychological dimensions** are central to our sense of well-being. Our capacities for thought and memory, for emotion and for anticipating the future reflect some of our most uniquely human qualities. These aspects are all part of the psychological dimension. This is undoubtedly the dimension where most attention is focused in relation to intervention in the aftermath of adversity, as explored in Chapters 4 to 6, in particular.

Gender is also part of the psychological dimension, as the classification of someone as masculine, feminine or androgynous arises not necessarily directly from a person's physical status as male or female, but from both innate characteristics and the social environment. Whereas sex refers to biological characteristics, gender refers to the complex interaction between individuals, societies and cultures regarding the expectations, identities and roles associated with masculinity and femininity. Thus, gender is a complex, socially constructed phenomenon, derived from multidimensional interactions across the lifespan.

A key aspect of the psychological dimension is the cognitive aspect. This includes our conscious cognitive capacity—our capacity for thought, for memory, and for the appraisal of events and ourselves. Across the lifespan, we experience changes in our cognitive capacity. Cognitive theorists such as Piaget (1995) and Vygotsky (1998) proposed that there are a series of cognitive stages across the lifespan. With the successful acquisition of each stage of cognitive development, higher levels of cognitive functioning are reached, to the point where individuals are capable of complex, abstract thought in adulthood. We develop critical memory, verbal capacity and reasoning skills, for example.

Other theorists propose that we each have an unconscious psychological life. This includes our dream life and our primary drives and motivations. These drives have been understood differently by theorists—for example, Freud argued for a theory of sexual drive and later the death instinct, Adler (1956, reproduced in Ansbacher & Ansbacher 1970), for a theory of power, Bowlby (1984) for a theory of attachment and Maslow (1968) for a theory of self-actualisation. Research in consciousness studies—for example, at the University of Arizona and Cambridge University—is also highlighting the impact on others of our unconscious life and the capacity to influence our environments, a view consistent with many Indigenous perspectives.

The capacity for memory and self-reflection means that we come to develop individual meaning structures, or schemas, (Kelly 1955) for how the world and our relationships operate. As a result of these cognitive schemas, we develop a sense of the world that is understandable and predictable, and we know how to act within it. In each of the chapters of this book, we explore aspects of these schemas. For example, we look at how young children develop an understanding of the mind (Baird & Sokol 2004) that becomes a foundation for empathic relational behaviour.

Another aspect of the psychological dimension is the emotional aspect—the feeling or mood responses a person has to their circumstances. Our distress, sadness, depression and anger are part of this emotional aspect, as is our capacity for the positive emotions of happiness, excitement and enthusiasm (Fredrickson 2000a; Fredrickson 2000b; Lyubomirsky 2000). Emotions and thoughts work together to form a sense of self-efficacy and agency (Kondrat 2002), factors that are explored in greater detail in Chapter 4. Ultimately, these dimensions also influence our moral reasoning, embedding our psychological responses in social attitudes and behaviours.

Many different theories have been used to explain our psychological dimensions and how they influence our behaviour. These include cognitive–behavioural, psychodynamic, existential and the more recent narrative theories. While each has a different focus, fundamental to all psychological theories is the belief that our thinking patterns, either conscious or unconscious, profoundly influence adaptation and well-being.

These theories are discussed in more detail in Chapter 5.

Spiritual dimensions

Discussion of the **spiritual dimensions** of human experience is frequently absent from texts dealing with human development and/or human experience. When it is present, it is often as an afterthought (see for example Garbarino & Abramowitz 1992a). While centuries ago in Western contexts, it was taken for granted that spirituality was a critical dimension in mental and physical well-being, social workers have only recently revived interest in this dimension and begun to actively research its influence in coping with adversity.

Of all the inner-world dimensions, spirituality is the most elusive dimension to define (Lindsay 2002; Rice 2002; Tacey 2003), although widely recognised as a universal dimension of human experience. Spirituality relates to our search for meaning and purpose in our own existence. Tacey (2003 p. 38) describes spirituality as:

> concerned with connectedness and relatedness to other realities and existences, including other people, society, the world, the stars, the universe and the holy. It is typically intensely inward, and most often involves an exploration of the so-called inner or true self, in which divinity is felt to reside.

The US National Institute of Healthcare Research defined spirituality as 'the feelings, thoughts, experiences and behaviors that arise from a search for the sacred' (as cited in George et al. 2000 p. 104). The sacred they defined as 'a divine being, higher power or ultimate reality'. Lindsay (2002 pp. 31–2) describes spirituality as relating to 'a search for purpose and meaning, and having a moral dimension which reflects a concern with relationships to others, the universe, and to some transcendent being or force'. For many of the world's indigenous cultures, such as the Australian Aboriginal culture, an intrinsic relationship with the land is core to a sense of the sacred. Spirituality has the capacity to connect people through fostering a sense of identity and purpose, creating ritual and building a sense of community and connectedness. Studies have shown a strong connection between spirituality and well-being, in relation to physical, psychological and social health (George et al. 2000).

Spirituality is somewhat different from religion (Tacey 2003), although researchers often confuse these concepts. **Religion** is considered to be the formal structures and doctrines of a faith tradition such as the Muslim, Christian, or Jewish traditions, whereas **spirituality** is defined as a more uniquely personal experience of a divine, spiritual or transcendent force, not necessarily requiring any formal structure or public expression. Spirituality has often been criticised for being a more individualised concept. This criticism is not necessarily accurate, as many people express their spirituality through a strong commitment to social justice and the environment. Research is consistently showing small to moderate positive correlations between spirituality and/or religion and better physical and mental health outcomes (George et al. 2000). This is discussed more extensively in Chapters 7 to 13.

Unlike the other dimensions, matters of the soul or spirituality continue to be considered cautiously, if at all, by social workers and other health professionals. In part, this is due to the very complex position of religion within the largely secular Australian community, the variety of spiritual perspectives and the difficulties experienced in researching this dimension of human experience. Nevertheless, spirituality is increasingly recognised for its significance across the lifespan, particularly in the aftermath of experiences of adversity.

An individual's outer world is multidimensional

In shifting a focus to the outer worlds, we look now at the many external dimensions, both direct and indirect, which influence experience.

Understanding the outer-world dimensions, or contexts, of an individual involves consideration of five key questions:

1   What relationships is the person involved in and what is the influence of these relationships?
2   How do these relationships interact as a social network, if at all?
3   What are the wider structural influences on a person's experience?
4   What are the cultural influences?
5   In what ways are the relational, social, structural and cultural dimensions influenced in turn by individuals and their families and communities?

Each of these four dimensions—relational, social, structural and cultural—is explored briefly below, and then discussed more comprehensively in Chapters 2 and 3.

Relational, social, structural and cultural dimensions

Urie Bronfenbrenner (1979) highlighted that an individual's experience was always occurring in a context of both direct and indirect social influence. He proposed four systems of major influence in individual behaviour, as part of an ecological approach—the microsystem, mesosystem, exosystem and macrosystem, all within a fifth system, the chronosystem, as represented in Figure 1.2

Other theorists have developed different interpretations of these layers or systems in the environment, referred to as the micro, mezzo and macrosystem (see, for example, Greene & Ephross 1991). Others, such as Thompson (2006) and Mullaly (2002) incorporate these dimensions into an anti-disciminatory or anti-oppressive framework, looking at a PCS (personal, cultural and structural) model. The visual representation of Bronfenbrenner's model indicates the embeddedness of each of these systems—that is, no one system can be interpreted without understanding the other four. Each system of the model is both influenced by and influences the others. In this model, the individual is seen as the central unit of analysis, although

FIGURE **1.2** Bronfenbrenner's systems of influence

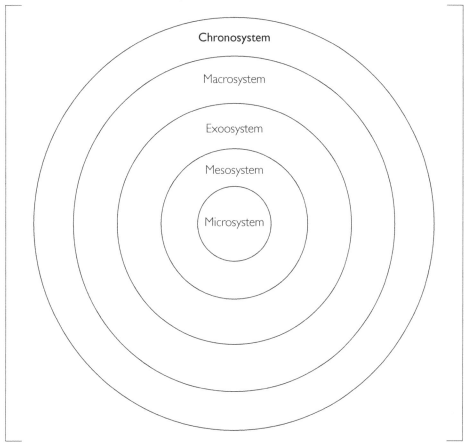

this need not be the case. Families could be seen as central (as Richmond first proposed in 1917; see Richmond 1945). It is important to think of it as a three-dimensional layering of systems with permeable boundaries between all of the layers. The model as it appears here is deceptively simple. In fact, the model is complex: it is not just about the person in their context and the influences the context has on an individual, family or group's experience; it is also about the ways in which individuals, families and groups change and influence contexts. *Both* are changed by each other. This way of thinking about the person and the environment informs interventions profoundly—intervention in any part of the complexity of factors will typically bring about change in others.

Bronfenbrenner's nested model of the environment continues to be profoundly useful. Social workers have drawn traditionally on his ecological theory, along with other systems theories, to understand the reciprocal influences of individuals on environments and vice versa. However, in recent years, developments in chaos theory and quantum physics have transformed understandings of systems, including human, as predictable and closed. There is often no clear cause and effect between human experience and environmental influences (Hudson 2000). In addition, some of the language of Bronfenbrenner's model (such as mesosystem and exosystem) has not readily been adopted in the practice context. A more contemporary perspective based on this model is therefore introduced in this book to place it within an Australian context in the twenty-first century. It also enables a deeper incorporation of the inner-world dimensions, often neglected within ecological perspectives. While Chapters 2 and 3 focus on these issues more specifically, we look briefly here at how each of these dimensions is understood.

Each one of us has unique relationships and connections with a variety of individuals and groups of people—with intimate partners, family members and friends, with peers and colleagues in the workplace or in educational settings, with health professionals or front-line staff in many organisations, and with many others in our world. We rely on these interpersonal relationships within our **relational dimensions** or context for our sense of well-being and identity, and, indeed, in many phases of our life, for our survival. They are the worlds, or settings, in which we live, work and play in some direct way, even if not on a daily or regular basis. Bronfenbrenner referred to these interpersonal relationships as our **microsystem**. Analysing microsystems is typically about analysing the face-to-face transactions that take place between the individual and each of their various worlds and examining their impact on the individual. Bronfenbrenner (1979 p. 22) defined a microsystem as 'a pattern of activities, roles and interpersonal relations experienced by the developing person in a given setting with particular physical and material characteristics'. This definition emphasises that these relationships determine for us a particular pattern or way of being that links profoundly with our sense of identity. This dimension of experience is understood by asking who the person interacts with and how they interact, as shown in Figure 1.3.

These relationships are initially dependent upon parental or caregiver networks. As a person moves from infancy into later stages of the lifespan, microsystems change too, as a result of the developing person and their changing contexts (Figure 1.4), and as a result of external influences on the microsystem. For example, in recent decades, the use of technology has enabled interaction beyond the face-to-face context.

Our adaptations do not rely only on our direct relationships and what goes on between them. When we shift our interest to consider the ways in which these various relationships interact with each other, we are analysing the **mesosystem**, the next layer in Bronfenbrenner's model. This is a layer of social connectedness, the layer of our **social dimensions** or networks. Rather than looking at the individual relationships a person has with each setting in their immediate environment, the

FIGURE **1.3** Relational dimensions

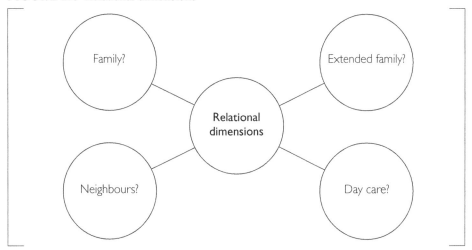

FIGURE **1.4** Relational dimensions change over time

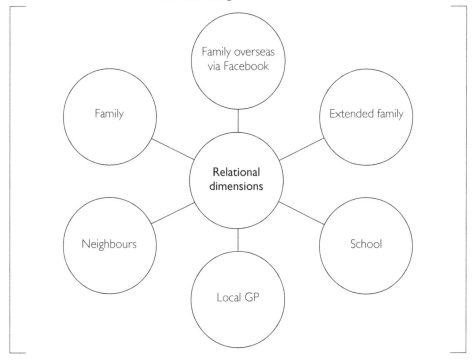

social network layer is about observing the interconnectedness or linkages *between* the settings themselves. While we are part of all worlds in a social network, the focus is on the interaction between these worlds, rather than our direct interaction with any of them (Figure 1.5).

FIGURE **1.5** Social dimensions (networks)

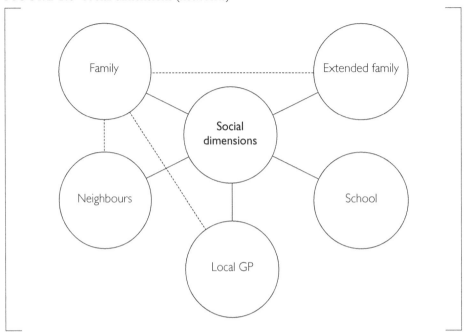

Each one of us also exists in broader **structural dimensions** (Figure 1.6), or contexts, or what Bronfenbrenner (1979) called the **exosystem**. We do not have direct, face-to-face relationships with the structural context. Rather, our individual experience and interpersonal and social contexts are all profoundly and indirectly shaped by these factors. Some key systems within our structural context include our political and legal systems. Resources such as the labour market, the transport system, income-maintenance structures, educational and health service systems are part of our structural context. Religious systems also influence many aspects of daily life. The structural context, like social networks, can be either a source of adversity or a vital resource in the face of adversity.

Giving shape to the experiences in our various relational contexts is the cultural dimension (Figure 1.7) or context in which we live. Bronfenbrenner called this the **macrosystem**, the social 'blueprint' (Bronfenbrenner 1979 p. 26). Our cultural context refers to the norms, principles or mores of a culture. Garbarino and Abramowitz (1992b p. 49) state that culture 'defines what is normal for one time and place'. The cultural context in which we live relates to our implicit assumptions about gender, generational cohorts, ethnicity, sexuality and sexual preference, religious and political beliefs. The dominant beliefs of a particular nation or community in relation to these issues, and many others, will profoundly influence an individual, family and community, as will the availability, beliefs and resources of subcultures.

FIGURE **1.6** Structural dimensions

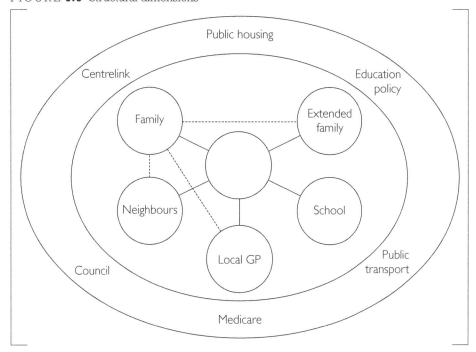

FIGURE **1.7** Cultural dimensions

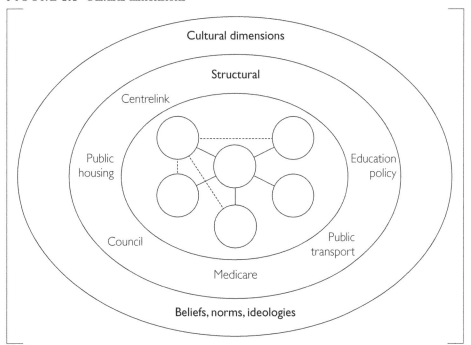

The cultural context is often hard to articulate or even to be aware of until we step into alternative cultural contexts or critically reflect on our core cultural assumptions. Shifting our thinking in relation to time and place can be one way of reflecting on what cultural assumptions are influencing our way of being and thinking. For example, marriage is an experience that exists in many parts of the world. However, in terms of both the rituals of marriage and the expectations of men's and women's roles within marriage, there is enormous variation between cultures. For example, in some countries, a husband can have multiple wives or gay and lesbian couples can marry—none of these forms of marriage are legal in Australia. An analysis of cultural influences also enables analysis of dominant cultural beliefs and the ways in which these connect with power and allow some groups to be priviliged while others are oppressed or marginalised.

At the time when Bronfenbrenner developed his ecological model, he was part of a more singular and ethno-specific understanding of culture, and thus talked about culture in the singular. With global mobility and technological developments, it is impossible to think of culture as a singular phenomenon, as we tend to be influenced by many different cultural contexts—both subcultures and dominant cultures. These issues are expanded on considerably in Chapter 3.

Like the inner world, the outer world can be understood using a variety of theories—theories that seek to understand what both causes adversity, and facilitates or impedes adaptation. These include feminist theories, systems theories (from ecological to chaos), conflict theories, and Marxist theories.

Time is multidimensional

Influencing all of the other dimensions discussed are the dimensions of time. Five significant time dimensions exist—biological, biographical, historical/social, cyclical and future time—forming what can be called the **chronosystem** (Bronfenbrenner 1979).

The **biological time** dimension is the chronological experience of being born and moving through various biological transitions and milestones across the lifespan until our death. It is a linear process. Certain biological processes occur because we are at a particular point in the biological timeline—we are born; we grow through infancy and childhood; we reach puberty and develop a reproductive capacity, we age and that brings about its own unique changes in functioning.

Closely associated with our biological time is the development of our own meaning structures or biography. Over time, we develop our own repertoire of coping methods and our understanding of who we are. Our individual sense and experience of time shapes our self-perceptions, our opportunities and our attitudes. This can be referred to as our **biographical time**. As Garbarino and Abramowitz suggest (1992a p. 18), our 'interest in development is really an interest in biography. We must discover how the lives of individuals and the lives of societies are interdependent'.

We are born into a particular generational **cohort** and, as a result, are exposed to cultural and historical adversities that shape our experience, which differ from those of people in other eras. Bronfenbrenner also emphasised **historical time**—human development is necessarily culture-bound and time-bound. These influences lead to the development of distinctive 'rules and expectations about how people at various ages should behave' (Peterson 1996 p. 14). This concept of historical time can also be understood as **social time**, referring 'to the incidence, duration and sequence of roles, and to relevant expectations and beliefs based on age' (Elder 1994 p. 6). For example, in the 1940s and 50s in Australia, a common path for professionals was to proceed from school to university to work, and then family and children followed, with many women required to resign from their employment and maintain the home and family. Only 8.6 per cent of married women were in the paid workforce in 1947 in Australia (Murphy 2002 p. 63). Today, most professionals do not follow this linear pathway, but participate in education, employment and family opportunities and responsibilities at different times throughout the lifespan.

Our experience of **cyclical time** is connected with both our own biography and historical time dimensions. Cyclical time refers to the patterns, seasons and anniversaries (Hutchison 1999 p. 22) that recur throughout our lives, which are unique to our own family, community, or religious context. For example, we celebrate or mourn at different times throughout the year, typically in memory of past events.

Our sense of **future time** is one that is often overlooked. The extent to which we anticipate a future significantly influences our present status. For example, young children and adolescents often have a sense of a long future ahead of them, but middle-aged and older people can be confronted by the shortening of their future time. People experiencing depression, trauma or grief often find it hard to engage with any sense of a future for themselves given their current state of mind.

Drawing all these dimensions together, a multidimensional approach can be presented in the following diagram (Figure 1.8).

FIGURE **1.8** A multidimensional approach

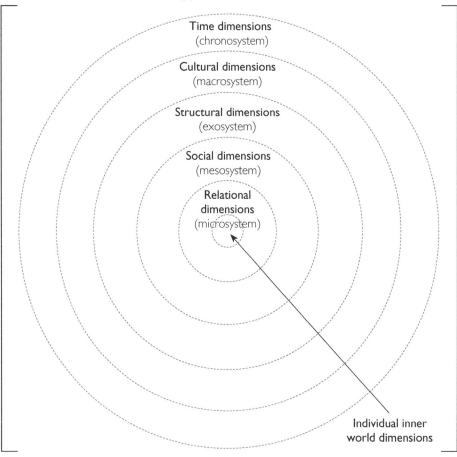

THEORY IN CONTEXT

A MULTIDIMENSIONAL APPROACH TO WORKING WITH SEXUAL ASSAULT

Kate, a social work student, describes how she found the multidimensional approach helpful in thinking about her work with a client in a sexual assault service.

Hoe, a Vietnamese mother, was interviewed at a children's sexual assault centre. Hoe's eleven-year-old daughter, Amanda, had been sexually abused by her stepfather, who at the time was in remand and about to go on trial for the murder of a person who was unknown to the family. An interpreter assisted at the interview, as Hoe's understanding of English was insufficient for the sexual assault centre staff to clarify information such as Amanda's safety or to explain the services that could be offered to Amanda and Hoe. The purpose of the interview was to put the circumstances of the incident in context, and to establish some practical strategies to initiate the beginnings of a holding process (to foster a sense of emotional security) upon which counselling would later build.

Because I think visually, I found it useful to apply theory to practice by thinking of theories in visual terms. For instance, planning how to question Hoe was assisted by using the multidimensional approach (see Figure 1.8) as a way of developing a client map. As information unfolded about Amanda's case, the external realities of her circumstances, such as her school, cultural links, other agencies involved and her extended family connections, were mapped out. The map evolved into a three-dimensional perspective, with exploration of the relationships between the connecting elements and theories such as attachment theory that were required to begin a deeper understanding of Amanda's internal world.

Questions

1 What is your personal reaction to this situation?
2 In what ways did Kate use a multidimensional approach to understand Hoe and Amanda's situation?
3 Are there other aspects of a multidimensional approach that you think could be usefully applied?

Human experience is multidimensional

Human experience is a combination of an individual's unique developmental trajectory and unique life events. An understanding of both the more normative tasks of development and the non-normative tasks provides a more holistic understanding of a person's adaptive capacities and resources.

Understanding human development is typically referred to as a **lifespan approach**. This is a normative approach, understanding individual experience and behaviour in the context of what most people within a particular cohort are experiencing in a particular context, using **prevalence** data as the basis for this understanding. For example, within the Australian context, longevity can be calculated for the population, and based on this calculation an expectation about how long we will live can be formulated. On the basis of difference or deviations from the normative developmental stages, policies and programs are put into place to provide individuals with resources. Thus, we understand human behaviour in the context of being at a particular age and stage in the human lifespan. There are some expectable transitions, aspects of healthy development, which are universal, although profoundly influenced by cultural and context. The strengths of this approach are that there is recognition of the needs of individuals and attempts can be made to resource and support them when these needs are not being met—for example, knowing the developmental milestones of infancy has enabled children at risk to be supported by early intervention programs when these milestones are not being reached. However, an obvious limitation of this approach is that it can lead to stigma and **othering** (Young 1990 p. 60) or to assumptions made by researchers and others that 'one size fits all'. There is also the potential for it to limit the capacity for individually or culturally appropriate strategies.

Another approach to understanding human experience is an adversity-focused approach, or a **life course approach**. This focuses on understanding human behaviour in specific contexts and experiences, particular adversities. It looks at particular events, stressors or traumas, and at the resources and deficits of individuals, families and communities. Individual developmental stages are acknowledged, but so too is the impact of these 'non-normative' life events that influence development and adaptation. The strength of this approach is that there is an understanding that single incidents do have a profound impact on subsequent human experience, right across the life course. Importantly, it recognises that what happens in adulthood is also influential. However, the limitation of such an approach is that it sometimes decontextualises coping and provides a sense that it is only the event and not the circumstances in both the pre-event and post-event context that influences coping.

Negative experiences are an inescapable aspect of being alive. Throughout this book, the term **adversity** is used as a way of referring generally to these negative life events. The adversities of life are the experiences that have the potential to harm us in some way; to cause distress and injury to many dimensions of our self. Adversity is experienced in many ways, arising from sudden and unexpected incidents or from lifelong burdens or states of being. An adverse event can profoundly influence one person yet seemingly have little or no impact on someone else. Some experiences of adversity, such as those of loss and death, are inevitable human experiences. Others are the result of particular environments and circumstances and are uniquely traumatic for those affected by them.

Adversity is referred to by many different terms, including threats, demands, stressors, structural constraints (Gottlieb 1997) and traumas. Marris (1986) refers to conditions of uncertainty, which lead to anxiety for individuals, families, groups and communities. Transition is another commonly used term (Germain 1991; Germain & Bloom 1999), although it is typically used in a more neutral way, to describe changes that have the *potential* to be negative, positive or indeed neutral in their impact. While all of these terms refer to negative human experiences or conditions, they differ slightly in their emphasis.

Adaptation and coping are multidimensional

Adaptation is the vital task for each person, in the context of our family, the groups to which we belong and our wider community. Yet, just as the causes of adversity are multidimensional, so too are the consequences—an understanding of the consequences of adversity for individuals, families and communities needs to incorporate the possibilities of both adaptation and **maladaptation**, and the range of experiences in between. **Adaptation** refers to our active responses to circumstances of change, with positive adaptations enabling the maintenance or re-establishment of health and well-being in their broadest sense (Bornstein et al. 2003). Querelt (1996 p. 17) describes adaptation as 'the continuous process of mutual accommodation between an active and evolving human being and the ever-changing settings within which the person functions'.

Adaptation is often a constant and even unrecognisable process, in that we must continually respond to the demands of each day. These daily adaptations tend to be gradual. Adaptation can also be a more radical process, under circumstances of greater adversity, when daily patterns of behaviour and beliefs are shattered by unexpected events. Adaptations are both conscious and unconscious processes.

In any adaptation, all dimensions of our experience are involved—the biopsycho-spiritual dimensions of our inner world and the socio-cultural dimensions of our outer world. More will be said about this in a moment. Driving our need for adaptation is our appraisal of what is going on for us—that is, do we perceive the experiences as being experiences of harm or loss, threat or challenge (Lazarus & Folkman 1984; Lazarus 1998)? Chapter 6 explores these issues more fully. When we are confronted with experiences outside of the familiar, we attempt to return to a recognisable and manageable way of being.

This adaptive tendency is often referred to as our self-righting tendency (Vaillant 1993). Adaptation processes are ideally about moving towards a steady state, or homeostasis, although not necessarily a stress-free one (Gottlieb 1997). Families and communities similarly seek to restore some sense of steady state. According to this line of argument, well-being occurs when there is an optimal balance between all dimensions. Positive adaptations depend on a degree of goodness of fit or compatibility between all of our lived dimensions. As Chapter 3 highlights, our cultural dimensions influence these adaptations profoundly.

For optimal mental health and well-being, research suggests that we need to maintain our meaning structures (Marris 1986) or a sense of coherence (Antonovsky 1979; 1987). We develop meaning structures in our own minds across the lifespan that reinforce for us who we are and how the world is—the world and our place in it develops some kind of predictability, even if this predictability is primarily negative. As Marris (1986 p. 2) suggests, we have a conservative impulse:

the impulse to defend the predictability of life is a fundamental and universal principle of human psychology. Conservatism in this sense is an aspect of our ability to survive any situation; for without continuity, we cannot interpret what events mean to us, nor explore new kinds of experience with confidence.

Others have suggested that not only can we adapt and cope well with stressful or traumatic life events, but we may be able to, as Carver (1998) suggests, thrive in the face of adversity, and come to an enhanced state of being, or we might experience what Tedeschi and Calhoun (1995; Tedeschi et al. 1998) term post-traumatic growth. This is a major shift in focus, away from a focus on maladaptation or the development of psychiatric disorders to focusing on the strengths and resilience that can also emerge in the aftermath of life experiences.

Central to the notion of adaptation in the aftermath of adversity is the process of coping. **Coping** refers to the specific psychosocial adaptations, the thoughts, behaviours and resources we use in our attempts to respond to stressors. That is, coping is about the thinking and doing that we engage in after an event in an effort to maintain or regain a sense of coherence or functioning. Similarly, families, groups and communities engage in various coping processes.

Moos and Schaefer (1986 p. 22) argue that coping capacity is dependent on a number of factors. These are:

» our demographic and personal characteristics, such as age, gender, socio-economic status or personality factors
» specific aspects of the crisis or transition itself
» the physical and social environment, and the resources it is able to provide.

Coping resources are therefore any of the above three factors associated with lowering our levels of distress or physical symptoms following experiences of adversity. As Moos and Schaefer highlight, dimensions of the environment are critical determinants of coping capacity.

The coping capacity of an individual is determined by complex interaction between the available resources in the inner and outer worlds of the individual. A range of factors determines an individual's response to a particular experience. These factors are often called **risk factors** and **protective factors**, although they may also be referred to as vulnerability and resilience factors respectively. Adaptation is a complex interaction between individual and environmental risk and protective factors.

Risk and protective factors
Within each of the dimensions of a person's inner and outer worlds, researchers have come to identify particular factors that can be understood as risk and/or protective

factors. The term 'risk' refers to the probabilities or likelihood of a future negative event. Applied to understanding responses to adversity, **risk factors** are a range of factors that *may* lead to poorer or negative developmental or biopsychosocial outcomes (Werner & Smith 1992). This cautious use of language is important. These factors may lead to negative outcomes, but many studies and autobiographical accounts are testament to the extraordinary resilience of human beings.

Some events can be understood as risk factors in themselves. They are risk factors in that, as events or experiences, they increase the likelihood of later difficulty in life for an individual. For example, the death of a parent in childhood significantly increases the risk of depression in adulthood (Parkes 1972). Similarly, child sexual abuse has been found to increase the risk of self-esteem and sexual difficulties in adult life (Mullen et al. 1996). Other risk factors can be thought of as factors that influence the processes of coping but are not the cause of the adversity themselves. Later biopsychosocial difficulties have been correlated with these factors also. For example, age is an associated (or proximal) risk factor, in that some events occurring at a particular age, such as separation or loss experiences, have a more profound impact than at another age. That is, age influences risk but is not the risk factor itself.

Discussion of risk factors raises two important matters. The first relates to the perceptions of risk, or dangers and hazards (Adam & Van Loon 2000). Who determines risk and for whom are crucial questions, with notions of risk closely associated with economic and political factors. For example, these issues are particularly relevant when we consider some of the issues of adolescent risk-taking.

The second matter relates to the fact that not everyone who is exposed to particular risk factors is adversely affected. There are varying degrees of effect. This raises the critical question as to what makes the difference, leading to attention being paid to the important role of protective factors. Werner (1995 p. 81) defines **protective factors** as the factors 'that moderate (ameliorate) a person's reaction to a stressful situation or chronic adversity so that his or her adaptation is more successful than would be the case if the protective factors were not present'. Protective factors are the buffers to the risk factors. For example, having a network of friends enables both practical and emotional support to be offered at times of high stress or loss. The loss might still occur, but the friends provide a buffer to its impact.

Therefore, a balancing act of risk and protective factors exists. Too many risk factors or too few protective factors can mean the difference between good and poor outcomes. The image of scales is sometimes used to denote this relationship (Gilligan 2000). This image is useful in that it highlights that positive experiences have the capacity to outweigh negative ones and that there is a need for a balance to be achieved between the two. We are not only looking to understand risk factors, we are also looking to understand why individuals in the face of adversity have not been overwhelmed. What protective factors are critical in enhancing their coping capacity? Another salient reminder exists in this image of scales: scales can only tolerate so much weight before they collapse altogether. This may hold true for humans too. The accumulation of risk factors does lead to higher risk of poor outcomes (Fraser et al. 1999). Ultimately, reducing risk factors to minimise the overall burden an individual carries is the most effective intervention.

While reducing risk is clearly important in enhancing the well-being of individuals, families and communities, there are some inherent challenges with this approach. The onus for prevention can very quickly fall onto individuals, families and communities—that is, risks are personalised and individualised—even when the risks stem from broader structural and cultural factors. For example, the current emphasis on obesity reduction can be seen as an individual responsibility involving diet and exercise (the primary approach) or a structural and cultural responsibility, involving limiting the marketing of junk foods and implementing strategies regarding the availability and pricing of healthy foods. A multidimensional approach brings an analysis of the person *and* their environments together simultaneously to avoid seeing risk management as the responsibility of individuals only.

Resilience and thriving

The increasing recognition that individuals in situations of high risk have not necessarily experienced the poor outcomes anticipated has led to a major shift in emphasis in understandings of adaptation at the end of the twentieth century. The new focus is on **resilience** (Rutter 1985; Werner & Smith 1992; Werner 1995; Fraser et al. 1999), thriving (Carver 1998) and strengths (Saleebey 1997). That is, research has focused on why it is that not everybody succumbs to adverse events and circumstances, and what factors either protect in the first place and/or enable people to recover and adapt positively in the aftermath of traumatic life events or extreme adverse conditions. While these notions are not necessarily new, with many writers such as Maslow (1968; 1996) writing about these issues in the 1960s, they continue to be taken up in the twenty-first century and incorporated into research, policy and interventions in a way never seen before.

WERNER AND SMITH: RESILIENCE

The notion of resilience gained particular recognition following the studies conducted by Emmy Werner and Ruth Smith on the Island of Kuaui, Hawaii. Werner and Smith followed 505 children who were born in 1955, from pre-birth to adulthood, 'monitoring the impact of a variety of biological and psychosocial risk factors, stressful life events and protective factors at birth, infancy, early and middle childhood, late adolescence and adulthood' (Werner & Smith 1992 p. 1). They found that one-third of this cohort was born into families where the odds were against successful development. The specific risk factors these children faced were:

» moderate to severe peri-natal stress (stress around the event of birth)
» chronic poverty
» having parents with little formal education
» living in disorganised family environments in which there was 'discord, desertion, divorce' and/or where parents were dealing with issues of alcoholism or mental illness (Werner & Smith 1992 p. 2).

Of this vulnerable one-third, two-thirds were encountering four or more cumulative risk factors by the age of two. They subsequently developed serious learning and behaviour problems by the age of ten or had a record of delinquencies, mental health problems or pregnancies by the age of eighteen. However, their key finding was that of the high-risk children, one-third (some ten per cent of the total cohort) had developed into 'competent, confident and caring young adults by the age of eighteen' (Werner & Smith 1992 p. 2).

The children in Werner and Smith's study were initially referred to as 'stress-resistant' or invulnerable, but they became more aptly described as resilient. This was in recognition of the fact that it was not that these environments had no effect, but that, in spite of these conditions of extreme adversity, these children had managed to reach normal developmental milestones. Resilience has therefore come to be defined as 'a successful adaptational response to high risk' (Fraser et al. 1999 p. 137; Luthar, Cicchetti & Becker 2000). Others have defined resilience as the capacity to 'bounce back' (Vaillant 1993) or achieve normal or optimal adaptation and development despite considerable threat to that development. Masten (2001 p. 235) has described it as coming from 'the everyday magic of ordinary, normative human resources'. In recent years, the view that resilience relates to a universal set of transferable inner- and outer-world human capacities has shifted. Rather, resilience is currently seen as 'a multidimensional construct, the definition of which is *negotiated* between individuals and their communities, with tendencies to display both homogeneity and heterogeneity across culturally diverse research settings' (Ungar 2008a p. 219). In a similar vein, Gilligan (2004 p. 94) suggests:

> While resilience may previously have been seen as residing in a person as a fixed trait, it is now more usefully considered as a variable quality that derives from a process of repeated interactions between a person and favourable features of the surrounding context in a person's life.

In thinking about how to promote resilience, some key factors have been identified. Three clusters of protective factors were identified by Werner and Smith (1992 p. 192) that differentiated the resilient group from other high-risk children who developed serious and persistent problems, both in childhood and in later life. These three clusters—involving intelligence, affectional ties and support systems—are presented in the box below.

WERNER AND SMITH'S CLUSTERS OF PROTECTIVE FACTORS

The three clusters of key protective factors are:

1 at least average intelligence and dispositional attributes that elicited positive responses from family members and strangers, such as robustness, vigour and an active, sociable temperament
2 affectional ties with parent substitutes, such as grandparents and older siblings, which encouraged trust, autonomy and initiative
3 an external support system (in church, youth groups or school) that rewarded competence and provided them with a sense of coherence.

Source: Werner and Smith 1992 p. 192

From a review of the literature on resilience, fifteen factors that appear to be key protective factors have been consistently identified (Fonagy et al. 1994). They are:

1 a good social and economic environment
2 an absence of organic deficits
3 an easy temperament
4 younger age for those who have suffered a traumatic experience
5 absence of early separation or losses
6 a warm relationship with at least one caregiver
7 the availability in adulthood of good social support
8 positive school experiences
9 involvement with organised religious activity, or faith
10 high IQ
11 superior coping styles
12 higher sense of autonomy and self-worth
13 interpersonal awareness and empathy
14 willingness to plan
15 a sense of humour.

What becomes evident from this list is the interaction between individual and environmental factors.

From more of an inner-world focus, Flach (in Granot 1996 p. 141) identified thirteen humanistic factors in psychological resilience:

1 insight into oneself and others
2 a supple sense of self-esteem
3 ability to learn from experience
4 high tolerance for distress
5 low tolerance for outrageous behaviour
6 open-mindedness
7 courage
8 personal discipline
9 creativity
10 integrity
11 a keen sense of humour
12 a constructive philosophy of life that gives meaning
13 a willingness to dream dreams that can inspire us all and give us genuine hope.

These critical protective factors are explored in later chapters.

In addition to a focus on resilience, researchers have begun to examine the issue of thriving. While resilience refers to a return to functioning or a bouncing back, **thriving** refers to being 'better off afterwards' (Carver 1998). Carver (1998 pp. 252–3) suggests that:

> psychological thriving appears to represent a kind of growth: growth in knowledge, growth in skill, growth in confidence, greater elaboration and differentiation in one's ability to deal with the world at large.

Experiences of resilience and thriving are context-dependent. Importantly, they are not about the absence of vulnerability—many situations are inescapable and enduring but individuals are able to display high levels of resilience. As Fraser et al. (1999) emphasise, resilience only emerges under conditions of risk—it is about a successful adaptational response to high risk. This viewing of resilience in context is critical, as some researchers are now critiquing it as an overly optimistic emphasis on the devastating effects of difficult life events. As Garbarino and Abramowitz suggest, 'the fact that humans can survive in the face of these risks should not be enough to excuse or rationalize the threats that these risks present' (Garbarino & Abramowitz 1992b pp. 63–4) or indeed become the basis for inaction. The risk with the notion of resilience is that a survivor can be expected to overcome difficulties, and a 'blame the victim' mentality can arise in that they are perceived to 'fail' in recovering. On the other hand, if the ultimate goal is about the enhancement of well-being at individual and social levels, we need to know far more about the experience of resilience and the ways of promoting it than we currently do.

In the Constitution of the World Health Organization, established by the United Nations, a statement is made about the principles that are 'basic to the happiness, harmonious relations and security of all peoples' (World Health Organization 2003). These principles are fundamental to how we think about well-being and resilience, both locally and globally, and are outlined below.

THE PRINCIPLES OF THE WORLD HEALTH ORGANIZATION

1 **Health** is a state of complete physical, mental and social well-being and not merely the absence of disease or infirmity.
2 The enjoyment of the highest attainable standard of health is one of the fundamental rights of every human being without distinction of race, religion, political belief, economic or social condition.
3 The health of all peoples is fundamental to the attainment of peace and security and is dependent upon the fullest cooperation of individuals and States.
4 The achievement of any State in the promotion and protection of health is of value to all.
5 Unequal development in different countries in the promotion of health and control of disease, especially communicable disease, is a common danger.
6 Healthy development of the child is of basic importance; the ability to live harmoniously in a changing total environment is essential to such development.
7 The extension to all peoples of the benefits of medical, psychological and related knowledge is essential to the fullest attainment of health.
8 Informed opinion and active cooperation on the part of the public are of the utmost importance in the improvement of the health of the people.
9 Governments have a responsibility for the health of their peoples which can be fulfilled only by the provision of adequate health and social measures.

Source: World Health Organization 2003, reprinted with permission

Attempts to theorise human development and adaptation should be multidimensional

Human experience, behaviour and adaptation can all be understood from multiple theoretical dimensions—theories of the inner world, theories of the outer world, and those that attempt to bridge the two. Rather than this seeming as if social workers do not have a firm theoretical base from which to work, to the contrary, a multidimensional approach acknowledges that there are many ways of understanding the complexities of the human experience and that these understandings constantly change and evolve. The task is to discern how we come to reach certain understandings and to work towards a 'goodness of fit' between the identified issues and the possible social work responses, particularly in our multicultural contexts.

A multidimensional approach helps in the identification of a range of factors that are influential in determining positive or negative adaptation. It gives the 'what' we should be alerted to in considering individual situations. Although many argue that it does not necessarily give the 'how' or the 'why'—that is, that it is not clinically useful (Wakefield 1996)—it does provide a map of the important experiential and contextual dimensions that shape and are shaped by adversity experiences.

A multidimensional perspective attempts to understand the influence of the critical dimensions of a person's situation. It extends beyond thinking about the individual causes and responses to considering interacting and competing issues as well. It encourages us to step out of our own comfort zones to think about problems in different ways—if we tend to think about individual adversity from an inner-world, or intrapsychic, point of view, we are encouraged to think more broadly in terms of the influence of the social and political environment. If we tend towards more structural theorising about adversity, we are reminded of the importance of individual factors in understanding a person's, family's or community's coping capacities.

Particularly at the individual casework level, it is argued that for intervention purposes more specific theories are required (Mattaini et al. 1998). These theories are referred to as domain-specific theories because they relate to specific domains or dimensions of human functioning, and they tend to be more explanatory of functioning in these specific domains. Some of the inner-world domain-specific theories include psychodynamic, cognitive–behavioural and narrative theories, each of which provides an explanation for the motivation of human behaviour. As you will see in later chapters, understandings of experiences of grief, stress and trauma tend to be viewed from theoretical perspectives that relate primarily to the inner world. Some of the outer-world domain-specific theories include Marxist, ecological (or systems), feminist, post-structural and chaos theories.

Human services responses must be multidimensional

In highlighting the many dimensions of both the inner and outer worlds that influence individual experience, it is apparent that a range of responses is essential in the human services. Responses must be multidimensional, including practices, programs and policies that incorporate prevention, intervention and postvention strategies. Research informs and evaluates all of these responses. If the various dimensions of an individual's world are constantly interacting to influence experience, changes in one dimension will potentially lead to change in others. This leads to a variety of considerations for practice.

Three different time dimensions influence the focus of human services practice. The Oxford Dictionary defines **prevention strategies** as 'the action of stopping something from happening or making impossible an anticipated event or intended act'. Prevention strategies have a future focus: they are devised on the basis of known risk factors. When we are referring to **intervention strategies**, we are referring to 'the action or an act of coming between or interfering, especially so as to modify or prevent a result' (Brown 1993 p. 1401). Thus, intervention strategies are present-focused in the face of risk having occurred, increasing the likelihood of damage occurring. In some instances, a further distinction is made, with **postvention strategies** referring to an action taken after an event, so as to modify or prevent *further* damage or disruption. This is most typically used in the trauma context, when arguably some psychosocial damage has already occurred and further damage is being prevented. In Chapter 5, critical incident stress management strategies will be introduced, giving examples of postvention strategies in the aftermath of trauma. Often within social work, it is necessary to start with intervention and postvention strategies in order to identify the critical risk factors and then begin to address issues from a preventive point of view.

Applying this, prevention strategies for mental health issues include many of the initiatives developed within primary and secondary schools in relation to self-esteem issues. Intervention strategies for mental health issues—that is, when they have become problematic for the person concerned—include the availability of mobile crisis assessment and treatment teams, designed to respond to people who are in the midst of acute and serious mental health problems. In this instance, the problem has occurred, but intervention is mobilised so as to prevent further negative consequences.

The method of prevention, intervention or postvention must be considered in the strategy. Social workers use a wide range of methods, including counselling, advocacy, liaison and referral, community development, policy development, information/ resource development and education and program development. Sometimes a distinction is made between direct practice and indirect practice methods. **Direct practice**, or casework, is typically delivered in a face-to-face context and can be focused on an individual, a family, a group or a community. With **indirect practice** methods, the person directly affected is not involved in the intervention but is influenced by it—for example, policy interventions are indirect practice methods.

In addition to considering the time frame of strategies and the methods used, a range of skills is required. The skills of engagement and attending, interviewing, assessment, intervention and evaluation are core to all practice. A detailed discussion of these skills is beyond the scope of this book; instead it focuses on the theoretical issues that then inform the interventions required.

Locating yourself: Engaging in reflective and reflexive practice

Many value-laden issues are inherent in a discussion of human development, relating to judgments about adaptation, coping and well-being, and conversely about maladaption or coping poorly. These terms may refer to developmental experiences as well as behaviours that are perceived by an individual or by others to be outcomes that are either good or bad or, more typically, somewhere in between. It is important to remember that much behaviour considered adaptive is culturally determined. It is not adaptive per se; it is only adaptive because of a particular context. Implicit in all research on human adaptation to adversity are assumptions about what it is to be human and what is the best expression of that humanity.

Our own values, based on our own experiences and contexts, become critical, therefore, in considering all of this material. We need to reflect on our own beliefs as to what it is to be human, what human rights are, what issues of adversity are, and how we understand their causation and their consequences. We need to be mindful of the ways in which our own experiences of gender, culture and class; of our biological, psychological and spiritual dimensions; and of our unique social networks and place come to influence these assumptions. It is important that we engage in critical reflection as to where we locate ourselves in relation to these matters. In turn, these reflections can enable us to change what we do and who we are. When our reflections transform our actions and change what we do, we refer to this as reflexive practice. It moves beyond our own reflective practice to effect change for others.

CHAPTER **SUMMARY**

Understanding human development and behaviour is an extremely complex yet necessary task for workers in the human services. A multidimensional approach highlights that there are many different ways in which human development can be understood. No single theoretical perspective can adequately account for the diversity of individual experiences and the many contextual dimensions that give rise to these experiences. Instead, a multidimensional approach invites us to think about the significance and interconnectedness of a person's biological, psychological and spiritual dimensions and their relational, social, structural and cultural dimensions. In this chapter, we have looked at how each of these dimensions can be conceptualised.

A multidimensional approach also encourages us to think about the ways in which these many dimensions can function as risk and/or protective factors, and later chapters will explore these more specifically. In examining risk and protective factors, we are considering the absence or availability of various resources for individuals in different contexts. The adaptation that each individual makes to particular circumstances is therefore dependent upon a unique combination of these inner- and outer-world resources. The shift in recent years to understand protective factors more fully has led to a focus on resilience and thriving, the positive developmental outcomes following experiences of adversity. Many questions remain in relation to the processes of fostering resilience—within individuals, families and communities.

APPLYING A MULTIDIMENSIONAL UNDERSTANDING

CASE STUDY

Mandy: Fifteen and homeless

Mandy is fifteen and has been homeless for the last six months. Since the age of twelve, her stepfather had been sexually abusing her. She had told no one about this, being terrified that she would be removed from the home if she said anything. Her mother found her diary and read of the abuse. However, she didn't believe Mandy and screamed at her for making up stories. Mandy left home after this argument and moves now between a friend's house, emergency accommodation and sleeping out on the streets.

Mandy has left school as well, although she occasionally keeps in touch with a teacher. She wants to finish secondary school but just can't get her life organised at present to return. She finds that she often feels overwhelmingly depressed, and has slashed her arms and legs on several occasions.

Her mother and stepfather have since separated, and her mother wants Mandy to come back and live with them again. She has a thirteen-year-old brother.

Questions

1 What is your personal reaction to Mandy's situation? Why?
2 Which dimensions of Mandy's experience do you see as risk or protective factors for her?
3 What about the risk and protective factors for her family?

4 In what way would your understanding of Mandy's experiences change if you knew that she lived in a rural or remote area?

5 What are some possibilities for intervention at a:
- direct-practice level?
- program level?
- policy level?

KEY TERMS

adaptation
adversity
biographical time
biological dimensions
biological time
biopsychosocial-spiritual dimensions
chronosystem
cohort
coping
cultural dimensions
cyclical time
direct practice
exosystem
future time
gender
health
historical/social time
indirect practice
inner world
intervention strategies
life course approach
lifespan approach

macrosystem
mesosystem
microsystem
multidimensional approach
normative
outer world
person:environment configuration
postvention strategies
prevention strategies
protective factors
psychological dimensions
relational dimensions
religion
resilience
risk factors
social dimensions
spiritual dimensions
spirituality
structural dimensions
subjective experience
thriving

QUESTIONS AND DISCUSSION POINTS

1 What are the three key dimensions of our inner worlds?

2 What are the four key outer-world dimensions that influence and are influenced by individuals?

3 What are the key dimensions of time?

4 What are risk factors and protective factors?

5 What is the nature of resilience?

6 Which dimensions of the human experience interest you most and why?

7 Think of your own context and how it influences your current life situation. Draw a map of your current relational, social, structural and cultural context, using Figure 1.8 as a guide.

8 What do you see as the strengths and limitations of a multidimensional approach to understanding human devleopment?

FURTHER READING

Bronfenbrenner, U. 1979, *The ecology of human development: Experiments by nature and design*, Cambridge, MA: Harvard University Press.

Germain, C. & Bloom, M. 1999, *Human behavior in the social environment: An ecological view*, 2nd edn, New York: Columbia University Press.

Gilligan, R. 2004, 'Promoting resilience in child and family social work: Issues for social work practice, education and policy'. *Social Work Education*, 23(1), pp. 93–104.

Hudson, C. (2000), 'At the edge of chaos: A new paradigm for social work?' *Journal of Social Work Education*, 36(2), 215–30.

Luthar, S., Cicchetti, D. & Becker, B. 2000, 'The construct of resilience: A critical evaluation and guidelines for future work' *Child Development*, 71(3), pp. 543–62.

Wakefield, J. 1996, 'Does social work need the eco-systems perspective? Part 1: Is the perspective clinically useful?' *Social Service Review*, March, pp. 1–32.

WEBSITES OF INTEREST

Australian Commonwealth Government: www.australia.gov.au
  This site provides you with access to a wide range of federal government policy and program frameworks, including both a research and a practice perspective.

Australian Institute of Health and Welfare: www.aihw.gov.au
  This site is an invaluable source of national health and welfare statistics and information.

Bronfenbrenner Lifecourse Center, Cornell University: www.blcc.cornell.edu
  This centre conducts research relating to the ecology of human development. The site contains research and program information, both past and present, and has useful links to other related sites.

The Children's Research Centre, School of Social Work and Social Policy, Trinity College, Dublin: www.tcd.ie/childrensresearchcentre

This site, compiled by Professor Robbie Gilligan, has an extensive publication list relating to resilience and excellent links to other resilience- and development-focused sites.

Embrace the future: www.embracethefuture.org.au

This site, developed by the Mental Health Foundation of Australia, provides information about resilience for young people.

Resilience Research Centre: http://resilienceproject.org

This site provides research by Michael Ungar and the International Resilience Project team, with a focus on multi-site, cross-cultural resilience research.

ResilienceNet: http://resilnet.uiuc.edu

This site was developed by the University of Illinois at Urbana-Champaign and has information about resilience, resiliency models and resilience research at a range of other centres.

The United Nations: www.un.org

This site provides extensive information about international human rights issues and global approaches to health and well-being.

World Health Organization (WHO): www.who.org

The World Health Organization is the health agency of the United Nations. This site has information, research tools, publications and links relating to international health topics.

Information for practice: World Wide Web resources for social workers: http://blogs.nyu.edu/socialwork/ip/

This jointly sponsored website of New York University's School of Social Work and the Division of Social Work and Behavioral Medicine and Mount Sinai's School of Medicine provides over 85,000 links to relevant electronic full-text journals, as well as to other scientific, technical and policy reports.

PART 2

The Critical Contexts
of Human Development

CHAPTER **2**

Relational and Social Dimensions

AIMS OF THIS CHAPTER

This chapter examines the ways in which our relational and social environments critically influence adaptation and development. It considers the following questions:

» How do we understand the relational dimensions of a person's context, particularly families?
» How do we understand social support and social capital?
» How do these concepts of social support and social capital link to well-being?

As emphasised in Chapter 1, we are all influenced by, and in turn influence, the many relational, social, structural and cultural dimensions in which we live. Within these various contexts, we experience the events of daily life, and these in turn give shape to who we are and how we live. These direct relational bonds and wider social networks are seen to provide or inhibit the social capital and social support for our optimal well-being. Yet relationships with other people are complex, and strong supportive networks are not always available to individuals and families. These realities raise questions as to what relational and social networks of support are needed for optimal development, and what shapes these networks of relationships. The network most strongly associated with our need for a sense of security and support, of being cared for and loved, as well as with the most instrumental provision of resources, is the **family**. In this chapter, we begin by exploring some definitions of the family and understandings of its structure and function. Then we look at peer relationships and other significant relational dimensions, before considering wider social networks and their role in providing social support. In Chapters 7 to 13 we then address specific aspects of relationships and social networks as they relate to each particular age group.

Relational dimensions

The family

The family network is considered to be far more critical than other social networks in influencing the well-being of individuals. Yet any research, policy or legislation that touches on the issue of the family immediately runs into the problem of defining it. The definitional disputes relate to how we think about the structure or composition of the family—who is in the particular family group, and what is its function.

One of the many ways in which the family can be observed is through the demographic data that is available from the national census. This enables comparison with other countries. For example, the demographic trends of Germany and the USA are similar to those of Australia. However, Italy, Japan and Greece have already reached a stage where there are more people in the older age groups than in the younger age groups, something Australia is moving towards in the next few decades

Changes in family forms in Australia over the past three decades have resulted in great variability between families. There are many significant gains, as well as possible losses, with this diversity. Of note is the continual increase in the number of single-parent families, particularly female-headed families. Table 2.1 shows some of the changes in the family forms in which children were raised between the years of 1997 and 2007.

While we can attempt to understand the family as a specific set of people, we need to be aware that there are limitations with this approach. The data is still skewed, in that it is unlikely to adequately represent minority family forms such as gay and lesbian families, as members may choose not to disclose their family identity to the census process, and the survey process itself does not have the sophistication to accurately measure all the family forms, such as the extended kinship networks among Indigenous Australian family groups. However, it does give us some important glimpses into the structure of households in Australia.

In Chapter 3, we look at some of the structural and cultural influences on family life.

TABLE **2.1** Australian family households

Living arrangements	1997	2007
Total households	6,910,000	8,187,000
Total families	4,899,000	5,751,000
Families with children under 15	2,130,000	2,240,000
Couple families	4,090,000	4,773,000
Couple-only families (of all couple families)	41.2%	47.1%
Couple families with children under 15	80%	78.3%
Lone-father families with children under 15 (of all families with children under 15)	2.3%	2.9%
Lone-mother families with children under 15 (of all families with children under 15)	17.7%	18.8%
Families with at least one child aged under 5 (of all families with children under 15)	47.8%	45.1%
Children under 15 living in one-parent families (of all children under 15)	18%	19.5%
Average family size	3.1	3.0

Source: Australian Bureau of Statistics (ABS) 2009a, *Australian Social Trends*, cat. no. 4102, Canberra: ABS.

Definitions

As McDonald (1995 p. 3) highlights, the *Family Law Act 1975* (Cth),

> … describes the family as the natural and fundamental group unit in society, but despite the level of importance it ascribes to the family, the Act does not tell us what the family is. The Act apparently presumes that what is meant by family is so well known that there is no need for a definition.

Previously dominant definitions or understandings of family have been on the basis of 'blood, adoption or marriage'. The problem with any definitions based solely on these criteria is self-evident. Such definitions do not view the single-parent family, the blended or remarried family, or the gay and lesbian couple with or without children as valid forms of family. Such definitions also fail to take into account the significant relationships that form within close networks, such as friendships and neighbourhoods, often essential relationships when families migrate by choice or become dislocated through civil unrest and war. The 'blood, adoption or marriage' style of definition relates primarily to a biologically determined family network, and certainly gives no recognition to the subjective experience of family relationships.

In order to acknowledge all the potential dimensions of family life, Hartman and Laird (1983 p. 30) propose a more inclusive definition of family. They suggest that:

> A family becomes a family when two or more individuals have decided they are a family, that in the intimate, here-and-now environments in which they gather, there is a sharing of emotional needs for closeness, of living space which is deemed 'home' and of those roles and tasks necessary for meeting the biological, social and psychological requirements of the individuals involved.

Many definitions of family either risk exclusivity, in that they lead to some living-together arrangements as deviant, or over-inclusivity, whereby the notion of family becomes meaningless (Germain 1991 p. 93).

So how do we come to understand the notion of the family? We can think about families as having unique structures and functions, which shift over time and across cultures. Family structures and functions are transformed as a result of their own internal, private changes, associated with the births, deaths, illnesses, migrations, separation and divorce experiences. They are by no means static entities. Gilding (2001) suggests that while a family might be analysed according to a specific set of people living together, it says nothing about the meanings of these attachments. As Don Edgar (2000 p. 21), founder of the Australian Institute for Family Studies, highlights:

> Because families are in themselves 'reality-constructing' institutions, it does not mean they share a stable or uniform worldview. Indeed they are the site of multiple realities: 'his', 'hers', 'the child's', view of marriage, family divorce, each different 'account' exposing a clear vulnerability to the shock of reality disjuncture.

They are also, at times profoundly, influenced by external factors: housing; health services; neighbourhoods; rural, remote or urban locations; employment opportunities; and poverty. The cultural norms that surround family life can render private relationships such as gay and lesbian relationships for fear of discrimination or attack.

For the first time in history, the family within Western cultures is increasingly freed from the domination of reproduction as its primary function (Giddens 2002). This has fundamental gains and challenges associated with it—on the one hand the freedom to determine relationships more on the basis of intimacy needs and choices, yet on the other, economic burdens individualised even further as more people choose or are forced to live alone. Some of the trends in the Australian context of family life are outlined below.

TRENDS WITHIN AUSTRALIAN FAMILIES

» Out of Australia's 4.6 million children aged under eighteen, three-quarters of these children live with both natural parents. One-quarter live with only one natural parent.

» Marriage is declining generally—in 1998, there were 110,600 marriages registered, down from 116,800 in 1988.

» People are marrying later in life—now twenty-one per cent of first-time brides are over thirty compared with only six per cent twenty years ago. The median marrying age for men is now thirty-one and for women twenty-nine years.

» In relation to marital status, 50.7 per cent of the population stated they were married compared with 31.6 per cent who stated they had never married. A further 3.4 per cent indicated that they were separated, 7.4 per cent divorced and 6.2 per cent widowed. There was a significant sex difference between men and women who were widowed, with 181,472 males (twenty per cent) and 738,432 females (eighty per cent).

» In 2001 seventy-three per cent of couples marrying had lived together prior to marriage.

» The mean household size within Australia is 2.6 persons.

» Single-parent and remarried households are increasing—one projection for 2021 estimates that thirty-one per cent of children aged zero to four will be living with one parent.

» Eighty-four per cent of one-parent households are headed by women.

» The elderly population is increasing significantly.

» Women's participation in the labour force has increased.

» Ethnic diversity is increasing.

Source: Australian Institute of Health and Welfare (AIHW) 2001

Functions

The family persists as a major organisational unit within Australian society, and indeed globally, raising the question as to why it prevails. Rather than solely focusing on who is present in the family structure and how this structure changes, we can also think about the family as being defined according to the key functions it performs.

These functions vary within and across cultures over time, and in the extent to which the family or other social institutions fulfil these functions. For example, in recent decades, births, aged care and deaths are increasingly managed within the health system, not the home. Similarly, child care is being shifted into more institutionalised forms of management, while deinstitutionalisation has seen care shifted for those with physical, psychiatric and intellectual disabilities back into families and the community. As Silva and Smart (1999 p. 7) note: 'In this context of fluid and changing definitions of families, a basic core remains which refers to the sharing of resources, caring, responsibilities and obligations'. Some of the dominant, current protective functions of the family are the bearing and rearing of children, the provision of intimacy and support, the construction of a sense of meaning and belonging, and economic and physical security. Yet the family also has the potential to function as a key risk factor and the potential for oppression and intimate terrorism.

Across all cultures, the family is seen to have the core function of bearing and raising children, providing the necessary attachment bond for development and giving attention to the physical needs of the infant. In Chapter 7, we will examine these aspects extensively. Within the Australian context, child rearing certainly occurs in the context of families. As noted in Table 2.1, nearly eighty per cent of all children under fifteen live in couple families. The long-term protective impact of positive early family life experiences is well documented—for example, in the Harvard Mastery of Stress Study (Ornish 1998; Vaillant 2002).

Many children live with gay or lesbian parents; however, limited information is available as to the number of gay and lesbian parents in Australia (Ray & Gregory 2001; McNair et al. 2008; Rawsthorne 2009). While there is often quite heated debate as to the effects of gay or lesbian parenting, studies of gay and lesbian parenting show no negative impacts, with some strengths emerging in terms of greater tolerance of diversity, and greater self-esteem and assertion skills. Stacey and Biblarz (2001) found, for example, in a meta-review that there were no differences of concern. They found that children with lesbian or gay parents showed:

» no differences in psychological or cognitive functioning
» similar levels of closeness and attachment
» less traditionally gendered behaviours and stereotypes
» greater likelihood to be open to homoerotic relationships
» modest and interesting differences, for example being more socially assertive
» that any differences were more associated with responses from the world around them, such as heterosexist social conditions, rather than any aspect of the parent–child relationship.

One of the greatest shifts towards the end of the twentieth century was towards the expectation that families, and particularly partners, provide psychological support and intimacy (Silva & Smart 1999 p. 7). One of the prevailing myths about marriage and family life is that they are considered more advantageous for men than women—both psychologically and practically. In looking at the mental health statistics and economic factors, marriage (or partnership of some form) seems as protective for women as for men, compared to single status (de Vaus 2002). The family is also seen to function as a site for meaning and identity construction. Through the experiences of family rituals, roles and rules, individuals form a continuing sense of self and self-worth within these significant relationships.

Related to these notions of intimacy and support is the family's function as a site for the provision of care. The provision of care within families remains a gendered role, with women providing the majority of informal health care within both the home and the community, often in addition to paid employment obligations (Draper 2000 pp. 340–1). As McDonald (1995 p. 1) comments:

> Families are by far the largest source of emotional, practical and financial support in our society, and most of this support is provided free of charge, in monetary terms at least. The value of emotional support provided by families is inestimable, but the financial value of time and effort provided by households to their members without cost has been calculated as being at least equal to the entire gross national product of the country.

The family as a structure, therefore, also provides economic and physical security, for both children and adults. The majority of women (seventy per cent) between the ages of twenty-five and fifty-four are now employed in the workforce (AIHW 2001). As Tongue and Ballenden (1999 p. 5) note, 'these changes have marked the end of the "male breadwinner" family model'. However, the changes have not meant full economic security for women. Women are still significantly disadvantaged in the workforce, earning on average three-quarters of the average male income. Research has shown that women who are economically able to are more likely to leave the marital situation (Noller et al. 2001). For both women and children, living in a two-parent family relationship provides more economic security than is the case when living in single-female-headed families, which constitute eighty-four per cent of sole-parent families (AIHW 2001). In this case, poverty is a major risk factor across the life course (Greig et al. 2003)—for children, linked with poor outcomes in relation to health, education and mental health, and for adults in relation to health and mental health. Hence, family life does provide an important economic safety net in relation to poverty.

However, families can be the site where much of life's adversity is experienced firsthand, through oppression and intimate terrorism. In these cases, rather than serving a protective function, the family itself becomes the risk factor in the life of a child, woman or, less frequently, a man. The major risk factor identified is family violence, which may include partner abuse or child abuse, or in situations where elderly parents are living with their children, elder abuse. For example, in 2005–06, '167,433 children aged 0–17 years across Australia were the subjects of one or more child protection notifications' (AIHW 2007, p. 50).

The nationally conducted Personal Safety Survey (ABS 2006a) showed that while men experienced more violence than women, 13.4 per cent of women respondents felt unsafe at home alone after dark compared to a significantly smaller number of men (see Table 2.2). Earlier, the Women's Safety Survey (ABS 1996) had found that 2.6 per cent of women who were married or in a de facto relationship had experienced violence perpetrated by their current partner in the twelve months preceding the survey and twenty-three per cent of women who had ever been married or in a de facto relationship had experienced violence in that relationship (Commonwealth Office of the Status of Women 2004).

TABLE **2.2** Experiences of violence and feelings of safety—during the past 12 months

	1996 Women's Safety Survey		2005 Personal Safety Survey			
	Women		Men		Women	
		%		%		%
Experienced violence	490,400	7.1	808,300	10.8	443,800	5.8
Physical violence	404,400	5.9	779,800	10.4	363,000	4.7
Physical assault	346,900	5.0	485,400	6.5	242,000	3.1
Physical threat	284,000	4.1	392,800	5.3	162,400	2.1
Sexual violence	133,100	1.9	46,700	0.6	126,100	1.6
Sexual assault	100,000	1.5	42,300	0.6	101,600	1.3
Sexual threat	44,800	0.7	*5700	0.1	34,900	0.5
Felt unsafe at home alone after dark	1,471,500	21.4	281,900	3.8	1,029,400	13.4
Felt unsafe using public transport alone after dark	384,800	5.6	404,600	5.4	544,800	7.1

* Estimate has a standard error greater than fifty per cent and is considered too unreliable for general use.

Source: ABS 2006a

The privacy of these experiences means that these figures grossly underestimate the extent of family violence, particularly given that psychological abuse is rarely reported due to the lack of substantiating evidence and differing perceptions as to what constitutes abuse.

Rather than focusing on finding a broadly acceptable definition of the family, a focus on those elements that are known to be abusive or destructive in any family formation would contribute more significantly to the well-being of Australians. As Kinnear states (2002 p. ix):

> In the new way of thinking, families are what families do. Rather than trying to ensure that family structure adheres to a preconceived ideal in the hope of greater 'stability', it is better to support all types of families in fulfilling parental functions competently, resolving disputes constructively, and ensuring economic viability and community attachment.

The family, therefore, can be understood as a vital social network. Yet discussion of the family in Western literature has focused primarily on the parental relationship with children; that is, the vertical understandings of the function and structure of family life. This reflects a bias in much of the Western literature available on family life, whereby other significant relationships within families are overlooked. These other significant relationships, less readily identifiable from the national demographic data, include those with siblings, grandparents, extended family networks (including cousins, aunts and uncles) and other groups. Research and policy are beginning to recognise the significant influence of grandparents and siblings in individual well-being, moving away from a focus solely on the nuclear family and on the vertical parent–child relationship. As Mitchell (2003 pp. 1–2) notes, 'Why should there be only one set of relationships which provide the structure of our mind, or why should one be dominant in all times and places?'.

Grandparents are increasingly becoming informal providers of child care to their grandchildren (AIHW 2001), for example. Siblings are now being incorporated more into research around grief and loss, and also into research around child abuse (McVeigh 2003), recognising the capacity for siblings to be perpetrators of abuse. As Cicirelli (1995 p. 2) notes, the sibling relationship is often the longest relationship of the lifespan, as parents die and peers change. He outlines five unique characteristics of the sibling relationship, briefly outlined below.

The role and experience of being a grandparent is explored in Chapter 13.

The sibling relationship is discussed in Chapters 7 to 13.

SIBLING RELATIONSHIPS: CHARACTERISTICS

Research has identified the following characteristics of sibling relationships:

1 They are potentially 'the longest relationship an individual will experience in a total lifetime'—this is increasingly significant as longevity increases.

2 'The sibling relationship is ascribed rather than earned'—unlike other relationships, 'there is no dissolution of the sibling status across the lifespan'.

3   During childhood and adolescence siblings are more people of 'intimate daily contact', whereas in adulthood, the relationship is 'more subject to change or disruption'.

4   A 'relative egalitarianism' exists—siblings establish understandings of equality based on their place within the hierarcy of siblings—with birth order often being a major influence on later psychosocial development.

5   'Sibling lives have in common a long history of shared as well as non-shared experiences.'

Source: Based on Cicirelli 1995 p. 2

Traditional Indigenous Australian family forms emphasise these relationships far more (Bourke & Bourke 1995; Bessarab 2000), with extensive relationships beyond immediate kinship ones being seen as family relationships. The nuclear family is 'one small part of the broader kinship system' (Bessarab 2000 p. 85), which also includes the wider Indigenous community, particularly its elders and other key members. The box below outlines some key features of Indigenous family structures,

FEATURES OF INDIGENOUS FAMILY STRUCTURES

Indigenous family structures are complex kinship and skin networks supporting people well beyond the nuclear family notions that underpin Western or Anglo-Celtic family structures.

The following extract is from *Working with ATSI and their communities* (Upper Hunter Community 2009; reproduced with permission):

A basic principle of this system in traditional societies is the equivalence of same-sex siblings. According to this principle, people who are of the same sex and belong to the same sibling line are viewed as essentially the same. Thus two brothers are considered to be equivalent. If one has a child, that child views not only his biological father as father but applies the same term to the father's brother. The same principle applies to two sisters with both being mothers to any child either one bears. As a father's brother is also identified as father, the latter's children will be brothers and sisters, rather than cousins. This system is known as the classificatory system of kinship because all members of the larger group are classified under the relationship terms. There is no need to expand the range of classifications or relationship terms. Several people are identified by an individual within each classification. Thus a person has several fathers, several mothers, and many brothers and sisters. A mother's brother, being on the same sibling line but of the other sex, is identified as an uncle. A father's sister is an aunt.

The structure of family life will continue to change as a result of individual, social, structural and cultural influences. One way of understanding these transitions is through the lens of a family life cycle (Carter & McGoldrick 1999)—that is, to look at the ways in which there are changes across time between partners, parents and children. Carter and McGoldrick (1999) described a simple model of the heterosexual family, with six fundamental transitions:

1 leaving home—the single young adult
2 the joining of families through marriage—the new couple
3 families with young children
4 families with adolescents
5 launching children and moving on
6 families in later life.

The inadequacies of models of the family life cycle become immediately evident when the statistics of Australian families are presented. The cycle does not accurately represent the experience for many people who live within any family structure other than the nuclear family, or the shifts in families that occur through separation and divorce. Nor does it reflect Indigenous and other collectively oriented family experiences and transitions. In the chapters ahead, we will look at the diversity of ways of thinking about families and our transitions within them. However, what a life cycle model does do is encourage thinking about what is happening for all members within a particular family structure within a particular context and the various role transitions or responsibilities at different times across the lifespan.

Another way of developing an understanding of the structure of an individual's family is to construct a **genogram**. In a genogram for a Western family structure, three generations of family structure are typically included, so that the visual representation gives an understanding of the horizontal and vertical relationships surrounding an individual. Some universal symbols are used to identify key aspects of family life, as Figure 2.1 indicates:.

APPLY YOUR UNDERSTANDING: GENOGRAM

Bianca is a twenty-six-year-old woman in a de facto relationship with Peter. They have just had a baby. Bianca has a child from a previous marital relationship with Shane, whom she divorced three years ago. Bianca's father died when she was ten years old and her mother remarried five years later. She has two brothers, one of whom is in a relationship and has one child; the other is single. Bianca's genogram typically looks like this:

FIGURE **2.1** Bianca's genogram

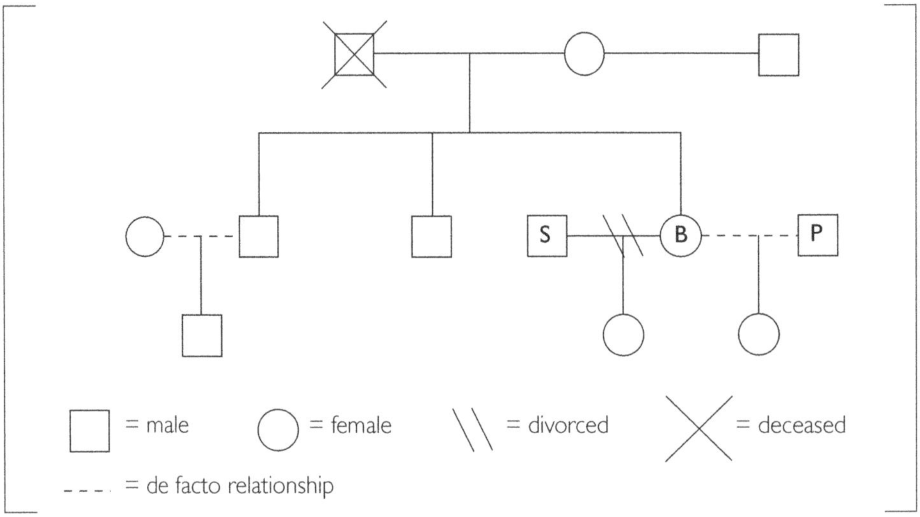

Questions

1   What information would you need to develop a genogram if Bianca was Aboriginal or Torres Strait Islander?
2   How useful do you think a genogram is in practice?
3   What are its strengths and limitations as a tool?

Peer relationships

The other key relationships, and often more intimate relationships, across the lifespan are the peer relationships we develop. While this influence has been noted for the teenage years, there has been less recognition of its influence on earlier development, or indeed on later development. Some peer relationships are enduring right across the lifespan. In recent years, there has been widening recognition that these other groups play a critical role in either improving or inhibiting development, particularly throughout childhood, but also in adulthood. This has arisen as the nurture assumption (Harris 1995; 2000) has been challenged. As Harris (1998 p. 2) argues, 'The use of "nurture" as a synonym for environment is based on the assumption that what influences children's development, apart from their genes, is the way their parents bring them up.' She cites groundbreaking yet unacknowledged research findings by Maccoby and Martin (1983 cited in Harris 1998 p. 38) that the 'correlations between the parents' behavior and the children's characteristics were neither strong nor consistent'—and concluded that 'parental behaviours have no effect, or that the only effective aspects of parenting must vary greatly from one child to the other within the same family'. Instead, she argues that the evidence points to children socialising each other, more so than parents socialising children.

Harris concludes that the influence of the peer group is critical, in terms of language, social and academic development. For example, children adopt the accents of peer group members rather than their parents from a very early age. While previously seen in the context of social networks, these relationships beyond the boundary of the parental relationships are being increasingly recognised as significant in identity formation and certainly in terms of support. In many studies of widows, for example, these networks of relationships have been found to be protective factors in the grief experience (Nelson & Burke 2002). Our intimacy and friendship needs can be met through many diverse relationships.

In Chapters 7 to 13, these relationships are examined more closely.

Wider social networks

People sustain many important ties with others beyond the boundaries of the family and immediate peers. Other networks that are critical include relationships within workplaces, within neighbourhoods and local community groups, volunteer networks, service clubs and other recreational and social settings. We know less about the supportive influence of these networks, because the focus in understanding well-being is so strongly on our intimate relationships (for example, on marital satisfaction). Yet, for those in the workforce, the majority of their waking hours are spent with people they do not necessarily choose to work with. These relationships tend to be regarded as very different from the primacy of home life, and yet these contexts critically influence who we are and how we are.

The importance of these wider connections, in conjunction with the importance of family connections, is shown in Table 2.3. This data is part of the Later Life Families Study conducted by the Australian Institute of Family Studies (Wolcott 1997). They conducted telephone interviews with 721 people aged fifty to seventy years. From the results it is evident that while family is still rated as very important by most men and women, friends and community are also rated as being at least somewhat, if not

TABLE **2.3** Social networks in the Later Life Families Study

	% men			% women		
	Very important	Somewhat important	Not at all important	Very important	Somewhat important	Not at all important
Family	65	31	4	84	15	1
Friends	45	49	6	55	43	2
Community	28	52	20	36	50	14

Source: Wolcott 1997

very, important. If we are concerned with the buffering effect of social relationships, it is critical that our discussions include these relationships as well.

Our **social networks** are comprised of the families, relationships, groups and communities in which we live. Like many sociological concepts, there are many technical definitions of a social network. Gottlieb (1981 p. 31) defines a social network as 'a set of nodes and a set of ties connecting these nodes—where the nodes may be persons, groups, corporate entities or other institutions'. Hirsch (1981 p. 160) defines a social network, as 'a personal community that embeds and supports critical social identities'. Whereas Hirsch's definition gives the impression of a more cohesive social context, Gottlieb's definition importantly allows for differentiation between ties. This differentiation is important, as our ties can vary from person to person or group to group within our networks, and the nature of these ties themselves varies depending on different circumstances.

A social network analysis is useful as a way of understanding our social connections. A common approach to understanding the nature of social networks is to analyse first their composition or structure. **Network composition** refers to the characteristics of network members or, more simply, who is in the network. Then, an analysis of network processes involves understanding the functioning and different attributes of the links between people in a network (Lein & Sussman 1983 p. 6). It involves an analysis of what happens between these people. We will now give an overview of both of these approaches.

Composition or structure

Our social networks can be analysed according to their structural properties, looking at features such as their size, their dispersion and their density (Gottlieb 1981 p. 203). Other factors, such as their heterogeneity or homogeneity, their reachability, or their segmentalisation, are also analysed as potential risk or protective factors.

One of the first aspects of our social networks that is considered is the size of them. That is, how many people do we, or could we, connect with in a direct way? The size of networks can range from limited to extensive (Stone 2001). Garbarino and Abramowitz (1992b) identify the size of a network as one of the key potential risk or protective factors in well-being. This is vividly illustrated in the case example found at the end of this chapter: 'Elsie'. There is no optimally sized social network, although the larger the network, arguably the wider the access to a variety of resources.

The size of an individual's social networks can also vary in terms of what might be considered its active size compared with its latent or dormant size: that is, those with whom we have regular contact and those networks we can activate if we need contact for specific purposes. Significant rituals such as Christmas or New Year are times when we frequently contact those with whom we sustain less contact but whom we would nevertheless see as being part of our social network. The critical question in relation to the optimal size of a social network relates to the adequacy of the available social network in meeting the needs of the individual.

Related to the size of networks is their **geographic dispersion** (Bowling 1997). Networks can range from household and neighbourhood networks to global networks, maintained by travel, telephone, email and the internet. Some people live within the confines of very localised networks, particularly at specific points in the lifespan—for example, when age and frailty may limit access to a widely dispersed network. Others live both physically and indirectly in the context of global communities (Giddens 2002). The risk in only occupying global networks may be that when specific resources are required—for instance those associated with becoming sick—the informal supports that exist at more local levels may not be available.

We may still tend to think of social networks as primarily face-to-face networks, based on the ongoing physical presence of various people. Yet the rapid expansion of social networking technologies has allowed us to communicate via the internet, mobile telephones and video conferencing. These technologies enable both professional and personal networks to be built and maintained in ways previously never thought possible. These technologies have enormous potential in facilitating the development of networks beyond the usual geographic and cultural boundaries we live within (Fook 2000 p. 22).

For example, email, Facebook and other social media networks have enabled the formation of global support groups, not only for socialising but also for people who want to connect with others experiencing a wide range of mental and physical health difficulties. These networks enable people to exchange vital information about their own experiences and the experiences of others, leading to better information, advocacy and support options. They enable the maintenance of contact between people that would not have otherwise been possible—including people with disabilities and elderly people unable to access the physical environment to the same degree as others. A question that remains unanswered is whether these virtual networks have the same capacity to support and enhance well-being that are known to be obtained through direct interpersonal contact.

Other challenges for these networks include their access and authenticity. Given the technology required to sustain these networks, these forms of networking run the risk of remaining the networks of the privileged. However, in the 2006 census, more than sixty-five per cent of all Australian households had direct internet access (ABS 2007b), reflecting a major shift in access from the 2001 census data. While it opens up vast networks of direct and indirect support for some, a small number of Australians cannot access this resource easily, further disadvantaging those with few resources in the first place.

Technology-based social networks may be at risk of exploitation. For instance, paedophiles have been able to gain access to children through establishing false online identities. This highlights the potential risks present without face-to-face contact, and also the need for personal and parental vigilance in their use.

Density (or multiplexity) refers to the degree to which network memberships overlap (Stone 2001 p. 21): that is, the extent to which people know and are connected with each other, forming a strong social web. This leads to a high degree of information exchange about an individual, and the maintenance of secrets becomes difficult or, as Hinde (1979) indicated, there is increased gossip potential across networks. When these networks are positive, this creates an ideal safety net—word gets around quickly in the face of adversity and there is a reduced need to explain what is going on. Rural communities, university residential colleges and boarding schools are examples where dense networks tend to operate. On the other hand, if the network is not supportive, the potential for exclusion or the loss of privacy is increased.

Heterogeneity and homogeneity factors refer to the degree of diversity or similarity among people in a particular network. The strength of a **heterogeneous network** is that it can provide a greater diversity of resources. Its limitation is that the person has to move between many different types of relationships and sustain relationships that may be incompatible with others. The strength of a **homogeneous network** is that there is consistency of relating and of the messages an individual may receive in relation to their identity. The limitations here are that there is a limited pool of resources to draw from and the risk of exclusion is higher. Different groups tolerate different degrees of heterogeneity at different stages of the lifespan. For example, the adolescent peer group tends to privilege homogeneity of networks and tends to be intolerant of much variation.

Reachability refers to how readily an individual can connect with another in the network, or beyond it by a process of referral. That is, how many steps does it take to reach appropriate information or support? For example, if someone needs legal advice, can they contact someone in their network who they know has a sister who is a solicitor, and thus, through a series of steps, quickly access this expertise?

Segmentalisation refers to the extent to which different groups of people are then compartmentalised within a person's network. A highly segmented network is one in which there are lots of distinctive groups of relationships that do not overlap; that is, social worlds do not collide. A network that has low segmentalisation is one in which everyone knows everybody else.

Networks can also be analysed according to the extent to which they are based on formal or informal ties, or according to whether they operate vertically or horizontally across age groups. The structure of a person's network is not a static structure. Social networks are fluid structures, often changing rapidly in response to individual experiences and changes in the social environment.

Processes or interactions

An analysis of the interactional properties of a social network involves an analysis of factors such as the frequency, reciprocity, complementarity, durability and intensity of social relationships, and the subjective experiences or content of them: that is, what happens within the structure.

Frequency refers to the number of contacts that occur between the individual and the people within the social network. We all interact daily with some people and see others rarely. However, frequency does not necessarily determine the significance or meaning of the relationship. While someone may spend all day with their work colleagues or a carer, the relationships that matter to them and provide them with the support they need are the social relationships they maintain outside of the workplace or home situation. This becomes a particularly significant factor if someone is spending most of their time in relationships that are not supportive or nurturing, an issue discussed later in this chapter.

Most relationships have some degree of **reciprocity**. As Hinde (1979 p. 79) notes, 'A reciprocal interaction is one in which the participants show similar behaviour, either simultaneously or alternately'. A simultaneously reciprocal relationship is one in which two people might listen to each others' difficulties and provide mutual support, whereas an alternately reciprocal relationship might mean that through one person's crisis time a friend is supportive, knowing that, in their own time of crisis, that person will be there for them. Reciprocity reflects the obligation or investment that typically binds relationships together.

Reciprocity is also used to refer to exchanges at different points—support in one form might be provided by a parent, which is later reciprocated in their old age by their own children. Reciprocity is often referred to as the 'social glue' (Silverstein et al. 2002), creating an insurance or investment in supportive relationships. In many instances, particularly family situations, **lagged reciprocity** occurs. This refers to a situation in which 'the provision of support to older parents was the fulfilment of an obligation to repay a social debt based on that parent's earlier transfers to the child' (Silverstein et al. 2002 p. S3). Around all of our relationships, therefore, are what can be termed the norms of reciprocity (Stone 2001). Different relationships can sustain different degrees of resource exchange—on an in-kind versus an in lieu basis, on a direct versus an indirect basis, or on an immediate versus a delayed basis. These are all questions relating to the degree of demand or expectation that can be placed on our different relationships.

In the Later Life Families Study (Wolcott 1997) mentioned earlier, reciprocity in relationships was examined. The giving and receiving of support was clearly evident between the generations, as Table 2.4 indicates. The perceptions of the older adults surveyed were that they were supporting and were supported by their adult children, across emotional, financial and practical dimensions, and that they were

TABLE **2.4** Reciprocity in later life

	Emotional		Financial		Practical	
	Men	Women	Men	Women	Men	Women
	%	%	%	%	%	%
Support to adult children	87	94	76	70	79	85
Support from adult children	70	89	14	30	72	82
Support to parents/in-laws	71	75	35	34	63	73
Support from parents/in-laws	39	47	17	22	22	34

Source: Wolcott 1997 p. 23

supported also by parents, although there seems to be lagged reciprocity evident in this relationship.

Complementarity has also been identified as an important interactional quality. It refers to the times when 'the behaviour of each participant differs from, but complements, that of the other' (Hinde 1979 p. 79). Mentor and mentee relationships are complementary relationships, where the investment in the relationship and the direction of the flow of resources differs but creates the basis for a working relationship.

Durability, or the extent to which relationships last over time, can be an indicator of the strength of the investment in a relationship. Family relationships are considered more durable than other relational types, where different norms around reciprocity and obligation tend to operate. Friendships are protective because of their capacity to provide a sense of meaning and coherence, in some instances right across the lifespan. However, the durability of the relationship may not necessarily indicate its significance. Under some circumstances, short-term relationships and connections can be particularly powerful protective factors, providing resources and support appropriate to the situation in which people find themselves.

These issues of reciprocity, complementarity and durability are connected with the strength or intensity of the ties within the network. Granovetter (1982), through his research into the ways in which people went about finding employment and the degree to which they were successful, proposed a theory of the **strength of**

weak ties. He found that those who relied on close family and friends took much longer to find employment than those who were able to make loose but purposive connections (that is, exert reachability) through their networks. Strong ties might be required in some situations, but Granovetter highlighted that weak ties also had a very significant role in others. For families who voluntarily or involuntarily migrate and find themselves without pre-existing networks and familiar personal linkages around them, the loss of both these weak and strong ties can constitute major losses and lead to vulnerability within their new communities.

Related to this issue of the strength of ties is the intensity of them. How obliged is an individual to participate in the relationship? Some relationships are loaded with far greater expectations and emotional investment than others. While they may not be networks in which there is regular interaction, the influence they exert can be profound.

The subjective experience of a social network refers to the perception and meaning a person has of their various relationships. This is sometimes referred to as the **content** of a social network, as it focuses on what is actually transacted or exchanged. We frequently distinguish between relationships in terms of what they provide for us. Some relationships are maintained because they are family relationships and seen to have a particular significance, quite different from other friendships. As Ornish (1998 p. 24) notes, 'While some studies measure the *number* or *structure* of social relationships, I believe that it is your perception of the *quality* of those relationships—how you feel about them—that is most important'. He proposes that the simple rating of whether we feel loved may be as effective as any complex network analysis if we are to understand whether our social networks are providing adequate support or not.

Toxic environments

Our social networks should not be thought of as being synonymous with support. They may be negative or positive, or vary in their capacity to be either negative or positive depending on specific circumstances. Gottlieb (1981 p. 30) comments on the 'romanticism and myopia that has seeped into research on the topic of social support'. His comment is a salient reminder to all that our social networks have the capacity to both enhance and inhibit our experience and our coping capacities. They are 'the source of demands and constraints on individuals, as well as supports and opportunities' (Lein & Sussman 1983 p. 4).

While a person might have an extensive social network around them, the impact of the network may be negative. This was affirmed in a recent study of young people who were involved in long-term psychotherapy following extreme childhood adversity and later difficulties in early adulthood relating to homelessness, substance abuse and relationship issues. While it was anticipated that these young people, through their earlier experiences of abuse and neglect and homelessness would have minimal social networks, particularly family networks, around them, they in fact reported strong social networks. However, these networks were characterised by criticism and conflict (Harms & McDermott 2003).

Social dimensions

Social support

In looking at the structure and properties of social networks, we have laid the basis for analysing the positive and sustaining resources that are exchanged within these networks, referred to as social support. Three types of **social support** are typically identified as being the resources exchanged within the context of relationships, however weak or strong—material, emotional and instrumental support.

Material support, or concrete support, as it is sometimes called, refers to the tangible resources that are exchanged. These resources might include financial resources or other resources such as food, housing, transport or clothing (McDonald 1995). They can be exchanged formally through welfare programs such as those offered by the Salvation Army and the Red Cross. These formal networks are identified as key providers of these supports in times of community crisis, with well-established structures and strategies for distribution of these resources. Local community groups also mobilise these resources through programs such as Meals on Wheels, for example. These resources can also be exchanged informally among family and friends.

Emotional support, also referred to as expressive or affective support, refers to the resources we receive when we are seeking validation, opportunities for ventilation, advice, consolation, comfort or a listening ear. Others describe this emotional support as including 'love, understanding and counsel' (McDonald 1995 p. 16). In many ways, this is a less tangible form of support than material support, but similarly it may be offered formally or informally. For example, following the Bali nightclub bombing, the Victorian Department of Human Services placed advertisements in the newspapers inviting people to attend debriefing sessions and giving those affected the opportunity to receive counselling support. In many workplaces, critical incident stress debriefings (CISD) are offered, a session of debriefing that is part of wider critical incident stress management (CISM) strategies (Robinson & Mitchell 1993). Such support might also be provided through mentoring programs such as the Big Brother, Big Sister program or

Canteen, the teenage cancer support group. Informally, we are sustained regularly by interactions and conversations with partners, family, peers, colleagues, neighbours and others who are able to provide this kind of support.

The group work literature is helpful in understanding what goes on between people in relation to the emotional support provided within the context of relationships. Irvin Yalom (1985), in his analysis of the therapeutic factors that operate in groups, identified eleven protective factors, which are outlined below.

YALOM'S ELEVEN THERAPEUTIC GROUP FACTORS

1 Instillation of hope: a confidence and optimism in the ability of the group and individual members to resolve issues and grow.
2 Universality: the sense that others share similar problems and feelings, and that one is not alone—the 'all-in-the-same-boat' phenomenon.
3 Imparting of information: leaders and group members sharing information and guidance about problems and concerns.
4 Altruism: the benefits experienced when one realises that one has helped another person.
5 Corrective recapitulation of the primary family group: the (re)experiencing of relationship patterns like those in the family of origin, while learning different approaches to relationships.
6 Development of socialising techniques: the examination of patterns of interacting with others and the acquisition of new social skills.
7 Imitative behaviour: observation of how other group members handle their problems and feelings, and recognition of how those methods apply to one's own situation.
8 Interpersonal learning: the process of learning about self through interaction with others.
9 Group cohesiveness: a sense of belonging that group members have ('we-ness'), and a sense of acceptance and support.
10 Catharsis: the sharing of deep and sometimes painful emotions with non-judgmental acceptance for group members.
11 Existential factors: the search for meaning and purpose in life.

Source: Yalom, Irvin D. 1985, *The theory and practice of group psychotherapy*, 4th edn, Basic Books, a member of Perseus Books, LLC; reproduced with permission.

Instrumental support, often referred to as task support, refers to the practical assistance that is offered, which might include assistance with negotiating systems (such as the Court Network program for those negotiating the court system), with transport arrangements (such as the Red Cross Patient Transport program) or child-care arrangements. Informally, instrumental support is exchanged through a multitude of ways, with family members assisting another family move house or through minding grandchildren.

As many authors note, attempts to distinguish between these types of support are often artificial (Scott 1992). Many gestures of instrumental or material support are arguably also gestures of emotional support, such as the cooking of meals following the birth of a new baby.

Social capital

Increasingly, **social capital** is a term appearing frequently in research and policy. This shift in emphasis to social capital is intended to increase and strengthen the resources of individuals, families and communities—and simultaneously, to decrease the reliance on governments and welfare structures for support. The notion is applied in a number of different ways. Robert Putnam (1995 p. 67), for example, states that:

> By analogy with notions of physical capital and human capital—tools and training that enhance individual productivity—'social capital' refers to features of social organization such as networks, norms and social trust that facilitate coordination and cooperation for mutual benefit.

From a social work perspective, Jack (2000 p. 7) describes social capital as social cohesion, more loosely seen in:

> … all the personal social networks of a particular community, the day-to-day exchanges between friends, relatives and neighbours, work colleagues, church members, political and social groups, community activities and official organizations.

While there are different ways of understanding social capital, there is some consensus that social capital refers to 'networks of social relations which are characterised by norms of trust and reciprocity' (Stone 2001 p. 4). These definitions resonate with the discussion in Chapter 1 about the degree to which there is a goodness of fit between the individual and their environment—where there is high social cohesion and cooperation, there can be mutual benefit.

Social capital is seen as residing in a number of levels within society—most commonly within communities or within nations and, to a lesser extent, within families. As distinct from social support, social capital is understood as having both negative and positive functions. In particular, it 'can explain much social exclusion, because the same ties that bind also exclude' (Narayan 1999 p. 5).

Three distinct types of social capital are recognised: bonding, bridging and building social capital. Bonding social capital refers to links within communities 'to people like you, for getting by in life'. Bridging social capital refers to links 'to people not like you, for getting on in life', and building, or linking, social capital refers to connections 'to people at a different step in the social ladder for obtaining access to resources and knowledge' (National Economic and Social Forum 2003 p. 4).

Social capital is seen as the property of communities and nations rather than the property of individuals. It 'exists only when it is shared' (Narayan 1999 p. 6). This highlights that social capital is seen as 'a resource between individuals, which inheres within and between social networks' (Stone 2001 p. 9). Thus, while a focus on social support tends to look at the degree to which an individual benefits from supportive networks, a focus on social capital looks at the way in which society also benefits.

The functions of social support and social capital

There are two dominant models outlining the way in which the social networks can operate as either a source of protection or vulnerability. They are the main effect and the stress buffering models (D'Abbs 1982; Noller et al. 2001).

The **main effect model** argues that social networks and connections 'provide us with regular positive experiences, and within the network, a set of stable roles (expectations about behaviour) enables us to enjoy stability of mood, predictability in life situations and recognition of self worth' (Hutchison 2003 pp. 146–7). Thus, because of the positive influence of social support, situations are not perceived as being threatening in the first place.

The **stress buffering** model proposes that social support is an intervening factor between the stressful life event and the perception of threat inherent in that event (Eckenrode & Gore 1981). Thus, a stressor is recognised, but the individual's analysis of the event is that there are adequate internal and external resources to manage the situation successfully. This perception of adequate coping resources intercepts the cognitive, emotional and physiological arousal caused by the stressor. Such a view is evident in Caplan's (1974 p. 6) definition of social support:

> The significant others help the individual mobilize [their] psychological resources, and master [their] emotional burdens; they share [their] tasks; and they supply [them] with extra supplies of money, materials, tools, skills, and cognitive guidance to improve [their] handling of [their] situation.

Thinking slightly differently about the function of social support, Martin (1997 pp. 164–7) has identified it as having four protective functions:

1 It provides 'an antidote to reduce the impact of stressors'.
2 It provides an important 'reality check'.
3 It 'protects us from dangerous self-neglect, denial and complacency'.
4 It promotes healthy behaviour.

Social support is recognised as a protective factor in both physical and mental health. One of the most outstanding studies that showed its protective function in physical health is the study conducted by Spiegel, Bloom, Kramer and Gottheil (1989), which examined the influence of participating in psychosocial support groups on the survival experiences of women with breast cancer. Women with advanced breast cancer were randomly assigned to two groups—one received ninety minutes of supportive, expressive group therapy a week for one year and the other did not. Five years later, all of the women in the non-intervention group had died, compared with fifty per cent of those who had participated in the social intervention group. This study is being replicated in Australia (McDermott 2002).

Other life experiences that have been studied in relation to the protective function of social support include pregnancy. Researchers found that women who had 'a higher quantity and quality of social support during pregnancy experience shorter and easier labours, deliver heavier babies in better overall condition and suffer from less post-natal depression' (Collins et al. 1993). Similarly, Frazier, Tix, Klein and Arikian (2000) found better adjustment among renal transplant recipients and their significant others who received support (and particularly when it enabled cognitive restructuring). They found that social withdrawal was associated with poorer adjustment.

Studies have also shown a protective link between mental health and social support. In relation to trauma experiences, Boscarino (1995) found that Vietnam veterans who had lower social support had higher rates of post-traumatic stress disorder (PTSD) and associated disorders, years after the trauma of war occurred. Studies such as this one raise important questions of causality—does low social support lead to experiences of PTSD or does the experience of PTSD lead people to withdraw from and find it difficult to engage in social relationships? Either way, the link between social isolation and ongoing mental health difficulties is a clearly established one.

Viktor Frankl's (1984) account of surviving the Second World War concentration camps vividly portrays the anchoring, if not survival, influence of social support. Frankl identified two key roles of social support. First, he described the continuation of social support, evident in the concern for the survival of fellow inmates, in the most impoverished of social conditions. Second, he described how received social support in the past is internalised and has positive reverberations in the future when the actual support is not there to be received in any active sense. By recalling his good relationship with his wife, he was able to maintain a strong sense of hope and optimism. Thus, past good experiences of social support become part of our inner world. Psychodynamic theorists talk about this as the internalisation of good inner objects. This highlights the importance of perceived support, as distinct from received support.

APPLYING YOUR UNDERSTANDING: AN ECOMAP

For the purposes of assessment and intervention, it is often useful to map out someone's social network visually. One way of indicating both the structural and interactional properties of a social network is by drawing an ecomap (Hepworth et al. 2002 pp. 346–7). An **ecomap** identifies all the significant relationships in an individual's environment: that is, the relational context. It then enables the social context to be described, as it portrays some of the qualitative aspects of these relationships and their interconnectedness. For example, some of the qualities that can be included in an ecomap are the strength or weakness of the relationships, the direction of them or degree of reciprocity involved, and their negative or positive qualities. It can be a creative map of an individual's immediate context that begins to highlight the risk and protective factors in the social environment.

An ecomap shows the immediate context of the individual. It does not show the broader structural and cultural layers of influence, as a multidimensional map might (see Figure 1.8). An ecomap can also be used to show changes over time, with both past and present connections being included in the map.

Andrew: a new start

Andrew is admitted to a youth drug and alcohol residential withdrawal service, following strong pressure from his girlfriend to attend. His heroin addiction is out of control and his girlfriend has threatened to leave him if he does not do something about it. They have recently moved from interstate, following a major argument with his two best friends, who allege that he owed them money. These friends are on drug-related charges and they suspect Andrew told police about their activities when he was questioned about a theft incident. The allegation in Andrew's case was dropped. He is now in the same state as his father, although his mother and older brother remain interstate.

Andrew is relieved to be away from his friends. He will be moving to new housing as a result of working with his Drug and Alcohol Worker, and he has been offered an apprenticeship through Centrelink. He sees this as a new start for himself.

Andrew's ecomap is shown in Figure 2.2.

FIGURE **2.2** Andrew's ecomap

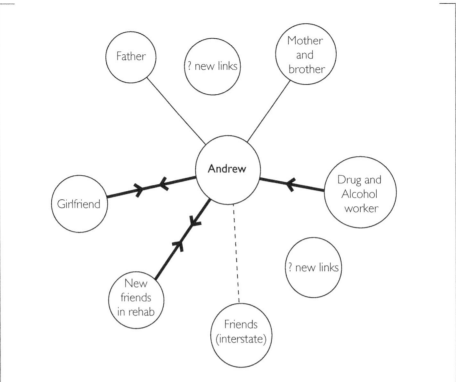

Questions

1 What formal and informal networks would you want to see Andrew creating to support himself more fully?
2 What difference would it make for you in understanding Andrew's networks, as presented in the ecomap, if he was either thirteen or eighteen?

MAPPING A CLIENT'S SOCIAL NETWORK WITH AN ECOMAP

Fill in connections where they exist. Indicate the nature of connections with a descriptive word or by drawing different kinds of lines for relationships that are:

» strong
» tenuous
» stressful

Draw arrows along lines to signify the flow of energy, resources, etc. Identify significant people and fill in empty circles as needed.

Factors influencing the availability of social support

The discussion so far has focused on the structure and functions of social networks. Whether or not these networks exist in the first place depends on a wide variety of factors, including the potential an individual has of forming social relationships in a particular context, and the availability of these social relationships within the outer world. These opportunities are influenced by factors such as age, gender, motivation, culture, social class, structural opportunity and physical location.

Our age, and with it our place in the family life-cycle, determines many of the opportunities for forming networks. Infants and young children are dependent upon others for provision of and access to social networks. In early and middle adulthood, the workplace is a ready provider of social interaction. Retirement often brings with it massive changes in social interaction and social support, given the absence of regular daily contact with others. The increased workforce participation of women has inevitably changed the nature of social networks and in particular the volunteer workforce. In late adulthood, networks often diminish through the death of peers or through diminished mobility.

Men's and women's support networks seem to differ greatly (Bell 1981; Lein & Sussman 1983 p. 4). Many studies have found that women participate in more extensive and more intimate social networks than men (for example, Hobfoll 1986), whereas men's friendship patterns are characterised more by sociability and task than by intimacy and relationship-building (Tannen 1996). As Noller, Feeney and Peterson (2001 p. 99) suggest, 'women tend to emphasize the importance of caring, interdependence and expressiveness'.

Other people are unable to participate in social networks for health or personality reasons. For example, following the experience of brain injury many people find that they are unable to sustain the social networks they had previously (Rowlands 1999). Similarly, diminished social network participation is noted in those with mental health difficulties such as schizophrenia and depression (Commonwealth Department of Health and Aged Care 2000 p. 13; Bloch & Singh 1997; Raphael 2000). This often leads to loneliness and depression, further compounding the difficulties already faced in adapting to a brain injury or mental illness.

CHAPTER SUMMARY

Human development and adaptation occurs in the context of social relationships. In this chapter, these social relationships have been interpreted as networks of connections, made up of the many complex and fluid links with other people. The family remains a notion and an experience that draws much heated debate from policy makers and practitioners alike. It can be understood in many ways—from conservative or liberal perspectives, from positive or negative perspectives, from structural and functional perspectives, and from the statistical perspective to the intensely personal and individualistic viewpoint of our own lived experience.

While the family continues to receive the most attention as the key relational context that influences experience, other critical relational and social dimensions exist that influence developmental experiences across the lifespan. These include relationships with extended family members, peers, neighbours and school or work colleagues. As households change in their structure and function, and as the current generation of young children—for whom child care, before and after school programs and family reformation are normal experiences—move into their adult life, very different understandings of the role and significance of many family functions will emerge.

One way of understanding these relationships and the degree to which they promote resilience or increase experiences of vulnerability and risk is to consider both the structural and interactional properties of these networks. Social networks are regarded as significant, given their potential to provide the necessary material, emotional and instrumental resources we need for our optimal development and well-being. What we do not know a great deal about yet is the impact of social support provided through very different means from previous generations—as the nature of community, family and work life changes, both in terms of structure and function, social support will be exchanged differently. With these social changes, as well as rapidly changing technologies, social support will be provided and distributed differently within local communities, and indeed globally.

Social support and social capital are important for the maintenance of physical and mental health and well-being. However, it is essential in any consideration of the structural and interactional properties of networks that promote resilience to recognise the subjective perceptions of these networks. The goodness of fit between what individuals want and need by way of social support and what they can access seems to be one of the critical factors underpinning these properties. Throughout the rest of this book, the protective potential of positive social support is discussed as a key resilience factor.

APPLYING A MULTIDIMENSIONAL UNDERSTANDING

Elsie: Forgotten, she died alone

The elderly woman at 203 McKinnon Road shut the world out so tightly that nobody noticed she was gone. Over the years, her circle contracted as she became distant from family and friends and finally pushed away her well-meaning neighbours, retreating into a few dim rooms at the back of the old dry-cleaning store. Those neighbours yesterday described Elsie Maude Brown as a 'very private person' who was estranged from her husband and, to their knowledge, never had any relatives or friends visit.

Last Wednesday, police found Mrs Brown's remains draped in a blanket on her couch. They believe her body may possibly have been there for twenty-three months. Newspapers and mail found inside her house date back to May 2001.

Mrs Brown owned two adjacent properties in Bentleigh—both with shopfronts and rear residences—in south suburban Bentleigh for at least 30 years. When Tina Murcia and her husband Jamie bought one of the properties from Mrs Brown four years ago, the property was blanketed in darkness. There were three layers of curtains inside and shade cloth was nailed across the windows outside.

On two occasions previously authorities feared for Mrs Brown. The second time, about two years ago, the Murcias had raised the alarm when broken glass remained on the pavement outside the home of their usually tidy neighbour and mail was visible at the front door. Mrs Brown only called out that she was OK when the police broke her door down.

This time, Ms Murcia notified authorities after receiving a phone call from Melbourne Water about Mrs Brown's outstanding bills. The discovery of her neighbour's corpse confirmed her worst fears.

'My husband and I always thought it would be this way … but it's still very sad', she said. 'She didn't want to be noticed. She didn't want anyone to know she was even in there. She didn't have lights on at night—never. It was like she wasn't there'.

The local council said Mrs Brown had never been on its books as someone needing care. 'Unless someone contacts us with some concerns, we have no idea who needs help,' a spokesman said.

Neighbour Maurice Hadley said he had not seen Mrs Brown, whom he knew as Betty, for about four years. 'When I was a kid we knew everyone in the street by name. Now you can live in a place for 27 years and you only know your neighbours on either side. I reckon it's an indictment on society,' he said.

Source: Gallagher & Murdoch, 2003, *The Age*, 17 March; reproduced with permission.

CASE STUDY

Questions

1   What is your personal reaction to her situation?
2   Which dimensions of individual, context, time and experience do you see as either risk and/or protective factors for Mrs Brown?
3   What could have prevented this situation, in terms of intervention at a:
   * direct practice level?
   * program level?
   * policy level?

KEY TERMS

complementarity

content

durability

ecomap

emotional support

family

frequency

genogram

geographic dispersion

heterogeneous network

homogeneous network

instrumental support

lagged reciprocity

main effect model

material support

network composition

reachability

reciprocity

segmentalisation

social capital

social network

social support

strength of weak ties

stress buffering model

QUESTIONS AND DISCUSSION POINTS

1   What are some key structural and functional properties of families?
2   Who would you include in definitions of the family and why?
3   Why are structural dimensions such major influences on family life?
4   In what ways do cultural dimensions influence family life?
5   Identify the structure of your own family network by drawing a genogram, using Figure 2.1 as an example.
6   What functions do you see your family performing?
7   What assumptions about the family do you think are implicit and explicit in the media?
8   What are some key structures and functions of social networks?
9   What is an ecomap?

10 What are the three types of social support?

11 In what ways do social capital and social support differ?

12 What factors influence the availability of social support?

13 What are some of the other groups and networks to which you belong that you see as being major influences in your life?

14 Thinking about a situation that has been particularly stressful for you, identify whether you thought there were social supports available to you and what some of these sources were. Develop an ecomap (using the example shown in Figure 2.2) showing your social network throughout this time.

15 To what extent do you see yourself located in local networks, based on geographic proximity?

16 In what ways have your networks changed since your childhood or adolescence?

FURTHER READING

Gilding, M. 2002, 'Families of the new millenium: Designer babies, cyber sex and virtual communities', *Family Matters*, 62, pp. 4–10.

Hepworth, D., Rooney, R. & Larsen, J. A. 2002, *Direct social work practice: Theory and skills*, Pacific Grove: Brooks/Cole.

Morphy, F. 2006, 'Lost in translation: Remote Indigenous households and definitions of the family', *Family Matters* 73, pp. 23–31.

Putnam, R. 1995, 'Bowling alone: America's declining social capital', *Journal of Democracy*, 6(1), pp. 65–78.

Stone, W. 2001, *Measuring social capital: Towards a theoretically informed measurement framework for researching social capital in family and community life*, Melbourne: Australian Institute of Family Studies.

WEBSITES OF INTEREST

Brotherhood of St Laurence: www.bsl.org.au

The Brotherhood of St Laurence is one of the major providers of welfare to the Australian community, through social action programs and research. The site provides information about many programs and research activities, as well as useful links.

The Community Portal: www.community.gov.au

This site provides information for Australian communities and community groups.

Department of Planning and Community Development: www.dpcd.vic.gov.au
   This site has information about creating 'liveable communities that are
   sustainable, connected and inclusive'.

Department of Sociology, University of Toronto: http://know.soc.utoronto.ca/
   This site contains direct links to research projects relating to social, structural
   and cultural risk and protective factors.

Domestic Violence Resource Centre (Victoria): www.dvirc.org.au
   This site provides information about domestic violence services and supports,
   as well as research and other links.

Infoxchange Australia: www.infoxchange.net.au
   This site provides information to the Australian community services sector.

Our Community: www.ourcommunity.com.au
   This site provides resources to build community capacity across Australia.

Robert Putnam's 'Bowling Alone' site: www.bowlingalone.com
   Robert Putnam is a key social capital theorist. His site provides useful
   theoretical material and links.

Stronger Families and Communities Strategy: National Evaluation: www.fahcsia.
gov.au/sa/communities/progserv/documents/sfcs_report/sec1.htm
   This site gives an overview of the Australian Government's Stronger Families
   and Communities Strategy.

The World Bank group: www.worldbank.org
   The World Bank is 'a development Bank which provides loans, policy advice,
   technical assistance and knowledge sharing services to low and middle income
   countries to reduce poverty'. The site has many links relating to research and
   projects to achieve this end.

Structural and Cultural Dimensions

AIMS OF THIS CHAPTER

This chapter explores the broad influences of the structural and cultural contexts in which we live, highlighting both risk and protective factors. It considers the following questions:

» What are key structural influences on the family, social networks and well-being?
» What are key cultural influences on well-being?

As emphasised in Chapters 1 and 2, we all have wider contexts of influence than just our immediate networks of relationships. These wider contextual factors can influence enormously both the exposure to various experiences and resources and the capacity of individuals to manage the demands inherent in these experiences. While inner-world factors play a major part in our development and experiences, a multidimensional approach to understanding human development encourages a focus on other dimensions—the wider structural and cultural dimensions of a person's context—as well. Social workers address inequalities and risks within these dimensions as often or more often than they address inner-world dimensions.

It is beyond the scope of this book to explore all of aspects of the structural and cultural dimensions in detail. However, in each of the chapters ahead, we will look at how the structural and cultural dimensions can be understood to influence development and experience broadly, and how to understand them as risk or protective factors. In this chapter, we look in an introductory and example-driven way at some key ways in which the structural and cultural dimensions influence some aspects of family and social support experiences and well-being more generally.

For further discussion of these dimensions, refer to Mullaly (2002), Thompson (2003) or Allan, Briskman & Pease (2009).

Structural dimensions

The structural dimensions of a multidimensional approach were introduced in Chapter 1 (pages 14–15) as the key systems which influence our individual, interpersonal and social contexts: for instance, political, labour market, transport, education and health systems and organisations. We do not have direct face-to-face relationships with these systems, but the decisions made within them influence our daily life profoundly.

On a daily basis, decisions made at the structural or policy level profoundly influence the resources and opportunities available to individuals, families, neighbourhoods and nations. Many resources and opportunities are provided through government and non-government sources, at all levels of the community, from the neighbourhood level to the national level. In this way, structural dimensions can either enable socially just resource distribution or institutionalise oppression and inequality (Habibis & Walter 2009). The availability of resources is critical for optimal individual, family and community well-being. A key focus for social workers in practice is understanding and working to alleviate the negative impact of structural dimensions—particularly experiences of oppression and exclusion that see individuals or families unable to participate in their community or the wider society in which they live due to a lack of resources and opportunities. Structural violence and oppression occur when:

> social divisions, practices, and processes, along with social institutions, laws, policies, and the economic and political systems, all work together to benefit the dominant group at the expense of subordinate groups (Mullaly 2002 p. 97).

While Mullaly highlights a single 'dominant group', structural violence and oppression often benefits many different dominant groups within a social context, thus adding to the complexity of alliances and influences on individual lives. This is seen, for example, in the structural dimensions influencing family life, the first focus of discussion.

Influences on the family

In Chapter 2, we looked at how significant relational and social networks are for promoting well-being. Here we look at how these relationships are influenced by wider structural dimensions. Three very significant influences on family life are the advances in medical knowledge and technology (and the influence of these advances on both reproduction and longevity), legislative changes and religion.

Increases in health funding, research and knowledge, leading to advances in medical technology, have led to some of the major shifts in recent decades in the forms families take. Australia's population is entering into a well-noted significant period of change, due to 'declining mortality rates and low levels of fertility over a long period' (AIHW 2001 p. 264). Medical knowledge and technology mean many people live with or are cured from illnesses that in previous generations would have led to earlier deaths. The result of this is that the median age of the Australian population will have increased from 34.3 years in 1997 to 'between 43.7 and 46.2 years in 2051' (AIHW 2001). In particular, this is related to the ageing of the non-Indigenous, post Second World-War baby-boomer generation.

Within the Australian context, one outcome of people living to increasingly older ages is that intimate partnerships and family relationships are sustained for longer than has ever been the case before, presenting new opportunities and challenges for family members. With life expectancy increasing, there are significant shifts—the increased length of relationships, the increased dependency burden in later adult life as more people live with more chronic health problems, and the increasing age of carers, with many sixty-year-olds and seventy-year-olds providing ongoing care and support for parents in their eighties and nineties respectively. The family and the structural context will adapt in new ways to these shifts.

Not only has medical knowledge and technology sustained the health of Australia's population in ways not previously seen; this knowledge and technology also enables the control of fertility and reproduction. In vitro fertilisation techniques have given infertile couples and single or lesbian women the opportunity to have children. More profoundly, however, the availability of the contraceptive pill in the 1960s radically altered women's ability to control pregnancy, and the separation of sexuality and reproduction became possible. Thus, changes in legislation relating to the availability of certain treatments or medications in turn influence the structures and functions of relationships, families and the wider community.

Legislative changes have also directly influenced the changing form of families. The amendments to the *Family Law Act 1975* (Cth) brought about the most significant changes, with its refocusing of the grounds for divorce on 'irretrievable breakdown' of the relationship, proven by a one-year separation period rather than the need to prove fault, as had previously been the case. This is in contrast to previous eras of history, when, some have argued, there was less need for divorce laws—for example, because there was the likelihood of the death of a spouse in a relatively short period of time (Phillips 1988 pp. 392–4). As the cultural expectations about the focus of family life shift to be more about the emotional needs of family members rather than exclusively about economic stability and reproduction, so too do the legal constraints.

Legal recognition of the status of de facto relationships and, increasingly, gay and lesbian relationships has provided many couples and families with the rights and securities previously afforded to married couples only. In Australia, debates continue about the rights of homosexual couples to access marriage and IVF treatment, forcing legislators and the community to reconsider what it is that defines the family and to confront the deeply entrenched homophobia in the wider community.

Organised religion has also had a profound effect in prescribing the rules and roles within family life (Phillips 1988). This includes the arrangement of marriages, expectations around reproduction (with, for example, the banning of the use of contraception within the Catholic faith tradition), and the determining of marital and parenting rights and obligations on the basis of gender roles. While many people in Australia are no longer affected as strongly by these doctrines as in previous generations, many others who live in more orthodox faith traditions continue to abide by them. Many migrant communities also bring strong religious faith and practices with them as they settle in Australia.

These changes cut across the belief of earlier generations that we are genetically programmed to form nuclear families (Gilding 2002). In fact, we seem to be emerging from a period of historical aberration—the baby boom after the Second World War (McDonald 1995)—the so-called 'traditional' nuclear family is now recognised as only one of many possible family forms. Thus, any consideration of the family needs to include the notion of families over time and in a particular context: families undergoing both their own transitions across the lifespan and transitions as a consequence of the wider cultural and structural environment.

HOUSEHOLD, INCOME AND LABOUR DYNAMICS IN AUSTRALIA (HILDA) SURVEY

The Household, Income and Labour Dynamics in Australia (HILDA) survey began in 2001 by interviewing 19,914 people from 7,682 households in Australia in an effort to track the influence of household, income and labour dynamics. Each year, household members are interviewed so that trends and changes in people's experiences can be identified.

Some key findings include:

» 'approximately 51% of all Australians were living in a couple with children household each year, while around 12% were in lone parent households and 10% lived alone'

» 'couple families are the most stable, with 91% who were in a couple only household in 2005 remaining in that category in 2006'

» 'Lone parent households are also quite stable, with 85% of individuals who were living in lone parent households in 2005 still living in a lone parent household in 2006'

Source: Wilkins et al. 2009 pp. 2–3, copyright Commonwealth of Australia; reproduced by permission.

Influences on social networks

Structural dimensions determine not only family experiences, but also other relational opportunities, through social networks. Research highlights that social class, and therefore structural opportunity, strongly influences the types of social networks that form (Greig et al. 2003). As Jack (2000 p. 709) notes, social support 'can be fatally undermined by inequalities and divisions or exclusions within a society, which act as barriers to the open and reciprocal interaction on which social cohesion thrives'. In a qualitative study of two housing estates in London, for example, it was found that 'a fear of crime and other indicators of a lack of trust deterred residents from making social contacts' (Cattell 2001 pp. 1507–8). Similar concerns have been raised in many large public housing estates in Australian cities. Yet in other settings, residents in state housing communities are engaged in strategies to address the issues of poverty and, by doing so, reduce social isolation through establishing very active tenants' groups (Quinn 2000) or community garden projects. Cattell concludes that 'deprivation can be both a cause of hopelessness and a spur to social action' (Cattell 2001 p. 1512).

Financial resources do, however, enable more diverse networks of support to be established. As mentioned earlier, access to mobile phone connections, the internet and social networking technology is not available to all Australians. Other differences on the basis of class have also been observed (D'Abbs 1982 pp. 32–4), such as:

» Middle-class adults maintain networks over a greater geographical area.
» In older working-class areas, relationships are multiplex and neighbours are more significant than in middle-class areas.
» Differences in perception about the meaning attached to specific types of relationships may exist.
» Outer-urban fringe dwellers are the most socially cohesive.

The influence of class and structural opportunities on the formation of social networks is evident in the 'Life Chances' study, conducted by the Brotherhood of St Laurence in Melbourne (Taylor & Fraser, 2003 Taylor & Macdonald 1998). The box on page 76 provides a brief overview of the study and some of the key findings when the children were six.

From both subjective and objective reports of social participation, families on lower incomes seem to be excluded from some of the known protective opportunities within social networks, such as safe neighbourhoods, peer networks and extracurricular activities.

In Chapter 9 we look at the subsequent report, 'Life at Eleven'.

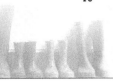

LIFE CHANCES PROJECT

Life at Six

The Brotherhood of St Laurence established the 'Life Chances' study in 1990 in Melbourne. The 'Life at Six' report details the findings from interviews with 148 families over six years, examining 'the changes in their families' lives since the birth of the children and the current situations of the children and families'.

Some of the key findings are:

» the families had high geographic mobility, with almost three-quarters of the families having moved away from the inner suburbs since the children's births
» seventy-four per cent of children had been living continuously with both their natural parents
» twenty-six per cent of the children had lived in sole-parent families at some stage
» almost one third of the children lived in families on low incomes.

Of those living on low incomes:

» mothers were more likely to say their children were only in fair health
» mothers were more likely than those in families not on low incomes to say:
   • they had quite a few problems managing the child
   • the child's father was not very involved with the child
   • they had experienced stressful life events over the previous twelve months (serious financial problems, serious disagreements with their partner, major health problems, serious housing problems)
   • the family's financial situation had a negative effect on the child
   • there were more difficulties affording schooling costs.

Fewer children of low-income families:

» lived in neighbourhoods their parents saw as excellent for them
» played with friends away from school
» were involved in sport, music or dance classes
» had been away on holiday in the previous year.

On average, the lower-income families were experiencing more difficulties.

Source: Taylor, J. & Macdonald, F. 1998, *Life at six: Life chances and beginning school*, Melbourne: Brotherhood of St Laurence, reprinted with permission.

Others have suggested that neighbourhood poverty is insignificant and that religious and friendship ties are more predictive of individual social resources and support (Barnes 2003).

The extent to which the external environment enables the formation of both formal and informal social networks is also critical. How and where we spend our daytime hours determines profoundly how we can develop relationships with others. Social networks are thus inevitably dependent on governments, whether local, state or federal, and the degree to which they prioritise community-building resources and strategies. Policies relating to working hours (and the degree to which they are family-friendly), to public transport, to the availability and safety of recreational facilities and to the structure and location of local shopping facilities, to list just a few, all profoundly influence where and how lives are lived.

Opportunities for connecting with others through more formal social networks provided by community health centres, neighbourhood houses, maternal and child health centres, for example, or through public events and the arts, are created through government funding. The websites listed at the end of this chapter highlight many of these initiatives. Churches, community groups and educational facilities, such as the Universities of Third Age (U3As) or the Councils of Adult Education (CAEs), also provide opportunities for individuals and families to join with others for a variety of purposes.

In the discussion to date, the emphasis has been on the financial and people resources required to create social support and social capital. Physical location is also a key determinant in the establishment of strong social networks. Geographic location determines the availability of many specific formal and informal networks of support—living in remote or rural Australia leads to very different social opportunities compared with living in the inner city. Living in high-density government housing is very different from living on the urban fringes in new growth corridors.. Each of these physical factors has the potential to be a protective or risk factor. For instance, on the one hand, living in high-density government housing can increase exposure to crime and violence, yet on the other hand, for recently arrived migrants, such living arrangements can lead to a strong sense of cohesion with other recently arrived migrants (Taylor & Macdonald 1998).

Optimising structural influences on well-being and safety

Many systems and structures influence both the experience of and resources to cope with both typical developmental experiences and particular experiences of adversity. To conclude this overview of the structural dimensions that influence and are influenced by individuals, we consider some key areas of structural influence that are the focus of social work practice.

One way to think about what the fundamental structural needs for individuals, families and communities are is to use the principles of the World Health Organization (WHO) along with the United Nations' Declaration of Human Rights. While these statements are criticised for their Western-biased view of human rights, they do provide universal statements and aspirations about human health and well-being. They emphasise the rights of individuals and families to access 'adequate health and social measures' (WHO 2003), which can be interpreted as adequate income maintenance, housing, transport, education, health and safety measures.

These principles are provided in Chapter 1.

For social workers, practice often focuses on addressing the causes and consequences of poverty. The consequences of poverty are multiple and often include poorer health, housing, educational and safety outcomes. As O'Brien (2009 p. 75) notes:

> Poverty is fundamentally the result of how we as a society distribute resources, how we decide who will get what in the way of income, and how income is distributed among groups in our society (for example, employers, managers and workers; beneficiaries and workers, men and women; adults and children; able bodied and disabled people).

Thus, a critical appraisal of the impact of our structural dimensions involves looking at beneficiaries and those who are excluded. It involves understanding the intended and unintended consequences of legislation, social policies and organisational structures. The following exercise encourages you to reflect critically on the inclusion and exclusion effects of various structural dimensions in our society.

APPLY YOUR UNDERSTANDING: CRITICAL REFLECTION

I   Outline the different (a) laws, (b) policies and (c) organisations that currently govern or influence people's experiences of:
   * health
   * fertility and/or adoption
   * disability
   * mental health
   * ageing
   * employment and income maintenance
   * violence against children or within the family
   * homelessness
   * drug and alcohol use
   * transport
   * migration
   * asylum seeking.

2 In what ways do you think social workers can make a difference in these areas of practice when oppression and inequalities are evident?

3 In Chapter 2 (p. 67) we looked at the story of Elsie Brown in relation to her social isolation. Consider, at this point, the ways in which the wider structural context in which she was living may have had an impact on her isolation and subsequent death.

   a What resources could have made a difference?

   b What are some of the challenges in ensuring these resources are available?

These broader decisions, be they policy, legislative or organisational, profoundly influence the daily experience of Australians. In turn, they are constantly influenced by the cultural contexts in which they are made.

Cultural dimensions

As highlighted in Chapter 1, culture is an elusive concept to define, and a vast literature is devoted to exploring definitions, concepts and critiques. For example, O'Hagan (2001) provides a useful discussion of the varieties of ways in which culture has been understood within the disciplines of anthropology, cultural studies, geography, sociology, psychology and medical anthropology.

The purpose of this discussion is to highlight some common ways in which our cultural dimensions are understood and the subsequent impact cultural dimensions have on well-being and development. In the same way that our relational, social and structural dimensions can enable, enhance or disable and destroy well-being, our cultural dimensions are pivotal influences on our well-being.

Culture can be broadly defined as our way of life or the influences on our life that are we take for granted. Our cultural context shapes our beliefs about what is 'right' and 'wrong', and ultimately becomes a way of setting priorities and limitations on acceptable behaviour by governments, communities and families. Our cultural context refers to all the tangible practices and intangible beliefs that govern our way of life and our sense of individual and collective identity. Our ethnicity, history, language, media and religion all powerfully influence our understanding of what it is to be human, and what our relationships with others and with the environment around us should be like. In our daily lives we experience the dominant culture and subcultures—these define our citizenship, our sense of self and our sense of belonging.

Sometimes looking historically and cross-culturally gives the strongest sense of the impact and influence of these dimensions on people's experiences. Cultural influences can exert subtle, intangible controls over behaviour, or can be used more overtly to control individuals and their responses. For some, this can lead to experiencing marginalisation, oppression and silencing; for others, it leads to power, privilege and access to all sorts of resources. The culture that one connects with, or feels marginalised by, can be the dominant culture or a subculture—both can be equally influential in a person's experience. In this sense, culture is not a singular phenomenon, but is necessarily pluralistic and contextual. We belong to many cultures, from national to family, from workplace to religious cultural contexts. This is in part because culture is now far less geographically prescribed. Rapid technological change and globalisation have changed so radically that our cultural identities are less driven by the daily, face-to-face interactions of the past. There is an expanded capacity to belong to or identify with more global cultures, leading to obvious difficulties and strengths.

Cultures determine the niche of each person. A niche 'is used as a metaphor for the status or social position occupied in the social structure of the community by particular groups' (Germain 1991 p. 50). Culture can have a devastating impact on those who are then seen to occupy niches different from the dominant or mainstream ways of life. One of the most devastating examples of cultural influence is described in the *Bringing them home* report (National Inquiry into the Separation of Aboriginal and Torres Strait Islander Children from their Families (Australia) 1997). Culturally biased views about Indigenous cultures were used as the basis for the most organised system of child abuse in Australia's history—the removal of Indigenous children from their families and communities. While the dissent of many was noted at the time (Reynolds 1998), the dominant cultural context and beliefs about Indigenous Australians were translated into a structural context that enabled the removal of many young Indigenous children from their families, to be placed in the care of white Australians, typically miles and cultures apart from their family of origin. This in turn led to devastating experiences of trauma and loss for individuals and families, with an intergenerational impact.

For example, in Chapter 13 we look at terror management theory, which proposes that culture is a way of managing death anxiety.

Cultural practices have been part of human communities since they began. Many different theories are proposed about the functions of culture. They include those that argue that culture ensures survival through social conformity, that culture enables the intergenerational transfer of knowledge, or that culture enables meaning making and provides a sense of coherence and belonging.

Culture and ethnicity

Culture and ethnicity are often used as interchangeable terms. However, a distinction is important. An **ethnicity** can be understood as a 'collectivity within a larger society having real or putative common ancestry, memories of a shared historical past, and a cultural focus on one or more symbolic elements defined as the epitome of their peoplehood' (Hutchinson & Smith 1996 p. 17). Using ethnicity as the basis for cultural identity, some challenges immediately emerge—in a multicultural context such as Australia, which ethnicity takes precedence as migrants settle into new communities and ways of living? People often hold multiple identities, and their self-ascribed ethnicity may differ from that ascribed to them by others.

AUSTRALIAN VALUES

All migrants are required by the Australian Government to sign the following national values statement (Commonwealth of Australia 2007 p. 4):

> To maintain a stable, peaceful and prosperous community, Australians of all backgrounds are expected to uphold the shared principles and values that underpin Australian society. These values provide the basis for Australia's free and democratic society. They include:
>
> * respect for the equal worth, dignity and freedom of the individual
> * freedom of speech
> * freedom of religion and secular government
> * freedom of association
> * support for parliamentary democracy and the rule of law
> * equality under the law
> * equality of men and women
> * equality of opportunity
> * peacefulness
> * a spirit of egalitarianism that embraces tolerance, mutual respect and compassion for those in need.

Ethnic identity formation is not a static experience, but rather a constantly changing one. It is also typically self-ascribed, and, as Rutter and Tienda note (2005

p. 53), 'self-designated ethnicity is a highly fluid psychological self-concept'. They also note:

> Religion, skin colour, nationality, language, country of origin and cultural affiliation may differ in their importance and meaning, depending upon social and political context, as well as stage of individual development.

As such, labelling people according to ethnic identities runs major risks of stereotyping and the development of racist attitudes. For example, in attempting to define particular ethnic practices in relation to grief, the risks are well stated by Shapiro (1994)—it can 'itself lead to ethnic tribalism in which groups that are complex, evolving psychosocial organizations are reduced to a few stereotypically generalized features'. In addition, individuals relate to these broader cultural contexts in unique and varied ways, with some people adhering strongly and in fundamentalist ways to particular ethnic practices (either religious or cultural) and others within the same ethnic tradition adhering quite loosely, if at all, to the codes of conduct. Thus, labelling by ethnicity is not always helpful and indeed can be the basis of racism and oppression.

However, the argument in favour of social workers having specific ethnic knowledge is that there are practices and protocols that differ profoundly between ethnic groups and a working knowledge of these practices leads to more culturally appropriate and responsive practice. The balancing act is described by Omi and Winant (2001 p. 372):

> From a racial formation perspective, race is a matter of both social structure and cultural representation. Too often, the attempt is made to understand race simply or primarily in terms of only one of these two analytical dimensions. For example, efforts to explain racial inequality as a purely social structural phenomenon are unable to account for the origins, patterning and transformation of racial difference.

Looking at race and ethnicity through both a structural and cultural lens enables social workers to take into account historical and current experiences of cultural diversity, marginalisation and oppression. For example, statistics on who is arriving under the humanitarian arrival scheme demonstrates profoundly where current war and conflict is occurring around the world. Table 3.1 shows those countries from where at least one hundred people arrived from in the financial year of 2008–09.

In Chapter 9, we look at the impact of war trauma on children.

It is also critical that we look at our own cultural history and current experiences and understand the ways in which these influence our worldviews. For non-Indigenous social workers, for example, in particular but not exclusively it involves a critical examination of whiteness (Sue 2004), acknowledging the privilege, opportunity and voice that comes with being a part of the dominant culture of Australia.

TABLE **3.1** Offshore visa grants by top ten countries of birth, 2008–09

Countries	Number of visas granted
Iraq	2874
Burma/Myanmar	2412
Afghanistan	847
Sudan	631
Bhutan	616
Ethiopia	478
Democratic Republic of Congo	463
Somalia	456
Liberia	387
Sierra Leone	363

Source: Department of Immigration and Citizenship 2010

Influences on family and relationships

Powerful messages as to what the family is, or what the family should be, come from a wide range of influences within the Australian community—from politics, religion, the mass media, legislation and economics, and from our continuing need for both support and intimacy as individuals, as well as the rearing of children. Many of these social forces often propose that the family is in decline; that it is under serious threat from liberal forces within the community (Gilding 2001). However, as many sociologists comment, the family as a social institution has been and always will be undergoing change (sometimes more rapidly than others), but is 'unlikely to decline' (McDonald 1995 p. 63) given its significance both at an individual and social level.

The family is a highly subjective and emotive topic of discussion. It often leads to fundamental clashes between conservative and liberal perspectives (Gilding 1997). The conservative position maintains that the family is a biological given, the natural order of things. From this perspective, the family structure is the heterosexual couple that forms to give birth to children. Its primary functions are reproduction and the nurturing of the next generation: the maintenance of the human species. There is a clear division of labour along gender lines. The liberal position maintains that families of all sorts of structures can meet the needs of its members and that families can have both reproductive and many other functions. Increasingly, gay and lesbian relationships and families are recognised in the law and in the community, although many people continue to live 'in the closet' for fear of discrimination in the workplace or violence in public. A major influence in changing attitudes has been the result of lobbying and social action by gay and lesbian groups, including through community events such as the Mardi Gras:

CHANGING ATTITUDES ABOUT SEXUAL IDENTITIES

Each year, the Sydney Mardi Gras grows as one of the largest international gay and lesbian pride celebrations. It began, however, in 1978 as a protest march. Being gay in Australia was illegal in many states and could lead to arrest and imprisonment. In its first year, 53 people leading the march were arrested. Over time, the Mardi Gras has grown and is a major Australian and international celebration of gay, transgendered and lesbian sexual identities. It took time, visibility, advocacy and voice for people to be aware of the discrimination experienced by many gay and lesbian young people and adults in the Australian community.

Influences on understandings of suffering and healing

Culture also carries powerful understandings for each one of us about human suffering and healing and which aspects of our human experience are most valued. Cultures 'teach their members to monitor bodily and emotional states' (Minas & Klimidis 1994 p. 14). As Kleinman, Eisenberg and Good (2006 p. 141) note, similarly:

> illness behaviour is a normative experience governed by cultural rules: we learn 'approved' ways of being ill. It is not surprising then that there can be marked cross-cultural and historical variation in how disorders are defined and coped with.

This has major implications for culturally responsive practice in relation to illness experiences, an area in which social workers are often engaged. For example, in Pasifika culture in New Zealand, the fonofale framework is used to integrate the importance of family, culture and spirituality in the lives of Pasifika people. Culture is described as 'all-encompassing in the sense that it characterises one's perception and experience of the spiritual, mental, physical and other aspects of well-being' (Mafile'o 2009 p.130), and is presented as the roof, 'the shelter of life' in the fonofale framework depicted in Figure 3.1.

FIGURE **3.1** The fonofale framework

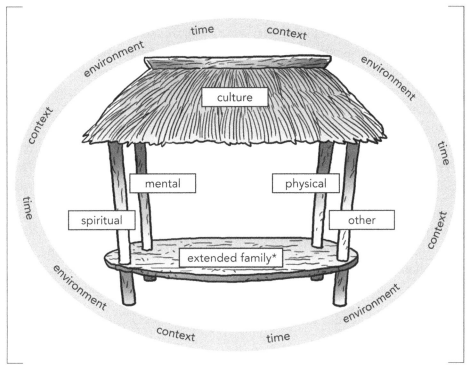

However, cultural context can also determine health and social inequalities. The current seventeen-year gap in longevity between Indigenous and non-Indigenous Australians, for example, is a result of many complex factors—including the intergenerational effects of colonisation, racism and marginalisation (Anderson et al. 2006; Gilbert 2009).

THEORY IN CONTEXT

WORKING WITH CULTURAL ISSUES

Pip, a non-Indigenous Australian social work student, reflects on how she began to integrate cultural understandings into her practice in the Anangu Pitjantjatjara Yankunytjatjara lands of South Australia.

Walking towards the house of a client in the remote Aboriginal community where I had my final placement, I had butterflies in my stomach. What use could I, a white city girl, possibly be in this completely foreign environment? Due to the chaotic nature of this Aboriginal community, my supervisor was unable to give the woman we were seeing typical whitefella-style counselling sessions; there was no way we would be able to have regular hour-long consultations in a quiet private room! However, squatting together in the red dust, with dogs and kids running around us, he managed to apply several theories in the fifteen minutes or so we had with her before her little kids demanded her attention. I learnt that theories do not need to be applied only in their purest form, but lessons can be learnt from them that inform the way we communicate with others, even in the space of a single sentence. For example, simply asking a grieving person 'what helpful advice might your mother have given you today to deal with these problems that you are facing?' is a way of applying the narrative approach of 're-membering'; to help a person find ways to think about their lost loved one in a positive way and to keep memories of them as a constructive part of their present life.

Questions

1 What is your personal reaction to this situation?
2 In what ways do you hear Pip using a cultural approach to understand the situation?
3 Are there other aspects of a cultural approach that you think could be usefully applied?

Culture is, therefore, determinative both of experiences of adversity and of how that adversity will then be interpreted and responded to. In the following chapters, the ways in which the cultural context can determine profoundly the types of developmental experiences and adaptations for individuals will be explored.

Structural and cultural change: Thinking about risk and resilience

For social workers, thinking about the risk and protective factors in the structural and cultural dimensions of people's lives is critical to effective practice. Rather than elaborate further on the complexities of structural and cultural understandings, in this book we focus on the need to develop culturally safe, competent and responsive practice.

One definition of cultural competence is that it 'implies a heightened consciousness of how clients experience their uniqueness and deal with their differences and similarities within a larger social context' (National Association of Social Workers 2007 p. 9). However, this definition falls short of 'reversing the gaze'—that is, bringing the focus back onto the worker to look at how we can develop a heightened consciousness of our uniqueness and how this may influence, both implicitly and explicitly, our worldviews, assumptions and prejudices. We are all different from each other in subtle and distinct ways—how we group those differences, draw distinctions and make judgments about capacities calls on a different skill set.

The notions of culturally safe and responsive practice have emerged as more useful terms in the Australian context—emphasising that it is in interactions and interventions, not in an acquired skill set or competency, that best practice emerges. According to Ramsden and O'Brien (2000 p. 4), **cultural safety** is concerned with:

> ... the life chances of people rather than their life styles. It is focused on the [practitioner], their attitudes and their power, and seeks the human commonalities which lead to trust.

Ramsden and O'Brien argue that the concept has not been well understood in New Zealand, where it originated in relation to nursing practice:

> ... in part due to its redefinition as transcultural nursing and the assumption that it is concerned with ethnicity. As a theory which has emerged from the experience and thinking of Maori, be assured it is concerned with power relations in health service delivery and is surely deserving of a category of its own.

Cultural safety is a relevant concept for both health and social service delivery, in emphasising that it is possible to be and express who you are when you feel culturally safe, either as a worker, client or patient. **Cultural responsiveness** refers to the way in which people's cultural diversity is respected, heard and integrated into appropriate interventions. It involves the listening to and careful use of language, including suspending an assumption of 'we', and a focus on the strengths and resilience inherent in many worldviews. It leads to recognising and respecting difference and diversity, as distinct from engaging in discrimination and oppression.

One useful way of thinking about the impact of the structural and cultural dimensions for cultural responsiveness and safety is to use Young's (1990) 'five faces of oppression', summarised below.

YOUNG'S (1990) FIVE FACES OF OPPRESSION

Iris Marion Young identified the following five experiences as critical aspects of **oppression**—sometimes experienced altogether and other times as single forms of oppression and domination:

» **Exploitation**—oppression 'through a steady process of the transfer of the results of the labor of one social group to benefit another' (Young 1990 p. 49).
» **Marginalisation**—oppression through people's exclusion from the system of labour and other forms of participation.

» **Powerlessness**—oppression through people's non-participation 'in making decisions that affect the conditions of their lives and actions' (Young 1990 p. 56).

» **Cultural imperialism**—oppression through 'the universalization of a dominant group's experience and culture, and its establishment as the norm' (Young 1990 p. 59).

» **Violence**—oppression through living 'with the knowledge that they must fear random, unprovoked attacks on their persons or property, which have no motive but to damage, humiliate, or destroy the person' (Young 1990 p. 61).

As social workers, we become part of a professional culture as well, as we complete social work education both within the university and under the supervision of experienced social workers throughout fieldwork placements. In many ways, this education is a professional inculturation process (whereby you are inducted into the values and role through an apprenticeship model of learning), as the values and knowledge of social work are imparted and integrated into new knowledge within new generations. Critical reflection on these processes is essential throughout our lifelong learning as social workers.

A multidimensional approach not only seeks to understand the impact of the structural and cultural context on us as practitioners and on the individuals, families and communities with whom we work. It seeks to understand how individuals, families and communities can bring about change and optimise well-being in the structural and cultural contexts in which people live. In the following example, Christine Fejo-King reflects on her experience of mobilising support for the National Apology to Indigenous Australians. For many Australians, Indigenous and non-Indigenous, the Apology has been a significant shift in both the cultural and structural responses to Indigenous experience. However, from the following account it is clear that strong advocacy in the face of apathy was essential for this transformation.

PRACTICE IN CONTEXT

THE NATIONAL APOLOGY

Social workers played a relatively unknown and unrecognised role in the social movement that resulted in the Apology to Australia's Indigenous Peoples delivered in the House of Representatives in Parliament House on 13 February 2008 by Prime Minister Kevin Rudd. Christine reflects on one incident where her social work role facilitated the promotion of the National Apology.

On Australia Day 2008, I went into the offices of Reconciliation Australia and found a number of the staff working. They were particularly concerned that the poll asking if the Apology should be delivered by the government was showing very poor results. In fact, the 'no' vote was receiving far more votes than the 'yes' vote. The concern was that the government, who are very polls-driven would say, as a result, that there was not the support from the community for the Apology to go ahead.

I asked if I could use their phone, opened my diary and began calling everyone in my networks in every state and territory of the nation, apologising for calling them on Australia Day and asking them if they were aware of the poll and what it was currently showing. I told them what was happening and requested that they go home, get onto their computer and vote for the Apology to proceed. These people were also asked to contact all the people they knew, including family, friends, work colleagues and others in their networks, and ask them to do the same so that we could change the poll. We achieved this goal in a relatively short time.

Questions

1 Values and attitudes play a very important role in the work we do as social workers.
    a   What values and attitudes are identified in this case study?
    b   How is strengths-based practice illustrated here?
2 What essential structural and cultural knowledge came into play?
3 Identify the skills utilised and discuss or think about how you might develop similar skills.

CHAPTER SUMMARY

In this chapter, specific aspects of the social environment, the structural and cultural dimensions, have been considered. The ways in which these dimensions determine the availability or absence of coping resources cannot be emphasised strongly enough. Issues of financial and employment security, housing and health services, and educational opportunity, as well as the different codes and rituals of conduct and experience embedded in our particular cultural contexts exert powerful influences over daily life. The influence of these outer-world dimensions on adaptation and coping will become increasingly evident in later chapters. We need to know a great deal more about the risk and protective qualities of these dimensions beyond the domain of individual and family life. Understanding the role of social policy, in particular, in effecting change at these levels is vital for social workers.

APPLYING A MULTIDIMENSIONAL UNDERSTANDING

CASE STUDY

The Ahmed family: Refugees in limbo

The Ahmed family arrived two years ago as refugees from Somalia. They have five children—three attending school, a three-year-old, and a one-year-old infant. They are living in shared housing with another family. They have been able to connect with the local school but miss many aspects of life back home. They have been able to build connections with other members of the Somali community.

They feel emotionally torn about their migration. They have left behind family and many friends. They are learning English but finding that it is still very difficult to fit into Australian culture. Being unemployed, they are also finding it difficult to afford the expenses of daily life.

Mrs Ahmed has found it much easier to connect with Australian life—she enjoys being in the shared house situation and the ways in which she can share the cooking and domestic duties with the other family with whom they live.

Mr Ahmed is frustrated by his difficulties in finding work. He sees himself as the one responsible for earning the family's income and feels deep shame that he has not been able to do this so far. He has become very withdrawn and depressed.

Questions

1 What is your personal reaction to their situation?
2 Which individual, relational and social dimensions do you see as either risk and/ or protective factors for the Ahmed family?
3 What do you see as some of the structural and cultural dimensions that will influence their experience?

KEY TERMS

culture
cultural safety
cultural responsiveness
ethnicity
exploitation
marginalisation
oppression

QUESTIONS AND DISCUSSION POINTS

1 Think about some of the social categories that may define you—either that you would use to define yourself or that others may use to define you—including the category of 'social work student'.
    a What are some of the consequences for you and for others of belonging to these categories?
    b If you wanted to change perceptions of yourself, what would you do?
2 Thinking about a situation that is causing stress for you at present, what are some of the structural and cultural determinants of that situation and your response to it?
3 In what ways do you see structural dimensions influencing your daily and family life?
4 In what ways do you see cultural dimensions influencing your daily and family life?
5 Thinking about a high-profile story in the media at present, what are some of the structural and cultural influences on:
    a what is going on (that is, the event itself)?
    b how it is being portrayed in the media?
6 What do you think about the values outlined on page 81 as reflective of Australian culture? What cultural assumptions are embedded in these values?
7 In what ways do you see Young's five experiences of oppression manifested in people's lives? What strategies would you propose to counteract these oppressions?

FURTHER READING

Gilbert, S. 2009, 'Aboriginal issues in context' in Connolly, M. & Harms, L., eds, *Social work: Practices and context*, 2nd edn, South Melbourne: Oxford University Press.

Greig, A., Lewins, F., & White, K. 2003, *Inequality in Australia*, Port Melbourne: Cambridge University Press.

Habibis, D. & Walter, M. 2009, *Social inequality in Australia: Discourses, realities and futures*, South Melbourne: Oxford University Press.

O'Hagan, K. 2001, *Cultural competence in the caring professions*, London: Jessica Kingsley Publishers.

Sue, D. 2004, 'Whiteness and ethnocentric monoculturalism: Making the "invisible" visible', *American Psychologist*, 59(8), pp. 761–9.

WEBSITES OF INTEREST

Australian Institute of Family Studies (AIFS): www.aifs.gov.au
This site provides a wealth of information relating to family-focused research and policy, including the online *Family Matters* journal. Links to many international research and policy centres, including major longitudinal studies, are provided.

Australian Bureau of Statistics (ABS): www.abs.gov.au
This site gives access to Australia's official statistics, including the annual Australian Social Trends data.

Australian Institute of Health and Welfare (AIHW): www.aihw.gov.au
This site gives access to Australia's health and welfare statistics and information.

Brotherhood of St Laurence, Ecumenical Migration Centre: www.bsl.org.au
Since the 1960s, the Brotherhood of St Laurence has run the Ecumenical Migration Centre (EMC), advocating for the rights of migrant communities. Follow the links on this site for 'Refugees and migrants'.

Department of Immigration and Citizenship: www.immi.gov.au/media/statistics
This site provides access to statistics for Australia's Migration and Humanitarian Programs.

Household, Income and Labour Dynamics in Australia (HILDA) Survey: www.melbourneinstitute.com/hilda/
The Household, Income and Labour Dynamics in Australia (HILDA) survey is a current major longitudinal survey of Australian households, looking at issues of household, income and labour dynamics.

Making multicultural Australia: www.multiculturalaustralia.edu.au
This website provides educational resources about Australia's multicultural history and contemporary debates and issues.

Reconciliation Australia: www.reconciliation.org.au
This site has extensive information about the reconciliation of Indigenous and non-Indigenous Australians, through such programs as Reconciliation Action Plans.

Stolen Generations Alliance (SGA): www.sgalliance.org.au
SGA aims to bring about healing, truth and justice. Their website includes information about the National Apology to the Stolen Generations.

Victorian Transcultural Psychiatry Unit (VTPU): www.vtpu.org.au
The VTPU provides services to mental health and psychiatric disability support services, in relation to culturally and linguistically diverse (CALD) consumers and carers. Their website contains extensive links to other sites.

PART 3

Adaptation following Specific Life Events and Experiences

In the following three chapters, we consider some of the ways in which adversity can have a negative impact on people's lives, referring to three broad types of adversity experiences—stress, trauma and grief. For each of these adversity experiences, we will examine the risk and protective factors that have been identified in relation to the events themselves, to individuals and to the environment. This separation of the three types of adversity experiences is somewhat arbitrary. To say that confronting the death of a person is a grief experience and not simultaneously a stress or trauma experience is counterintuitive. However, while there are areas of conceptual overlap, there is also distinctive literature and distinctive research bases for each of these areas, and so each will be considered separately.

CHAPTER 4

Coping with Stress

AIMS OF THIS CHAPTER

This chapter examines concepts relating to stress. It considers the following
questions:

» What is stress?
» What are some of the definitions of stress?
» What is the subjective experience of stress?
» What are the risk and protective factors associated with stress management?
» What are some of the ways of coping with stress?

From infancy through to late adulthood, various demands are placed on each one
of us. At one end of the spectrum, there are those who face so many demands that
there seems to be no way of meeting them. There is too little time in which to do
too much. For others, each day spreads before them as a vast vacuum. Nothing is
happening, and there is no one with whom to engage. For others, the day is full.
There are many things that have to be done, but there is an energy and excitement
about these experiences. There are demands, but there are sufficient resources
to meet them. Each of these scenarios is talking about the role of **stress**—as an
overwhelming, underwhelming or optimal presence. What causes one person to
feel totally psychologically and physically overwhelmed may cause another to feel
elated. The stress experience is a complex interplay of individual and environmental
factors (Haggerty et al. 1996).

Stress is essentially about the demands and pressures we experience in our
everyday living. Stress management refers to our capacity to deal with those demands

through the use of coping resources. The demands may arise in our interactions with others, in relation to our performance in the outer world or capacity to negotiate this outer world, or it may arise as a result of the internal demands we place on ourselves, our self-talk.

Unlike trauma and grief experiences, stress is not an inherently negative human experience, even though this is how it is frequently portrayed. As Martin (1997, p. 146) states, 'Sweeping prejudice aside and looking more calmly at the scientific evidence reveals that stress is by no means all bad. Relatively mild and controllable stress can be stimulating and enjoyable'.

This chapter explores some of the factors that influence whether stress has a negative or positive effect.

Subjective experiences of stress

When we experience increasing demands, we have what is termed a **stress response**, the common physiological response to stress (Selye 1987). In the 1950s, Selye identified the General Adaptation Syndrome, which includes the three stages of non-specific physiological response outlined below. He argued that the stress response is non-specific in that the physiological response is the same, regardless of the source. Research over many years has identified two major systems as playing key roles in the stress response: the sympathetic nervous system and the hypothalamus–pituitary–adrenaline system. The sympathetic nervous system initiates the **fight-or-flight response**. With the release of noradrenaline and adrenaline from the hypothalamus, the heart rate increases, as does our blood pressure, sugar is released into the bloodstream, the blood flow increases to our legs and vital organs, our breathing rate increases, as does our sensory arousal of hearing and sight. While these systems switch into a heightened state of functioning, other systems, such as the digestive, immune and sexual/reproductive systems, shut down. The hypothalamus–pituitary–adrenaline system then helps to convert the body's energy reserves into a form ready for immediate use. The changed biology of the stress response ensures that the human body is prepared for action—either to flee quickly from the threat, or to fight the imminent threat (Resick 2001). A third response, the **freeze response**, has also been identified, whereby we are so overwhelmed by the stress that we become immobilised, unable to respond in any way. This is more consistent with the dissociative reaction, discussed in Chapter 5.

The three phases of the stress response that Selye identified are: first, an alarm and mobilisation reaction, when hormones are mobilised for action; second, a stage of resistance, when response systems are activated to return the body to homeostasis;

and third, a stage of exhaustion, when the demands on the body's systems can be sustained no longer. The stress response, biologically speaking, is intended to be a short-term response, 'associated with ingrained and immediate reactions over which we have no control that were originally designed to be beneficial' (The American Institute of Stress 2006). As documented by The American Institute of Stress (2006), the reactions include an increase in heart rate and blood pressure 'to increase the flow of blood to the brain to improve decision making'; an increase in blood sugar, enabling the creation of more 'fuel for energy as the result of the breakdown of glycogen, fat and protein stores'; a decrease in blood flow to the stomach, decreasing digestive processes; an increase of blood flow to the 'large muscles of the arms and legs to provide more strength'; and blood clotting 'occurs more quickly to prevent blood loss' should lacerations occur. This response was particularly adaptive for humans thousands of years ago, when threats were dinosaurs or invaders, requiring an immediate physical response. Stressors we experience today, such as poverty, relationships or even essays, do not typically require a physical solution, yet the response is the same. We can exist in these states for short periods of time with little effect, but if we remain in these aroused states for prolonged periods of time, health difficulties arise, primarily in relation to the systems that have shut down.

The stress-performance curve illustrates this effect of long-term demand on an individual. The curve shows that for an optimal performance, a degree of increased demand is required. However, over time, and with sustained demand, our capacity to perform optimally is negatively affected.

The stress response has a critical survival function—it readies us for action. It enables us to reach optimal physical and psychological concentration and performance standards. It enables us to tap into our capacity to function at an optimal level. As a consequence, when stress connects us with these capacities, we begin to enter into a positive spiral—there is an engagement with a sense of accomplishment, a positive self-regard, and a sense of mastery and competence. These experiences then often spiral into our relationships and our future plans (Updegraff & Taylor 2000). As Wheaton (1997) emphasises, stress is not only about the expenditure of coping resources, but also about developing coping resources for the future.

This emphasises that stress is a normal part of human experience, and that different stress levels then have different impacts. Selye (as cited in Atwater 1990) distinguished between four types of stress:

1 **distress**, arising when stress has a harmful effect on us
2 eustress, being the stress that has a beneficial effect
3 hyperstress, referring to an excessive amount of stress
4 hypostress, being insufficient stress.

Each of these distinctions is important in considering how people are adapting to the adversities that they face. Thus, stress does not necessarily mean dysfunction or distress. A moderate level of stress is necessary for motivation and for a heightened performance, as the widely accepted performance curve in Figure 4.1 suggests.

The issue of when stress becomes distress is a critical one. Each individual, depending upon their internal and external resources, differs as to when the demands become too much. Researchers have suggested that there is an optimal stress point for each person, beyond which stress becomes counterproductive and our coping capacities are affected. When an individual's coping resources are overwhelmed, we refer to such a severely stressful situation as a **crisis**. Extreme stress reactions are diagnosed according to *The Diagnostic and Statistical Manual of Mental Disorders IV-TR* (American Psychiatric Association 2000). The specific diagnosis that exists for a stress condition is acute stress disorder (ASD).

Stress reactions are the observable consequences of the stress response. They are, therefore, not the immediate physiological phenomena, but the adverse health and behavioural problems that result from the difficulties in adapting effectively to the environmental demands. Stress reactions can occur in the physical, psychological, social and/or spiritual dimensions of our lives. Many studies have demonstrated the impact of stress on both mental and physical health. From a mental health point of view, stress can lead to depression and helplessness. This can have a significant impact on relationships. The social consequences of stress can leave an individual in a withdrawn, disengaged state, lacking the energy and motivation to connect

Acute stress disorder is discussed further in Chapter 5 in the context of post-traumatic stress disorder (PTSD).

FIGURE **4.1** The stress–performance curve

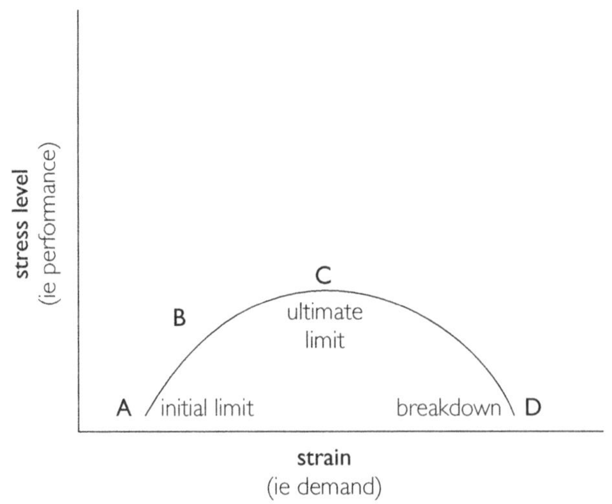

Source: adapted from Gottlieb 1997

with others. A vicious cycle is established whereby increased isolation leads to more stress, which in turn leads to increased isolation.

From a spiritual or existential point of view, stress can lead to feelings of aimlessness and meaninglessness. There is a loss of energy to invest in the enjoyable activities of life and in relationships. The term 'burnout', used to describe a loss of meaning or loss of a sense of coherence, captures very evocatively the sense that someone feels there are no longer resources to deal with the demands they are confronting.

The longer-term consequences of stress on the human body have been well documented. Stress is recognised as leading to headaches and digestive and reproductive difficulties (Martin 1997). Stress has been associated with life-threatening diseases such as cardiac disease and cancer (Ornish 1998). On the other hand, as Selye noted in his early conceptualisation of stress, it leads to positive outcomes as well. Our optimal performance relies on the stress response, and thus some of the positive outcomes of stress can include an enhanced sense of self-esteem when a goal has been successfully attained. It can also foster a strong sense of relationship and connection when stressful situations have been mastered collectively.

Risk and protective factors

If stressful events have the capacity to evoke these sorts of negative and positive consequences, the risk and protective factors that influence the experience need to be examined. These risk and protective factors can involve inner- or-outer world dimensions, or dimensions of the event itself.

Dimensions of stress events

A **stressor** is defined as the stimulus that provokes a stress response. That is, something happens that begins to place increased demand on the coping capacity of an individual. From Selye's work, the conclusion was that if people had a similar stress response to whatever type of stressor, the type of event did not predict the *severity* of response someone might have. People could have as acute a stress response and reaction to an essay as to a life-threatening car accident. This notion has been under considerable scrutiny since it was first proposed.

In the 1960s, Holmes and Rahe (1967) proposed a ranking of relativity of **stressful life events**. They developed the Social Readjustment Ratings Scale, which ranked a range of expectable life experiences according to the perceived stress associated with each one. With this model of stress, the emphasis was on the event rather than the inner world of the individual. There was an assumption that for all people the death of a spouse was the most stressful life event to be experienced, and that other events could similarly be ranked for their relative stress levels. They included events that might not have been recognised previously for their capacity to evoke stress—such as holidays or an outstanding personal achievement—as well as other expectable stressors such as illness, retirement, family difficulties and other major transitions. The difficulty for Holmes and Rahe was that when they examined stress responses, people did not in fact respond predictably, but were responding in a variety of ways to the same types of events. Thus, individual differences *did* influence both the stress reactions and coping capacities.

Other researchers and clinicians have argued that, rather than thinking about the events or transitions themselves as having the capacity to create stress, there is a need to think about the aspects of events, experiences or transitions that create stress—typically their duration, timing, predictability and controllability (Martin 1997). This is particularly important given that 'stressors are rarely single events, but instead are parts of complex environmental and transitional influences' (Haggerty et al. 1996 p. xvii).

Our stress experiences can be acute in that they are short in duration but intense in nature, or chronic, in that they are long-term and pervasive. Chronic stress situations present unique difficulties in understanding stress responses and reactions. As Gottlieb (1997 p. 10) suggests:

> When persistent demands are woven into the tapestry of life, it is virtually impossible to bracket off coping from all the other thoughts and behaviours that people employ to maintain their equilibrium and stay productively engaged in their role repertoires.

Given this, it is suggested that coping with chronic stress is a very different process from coping with acute stress. Wheaton calls for a distinction between nine forms of chronic stress, given that 'chronic stress presents itself as an ongoing, open-ended problem located in the structure of the social environment' (Wheaton 1997 p. 57). He describes chronic stress as involving threats, demands, structural constraints, complexity, uncertainty, conflict, restriction of choice, under-reward and resource deprivation (Wheaton 1997 p. 65). Situations where someone is caring for another with a severe disability or chronic illness are often characterised by many of these features.

The timing of these various stressors is also important. Stressors in rapid succession of each other can lead to coping capacities being overwhelmed, as they can at different points in the lifespan. While some stressors are readily predictable in these ways, such as the stress associated with completing the final-year exams of secondary school, many stressors, such as accidents or illnesses, are unpredictable and unanticipated.

In focusing on chronic stress as an intense and enduring experience and the timing of stressors, others have drawn attention to the stressful nature of **daily hassles** (Lazarus & Folkman 1984; Lazarus 1998). These seemingly smaller stressors are more closely linked with health problems than major undesirable life events, given their potential to evoke chronic arousal and irritability. Like major stressors, daily hassles are typically uncontrollable and are often unforeseeable events and circumstances. They can accumulate to create a host of competing demands. Missing the train for work, having to pay bills in a short lunch break, having to pick up children from school and being stuck in a traffic jam, or having to find missing keys when in a hurry are all the kinds of hassles that increase frustration across the day.

Many studies have noted that lack of a sense of control over the demands leads to increased stress levels. For example, a study of blue-collar workers and the impact of being at different levels in the workplace hierarchy found that they were at greater risk of stress-related illness when they experienced status inconsistency, job insecurity and work pressure, and they could not establish a sense of control (Siegrista et al. 1990). The loss of options seems to be a critical stressor. The controllability of life events also relates to the absence of events. We can become stressed when things are not happening as they could be. So rather than the emphasis being placed on a particular event that happens to us or around us, we become stressed because we cannot find the lifelong partner we think we should have, because we cannot make the changes to our workplace that we would like to see happen, or because we experience infertility. Our inability to act or to influence change can become the source of stress, related to our needs and desires both in the present and in the future.

Inner-world risk and protective factors

In understanding the risk and protective factors associated with the stress response, most of the research has focused on the inner-world dimensions, particularly the psychological dimension, to explain variation. Researchers have tried to identify the key personality traits or states of people that either succumb to stress or rise above it. Some of the aspects that have been particularly analysed include cognitive appraisal, the **hardy personality**, optimism, self-esteem and the notion of the stress-resistant personality.

Cognitive appraisal

Encapsulated in Shakespeare's often-quoted phrase from Hamlet 'There is nothing either good or bad, but thinking makes it so' is the notion that it takes a process of **appraisal** to assign meaning to any event that takes place. Events themselves are meaningless. Events can be perceived to have entirely contradictory qualities, dependent upon the positioning of the individual in relation to those events. From this understanding it follows that how an individual appraises an event determines whether they perceive it to be stressful or not. This focus on the individual's appraisal of the stimulus is not without its pitfalls (Aldwin 1994)—for example, it could be concluded that poverty is not stressful if not *perceived* as stressful and governments therefore should not be made to alleviate it.

Richard Lazarus, Martin Seligman and others are renowned for their work with the cognitive factors that underlie stress and, in particular, the notion of cognitive appraisal, which is the individual's appraisal of the threatening condition and the potential avenues for solution and mastery (Lazarus & Folkman 1984; Lazarus 1998). The primary appraisal is of 'what is at stake'—that is, whether the event involves a loss, a threat or a challenge. The secondary appraisal involves consideration of 'what coping resources and options are available, so that the event can be changed or accepted' (Folkman & Lazarus 1980 p. 223). When an individual appraises a situation as causing harm or loss, damage has already occurred. An appraisal of a threat indicates the anticipation, but not experience, of loss. An appraisal of challenge involves a judgment for harm and gain.

From this understanding, Albert Ellis (1995) developed his theory of rational emotive therapy and the ABC model, the basis for cognitive behavioural therapy (Alford & Beck 1997). The theory proposes that there are three fundamental stages in an event: A + B = C (Ellis 1995 p. 12). In this equation, 'A' represents the activating event, 'B' represents the beliefs that an individual forms about that event, and 'C' represents the consequences, both behaviourally and emotionally, that an individual experiences. The theory is focused on the perception of the event. Ellis then proposed that unhelpful beliefs could be changed about an event, thus reducing its impact on an individual and its capacity for stress.

Applying this model, two students who face an exam (A) situation in a few hours might feel and behave very differently (C). Student X, who has been preparing for weeks, and believes they have adequately covered the material (B), will be feeling and behaving very differently from student Y, who also has been preparing for weeks, but sees exams as awful experiences and a time when they cannot concentrate at all on the task at hand (B). The beliefs about the exam, in spite of their equal readiness for it, according to this perspective, will determine greatly the behavioural and emotional consequences for X and Y. In this example, X and Y were viewing the exam as a challenge and a threat respectively.

Neuroscience has expanded our understanding of cognitive appraisal further, by highlighting the different ways in which the human brain encodes information in the first place. That is, the information taken in and processed varies depending on whether a person is more dominant in right- or left-brain functioning. One test, for example, highlights that people watching a computer screen with a figure constantly rotating on the spot will see the figure turning in either a clockwise or anti-clockwise direction and sometimes changing direction or not. Each person is convinced that their perception is correct, when what the study highlights is that people see the figure turning in the direction they do because of the dominant side of their brain used at that time. This critical step of perception underpins what then becomes a cognitive appraisal, and it highlights that we are highly unlikely to all perceive an event similarly.

The difficulty with this approach is that it tends to over-psychologise stress rather than focus on the outer-world dimensions that can mediate if not eradicate stress experiences. While the impact of exams (or indeed other stressors such as poverty) might be different depending on whether someone views them as a short-term stressor over which they have no control, it may well be the exam itself (or poverty), not the individual stress in relation to it, that should be addressed. This is where a multidimensional perspective is critical in maintaining both an inner- and outer-world focus of understanding. These structural issues will be explored more fully later in the chapter.

Explanatory style: Optimism or pessimism?

The way we interpret and explain our experience of the world, both for ourselves and with others, is understood to reflect our explanatory style. The two key styles that are identified are an **optimistic style** and a **pessimistic style** (Seligman 1992). Optimists tend to appraise events positively, often overlooking aspects of events that contradict this positive appraisal, whereas pessimists tend to appraise events negatively. Interestingly, pessimists are understood to carry a more accurate perception of events, and therefore have been thought to have the more 'accurate' response, suggesting that optimists may indeed be accused of wearing 'rose-coloured glasses'. While arguably optimists are viewing the world in a less than accurate way, there is an argument for maintaining this degree of illusion (Taylor 1983, 1989; Taylor & Armor 1996) or denial. There is one simple reason—optimists tend to live healthier, happier and longer lives! (Taylor et al. 1984; Peterson et al. 1988; Taylor & Brown 1988; Taylor 1989; Seligman 1992; Taylor & Armor 1996)!

This finding has been known for a number of years now. It is leading to is a wider interest in avoidance or repression as an adaptive coping strategy rather than as a maladaptive one. It may in fact be harmful to be forced to confront the harsh realities that the pessimist sees so clearly. The emphasis in dealing, not only with stress situations, but also with grief and trauma, has been on the ventilation and retelling of stories of stress and loss, in order to release the emotional distress and to re-establish an understanding of what has happened. This finding about optimism combined with an appreciation of the protective or survival function of avoidance may radically alter that approach.

Locus of control

Rotter (1966) proposed that individuals tended to appraise their capacity to control their circumstances using one of two distinctive styles, an internal or an external **locus of control**. With an internal locus of control, individuals perceive themselves to have power over their situation and believe that their actions will influence the outcomes of their situation. With an external locus of control, individuals perceive themselves to have little power to influence events. They perceive others to have more influence. Studies over many years have shown that an internal locus of control is more consistently connected with more positive outcomes. In some studies, an external locus of control has been associated with higher levels of depression (Azar et al. 2003; Saade & Winkelman 2002). However, cultural context is a critical determinant of this experience, with Western cultures typically reinforcing notions of agency and independence.

Learned helplessness

The concept of **learned helplessness** was developed by Martin Seligman (Peterson & Seligman 1983; Seligman 1992; Peterson et al. 1993), based on research conducted initially with dogs in laboratory situations. He and his colleagues subjected animals to painful stimuli that they initially attempted to escape from but from which they could not, given the physical space they were contained within. When these dogs were subsequently exposed to painful stimuli that they could escape, some of them made no attempt to do so. In a short period of time, they had 'learned' that they were powerless to change their situation and their experience of pain. This learned helplessness was then translated into other settings as a pattern of behaviour. Seligman expanded his experiments to see if they explained human responses to adversity, and has consistently found evidence to support this. From this research, there has been further exploration as to how social conditions can be changed to enhance, not inhibit, a sense of personal control.

Self-efficacy

A sense of personal competence, or **self-efficacy**, is a notion considered integral to a capacity for self-regulation and motivation (Bandura et al. 2003), capacities vital in the aftermath of adversity. Bandura and his colleagues (2003 p. 769) describe the effects of a strong sense of self-efficacy as follows:

> Beliefs of personal efficacy influence what self-regulative standards people adopt, whether they think in an enabling or debilitating manner, how much effort they invest in selected endeavours, how they persevere in the face of difficulties, how resilient they are to adversity, how vulnerable they are to stress and depression and what types of choices they make at important decisional points that set the course of life paths.

People arrive at beliefs of self-efficacy by attending to four sources of information: acquiring a history of actual successes or failures; being encouraged by watching others succeed or fail (modelling); by exhortation or persuasion; and by the physiological feedback accompanying our actions (Peterson & Bossio 1991 p. 47). This highlights that a sense of self-efficacy is dependent upon the constant interactions with the social environment, and therefore is a factor that is likely to be negatively influenced by experiences of oppression and powerlessness.

A sense of coherence

A **sense of coherence** is understood to be:

> the pervasive, enduring, though dynamic feeling of confidence that internal and external environments are predictable and there is a high probability that things will work out as well as can reasonably be expected (Antonovsky 1987 p. xiii).

A sense of coherence has three underlying dimensions: meaningfulness, manageability and comprehensibility. Stressful life events, as well as trauma- and grief-related events, have the potential to bring these three areas of coherence into disarray. This notion is being increasingly investigated in research studies, to see the extent to which a coherent meaning or value system is protective of one's well-being.

Personality and temperament

Definitions of personality, temperament and character differ throughout the literature on human development. In looking at personality development, we are focusing on a belief that 'personality is fundamentally a matter of human individuality', or 'individual differences' (Haslam 2007 p. 5). For example, Susan Kobasa (1979) developed the notion of the **hardy personality** as a way of recognising that there seemed to be what she termed a steeling effect for many people from past experiences of adversity. She argued that this personality style was characterised by three 'Cs'. The first factor is a sense of control—a tendency to feel and act as if one is influential rather than helpless. The second factor is a sense of commitment—a tendency to be involved and find purpose and meaning rather than feeling alienated from life's events and encounters. The third factor is a sense of challenge—a belief that change is normal in life and that anticipation of change is an opportunity for growth rather than a threat to well-being. As with self-efficacy, it is vital to get behind these factors to ask what influences them. Good networks, positive experiences and the availability of resources would all seem critical influences on these inner-world capacities.

Studies of stress and coping typically emphasise five major personality traits on which individuals vary. These traits have come to be known as the 'big five', from the five factor model (McCrae & Allik 2002; McCrae & John 1992). The five factors are outlined below, along with some of the adjectives commonly used to describe these qualities in lay terms. A neurotic personality style is frequently identified as the 'usual suspect' in poorer outcomes.

TABLE **4.1** The five factor model of personality traits

Extraversion (E)	active, assertive, energetic, enthusiastic, outgoing, talkative
Agreeableness (A)	appreciative, forgiving, generous, kind, sympathetic, trusting
Conscientiousness (C)	organised, efficient, planful, reliable, responsible, thorough
Neuroticism (N)	anxious, self-pitying, touchy, tense, unstable, worrying
Openness (O)	artistic, curious, imaginative, insightful, original, wide interests

Source: McCrae & John 1992 pp. 178–9

By distinction, Haslam (2007 p. 9) notes that:

> Temperament usually refers to those aspects of psychological individuality that are present at birth or at least early in child development, are related to emotional expression and are presumed to have a biological basis.

We look at temperament constellations in Chapter 7.

Spirituality

In Chapter 1, spirituality was defined as the search for meaning and purpose in life, particularly through experiences of transcendence. George et al. (2000 pp. 105–6) outline the aspects of religion or spirituality that may function as protective factors in the face of stressful life events. These aspects, listed below, are a combination of inner- and outer-world dimensions.

THE DOMAINS OF RELIGION OR SPIRITUALITY CONNECTED WITH HEALTH OUTCOMES

1   Preference or affiliation—membership in or affiliation with a specific religious or spiritual group.
2   History—religious upbringing, duration of participation in religious or spiritual groups, life-changing religious or spiritual experiences, and 'turning points' in religious or spiritual participation or belief.
3   Participation—amount of participation in formal religious or spiritual groups or activities.
4   Private practices—private behaviours or activities, including but not limited to prayer, meditation, reading sacred literature, and watching or listening to religious or spiritual radio or television programs.

5   Support—tangible and intangible forms of social support offered by the members of one's religious or spiritual group.

6   Coping—the extent to which and ways in which religious or spiritual practices are used to cope with stressful experiences.

7   Beliefs and values—specific religious beliefs or values.

8   Commitment—the importance of religion or spirituality relative to other areas of life and the extent to which religious or spiritual beliefs serve to affect personal values and behaviour.

9   Motivation for regulating and reconciling relationships—most measures in this domain focus on 'forgiveness', but other issues may be relevant as well (for example, confession, atonement).

10 Experiences—personal experience with the divine or sacred as reflected in emotions and sensations.

Similarly, Ellison and Levin (1998) have identified seven ways in which spirituality works as a protective factor in stressful life circumstances:

1   regulation of individual lifestyles and health behaviours
2   provision of social resources
3   promotion of positive self-perceptions, such as self-esteem and feelings of mastery
4   provision of specific coping resources
5   generation of other positive emotions, such as love and forgiveness
6   promotion of health beliefs
7   additional hypothesised mechanisms, such as the existence of a healing bio-energy.

Sex and gender

In most studies of stress, women consistently report higher levels of stress and distress than men. This has led to a lot of debate about sex differences in coping behaviour, and to arguments that women cope less well with stress than men. This is a complex and controversial debate. There is a well-recognised difference between the sexes in their experience of distress and depression (Stoppard 2000). This has been linked with different socialisation processes, the relative exposure to stressful events in daily life and/or different coping resources. Sex differences in access to financial resources are also a major contributor to stress levels, both in relation to the impact of limited financial resources and the management of this on a daily basis, and in relation to what is also secondary to this.

Differences on the basis of gender are evident in coping strategies (Prior 1999). Men are more likely to describe themselves using action-oriented, task-focused or avoidance strategies. Women are more likely to seek social support and positive reappraisal (Nelson & Burke 2002), both considered to be more emotion-focused coping strategies.

Age

Individuals acquire different coping capacities and resources across the lifespan as a result of their biopsychosocial–spiritual development. The presence or absence of resources profoundly influences the risk and protective capacities of children and adults in the face of situations of stress.

During infancy stressors are primarily within the immediate context of the family relationship, to do with the availability of attachment figures. Stressors can arise as a result of the prenatal environment, the event of birth itself or as a result of a high-stress and non-supportive environment in which the baby develops (Lobo 1990)—that is, as a result of a lack of goodness of fit between the infant and their environment. In early and middle childhood, the stress experience is increased by the child's movement into a wider social network, but this also potentially offers them greater protection from stress. Adolescence typically brings with it new stressors, both in terms of identity formation and in terms of the various demands of the education and employment sectors in which young people participate. During adulthood, the increase in demands is well noted, with adults frequently juggling both the daily hassles of family and work life and many of the major life stressors, such as illness, financial difficulty and parental loss.

Many of these age-related issues of stress are discussed more specifically in Chapters 7 to 13.

Outer-world risk and protective factors

The stress literature has extensive information about individual risk and protective factors. However, each one of these factors is a result of the individual's interaction and experience in the social environment, so it is critical to maintain a focus on these in any understanding of stressful experiences. The focus in research tends to be on the inner-world resources that a person uses to cope with a stressful situation; the factors that both cause and perpetuate stress in the social, structural and cultural contexts need to be more fully understood. As discussed earlier in this chapter, stress reactions typically arise when the demands of the outer world exceed the resources of our inner world. Chapters 2 and 3 examine extensively the risk and protective factors in social networks, so the remainder of this chapter focuses briefly on the risk and protective factors for stress in our structural and cultural contexts.

Structural and cultural dimensions of stress

Both the daily hassles and the chronic stressors arise from the pressures of modern life—for example, the long hours of work that those who have employment are expected to sustain, or the juggling of many aspects of family and work life. Alternatively, these stressors can be understood as arising as a result of social, structural and cultural inequalities—for example, financial, racial, political or gender-based inequalities.

The availability of appropriate structural supports to both prevent stress, and to buffer stress if it occurs, becomes critical. The cycles of stress, poverty and **marginalisation** are well recognised (Mullaly 2002; Greig et al. 2003). Thus, factors such as whether or not the Australian Government adequately provides welfare support through Centrelink payments for people facing unemployment or long-term care situations, whether child care places are available within the workplace or in the community, or whether there is adequate maternity leave all influence the daily lives of those affected by these issues.

As highlighted in Chapter 3, poverty is one of the major sources of stress. Research consistently finds strong links between poverty and higher levels of reported stress. Economic resources influence the exposure to particular stressors in the environment, creating cycles of stress and adversity—for example, poor housing conditions are connected with poor health conditions; and lower socio-economic status is connected with lower educational attainment, and therefore with lower employment opportunities. Poverty for some families is short-term and transitional. For others, poverty is long-term and chronic, and for many within this experience, intergenerational (Serbin and Karp 2004). Thus, both the exposure to particular stressors and reduced access to other resources arise as a result of inequalities in income and a lack of income maintenance.

One of the key issues with poverty and stress is the issue of power—power and control over a person's own life, whether their working life or home life. An internal locus of control has been found to be more common among middle- and upper-class individuals, where control over the outer world is a possibility, thus reinforcing a sense that they can influence their environments and effect change.

Another critical element shaping the subjective experiences of stress is the degree to which the wider cultural context acknowledges or validates the stress of the individual. Issues of discrimination further isolate individuals. For those living with serious mental illnesses or other disabilities, not only does the lack of opportunity to earn an income mean that housing and health opportunities are limited, it means living with stigma. The cultural context is highly significant in shaping whether individuals perceive situations to be threatening or not. As Blankenship (1998 p. 5) notes:

> closely connected to the importance of recognising that the kinds of challenges people face are partly dictated by their location in the social hierarchy is the importance of recognising that what is profound and extraordinary in one context may be routine and ordinary in another.

We explore this theme further in Chapter 5, when we look at notions of the relativities of trauma.

PRACTICE IN CONTEXT

STRESS IN MILITARY LIFE

In the following example, Lisa describes a case that typifies the stress of military life:

Jane presented for relationship counselling with her partner John. They have been in a relationship for eight years and together have three children, aged one, five and seven. John is a member of the Australian Defence Force and has served overseas on both peacekeeping and war missions. John returned home to Australia four months ago, following a six-month deployment to a war zone.

Jane described this separation as being particularly stressful with a new baby and having relocated to another city in the month prior to John deploying overseas to a war zone. Following his return, she expected that they 'would just come back together' as they have done in the past. Since John has been home he has spent significant periods of time socialising with his work colleagues.

John agreed to relationship counselling because the couple's relationship had reached a crisis point and was on the verge of breaking down. John found it difficult to talk about what was happening for him. Since returning to Australia, John described 'feeling different' and having encountered difficulty adjusting and reintegrating into home life. He said that he needs to be with his mates who understand. He revealed an inability to sleep and the onset of nightmares.

Questions
1   What is your initial reaction to their situation?
2   What stressors do you think Jane and John are experiencing?
3   What risk and protective factors do you think are evident in this situation?
4   What would you see as some of the important priorities for intervention in this situation?

Coping with stress

Over the course of a lifetime, we learn many different ways of coping with stress and other events in the environment. As a result of both personality styles and life experience, a repertoire of coping is developed. What has become increasingly apparent is that different kinds of **coping strategies** are required for different stressful situations. For example, Coyne, Aldwin and Lazarus (1981) found that in dealing with depression, it was not that depressed people use any less coping responses—in fact, depressed people often used more coping strategies. The problem was that they were inappropriate ones that did little to change the situations or their capacity to cope with them.

Two major styles of coping have been identified—**approach** and **avoidant coping** (Schaefer & Moos 1992). **Approach coping** involves 'trying to analyse the crisis in a logical way, reappraising the crisis in a more positive light, seeking social support and taking actions to solve the problem'. **Avoidant coping** involves 'trying to minimise the problem, deciding that nothing can be done to change the problem itself, seeking alternative rewards and venting emotions' (Saade & Winkelman 2002; Beekman et al. 2000). These styles have also been called task-focused and emotion-focused coping strategies, respectively. Up until recently approach coping has tended to be favoured over avoidant coping. However, several recent studies have suggested that avoidant coping may be an adaptive response that leads to more favourable outcomes than approach coping. Ginzburg, Solomon and Bleich (2002) found in their study of those who had survived myocardial infarction that a repressive coping style led to less acute stress disorder and post-traumatic stress disorder. Thus, a distinction may need to be drawn between what characterises a healthy versus an unhealthy avoidance coping style, given the type of stressor faced and in what circumstances.

Researchers are careful to distinguish between a **coping style**, which is a relatively stable characteristic of individuals and typically identified as being either the approach or avoidant style, and coping strategies (or processes), which, given a particular situation, may vary from the general coping style.

Expanding on the notions of approach and avoidance strategies, Lazarus and Folkman (1984) proposed that there are eight basic ways of coping, which individuals incorporate into their own repertoire of coping with stress. These are outined in the following box.

THE EIGHT WAYS OF COPING

1 Confrontive coping: expressing anger or other emotions, recognising that there is a problem.
2 Distancing: making light of the situation, minimising the threat.
3 Self-controlling: keeping feelings to oneself.
4 Seeking social support: telling someone about the situation.
5 Accepting responsibility: acknowledging own agency or blaming self.
6 Escape-avoidance: wishing the situation would go away.
7 Planful problem-solving: making an action plan and following it.
8 Positive re-appraisal: seeing oneself as having grown or changed in a good way as a result of the situation.

Source: Lazarus and Folkman 1984

Importantly, none of these ways of coping is more effective than others. The critical issue is the degree of fit between the problem and the strategy used to deal with it. For example, escape-avoidance may seem like a strategy based on denial, but as a short-term strategy for dealing with overwhelming news about health, it is very functional. Emphasis is placed on having a repertoire of ways of coping, not just one style, and having the capacity to determine which problems require which strategies.

As distinct from these conscious coping mechanisms described so far, psychodynamic theorists propose that there are unconscious ways in which we protect ourselves from the experience of anxiety. These unconscious mechanisms deny, distort or restructure our experience of overwhelming emotion in order to protect the self when it is under threat. We remain less aware of our **defence mechanisms**, because they have been developed across the lifespan as automatic responses to overwhelming anxiety. Defence mechanisms are seen as a normal defence against anxiety, not necessarily something problematic or pathological. Denial, for example, is very important in enabling normal functioning and engagement in daily life in the face of life stressors.

Anna Freud identified nine defence mechanisms—regression, repression, reaction formation, isolation of affect, undoing, projection, introjection, turning against the self, and reversal (Freud 1937; Sandler & Freud 1985). She, and others, argued for a hierarchy of defence mechanisms, from 'primitive' to 'mature' (Harari & Meares 2001). These have subsequently been added to and include the mechanisms outlined below. For example, Vaillant (2002 p. 63) identifies sublimation, humour, altruism and suppression as adaptive coping strategies and mature defence mechanisms. For a more comprehensive discussion of these issues, refer to Freud (1937; Sandler & Freud 1985), Vaillant (1993) and Goldstein (1995).

SOME OF THE KEY DEFENCE MECHANISMS

1 Repression—keeping unwanted thoughts and feelings out of awareness.
2 Reaction formation—replacing an impulse in consciousness with its opposite.
3 Projection—attributing unacknowledged feelings to others.
4 Isolation of affect—repressing feelings associated with a particular context or ideas associated with certain emotions.
5 Undoing—nullifying an unacceptable or guilt-provoking act.
6 Regression—returning to an earlier developmental phase and level of functioning.
7 Introjection—turning feelings towards the self rather than directly expressing powerful emotions.

8 Idealisation—overvaluing another person, place, family or activity beyond what is realistic.

9 Denial—non-acceptance of important aspects of reality.

10 Somatisation—converting anxiety into physical symptoms.

11 Reversal—altering feelings or attitudes into their opposite.

12 Sublimation—converting a socially objectionable aim into a socially acceptable one.

13 Intellectualisation—thinking about the experience or emotion rather than experiencing it directly.

14 Rationalisation—using convincing reasons to justify certain ideas.

15 Displacement—shifting feelings or conflicts about one person or situation onto another.

Source: based on Goldstein 1995; Vaillant 2002

Other stress management strategies involve intervening with the physical stress response—that is, mediating the fight-or-flight response. This lowering of the physiological arousal can be achieved using meditation or relaxation techniques, which principally focus on regulating and slowing the breathing and on relaxing muscles. These techniques, when used proactively, have led to a range of positive physical and mental health outcomes. Like supportive social networks, these strategies seem to have both a stress-buffering effect and a positive overall effect on health.

Others have argued that 'psychological stress is simply a reaction to losses (or threatened losses) in resources' (Resick 2001 p. 58). Stress management therefore involves addressing the losses that have been sustained or are threatened in order to conserve resources.

This is consistent with a **conservation of resources (COR) theory** of stress, although COR theory goes one step further than this. Hobfoll (2001 p. 341) proposes that 'the basic tenet of COR theory is that individuals strive to obtain, retain, protect and foster these things that they value'. As individuals, groups, families and communities, we develop 'caravans of resources' or **assets**; that is, a diversity of inner- and outer-world resources that enhance or inhibit our functioning and well-being. Four resource types are identified (Hobfoll et al. 2000):

1 object resources, such as cars, houses, or clothes
2 condition resources, such as social support or environmental resources
3 personal resources, such as self-esteem, confidence, an internal locus of control, or intelligence
4 energy resources, such as time and sleep.

In particular, Hobfoll (2001 pp. 341–2) notes that 'stress will occur:

» when individuals' resources are threatened with loss
» when individuals' resources are actually lost, or
» where individuals fail to gain sufficient resources following significant resource investment.'

The theory proposes that both losing and *gaining* these personal and/or environmental resources can lead to stress, in that both potentially place demands on individuals, families or communities to change as a result. It also highlights that changes can occur in one or more resource domains, and that experiences can lead to both gain and loss. It expands, therefore, the earlier theory of stress proposed by Holmes and Rahe, in that it refines the particular aspects of experiences that are losses or gains and sees both as placing demands on individual, family and community coping capacities. The notion of 'caravans' of resources, or the accumulation of resources, also connects strongly with intergenerational understandings of risk and resilience—with an accumulation of extensive resources protecting against the transmission of intergenerational risk and vulnerability (Serbin and Karp 2004). The theory also highlights that for people experiencing major transitions, such as migration or adapting to illness and injury, multiple resources may be lost or under pressure. For Indigenous Australians living in remote communities, many resources available to others living in urban contexts may not be accessible at all.

COR theory shifts away from a solely inner-world focus to a recognition that many sources of stress are located in the outer world and that attending to them may have a more significant impact than developing inner-world strategies. The structural context is crucial. For example, where there is a welfare state that adequately supports vulnerable individuals and families in relation to employment, benefits, housing and health, stress can be minimised. The outer-world causes of stress, rather than the inner-world consequences, may be the more influential site of intervention.

Resilience: Adapting to stress

Moos and Schaefer (1986 p. 11) outline five possible or expectable adaptations for individuals to stress:

» Establish the meaning and understand the personal significance of the situation.

» Confront the reality and respond to the requirements of the external situation.
» Sustain relationships with family members and friends as well as others who may be helpful.
» Maintain a reasonable emotional balance by managing upsetting feelings aroused by the situation.
» Preserve a satisfactory self-image and maintain a sense of competence and mastery.

In a multidimensional approach, however, structural adaptations should be considered also, along with an appreciation of coping within specific cultural contexts. For example, stress often results in politicised responses through community advocacy (Blankenship 1998) and group movements (Tummala-Narra 2007). In turn, these factors influence collective resilience and hope (Tummala-Narra 2007).

CHAPTER SUMMARY

Any discussion of stress and stress experiences needs to take into account all of the dimensions of experience that have been discussed in this chapter—the individual, relational, social, structural and cultural dimensions. Stress can clearly be understood in many different ways, as a physiological state, a psychological experience, or as a phenomenon of the outer world, of relationships, of resources and of culture.

Within the Australian context, Western attitudes towards stress tend to be reinforced. Stress tends to be psychologised and rendered a private, inner-world experience. An understanding of both the conscious and unconscious coping processes and strategies of individuals is important. Explanatory styles, optimism and hardiness clearly play a part in protecting individuals from the debilitating effects of stress. Yet in viewing stress from this perspective only, stress experiences become highly individualised, even though the source of stress typically lies in dimensions beyond the control of the individual. This bias also tends to overlook the vulnerability that particular individuals experience as a result of their position within the social hierarchy. Thus, an understanding of the outer-world factors that give rise to the demands or the loss of resources in the first place that trigger the stress response is critical, recognising the structural and cultural context of stress.

APPLYING A MULTIDIMENSIONAL UNDERSTANDING

Sandra: Confronting poverty

Sandra, a thirty-year-old woman, has three children—Simon (twelve), Greg (nine) and Amanda (seven). Simon's father no longer has any contact with her. He's been in and out of prison over many years, and she has removed herself and the children from the chaos of his involvement. Greg and Amanda's father lives in the same suburb and has them over to his place with his new partner every second weekend. He and his partner have a child of their own.

Sandra receives Centrelink payments, with which she tries to meet all the family's financial commitments. Their housing commission flat is tiny, and Sandra is concerned about Simon's increasing involvement with a gang of older children in the flats. She wants to move, but the waiting list is vast, with about a four-year wait. In the next week, Sandra has to find enough money to pay for the school fees and books. She has $15 to last the next two days, until pension day.

Val and Roy: Physical impairment

Val and Roy, both aged forty-eight, live on a remote station, about two hundred and seventy kilometres from the nearest small town. They have lived there for ten years, working as labourers for the property owners. Recently, Roy fell and injured his back. While he has recovered considerably, he is no longer able to do the lifting required in his job. His boss called him in last week and told him, reluctantly, that he would have to discontinue his employment. Roy and Val are in crisis—they have no family other than their community on the property, apart from Val's father, who is in a nursing home. They have two weeks to find a new home and other employment. Roy's back has been worse in the last few days and he doubts anyone will ever employ him again.

Questions

1 What is your personal response to these situations?
2 What are the potential individual and family stressors in these situations?
3 Which inner- and outer-world dimensions do you see as either risk and/or protective factors?
4 What additional demands emerge:
   * if Sandra and her family are from a non-English speaking background?
   * if Roy is fifty-eight rather than forty-eight years old?
   * if Roy had experienced a major depressive episode as well as a back injury?
5 What are the possibilities for intervention at a:
   * practice level?
   * program level?
   * policy level?

KEY TERMS

appraisal	freeze response
approach coping	hardy personality
assets	learned helplessness
avoidant coping	locus of control
conservation of resources (COR) theory	optimistic style
	pessimistic style
coping strategies	self-efficacy
coping style	sense of coherence
crisis	stress
daily hassles	stressful life events
defence mechanisms	stressor
distress	stress reactions
fight-or-flight response	stress response

QUESTIONS AND DISCUSSION POINTS

1 What is the stress response?
2 What are the key inner and outer world effects of stress?
3 What dimensions of stressful events are considered to be risk or protective factors?
4 What are some of the key ways of coping with stressful life events and circumstances?
5 Reflecting on stressful situations you have been in yourself, identify your familiar stress responses and reactions. How do these differ from your family and friends?
6 What strategies for coping with stress work well for you and what are the strategies that you see others using?

FURTHER READING

Aldwin, C. 1994, *Stress, coping and development: An integrative perspective*, New York: The Guilford Press.

Bandura, A., Caprara, G., Barbaranelli, C., Gerbino, M. & Pastorelli, C. 2003, 'Role of affective self-regulatory efficacy in diverse spheres of psychosocial functioning', *Child Development*, 74(3), pp. 769–82.

Hobfoll, S. 2001, 'The influence of culture, community, and the nested-self in the stress process: Advancing conservation of resources theory' *Applied Psychology: An International Review*, 50(3), pp. 337–421.

Lazarus, R. & Folkman, S. 1984, *Stress, appraisal, and coping*, New York: Springer Publishing Company.

Seligman, M. 1992, *Learned optimism*, Milsons Point: Random House.

WEBSITES OF INTEREST

Albert Ellis Institute: www.rebt.org

The Albert Ellis Institute is a world centre for mental health research, training and clinical practice. This site contains a useful bibliography and information about rational emotive behaviour therapy.

The American Institute of Stress: www.stress.org

This site was established at the request of Hans Selye, and provides an updated library of information relating to stress, and a monthly newsletter, *Health and Stress*.

Beck Institute for Cognitive Therapy and Research: www.beckinstitute.org

This site contains useful background information about Aaron Beck's work and extensive research and resource material.

BeyondBlue: www.beyondblue.org

This site provides research and services information about depression- and anxiety-related disorders.

Centrelink: www.centrelink.gov.au

This site provides multilingual access to Centrelink's range of Australian Government services for individuals and the community.

Gawler Foundation: www.gawler.org

This site provides information about complementary health and stress management techniques, including meditation.

Positive Psychology Center: www.ppc.sas.upenn.edu

This centre is directed by Martin Seligman at the University of Pennsylvania. The site contains extensive research materials and links.

CHAPTER **5**

Coping with Trauma

AIMS OF THIS CHAPTER

This chapter explores experiences of and responses to psychosocial trauma. It considers the following questions:

» What is trauma?
» What are some of the definitions of traumatic stress?
» What is the subjective experience of trauma?
» What are the risk and protective factors associated with trauma recovery?
» What are some of the ways of coping with trauma?

In Chapter 4, we considered the consequences of stressful life events and circumstances and some of the ways in which coping capacity is affected by the presence or absence of various internal and external resources. While there is a considerable degree of overlap in the use of the terms 'stress' and 'trauma', they do differ conceptually. Stress typically refers to everyday instances of demand and resource, where our coping capacity is stretched to the limits, and sometimes beyond. **Trauma** refers to situations where a person is confronted with situations that exceed and overwhelm their coping capacity. These situations threaten the physical or psychological integrity of the person and cause an intense reaction of horror. Typically, there is a significant impact on at least immediate, if not long-term, functioning, involving distress and disturbance and, for some, disorder. Thus, stressful events and traumatic events are distinguished by severity, and most typically by frequency and exposure.

Some key terms

Like the word 'stress', 'trauma' is a word that is used in everyday language to refer to a wide variety of experiences that disrupt and punctuate our lives. However, in literature about psychological trauma, there are very technical definitions for specific categories of disorder. We consider these, as well as the everyday uses of the term, in this chapter.

The word 'trauma' is derived from the Greek word 'traumata' meaning 'to wound'. It conveys a strong sense that a wounding or injury, rather than just a disruption, has occurred to all dimensions of the person. As with a physical wound, in many instances there is a need for intervention. But in the image of a wound we can also recognise the fact that human beings, like many wounds, are capable of self-healing, given the right conditions. Therefore, individuals who experience psychological trauma may be able to spontaneously recover, or may need intervention.

Tedeschi and Calhoun (1995) identify from the research literature four key characteristics of traumatic events. Traumatic events are typically sudden and unexpected, so that the individual is unable to prepare psychologically for the event. They are perceived as being out of one's own control. They are out of the ordinary for the individual and as a result the individual affected is unable to draw on past experiences in an attempt to cope. They also typically create long-lasting problems. Others have described traumatic events as being characterised by being 'too much' (Laub & Auerhahn 1993)—too much to bear or to manage in any way. The *Diagnostic and Statistical Manual of Mental Disorders IV-TR* (American Psychiatric Association 2000), commonly referred to as the DSM-IV, using a different framework, puts forward strict criteria for trauma reactions, under the diagnostic labels of post-traumatic stress disorder (PTSD) and acute stress disorder (ASD), explored more fully in the following pages.

The variety of trauma experiences

Traumatic events have occurred continually across time within all human communities. Many of these events become the defining moments of human history, both individual and collective. Aldwin (1993), a key trauma researcher, has classified three types of traumatic event. First, there are the natural disasters—such as bushfires, floods and droughts, and technological disasters such as the Chernobyl nuclear reactor disaster and the Coode Island fires. Second, there are wars and related events such as the Holocaust or the genocide experienced in Srebrenica, Rwanda and other places. Wars lead to all sorts of ongoing traumas of daily life. Aldwin defines these as expectable traumas, where there is some forewarning. It is important to note that many aspects of war, such as terrorist acts, are totally unexpected. Third, she identified individual traumas—individual acts of violence perpetrated within the privacy of the home towards children and adults, or acts of rape, murder or suicide; car or work accidents; and sudden deaths. Some traumas are inflicted by individual human beings or by governments or particular community groups. Other traumas are caused by nature and are beyond human control.

The single thread that unites all these experiences is their capacity to cause acute distress and horror and massive disruption to a person's physical, psychological, spiritual and/or social functioning. For some people, their families and their communities, this disruption is a lifelong experience.

Over the past two decades or so there has been renewed interest in the psychosocial consequences of trauma—the aftermath reactions for individuals and communities. While the interest is renewed, as many books on trauma now document, there is a long history of understanding how it affects individuals and communities, with different historical eras recognising trauma experiences more than others (Wilson 1995).

Some of the key developments over the past two centuries include the understandings that arose from Freud's notions of the trauma neurosis associated with childhood sexual abuse, the psychiatrists of the First World War who developed notions of shell shock, and the existential understandings that emerged from writers following the concentration camps of the Holocaust. From the 1960s onwards, lobbying by veterans occurred, following the traumas of the Vietnam War, and by feminists, in relation to domestic violence and rape issues. The effects of trauma were more systematically identified following recognition in 1980 of post-traumatic stress disorder as a psychiatric condition. During the 1980s and early 1990s, intense debate developed around the existence of repressed memory of childhood sexual trauma. From the 1990s onwards, interest has focused on the neurobiological processes involved in trauma responses. These movements of social and medical interest in trauma reflect the different impact of cultural and historical understandings.

Subjective experiences of trauma

As a result of intense lobbying by Vietnam veterans and feminists (who wanted the aftermath reactions of war and domestic violence, respectively, publicly and structurally recognised), the diagnosis of PTSD was included in the *Diagnostic and Statistical Manual of Mental Disorders IV-TR (DMS-IV)* for the first time in 1980. The current criteria statement for PTSD (American Psychiatric Association 2000 p. 463) recognises that:

The essential feature of Posttraumatic Stress Disorder is the development of characteristic symptoms following exposure to an extreme traumatic stressor involving direct personal experience of an event that involves actual or threatened death or serious injury, or other threat to one's physical integrity; or witnessing an event that involves death, injury or a threat to the physical integrity of another person; or learning about unexpected or violent death, serious harm or threat of death or injury experienced by a family member or other close associate.

Post-traumatic stress disorder (PTSD) can be diagnosed as being acute (less than three months), chronic (symptoms last for more than three months) or with delayed onset (more than six months since the event). The lifetime prevalence is estimated to be one to fourteen per cent, although other studies have indicated prevalence rates ranging from three per cent to fifty-eight per cent for high-risk populations (American Psychiatric Association 2000 pp. 425–6).

The diagnostic criteria (outlined in the box below) include the:

1 exposure to a traumatic event
2 persistent re-experiencing of the event
3 persistent avoidance of stimuli associated with the event, and numbing
4 persistent symptoms of increased arousal
5 persistence of these symptoms for a period of more than four weeks.

CRITERIA FOR POST-TRAUMATIC STRESS DISORDER

The person has been exposed to a traumatic event in which the person experienced, witnessed, or was confronted with an event or events that involved actual or threatened death or serious injury, or a threat to the physical integrity of self or others and the person's response involved intense fear, helplessness or horror.

The traumatic event is persistently re-experienced in one (or more) of the following ways:

1 recurrent and intrusive distressing recollections of the event, including images, thoughts or perceptions
2 recurrent distressing dreams of the event
3 acting or feeling as if the traumatic event were recurring (includes a sense of reliving the experience, illusions, hallucinations and dissociative flashback episodes, including those that occur on awakening or when intoxicated)
4 intense psychological distress at exposure to internal or external cues that symbolise or resemble an aspect of the traumatic event
5 physiological reactivity on exposure to internal or external cues that symbolise or resemble an aspect of the traumatic event.

The individual also has persistent avoidance of stimuli associated with the trauma and numbing of general responsiveness (not present before the trauma), as indicated by three (or more) of the following:

1   efforts to avoid thoughts, feelings or conversations associated with the trauma
2   efforts to avoid activities, places or people that arouse recollections of the trauma
3   inability to recall an important aspect of the trauma
4   markedly diminished interest or participation in significant activities
5   feeling of detachment or estrangement from others
6   restricted range of affect (e.g. unable to have loving feelings)
7   sense of a foreshortened future (e.g. does not expect to have a career, marriage, children or a normal life span).

Persistent symptoms of increased arousal (not present before the trauma), as indicated by two (or more) of the following:

1   difficulty falling or staying asleep
2   irritability or outbursts of anger
3   difficulty concentrating
4   hypervigilance
5   exaggerated startle response.

The disturbance, which has lasted for at least a month, causes clinically significant distress or impairment in social, occupational or other important areas of functioning.

Source: Reproduced with permission from the *Diagnostic and Statistical Manual of Mental Disorders IV-TR*, Text Revision, Copyright 2000, American Psychiatric Association, pp. 467–8.

The key features of this diagnostic category are the disturbances of cognitive processes as a direct result of exposure to a traumatic event. It is believed that fear networks are established within thought processes, which dominate cognitive functioning at least in the short term, if not the longer term (Salmon & Bryant 2002 p. 168). **Acute stress disorder (ASD)**, or acute stress reaction (ASR) as it is also referred to, has all the same diagnostic criteria as PTSD except that it has a shorter time frame of onset and resolution (within one month following a traumatic event).

The widespread appeal of the PTSD diagnosis is at least two-fold. First, it gives a clear checklist of symptoms on an individual basis and provides a generalisable yardstick for those involved in subsequent compensation, legal and research processes. Second, it provides a label for very distressing experiences, which potentially validates the experiences people have been through. While the act of labelling places it within a psychiatric category, doing so identifies an external source of causation rather than an intrapsychic cause of psychiatric disturbance. Many people have reported being greatly relieved to have a label and a language that fits their subjective experience and gives them access to treatment and litigation processes as a result. It has enabled the development of effective therapies and treatment strategies, such as those outlined in the *Australian Guidelines for the Treatment of Adults with Acute Stress Disorder and Posttraumatic Stress Disorder* (Australian Centre for Posttraumatic Mental Health 2007).

Counteracting the widespread appeal of the PTSD diagnosis, numerous criticisms have been raised. These include the following:

1 The diagnosis fails to capture anything but the cognitive experience of distress, ignoring the vast social, spiritual and meaning disturbances or effects of trauma.
2 It does *not* identify people who are having a normal reaction to an abnormal event. PTSD is a rare diagnosis in the aftermath of trauma, and is not the normal response (Yehuda & McFarlane 1995; Young 1995; Ellard 1997).
3 It has been shown to have high co-morbidity rates with other psychiatric diagnoses.
4 While it argues that it is the event that is the causative factor and that any traumatic event has the capacity to affect an individual in this way, it bases its criteria on the cognitive processes of the individual and ultimately comes to pathologise the individual for their reaction (McFarlane 1995; Yehuda & McFarlane 1995; Bowman 1997).

Thus, as Norris (1992) suggests, PTSD represents only the tip of the iceberg of the experience of trauma. It is one lens, among many, with which the aftermath experience might be understood. The reactions to trauma that frequently present in counselling settings, not included in the PTSD criteria and often not emphasised in the literature, include the feelings of intense or even unspeakable rage, revenge, a sense of injustice and violation, guilt and distress. Another way of identifying the distress of trauma is by using Macnab's eight factors. He argues that, in order to assess the distress of trauma, the subjective reports of the intensity of the distress in relation to the nature of the trauma and the known resources and history of the person; the duration of the distress; the coherence of the distress; the controllability of the distress; and the direction, language, consequences and accessibility of the distress all need to be recognised (Macnab 2000 pp. 15–16).

Survivors of traumatic life events frequently report, in addition to the experiences described above, experiences of positive, unanticipated change and growth in the aftermath of these events. Since the 1980s at least, concepts have been evolving around the notion of the possibility of positive outcomes from trauma. As Tedeschi et al. (1998 pp. 2–4) note, these positive changes have been variously referred to as positive psychological changes (Yalom & Lieberman 1991), perceived benefits or construing benefits (Calhoun & Tedeschi 1998; McMillen et al. 1995; Tennen et al. 1992), stress-related growth (Park et al. 1996), thriving (O'Leary & Ickovics 1995), positive illusions (Taylor & Brown 1988), positive reinterpretation (Scheier et al. 1986), drawing strength from adversity (McCrae 1984) and transformational coping (Aldwin 1994). The possibility of positive outcomes is also an implicit component of the strengths perspective (Saleebey 1997; Rapp 1998), which emphasises individual strengths rather than deficits in human coping and adaptation.

While each of these notions differs slightly, they each capture in some way that individuals are able to notice positive changes in the aftermath of various life traumas that they had experienced; that there had been some kind of enhanced experience. These positive consequences are most consistently reported in three areas: changes in self-perception, changes in relationships with others and changes in worldview (Taylor 1983).

According to Schaefer and Moos (1992), changes in self-perception occur in two ways—enhanced personal resources and enhanced coping skills. In relation to enhanced personal resources, they identify the following factors: more cognitive differentiation, assertiveness, self-understanding, empathy, altruism and maturity. It then follows that enhanced coping skills include such factors as the ability to think through a problem logically, to seek help when needed and to regulate emotional affect.

Others such as Tedeschi and Calhoun (1995) see that positive changes in self-perception include an increased sense of self-reliance and a sense of being a stronger person. This leads to self-evaluations of greater competence in difficult situations and therefore greater confidence. McMillen and Fisher's (1998) study identified different personal changes again, with the aspects of personal growth including perceptions of becoming a nicer person, stronger and more spiritual and making changes in life priorities. A strong cyclic link can be seen to occur between using an enhanced coping skills repertoire and subsequently experiencing personal mastery and insight (Argyle 1987).

The enhanced relationships with others identified by McMillen and Fisher (1998) included an increased closeness to others, as in becoming closer to family and friends, as well as experiencing an increased sense of community closeness. Schaefer and Moos (1998 p. 101) view enhanced social resources as relating to better relationships with family and friends and to building new support networks and confidant relationships. For example, often the network of support available to road trauma survivors is expanded by meeting other survivors in the rehabilitation setting. The unique bond of being inpatients together creates a strong network during the initial recovery time and often afterwards.

Tedeschi et al. (1998 p. 12) see this enhancement of personal relationships as arising through the continuing need for discussion of the consequences of events and the need for self-disclosure. They argue that this self-disclosure may provide an opportunity for testing out new relating behaviours. Recognition of individual vulnerability may lead to more emotional expressiveness and to a willingness, therefore, to accept help and use social supports that had previously been ignored. This latter theory is at the heart of Caplan's (1974) crisis theory and the 'malleable state' of the individual in crisis. This vulnerability and malleability justifies the work of crisis intervention by health services professionals in the early days following trauma.

Through this increased self-disclosure or emotional expressiveness, it is argued that people also regard themselves as having an enhanced sense of compassion towards, and empathy with, others, and that this in turn leads to an increased desire to give to others or perception of themselves as giving to others—an increased sense of altruism. Consistent with these notions, Blankenship calls for the positive consequences of trauma to be considered from this community reconnection perspective, arguing that 'thriving sometimes manifests itself in an other-directed commitment to community advocacy' (Blankenship 1998 p. 395).

Some people talk about their experience of trauma as being like a 'wake up call' (McMillen et al. 1997 p. 738) or a major turning point in their life. As a consequence, the crisis causes them to confront issues of their own mortality and their life's purpose and meaning, their worldview. In doing so, people frequently report positive changes in their priorities in life and their sense of appreciation of life. For many, this involves questioning issues of religion and spirituality (McColl et al. 2000), or developing a general philosophy of life or worldview that provides new meaning (Silver et al. 1983).

Maslow (1968 p. 206) argued that 'the state of being without a system of values is psychopathogenic' in that all people need a 'framework of values, a philosophy of life, a religion or religion-surrogate to live by and understand by'. Growth is considered to have taken place when these beliefs about the world and the self and any transcendent aspects of daily life are strengthened, giving the individual an 'increased sense of control, intimacy and of finding meaning' (Tedeschi & Calhoun 1996 p. 458). Enhancement, or the perception of enhancement, in this area is considered to be a potential buffer against the ongoing disorganisation and distress of trauma, in that it provides a stable assumptive world.

A more specific area of perceived benefits or growth is enhanced health awareness—awareness of the need to attend to physical health needs, in terms of diet, exercise and other aspects of physical and mental health, such as meditation and relaxation. For example, Affleck et al. (1987) noted that men who had experienced heart attacks reported being 'taught a lesson' about the importance of health behaviour practices to live a long life. They found that those who perceived benefits seven weeks after their initial coronary episode were more likely to have avoided further coronary episodes at a follow-up eight years later. This benefit may well connect then with the perceived benefit of appreciating life more, and thus the cycle of growth begins. A 'second chance' or a crisis of health seems to promote a re-evaluation of health practices.

Changes occur beyond the inner world, with benefits also occurring in social and structural dimensions. For example, McMillen et al. (1997) found that renal transplant survivors also reported improvements in the areas of material gains, becoming a focus on or attaining entertainment value, becoming better at a job, better work conditions and changes in laws and policies. These may be important sources of growth in other areas—for example, the sense of mastery in becoming better at a job may well enhance self-perception.

Risk and protective factors

A range of risk and protective factors has been considered influential in determining either the negative, positive or neutral consequences of trauma. These include both inner-world and outer-world factors, as well as the dimensions of the event itself. These are discussed blow.

Dimensions of traumatic events

The severity of a traumatic event is assessed on the basis of a number of factors. According to Harvey (1996 p. 8), they include 'the frequency, severity and duration of the event/s experienced, the degree of physical violence and bodily violation involved, the extent of terror and humiliation endured and whether the trauma was experienced alone or in the company of others'. Carlson (1996) argues similarly, in considering the severity of an event, that it 'includes a number of variables such as the number of events experienced, the intensity of the event/s, the nature of the trauma and the duration of the trauma'. The research findings are contradictory in relation to the impact of the severity of the stressor event on subsequent negative psychological outcomes, for example in relation to road trauma (Green et al. 1993; Kleber et al. 1995; Jeavons et al. 1996; Blanchard & Hickling 1998). In part, this may be due to the fact that there are often a number of traumatic experiences that flow from a trauma like a road accident and its aftermath.

McFarlane (1995a p. 40) highlights the evidence that does not confirm 'the powerful relationship between the stressor and subsequent symptoms'. He also argues that there has been 'little systematic examination of the different dimensions of a traumatic experience and their interrelationship'. As with age and sex, there are some studies that identify the importance of the nature of the event itself. Yehuda and McFarlane (1995 p. 5) therefore conclude: 'Indeed it is likely that some types of events are more traumatic than others and produce different rates of PTSD'. It is also possible that events experienced as traumatic by one person are not experienced that way by another. In recognition of this, the *Australian Guidelines for the Treatment of Adults with Acute Stress Disorder and Posttraumatic Stress Disorder* (Australian Centre for Posttraumatic Mental Health. 2007) refer to **potentially traumatic events (PTEs)** rather than assuming all events are traumatic and/or are experienced as such by all people who encounter them.

There is some evidence to suggest that certain kinds of traumas are more likely to lead to positive outcomes. For example, McMillen, Smith and Fisher (1997) studied survivors of three different trauma events—a tornado, a mass killing and a plane crash. They found that perceived benefits were observed most among survivors of the tornado, followed by the survivors of the mass killing and least of all among the survivors of the plane crash. This study suggests that there may be some differences in the recovery processes and outcomes between natural disasters and traumas where human responsibility plays a major part. It is argued that where more human responsibility is evident in causing the trauma, the victim or survivor feels greater anger and a sense of violation and this complicates recovery experiences, whereas surviving a natural disaster may enable people to develop a sense of survivorship and resilience more readily.

There is only minimal research on whether the severity of an event affects **post-traumatic growth**, with Tedeschi and Calhoun (1996 p. 466) proposing that, theoretically, the more severe the trauma, the more growth there should be. This proposal is supported by their comparison of those who had experienced one or more severe traumas in the past year with those who had not.

The severity of the event raises a number of issues. First, there is the question of what the source of the trauma response is. As Reiter (2000) notes in relation to survivors of the Holocaust, there are often multiple stages of a traumatic event. Even in one as typically brief as road trauma or rape, what actually is perceived as the stressor event is difficult to determine.

Related to this is the second issue of what aspect of the event is considered traumatic. A number of counterintuitive findings have emerged in relation to the effect of proximity to the stressor on distress outcomes. This has primarily emerged from studies of Vietnam veterans which have shown that those with least proximity to the traumatic events were the most traumatised (Boscarino 1995). Similarly, McFarlane (1992) in his follow-up of 469 firefighters at four, eleven and twenty-nine months after the Ash Wednesday bushfires found that, 'neither the magnitude of people's losses nor the intensity of their exposure was a direct cause of disorder'. On the other hand, Biernat and Herkov (1994) found in a study of student reactions to campus murders that negative consequences were related to proximity to the stressor. Those closest to the event experienced greater levels of distress.

Third is the question of the role of the passage of time. The role of time in leading to natural recovery from negative psychological consequences remains unclear, as does its role in promoting growth reactions. Tedeschi and Calhoun (1996 pp. 467–8) found no association between the length of time since the traumatic event and the subsequent growth experience, although they do hypothesise that growth will not be seen in the very early phase of trauma recovery.

In relation to distress, there has been some effort to distinguish the types of trauma that lead to more protracted recovery experiences than others. For example, Biernat and Herkov (1994 p. 311) discuss the way in which crime victims are thought to resolve their trauma within six to twelve months, compared with other victims such as child abuse and sexual assault victims, who may experience much more long-term reactions, given the degree of physical and sexual violation.

Traumatic events are often community or even national events, and can be either natural or human-made. In recent years, some significant disasters have included the September 11 attacks on the World Trade Center in New York, the 2001 invasion of Afghanistan and the 2003 invasion of Iraq, the 2004 Boxing Day Indian Ocean earthquake and tsunami, the Black Saturday bushfires in Victoria in 2009, and civil wars in the Democratic Republic of the Congo, Somalia and Sudan, where children are torn away from families and rape is frequently used as a weapon of war. Each of these situations have left hundreds, if not thousands, of people dead or experiencing dislocation, physical injury and/or trauma. Reactions to disaster are often compounded by experiences of dislocation and loss of community infrastructure. The communication of essential information can be problematic or non-existent and the coordination of disaster recovery and relief efforts complicated and often delayed.

For example, studies of the impact of the Boxing Day Tsunami showed that those who experienced the most traumatic stress were those who experienced exposure to death (as did most people) but also physical dislocation and relocation in the aftermath of the trauma (Silove 2007; Van Griensven et al. 2006). These experiences highlight how important a multidimensional approach is in responding to trauma. Loss of the structural context compounds trauma and inhibits timely responses. A multidimensional approach encourages a broad focus on all of the personal and environmental factors that influence both the events in the first place and the aftermath environment.

Inner-world risk and protective factors

Perceptions of the traumatic event

The considerations above lead to the issue of whether it is the objective or subjective perception of the event that is more influential. It has become increasingly evident that one of the key determinants is the subjective perception of these events, rather than the objective 'reality' of the event (Green et al. 1993; McFarlane 1995a; Harvey 1996 p. 8; Holtz 1998). Consistent with stress theories, appraisal is considered to be a critical risk or protective factor. That is, how the individual affected by the trauma perceives their experience, particularly in relation to a threat to life or perceived threat to life (Lifton 1988; 1993), is critical to the way in which a trauma response develops. It is one of the central diagnostic criteria for PTSD. The reasoning behind this is that the greater the perception of threat, the greater the level of disturbance or disruption this perception creates, hence, the greater the potential for a traumatic stress response. For example, Mayou et al. (1993) found that the initial intrusive and horrific memories of road accidents were related to the development of PTSD.

However, as Richmond and Kauder (2000) note, it is not only the perceived threat to life that a critical risk or protective factor, but also the perceived 'violation of their social and personal integrity, resulting in feelings of stress and vulnerability, as they confront the possibility of their own mortality'. The subjective construction of the event is thus of critical importance. Along with a perceived threat to life, a range of other disturbing perceptions and experiences can be heavily influential in the survivor's recovery experience—the perception of the loss of personal control; the perception of the future and self-determination; the perception of systems and the social environment and their helpfulness or unhelpfulness.

One of the other key perceptions may be whether the event is in fact traumatic or not. There is the presumption in using the language of trauma that if the event is considered generally to be of a potentially traumatic nature, then all trauma survivors will experience it as such. However, research with firefighters following the bombing in Oklahoma City in 1995 (North et al. 2002) showed, for example, that the disaster, rather than leading to high levels of traumatic stress, led to feelings of affirmation and efficacy of their role. This is the reason for the adoption of the term potentially traumatic event (PTE) in place of the presumptuous 'traumatic event' terminology.

There is also the issue of the relative traumatic nature of the trauma experience. Does the experience of previous trauma lead to a minimising of the perception of trauma experiences, consistent with Kobasa's arguments about the 'steeling effect' (Kobasa 1979) of a history of traumatic experiences, or does prior traumatic experience lead to other perceptions of vulnerability? Recent research has focused less on the conscious appraisal aspects of trauma processing, and more on the neurobiology of traumatic responses and memories, an issue we explore later in this chapter.

Another key perception that has been examined is the perception of blame and responsibility for the trauma itself. This is particularly pertinent in the experience of road trauma where typically there is an issue of human error or fault (Wheat & Napier 1997). Dohrenwend (1998 p. 5) reinforces the importance of assessing the issues of blame and personal responsibility, in stating 'we must face the fact that the individual's behaviour plays a large part in the occurrence of many of these events and, that, to the extent that it does, individuals can create the "calamitous circumstances" to which they are exposed'. Many traumas are preventable incidents, occurring through human error or recklessness. This leaves many survivors grappling with issues of guilt, anger and blame, whether directed towards themselves or towards others.

A number of researchers have examined the impact of perceived responsibility, and therefore perceived control, for the trauma on recovery outcomes. This is in relation to road trauma recovery (Bulman & Wortman 1977; Delahanty et al. 1997), rape (Frazier & Schauben 1994) and other trauma experiences. Delahanty, Herberman, Craig, Hayward, Fullerton, Ursano and Baum (1997), and later Hickling, Blanchard, Buckley and Taylor (1999), have shown, perhaps counterintuitively, that those who blame themselves for the accident and fulfil criteria for PTSD are 'less symptomatic initially, and recover more rapidly in the first six months than those with PTSD who blame another party for the accident' (Hickling et al. 1999 p. 345). Similarly, Bulman and Wortman (1977) found in an earlier study of survivors of spinal injuries that those blaming themselves for the accident were perceived by social workers and nurses to be coping better than those who were blaming others. Frazier and Schauben (1994), along with others such as Janoff-Bulman (1979) and Herman (1992), have examined the ways in which characterological and behavioural self-blame influence outcomes from trauma. Frazier and Schauben (1994) found that some behavioural self-blame might be protective. It may enable the individual to feel confident and in control of how they act in the future, and feel that by changing their behaviour they can restore a greater sense of safety.

The final area of perception that has been examined in relation to trauma has been perceptions of coping and recovery. One of the phenomena noted is the process of downward comparisons—'comparing oneself to those who are worse off is a productive way to interpret one's own situation' (Harvey & Miller 2000). It is argued that in minimising one's own injuries or difficulties, the ability to cope with the traumatic event is heightened.

Age

Age is intimately connected with the developmental stage of the individual, and therefore intimately connected with the adaptive tasks of the individual in the aftermath of trauma. Assumptions about the impact of age on recovering from trauma vary considerably. One belief is that younger people cope better with trauma because of their innate resiliency and capacity to bounce back. This is in view of the fact that they are considered to have more of a future focus than a retrospective one. Other research has found the opposite—that older age is a protective factor. This is based on the belief that older people cope better because of their working through of existential and death-related matters. For example, Northouse (1994) found that older women tended to experience less emotional distress than younger women with breast cancer.

However, age can be a significant influence on the exposure to different traumatic life events and the availability of support within the environment. Age also influences the coping capacities of the individual, in terms of both their inner-world and outer-world risk and protective factors. Chapters 7 to 13 explore these issues in detail.

Sex and gender

Refer to Table 2.2 on p. 46.

Sex is a risk factor both for the prevalence of certain traumas and for the recovery trajectories. For example, sexual assault and rape are traumas experienced more commonly by women, as the Personal Safety Survey (ABS 2006a) demonstrates. Across a range of trauma experiences, females tend to report more psychological effects. This reporting includes both negative consequences (Norris 1992; Biernat & Herkov 1994; Koopman et al. 1996 p. 535; Blanchard & Hickling 1998) and positive consequences (Lehman et al. 1993; Tedeschi & Calhoun 1995 p. 114; Park et al. 1996 p. 710; Polatinsky & Esprey 2000; Cordova et al. 2001; Weiss 2001). For example, Wallerstein and Blakeslee's (1989) study, found four times as many females than males reported psychological growth.

In relation to distress, the findings are similar. For example, Kenardy, Webster, Lewin, Carr, Hazell and Carter's (1996) study of the Newcastle earthquake that occurred in 1995 found that males and younger individuals experienced less distress than females and older individuals. The stronger connections with roles and the locality base were more disrupted for women.

Other studies that have set out with the question of gender specifically as the focus of their research have failed to show any significant differences in outcome. For example, Polatinsky & Esprey (2000 p. 715), in their study of sex differences in the perception of benefit resulting from the loss of a child, found no evidence of significant sex differences.

Sex or gender as a potential protective or risk factor is a problematic area for a number of reasons. First, more reporting may not indicate more distress. It may relate more to females' socialised communication abilities around areas of emotional distress rather than actual difficulty resolving such emotional distress (Gilligan 1993; Tannen 1996). Second, there are problems in relation to the possible gendered nature of trauma responses. While research highlights that men tend to use coping styles that are problem-focused or behavioural and women tend to use coping styles that are emotion-focused and relational (Thoits 1991), many trauma measures continue to overlook coping behaviours such as increased drug and alcohol use or changes in work commitments that may highlight a more complex interplay of these coping styles. Third, there is an argument that females are exposed to more stressors generally and therefore are more traumatised (Thoits 1991 p. 107). Finally, in most areas of general community trauma research, females are over-represented. This has important implications for the research into trauma, as conclusions based on female trauma samples may be inappropriately drawn for males recovering from trauma.

Hope and optimism

The important roles of hope and optimism in individual well-being and, indeed, often in survival, are frequently acknowledged. For example, Frankl (1984 pp. 96–7) observed the role of hope in the survival of concentration camp inmates when he stated: 'Those who know how close the connection is between the state of mind of a man—his courage and hope, or lack of them—and the state of immunity of his body will understand that the sudden loss of hope and courage can have a deadly effect'. Yet until the last decade, although there was awareness of this connection, hope and optimism have been neglected by many disciplines, including psychology and psychiatry (Stotland 1969), as well as social work, in understandings of the mediating variables in a range of critical life events.

While there are many ways in which **hope** is understood (Stotland 1969; Averill et al. 1990; Brackney & Westman 1992; Briton & Jackson 1996), a prevailing understanding is that it is related to 'an expectation about goal attainment' (Stotland 1969 p. 17). As Godfrey suggests, 'hope thus involves beliefs about the possibility and the worth of what is hoped for' (Godfrey 1987 p. 29). In terms of recovery from trauma, hope is seen as a vital factor in being able to connect or reconnect with future possibilities and become freed from the focus on the past that trauma imposes (Freud 1982; Macnab 2000 pp. 25–32).

Snyder and others (Snyder et al. 1991; Snyder 2000) propose that hope, when compared with optimism, has two distinguishing features. They argue that hope has:

» an inherent sense of agency—that is, an individual's sense of expectation about achieving goals
» an inherent sense of pathway, in that there is an ability 'to sustain movement along the imagined pathways to goals' (Snyder 2000 p. 13).

This model of hope, unlike others, emphasises thinking rather than viewing hope as more of an emotion-based concept.

Optimism is conceptually similar to hope in that it is understood to be the generalised expectancy for positive outcomes (Scheier et al. 1994) or a confidence in the future. Averill et al. (1990 p. 95) propose that optimism is a more morally neutral and non-emotional concept than hope, and that claims of optimism can be 'based on evidence that can be judged in terms of rational criteria'. They also conclude that hope can be maintained under conditions when optimism can no longer be sustained. This explains the predominance of hope, rather than optimism, in the research into mediating variables in areas such as terminal illness. Thus, some researchers have concluded that hope is a more 'flexible' or 'open' construct than optimism.

Hope and optimism have been strongly linked with the notion of post-traumatic growth. In a study examining the impact of hope and optimism on growth for patients living with chronic pain caused by fibromyalgia, re-evaluations of the relationship between growth and optimism (measured by the Post-traumatic Growth Inventory and the Life Orientation Test—Revised) have shown no relationship between the two. However, a significant relationship was found between growth and hope (Tedeschi et al. 1998 p. 72). It would seem logical that hope or optimism would be required to motivate a process of personal growth and that some relationship would therefore be demonstrated between growth and these two variables.

The major areas in which hope and optimism have been researched are performance, adjustment and health (Snyder 2000). Hope has been found to be a positive influence in terms of coping with spinal cord injury, burns during adolescence, breast cancer, HIV/AIDS and with fibromyalgia. Darlington and Bland (1999) found hope to be an important factor in living with serious mental illness. Elliott et al. (1991), in an earlier study, examined the role of hope in adjusting to physical loss and found that those who had a high sense of agency were more 'psychologically buoyant'.

Hope and optimism are beneficial in coping with these adverse life events because they motivate individuals towards action or, as Averill et al. (1990 p. 100) argue, when action is not possible, hope serves a 'regulatory' role, maintaining a 'sense of coherence'. These functions assist in approach coping. In coping with the aftermath of trauma, task-focused coping or approach coping have been identified as more successful coping strategies than emotion-focused coping or avoidant coping styles (Aldwin 1993). Importantly, given the data that suggests females adopt more emotion-focused coping styles and males adopt more task-focused coping styles, no gender differences have been noted in patterns of hopeful thinking to date (Snyder 2000 p. 21).

Spiritual, religious and existential factors

As well as increased interest in the psychological resources of optimism and hope, there has been increasing attention paid to the buffering effects of spirituality and religion. As George et al. (2000) note, people frequently report that spiritual beliefs and practices are major sources of personal strength and recovery, although this phenomenon remains little understood in most of the health and mental health sector.

While literature about stress is relatively devoid of any reference to the importance of spirituality, an extensive body of research is emerging that demonstrates strong links between matters of the spirit, trauma experiences and subsequent psychological and physical health. As Blanchard and Hickling state (1998), persistent pain, limited activities and injury are constant reminders of an accident and of the trauma associated with the accident. Therefore, in such cases, there is cause to constantly search for a reason why and look for a way to draw meaning from an event.

It is argued that religion and/or spirituality affect health in at least three ways (George et al. 2000; Loewenthal 2000). First, religion or spirituality promote health behaviours—in two ways. The first is in the specific prohibitions against the behaviours that place health at risk, such as drug and alcohol use, sexual promiscuity, smoking and violence (George et al. 2000 p. 110). The second is through the encouragement of health promotion as a result of viewing the human body as having spiritual and material significance (George et al. 2000 p. 110). Second, religion or spirituality promotes social support. It is argued that religious or spiritual affiliation encourages the development of close social bonds outside the nuclear family, and in turn the establishment of a social network that can be depended on in times of trouble. However, it is interesting to note that social support only explains five to ten per cent of the relationship between religion and health (George et al. 2000 p. 111). Third, the most strongly supported health-promoting aspect of religion or spirituality is understood to be its provision of a sense of coherence and meaning for people. It is argued that through participating in a faith tradition, 'people understand their role in the universe, purpose of life and develop courage to endure suffering' (George et al. 2000 p. 111). This theory of the buffering effect of spirituality is linked with the trauma response. If trauma shatters worldviews, narratives and core assumptions, as argued in Chapter 1, and if religion provides an overarching experience of coherence or preservation of a sense of coherence, then spirituality or religion may well function as protective factors.

Premorbid factors

Premorbid (or pre-existing) factors, such as personality style and existing social supports, are important and influential factors in coping with the aftermath of a traumatic event. But the extent to which they are considered influential varies enormously. Bowman (1997) argues strongly for premorbid personality styles to be acknowledged as the key determinant of recovery outcomes. There is some evidence to support this view. For example, Frazier et al. (2000), in studying transplant survivors, found that coping styles, as well as enduring social supports, were predictive of later coping and adjustment. There is, however, also evidence to the contrary: 'Eitinger (1961) in his study in Norway and Israel, inquired about premorbid factors and concluded that personality characteristics did not play a part in the after effects of the trauma' (Dohrenwend 1998 p. 24). Research on massive psychic trauma has consistently hypothesised that 'the more stressful the circumstances, the lesser the role played by premorbid factors' (Dohrenwend 1998 p. 29). Bowman (1997) provides an extensive critique of the role of personality.

Another premorbid factor taken into account is the role of prior psychological difficulties. Breslau et al. (1991) found that prior trauma and prior PTSD predicted PTSD when there was a new trauma with which to cope.

Co-morbidity

Continually debated among the PTSD researchers is the issue of co-morbidity, or the co-existence of other difficulties. Evidence suggests that there is a high level of co-morbidity, or coexistence, of PTSD with other psychiatric and psychological disorders, particularly depression, causing many to question the validity of the PTSD notion. Some, such as Yehuda and McFarlane (1995) and Keane and Wolfe (1990), suggest that 'anywhere from 50% to 90% of individuals with chronic PTSD also meet diagnostic criteria for another psychiatric disorder, including substance abuse' (Yehuda & McFarlane 1995 p. 7).

Outer-world risk and protective factors

> One of the most vital elements of the healing process following trauma is the quality of human compassion for another person's suffering, regardless of the nature of the trauma. (Raphael & Meldrum 1994 p. 1)

To date, the discussion has focused on the research that examines the role of physical and psychological risk and protective factors. This part of the chapter examines the significance of the social context of trauma and recovery, and its capacity to function as either a protective or vulnerability factor. For, as Kleber et al. (1995 p. 1) suggest, traumatic experiences do not occur in a vacuum. Each person, before and after their trauma experience, is both influenced by and influencing social relationships and support.

Social dimensions

The most frequently examined aspect of social support, in both the research and practice context, is that of immediate, close associates or informal networks of family and friends.

In the aftermath of trauma, many people recount the experience of losing a sense of understanding or connectedness with their social support networks, of feeling major changes within their intimate relationships and a sense of abandonment by society's institutions that present impersonal, devaluing responses to their predicament (Durham 1997). Likewise, Gottlieb (1981) warns against romanticising the support available to individuals from families and friends, when as Martin (1997) highlights, many families and friends are not in a position to be offering support, be it emotional, instrumental or material.

Discussions about the impact of trauma on communities are diverse, with some arguing that trauma brings a community together through the shared experience of loss and grief, and others seeing communities shattered by their experiences. Herman (1992 p. 214) talks about the devastating impact of trauma on interpersonal relationships and sources of social support—'Traumatic events destroy the sustaining bonds'—arguing that reconnecting with groups is a necessary part of the healing and recovery process. Erikson (as discussed in Caruth 1995), in his follow up of the Buffalo Creek flood survivors, found that this was not possible within the community itself. Numerous fields of inquiry have led to the development of broader definitions of social support and its vital protective function. It certainly cannot be claimed to be an area of new knowledge, in that the beneficial aspects of social support, both in relation to physical and psychological health, have long been recognised. Some of the existential writings from Holocaust survivors, for example, portray vividly the life-saving quality of social support. Bettelheim's (1991 p. xvi) recognition of the importance of human links flows through his work:

> The strongest motive for staying alive is that one has something for which one is determined to remain alive at all costs, at all risks. This is no problem as long as one has strong attachments to others, for whose sake one wishes to remain alive.

However, it is only relatively recently that detailed research has been undertaken in an effort to demonstrate the significant impact on mind and body of supportive relationships with others. A number of critical studies legitimised this focus, including Spiegel, Bloom, Kraemer and Gottheil's (1989) now famous study of women with metastatic breast cancer and the life-enhancing impact of belonging to a support group, and Peterson, Seligman and Vaillant's (1988) Harvard Mastery of Stress study, which examined the impact of perceptions of earlier parental relationships on mid-life health status.

Consistent with this, Perry et al. (1992) found that social support was more predictive of psychological outcome from a burns injury than was the severity of the injury. Conversely, studies of Vietnam veterans have found that 'lower social support was associated with all disorders, except drug abuse' (Boscarino 1995 p. 317).

Some studies have examined the effects of more formal support networks established throughout trauma recovery phases. Jeavons et al. (1996 p. 32), for example, found that twenty-two per cent of their sample of road trauma survivors had received counselling. One-third reported that counselling had been helpful, forty-four per cent found that it helped a little, and twenty-two per cent reported that it had not been helpful. They also examined who the survivors would have liked to talk to. Thirty-five per cent would have liked to talk to a professional counsellor, three per cent a volunteer, nine per cent somebody else; forty-seven per cent nobody, and six per cent did not know. Thirty-six per cent said that they still thought they needed help for the medical, psychological, social or economic consequences, which they were not receiving. Twenty-six per cent specifically thought that there had been a lack of opportunity to talk about feelings.

Other studies have examined the effects of counselling from a different perspective. Rather than seeking subjective opinions as to the helpfulness of counselling, they have measured the course of PTSD development over a period of time. Some studies have actually shown increased PTSD rates for those who received counselling than for those who received no intervention (Hobbs et al. 1996), fuelling debates as to the efficacy of trauma counselling and post-trauma interventions (Robinson & Mitchell 1993; Raphael & Meldrum 1994; Robinson & Mitchell 1995; Kenardy 1996; Kenardy et al. 1996). Others have argued that those who seek counselling in the first place are more likely to represent only the most distressed group of survivors (Holman & Silver 1996 p. 333), thus biasing any research findings.

Like many studies of counselling intervention and psychotherapy, these studies vary in their assumptions—who provided the counselling, what theoretical model was used if any, how long the counselling continued, at what point counselling was initiated, and at what point the assessment of the counselling process was undertaken. For example, Watts (1994 p. 32) found in his sample of bus accident survivors that only one participant, in retrospect, reported feeling the need for counselling during the first two weeks. In contrast, fifty-nine per cent felt the need for counselling in the subsequent year.

CORE TASKS WITHIN CRITICAL INCIDENT STRESS MANAGEMENT (CISM)

Federal and state governments, and many other organisations, offer **critical incident stress management (CISM)** following traumatic events. In media reports, this is often referred to as 'counselling' for victims of trauma.

CISM typically involves a range of interventions, including:

» defusing (immediately discussing and expressing feelings and thoughts in a safe environment).
» formal debriefing: a five-stage process that involves establishing the facts, behaviours, thoughts and feelings about the event and moves to an educational and preventive focus, typically taking two to three hours
» education: typically about possible short-term and long-term trauma responses and about coping strategies
» counselling: typically a longer-term response, responding to people who wish to address more individual and therapeutic aspects of the trauma
» referral: typically to a wide variety of health and mental health services.

Building on the recognised need to provide some kind of intervention in the aftermath of trauma, early intervention now focuses on providing **psychological first aid**. This is in recognition that the first people on the scene of many traumas and disasters are not social workers or other health professionals but that useful early intervention can be provided in the form of informal, conversational care (Litz 2008). Five essential elements of early trauma responses, particularly in the wake of mass disasters, are outlined by Hobfoll et al. (2007) in the following box.

FIVE CORE ELEMENTS OF EARLY TRAUMA RESPONSE

An article written by a panel of world experts on trauma provides a summary of their 'view of the distilled version of best intervention practices following major disaster and terrorist attacks for the short-term and mid-term period, a period that [is defined] as ranging from the immediate hours to several months after disaster or attack' (Hobfoll et al. 2007 p. 284):

1 Promote sense of safety.
2 Promote calming.
3 Promote sense of self- and collective efficacy.
4 Promote connectedness.
5 Promote hope.

Structural dimensions

The structural context determines an individual's positioning in the social hierarchy, and, as Marris suggests, their 'vulnerability to uncertainty … The distribution of uncertainty, therefore, affects both vulnerability and the response to it, affecting vulnerability in the future' (Marris 1993 p. 81). In this way, the structural context can be a major risk factor for exposure to trauma, as well as a risk factor in the aftermath experiences.

For optimal trauma recovery to occur, formal systems of support are crucial. These include the quality and quantity of support available to the individual from health and welfare systems, and, in many trauma situations, from appropriate legal and compensatory systems. Yet the formal systems of care are rarely accounted for in the examination of how individuals recover from their trauma experience.

Freyd, Deprince and Gleaves (2007) propose a **betrayal trauma theory** as one way of understanding the complex aftermath of trauma responses. This theory proposes that two processes affect the individual in trauma experiences— the extent to which a social betrayal occurs in relation to the traumatic experience and its aftermath, and the extent to which the trauma is terror- or fear-inducing. This is illustrated in Figure 5.1

This way of understanding the consequences of trauma, as a sense of violation, resonates with Atkinson's findings in working with Indigenous community members affected by the intergenerational traumas of the Stolen Generations, about which she concluded, 'people feel victimised, which is different to bereavement' (Atkinson 2003 p. 91).

Much of the push behind the psychiatrisation (Davis 1999) of the post-trauma effects has come from the litigation processes that have surrounded trauma experiences, particularly driven by Vietnam veterans and survivors of domestic and sexual violence. Not only was the legal process a major aspect of the movement to get PTSD formally recognised as a psychiatric disorder, increasingly legal processes

FIGURE **5.1** Guide to betrayal trauma theory

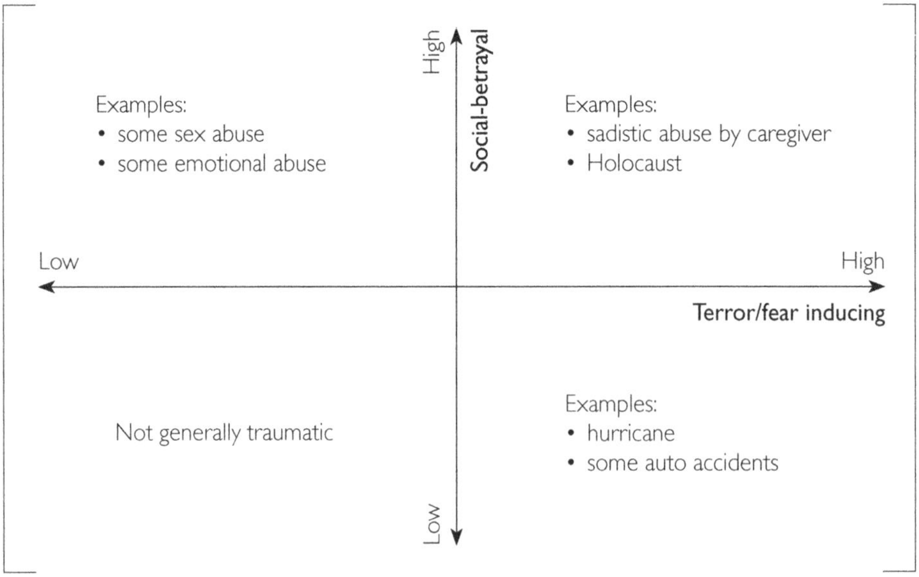

Source: Jennifer J Freyd 1996, reprinted with permission

are a part of the individual survivor's recovery process. Indeed, many have seen it as a necessary step in the recovery process (Herman 1992; Blankenship 1998).

However, legal processes are acutely stressful processes for the individual to negotiate, and little attention has been paid to the fact that this is an ongoing stressor for many who experience it. While research has been conducted around the possible impact of legal processes on an individual's recovery in terms of malingering (Blanchard et al. 1998; Fontana & Rosenheck 1998) and compensation-seeking, little if any research acknowledges the very real impact of negotiating a stressful legal process. Thus, litigation and dealing with impairment processes have not been recognised or acknowledged as additional and ongoing sources of stress and trauma in themselves.

Cultural dimensions

Trauma goes beyond the individual. It has a far wider context. We interpret war, loss, violence and disasters in ways shaped by our culture, by our society, and by its values and norms. We cope with serious life events in ways provided and approved by our surroundings. Traumatic stress does not occur in a vacuum. (Kleber, Figley and Gersons 1995 p. 1)

The extent to which a community regards an experience as traumatic will be, in part, reflected in the way in which it provides social, legal and financial resources to ameliorate the effects of the trauma. It will be reflected in the rituals and memorials it establishes and in the acknowledgment it gives to the ongoing **memory** of the experience. It will determine 'the way survivors talk about their disaster concerns' (Gist & Lubin 1999 p. 329), if at all, in establishing a public discourse of the experience.

Cultures therefore come to recognise different experiences as traumatic and are changed themselves by that perception. As Minas and Klimidis (1994 p. 140) note: 'Each culture provides distinctive understandings of human suffering and of healing'. They highlight the variation in the ways in which cultures teach their members to monitor bodily and emotional states. This is evident in the way in which Western understandings, and particularly American understandings as conveyed in the DSM-IV, are primarily related to psychological responses rather than the ways in which the somatising of trauma would be understood in Asian or Eastern cultures.

Conflicting agendas frequently exist between a society and an individual and the task of remembering (van der Kolk et al. 1996 p. 27). Trauma shatters the sense of coherence and peace in communities, as it does in individuals, so to some extent the resumption of 'normal' life is critical for the survival of the community.

Yet when a community or nation does not validate the experience, the consequences can be disastrous. Following the Vietnam veterans' return from what was perceived to be an unpopular and unjustified war, they were targets of hostile reactions in their home country. The suicide rate following the Vietnam War was higher than the casualty rate during the conflict. The lack of recognition for the horrors they had experienced is seen as a major contributing factor in this outcome.

However, there are other ways in which a society responds to trauma. Current social commentators note the 'public emotions' surrounding grief and loss, and the powerful expectation, for example, that the individual should resume their normal life and put the traumatic experience behind them (Tacey 1995; Little 1999). In recent years, the ANZAC Day memorial services and the Gallipoli dawn services have experienced greater levels of support and attention than ever before. Similarly, the Sorry Day and Reconciliation marches drew out thousands of people to march in recognition of Indigenous peoples' experiences of oppression and devastation throughout the history of Australia, and on the 14 February each year the National Apology to Indigenous Australians is commemorated. The social remembering and forgetting of trauma are political processes which highlight the costs of trauma, both individually and socially.

PRACTICE IN CONTEXT

TRAUMA AND ITS CONTEXT

In this case example, Sam describes the many impacts on a client's life of domestic violence and sexual assault.

Helen is thirty-two years old. She is known to welfare and health services. She has multiple psychiatric diagnoses. Helen wants a 'normal' life but does not see how this is possible. Helen was four when her mother (Joan) took her and her two siblings to a refuge following extensive domestic violence from their father. Joan later remarried. Frank (Helen's stepfather) regularly sexually assaulted her. Helen began cutting herself when she was eleven and binge drinking when she was fourteen. Helen left home at fifteen and began using any drug she could obtain. Helen has been assaulted by multiple perpetrators throughout her adult life. Helen feels worthless, cries often and is socially isolated. Helen has alluded to experiencing childhood sexual assault to health and welfare professionals but she has felt unable to discuss the extent or impact of the abuse. It is December and Helen is planning to kill herself.

Questions
1   What is your initial reaction to Helen's situation?
2   What traumas do you think Helen has experienced?
3   What risk and protective factors do you think are evident in this situation?
4   What would you see as some of the important priorities for intervention in this situation?

Coping with trauma

Understandings of the aftermath reactions of trauma and their causes are varied, and tend to be interconnected across a number of theories. The dominant theories of the negative consequences of trauma include psychoanalytic, cognitive and cognitive–behavioural, narrative, existential, neurobiological and multidimensional views (see Table 5.1). Each of these theories will be briefly overviewed in the following pages.

Psychoanalytic views

The psychoanalytic view is the earliest and most extensively incorporated understanding of the negative consequences of trauma. This diverse body of theory provides the foundation for the current understanding of the trauma experience as causing disturbances to the ego. The development of this theory is largely attributed to the work of Freud, although it was significantly influenced by others, such as Charcot and Breuer (Gay 1988). The complexities and controversies surrounding it, from both an historic and theoretical perspective, are beyond the scope of this book but are well documented elsewhere.

Freud (1982; 1984) proposed that there were four core disturbances of trauma:

1 The protective shield around the ego is breached, due to lack of preparedness for the anxiety evoked by the event.
2 The person becomes fixated on or preoccupied by the event, and as a consequence becomes separated from both the past and the future.
3 Freud adopted an 'economic' view of mental processes, arguing that the overwhelming nature of the traumatic encounter, in presenting too powerful a stimulus in the first place, then leads to permanent ongoing disturbances of energy in the individual's psyche.
4 He argued that there is an accompanying loss of libido—the future fantasy is lost. There is an abandoning of all future interest, as noted frequently in today's grief and trauma literature (Tedeschi et al. 1998 p. 2).

Defence mechanisms, as described in Chapter 4, particularly repression and regression, are evoked to manage the overwhelming anxiety that characterises trauma. While Freud later (in 1897) infamously retracted his sexual theory of the origins of the trauma response, his work on the traumatic neurosis became heavily influential in the treatment of traumatised soldiers from the First World War, and remains influential today. Many of these Freudian notions can be seen as implicit notions in both conceptual models of the trauma and grief response and in therapeutic models.

TABLE **5.1** A summary of theoretical understandings of trauma

Theoretical framework	How the negative consequences of trauma are understood	Implications for recovery
Psychoanalytic	• a breach of the protective shield around the ego • a fixation on the traumatic event, disconnecting the individual from the past and present • a permanent disturbance of energy due to overwhelming nature of the trauma stimulus • a loss of libido—future fantasy is lost	• conscious connection with the memory • cathartic release of appropriate emotion
Cognitive	• the trauma is too overwhelming to be processed in the same way as other experiences • cognitive processing of the traumatic event occurs slowly over time through the oscillating experiences of intrusive and avoidant thoughts • memory of the event is stored via different memory processes • memory retrieval is therefore different • the inner schemas, or worldviews, of the individual are shattered	• integrating memory of the event • appropriate effect accompanying the memory • developing a new worldview that incorporates the traumatic event
Narrative	• disruption of the individual's way of understanding their place in the world • loss of role and identity • loss of meaning and a sense of coherence	• redeveloping an integrated narrative of the self that includes the traumatic event • bearing witness to the subjective experience and validating the story • social validation required
Existential	• confrontation with mortality, isolation, anxiety, meaninglessness in the unexpected life-threatening traumatic event	• restoring hope and meaning • restoring connections with others • confronting death • involving wider social justice or humanitarian issues

Theoretical framework	How the negative consequences of trauma are understood	Implications for recovery
Cognitive behavioural	• event is appraised in particular ways and usual coping strategies are initially applied • usual coping mechanisms are found to be redundant in dealing with the trauma • coping efforts are challenged	• moving towards new ways of coping, primarily problem-focused ways of coping • finding appropriate coping strategies for the given situation
Neurobiological	• exposure to stressful situations overstimulates the amygdala and hypothalamus, leading to endorphin excretion • memory storage processes are different as a result	• uncertain, given hypotheses of permanent damage to neurobiology
Ecological	• trauma interrupts all the domains of an individual's life—the biological, the psychological, the social and the spiritual • active adaptation is required to maintain homeostasis of functioning	• return of balance to all areas of functioning

Cognitive views

There is a range of cognitive theories about the negative consequences of trauma, sharing core themes. These core themes are, first, that the event is so cognitively overwhelming it cannot be processed in the same way as other experiences. Therefore, the cognitive processing of the event occurs slowly over time through the oscillating experiences of intrusive and avoidant thoughts (Horowitz et al. 1979; Horowitz 1992). Second, the event is so cognitively overwhelming that the memory of it is not encoded in the same way as normal event memory (van der Kolk 1994; Schacter 1996). Therefore, both different memory storage and retrieval mechanisms apply. Third, the event, through its unfamiliarity and unpredictability, shatters the assumptions or inner schemas of the individual, so that the worldview that the individual previously held, no longer holds (Janoff-Bulman 1979; Marris 1986; 1996).

From a cognitive perspective, the key to the victim's recovery is the re-establishment of an integrated memory of the event and a newly organised set of basic assumptions or schemas. In order to do this, the individual oscillates between intrusive memories, thoughts and flashbacks of the experience, and avoidant thoughts, until the traumatic event can be assimilated into the survivor's cognitive world (Horowitz et al. 1979; Horowitz 1992; McFarlane 1992). Intrusions are the 'unbidden thoughts and images, troubled dreams, strong pangs and waves of feelings, and repetitive behavior' and avoidance refers to 'ideational constriction, denial of the meanings and consequences of the event, blunted sensation, behavioral inhibition or counterphobic activity, and awareness of emotional numbness' (Horowitz et al. 1979 p. 210). This state of oscillating between intrusive and avoidant thoughts is matched by a hyperarousal, a readiness for the unexpected event to occur again. Horowitz argued that, over time, the individual was able to incorporate the event into everyday life, as part of an innate human 'completion tendency'. Horowitz's notions of intrusion and avoidance, and later hyperarousal, formed the key symptoms of a trauma response, PTSD.

Narrative views

Hyer et al. (1996) highlight a dilemma for survivors: the pre-trauma 'world' and its values can be changed fundamentally as a result of the trauma experience. This change, it is argued, is what causes disruption for the individual, as the 'world' is suddenly unpredictable and unknowable (Janoff-Bulman 1979; Marris 1986, 1996; Parkes et al. 1993). Given this new unpredictability and instability, the individual's previously held understandings and assumptions no longer help them make sense of what has passed and what is now their present reality.

The underlying conceptual basis for this argument is found in ego psychology and psychoanalytic models (Howe 1995). As we will explore in Chapter 7, it is argued that in the early attachment phase of infancy, normal human functioning arises when the infant can develop a stable, inner representational model of the 'world' and their role in it (Bowlby 1980. The stability of the availability of caregivers and the meeting of physical and affective needs is crucial. Stability and vitality as an adult are dependent upon 'good enough' experiences of predictable, close attachments with primary caregivers in infancy and early childhood (Winnicott 1968).

In this sense, there is an argument for a conservative impulse (Marris 1986 pp. 5–22)—that is, that human beings strive to keep the world as predictable and knowable as possible, in order to minimise anxiety and to maximise successful functioning. In view of these underpinning notions, two major areas of thought have addressed these disturbances.

First, Janoff-Bulman (1992) developed her widely accepted notion that individuals hold three core assumptions and that the trauma experience shatters some or all of these. This concept is referred to as **shattered assumptions**. The three fundamental assumptions she outlines are: the world is benevolent, the world is meaningful, and the self is worthy. However, there are difficulties with this model. Leys (2000) points out that there are difficulties in verifying that these three assumptions are, in fact, the core assumptions that individuals carry with them and that in turn they are 'shattered' by the experience of trauma.

Second, consistent with this model of disturbed inner schemas, increasing attention has been paid to the importance of developing a testimony or a coherent narrative of the traumatic event (Caruth 1995; Neimeyer & Stewart 1996; Harvey & Miller 2000; Reiter 2000). Similar to the notion of shattered assumptions, Neimeyer and Stewart (1996), for example, propose that the event is initially beyond words and beyond meaning for the survivor. Thus, the event creates a discontinuity in the individual's narrative of themselves and their place in the world. The event literally does not fit in the worldview that has been held up until this point.

The testimony, Gist and Lubin (1999) argue, is about seeing that: 'Telling one's story is more than merely recounting the events of one's personal encounter with disaster; it is a complex, multi-faceted, coping strategy that should not be discounted as unnecessary or minor in the often chaotic wake of such events'. The testimony not only includes the individual story of the survivors, but also aims to include the historical and sociopolitical context in which the experience took place.

At an individual level, the two central tasks of recovery are addressing the basic psychological processes and joining the traumatic self and the associated narrative with the pre-existing selves and the primary narrative (Neimeyer & Stewart 1996). Both Herman (1992) and Laub (1995) explore the notion that recovery is dependent on the development of a testimony or, as Laub defines it, an internal witness. This is encapsulated in the words Herman (1992 p. 202) proposes could stand as an emblem and final stage of recovery—'I know I have myself'.

This process is argued to involve more than just a strong internal witnessing. At a social level, it is often about addressing the external inequities in a public manner. Herman (1992 p. 181) argues that the trauma and the recovery must become a source of a survivor mission, whereby there is some form of externalising the internal recovery process: 'Testimony has both a private dimension which is confessional and spiritual, and a public aspect, which is political and judicial'. Thus, the role of the recovery environment is also critical.

Existential views

For survivors, the experience of trauma is perhaps most sharply marked by the distress and suffering it leaves in its wake. There is the horror and shock that define the reactions to the event, and there is the continuing distress and suffering in the aftermath. Yet this human experience of suffering tends to be either curiously absent or a sanitised element of much of the trauma discourse. Its absence is curious because so widely accepted as central to the definition of trauma is the notion that there has been, if not a real threat to life, a perceived threat to life. Thus, immediately, existential themes seem central. For example, road trauma presents the individual with the experience of threat to life and the confrontation with death. In the wake of this experience, there is frequently a reviewing of the purpose of life and its inherent as well as specific meanings.

Yet, a language of trauma symptoms and behaviours characterises the trauma research, rather than a language of human suffering and distress. The existential discourse is typically sidestepped by many of the dominant researchers who have tended to focus on the far more readily quantifiable cognitive reactions (Blanchard & Hickling 1998 p. 292).

The existential discourse has primarily grown out of the recent literature focusing on survivors of the Holocaust and survivors of other forms of mass human destructiveness. The theorising revolves around the subjective works of survivors such as Frankl (1984) and Bettelheim (1991). Eitinger's (1961) later study on the effects of prolonged, deliberate trauma and torture inflicted during the Holocaust, and, most specifically, through the concentration camp experience, has also been influential. This is a discourse that has emerged from the very survivors of those experiences, rather than from some of the more objective, quantified bodies of research. It is also reflected strongly within individual survival accounts of road trauma, such as those provided by Durham (1997), Eisendrath (1997), Moore (1991) and Traynor (1997).

This existential perspective offered a significantly different exploration of the trauma response and the possibilities for recovery, placing hope, the search for meaning and human connectedness at the centre of its theory. The existential discourse offers a language of experience or suffering that defines human attempts to come to terms with four major themes often disturbed by trauma—death, freedom, isolation and meaninglessness (Lifton 1988; Yalom & Lieberman 1991). The key areas of an existential focus include the nature of human suffering, the will to live (Kahana et al. 1995) and the search for meaning in such suffering (Marris 1986; 1996).

The implications for recovery are that the core task is the restoration of the continuity of meaning (Marris 1996 p. 48) or a coherent worldview that incorporates the traumatic experience. There is also an argument that recovery and restoration of meaning leads to a wider connection with humanity—as Lifton (1988 p. 8) suggests, 'we find in each case a struggle to reinstate a larger human connectedness or a sense of being'. Thus, there may be a new connection with or concern for others (Macnab 2000 pp. 10–11), or an involvement in community advocacy (Herman 1992; Blankenship 1998).

While there has been acknowledgment of the central importance of existential issues (for example, threat to life or perceived threat to life is one of the core diagnostic criteria for PTSD), there has been little attention paid to these issues within research methodologies. This is no doubt a result of the perceived difficulties in putting terms associated with existential concerns into operation. Unlike the checklist notions associated with PTSD symptomatology, the existential domain presents a multitude of challenges to the researcher.

Cognitive behavioural views

In addition to disturbing the experience of self and the world, trauma disturbs the usual coping mechanisms; thus, usual or known coping efforts are often redundant in the face of trauma. This has focused attention on what types of coping effort are most adaptive. Research has consistently found evidence that active, approach-oriented coping strategies, discussed earlier in Chapter 4, lead to better levels of adjustment, in contrast with passive, avoidant coping strategies.

In examining the coping strategies of trauma survivors, for example war veterans, it has been found that the majority tend to use emotion-focused and avoidant coping strategies (Hyer et al. 1996 p. 307), leading to poorer coping outcomes. Hyer et al. also found that planful problem-solving (ten per cent), seeking social support (nine per cent), and positive reappraisal (seven per cent) were the least frequently used coping methods.

Coping mechanisms are activated after an initial appraisal of the event—thus, according to Lazarus and Folkman (1984): 'Stressful appraisals include whether the situation involves threat, harm, and/or loss, and are a function of both the person (beliefs, values, commitments, and personal preferences) and the situation (e.g., its controllability)'. There is inevitably a close and complex relationship between personality and coping mechanisms. However, social workers and others working in the trauma area, clearly do not believe that recovery is solely a matter of personality. There is belief in the effectiveness of intervention at an intrapsychic, interpersonal and social level, and knowledge of its possibilities. While undoubtedly personality plays an important role, it does not account entirely for the picture of recovery that is seen. The assumption that recovery is largely a matter of personality is both counterintuitive and counter-experiential.

Neurobiological views

Extensive work has been undertaken in recent years to understand the biological and neurobiological processes involved in the trauma experience. This has in part been driven by the debates around false memory syndrome and the differences between traumatic and non-traumatic memory storage and retrieval processes (Schacter 1996). The research has focused on the role of, particularly, the anterior hypothalamus, the amygdala and the hippocampus (van der Kolk 1994; Schacter 1996). Of particular interest has been the way in which exposure to certain stressful situations activates these receptors, resulting in endorphin secretion, raising the possibility that the trauma response is a hormonal response. Schacter (1996) and van der Kolk (1994) argue that a unique form of memory storage then takes place, with normal memory-processing pathways being overwhelmed by the trauma experience. These findings have significant implications for traumatic memory recall. While earlier psychoanalytic views proposed that traumatic memory was repressed, neurobiological views propose that traumatic memory is encoded in ways that often bypass usual cognitive processing and are encoded using more emotionally focused parts of the brain (LaBar 2007). Thus, traumatic memory is more likely to be fragmented and incomplete and emotionally experienced.

Trauma in infancy is the developmental stage where this neurobiological approach is most focused, given the devastating impacts on neural development trauma and neglect that have been demonstrated (Shonkoff & Phillips 2000). As Leys (2000) notes, it is a popular theory due to its strong links with neuroscience and neurobiology, away from the subjective domains of interpretation and meaning.

In Chapter 7, we look at this research in more detail.

Multidimensional views

To a much lesser extent, the negative impact of trauma is viewed as multidimensional or ecological (Harvey 1996; Herman 1992; Caruth 1995; Tedeschi & Calhoun 1995; Tedeschi et al. 1998). In addition, the attempts to be multidimensional (or ecological) remain unsatisfactory. Most trauma models focus solely on the nature of the event and the individual's capacity to psychologically respond and recover. There are, however, a number of models that take account of the fact that the trauma and the individual is never occurring outside a social context. This context includes a vast range of cultural, financial, political and sexual factors. How the individual is incorporated within this context post-trauma will have a significant impact on their recovery and thus both multidimensional and ecological models emphasise the 'post-crisis environment' (Tedeschi et al. 1998), social support, access to resources, and stability of functioning from the pre-crisis environment.

THEORY IN CONTEXT

In the following case scenario, Susie reflects on how she integrated these theoretical understandings into her practice at a large trauma hospital.

While on final placement at a major trauma hospital, I was involved with a patient who had experienced a high-speed car accident. Stephanie, a 20-year-old female, was the driver of the vehicle and sustained significant lower body injuries. After my initial assessment, it was clear that Stephanie was experiencing symptoms consistent with an acute stress reaction (ASR) following this traumatic event. With the criteria for post traumatic stress disorder (PTSD) in mind, I was able to recognise that Stephanie was re-experiencing the accident through vivid dreams and flashback episodes. She was also suffering severe nausea and a constant tremor. Stephanie could not recall the accident at first, and avoided talking about the incident stating, 'I don't want to think about it'. She reported difficulty sleeping, as she would experience nightmares of the accident.

In order to help Stephanie understand why she was experiencing these feelings, I provided her with information about symptoms of ASR. We then discussed these responses and explored her thoughts surrounding them. Over the course of the next few days Stephanie and I were able to discuss the accident at her own pace, as she began to feel more comfortable about her responses to the trauma.

Trauma theory enabled me to understand how trauma can affect a person in all facets of their life. Stephanie was experiencing physical, psychological and social distress, and the theory enabled me to understand the reasons behind this, and to address them in a way that was effective for her. Understanding the theory behind ASR and PTSD allowed me to acknowledge that my patient was experiencing these symptoms, and I was thus able to tailor my interventions accordingly. I was also able to assess and screen for the possibility of PTSD developing, and inform the rehabilitiation social worker if I thought this was a concern.

Questions

1 What is your personal reaction to this situation?
2 In what ways did Susie use trauma theories to understand Stephanie's situation?
3 Are there other aspects of trauma theories that you think could be usefully applied?

Recovery from trauma

The origin of the word 'recovery' is the French verb 'recoverer' meaning 'restore to health, strength or consciousness', quite distinct from the notion of going back to or returning to some former state, frequently reported by survivors of trauma (Harms 2002). This is about establishing a restored sense of self, and of the new reality.

Herman (1992 p. 155) proposes a three-stage model of recovery. The central task of the first stage is the establishment of safety. The central task of the second stage is remembrance and mourning. The central task of the third stage is reconnection with ordinary life. One of the markers of the final stage of recovery from trauma, she argues, is that the survivor has made a community connection, or a connection beyond the individual context, to become involved in advocacy or community development activities. This model of recovery fits with a multidimensional approach, in that it recognises the significant processes and resources in both inner and outer worlds that influence coping and adaptation. It recognises that resilience is not an individual quality, but arises through dynamic individual and environmental processes and interactions over time.

CHAPTER **SUMMARY**

Trauma responses, like stress responses, can clearly be conceptualised in many different ways, ranging from being understood as part of a psychiatric condition or a neurobiological response, to being understood as a complex psychosocial interaction particularly creating massive uncertainty or a loss of meaning or sense of coherence. It is all of these things and more. Post-traumatic growth and thriving are now recognised as possible outcomes from trauma, expanding the understandings of the effects of trauma even further.

Given the capacity of trauma to cause such inner- and outer-world chaos, traumatic life events tend to be associated with poorer developmental outcomes than stressful life events. Specific aspects of traumatic events are associated with different outcomes. The perceived threat to life seems to be one of the key risk factors for some people. The age of the survivor influences both the cognitive appraisal of the events and the availability of appropriate coping resources.

The interest in resilience has developed from the recognition of resilience under conditions of extreme adversity. The protective factors that are mentioned recurringly in the literature are a sense of coherence, of trust and of optimism, in the inner-world dimensions. The outer-world dimensions again exert a profound influence on recovery pathways. Trauma experiences are typically not about one single event, but a series of events and conditions. How the social, structural and cultural dimensions mediate these experiences, by acknowledging and validating an individual's suffering, has been identified as a key potential risk or protective factor. Similarly, an individual's position in the structural and cultural context will determine their exposure to various traumas.

Questions remain as to how we can really hear and understand another's suffering, and come to understand the damage to the self that trauma so frequently creates, and how we can more fully understand experiences of resilience in the aftermath of trauma.

APPLYING A MULTIDIMENSIONAL UNDERSTANDING

Sam: Road trauma

Sam is in a rehabilitation hospital following a major car accident. He was the passenger in a car that swerved off the road late at night, hitting a tree. His friend, who was driving, was killed instantly. Sam has sustained serious injuries. He has a badly broken leg and needed surgery to have his right arm amputated. He will be in rehabilitation for another week, and then continue as an outpatient for months afterwards.

Sam is twenty-four and his girlfriend of two years left him a week after the accident. She was tired of his drinking and his marijuana use, and wanted him to sort himself out. Sam's parents have cleared out his flat and moved his things back to their house. He was behind in his rent payments anyway, and they want him to come home to recover, then find work and move out later.

Sam is furious about all these decisions being made for him. He smashes furniture in his hospital room. The police have made an appointment to see him.

Community: Bushfires

Every house in the town was burnt to the ground, with the exception of two. The community had been advised that they were relatively safe from the fires, which were burning kilometres away, but the wind changed suddenly and within several hours, the whole town was razed to the ground. Some families had evacuated and were directed to community halls in neighbouring towns. Some people had been able to gather up possessions but others had not had the chance. The fire took everything they owned. Some families had stayed to defend their properties and died, through the intensity of the heat and the choking fumes. Other people were caught on the roads and died in their cars, unable to flee from the fire quickly enough. At the relief centres, basic physical needs such as food, shelter and clothing were available, and psychological first aid was also being offered.

Questions

1. Adopting a multidimensional understanding, what trauma reactions do you think each of these individuals and families will experience?
2. What are the risk factors in these scenarios?
3. What response and resources do they need to cope? Who should provide it?
4. What reactions would you expect over time, from these individuals, their families and the wider community?

CASE STUDY

KEY TERMS

acute stress disorder (ASD)

betrayal trauma theory

critical incident stress management (CISM)

hope

memory

optimism

post-traumatic stress disorder (PTSD)

post-traumatic growth

potentially traumatic events (PTEs)

psychological first aid

shattered assumptions

trauma

QUESTIONS AND DISCUSSION POINTS

1   What are the three symptoms of post-traumatic stress disorder?
2   What are the key biopsychosocial and spiritual effects of trauma?
3   What dimensions of traumatic life events are considered to be risk or protective factors?
4   What are the inner world risk and protective factors associated with trauma?
5   What are the outer world risk and protective factors associated with trauma?
6   What are some of the key ways of coping with trauma?
7   In what ways has trauma impacted upon your life?
8   What rituals are you aware of that occur in the aftermath of trauma?
9   Some traumas are more validated within communities and cultures than others. Think about the different trauma experiences that are validated or not within the Australian context.

FURTHER READING

American Psychiatric Association 2000, *Diagnostic and statistical manual of mental disorders IV-TR*, Washington: American Psychiatric Association.

Gist, R. & Lubin, B. eds, 1999, 'Response to disaster: Psychosocial, community and ecological approaches', *The Series in Clinical and Community Psychology*, Philadelphia: Brunner/Mazel.

Harvey, J. & Miller, E. eds, 2000, *Loss and trauma: General and close relationship perspectives*, Philadelphia: Brunner-Routledge.

Leys, R. 2000, *Trauma: A genealogy*, Chicago: University of Chicago Press.
Tedeschi, R., Park, C. & Calhoun, L. 1998, *Posttraumatic growth: Positive changes in the aftermath of crisis*, London: Lawrence Erlbaum Associates.

WEBSITES OF INTEREST

The Australasian Society for Traumatic Stress Studies: www.astss.org.au
This site includes excellent links to international trauma research sites.

Australian Centre for Posttraumatic Mental Health: www.acpmh.unimelb.edu.au
This site also provides excellent resources relating to research, clinical practice guidelines, consumer information and international links.

David Baldwin's Trauma Information Pages: www.trauma-pages.com
This is an excellent website developed by a psychologist in the USA, providing research and clinical services links. In addition, there is easy access to the database PILOTS (Published International Literature on Traumatic Stress) under the 'trauma resources' link.

International Society for Traumatic Stress Studies (ISTSS): www.istss.org
The ISTSS is the international organisation set up to address trauma treatment, education, research and prevention.

National Center for PTSD—USA: www.ptsd.va.gov
This site is an educational resource site for PTSD and other longer-term consequences of traumatic stress, established by the US Department of Foreign Affairs. It includes the PILOTS (Published International Literature of Traumatic Stress) database.

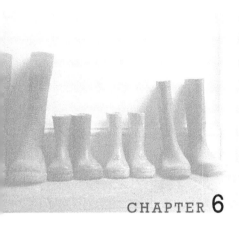

CHAPTER 6

Coping with Loss

AIMS OF THIS CHAPTER

This chapter explores experiences and understandings of loss and grief. It considers the following questions:

» What is grief?
» What are some of the definitions of grief?
» What is the subjective experience of loss and grief?
» What are the risk and protective factors associated with grief recovery?
» What are some of the ways of coping with loss?

Experiences of attachments to people, places and ideas are critical to our survival and our sense of well-being, right across the lifespan. When we inevitably lose some of these attachments, we typically feel intense and distressing reactions to their absence. Theories about these reactions are different from the understandings of stress and trauma, although there are points of commonality.

Most of the grief literature describes experiences that are associated with the loss of relationships with other people, most typically with the death of a significant person. Death takes many forms—from the sudden death of someone to an anticipated death following chronic illness. These deaths are sometimes in the context of relationships that have spanned lives, such as siblings who have known each other for eighty years or more, and partners who have been together some fifty or sixty years. Other deaths take place in the context of extremely short-term but nevertheless significant relationships—with the birth and death of a child, for example.

Other interpersonal losses occur as a result of separation. Where a relationship has become stagnant or toxic, a person goes missing, an affair has occurred or there is mutual agreement that the relationship has run its course, experiences of loss can be profound. Other losses come about as a result of separation because of various life events—migration, moving communities, changing jobs, or moving to a nursing home.

Losses can be associated with place and possessions, as a result of changes in both the social and the physical environment. Peter Read (1996), in his book *Returning to Nothing*, portrays vividly the loss of place for various Australians, for example through Cyclone Tracy, which devastated the city of Darwin on Christmas Day 1974. Many other significant losses of place are part of the Australian psyche—the bushfires of Ash Wednesday in 1983, of Canberra in the summer of 2001, and of Black Saturday in Melbourne 2009, and the Newcastle earthquake, to name a few. In these instances, both the physical and social fabric of the communities involved has been significantly damaged. Along with this loss of the physical environment can come a profound loss of a sense of belonging and connectedness. The reminders of past history can be gone in a matter of minutes during a bushfire.

Losses can occur also within the inner worlds we occupy, often invisible to those around us. We can experience the loss of dreams and hopes, the loss of a worldview or a good sense of spirituality and connectedness. We can feel very profoundly the loss of an anticipated social role, through unemployment, or the death of a child or grandchild, or by missing a place at university. We can experience the loss of part of our bodily self or function, through injury, incapacity or ageing.

Some key terms

Within the grief literature, four key terms are frequently used, often interchangeably, in relation to these experiences: loss, grief, bereavement and mourning. According to Weiss (1988 p. 38), 'loss is an event that produces persisting inaccessibility of an emotionally important figure'. This definition can be expanded to include the persisting inaccessibility of an emotionally important place, object or role. Additionally, it may not be about a single event as much as a change of attitude or inner-world experience. Inaccessibility is the key feature of the loss experience—the inaccessibility of a relationship or a dream or whatever is desired—that makes loss so overwhelming and seemingly unbearable. What is loved, yearned for or familiar is no longer there and typically cannot be there again. Even though continuing connections with many aspects of the experience may be possible, loss brings about a new reality (Freud 1984; Macnab 1989; Worden 2003).

In response to these loss experiences, we have what is termed a **grief reaction** (Parkes 1972). Marris (1993 p. 81) notes that 'any loss which fundamentally disrupts the central purpose of our lives will normally provoke severe and long-lasting grief'. This reaction is a complex biopsychosocial–spiritual one, determined by the nature of the loss, the context of the loss, and our own inner- and outer-world resources. Marris (1993 p. vii) describes grieving more specifically as referring to 'a process of psychological reintegration, impelled by the contradictory desires at once to search for and recover the lost relationship, and to escape from painful reminders of the loss'. Consistent with theories of trauma, grief is an experience of both avoidance and intrusion. **Bereavement** refers to the experience of having lost someone or something, as a result of death or separation. That is, someone who is grieving is bereaved.

Sometimes, a distinction is made between **grief**, referring to the emotional response to the loss, and **mourning**, as the behavioural and social processes that occur following grief (Raphael 1984).

A distinction is made also between bereavement and traumatic bereavement (Raphael & Meldrum 1994), an important distinction in light of the discussion in the previous chapter. **Traumatic bereavement** emerges in the aftermath of trauma incidents, and it is argued that the reaction is more consistent initially with a trauma response in these instances, with grieving processes emerging later in the recovery experience.

Subjective experiences of grief

> For some people, initial grief is a raw and unpredictable pain. For others pain filters through more slowly, a little at a time as the body can bear (Deveson 2003 p. 259).

The lived experience of grief is most vividly portrayed in our art, poetry, literature, dance and music, where the experiences of despair and suffering can find their visual, aural and verbal expression. The language of grief tends more to be a language of feelings, related to the heart and soul, than the language of trauma and stress, which relates more to matters of the mind. In contrast, the language of our textbooks sanitises significantly the experience of grief, making it sound like an experience that is somehow much more contained and understandable than the existential crisis that it so often is. Some even medicalise it to such an extent that it sounds like a medical condition, not a response to psychosocial loss. This raises the critical question as to when, if ever, grief becomes a condition, requiring treatment and intervention.

Lindemann (1944), an American psychiatrist, was the first to systematically study the acute grief reactions of individuals. In his frequently cited article of 1944, he documented five acute grief reactions experienced by those he studied. Included in his sample of 101 people were survivors of a range of grief and loss situations, including thirteen of the survivor group from the Cocoanut Grove Fire, a fire that burned down a Boston night club, killing more than five hundred people and injuring many others.

Lindemann documented systematically a range of feelings, cognitions, physical sensations and behaviours experienced by directly affected individuals and their family members. He identified five features of acute grief—somatic distress, a preoccupation with the image of the deceased, feelings of guilt, feelings of hostility, and a loss of patterns of conduct. He noted that these reactions tended to resolve after four to six weeks following the loss experience. This led to an understanding that the grief reaction was a relatively short phenomenon. However, research over the past decade has shown that this is not the case, with a number of studies highlighting both the long-term nature of grief (Lehman et al. 1987) and often even the intergenerational nature of grief. In this sense, Lindemann's observations need to be seen as the acute grief reaction, and many would still argue, consistent with crisis theory, that the first two months are when the most acute, particularly physical, manifestations of a grief reaction are experienced. Bonanno and Kaltman (2001 p. 709) reviewed a number of studies and concluded that:

> depending upon the measures used, between 50% to 85% of the bereaved individuals in these studies appeared to exhibit a common grief pattern consisting of moderate disruptions in cognitive, emotional, physical or interpersonal functioning during the initial months after a loss.

Shapiro notes that: 'The initial sensations of grief in adulthood are profoundly and simply physical and physiological' (Shapiro 1994 p. 21). She highlights the way in which the loss of a significant relationship leads to a loss of capacity for the regulation of our experience, arguing that relationships typically provide the anchor for this biological and emotional regulation. Some of the physical reactions described by people who are bereaved include a feeling of hollowness in the stomach, as if they have been punched in the stomach, and a tightness in the chest and throat. This often includes breathlessness and a dry mouth, a feeling of weakness in the muscles and an overall lack of energy. Other reactions include an oversensitivity to noise and a sense of depersonalisation (as if the world is happening around them, but they are not in their body experiencing that world directly).

The psychological dimension of grief is often a complex cluster of reactions. People frequently describe the overwhelming nature of the emotions of grief. The feelings described include shock, numbness, sadness and anger. Connected with these feelings are others of guilt, anxiety, profound exhaustion, helplessness and yearning. For some people, there are also feelings of release and relief. For others, the emotional loneliness (Weiss 1973; Stroebe et al. 1996) rather than a social loneliness, is one of the hardest aspects of the psychological dimension.

The cognitive dimensions of grief that people describe include disbelief and confusion, particularly in the early days following a loss. Others describe an ongoing preoccupation with the person or object that has been lost—ruminations, similar to the trauma reaction. Some also report a sense of the presence of the person who has died, something that is not always easily understood by those around them, and other experiences of hallucination, either auditory or visual.

The behaviours that people experience include sleep and appetite disturbances, absent-minded behaviours, social withdrawal, taking care to avoid reminders, searching and calling out, a restless overactivity and crying. However, rather than avoid reminders, others describe wanting to visit places that carry special memories, or wanting to surround themselves with reminders of the person, often treasuring objects such as clothing that belonged to them or their cremated ashes. These behaviours vary enormously and are perceived as 'normal' or not depending on the particular socio-cultural context.

While not everyone will experience these grief reactions, it is important to note that over hundreds of years, these have been the aspects described by people, both in the context of clinical practice and research and also in music, poetry, art and literature. While a very strong emphasis is placed on the subjective experience of each individual, and there is a movement away from universal theories of grief, it is because there is now this well-established awareness of some of these common experiences of grief within particular socio-cultural contexts. In previous times, many of these experiences were not recognised at all, leaving many people isolated in their experiences, wondering if they were quietly going mad. Information and education about expectable experiences in the aftermath of loss experiences has made major changes to people's experiences.

One of the questions people frequently ask in the aftermath of loss is how long their grief will last. Bonanno has emphasised that grief is not a persistent state, in reporting that it is 'overwhelming at times and often quite manageable at others' (Bonanno 2001 pp. 718–25; Bonanno & Kaltman 2001). Increasingly, recognition is being given to the long-term nature of grief, an issue discussed later in this chapter.

Where more of the current research and controversy lies is in the identification of complicated or prolonged grief reactions. Unlike experiences of stress and trauma, grief has not, to date, been included in the *Diagnostic and statistical manual of mental disorders IV-TR* (American Psychiatric Association 2000), commonly referred to as the DSM-IV, as a separate diagnostic category. Even though grief has been recognised for its potential to cause significant disruption of our biopsychosocial–spiritual dimensions over periods of time, it has been regarded as a normal reaction to normal human experience. As Freud (1984 p. 252) wrote:

It is also well worth notice that, although mourning involves grave departures from the normal attitude to life, it never occurs to us to regard it as a pathological condition and to refer it to medical treatment. We rely on its being overcome after a certain lapse of time, and we look upon any interference with it as useless or even harmful.

Grief has been referred to only in relation to major depressive disorder, following a period of two months between the loss experience and the diagnosis of depression (American Psychiatric Association 2000). It is proposed that the next edition of the DSM will include a category of **prolonged grief disorder** (Stroebe et al. 2000), and there are strong arguments for and against its inclusion.

The main argument for a diagnosis is that since the initial writings on grief, less common grief reactions have been observed. These are defined as **complicated grief** reactions or pathological grief reactions. They are sometimes referred to as abnormal or severe grief reactions. Some of these, first identified by Lindemann (1944), include the distorted or delayed reactions. Bowlby (1980) described three different types of complicated grief reaction. The first he distinguished was chronic mourning (compared with Lindemann's reference to distorted mourning), where the phases of yearning and searching, and disorganisation and despair seem to be distorted and to continue beyond expected time frames (Bowlby 1980 p. 139). The second type of complicated grief reaction he distinguished as the prolonged absence of conscious grieving (compared with Lindemann's reference to absent, delayed, inhibited and suppressed grief reactions), where the phase of numbing seems to be prolonged, with an eventual but significantly delayed point of breakdown (Bowlby 1980 p. 138). The third, and less common, complicated reaction, he identified as euphoria (Bowlby 1980 p. 139).

Bowlby argued that these complicated grief reactions led to physical and mental ill health. These 'variants' could be assessed according to the 'extent to which they influence a part only of mental functioning or come to dominate it completely' (Bowlby 1980 p. 140), and the extent to which someone could both 'make and maintain love relationships' and organise the rest of their life (Bowlby 1980 p. 137). For this reason, and to enable access to mental health services (particularly in the USA), establishing a diagnosis has been seen as an important step to ensure people who experience prolonged grief reactions are properly supported.

These descriptions have the potential to be deeply pathologising of individual experience. Diagnosis of a complicated grief reaction has been seen as intensely political and fraught. Yet the reality is that grief does strike some people harder and more profoundly than others. For those diagnosed with complicated grief reactions, there is a strong connection with other mental health difficulties, particularly depression. It raises the question as to whether pathological grief is a form of extreme stress, depression, various other typologies or a distinct phenomenon in its own right (Stroebe et al. 2000). Prigerson and Maciejewski (2006) and others have been arguing the case for the prolonged grief disorder diagnosis to be part of the next edition of the DSM. Their proposed criteria for prolonged grief disorder are outlined below.

PROPOSED CRITERIA FOR PROLONGED GRIEF DISORDER FOR DSM-V

» Criterion A: Yearning, pining, longing for the deceased. Yearning must be experienced at least daily over the past month or to a distressing or disruptive degree.

» Criterion B: In the past month, the person must experience four of the following eight symptoms as marked or extreme:
  • trouble accepting the death
  • inability trusting others since the death
  • excessive bitterness over the death
  • feeling uneasy about moving on with one's life (e.g. difficulty forming new relationships)
  • feeling emotionally numb or detached from others since the death
  • feeling life is empty or meaningless without the deceased
  • feeling the future holds no meaning or prospect for fulfilment without the deceased
  • feeling agitated, jumpy or on edge since the death.

» Criterion C: The above symptoms cause marked dysfunction in social, occupational or other important domains.

» Criterion D: The above symptom disturbance must last at least six months.

Early attachment styles are explored in Chapter 7.

These criteria have strong links with early attachment styles.

Unlike the research focus in both the stress and trauma fields, there has been less of a focus on the possibilities for positive consequences of grief experiences. Yet in the aftermath of loss, many people come to report experiences of change and growth that are positive. The Stanford Bereavement Project (Davis & Nolen-Hoeksema 2001), in following up some 280 bereaved individuals up to eighteen months following the death of a family member, found that seventy to eighty per cent of their sample reported some perception of benefit—whether in relation to growth in character, a gain in perspective or a strengthening of relationships. The capacity to perceive benefits did lead to reduced emotional distress. Importantly, their study did not find a similar pattern with the experience of making sense of the loss. As they state, 'whereas making sense of loss involves the task of maintaining threatened worldviews … finding benefit seems to involve the task of maintaining or rebuilding a threatened sense of self' (Davis & Nolen-Hoeksema 2001 p. 737).

Experiences of loss, like trauma, have also been the catalyst for major environmental change, often leading to the prevention of further loss. This has been in relation to the establishment of support groups and lobby groups— coming together in recognition that instead of pathologising and privatising the individual grief experience, it can be publicised and politicised. This transforms the experience for both the individual and social environment. For example, the changes to the federal legislation around gun laws arose as a direct result of intense lobbying following the deaths of thirty-two people at Port Arthur, shot by Martin Bryant in 1996. As Allan notes, 'healing, education, awareness-raising, attitudinal and social change' arise as a result of activism, which 'can occur through lobbying and campaigning for legal and other reforms, public rituals, speaking out on issues, public storytelling, setting up new support or action groups and publishing' (in Allan et al. 2009 p. 225).

Risk and protective factors

Much attention has been paid to what influences these grief experiences, particularly risk factors that could be considered predictive of more complicated grief experiences. Bowlby (1980) identified five categories of variables that influenced the course of mourning, including the identity and role of the person lost, the age and sex of the person bereaved, the cause and circumstances of the loss, the social and psychological circumstances affecting the bereaved about the time of and after the loss, and the personality of the bereaved, with special reference to their capacities for making love relationships and for responding to stressful situations (Bowlby 1980).

Marris (1996 p. 48), in reviewing the available literature on the conditions that influence the experience of bereavement, identified four key factors:

1 poorer experiences of attachment during childhood
2 the nature and meaning of the relationship that has been lost, particularly when it was conflicted, doubtful or unresolved
3 the circumstances of the loss, particularly when there has been less opportunity to prepare for the loss and the circumstances around the loss event were less predictable or meaningful, leading to more traumatic structural disruption
4 the events after the loss that support or frustrate the processes of recovery.

Parkes (1972) similarly identified factors that affected the outcome, according to whether they were antecedent, concurrent or subsequent to the loss experience. The antecedent factors include childhood experiences, later experiences, previous mental illness, life crises prior to the bereavement, relationship with the deceased, and the mode of death. The concurrent factors he identified as the sex of the bereaved person, their age, their personality characteristics, their socio-economic status, nationality, and religious and cultural factors. And the subsequent factors he identified as social support or isolation, any secondary stress factors and emergent life opportunities.

These factors, identified by Parkes, Marris, Bowlby and others reinforce that the individual's biopsychosocial-spiritual grief reaction must be understood as inextricably linked with the socio-cultural context in which they find themselves and in which they experience that loss. The context of grief is critical in shaping the expectations and resources for the individual.

Dimensions of loss and grief experiences

Many studies have highlighted specific event-related factors that seem to influence subsequent bereavement experiences to a greater or lesser degree—whether the loss is recognised, whether there is forewarning of its occurrence, whether it is an ongoing loss, and whether there are specific losses that are inherently more traumatic or stressful than others.

Disenfranchised grief

Not all loss experiences are acknowledged or validated by those around us. The expression **disenfranchised grief** was popularised by Doka (1989), in recognition of the fact that many people experience private losses that are not validated by the wider social environment. As Peskin (2000 p. 102) states, the 'right or permission to grieve is more essential to the process of mourning than we usually let ourselves know'. The impact of disenfranchised losses gained substantial recognition during the AIDS crisis, when so many gay men were excluded from care situations or from funerals because their gay partnerships were either not known about or were invalidated by the family members of the person who had died.

Other situations of disenfranchised grief have been identified in relation to the experiences of infertility, death in situations of an extra-marital affair, or the loss of a pet—all experiences that are generally overlooked in terms of their significance by the wider society of which the person in grief is a part. Part of this overlooking is related to the social recognition of such relationships and taboos that surround some relationships and not others. One of the most horrific examples of this within Australia's history is the loss experience of the Stolen Generations. Based on federal government policy, Indigenous children were forcibly removed from their family homes, based on the fallacious belief that these children would be better off fostered into other homes within mainstream, white Australia. The aftermath of such widespread, sanctioned dislocation has been devastating, and is documented to some extent in the *Bringing them home* report (National Inquiry into the Separation of Aboriginal and Torres Strait Islander Children from their Families (Australia) 1997). This dislocation involved separation from primary attachment figures, from place, from culture and from identity, followed by the traumatic experiences encountered in many of the foster homes and institutions.

Anticipatory grief reactions

> One minute we had sat with a man who was thinking, moving, feeling. Then the man died, and in his place there was a body, warm for a few minutes and then alarmingly cold. Such a fine thread that connects us to life. Such a brief moment of time that takes life away. Although I had all that time to prepare for Robert's death, I still went into some kind of shock. At the same time I felt immensely tired. (Deveson 2003 p. 258)

Another experience of grief that has been described and debated within the literature and clinical worlds is **anticipatory grief**. Anticipatory grief is observed as the process prior to the impending death or loss of a person. Rando (1986 p. 24) defined anticipatory grief as:

> the phenomenon encompassing the processes of mourning, coping, interaction, planning and psychosocial reorganization that are stimulated and begun in part in response to the awareness of the impending loss of a loved one and the recognition of associated losses in the past, present and future.

Anticipatory grief has been explored in relation to many chronic illness situations. The understanding of anticipatory grief is that the knowledge of an impending death leads to a different grief reaction than if the loss experience has been sudden and unexpected. The argument is that the grief work has already begun prior to the death. It was therefore anticipated that those who were grieving as a result of anticipated situations might have a less severe grief reaction once the death occurred. Rando (1986 p. 24) suggests that the griever in this situation is 'pulled in opposing directions', with the task being to 'balance these incompatible demands and cope with the stress their incongruence generates' (Rando 1986 p. 25). Others suggest that it is a more specific reaction, mourning parts of the relationship and/or roles, but maintaining an ongoing investment in the relationship and grieving its loss only after the death of the person.

Chronic sorrow and non-finite grief

Some situations of loss are considered to be more ongoing than others, with a capacity to involve persistent grieving. One area where this has been perceived to be relevant is in the experience of disability, where parents are reminded continually of what could have been and what has been lost. Olshansky (1962) developed the notion of **chronic sorrow** to refer to this experience of people living with constant loss and grief. This term has been reinterpreted by Bruce and Schultz as **non-finite grief**. This notion refers to grief that is recurrent throughout the lifespan in response to the losses associated particularly with disability. That is, they are the grief reactions evoked in response to 'what should have been' that are reawakened through anniversaries, significant developmental milestones and the 'lack of synchrony with hopes, wishes, ideals and expectations' (Bruce & Schultz 2001 p. 7).

The research supports these notions to some extent, although Hewson (1997) has argued for a model of episodic stress response rather than regarding the experience as primarily one of grief.

Public grief

In contrast to the very private nature of disenfranchised grief, public grief has also gained researchers' attention. Public grief situations often create an overwhelming outpouring of grief and distress (Little 1999). Princess Diana's death in 1997 was much analysed for its capacity to draw millions of people into a grief reaction on an enormous scale. The September 11 attacks and the Canberra and Black Saturday bushfires have also given rise to very public expressions of grief, through community rituals and memorials in particular. These events become part of the history and culture of communities and nations, and wider recognition is now given to the importance of publicly acknowledging experiences of significant loss.

Characteristics of specific loss events

Some specific characteristics of events are frequently examined for their potential to be risk or protective factors, primarily in relation to loss situations involving the death of a significant person. These factors include the suddenness and unexpectedness of loss, the violence involved, whether the death was a result of suicide, and the perceived timeliness of the death.

Deaths that are sudden and unexpected are regarded as causing greater difficulty in the mourning process. Whereas, as argued earlier, anticipated deaths prepare people in some ways for what will inevitably occur, sudden deaths occur with no warning and no time for such preparation. A sense of unfinished business and regret often lingers.

The perceived cause of the loss is also important. Loss can be viewed as being either a result of persecution or random events. Particular populations of people at different points throughout history have been persecuted or victimised and have been affected extremely by loss as a consequence. Other losses occur through more random and uncontrollable events. Following loss experiences, searching for answers to the question 'why?' is a common process. Where there has been a violent death as a result of homicide or suicide, the questions of why, and the trauma associated with such a death, are seen to be complicating factors in the mourning process (Currier, Holland & Neimeyer 2006).

As individuals and communities, we tend to hold assumptions about age- and stage-appropriate life events, particularly in relation to death and dying. That is, we tend to believe that there is a correct life sequence (Berger & Luckman 1966; Neugarten 1996), both for ourselves and for others. The death of a ninety-year-old patient in a nursing home is viewed significantly differently by society than the death of a three-year-old child, for example. We carry in our minds a sense of the 'correct' life sequence—parents predecease their children, older people predecease younger ones. This is sometimes referred to as the ranking of grief. Peskin (2000 p. 104) argues that 'we all carry within us monologues of comparative bereavement wherein we take measure of our own need to mourn against our own right to mourn and do in light of others' needs and rights'.

Consistent with many of the theoretical notions of grief and coping with grief, these events characteristics are factors in which our meaning structures (Marris 1996, p. 26), both individual and cultural, are potentially significantly disrupted. These factors highlight the ways in which different cultural contexts influence bereavement. In communities where infant mortality rates are very high, for example, very different cultural expectations around death and bereavement exist. Western cultures have come to expect that, with such significant advances in medical technology, death can be avoided, particularly in infancy and childhood. Similarly, with so much death and dying removed from everyday experience within many Western cultures, and managed within the context of hospitals and hospices, very few people come to witness death as a natural part of life.

Increasing recognition is being given to the impact of intergenerational loss experiences, primarily through the experiences of the Holocaust survivors and Australia's Indigenous populations (Raphael & Swan 1997). These experiences of oppression and persecution, involving the multiple losses of people, places and a sense of identity, have reverberated through to the next generation. Losses of this magnitude continue to occur around the world, where political and social forces have a profound impact on the well-being of individuals.

Some theorists have called for further work on the issue of what distinguishes a major loss from a relatively minor one. For example, Harvey (2001) argues that major losses are relative and cumulative, and that they lead to identity change and the need to adapt to loss of a sense of control. They also have the potential to lead to the creation of new meanings and often the externalising of those new meanings through social action.

Another key psychosocial dimension of the event is its impact in financial and legal terms. While the focus in the literature, and often in practice, is predominantly on the psychological and social dimensions of loss, many loss experiences carry with them other costs. For example, Stebbins and Batrouney (2007) looked at the costs for families where a child had died. The average cost was estimated to be $16,000 per family, taking into account unpaid leave that had to be taken, decreases in employment hours and loss of work opportunities, along with other care cost factors.

Our own death

The literature tends to focus on the experience of grief in the prelude or aftermath to someone else's death or to some external loss experience. Elisabeth Kubler-Ross, a Swiss psychiatrist who migrated to the USA, however, was a pioneer from the late 1960s onwards in highlighting the grief individuals experienced when facing their own death. Broaching issues that were previously taboo within the medical profession, she spoke with hundreds of dying patients and raised a critical awareness of the inner worlds of the dying person. She observed five stages of grief experience that many patients seemed to experience, described later in this chapter (pages 175–7). While many practices have changed for individuals in the final phase of life, and for the ways in which hospitals and other health systems respond to them, there are still major taboos surrounding death and dying. Terror management theory (Pyszczynski, Greenberg & Solomon 1999) has been proposed as a way of theorising these taboos and responses, in looking at how people manage the knowledge that we will inevitably die.

These issues are explored further in Chapter 13.

Inner-world risk and protective factors

Many of the risk and protective factors identified in relation to stress and trauma apply for grief as well. The personality characteristics raised in relation to stress and trauma consistently emerge in the grief literature also. Hope, optimism and humour have all been examined for their capacity to be protective factors in the face of grief. However, some specific inner-world risk and protective factors are associated with grief and are considered below.

The nature of the relationship prior to the loss

The nature of the relationship is a factor that is considered crucial to the grief experience. Zisook and Lyons (1988) looked at reactions to different relationship losses within families, and found that, within their sample, grief was most unresolved when they were mourning their child's death and most resolved in relation to the death of parents. They noted also high levels of unresolved grief with sibling loss, an often underestimated loss. Irrespective of the nature of the relationship in terms of kinship, the more ambivalent the relationship prior to the loss, the more complicated the grief reaction seems to be, 'because its meaning, unresolved in the past, is all the more difficult to resolve in the future' (Marris 1993 p. 49).

The assumption and role of love in these discussions of a loss of relationship is important to note. Much of the grief literature refers to the loss of 'loved ones', assuming that this is the nature of the relationship. Some exploration of this is required. Hobfoll, Ennis and Kay (2000) importantly highlight the fact that not all relationships are built on a basis of love, but may have functional elements as more primary motivations for their existence. However, absent from their discussion also is the fact that many relationships exist on the basis of a complicated confusion of hatred and love—high levels of ambivalence are experienced. Family violence situations are an example of very ambivalent and complex attachments. Alternatively, in the instance of some relationships that involve heavy care burdens, when they end, the reaction is not necessarily one of bereavement but of release and relief, both for themselves and the person who has died. The idealisation and romanticisation of many relationships makes the language of grief devoid of many of the complications and hostilities of everyday relationships. Another frequently unacknowledged aspect of grief relates to the reality-base versus the fantasy-base of many relationships. These taboos or oversights mean that many important dimensions of the grief experience are often not explored.

Sex and gender

Many of these understandings of the grief experience are in fact heavily gender-biased understandings, arising from studies with women who have experienced the death of a partner or of their children. This is in part due to the fact that women experience widowhood more frequently than men do, given the longevity differences between the sexes, and are more likely to be within clinical, or help-seeking, populations, which in turn become research populations (Stroebe et al. 2003). Others have argued, similar to the stress issues discussed in the previous chapter, that women have an increased exposure to loss and grief experiences, through their child-bearing and rearing roles, through roles of immediate care for children and other family members, and through a strong connection with home and place.

Some of the studies into the impact of gender on grief reactions have found that there are differences between the sexes. For example, mortality rates following the death of a spouse tend to be higher for men than for women (Christakis &

Iwashyna 2003), in part attributed to the lack of alternative social networks (Davidson et al. 2003). For women, loss of a partner often brings with it a series of different changes, particularly relating to socio-economic status and social role. Thus, factors in the outer world associated with gender status influence subjective experiences. The social context is a critical determinant of the protective factors that are available to the grieving person.

Age

As with stress experiences, the age of an individual can determine both the exposure to different types of loss and grief situations and the availability of various coping resources. For example, when attachment relationships have been lost as a result of death or separation during infancy, there seems to be a lifelong effect on mental health outcomes (Parkes 1972). The availability of other attachment figures and social support becomes critical as a protective factor in the grief experience (Rutter 1987) right across the lifespan. Similarly, studies highlight that the availability of supportive structural and cultural dimensions is a key protective factor.

Chapters 7 to 13 explore these age-related dimensions in detail.

Outer-world risk and protective factors

The context in which grief occurs is enormously influential in the immediate and long-term experiences of someone who has experienced significant loss. Parkes (1972) identified a number of factors in the aftermath environment that were influential—religious factors, social relationships, socio-economic status and secondary stressors, and emergent life opportunities. Bowlby (1980) identified the living arrangements, the socio-economic provisions and opportunities, and the beliefs and practices facilitating or impeding healthy mourning.

Social dimensions

Our social networks in the aftermath of grief are a critical influence in recovery. Yet grief typically disrupts social networks, either directly by the loss of relationships within it, or indirectly through the changes that such losses inevitably bring about. The difficulty of maintaining high levels of social participation in the aftermath of loss is a frequently reported effect of grief, leading to the emotional isolation of grief. As Shapiro (1994 p. 221) states, 'it is an experience that places us outside our existing social constructions and categories while we reclaim and re-establish our place in the social world'. It is a socially dislocating experience. Whether the loss is the death of a significant person or the loss of a job, a particular world, with its roles and routines is changed.

Difficulties arise within social networks not just as a result of the inaccessibility of the significant person or role. These losses impact on others, and the complexity of different grieving styles is encountered. In the aftermath of loss, new ways of relating and finding meaning need to be negotiated, leading in some instances to the question as to whether relationships are able to be maintained.

Friendships are often profoundly affected as a result of the death of a partner, as people find it increasingly difficult to maintain an ongoing relationship, or the workplace finds it difficult to know how to respond to someone who is bereaved in their private life. In the aftermath of divorce, some family members and friends lose contact with certain members of the separating family.

While it is widely acknowledged that social support is critical in the aftermath of grief, it is important to consider what kind of social support people find useful. These distinctions are highlighted in Chapter 2.

However, experiences of loss and grief can lead to the development of new connections and the widening of social relationships. The availability of new networks, through the many community support groups, such as Solace, Compassionate Friends, Road Trauma Support Team and SIDS and Kids, discussed broadly in the next section, offer the specific social support that individuals and families require. For some people, connecting with religious communities is helpful in the process of finding a new meaning and purpose in life.

Structural dimensions

The availability of the formal, and even some informal, social networks of support depends upon the resources and the commitment within the wider structural context. The structural response to loss varies enormously, dependent upon the nature of that loss, linking with the earlier notions of disenfranchised grief. For example, in the aftermath of the death of a partner or close family member, there is typically provision in Australian workplaces for compassionate leave. This is typically one to two days of leave, to attend to the immediate tasks associated with a death, primarily the funeral and burial or cremation. In the context of the previous discussion, this does not even correlate with the acute grief phase. It is also granted on the basis of particular relationships; thus, other losses, which may be equally devastating, are not recognised. The hierarchy of loss that is socially and structurally recognised is often quite incompatible with the subjective experience of loss an individual encounters.

In the aftermath of many losses, there are institutions and systems with which the bereaved person needs to interact (Allan et al. 2009). Death is regulated by a range of legislative processes, such as the Coroners Court, the funeral industry, cemetery regulations and laws relating to wills and estates. In the event of divorce, similarly, legal processes are required to annul the marriage and often to establish new boundaries around access rights between parents and children. In the event of loss of property through bushfires or through drought, the government and organisations such as The Salvation Army and Red Cross ensure the availability of disaster relief programs. The availability of insurance or government-funded emergency relief critically influences the degree to which secondary stressors and emergent life opportunities (Parkes 1972; Allan 2009) are part of the recovery experience.

The socio-economic status of the individual, family and community also leads to a range of general opportunities and options, which can either compound or relieve the loss situation—access to financial safety nets through Centrelink, access to health care through Medicare, or access to funded counselling through community health centres. Structural dimensions also determine the availability of specific grief supports and resources—counselling support and published material, for example, for those who are bereaved. Decisions at a structural level determine whether there is government or philanthropic funding for services such as Compassionate Friends, the Australian Centre for Grief and Bereavement, or the Road Trauma Support Team.

The structural context is also a source of risk for initial and subsequent loss for individuals and families. Certain socio-economic conditions or geographic contexts lead to more exposure to loss experiences than others. For example, with the increase in the ageing population within Australia, the structure and affordability of care arrangements will mean people will either need to leave their neighbourhoods when their health needs become insurmountable or care will need to be structured such that they can be more fully cared for in the home. Aged care facilities in turn can promote or reduce loss experiences by the ways in which the care of couples can be provided in the same facility.

Cultural dimensions

Our socio-cultural dimensions influence both our exposure to loss experiences and also how we are expected to respond in its aftermath. Every culture has its own norms and beliefs for understanding loss and how it is ritualised or not. In the aftermath of death, for example, different faith and ethnic traditions prescribe all sorts of observances about the dying process, the management of the body of the deceased person, and the funeral rituals and rites. Similarly, the mourning period is frequently socially prescribed for individuals. In the multicultural context of Australia, awareness of these cultural differences and needs is critical. Nelson-Feaver and Warren (1994 pp. 156–7), for example, note that:

> Many Greeks view death as personified—that death's physical form is that of a man, his character being cold, objective and impartial; while Sikhs view death as an illusion. Australian Aborigines view death as a natural passing on from one spiritual world into another, while Muslims believe that a person's soul does not

die but merely returns to its original home. Roman Catholic Italians believe that the soul is immortal, while Vietnamese Buddhists believe that birth and death are predestined—everyone is born, dies, decays and is born again.

From an Australian Indigenous perspective, the death of a family member leads to sorry business. In sorry business, the community comes together to mourn and remember the person. Some of the rituals that are part of sorry business include:

» payback
» no longer naming the person who has died.

However, while some broad understandings of different cultural understandings of death can be developed, it is arguably more important to listen to each individual's and family's perspective, given how limiting it is to generalise across cultural groups as to what beliefs and practices might look like in the aftermath of loss, when in reality, culture for each one of us is a constantly changing and individually experienced phenomenon. In this multicultural Australian context, where migration has been so influential on the growth of the population, 'complex cultural shifts' (Campbell et al. 2000 p. 69) occur for individuals, families and ethnic groups.

While Australian culture has been characterised by its secular nature, of the 102 families who took part in a Melbourne family grief study, seventy-seven per cent used religious funeral rites to farewell their dead (Kissane 2000 p. 62). Shapiro (1994) notes that in times of crisis or grief, we tend to revert to long-held cultural practices and beliefs, even if they are not seemingly part of our everyday experience.

Our perceptions of loss, beyond just consideration of circumstances of loss as a result of death, are profoundly shaped by our wider cultural and historical context. This context will influence whether we regard grief as a private or a public experience. Our beliefs about love and loss, about relationships and their significance will influence the pressure that will be exerted on someone to 'get over their loss'. Whether we believe it is possible to get over loss or whether we believe loss casts a lifelong and inescapable veil over our lives will influence how we understand an individual's experience. These cultural beliefs will profoundly influence the tolerance and support shown to somebody in their grief experience.

Certain cultural beliefs also lead to loss experiences. The acts of removing the children of our Indigenous population, described earlier in this chapter, were a direct result of racially prejudiced beliefs. The gay community suffered, and continues to suffer, intense discrimination and hostility as a result of the HIV/AIDS crisis of the 1980s and of religious beliefs and conservatism. Thus, the cultural context in which loss occurs is a critical influence on the recovery experiences of individuals and families, but it is also a critical determinant of who is exposed to loss and who is potentially ostracised further as a result.

THEORY IN CONTEXT

THE MULTIPLE IMPACTS OF LOSS

In the following case scenario, Kirsten reflects on how she integrated theoretical understandings into her practice at a family support service.

At the age of seventeen, Melissa suffered the loss of her mother to cancer after an ongoing struggle with the illness for two years. A few months later, she was tragically involved in a car accident in which she witnessed her father and brother die at the scene. This left her with no immediate family. A year later, her first child was born with a life-threatening condition and died when a few weeks old. Melissa remained in the relationship with the father of this child, and later had another child to him, without complications. However, the relationship was a violent one. The child was removed from the parents' care at four months, due to the violence and Melissa's suicide attempt. She separated from her violent partner and was reunited with her child some years later.

Melissa has experienced an accumulation of traumatic events and suffered much loss in her life. It was not surprising to me, then, that many of the practical interventions were limited in their ability to facilitate long-lasting change. With an understanding of past trauma, I hypothesised that the reason for environmental neglect was not due to a lack of her understanding of home management, but perhaps imbedded deeper in her own internal turmoil.

Trauma and loss would have disrupted her adolescent developmental processes and it appeared that in the case of this mother the ability to form positive intimate relationships, plan for the future and accept adult roles and responsibilities was limited or lacking. With my knowledge of the mother's past traumas and the times at which they occurred, I asked at a case conference how Melissa presented herself, and it was reported that she presents like a teenage girl. This struck as me extremely interesting considering that she was seventeen years old at the time of her first and most significant loss.

It was of particular interest to me that one of the identified needs by Melissa was work to improve her self-esteem. This indicated to me that many of the presenting problems were actually rooted deeply in her history of loss and trauma, which led me to hypothesise that long-term therapeutic work might be more effective than short-term practical support.

Questions

1 What is your personal reaction to this situation?

2 In what ways to you hear Kirsten using grief theories to understand Melissa's situation?

3 Are there other aspects of grief (and trauma) theories that you think could be usefully applied?

Coping with grief

> Life has returned to its normal beat, almost as if nothing had ever happened—but not quite, because I am different (Deveson 2003 p. 266).

The last one hundred years have seen some major shifts in our thinking about coping in the aftermath of grief experiences, beginning with the work of Freud and continuing to evolve through the work of Bowlby, Parkes, Marris, Kubler-Ross, Neimeyer, Silverman, Kellehear and others. In addition to these Western theorists, grief understandings from other communities around the world have begun to influence practices and responses in the West. The rest of this chapter gives an overview of some of these understandings.

Grief work and the breaking of bonds

Central to the writings of Freud was the notion of grief as 'work', which demanded the time and energy of the bereaved person. From this Freudian perspective, 'the goal of grief work is to break the bond which exists between the griever (the subject) and the deceased (the object)' (Leick & Davidsen-Nielsen 1991 p. 9). Freud (1984 p. 253), in his paper *Mourning and Melancholia*, described mourning as the gradual release of memories and expectations of the lost relationship, arguing that 'when the work of mourning is complete, the ego becomes free and uninhibited again'. The person who is bereaved is then able to reinvest the energy that they had in the previous relationship into present relationships and possibilities. While Freud's notion of grief work and breaking the attachment bond seemed to be supporting a notion that grief work can be finished or resolved, he came to think that this was unlikely, particularly as he encountered his own experiences of loss and death within his family.

Attachment bonds

Bowlby also significantly contributed to theoretical understandings of grief in outlining the phases he observed young children moving through in response to prolonged separations from attachment figures. Bowlby (1980) described the phases of the grief response as involving the shock of the initial impact (phase one), the experience of acute separation pain and protest (phase two), and the undoing of the bonds (phase three). He applied these observations of grief and separation in children to adults, and noted that the same phases were typically occurring.

In Chapter 7, we look at the different attachment styles and in later chapters we explore the links between attachment styles and grief in adulthood.

Stages of grief

Kubler-Ross (1970), mentioned earlier in this chapter, was another pioneer in relation to grief theory. Rather than focusing on those who were grieving the death of someone, she was the first to document something of the collective experience of those who were dying. She wanted to give voice to what it was like to confront the impending reality of death, given the social taboos surrounding any discussion of this critical experience at the end of the lifespan. Using interviews with terminally ill patients in the hospital where she worked as a psychiatrist, she came to identify five 'stages' of the dying experience—shock, denial, bargaining, anger and acceptance. She identified that immediately following diagnosis, patients seemed to be in a state of numbness and shock and were frequently in denial of their illness. She argued that the need for denial existed in every patient at times, and more so at the beginning of the dying experience than at the end (Kubler-Ross 1970 p. 37). This is consistent with our understandings of the trauma reaction, with denial and shock being commonly reported experiences in the immediate aftermath of an incident.

The second stage she identified as one of anger, where the patient questioned, 'why me?' (Kubler-Ross 1970 p. 44). She highlighted that health professionals and family and friends do not often think about why the dying person has cause to be justifiably angry.

The third stage she called the stage of bargaining, where the dying person enters into some sort of agreement in an attempt to postpone their death: 'it has to include a prize offered "for good behaviour", it also sets a self-imposed "deadline"... and it includes an implicit promise that the patient will not ask for more if this one postponement is granted' (Kubler-Ross 1970 p. 73). She made a comparison with the child who says they will not fight again with their sibling—the promise is not kept! Importantly the issue of the things that are still left undone is implicit in this bargaining process, and she made a link with guilt that might be felt about this (Kubler-Ross 1970 p. 74).

The fourth stage she identified was a period of depression, which she saw as a preparatory depression rather than a reactive one. She raised awareness of the importance of this taking into account of the impending losses, and argued that it was not a depression to be positively reframed but confronted (Kubler-Ross 1970 p. 76). The final stage she identified as one of acceptance, emphasising that: 'Acceptance should not be mistaken for a happy stage. It is almost void of feelings. It is as if the pain had gone, the struggle is over and there comes a time for the "final rest before the long journey" as one patient phrased it' (Kubler-Ross 1970 p. 100). She identified the ways in which the dying person's circle of interest diminishes.

Kubler-Ross has been widely criticised for her stage theory of grief, at the expense of recognising the significance of her work in numerous ways. The criticisms are primarily in relation to the perceived 'linear' emphasis of her theory although she was clear in highlighting the cyclic nature of these experiences and, in many cases, the absence of many of these stages. Her theory of stages of the dying process raised questions as to whether there are so-called 'normal' or expectable phases of grief—or whether everyone's grief reaction is so profoundly unique that a generalised model or theory cannot be proposed. Her theory has also been misinterpreted as a theory of how people grieve after loss, when it is specifically a theory describing the subjective experience of dying.

Regardless of the criticisms, one of the most significant contributions Kubler-Ross made was to raise awareness of the inner world of dying patients. Along with this came a new emphasis on the need for appropriate personal and structural support for the dying experience—the need for open communication with not only the patient but also with their family and friends, and the need for medical and nursing care appropriate to the patients' needs.

The tasks of grief

Many clinicians and theorists have proposed various pathways towards recovery from grief experiences, shifting away from the earlier stage theory outlined above to more task-focused theories. For example, Leick and Davidsen-Neilsen (1991) have described the four tasks as involving the acceptance that the loss is a reality, an entering into the emotions of grief, the acquisition of new skills, and the reinvestment of energy in new ways. Worden (2003) sees these similarly as accepting the reality of the loss, working through the pain of grief, adjusting to an environment in which the deceased is missing, and emotionally relocating the deceased and moving on with life. This last task was consistent with the Freudian notions of grief work but was amended later to reflect the more contemporary thinking that the bond needs to continue somehow rather than be severed.

Through the Child Bereavement Project conducted by Worden (as cited in Currer 2001; Worden 2003) and also described by Klass et al. (1996), the four tasks above were confirmed as the tasks children similarly worked through, with recognition that there were six factors in the person:environment configuration that were of significance:

1   the death and the rituals surrounding it
2   the relationship of the child with the deceased parent, both before the death and afterwards
3   the functioning of the surviving parent and his or her ability to parent the child
4   family influences such as solvency, style of coping, support and communication, as well as family stressors and changes and disruptions in the child's daily life
5   support from peers and others outside the family
6   characteristics of the child, including age, gender, self-perception and understanding of death (Worden 1996 p. 17, cited in Currer 2001 p. 109).

The importance of continuing bonds

Whereas Freud's notion of grief work emphasised the relinquishing of the bond between people, in order to move into the new reality and form new relationships, recent theorists have emphasised the reality and need for people to maintain some kind of enduring link with what has been lost. Shapiro (1994 p. 41) suggests that 'the end point of successful grief work is not the relinquishment of the lost relationship but the creation of a new bond, one that acknowledges the enduring psychological and spiritual reality of someone we have loved and made a part of ourselves'. Similarly, this idea of **continuing bonds** is reflected in the work of Klass, Silverman and Nickman (Klass et al. 1996; Klass 2001), where they have argued that 'the process does not end, but in different ways, bereavement affects the mourner for the rest of his or her life. People are changed by the experience; they do not get over it, and part of the change is a *transformed but continuing relationship* with the deceased' (Klass et al. 1996 p. 19). There is an important balance to be established between the reality of the inaccessibility of what has been lost and the reality of the capacity to form ongoing related connections or bonds with both what has been lost and what is now possible.

Finding new meaning

Increasingly mindful of wide individual variation in the grief reaction, theorists have more recently turned their attention to the meaning or significance of the loss for individuals, irrespective of the 'objective' nature of such loss. The individual's perception of events becomes the most determining factor in the grief experience, a significant shift away from Holmes and Rahe's (1967) notion of some life events carrying more significance than others as a result of their objective nature, discussed in Chapter 4. In analysing the risk and protective factors earlier in the chapter, it is evident that the meaning or significance of the loss is integral to each of them.

There are layers of meaning, however, which need to be emphasised. As Gilbert (2006 p. 63) highlights, grief is about our alternate lives and how things were and could be in the past, present and future. One of the implications of the subjective experiences of grief is that individual, family, community and cultural meanings may all differ significantly, leading to a lack of goodness of fit between family perceptions and community perceptions, for example.

Marris's work has further expanded these notions, with his emphasis on the loss of meaning, and the subsequent insecurity that arises, for individuals who face loss situations when there is insecurity of meaning. Marris (1996) argues that with the experience of severe loss, there is a loss of continuity of meaning. Individuals can no longer make sense of themselves in the context of this loss, and thus the work of recovery is about restoring or redeveloping a sense of continuity of meaning. Neimeyer and Stewart (1996), in their work around the 'narrative emplotment of loss' (that is, mapping the story of grief) argue similarly that meaning reconstruction is central in the process of grieving. These meanings, however, are not static, and any understanding needs to 'focus not only on people's perceptions and stories of loss, but also on how their perceptions and stories change over time' (Liiceanu 2000 p. 113).

One key example of this was when, in 2007, the Prime Minister Kevin Rudd apologised to Indigenous Australians for the grief and trauma caused by the government's policies of the forcible removal of Indigenous children from their families and communities. This public apology enabled a new meaning to emerge for all Australians, Indigenous and non-Indigenous, in that their experiences were being recognised for the first time in this formal, national way. As the homepage of the Stolen Generations Alliance states:

> The 'Sorry Day', recommended in *Bringing Them Home*, provided the opportunity for all Australians to express their sorrow at the tragic events spanning such a long time of our shared history and, then, to celebrate the beginning of a new understanding. The wider Australian community was being invited to remember those affected by removal, so that the nation could continue the process of healing together. Indigenous people participate in the day dedicated to the memory of loved ones who have never come home or are still finding their way home.

These public, formal acknowledgments of loss have been increasingly recognised as providing significant healing for people in their grief—acknowledging both that they matter and that what has happened to them matters. Meaning making, therefore, is not just an individual, private process of restoration but one that is profoundly influenced by and influences broader social experiences.

A dual process approach

Stroebe and Schut's (1999) **dual process model** is currently a dominant model in grief research and counselling. It incorporates many threads of these latest developments in grief theory. The model proposes that there are two major orientations in grief —a loss orientation and a restoration orientation process. The work of **loss orientation** is the focus on what has gone and what is remembered from the past—the grief work of old. This involves both positive and negative reminiscences and finding a way of dealing with the realities of the losses experienced. The **restoration orientation** is associated with the person having to face the challenges of the new realities in the absence of the person who has died. This has a present and a future focus, and again, both negative and positive possibilities. These two processes, of loss and restoration, can oscillate for the person and gradually over time should lead to a resolution of the intensity of a loss orientation.

In addition, the model enables an understanding of different grief reactions between people, whereby someone may be immersed in a loss orientation and another in a restoration one, over different lengths of time or at different points in time. Gender differences have been accounted for in this model too, with some arguing that women are more likely to adopt a loss orientation and men a restoration orientation. Some research has shown that therapeutic outcomes are reached when someone is supported in actually engaging in the work of the other orientation to their dominant one (Schut 2008). Figure 6.1 shows the interrelationship of these orientations and the various characteristics of each.

Thus, the model does attempt to address two of the major deficits of previous models—issues of culture and of gender and their influence on both gendered and cultural factors in grief (Currer 2001). The model can also be used to understand the diversity of grief experiences within families and communities, as experiences of loss and restoration vary over time and among individuals.

Research is also focusing on the link between attachment styles and the dual process model (Mikulincer & Shaver 2008), an issue we will return to in later chapters when looking at adult grief experiences.

FIGURE **6.1** The dual process model

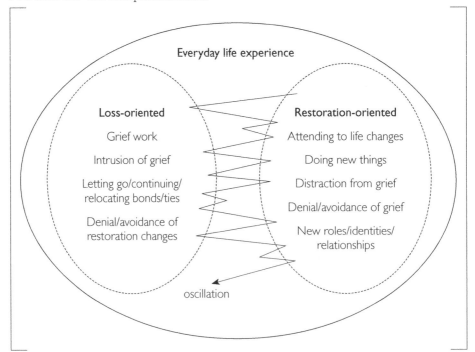

PRACTICE IN CONTEXT

PARENT BEREAVEMENT SUPPORT GROUP

Jane describes some of the sharing within a parent bereavement support group she facilitated as a social worker in a paediatric hospital.

One of the hopes of a parents' bereavement support group is that parents will make supportive, encouraging connections among themselves. The authentic sharing of ongoing personal stories with all their distress, tribulations, achievements and adjustments, can offer mutual validation and aid. In some ways the parents are human resources for each other. They offer a unique understanding based on shared yet individual experience. However, the exchanges and interactions within a potentially vulnerable and sensitive group of individuals, each with their own unique personality and history, can be perilous. They can be positive or hurtful. The following vignette illustrates this.

A father whose school-aged daughter died several years ago attends a parent bereavement support group regularly. He makes occasional spoken contributions in the group but mostly he listens. Out of compassion and understanding, an informal role that he has adopted is to connect with newcomers to the group and especially with other grieving fathers. He does this quietly, unobtrusively and naturally before the group and over supper. Other parents warm to his introducing himself, to his gentle asking about their situation and occasional reflections on experiences and the group. The father has spoken with the group facilitators about his feelings for newcomers and his particular empathy for fathers. As facilitators, we are mindful of our responsibility for *both sides* in these interactions and have discretely listened in. What we have heard is an *other focused* gesture of support which is at the core of such groups.

Having the opportunity and choice to make connections beyond the group are empowering aspects of a parents' support group. In an open group there is no control of who a parent may find as a fellow participant in the group. There is the opportunity over refreshments, to make a deliberate choice to catch up with other parents. Parents can talk more privately after a group and can decide to exchange phone numbers or to ask the facilitator to pass their contact details on to another parent and offer to be available to meet if further contact is sought. Potentially there may be a risk, as there is in all human interactions, of unintended negative consequences. For example, an imbalance in the relationship, with one parent overwhelming the other. However, the autonomy and self-determination of parents and their capacity to deal with unexpected consequences needs to be respected and availability of facilitators to be called on to intervene if needed.

Comparison of experiences in parent bereavement support groups is natural. It may be overt and articulated or thought and silent. A challenge to group members and facilitators is when one parent names their grief as worse than everyone else's. Understandably this can bring an angry response from other group members: 'You can't quantify grief!' 'You can't say yours is worse than ours!' 'You don't know what we've gone through!' Confrontation between group members can strain the atmosphere in the group. Awkwardness can constrain continued sharing.

Parents who have experienced the death of a loved child can find themselves re-examining religious, spiritual and philosophical beliefs. For some, beliefs are affirmed, while for others they are shattered. Old views of life or priorities may give way to new ones. Often there is a vacuum, a nothingness. Such subjects are frequently raised and explored by parents in bereavement support groups. While from the outset it is noted by the facilitators that each parent's views are to be respected, when there is strength of conviction about beliefs it can be difficult for group members to acknowledge the legitimacy of other opinions and facilitators to guide the discussion.

'The only meaning is that there is no meaning ... there's nothing beyond here,' a father once shared with the group when the conversation touched on this area. His words evoked a powerful response for a deeply religious member of the group. With almost a proselytising zeal, she embarked on a monologue to change the father's view. The father listened but replied that he just could not relate to her words and did not and could not believe in life after death, a belief held by the mother and her child who had died. The mother countered with 'Can't you just leave room for the possibility?' Silence was the response.

Questions

1 Imagine you are a facilitator. What are your thoughts about what is going on in this group?
2 What words would you use?
3 What aspects of grief theory seem useful in understanding this situation?

Resilience after grief

In recognition of the 'enduring nature of severe grief reactions' (Bonanno & Kaltman 2001 p. 711), the following have been suggested as 'reasonable expectations' (Weiss 1988 pp. 44–5) for recovery from grief and loss:

» an ability to give energy to everyday life
» an ability 'to find psychological comfort (as demonstrated by freedom from pain and distress)'

» an ability 'to experience gratification (to feel pleasure when desirable, hoped-for or enriching events occur)'
» a sense of 'hopefulness regarding the future'
» 'being able to plan and care about plans'
» an 'ability to function with reasonable adequacy in social roles as spouse, parent and member of the community'.

Importantly, Weiss (1988 p. 50) emphasises that rather than being either complete or absent, recoveries 'tend to be either more or less adequate'. These expectations leave open the possibility that grief will be ongoing but a reconnection with the good experiences of life will also be possible.

Researchers are making important links between positive emotions and resilience after grief. Bonanno and others have studied the expression of positive emotion in the months after a loss, and found that those able to engage in positive emotions, and particularly laughter, seem to experience more positive outcomes in the months and years post-bereavement. They argue that laughter provides a very necessary respite from the intensity of grief, and the overwhelming negative emotions of a loss orientation (Bonanno & Keltner 1997).

Weiss's expectations place recovery within the psychological dimension primarily, and need to be expanded to take into account the significance of the spiritual and socio-cultural dimensions. They also do not emphasise the ways in which people's grief becomes a motivation for wider changes within the community (Allan 2009), thus transforming environments as well as individuals and families.

CHAPTER **SUMMARY**

Grief and loss experiences will touch all of our lives, as people, places and personal issues change across the lifespan. Yet, as this chapter has examined, each one of us will be affected in very different ways, depending upon the nature of the loss experience and our particular inner- and outer-world context. The physiological effects of grief, the shock and numbness that characterise the early recovery experience, are common for many people, but the expression of grief and mourning is diverse and context-dependent.

One of the key risk factors identified for poorer outcomes following a loss is a more complicated or ambivalent relationship with the person who has died or who is no longer accessible. This connects with one of the other key risk factors, the inability to establish any meaning of the loss. Other potential risk factors such as age, sex or gender tend to be mediated by other factors in the environment—for example, the availability of other attachment figures or structural supports.

Some of the key protective factors, similar to stress and trauma experiences, are the availability of supportive relationships and appropriate resources, both emotional and material, and a sense of coherence or meaning, which is both an inner state and reflected in the external environment.

Unlike in the stress and trauma literature, the importance of the socio-cultural dimensions of grief in creating the meaning of the experience for individuals, families and communities is emphasised heavily in the research literature. This influence is reflected in the different ways that grief reactions have been understood over the last century, moving from the notion of grief work as something that can be completed and moved on from, to something that becomes an integrated and enduring experience of our inner worlds. Grief and mourning will continue to be understood differently in the future, as they are shaped so profoundly by the cultural context in which they occur.

APPLYING A MULTIDIMENSIONAL UNDERSTANDING

CASE STUDY

Jan: Sudden death

Jan tells her counsellor that she feels as if she is going crazy. It was eleven months ago that her mother, Ella, died suddenly at a family gathering. They had been in the kitchen preparing the meal when Ella collapsed to the floor and died from a heart attack. Jan recalls the horror she felt when she realised what had happened, and can only recall certain moments in the chaos that followed, as an ambulance was called and her mother was taken to hospital. The funeral, she remembers, was a tense and anxious time, as it meant an encounter with her former husband, with whom she had maintained no contact. Since then, Jan has experienced difficulty sleeping, as she often wakes after nightmares. She experiences flashbacks in the kitchen, and feels as if it is all happening again: 'It's as if she's there in front of me'.

The handling of the estate has been problematic, as Jan's brother and wife are contesting the will. They feel entitled to half the estate, even though it had been the expressed wish of Ella for them to receive one-quarter. Jan's children tell her not to worry about the money, and to get on with living. They say she was old and it could have happened at any time, but Jan keeps remembering the events of the day her mother died.

Tran: Anticipated death

Tran was diagnosed as being HIV-positive eleven years ago, when he was twenty-two years old. He developed AIDS two years later and for nine years had been taking medication daily to keep him well. Over the past year, his body seemed to develop a tolerance to the medication and he rapidly deteriorated. Tran's partner, Josh, was with him at the time of his death. He had been at home, with the palliative care service visiting regularly. This had been where he had wanted to die.

The day before he died, his mother came to see him, but his father stayed away. He had stopped all contact with Tran when he heard he was HIV-positive, about five years ago. Tran had a strong relationship with his mother and three sisters, but in the days prior to his death, his father had insisted that they not come to see him. Tran and Josh had a wide network of friends, who had supported them through the last few months.

Tran and Josh had been together for six years, and Josh had known from the beginning of their relationship that Tran had AIDS. In recent weeks, they had planned the funeral together and spoken about the need for Josh to move on into other relationships. Josh feels empty and numb following the events of the past few days. He thought he had prepared himself for this time and what he would need to do, but he finds himself unable to concentrate or to even think about anything as being important.

Questions

1 What dimensions of grief are these people experiencing?
2 What key issues do you think each of them faces?
3 What changes in our understanding of the experiences occur if the gender of the people in each of the above scenarios is different?
4 What are possible interventions:
   • at a practice level?
   • at a program level?
   • at a policy level?
5 What factors could influence the grief experiences of these individuals if we think of these events occurring within a Jewish, Christian, Islamic, Buddhist, Indigenous or atheist family context?

KEY TERMS

anticipatory grief

bereavement

chronic sorrow

complicated grief

continuing bonds

disenfranchised grief

dual process model

grief

grief reaction

loss orientation

mourning

non-finite grief

prolonged grief disorder

restoration orientation

traumatic bereavement

QUESTIONS AND DISCUSSION POINTS

1 What are the key biopsychosocial and spiritual effects of grief?
2 What dimensions of grief experiences are considered to be risk or protective factors?
3 What are some of the key ways of coping with grief?
4 Reflecting on your own experiences of loss, identify the similarities and differences with the theoretical material outlined in this chapter.
5 What rituals do you see occurring around loss experiences—in your family and in the wider community?
6 What resources do you consider to be essential for people who are faced with grief situations?
7 In what ways do you see cultural factors influencing the grief experience in the wider community?

FURTHER READING

Bowlby, J. 1980, *Loss: Sadness and depression*, Ringwood: Penguin.
Klass, D., Silverman, P., & Nickman, S. 1996, *Continuing bonds: New understandings of grief*, Washington: Taylor & Francis.
Marris, P. 1996, *The politics of uncertainty: Attachment in private and public life*, London: Routledge.
Prigerson, H. & Maciejewski, P. 2006, 'A call for sound empirical testing and evaluation of criteria for complicated grief proposed for DSM-V', *Omega*, 52(1), pp. 9–19.
Stroebe, M. & Schut, H. 1999, 'The dual process model of coping with bereavement: Rationale and description', *Death Studies*, 23(3), pp. 197–224.

WEBSITES OF INTEREST

Australian Centre for Grief and Bereavement: www.grief.org.au
This site contains links and resources relating to a wide range of grief experiences.
The Australian Child and Adolescent Trauma, Loss and Grief Network: www. earlytraumagrief.anu.edu.au
This site is based at the Australian National University and provides links to a range of trauma, loss and grief resources relevant for working with children and adolescents.

Compassionate Friends: www.thecompassionatefriends.org.au/TCFAustralia.htm
> This site contains links and resources relating to this international support group for those affected by grief.

Faculty of Social and Behavioural Sciences, Utrecht University: www.uu.nl/EN/faculties/socialsciences/Pages/default.aspx
> Search this website for the research and publications of Margaret and Wolfgang Stroebe and Henk Schut.

Kings College Centre for Education about Death and Bereavement: www.kings.uwo.ca/thanatology/
> This site, based at the University of Western Ontario, Canada, has excellent resources relating to courses and research relating to grief.

Robert Neimeyer and meaning reconstruction: http://web.mac.com/neimeyer
> This site is the home page of Robert Neimeyer and his meaning construction approach to grief. The site hosts his presentations, research and writings.

SIDS and Kids: www.sidsandkids.org
> This site contains excellent national and international links relating to sudden infant death syndrome and a range of other childhood death issues.

Stolen Generations Alliance: www.sgalliance.org.au
> The website for the Stolen Generations Alliance contains the full text of the report *Bringing them Home: Report of the National Inquiry into the Separation of Aboriginal and Torres Strait Islander Children from their Families* (1997), as well as resources relating to Sorry Day.

PART 4

Development and Adaptation across the Lifespan

Many theorists have identified particular **developmental tasks** and **psychosocial stages** across the lifespan. In this part, we look at the dominant stages, tasks and theories that are relevant to the human services. It is impossible to be comprehensive in such a discussion. Every topic discussed has extensive literature and research which can be explored. The aim of these chapters is to raise awareness of some of these dominant stages, tasks and theories for practice, and to encourage you to think more about them.

CHAPTER 7

Infancy

AIMS OF THIS CHAPTER

This chapter explores development in the earliest phase of the lifespan, infancy. It considers the following questions:

» What are the biopsychosocial-spiritual developmental tasks and transitions of infancy?
» What are the experiences and impacts of stress, trauma and loss in infancy?
» How is resilience in infancy understood?

As infant researcher Field (2007 p. 161) notes, 'It is truly amazing that in the short space of two years, infants learn to hold their head up, roll over, sit up, crawl, stand, walk, run, climb, throw a ball, and jump with their bodies, as well as to imitate'. In addition to these physical mobility capacities, infants learn to talk, engage socially, distinguish themselves from others, express emotion and develop memories.

This chapter focuses on these transitions from birth through the first year of life. The term **infancy** is often used to refer to this period of development, differentiated from **toddlerhood**, typically used to define two- to three-year-olds. The chapter begins with an exploration of the birth and biological dimensions of infancy, before we look more closely at the specific psychosocial developmental tasks and transitions associated with this part of the lifespan. We then look at some of the known risk experiences, as well as the protective factors that enhance resilience in infancy.

Over the past forty years, the World Health Organization (WHO) has developed the Global Database on Child Growth and Malnutrition, a database that has collated global information about children's health and well-being, including height, weight, motor development and nurtrition status. These normative measures of development are useful guides for expectations about health and well-being, and for identifying risks and problems in many different cultural contexts. While these developmental experiences are influenced by and influence the environments into which infants are born, and the opportunities and resources they encounter, the WHO has identified enough commonality to establish a global or universal understanding. For social workers, knowledge of these milestones is important, as failure to reach these milestones may be indicative of difficulties. These and some of the other normative developmental tasks of infancy that are commonly assessed when looking at infant well-being are explored below.

Key developmental tasks and transitions

In the chapters that focus on the early stages of the lifespan, you will notice that there is an emphasis on biological and behavioural milestones. Later in the lifespan, self-report of differences and difficulties means that less attention is paid to these normative notions of development. Increasing individual diversity in human experience makes normative understandings of adult experience both less possible and desirable.

Biological dimensions

Birth

The Australian birth rate has been the focus of much discussion in recent years. It was in steady decline from 1981 onwards. However, since 2005, the trend has reversed, with the highest number of births ever recorded in Australian history occurring in 2007, when 285,200 babies were born (ABS 2007a p. 6). Approximately three point seven per cent of all these babies have an Aboriginal or Torres Strait Islander mother (AIHW 2008a p. 271). As in other developed countries around the world, more male (approximately fifty-one or fifty-two per cent) than female babies are born each year (AIHW 2008a p. 273).

Typically, infants are born after thirty-seven to forty-one weeks of development in utero. It is important to remember that babies have already experienced nine months of life, albeit in a different environment, before they come into the world (Brazelton 2009 p. 1). They have experienced sleep, movement, sound and the emotional environment created through the maternal experience.

For some infants, the prenatal environment is a stressful environment—with particular risk factors including maternal experiences of drugs and alcohol, violence, stress and poor nutrition. For some infants, this leads to a low birthweight, and birth involves withdrawal from maternal substance use. For these reasons and others, some infants are born prematurely.

A premature birth is one that occurs prior to thirty-seven weeks, and has been associated with a range of developmental difficulties. Babies born at twenty weeks onwards, irrespective of survival, are regarded as legal births. Prematurity, and the associated low birthweight of such young infants, are associated with higher morbidity and mortality rates in infancy, and 'long-term physical and developmental disabilities, which can profoundly affect them for the rest of their lives' (Connor and McIntyre 2002 p. 131).

Before we look at the developmental aspects of infancy, it is important to note that hundreds of babies do not survive the birth experience each year. For example, 'in 2006, there were 2091 fetal deaths reported … resulting in a fetal death rate of 7.4 per 1000 births' (Laws & Hilder 2008 p. 68). Higher death rates were reported for younger mothers. They were also reported for Aboriginal and Torres Strait Islander mothers—a rate of 11.7 deaths per 1000 births compared with 7.2 deaths per 1000 births for non-Indigenous mothers—and this was linked with a higher fetal death rate for mothers living in the Northern Territory (Laws & Hilder 2008). Most child deaths occur in the first year of life (seventy-one per cent in 2005; AIHW 2008a p. 277), as a result of 'conditions originating in the perinatal period (51% of all infant deaths), congenital malformations (24%) and sudden infant death syndrome (7%)' (AIHW 2008a p. 277). Gains have been made in the past twenty years or so, with the death rate halving in that time from ten deaths per 1000 live births to five deaths. Nevertheless, Australia's infant death rate remains higher than nineteen other OECD (Organisation for Economic Cooperation and Development) countries (AIHW 2008a p.277). These losses often cause lifelong and sometimes intergenerational grief and distress for parents, caregivers and extended family members.

Ninety per cent of children living in Australia today were born here. Of the ten per cent of children born overseas, six per cent come from non-English-speaking countries and four per cent from English-speaking countries (AIHW 2007 p. 19). Since the last census, an increase in the proportion of children born in Sudan has been noted ('from 0.1% of all overseas-born children and young people in 1996 to 2.4% in 2006'), as well as an increase in children from Kenya, Afghanistan and Iraq (AIHW 2007 p. 19).

Weight and height, and nutrition

A healthy birthweight is considered to be a weight of 2500 grams and above (AIHW 2008a p. 270). Australian records from 2005 show that 'the average birthweight of liveborn babies … was 3369 grams, ranging from 3246 grams in the Northern Territory

See Field's excellent book, *The amazing infant* (2007), for information about the prenatal period of development.

Chapter 11 focuses on the transition to parenthood and also the grief associated with pregnancy or infant loss.

to 3395 in Tasmania' (AIHW 2008a p. 270). Male babies are typically around four per cent higher in weight than females.

About eight per cent of babies are born with a low to extremely low (less than 1000 grams) birthweight each year. Some of the known causes of low birthweight and prematurity are maternal health and mental-health difficulties, maternal drug (including cigarettes) and alcohol use, and poverty. Optimal infant well-being is dependent on maternal well-being, which in turn is dependent on social, structural and cultural dimensions. It is critical to see these issues in a broader structural and cultural context, rather than just regarding them as individually situated mother–child problems.

The transition from the prenatal environment brings about massive changes for infants. Feeding is one of these changes, with infants relying on the availability of nutrition through breastfeeding or alternate sources. How babies receive their nutrition can have an impact on their longer-term developmental outcomes. The Longitudinal Study of Australian Children (LSAC) has found that 'breastfeeding is associated with better health' for infants and for the follow-up child cohort aged four and five years. Breastfeeding is advocated as the preferred way of providing nutrition to infants, as breast milk has been found to be integral to 'protecting infants against infection and chronic diseases such as diabetes and asthma, and it has been suggested that it also reduces the risk of obesity in childhood' (AIHW 2008a p. 278). For example, the LSAC study found that more than six months of breastfeeding 'reduced the risk of wheeze in the infant cohort' and 'asthma was strongly predicted by the duration of breastfeeding in the child cohort' (AIHW 2008a p. viii). Despite the benefits of breastfeeding, the majority of mothers in the LSAC study had not exclusively breastfed their babies for the recommended first six-month period of life, for a wide range of reasons. These include difficulties with breastfeeding and the need to return to employment.

In addition to the health arguments for breastfeeding, arguments have also been made about the relationship benefits of breastfeeding practices. One study of 7223 Australian mothers and infants found that breastfeeding may help to protect against maternal neglect (Strathearn et al. 2009), although a meta-analysis recently confirmed the health but not the relational effects of breastfeeding (Jansen et al. 2008).

From three months onwards, infants can be introduced to solid foods, and they begin to explore a world of new tastes and textures. By two years of age, children typically weigh in the range of nine to fifteen kilograms (WHO 2009) and are quadruple their original birthweight and double their height (Woody 2003b p. 118).

Details about the LSAC are provided on p. 237 in Chapter 8.

Brain development

In recent years, major attention has been paid to the ways in which an infant's brain develops, enabling new understandings to emerge of both the infant experience and the lifelong consequences of this early brain development, particularly for infants experiencing severe trauma and/or neglect. As Joyce (2005 p. 31) notes:

> At birth the human brain is remarkably unfinished in its development: more than 75 per cent of the neuronal connections in the brain develop after birth in the first year, in direct relationship with the external environment, and the emotional tone of this environment is as crucial as other aspects of stimulation

With advances in neuro-imaging, it has been possible to gain a deeper understanding of the ways in which the 'hardwiring' of the brain occurs—that is, how the neural pathways develop. As noted by paediatric researchers:

> during fetal development and early childhood, brain growth is regulated by genes but is critically influenced by sensory stimulation and experience. Neuronal connections are formed and modified by repetitive, patterned stimulation of the neural system in a 'use-dependent' manner. (Strathearn et al. 2001 p. 149)

What a lot of this research confirms are long-held theories about the importance of relational and social interactions and the impact of physical environments on well-being and development. It provides evidence for the permanence but also the plasticity of the developing infant brain (Brehmer et al. 2007), and subsequently on their capacity to engage with the world around them. We return to this later in the chapter when we look at the impact of trauma on infants.

Sleep

Across the lifespan, sleep serves a critical function. Getting adequate sleep in infancy is critical for health and well-being, both for the baby and for the parents. Young infants spend about three quarters of the day asleep during the early weeks of life. It is believed that during this 'down' time significant brain development continues in the first months of life as babies adapt to their world. Sleep patterns change rapidly through the first weeks of life, when, 'the total length of sleep typically decreases from 16 to 17 hours a day in the newborn to 14 to 15 hours by 16 weeks and 13 to 14 hours by six months' (Adams et al. 2004 p. 96). A study by Adams et al. (2004) found that in a sample of 511 infants, by eight weeks fifty per cent were sleeping through a whole night without waking and by twelve weeks, seventy-five per cent were doing so. While most infants begin to move into some routine regarding sleep, for others, unsettled and non-routine sleep patterns continue throughout their early years.

An infant's sleep patterns have a direct impact on their parents and primary caregivers. New parents often face significant sleep deprivation, particularly in the early weeks following birth, sometimes misinterpreted as post-natal depression (Armstrong et al. 1998). Routines around sleeping times and behaviours assist enormously with establishing a sleep pattern for infants.

Toileting skills

From initially having no control over toileting behaviours, older infants start to independently control their toileting. Variation occurs across cultures around the timing of toilet training, with Asian and African communities typically encouraging toilet training at a much earlier age, beginning around one to three months and completed around one year, compared to Western communities tending to start toilet training around eighteen months (Sun & Rugolotto 2004). Regression in toileting skills can often be a sign of trauma, stress or loss, something we return to later in this chapter.

Crying

Babies communicate many of their needs through crying, in particular their need for food or fluids, for sleep, for temperature regulation and for human care and contact. From birth, infants cry increasingly, peaking at about six to eight weeks and declining by three months of age. Crying tends to peak during this time in the evening. From cross-cultural studies, it would seem that this pattern of infant crying in the first two months of life is universal (St James-Roberts 2007). While young infants are similar in early crying patterns, studies have shown that cultural responses shape crying behaviours after these first few months of life (St James-Roberts 2007), with infants in Western countries tending to cry more than those growing up in non-Western countries. Beyond these first few months, infants vary enormously in the amount of time they cry, from minutes per day and up to three hours a day (Evanoo 2007). Persistent crying has been studied extensively, with both physical and psychological causes being proposed. In one randomised control trial (Jordan et al. 2006), 103 infants with persistent crying and their mothers were assigned to one of three groups: medication, placebo or mental-health intervention only. Only the group that had active mental-health intervention experienced a reduction in admissions to a mother–infant unit, highlighting the complex interaction of factors in an infant's crying behaviour.

As with sleep behaviours, crying has an immediate impact on parents and caregivers. As Evanoo (2007 p. 333) summarises:

> Many parents find inconsolable crying to be particularly difficult because the use of soothing techniques to comfort the infant seems futile. Parents also may view infant crying as a negative reflection on their ability to parent, increasing their distress.

For this reason, it is important to address sleep problems early, so that secondary cycles and difficulties do not emerge in relation to the stress of infant crying. Specialist mother–infant units are designed to support mothers and babies settle into better sleep routines or identify particular sleep disorder issues that may be related to other health issues.

Reflexes and motor skills

Infants are born with a number of reflexes, enabling them to react to different stimuli. Over time, these reflexes diminish and are superceded by consciously controlled motor skills. These skills enable infants to sit and eventually mobilise by rolling, crawling, walking, and, by age two, being able to run and engage in a host of physical activities such as drawing, reaching and lifting.

Disability, injury and diseases

The first year of life can be a time of injury and illness for many infants, and for some, as outlined earlier, a time of death. Around one quarter of all hospitalisations for zero- to fourteen-year olds, for example, are for children under one year of age (AIHW 2008a), with the most common conditions being respiratory (twenty per cent) or **perinatal** (eighteen per cent). For others, it is about beginning a life of disability and learning to adapt to its consequences. Around seven per cent of all Australian families have a child with a profound or severe disability (AIHW 2004). Developmental delay in one or more of the physical milestones that we have discussed is often the key indicator that a child has a disability of some sort.

One condition some infants experience is non-organic failure to thrive (NOFTT). Infants with this condition are not reaching the normative physical developmental milestones such as weight and height gain, even though there is no apparent physical cause. This condition is commonly seen in infants where there is abuse or neglect, and appears to be connected with a stress response. It requires careful assessment and the ruling out of other organic causes.

For all of these biological and physical developmental experiences outlined so far, infants are utterly dependent on the adult caregivers around them to provide the necessary care and support. Coping with warmth and cold, hunger and thirst, fatigue and physical mobility are all beyond the immediate capacities of infants, and thus they rely on the availability of adults in the immediate environment. By the age of two, young children are able to verbalise these needs and independently manage many of them, as we shall see in Chapter 8.

Psychosocial-spiritual dimensions

As the previous discussion has highlighted, in many ways, this is the most vulnerable stage of the lifespan, in that infants are utterly dependent on their relational contexts for survival and growth. However, from the first minutes of life onwards, infants are active agents, engaging with primary caregivers and interacting with their environments.

Optimal psychosocial development occurs through the development of:

» sensory, perceptual and motor functions
» attachment capacity
» sensori-motor and early causal (or explanatory) schemes
» an understanding of the nature of objects and creating categories
» emotional development (Newman & Newman 2003).

All these developments enable the infant to move towards knowledge of the world and their capacity to be an independent actor in their world.

Throughout infancy, rapid changes are seen also in psychosocial functioning. In this next part of the chapter, we will look at how some of the capacities and skills developed throughout this time relate to an infant's cognitive, emotional and relational dimensions.

Cognitive development

Many different aspects of an infant's cognitive development have been studied. However, a persisting theory of cognitive development is Piaget's (1995) model of the stages of cognitive development. This theory remains widely accepted because of its capacity to propose a general and holistic understanding of the ways in which people acquire knowledge of the world around them. He proposed a four-stage model of development from birth through to adulthood. The first phase he described as the **sensori-motor phase**, from birth until around eighteen months, during which time the infant develops 'increasingly complex sensory and motor schemes', which enable them 'to organize and exercise some control over their environment' (Newman & Newman 2003 p. 71). As Bremner (1994 p. 121) notes:

> The infant is seen as constructing progressively more complex, cognitive action-based structures through operating on the world, and the end-point of this construction process is marked by the emergence of mental activity divorced from action, in other words, representational activity.

While Piaget saw this development as motivated by inner-world tension and change, other cognitive theorists have argued for more social models of cognitive development (Meadows 1993; Vygotsky 1998). That is, the infant is influenced by the immediate relational context and is socialised into the various cognitive tasks of development. This model is in keeping with a multidimensional approach. It is also consistent with another major theoretical framework for understanding an infant's psychosocial development: attachment theory.

See pp. 200–4 for a discussion of attachment theory.

With cognitive development comes linguistic ability, as the infant moves from vocal imitation to a capacity to use words. From nine months through to sixteen months, infants may be making their first word or two-word utterances, and by the time they reach the age of two years, may have between fifty and one hundred words in their vocabulary.

Perceptual development

In the early weeks of life, babies' visual capacities are markedly different from adults, with studies showing that images for infants are blurred and indistinct until several months into life. From six weeks onwards, babies can visually fix on an object and begin to visually follow it. Interactions with parents, and the primary caregiver in particular, become of central importance around two to three months of age, with the mother's or primary caregiver's face, in particular, being an important stimulus as connection is sought out. Studies have shown that infants become distressed if they have a 'still-faced' interaction with a caregiver who is usually warm and responsive (Weinberg & Tronick 1996), a finding that has implications for infants whose mothers are experiencing significant depression or emotional unavailability.

Infants from this time onwards can also smile, although initially not discriminating who they are smiling at. Around two to three months, they are much more preferential and consistent in their smiling. The significance of both infant and maternal smiling for the building of relationships has been tracked in one study. For first-time mothers when shown their own infant's face, 'an extensive brain network seems to be activated', with reward centres in the brain activated specifically in response to happy infant faces (Strathearn et al. 2008). These findings highlight the neural underpinnings of mother–infant attachment, something we explore in the following pages.

Relational development

From a survival perspective, the infant must be part of a social network of some sort given that they have no capacity to physically care for themselves. Each infant is born into some family configuration, and irrespective of the nature of this configuration, infancy is typically a time of transition for the infant, parents and any siblings or extended family network.

The development of secure attachments, a sense of basic trust in the world and a sense of self are seen as the critical protective factors to be developed during these first few years of life. Interactions with parents or caregivers, and environments, profoundly influence these dimensions.

In Chapter 8, we focus more specifically on parenting styles and child-rearing practices. We also look at these in their structural and cultural contexts.

Primary caregivers

In relation to family environments, as noted in Chapter 2 (Table 2.1), most children live with their mother and father, although the number of female-headed single-parent families continues to increase. While difficult to confirm because of the absence of statistics, it is estimated also that around twenty per cent of Australian lesbians, gay men and bisexuals have children (McNair et al. 2002 p. 40).

Historically, adoption was the way many infertile couples were able to have their own children. According to the *Adoptions Australia 2006–07 report* (AIHW 2008a p. vii), the pattern of adoption has changed dramatically in Australia, with a reduction in local adoptions and a major increase in recent years in intercountry adoptions. The box below shows some of these trends.

ADOPTIONS IN AUSTRALIA 2006–07

» There were 568 adoptions in Australia—71 per cent were intercountry, 10 per cent were local and 18 per cent were 'known' child adoptions (adoption of a child already known to the adopting parent—for example, a stepchild).

» Almost two-thirds of intercountry adoptions were from China (31 per cent), South Korea (20 per cent) and Ethiopia (12 per cent).

» For 'known' child adoptions, 76 per cent of adoptions were by step-parents and 21 per cent by carers.

» In local and intercountry adoptions, nearly all children were less than five years old (92 per cent), whereas for 'known' child adoptions, most were aged ten years and over (71 per cent).

» Around half of the children in local and intercountry adoptions were adopted into families with no other children, and three in every five had adoptive parents aged 40 years and over.

Source: *Adoptions Australia 2006–07* (AIHW 2008a)

Some infants begin their lives in the care of the State, as protective concerns lead to their removal from their biological parents. An increase in out-of-home care-services has been noted in the past six to seven years, with some 25,454 Australian children in 2006 in out-of-home care-arrangements, including an over-representation of Indigenous children (AIHW 2007 p. 52). Recognising the significance of cultural identity, protocols between protective services and Aboriginal community agencies are now in place to try to ensure that all Indigenous children removed from their immediate family are placed in culturally appropriate care.

All of these demographic factors highlight the diversity of the experiences of growing up in particular contexts, in both diverse family situations and diverse communities and cultures. Within each of these contexts, optimal well-being is achieved through secure attachments in the key infant–adult relationships.

Attachment theory
Attachment theory has dominated the last fifty years of research into the experiences of infants and children, and has moved into the domain of adult

well-being and mental health as well. It also forms much of the basis for our understandings of grief reactions.

Attachment theory developed in the middle of the twentieth century, from the work of British researchers such as Rene Spitz and John Bowlby, and the cross-cultural work of Mary Ainsworth (1985). Spitz was the first to provide a language of attachment after examining what he termed 'emotional deprivation syndrome' through 'hospitalism' (Spitz 1965 pp. 274–84). Observing children who were in hospital for long periods of time, he monitored the influence of a lack of supportive, animate caregivers. Children deprived of supportive, animate care were found to exhibit five characteristics: egocentricity, a superficiality of attachments, an inability to give and/or receive affection, aggression, and speech delay.

Attachment relationships are considered unique from the range of relationships an individual may develop. Four aspects of attachment relationships create this uniqueness (Allen 2003). The first is its protective function. The infant, in being so utterly dependent on the availability of a primary caregiver for survival must be able to elicit this unfailing protection from a more powerful figure in the environment. The second is its function of assisting with physiological regulation. The third is its function of assisting with emotional regulation. And the fourth is the important process of teaching the child to mentalise. This capacity to mentalise is part of what is termed **theory of mind**—the essential capacity an infant must develop in order to recognise that other people are separate and different from him or her. This capacity to develop an awareness of the mind of another person is a key factor in relationships and empathy: the ability to see things from another's point of view. For infants, 'pretend play, or the infant pretending to be someone else, is an index of the theory of mind' (Field 2007 p. 179).

The characteristics that distinguish attachment from other relational bonds (Bowlby 1984 pp. 177–234) include:

1 *proximity seeking*—the child will attempt to remain within protective range of parents, with the range decreasing in strange, threatening situations. When situations are perceived to be threatening, the child seeks closer proximity to their attachment figure.

2 *the secure base effect*—the presence of an attachment figure fosters security in the child, which results in inattention to attachment considerations and in confident exploration and play. The securely attached child can feel safe enough to explore the environment and attend to other matters without having to scan the environment for risks or threats. The argument behind this is that the notion of a secure base becomes internalised over time, enabling the child to rely on themselves once they have been part of a safe, predictable attachment relationship.

Chapter 8 outlines how attachment theory is the basis of our understanding of grief reactions.

3 *the separation protest*—threat to the continued accessibility of the attachment figure gives rise to protest and to active attempts to ward off the separation (Parkes et al. 1993).

John Bowlby, in his profoundly influential three-volume series on attachment and loss, proposed that attachment behaviour was as innate and significant a need as feeding and the sexual needs of the infant. He argued that social attachments were essential for the infant's survival and, indeed, for well-being right across the lifespan, 'from cradle to grave' as he termed it. He wrote: 'Attachment behaviour is conceived as any form of behaviour that results in a person attaining or retaining proximity to some other differentiated and preferred individual' (Bowlby 1980 p. 39). He argued that any threat to the individual or to the attachment figure led to the display of attachment behaviour, behaviour designed to regain proximity and relationship with the attachment figure.

After observing children under the age of three who were separated for significant periods of time throughout hospitalisations from their primary caregivers, Bowlby theorised that there were three phases of reaction. Protest is the first phase, an intense initial reaction following separation, in which the child expresses their distress either physically and/or verbally in an attempt to be reunited with the caregiver. Despair is the second phase, when some days after the separation, there is a depressive affect and withdrawal. While the child may seem depressed, they are still preoccupied by the caregiver's absence (Bowlby 1984 p. 27). As Bowlby describes, it is as if the child is 'grief stricken'. Detachment characterises the third phase, whereby, following a week or more of separation, there is a superficial change in the interactiveness and mood of the child (Bowlby 1984 p. 28), and even an increase in responses to other people in the environment, but the child is generally unresponsive to their environment given the lack of an attachment figure.

Ainsworth put Bowlby's theory into operation through the establishment of a laboratory test, the 'strange situation'. This was a laboratory experiment in which, through a series of separations and reunions with the mother, the infant's attachment behaviour could be monitored. Ainsworth concluded from these experiments (the findings of which she validated in the home environments of the children), that infants at about twelve to fifteen months demonstrated one of three major attachment styles or strategies: secure, insecure and avoidant, or insecure and disorganised.

The majority of her sample (approximately sixty-six per cent) showed **secure attachments**. As Ainsworth (1985 p. 16) describes:

> Infants in this group behaved in the strange situation just as one year olds were expected to behave when the procedure was designed. When they were alone with their mothers, they explored actively, showing very little attachment behaviour. Most of them were upset in the separation episodes and explored little.

All of them responded strongly to the mother's return in the reunion episodes, the majority seeking close bodily contact with her, and all at least displaying keen interest in interacting with her.

The second group, comprising about twenty-two per cent of the sample, she described as having **insecure and avoidant attachments**. These children behaved unexpectedly, in that:

In particular, they showed little or no distress in the separation episodes, and, most important, they avoided contact, proximity or even interaction with the mother in the reunion episodes. Some steadfastly ignored their mother, refusing to approach her or even look at her when she coaxed the child to come. Others mingled attachment behaviour with avoidance.

The third group, about twelve per cent of the sample, were described as having **insecure and ambivalent attachments**. These children were noted to be anxious prior to their separation experiences. Ainsworth (1985 p. 16) noted that: 'All were very upset by separation. In the reunion episodes they wanted close bodily contact with their mothers but they also resisted contact and interaction with her'.

Attachment theory was later expanded to include a fourth type of attachment behaviour, which was termed **insecure and disorganised** and **non-attachment** (Howe 1995). The parenting styles associated with each of the attachment styles were as follows:

» secure attachment—the parent is available, helpful, responsive, sensitive and attuned
» insecure, or anxious, attachments—the parenting style is marked by uncertainty, inconsistency, misinterpretation of signs, frequent separations and rejections
» insecure, disorganised attachments—the parenting involves excessive early deprivation or absences.

Another way of conceptualising attachment is from a two-dimensional perspective (Mikulincer & Shaver 2008; Mikulincer 2008), with people varying along both a low to high avoidance axis and a low to high anxiety axis, as illustrated in Figure 7.1.

Since the beginnings of attachment theory, a number of criticisms have continued to be raised. The first is in relation to the gender assumption underlying the theory: that the primary caregiver is the mother. Related to this is the second criticism of it as a culture-specific theory, not relevant to other cultures where less nuclear forms of family structure are apparent. Much of Ainsworth's research was conducted in Uganda, as well as more Westernised communities, which would suggest some early evidence for the cross-cultural relevance of this theory. On the other hand, Ainsworth herself (in Parkes et al. 1993) has argued the need for more cross-cultural

FIGURE **7.1** Attachment from a two-dimensional perspective

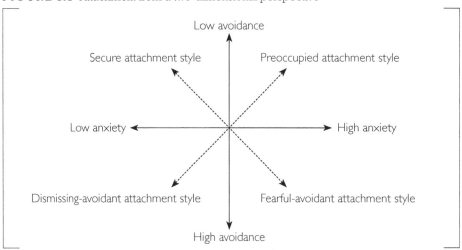

research before conclusions about its universal applicability can be drawn. The third question relating to the universality of attachment theory is in relation to whether there are critical attachment periods, as the theory seems to suggest. Some of the research findings from a follow-up of children adopted from Romanian orphanages (which had a profound lack of stimulation) seems to suggest that there is a positive correlation between the length of time in these impoverished environments and later developmental and psychiatric disturbance (Rutter & English and Romanian Adoptees study team 1998; Gunnar et al. 2000; Maclean 2003). Others have suggested that around twelve months is a critical period of insecurity for infants, and, for example, should be avoided as a time when infants begin day care and day-long separations from primary caregivers.

PRACTICE IN CONTEXT

WORKING WITH INFANTS

Fiona works as a manager of a high-risk infant service and reflects on the way in which attachment theory assists her in her practice with families.

Whenever I meet a new family with an infant, Bowlby's theory of attachment is always at the forefront of my mind, particularly the way in which he outlined the attachment activation behaviours of crying, clinging, following and smiling. Holding Bowlby's theory in mind while observing the infant in his interactions with others is not only a way of linking a theoretic perspective to the practice of assessment, it also indicates and informs the intervention. Understanding that an infant's repertoire of attachment behaviours are initiated by the infant not only to ensure the closeness of his caregivers and therefore receive care, but also as an infant's rudimentary way of initiating relationships, gives depth and perspective to my observations and assessments of both the infant's and their family's functioning. This in turn often reveals the pathway to intervention. For example, in my work with high-risk families, I notice many parents do not realise their baby has such wonderful abilities, and some parents either miss or misinterpret their baby's cues or cries. Sometimes just the simple act of helping parents understand that these cues are their infant's way of seeking out their love and care helps them see their baby in a new light and can add to the attachment relationship, even if the infant is not in the parent's care.

Questions

1 What is your initial reaction to Fiona's observations?
2 What risk and protective factors do you think she is listening for in her understanding of infancy?
3 What would you see as some of the important priorities for intervention with 'high risk' families?

While attachment theory focuses on the formation of this attachment bond in infancy, and hypothesises that this determines adult attachment style, there has been increasing recognition that attachment styles are not rigid, lifelong styles, but are open to both positive and negative influences across the lifespan. Many factors in later childhood and adulthood can buffer the effects of early negative attachment experiences.

Current studies are confirming this finding that early attachment disturbances can be repaired in adulthood and, similarly, that a capacity to form secure attachments early in life can be disrupted by the accumulation of traumatic events in adulthood (Hamilton 2000; Waters et al. 2000).

Another important question relates to the degree to which attachment is to one person alone (typically to the maternal attachment figure) or to multiple people— fathers, grandparents or other significant relationships within wider kinship networks, for example within Indigenous family networks. An underestimation of other direct relationships is often perpetuated through regarding attachment as a maternal phenomenon only. Some child- and family-welfare experts have seen this as the creation of 'ghost fathers', referring to 'the paradox of father presence and absence in child welfare', where fathers are often seen as uninvolved or invisible even when they are present in child-welfare contacts (Brown et al. 2009). Infants are dependent not only on their direct relationships with parents and caregivers, but also on their parents' or caregivers' connectedness or social networks in ways

In Chapter 11 we look at the transition to parenting for mothers and fathers, and in Chapter 13 we look at the grandparent role.

unlike other stages of the lifespan. The extent to which an infant's parents or family are supported emotionally and practically will inevitably have an impact on the individual experiences of infants. Attachment is a critical concept for the infant–parent relationship and parental relationships more widely.

Psychosocial development

The newborn infant is not a blank slate (Pinker 2003), but an emergent being, ready to influence and be influenced by the outer world into which they are born. Various theorists have proposed phases of development in relation to psychosocial skills, in the context of this primary attachment relationship. Building on the work of Freud in relation to early developmental phases, but disagreeing with this emphasis on sexual drive alone, Erikson (1959; 1963) proposed an eight-stage model of psychosocial development, recognising the importance of the wider social context of an individual. While five stages still occur in childhood, Erikson's model attempted to identify the core tasks right through to adulthood, unlike Freud's model, which saw the core tasks as occurring in infancy. Erikson proposed that significant growth and development occurred right across the lifespan. He argued that each developmental transition was like a crisis for the individual, and that healthy development required the successful completion of each task before proceeding to the next phase of healthy ego development. The failure to negotiate each crisis successfully led to psychopathology. These phases have been extended by Vaillant to include a further two phases of adult development, discussed in Chapter 12. An overview of Erikson's crises is provided below in Figure 7.2, and we look at each of these stages in more detail in the relevant chapter. The successful mastery of each 'crisis' in development lays the foundations for mastery of the next (Erikson 1978 p. 25).

FIGURE **7.2** Key psychosocial theory

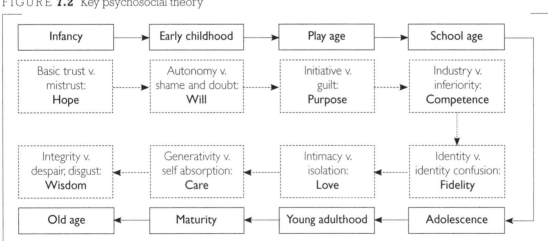

Erikson saw the first task or crisis as one of developing a sense of **basic trust**. Occurring during the first year of life, the infant, if able to develop this sense of basic trust, feels a sense of hopefulness. This leads to a basic conviction in the predictability of the world and its fulfilment of their needs and enables a sense of hope to be fostered. When an infant fails to develop a sense of trust, they are likely to be withdrawn and to have a lack of drive and/or hope, and the incapacity to form intimate relationships.

With a sense of basic trust, or secure attachment, infants are able to engage with and explore the world around them. In these tasks, 'emotion acts as a means of achieving environmental goals and of regulating social interaction' (Bremner 1994 p. 192). Many infants have been shown to have a high sense of 'empathic arousal', tending to cry when other infants do, and in doing so, discriminating the emotional states of others (Roth-Hanania, Busch-Rossnagel and Higgins-D'Alessandro 2000).

Through attachment relationships, infants learn the critical life skill of affect or emotion regulation (Schore 2002), which 'is the ability of infants to control their emotional reactions' (Field 2007 p. 122). Affect regulation is essential for self-regulation and ultimately is part of an essential social interaction skill set—being able to control anger or express empathy towards someone else is essential for the maintenance of social relationships. Being able to self-soothe is also a critical lifelong skill. In Chapter 8, we look at this further in relation to the expected temper tantrums of early childhood.

Personality and temperament

A factor that influences attachment and relationship capacity is temperament—of both the caregiver and the child. **Temperament** can be defined as the 'constitutionally based individual differences in behavioural style that are visible from early childhood' (Rothbart & Bates 1998). Three temperamental constellations (or groups) have been identified from infancy (Chess & Thomas 1996). They are the difficult, easy and slow-to-warm-up temperamental styles, distinguished on the basis of nine different factors. Children identified as having difficult temperaments were found to have a combination of withdrawal, intensity of mood expression, slow adaptability to change and negative mood. Children with easy temperaments were found to have a combination of ability to approach new situations, quick adaptability, low or moderate intensity of mood expressions and predominantly positive moods. Children with slow-to-warm-up temperaments were found to have a combination of a tendency to withdraw from new situations, slow adaptability and mild intensity of mood expression. However, in their original study, Chess and Thomas found that these three constellations only accounted for about sixty-five per cent of their sample, with the remaining thirty-five per cent of infants showing a combination of these temperament types.

Another way of thinking about temperament, clearly based on the above concepts, is to consider the degrees of:

1 negative reactivity ('high intensity negative reactions such as irritability, whining and whingeing')
2 approach/inhibition ('the tendency of a child to approach novel situations and people, or conversely to withdraw and be wary')
3 persistence ('the ability to stick at one task for some time and sustain organised play') (Hemphill & Sanson 2001 p. 42).

A national survey in Canada used the Infant Characteristics Questionnaire (ICQ), which measures four dimensions of infant temperament: good-natured, independent, consistent and adaptable (see Table 7.1). They interviewed the 'person most knowledgable' to assess the infant's temperament. They measured temperament across a large sample of infants, with two key findings emerging: first, that 'children's temperament can be assessed reliably as early as the first year of life' (Japel et al. 2002, p. 116) and 'measures of children's temperament are only weakly related to markers of vulnerability at the individual level' (Japel et al. 2002, p. 117). Second, and importantly, they also identified that younger mothers, in their teenage years, were 'more likely than any other group to report that their child has a difficult temperament' (Japel et al. 2002, p. 118).

The largest scale study of temperament in Australia was commenced in Victoria in 1983—the Australian Temperament Project (ATP) (Prior et al. 2001). Two thousand four hundred Victorian infants (born in 1982–83) and their families were recruited into the study, which has researched their temperament over the eighteen or so years of their lives. The study analysed nine dimensions of temperament, using a variety of methods, although primarily questionnaires. These dimensions are sociability, adaptability, mood, intensity, distractibility, persistence, rhythmicity (a sense of rhythm or regularity), reactivity and activity. The LSAC, mentioned earlier, is following two later cohorts, having recruited one cohort of zero- to one-year olds (born in 2003–04) and a second cohort aged four to five years (born in 1999–2000). We look at how these dimensions affect experiences later in childhood in Chapter 9.

In view of cultural criticisms, what is recognised now more fully is the importance of a goodness of fit or compatibility between the temperament of the parent or caregiver and the child, and also beyond, between the temperament of other caregivers and the broader cultural context. A significant finding from one study is that where there is not a good fit between the parent and child, a parent is likely to exaggerate their perceptions of the difficulties between themselves and their child (Hemphill & Sanson 2001). Temperament, as a risk or protective factor, figures significantly in studies of coping resources and capacity throughout infancy and early childhood.

TABLE **7.1** Infant Characteristics Questionnaire measures of the temperament dimensions by age group

Temperament dimensions	3–11 months	12–23 months
Good-natured	Easy or difficult to calm or soothe when upset How many times per day fussy and irritable How much crying and fuss in general How easily upset When upset, how vigorously crying and fussing What kind of mood generally How changeable mood Overall degree of difficulty	Easy or difficult to calm or soothe when upset How many times per day fussy and irritable How much crying and fuss in general How easily upset When upset, how vigorously crying and fussing What kind of mood generally How changeable mood Overall degree of difficulty
Independent	Wants to be held How much attention other than for caregiving When left alone, plays well	How much attention other than for caregiving When left alone, plays well
Consistent	Easy or difficult to predict sleep and wake-up Easy or difficult to predict when hungry Easy or difficult to know what is bothering when cries	Consistent in sticking with sleeping routine Consistent in sticking with eating routine Response to new foods
Adaptable	Reaction when being dressed Response to changes in everyday routine Response to first bath	Response to changes in everyday routine Response to new playthings Response to new person Response to new place How well adapts to new experiences

Source: Japel, Normand, Tremblay and Willms 2002, p. 110; reproduced with permission.

Gender and sexuality awareness

In utero and from birth, males and females differ in many ways. More boys are born but they are more likely to die in the first year of life. Boys are heavier in weight at birth and taller. Over time, these sex differences are influenced further by gender differences.

Prior to the past decade, it was thought that children became aware of gender and race cues around three to four years of age. There is now evidence to suggest that infants respond to male and female adults differently (for example, they condition more readily to and prefer high-pitched voices), and that by six months, they are cuing to both gender and race issues (Katz & Kofkin 1997; Serbin et al. 2001).

Studies have shown significant differences in the ways in which adults respond to babies and the ways babies are socialised into gender identities, based on assumptions about their sex. Simply dressing babies in either blue or pink clothing elicits strong behavioural differences between the treatment of boys and girls. Boys tend to be held upright and talked to assertively whereas girls tend to be held in a lying position in an adult's arms and talked gently to—engaging young infants in very different 'display rules' regarding emotional expression and gender identity (Brody 1999). These socialisation experiences profoundly shape behaviours and experiences of behaviour, and so gendered expectations are reinforced from birth or, in situations where the sex of the baby is known, throughout the prenatal period.

Spirituality

Chapter 1 explores definitions of spirituality.

If spirituality in adulthood is little understood by many, spirituality in infancy is even less so. In part, this is due to the absence of verbal capacity and report during this time. Children aged three and above have been able to report their worldviews and we will explore this in Chapter 8. Therefore, whether spirituality is an innate human experience or a socially and culturally constructed one becomes a key question for this lifespan stage. Fowler and Dell (2006) described zero to three years as the 'undifferentiated' stage of faith development. McSherry and Smith (2007 p. 19) argue that the 'positive experiences of love and affection, and a stimulating environment may foster aspects of spirituality such as hope and security in an infant'.

Spirituality does intersect with infancy through family views of the spirituality of this phase in the lifespan. Many religious and spiritual traditions see the experiences of birth and infancy as signifying the miracle of human life, and so in this sense, infants play a key role in people's sense of new life and hope. In one study, the spiritual meanings of childbirth for Mormon and Jewish women were explored, and the 'importance of personal connectedness with others and with God' and the spiritual dimensions of their birth experiences were noted (Callister et al. 1999). Spiritual meanings are used in other ways too—for example, when an infant dies, many people refer to him or her using religious and/or spiritual symbolism, such as referring to them as an angel (Capitulo 2004).

PRACTICE IN CONTEXT

REFLECTING ON INFANCY

Melissa, a social worker, reflects on her observations of her daughter Isabel's growth in her first two years.

My daughter, Isabel, has just had her second birthday. Isabel weighed 2.855 kilograms at birth and was 47.5 centimetres long. She now weighs almost 10.8 kilograms and stands at 81.6 centimetres tall. She has gone through five clothing sizes, from a '0000' to a '1'. When I went shopping before she was born the '0000' and '000' clothes seemed so small I assumed they were for premature babies only. I consequently initially had nothing small enough to fit her and my daughter spent her first two months in borrowed blue clothes brought round by a girlfriend.

For her first six months Isabel consumed nothing but breast milk, after which she was gradually introduced to different solid foods: from rice cereal, potato and pumpkin, to greens, and eventually to meat, eggs and food containing nuts. She weaned herself from the breast at fifteen months, wanting the freedom to walk around and look at things between mouthfuls and to manipulate plastic cutlery herself.

At eight weeks, supine (on her back), Isabel could move her arms and legs about and turn her head, and prone (on her belly), she could lift her head. By four months she could roll over, and by six she could sit up. By eight months Isabel was confidently crawling on all fours and could pull herself to standing against the couch or a low table, she got her first tooth, and she could communicate with single syllables like 'ba' and 'da'. By eighteen months Isabel knew and used about eighty words. Now, at two, she can form four- and five-word combinations that even show a sense of temporal understanding, such as 'Daddy coming later' prior to his return from work, and 'Me want more apple now'.

Isabel now loves the park, the swings and slide, to jump, to pretend to wash and feed her baby doll and put it to sleep, to draw and paint, and to avoid going to bed at night for as long as humanly possible. She is the most amusing, spirited and joyous person I have ever known. The challenge now is to help her manage her fierce need to be independent and her frustration with herself if she can't do things straight away when she attempts them.

Questions
1 What is your reaction to this scenario? Why?
2 What are some of the questions this situation raises for you?
3 What are some of the structural and functional strengths and limitations in this family and social network?
4 What is the influence of ethnicity, if Melissa and Isabel are of Middle Eastern, Greek, Indigenous or Anglo-Australian background?

Coping with risks and adversities

Infancy is a time of unique transitions and potential adversities. While we have looked at normative developmental milestones so far in this chapter, we now look at specific risk and protective factors in the face of stress, trauma and loss. This starts to build a more complex understanding of the lives of infants—incorporating the 'universal' developmental experiences with the unique and particular experiences of human lives. As with each of the stages of development, it is impossible to explore here the full range of experiences. The stress, trauma and loss experiences that are explored reflect some of the key issues that emerge in social work practice. It is useful to think about all of these experiences multidimensionally—taking into account what we know about their incidence and prevalence, their effects on individuals, families and communities, and how they are understood in the wider social and cultural contexts in which they occur.

Stress

Refer to Chapter 4 for further discussion of the stress response.

As highlighted in Chapter 4, stressors in infancy can arise as a result of the prenatal environment, the event of birth itself, or as a result of developing in a high-stress and non-supportive environment (Lobo 1990), one in which there is a lack of goodness of fit between the infant and their environment. What remains relatively unknown is the subjective experience of stress within these contexts, and its impact. For example, 'while a degree of stress can be viewed as positive for the adult, and even for the older child, it is not known whether the presence of any stress can be positive for the infant' (Lobo 1990 p. 179). The critical question emerges as to what level of exposure to high-risk situations has a negative impact on development and well-being.

The impact of stressors in infancy is difficult to assess, given that there is no capacity for verbal self-report. Rather, infants under stress are identified on the basis of observational data, monitoring for irritability and distress, and physiological indicators of stress (Lobo 1990). For example, studies monitor levels of cortisol, the stress hormone, to assess stress states. However, this is often difficult, given that infants spend most of their time within a limited number of relationships and in non-clinical settings. The stressors of infancy arise in relation to both particular events and this dependence on immediate social relationships for survival and the meeting of immediate needs.

Tolerance or resistance to stress is a complex interaction of both the environment and the infant—the different temperaments and personalities of infants are discernible from a very young age and are a critical part of the interactions with their environments. Physically too, compared to adults, infants have a limited tolerance to heat and cold, to disease as their immune system has not yet developed, and to hunger and fatigue. All of these factors interact in any stress response.

Many infants have already experienced significant stressful events prior to birth. As Field (2007 p. 25) notes, 'prenatal stress comes in many forms, including the daily hassles, depression, anxiety, anger, panic disorder, post-traumatic stress disorder, and even optimism/pessimism experienced by the pregnant woman'. These experiences have then been linked with labour difficulties, decreased birthweight and slow growth rates (Field 2007 p. 29), as have experiences of lower social support and lower socio-economic status. The social, structural and cultural environments supporting women play a key role in preventing these experiences.

For some infants though, home environments are not safe, nurturing environments. Some parents are unavailable and inconsistent with their attention to infants, as a result of mental health problems and/or through substance abuse. Stress for infants inevitably arises in these contexts, as the consistency and responsiveness they require for healthy development are not available to them, nor are they able to be accessed independently from others. Stress for infants can arise, therefore, through acts of neglect too. Many environmental factors influence the capacity for stability, consistency and responsiveness. For families living with the daily stress of poverty and its consequences as well as raising young children, this stability can be hard to find and to maintain; this reality affects large numbers of infants. For example, 'nearly half of all the children accompanying parents to housing services following experiences of homelessness (44% of 22,000) were aged 0–4 years' (AIHW 2007 p. 55).

As noted earlier in this chapter, in recent years in Australia there has been an increase in the number of children born in Sudan, Kenya, Afghanistan and Iraq (AIHW 2007 p. 19), countries where war, famine and traumas have been rife. Parents arriving in Australia are adapting to a new culture and language, often facing poverty and social isolation. These major transitions can lead to stress and conflict between parents and across cultures around perceptions of childhood, child treatment and maltreatment.

Home is not the only potential source of stress, however, with many infants experiencing illness and disability, with their unique impacts, interventions and consequences, such as frequent hospitalisations and/or painful procedures.

Separations from parents and primary caregivers can be significant stressors. In the last decade, there has been a major shift to out-of-home day care, meaning that parents are not spending the same amount of time in direct child care as in previous generations. Typically, with both parents working, many children are spending the majority of the week in day care centres, family day care or with other informal carers (often grandparents). The research into the effects of child care on the well-being of children suggests that there are some critical factors that have an impact on the stress levels experienced in care—primarily the age at which children enter such care (Brazelton & Greenspan 2000; Zigler & Finn-Stevenson 1995), the ratio and quality of the care, and the number of hours across the week the child spends in care. A major American study of the impact of child care (NICHD Early Child Care Research Network 2003, 2006) found that thirty or more hours of day care per week had a negative impact on the psychological health of young children. Other studies have looked at cortisol levels and found elevated levels in infants separated from their parents through child care arrangements (Dettling et al. 1999). This is only part of the picture though. In the Australian context, the LSAC has identified two key findings for infants in relation to care experiences, as identified below.

KEY FINDINGS FROM THE LSAC

» Children in the infant cohort participating in group-based child care programs were at most risk for impaired physical outcomes in the first year, probably due to exposure to infectious diseases.
» Children in the infant cohort who experienced only informal care tended to have higher learning scores than infants not in care.

Source: Wake et al. 2008 p. viii

Positive impacts of child care are consistently found, not only in relation to higher learning scores but also in relation to social skills. This highlights that stress and demands, as for adults, are an essential part of building coping capacities and new skills, but that there are limits to the positive tolerance of stress.

The debates surrounding the impact of child care are strongly connected with cultural beliefs and assumptions about attachment and the role of parents in providing this attachment bond. The positive findings suggest, however, that infants can feel secure with a range of adult caregivers, and thus that wider networks of support in the community can also adequately respond to these needs.

PRACTICE IN CONTEXT

WORKING WITH INFANTS

Julie reflects on how she thought about the theoretical rationale for a group with infants and toddlers.

The task was to identify a way to evaluate a group pre-reading program for infants and toddlers, involving singing and storytelling. The program was aimed at encouraging mothers and infants to spend interactive time reading, singing and listening to each other in order to foster pre-reading skills like word recognition, listening and turn-taking among the children and to develop parents' confidence in playing and interacting with their infants in ways that are positive and enjoyable for both parent and child. The group setting provided an environment that was safe and friendly, created opportunity for networking and the potential for peer support away from the program. Ultimately the desire was to promote secure attachment and robust social connections as a way of preventing situations of risk for families.

Questions

1 In what ways does Julie use theories of infant development to inform her work?
2 In what ways do you think she is understanding stress in early childhood?

Trauma

Some common traumas for infants relate to their birth experiences and their subsequent physical and psychological vulnerability. For example, for around fifteen per cent of babies, life at birth starts with health crises and admissions to 'a special care nursery (SCN) or neonatal intensive care unit (NICU)' (AIHW 2008a p. 271). Experiencing these environments often involves invasive medical procedures and highly technological, stimulating environments. While PTSD is noted for mothers in birth and hospitalisation experiences, the trauma some infants experience through the birth process and its immediate aftermath is unknown. Studies have shown, however, that physical pain levels can be very high (Harrison et al. 2006) and this experience alone carries with it a psychological and relational response.

Other traumatic events relate to experiences of family violence, both experienced directly by infants and indirectly through their witnessing of other forms of family violence. National child protection statistics indicate that children aged less than one 'accounted for between 10% and 16% of all substantiations across the jurisdictions—a rate of between 4.0 and 23.6 substantiations per 1000 children aged less than 1 year' (AIHW 2007 p. 53). Infants' physical tolerance of neglect and physical abuse is lower than that of older children, and the capacity to actively seek out other support is not yet developed. One argument why these high rates of abuse in infancy exist is that they are due to the growing awareness of the lifelong implications of experiences of early trauma and neglect and the need to intervene early to prevent this trajectory. The lifetime trajectory of early trauma is well-documented, with studies showing that early traumas impact on biopsychosocial-spiritual well-being (Briere & Scott 2006 p. 150). Psychoanalytic theory has always proposed this stance and the internal mechanisms by which this disruption occurs. Recent neuro-imaging studies have provided further evidence of this internal disruption, and have shown that 'for relatively extreme levels of deprivation, early experience does not require continuity to have its impact' (Fonagy 2001 p. 45). One study found, for example, that in infants with extremely low birthweight who had experienced neglect, cognitive development was significantly impaired compared with other infants with low birthweight (Strathearn et al. 2009).

While many children in the first two years of their lives are exposed to traumatic events, given their developmental age it is difficult to assess the impact of such experiences. Infants' reactions are primarily physical and behavioural. Infant distress tends to be reflected in:

> sensorimotor disorganization and disruption of biological rhythmns, as shown for example in frequent and prolonged crying, unresponsiveness to soothing, muscle flailing, rigidity, agitation and restlessness, feeding disturbances, sleeping disorders, lack of interest in the environment and various somatic problems with no detectable organic cause (Lieberman & Knorr 2007 p. 212).

These reactions can be indicative of the symptoms of PTSD (intrusion, avoidance and hyperarousal), exhibited behaviourally rather than reported as cognitive states, and often through 're-experiencing in response to traumatic or loss reminders, exaggerated avoidant symptoms and traumatic estrangement' (Cohen et al. 2002 p. 308). Some of the commonly observed trauma reactions include sleep disruption, irritability, loss of acquired motor and communication skills, lowered immunity, loss of appetite and eating skills, regression in behaviours such as toileting, heightened separation anxiety and hyperarousal. Some young children can become indiscriminate in their attachment behaviours or disengage from relationships.

Infants are exposed to many of the traumatic events adults experience. The profound difference is that they have the protective shield of adults as a mediator in ways that are more significant than at other times in life. Trauma reactions in infancy relate not only to the traumatic event itself, but also, arguably more importantly, to the quality of or impact on the attachment relationship. Infant trauma experiences are mediated by the ongoing availability of responsive, nurturing adults. However, in some instances parents and/or other adults in the infant's world are the perpetrators of the traumas themselves and are the source of fear. When the attachment relationship is the source of the trauma, the consequences are profound. Betrayal trauma theory (Freyd et al. 2007) is one theory that addresses the processes involved in this trauma reaction. The box below expands on some of the key tenets of this theory and highlights the double bind that survivors experience in infancy, when the perpetrator is a carer.

See Figure 5.1.

BETRAYAL TRAUMA THEORY (BTT)

From her work with survivors of childhood sexual assault, Jennifer Freyd has proposed BTT as a way of understanding the inner-world reactions of these survivors. Betrayal trauma 'occurs when the people or institutions on which a person depends for survival violate that person in a significant way'. The theory:

» 'proposes that the way in which events are processed and remembered will be related to the degree to which a negative event represents a betrayal by a trusted, needed other'
» 'argues that victims, perpetrators, and witnesses may display betrayal blindness in order to preserve relationships, institutions, and social systems upon which they depend' (Freyd et al. 2007 p. 311).

Loss

The focus of grief understandings is the reporting of biopsychosocial-spiritual distress and disruption. The limited cognitive and verbal capacities of infants mean that this distress and disruption is little understood. While trauma experiences and their impact have been extensively studied in infancy, relatively little research has been done with children under the age of two to three in relation to grief experiences. Where research has focused is on children's understandings of death (Grollman 1969; Bluebond-Langner 1978), an issue we explore in Chapter 8. What is known from research on adult mental health generally and adult grief experiences more specifically is that early childhood loss experiences, particularly parental loss, lead to more complex adult outcomes (Parkes 1972). There is a lifelong connection for many between early loss and later-life mental health experiences.

Promoting resilience

For infants, optimal well-being and resilience are best promoted through protective and nurturing relationships with adult caregivers and the environments around them. Historian Janet McCalman (2005 p. 36) notes that, historically, in Australia, an infant's:

> best chance of reaching their first birthday lay in having a health, happy supported mother; and that meant a stable marriage, a regular income, an adequate house, clean water, and ideally a close-knit community of relatives and friends.

While parental relationships and care-giving roles have shifted dramatically since the nineteenth century, about which McCalman was writing, many of these critical factors in ensuring both the physical and psychosocial survival and thriving of infants remain the same in the twenty-first century. What has also shifted is the recognition of how the structural and cultural dimensions help or hinder families and individuals in these tasks. Therefore key protective factors are:

» an available, constant, responsive, healthy, happy and well-supported primary caregiver
» financial security
» housing, clean water and good nutrition
» safe and supportive networks of family and friends
» safe and supportive neighbourhoods and community resources

The availability of resources in the structural and cultural contexts in which infants are living is essential. It helps prevent the occurence of trauma, stress and loss in some instances and ameliorates the effects when they do occur. Infants rely on having their basic needs met immediately—that is, they need food, clothing, shelter and sleep and a sense of love and security maintained through a routine that is re-established as soon as possible. To bring these about, and to support parents in providing these resources, communities need good maternal and child health services, maternity/paternity leave provisions, safety and spaces to play, and adequate access to the basic resources of food, clothing and shelter. Communities also need support through adequate child and family services that provide early intervention and protection. Infants need to be in environments where they are valued as citizens and parenting is valued.

At a cultural level, this means a shift to seeing children as citizens with rights. The Convention on the Rights of the Child outlines these critical dimensions, reflecting a universal understanding of these resources.

CONVENTION ON THE RIGHTS OF THE CHILD

» Recalling that, in the Universal Declaration of Human Rights, the United Nations has proclaimed that childhood is entitled to special care and assistance,

» Convinced that the family, as the fundamental group of society and the natural environment for the growth and well-being of all its members and particularly children, should be afforded the necessary protection and assistance so that it can fully assume its responsibilities within the community,

» Recognizing that the child, for the full and harmonious development of his or her personality, should grow up in a family environment, in an atmosphere of happiness, love and understanding,

» Considering that the child should be fully prepared to live an individual life in society, and brought up in the spirit of the ideals proclaimed in the Charter of the United Nations, and in particular in the spirit of peace, dignity, tolerance, freedom, equality and solidarity

Source: United Nations, Convention on the Rights of the Child, www2.ohchr.org/english/law/crc.htm

A rights discourse for infants is challenging in that it assumes two things—that the rights can be actively claimed and that there is someone who will ensure that they are if they are not able to be directly claimed. For an infant, both these assumptions can be compromised. Goodin and many others advocate, therefore, for a child-centred approach to infant well-being: 'Rather than focusing on what is good for society, or for particular adult members of society, this model has us focusing on what is good for the child' (Goodin 2005 p. 77). This requires bringing together the knowledge we have about risk experiences and protective factors in each of the individual, relational, social, structural and cultural dimensions.

CHAPTER SUMMARY

In this chapter, we have explored some of the key biopsychosocial-spiritual dimensions of infancy. From birth through the first year or so of life, most infants grow from weighing little more than 2500 grams to weighing around fifteen kilograms. They also move from not being able to mobilise to being able to move independently and fast, using a range of fine motor skills; from crying to express needs and reactions to talking about their worlds; and they form secure attachments with primary caregivers and friendships with peers. Infancy is a time of unique dependence and vulnerability, resulting in specific health and social risks. Tthe key resources that promote optimal development and growth throughout this foundational time of life are adequate sleep and nutrition; secure relationships that are responsive, warm and positive and environments free from major stressors, losses and traumas, To this end, environments and cultures that support parents and care-givers are also essential. Some of these experiences will be addressed further in Chapter 8, as we move to consider the experiences of early childhood.

APPLYING A MULTIDIMENSIONAL APPROACH

CASE STUDY

Zac: Sleep problems

Zac is six months old. He has had multiple hospital admissions over the first months of his life, as he has had enormous difficulty settling into any sleep routine and gaining weight. He is well underweight for his age, and his parents are anxious about his well-being. They are increasingly frustrated by a lack of a diagnosis of problems. They think he has some kind of allergy. They feel very distant in their relationship with him, as they feel that nothing they do soothes him or helps in any way. Their sense of desperation and incompetence as parents is growing. Everyone around them seems to do it so easily and they thought parenting would be so much easier.

Questions

1 What is your initial reaction to this situation?
2 What do you think are the key stressors for everyone involved in this situation, including hospital staff?
3 What relational, social, structural and cultural information would you want for a comprehensive assessment?
4 What are the possibilities for intervention using a multidimensional approach?

KEY TERMS

attachment theory

basic trust

infancy

insecure and ambivalent attachments

insecure and avoidant attachments

insecure and disorganised attachments

non-attachment

perinatal

secure attachments

sensori-motor phase

temperament

theory of mind

toddlerhood

QUESTIONS AND DISCUSSION POINTS

1   What are some of the key biopsychosocial-spiritual developmental tasks of infancy?
2   What are some of the different risk and protective factors in this earliest lifespan stage?
3   What are some of the structural and cultural dimensions that influence understandings and experiences of this stage of life?

FURTHER READING

Bowlby, J. 1984, *Attachment*, London: Penguin.
Bremner, G. & Slater, A. eds, 2004, *Theories of infant development*, Carlton: Blackwell Publishing.
Field, T. 2007, *The amazing infant*, Carlton: Blackwell Publishing.
Kochanska, G., Friesenborg, A., Lange, L. & Martel, M. 2004, 'Parents' personality and infants' temperament as contributors to their emerging relationship'. *Journal of Personality and Social Psychology*, 86(5), pp. 744–759.
Wake, M., Sanson, A., Berthelsen, D., Hardy, P., Misson, S., Smith, K. et al. 2008, *How well are Australian infants and children aged 4 to 5 years doing? Findings from the Longitudinal Study of Australian Children Wave 1*, Canberra: Department of Families, Housing, Community Services and Indigenous Affairs.

WEBSITES OF INTEREST

Adult Attachment Lab, University of California, Davis: http://psychology.ucdavis.edu/Labs/Shaver/PWT/index.cfm
This site provides an overview of the Adult Attachment Lab and has links to the attachment research of Shaver and Mikulincer.
Australian Indigenous HealthInfoNet: www.healthinfonet.ecu.edu.au
This site provides information and links relating to the health of Indigenous Australians.
Australian Institute of Family Studies (AIFS): www.aifs.org.au
The AIFS site provides extensive links to longitudinal studies of children within Australia, New Zealand, Europe and North America, including the Longitudinal Study of Australian Children.
Australian Research Alliance for Children and Youth (ARACY): www.aracy.org.au
This site provides information and links about ARACY, which is a national collaboration of researchers, policy makers and practitioners that focuses on children's and young people's well-being.

The Brazelton Institute: www.brazelton-institute.com

This site is run by the Harvard Medical School and Children's Hospital, Boston. The Institute looks at child well-being and includes the Brazelton Neonatal Assessment Scale.

Campbell Collaboration: www.campbellcollaboration.org

This site provides access to systematic reviews of social care interventions.

Cochrane Collaboration: www.cochrane.org

This site provides access to systematic reviews of health care interventions.

The Erikson Institute: www.erikson.edu

The website of this applied research centre for child development based in Chicago, USA, has links to infant and child development research and training materials.

National Association for Prevention of Child Abuse and Neglect (NAPCAN): www.napcan.org.au

This site provides information and links relating to child abuse and neglect in Australia.

Child Welfare Information Gateway: www.childwelfare.gov

This site is a US gateway for information relating to child abuse and neglect.

Parenting Research Centre: www.parentingrc.org.au

The Parenting Research Centre is a national, and independent, parenting research organisation.

Victorian Government, Department of Education and Early Human Development's Best Start Strategy: www.beststart.vic.gov.au

The website for this program includes reviews of the demonstration projects associated with this strategy, as well as extensive international program and research links.

Zero to Three: www.zerotothree.org

This site has extensive information about the first three years of life, including details of infant development month by month in their newsletter *From Baby to Big Kid*.

CHAPTER **8**

Early Childhood

AIMS OF THIS CHAPTER

This chapter explores the developmental experiences of early childhood. It considers the following questions:

» What are the biopsychosocial-spiritual developmental tasks and transitions of early childhood?
» What are the experiences and impacts of stress, trauma and loss in early childhood?
» How is resilience in early childhood understood?

The developmental stage of **early childhood** typically includes children between the age of two to four or five years, the pre-school years beyond infancy. Many of the important foundational developmental tasks that commenced in infancy continue throughout this period of the lifespan. By comparison, though, it is a time of newfound independence, physically, psychologically and socially, as young children expand their networks through child care and kindergarten. As with infancy, in recent years research has focused particularly on this period of development, in recognition that it is so foundational for well-being later in life (Richardson & Prior 2005 p. 4). This chapter focuses on the dimensions of early childhood that are linked with well-being throughout this stage for its own sake, as well as linked with well-being outcomes in later life. The discussion focuses on the biopsychosocial-spiritual transitions and the experiences and impacts of risk, adversity and resilience that typically mark this period. Much of the emerging research demonstrates that many of life's chances and opportunities can be determined by the age of four to five.

Key developmental tasks and transitions

Biological dimensions

Weight and height, and nutrition

During early childhood, children continue to increase in height and weight. While these weights and heights vary depending where in the world children are living, the World Health Organization's (WHO's) standardised tables propose that boys on average change from 87 centimetres in height around age two to 110 centimetres around age five. Girls change from 86 to 109 centimetres in the same time. In relation to weight, the WHO proposes that boys on average increase from weighing 12.2 kilograms at age two to 18.3 kilograms at age five. Girls typically weigh around 11.5 kilograms at age two and increase to 18 kilograms by age five. In recent years, obesity rates for Australian children have risen markedly, and increasingly obesity has its onset earlier in the lifespan.

We look at obesity more closely in Chapter 9, as more evidence is available for school-aged children.

However, for some children poor nutrition leads to malnutrition rather than obesity. For example, Indigenous children living in remote communities experience malnutrition at much higher rates than non-Indigenous children, often as a result of limited food availability coupled with very high cost, particularly for fresh fruit and vegetables. Malnutrition leads to a range of significant consequences—poor growth, reduced immunity and reduced concentration—all of which influence well-being and the capacity to engage in learning tasks. Food security (the stability of supply of food) is a key issue not only in remote parts of Australia, but for many families living in poverty in urban areas.

Brain development

As with infancy, a recent research emphasis has been on brain development, demonstrating crucial links between optimal brain development and optimal physical, relational and social development. As Stanley (as cited in Nancarrow 2004 p. 4) notes:

> We now know that children's brain development is an exquisite interaction between genetic potential and environment, not just physical environment but intrauterine environment and emotional environment. By four or five, most of these things have come together. Or not.

Patterns of reactivity become established through the development and usage of particular neural pathways, profoundly influencing a child's capacity to concentrate, to process and retain information, and to develop a sense of self. The relational aspects of this brain development have been emphasised through studies showing that the right brain hemisphere matures through experience-dependent processes. Secure attachment fosters this maturation process. Relational traumas up to the ages of two or three disrupt it, such that 'control of the vital functions that support survival and the human stress response' is damaged (Schore 2002 p. 236). That is, children become neurobiologically adapted to the environments in which they are living, and the level of stress to which they are exposed.

Sleep

By early childhood, most children are sleeping through the night and not needing daytime sleep at all (Adams et al. 2004 p. 96). Compared with previous generations, though, many young children (as well as adults) do not get adequate sleep, with a number of significant consequences for health and well-being. Sleep hygiene refers to the practices that support good sleep experiences—including factors in the child's and caregivers' environments, the routines associated with going to sleep and daily activities that precede sleep (Mindell et al. 2009). For many young children, sleep hygiene is poor as a result of watching television, not having consistent rules around routines and sleep times, and/or having disrupted sleep patterns through loud or stimulating environments.

While an overall lack of reliable information about pre-school children and their sleep patterns has been noted (Hiscock et al. 2007 p. 86), the first wave of data from the Longitudinal Study of Australian Children (LSAC; interviewing 4983 families with four- or five-year-olds about their children's sleep problems) found that difficulties were common. During these years, children frequently experience dreams, nightmares and night terrors. Nightmares tend to peak at about four to six years (Rutter 1987). Some estimate that about one in ten children throughout this age period experience sleep difficulties (Bloch & Singh 1997 p. 204). The LSAC found that the 'children with sleep problems had poorer child-health-related quality of life, more behaviour problems, and higher rates of attention-deficit/ hyperactivity disorder' (Hiscock et al. 2007 p, 86). The sleep problems associated most strongly with these outcomes were difficulties going to sleep and morning tiredness.

Motor skills

In early childhood children gain independence of mobility and continue to refine their motor skills through play. They move from broad capacities to specific skills, including toilet training (discussed below). By the age of four, most children have not only grown significantly in height, weight and stature, but they are also able to demonstrate a range of fine motor skill capacities such as playing musical instruments, using computers and mobile phones, drawing, and playing with more complex toys. It is a time of rapid development.

Toileting skills

Most children by the age of five have learnt to control their bladder and bowel functions, although, as Rey, Hazell and Walter (2007) note, about seven per cent of boys and three per cent of girls aged five years will experience enuresis (loss of bladder control). To a lesser extent again (about one per cent of five year olds), some children experience encopresis (loss of bowel control) on occasion. Boys are more likely than girls to experience enuresis and encopresis. A persistent regression in the management of these functions is often associated with stress, trauma and grief experiences, and so changes such as these can be important indicators of distress. Losing bowel or bladder control can also lead to significant social embarrassment among peers.

Tantrums and tears

Early childhood is seen as an emotionally turbulent time, when children experience often very intense and labile moods (Rutter 1987 pp. 83–4). These mood swings are often displayed through disinhibited expression, as the child has not yet learned socially acceptable ways of expressing displeasure or frustration. It is particularly noted that two- to three-year-olds experience an increase in **negativism**—that is, the capacity to refuse to do things, to say 'no' and to refuse adults, through both verbal and physical tantrums. The two-year-old period is sometimes referred to as 'the terrible twos' (Germain 1991 p. 265), as a reflection on both the behaviour of two-year-olds and the experience for parents! Tantrums during early childhood, particularly for two- to three-year-olds, can occur daily as rules and boundaries are negotiated with parents or caregivers. From a developmental perspective, children are learning to manage their emotional life, and their distress, anger and frustration in particular:

> They have new skills and behaviours to learn and remember, feelings to grapple with, and these can be overwhelming. They can wait a little while ... but not for long. They can hold strong feelings inside a litte, but these can burst out in a rush. (Child and Youth Health 2009 p. 7)

The skills of **affect regulation** are linked with a range of other critical skills—participating in social relationships, being an autonomous individual, and expressing and managing wants and needs. All of these experiences are ways a young child begins to negotiate and understand themselves and their unique social context. **Aggression** can become a more problematic behaviour among young children—, for example, studies have shown a link between aggression and sibling interactions (discussed later in this chapter) as well as television viewing habits and parental interactions.

In Chapter 9 we look at these issues more closely.

Disability, injury and diseases

Children under the age of four are most commonly admitted to hospital for respiratory or perinatal conditions, and asthma and allergies continue to be the major ongoing health conditions (AIHW 2008a p. 275). While mortality rates continue to decline for this age group, injury (through road trauma or drowning) continues to be a major cause of death for young children, along with cancer or neurological diseases. For Indigenous children, the mortality rate 'is around three times that of non-Indigenous children (41 deaths compared with 14 per 100,000 children aged 1–14 years in 2003–2005' (AIHW 2008a p. 275).

By the age of three, some of the developmental disorders of early childhood have become apparent, as particular physical, social and linguistic milestones are not reached. The developmental disorders of autism and Asperger's syndrome, in particular, become diagnosable around this age (Bloch & Singh 1997 p. 207) when children do not achieve the expected cognitive, social, emotional and behavioural milestones. While many parents report concerns about developmental issues earlier than this, diagnosis is often not possible because of the need to assess particular skills—for example, social and verbal skills.

Psychosocial-spiritual dimensions

Throughout the early childhood years, children are seen as engaging in a very active 'phase of language development, of growth of play, of identification and emergence of guilt, of gender identity and locomotion' (Rutter 1987 p. 73). As distinct from infancy, when most aspects of a child's well-being are being cared for by adults, during this time of life young children are learning to participate in all sorts of activities independently and to express their needs and wants. By the age of five, most young children are at school. However, as Punch (2003) notes, this is the experience for most Australian children, who are theoretically part of the world's 'minority' experience of childhood. For the majority of the world's children, growing up in Latin America, Asia and Africa, and for many Indigenous Australian children, childhood does not necessarily bring the opportunities of play and school. It is with this in mind that some of the psychosocial-spiritual changes over these early years of the lifespan are now considered.

Cognitive development

Within this preoperational phase of cognitive development (Piaget 1995), the child is at a pre-conceptual stage, which:

> begins when the child learns a language and ends about age 5 or 6. During this stage, children develop the tools for representing schemes symbolically through language,

imitation, imagery, symbolic play, and symbolic drawing. Their knowledge is still very much tied to their own perceptions. (Newman & Newman 2003 pp. 71–2)

In this sense, a child's view of the world is relatively egocentric—with them at the centre of causation of events. The belief that they control or cause what happens tends to mediate their perceptions of the world around them, as they are unable to engage in abstract or hypothetical thought. Notwithstanding this, children are developing a coherent worldview based on their experiences—developing a sense of predictability at the same time as beginning to appreciate the existence of others. This predictability and coherence is, however, mediated by significant others around them, primarily adults. Recognition of the importance of this has come from another theory of child development, Vygotsky's, which focuses on the social embeddedness of these developments. Rather than seeing cognitive development as a series of stages, reliant upon the child's readiness to engage in the skills of each, he argued that there are two key pivotal processes of mediation in the child's development of new tools and capacities: 'Adults mediate the child's acquisition and mastery of new psychological tools, which get internalized and come to mediate the child's mental processes' (Karpov 2006 p. 20). Thus, cognitive development is about both a child's capacity to engage in increasingly complex cognitive tasks *and* the stimulus with which the child is provided to do so.

Intelligence

One of the protective factors that consistently emerges in developmental research is intelligence. Werner and Smith (1992) first highlighted this in their study of children who were growing up in circumstances considered to be high risk—where their parents were poorly educated, had mental illnesses or were in families with high discord and violence. In this study, three key protective factors were identified for young children—having at least one adult to whom they mattered, being engaged in extracurricular activities with supportive adults outside the home and having above-average intelligence. Increased intelligence offers a child a number of resources, including the capacity to think through situations and engage in problem solving; to know the world around them and begin to make sense of actions and their consequences; to engage in learning experiences easily; and to receive positive feedback from others for their intellectual achievements.

Intelligence is now recognised as a multidimensional construct, in that children and adults have academic, social and emotional intelligences, all of which can develop in different ways (Gardner 2004). Children require a repertoire of intelligences to succeed in their relationships and in their educational experiences, and schools now actively encourage the development of social and emotional intellegence in their curricula. Within the home, parents are encouraged to enhance their child's academic intelligence further through activities such as regular reading together. Studies affirm that children whose parents read with them throughout early childhood develop stronger intellectual capacities (Sénéchal & LeFevre 2002). Whereas by the end of the infant period children are beginning to put a couple of words together into a sentence, by the end of early childhood most children are beginning to write and have a vocabulary of spontaneous language. Complex and compound sentences are able to be used, and children can distinguish between yesterday, today and tomorrow (Child Development Institute 2009). However, reading itself may not be the only stimulus to intelligence—when reading together, children are interacting positively with parents, typically in a close, supportive and nurturing relationship, enabling the child to develop a strong sense of trust and knowledge of the world.

Personality and temperament

As described in Chapter 7, temperaments differ according to each child's integration of the qualities of reactivity, sociability and self-regulation (both of affect and behaviour) (Smart 2007 p. 1). The Australian Temperament Project (ATP) and the LSAC project have provided unique insights into the temperament experiences of children throughout these years, and unique opportunities to compare children in two cohorts, twenty years apart.

See Chapter 7 and p. 237 for a brief overview of these studies.

In the comparison of two- to three-year olds in the ATP (born in 1982–83) and LSAC cohorts (born 2003–04), mean scores showed that most children were 'usually sociable, frequently persistent and usually not reactive and intense' (Smart & Sanson 2008 p. 56). However, some significant differences were found in comparing the temperaments of young children across the twenty-year age difference. The ATP children 'were reported to be significantly less sociable, less persistent and more reactive than LSAC children' (Smart & Sanson 2008 p. 54), indicating that young children today are tending to do slightly better than those in the 1980s by way of temperament. For school-aged children, however, some other differences emerged, which will be discussed in Chapter 9.

In another study of 182 Australian pre-schoolers, the link between temperament and peer acceptance was analysed. The study found that 'rejected children displayed a more difficult temperament than popular children in terms of higher activity levels, higher distractability and lower persistence' (Walker et al. 2001 p. 177) and that boys were more likely to be rated with these traits. The other critical aspect of temperament is the goodness of fit with parents (Kochanska et al. 2004) and/or caregivers. Some research has shown that parents under stress more typically see their children as having 'difficult' temperaments when this is not objectively the case. Thus, interaction with parents, siblings, peers and carers is a critical influence on how both personality and temperament are perceived and shaped throughout early childhood.

Emotional development

As discussed in Chapter 7, Erikson, the developmental theorist, proposed that infants were psychosocially engaged in building a sense of basic trust through secure relationships with parents and/or caregivers. He regarded basic trust as the initial building block, or crisis, of development that enables or precipitates moving to the next developmental crisis, the crisis of **autonomy** versus shame and doubt. In this stage, the young child is more active in exploring their world and in establishing their ability to act as an independent entity. They are striving towards autonomy yet having to balance their ongoing dependency needs. Erikson proposed that those who are unable to develop a strong sense of autonomy are likely to experience shame and doubt, where there is a fear of the loss of love, leading them to become overly concerned with their parents' approval, and self-conscious. The failure to develop a sense of autonomy means that the child does not develop a sense of will power—that is, a sense that they have any capacity to change or influence the environment around them. The individual emphasis within these skills raises important questions of cultural context; not all communities and cultures within Australia and New Zealand, and beyond, emphasise these skills. It does seem important, however, cross-culturally, that children acquire a sense of basic trust with those around them.

Later in early childhood, from around the ages of three to five, Erikson proposed that the developmental 'crisis' is one of **initiative** versus guilt. That is, learning to trust oneself enough to begin to act in the world around them. The ability to acquire a sense of initiative leads the child to develop a sense of purpose. Those who are not able to acquire a sense of initiative are left plagued with guilt, confused about gender and family roles, self-centred and overly anxious. In this third phase, Erikson saw that there was either successful identity formation or role diffusion. That is, the individual either developed a clear sense of who they were, developed boundaries around the expression of that self, or was unable to distinguish themselves from various people around them such as peers or family.

Having gained autonomy, the young child strives to find out the kind of person they want to be—searching out others with whom to identify. During early childhood, children typically identify very strongly with adults and idols around them. Children are also attracted to those who seem powerful and competent, and with whom they share a warm and loving relationship. For boys, this is more so than for girls, and they often identify strongly with superheroes, such as Superman, or sports figures (Holub et al. 2008). Through this process of identification, children develop a sense of mastery and control, through identifying with figures that can overcome all sorts of dangers in the worlds around them. They also provide 'children with a way to understand their culture and place in society' (Holub et al. 2008 p. 567). In middle childhood this changes, as fears and worries increase in response to greater insight as to the reality of these threats. Marketing campaigns influence and foster these identifications in early childhood, with children and their parents flooded by images of products through the television and internet (Pine & Nash 2003).

Relational development

Attachment behaviour and the ongoing experience of secure attachments remains important. For this age group, relationships with parents continue to be crucial, and thus research focuses on both temperament and personality styles, as well as parenting style or quality of parenting. While parenting skills are clearly something that emerges in caring for an infant, they are perhaps more exerted and obvious in interactions with children's increasing autonomy in early childhood.

See Chapter 7 for attachment theory.

Styles of parenting differ in the extent to which there is high or low warmth present in the parent–child relationship, and the extent to which children experience rigidly imposed or negotiated rules. Baumrind (1971; 1995; Aunola & Nurmi 2005) set out three types of parenting style—the authoritative, the authoritarian and the permissive style (see box below). She, along with many others, has advocated for the authoritative parenting style, with its qualities of high warmth and high negotiation of rules, arguing that this is the style most likely to foster a sense of mastery and competence in children, which leads to a sense of mastery and competence in later life.

BAUMRIND'S (1971) THREE PARENTAL DISCIPLINE STYLES

1 **Authoritarian:** Parents who use this type of parenting are rigid and controlling, rules are narrow and specific, with little room for negotiation, and children are expected to follow the rules without explanation.
Type of discipline: cold and harsh, physical force, no explanation of rules.
2 **Authoritative:** These parents are more flexible. Their rules are more reasonable, and they leave opportunities for negotiation and compromise.
Type of discipline: warm and nurturing, positive reinforcement, sets firm limits and provides rationale behind rules and decisions.
3 **Permissive:** The parents' rules are unclear and children are left to make their own decisions.
Type of discipline: warm and friendly towards their children, no direction given.

As children from much younger ages now enter into different care arrangements during the day, questions about disciplinary style extend to the social networks of the child and the extent to which the child moves between compatible or incompatible styles of discipline and expectations about behaviour—between grandparents and parents, for example, or between day care workers and parents.

Preferred parenting style may also reflect the Western cultural context, though, as some suggest that there is variation across cultures (Prior et al. 2001 pp. 17–18). For example, some have argued that authoritarian parenting is more typical in collectivist cultures and authoritative in more individualistic cultures. However, an analysis by Sorkhabi (2005) found that there was little evidence of these patterns, and that, irrespective of cultural context, optimal academic and psychosocial adjustment was consistently found with authoritative parenting across many cultures, both collectivist and individualistic.

However, the overall influence of parents on children's development and, in particular, personality has been questioned by some. Harris, for example, has claimed that this emphasis on parents as the main influences constitutes a 'nurture assumption'—that is, 'the assumption that what influences children's development, apart from their genes, is the way their parents bring them up' (Harris 1998 p. 2). She undertook a systematic review of the available developmental literature, asking three key questions (Harris 2000):

1 Do parenting behaviours have any lasting effects on child outcomes?
2 Are learned social behaviours specific to the social context in which they were learned?
3 What are the experiences that do have lasting effects on child outcomes, and what roles do peers play in these experiences?

She concludes that there is little evidence to suggest the profound impact of parents on children's development that is often assumed. Instead, she proposes a group socialisation theory, a theory that sees the key influences on children's immediate behaviour as arising from the peer group in which they are living and relating. Research highlights that children are, from a very early age, able to distinguish the rules of the particular setting in which they find themselves and can adjust their behaviour accordingly. She cites as one source of evidence for these wider rules of significance the example of children who migrate to other cultures and quickly adjust their behaviour to fit into the group. The resilience of children seems to be in their capacity to engage appropriately within the worlds they occupy, being able to move flexibly across relationships as required. This hypothesis, that group socialisation rather than parental influence has a more profound impact on development, fits with the stress and adaptation literature that suggests it is the child's capacity to build a repertoire of coping behaviour and demonstrate the knowledge of and flexibility to respond to whatever situation they find themselves in that leads to better coping outcomes.

Siblings become critical influences in these coping repertoires. Siblings share contexts and histories in unique ways, and the sharing of multiple, significant relationships can be the source of particular rivalry and tension. Sibling rivalry peaks around the age of two to four years (Rutter 1987). Sibling relationships, in many ways, serve as a microcosm of the wider social networks into which children will function throughout their lives and are thus important learning grounds and experiences in and of themselves. In one study, undertaken by McIntosh and Punch (2009) with ninety children from thirty families, they discovered that from a very young age, siblings learn to use bartering, deals, bribes and threats in their relationships with each other, skills that are then generalised into other relationships. Importantly they found that gender was not the key determinant of these interactions, but birth order; that is, older siblings controlled the outcomes of younger siblings.

Given that sibling relationships are a significant influence in the development of relationship and negotiation skills, sibling aggression has been studied extensively. Sibling relationships are a common site for the expression of tensions, both verbally and physically, and for learning how to resolve them. The other reason for a focus on siblings rather than other peers or relationships, in relation to the development of aggression management skills, is that siblings often hold a unique degree of intimacy or shared history, with siblings acquiring 'embarrassing stories, secrets and knowledge of the most painful buttons to push' (Stauffacher & DeHart 2006 p. 236). One study of aggression found that 'during preschool age, children engaged in little relational aggression with their friends but there were high levels of relational aggression observed with their siblings (Stauffacher & DeHart 2006 p. 229). The relative permanence of the sibling relationship enables the expression of more open aggression, as there is little threat of losing the relationship because of it. It provides an opportunity to develop the skills of aggression, and importantly, aggression management, for more selective use in friendships later in middle childhood (Stauffacher & DeHart 2006 p. 236).

Young children also spend waking hours with others, not just siblings and parents. What this means is that parenting style and siblings are not the only influences on children's development. With young children spending so many hours in the care of others, day care workers, kindergarten teachers, grandparents and other carers become significant attachment figures in the lives of children. In the LSAC, for example, only 1.2 per cent of children had no grandparents, and 2.6 per cent had no contact, compared with 74.9 per cent who had contact at least every month— among these high-contact grandparents, 44 per cent of the four- to five-year-olds had contact every week (44.8 per cent) and 12 per cent every day (Gray et al. 2005).

Wider relational opportunities seem to lead to greater benefits, particular when the home environment may not be optimal for many children. For young children, the LSAC identified:

> Children in the child cohort attending pre-Year 1 early education programs had
> higher overall and learning outcomes than children who had only informal care

In Chapter 2 we looked at the characteristics of sibling relationships.

arrangements. These results highlight the possible beneficial effects of attendance at programs with more strongly focused educational curricula. (Wake et al. 2008 p. viii)

During this age, children's social networks do increase rapidly at a peer level, and play and recreation fosters them. Whereas during the first year of life most play is solitary, from the second year of life children increasingly pay attention to others such that they will now play alongside each other. By the third year of life, children are moving into associative play and the degree of cooperative play increases (Newman & Newman 2003 pp. 191–8). Repetition and routine are vital parts of this play, leading to a sense of security and meaning. Three- and four-year-olds show a rapid increase in the use of imaginative or pretend play (Woody 2003a pp. 175–7). Any real object can become an imaginary object, as children experiment with new roles and rules. Play in pre-school offers children free activity separate from their world with adults and a place where social and cultural rules are enacted and negotiated. As Vygotsky (1978 p. 99 as cited in Karpov 2006 p.157) stated:

> Play continually places demands on the child to act against immediate impulse. At every step the child is faced with a conflict between the rules of the game and what [s/]he would do if [s/]he could suddenly act spontaneously ... A child's greatest self-control occurs in play.

Play allows the child to explore emotions, to lessen fears, and to come to understand an event by taking things apart and finding out how things work. Play enables imagination and creativity to come to the fore. Others propose that play enables children to engage with the adult world, even though they cannot do this in reality—'they "penetrate" the world of adults by imitating and exploring social roles and relations in the course of sociodramatic play' (Karpov 2006 p. 140). Having the space and opportunity to play, in unstructured ways in particular, is an increasingly problematic issue in urban areas, as the opportunity for friendships to form outside of the home depends upon the availability and access to playgrounds and other opportunities for safe and stimulating activities with others. In the Australian context, children's play has become increasingly restricted and indoors, leading to a range of consequences. In previous generations, children played freely at each other's houses and in the streets, but with increasing concern about risk management (preventing injuries or the risk of child maltreatment, for example) and the simultaneous developments in technology, children's play tends to be passive, taking place indoors and using computer technology.

Gender and sexual identity

The processes of gender identity formation have been the focus of extensive research, incorporating an emphasis on the influence of both cognitive development and socialisation processes. By the age of two, children are able to distinguish gender differences.

By about the age of two to two-and-a-half years, children are beginning to identify themselves as gendered, use gender-differentiating language and identify toys and peers according to a gender identity (Martin et al. 2002; Ahmed et al. 2004). This is not always an accurate process, though, with studies reporting that children aged three, while likely to identify their own gender, may not be able to correctly identify that of their peers (Katz & Kofkin 1997 p. 58).

From infancy onwards, children experience the sexuality of their bodies. These experiences are mediated by the familial, social and cultural messages about sexuality. Throughout early childhood, interest in sexuality and sex differences becomes heightened, and sexual exploration increases. Around the ages of four to six years, 'children are generally showing a good deal of curiosity about sex and play' (Rutter 1987 p. 83) and play often involves undressing and sexual exploration (Woody 2003a p.174). As Family Planning Queensland resources (2007 p. 1) state:

> Sexual play such as 'Show me yours and I'll show you mine' is quite common. It is also common for children to role-play relationships and gender roles that they observe around them.

Children receive many messages about the social acceptability of their sexuality, and are introduced through these messages to the complex interaction of the body with all the other dimensions of experience—relational, social and cultural, in particular. Within family cultures and wider cultural groups, perceptions differ as to when sex education should be provided. Given concerns about sexual abuse and exploitation, much of the emphasis on children's sexuality is typically related to these concerns, rather than understanding sexual expression in context. When young children show a seemingly precocious knowledge of sexual behaviours, this can be a possible indicator of sexual abuse.

Sex education is explored more fully in Chapter 9.

Moral and/or spiritual development

Many different theories of young children's moral and spiritual development have been proposed. Moral development theories have focused on trying to understand how and when children acquire a sense of what is right and wrong, and how they modify their behaviour or not as a consequence. They have tended to emphasise either cognitive developmental influences or environmental ones.

In relation to moral development, both Kohlberg's and Gilligan's theories have continued to have resonance. Kohlberg proposed a three-stage model of **moral development**. He argued that as children's cognitive capacities increased, they moved from what he termed to be pre-conventional to conventional, and in adulthood through to post-conventional, moral decision-making processes. Pre-conventional moral reasoning (Stage 1) is seen as ego-centric, and reinforced by parental limits and punishments. The next stage, Stage 2, sees shifts with maturity whereby children become focused on 'pragmatic exchanges with like-minded others' (Lapsley 2006). With pre-conventional reasoning, the focus is on 'an exchange system of favors, goods and sanctions that are engaged to meet selfish concrete-individualistic goals' (Lapsley 2006 p. 46). With conventional moral reasoning, children become aware of their group membership and eventually of the importance of shared relationships. In the later stages of development, Kohlberg proposed that children and adults came to identify with morals over and above laws; that is, beyond the conventional. This typology developed from presenting children and adults with moral dilemmas in case scenarios and asking them about the reasoning behind the decisions they made as to whether particular behaviours were wrong and in what ways. He claimed these stages were universal and evident across cultures, although his stages 5 and 6 came to be seen to reflect particular Western philosophies (ways of thinking that were rare even in Western contexts) and to be unachievable. Gibbs, Basinger, Grime and Snarey (2007 p. 491), in their meta-analysis of Kohlberg's claims across twenty-three countries, conclude that Kohlberg was 'in principle correct regarding the universality of basic moral judgment development, moral values, and related social perspective-taking processes across cultures'. By contrast, Gilligan (1993) proposed that Kohlberg's model privileged a traditionally male orientation and thus missed out on understanding female experiences and processes of moral development.

The developing cognitive and verbal capacities of children in early childhood make it possible to explore issues of spirituality from their own point of view. In the United Kingdom, the Association for Children's Spirituality is undertaking a study in which children's worldviews are being explored in their own right through qualitative, narrative methods. In the United States, the Search Institute is undertaking similar research. Much of the research tends to be retrospectively focused, in that it asks adults about their childhood experiences of spirituality. These experiences tend to be memories of moments of bliss, happiness, extreme clarity or love, and often within the context of relationships or in the environment.

Many different theories are proposed about children's spirituality, including theories that argue that children are innately spiritually developed and advanced and that to see them as 'developing' is to overlook their inherent spirituality that is given and present. Fowler and Dell (2006) described faith development from the ages of four to seven as being 'intuitive-projective'. What they mean by this term is that, in:

> lacking simple perspective taking and the ability to reverse operations, young
> children may not understand cause-and-effect relations well. They construct

and reconstruct events in episodic fashion. Fantasy and make-believe are not distinguished from factuality. (Fowler & Dell 2006 p. 38)

The question continues across these early years as to whether spirituality is experienced cognitively or as a more all-encompassing emotional and transcendent experience.

Coping with risks and adversities

Stress

For young children, stress continues to occur primarily in the context of their relationships with primary caregivers and their family. Major stressors identified for this period include experiencing illness and disability, poverty and major separations from primary caregivers.

The impact of poverty on young children has been well-documented through lifespan studies and, according to the LSAC, has more impact on development in this phase of the lifespan than in infancy. The box below highlights some of the key findings to date.

Some findings from this study were referred to in Chapter 7.

LSAC: FIRST ANALYSIS

This study is tracking the experiences of Australian children, to identify risk and protective factors for well-being. The first wave of data analysis has been completed, comprised of 5,107 children in what is termed the infant cohort, and 4,983 four- and five-year-old children in what is termed the child cohort.

Five aspects of the children's experiences have been analysed:

1 key sociodemographic characteristics covering the child, mother, family and neighbourhood
2 non-parental care experiences
3 child health—pre-natal and post-natal experiences and exposures
4 maternal physical and mental health
5 the early educational experiences of the child cohort in the home and in out-of-home contexts.

Some key findings from this first analysis are as follows:

» Most children are doing well and few have pervasive difficulties.
» Sociodemographic factors are more strongly related to child than infant developmental outcomes.

» Different forms of non-parental care and early education programs have differential effects on developmental outcomes.

» Child health variables affect developmental outcomes.

» Breastfeeding is associated with better health in both cohorts.

» Maternal physical and mental health affects child outcomes.

» Family learning environments are strongly associated with children's learning outcomes.

While the first wave of data from the LSAC has demonstrated that 'most children are doing well and few have pervasive difficulties' in the early childhood cohort (4,983 children aged four and five), it demonstrates that 'sociodemographic factors are more strongly related to child than infant developmental outcomes' (Wake et al. 2008 p. vii). That is, by the age of four and five, Australian children, 'were more likely to have positive outcomes in the context of higher maternal education, higher family income, higher parental occupational status, and in the absence of financial stress' (Wake et al. 2008 p. viii).

Poverty is a major stressor, in that it can both determine the environments in which children are living, depriving them of opportunities to play and interact with others in safe, resourced neighbourhoods, and the parenting style, in that parents faced with financial strain and pressure are often less able to respond fully to a child's demands. For many families, this stress and strain is intergenerationally experienced, whereas for others, it can be transitional and relatively short-term.

Poverty and its impact on children is explored in more detail in Chapter 9.

Many other parent-related and broader social problems have an impact on children. For example, it is estimated that in about eighty-five per cent of all families where there is a substantiated child protection notification, parents are adversely affected by substance abuse. This means that children's parents are often episodically, if not more persistently, unavailable to care for their children and ensure their basic needs such as food and adequate clothing are met. The trauma impacts of these situations are discussed in the next section of this chapter.

For another group of children, migration is an early childhood experience. This can often involve language differences and difficulties, and housing and employment difficulties for their parents, which inevitably have an impact on them too. The embeddedness of their family within the wider social and cultural contexts can make a major difference to their sense of social isolation and/or connectedness.

Trauma

In the Australian context, major traumas for young children include accidents, disasters and family violence or neglect. In this chapter, we look at the traumas of child abuse and neglect. In Chapter 9, we look at the traumas of sexual abuse, natural disasters and war.

According to statistics from the Australian Institute of Health and Welfare (AIHW 2009b), child protection notifications have increased significantly in each annual period since 2003–04. For example, in 2003–04, the number of notifications was 219,384 but it increased to 317,526 in 2007–08 (AIHW 2009b p.viii). Substantiations have also increased. However, these figures are a reflection of a complex system of child protection, and are influenced by different legislation across each of the states and territories, as well as by the resources of the child protection system to adequately respond to notifications. Notwithstanding these issues, thousands of Australian children are experiencing violence or neglect in various forms, with emotional abuse the most common type of maltreatment substantiated in five states and territories, and the second most common type behind neglect in the other three (AIHW 2009b p. 26). Within all of the child protection systems, Aboriginal and Torres Strait Islander children are significantly over-represented (AIHW 2009b p. 30), both in terms of a substantiation of abuse or neglect and in relation to being removed into state care. Complex factors lead to this over-representation, including the enduring and intergenerational impacts of colonisation, loss and trauma, the continuing health and social inequalities, and continuing racism.

Table 8.1 shows the rates per 1,000 children of substantiations of notifications for children aged between one and four years, in each of the states and territories, in 2008–09.

TABLE **8.1** Rates of substantiations by child protection services

Age	NSW	Vic.	Qld	WA	SA	Tas.	ACT	NT
1–4 years	10.3	5.6	7.1	3.3	7.9	11.0	8.7	16.4

Source: AIHW 2010 p. 19

Early childhood trauma does have an impact on children's well-being, both at the time and in later life. As with infancy, the processes leading to the impact of trauma on young children are not as well understood as the impact of trauma in adulthood. Unlike infants, children in this stage have verbal capacities, even if limited, to report their experiences much more readily. Generally speaking, young children seem to show some similarities with an adult post-traumatic stress reaction, although their reactions are more likely to 'include more behavioural symptoms such as play reenactment, separation anxiety, nightmares and aggression' (Salmon & Bryant 2002 p. 168). Whereas adult trauma reactions are understood primarily in relation to the disruption caused to existing cognitive schemas by trauma-related information,

PTSD is defined
and discussed in
Chapter 5.

for children, these cognitive schemas are not as developed. Given this, 'the child's knowledge base and language development influence how both traumatic and non-traumatic events are encoded, appraised and represented in memory' (Salmon & Bryant 2002 p. 169). For each child, these events and their aftermath are unique.

Many young children's reactions to trauma continue to be interpreted through physical indicators, with regressive behaviours being a major indicator. Some of the possible indicators include sleep disturbance or distress, behaviour and mood changes, specific fears and generalised anxieties, and regression in developmental capacities. No expectable pathway exists for children and their reactions to trauma. Each situation requires a careful consideration of the unique capacities and changes for each child. Many trauma experiences for young children are compounded by significant losses and changes. For example, in one study of children where a parent had murdered the other parent, not only did the child lose a parent through highly traumatic circumstances, nearly one half of the children had at least three placements with different carers, and some had up to six placements (Kaplan et al. 2001 p. 12).

PRACTICE IN CONTEXT

WORKING WITH TRAUMA IN EARLY CHILDHOOD

In this case example, Jill reflects on her work with a young boy. The strong interaction between trauma, loss and change is highlighted.

Adam is now five. His mother Sarah is in her thirties and African in origin. She is divorced from her Spanish husband, who is repartnered and has a daughter from this relationship. Sarah and Adam were referred to counselling after a lengthy involvement with child protection services. The counsellor was informed that this case was particularly difficult because the mother was suspected of making up allegations of sexual abuse by Adam's father to ensure that he would not again see his son.

When Adam first came to counselling he was speech-delayed and very angry. Sarah was very wary of yet another worker and immediately asked how I would be different from the countless workers who had disbelieved and harassed her and her son over the past three-and-a-half years. In counselling, I began by telling Adam that I was there to make a book with him. Adam loved drawing and began with a story about his father losing his temper and then leaving. He then drew in detail the story of him and his mother moving to a new home because of the fighting in the old house. By our third meeting, Adam was talking much more clearly and drew and told me about inappropriate sexual behaviour that had occurred on access visits with his father. He said that he was scared and did not want to visit his father again. The child had an infection but there was not clear evidence that this was related to any abuse. I reported this to Child Protection who took my details but said that the case was suspended and not open to the protective worker taking my report. I discussed the issue with Sarah and suggested that she go to the police and let them know that she was not prepared to send Adam on access. They did not want to take Sarah's statement. She said this was because they had heard from her too often in the past. Both Sarah and I contacted the children's hospital workers who knew the case and reinforced the need to follow reporting procedures. After some deliberation she phoned the father herself and explained why she would not send Adam. His phone calls stopped.

The matter was taken to the Family Court again, but the case was dismissed as the mother had not yet been tested psychologically. This assessment was arranged and both mother and child went. I accompanied Adam because he was afraid to see his father without someone he trusted to support him. When he saw his father, after a six months break he was excited to see him again. The assessing professional was confused. So was I. I asked Adam about this after the visit and he said he loved and missed his father but he didn't want to be hurt. He wanted to see his father again. Could someone cut off his father's hands so that Dad could stop hurting him?

Changes in Adam

Adam now speaks well. He rushes up and welcomes me whenever I arrive. He discusses things with me in a very adult manner. He loves singing with me, enjoys acting out feelings and loves it when we say BOOO to the scary things under his bed. His tempers are less frequent and he is able to understand why he gets angry. He now knows how to talk about his nightmares and they happen less frequently. Adam no longer talks about his imaginary friend. In the beginning of therapy this friend took over when ever things got tough. Adam wets the bed less often now but still has a slip-up now and then. He is looking forward to school next year. He loves making the appointments with me at the end of each session. We compare diaries and negotiate suitable times together. We have an agreement that he can call and leave a message if scary things happen between appointments. He has phoned me once.

Questions

1 What is your personal reaction to Adam and his family?
2 What is your reaction to Jill's reflections on her work with this family?
3 What are the developmental issues that stand out for you in considering Adam's situation?
4 What trauma concepts seem relevant for you in thinking about working with Adam and his family?
5 How does a multidimensional approach help you to think about interventions other than counselling for Adam and his family?

Loss

Each young child's experience of loss is different, particularly so because it occurs at unique points in their biopsychosocial-spiritual development. While young children may not be able to verbalise their distress and their experiences, their grief often manifests in a range of physical and behavioural responses. Factors that influence a child's understanding include their verbal and cognitive capacities, as well as their exposure to information about the loss that has occurred and the reactions of those around them. Experiences of loss during early childhood collide with a stage of development when a language of the child's emotional life is only beginning to emerge and they are trying to master and manage that emotional life.

Through observation and discussion with children as young as three, it has been discovered that they are acutely aware of death and dying. Children comprehend far more about death than is commonly believed (Bluebond-Langner 1978; Kubler-Ross 1970). Children tend to express grief differently, through behavioural reactions and regression rather than through language, with often a delayed period of time between the time of loss and the onset of difficulties. One of the reasons for the delayed reaction is that children seem to wait for their immediate parents or caregivers to be through the most distressing phase of their grief reactions (Worden 2003) and express their distress more fully when this parent or adult is available emotionally to support them through their experience. Other reactions occur because new skills have been developed, particularly cognitive and linguistic skills, enabling their experience to be understood in new ways.

In the meantime, young children will often create a story or fantasy as to what has occurred in their efforts to build a coherent narrative. However, this narrative often has them as the central cause of what has occurred. Studies have also highlighted the egocentricity of young children's understandings, with children often believing they have been somehow responsible for deaths or other losses that have occurred (Lieberman & Knorr 2007).

For many children, the loss experienced is the death of a parent. As Edelman (1998 p. 6) notes, many children do not have the psychological and emotional capacities that facilitate adaptation:

> a full understanding of death; the language and encouragement to talk about their feelings; the realization that intense pain won't last forever; and the ability to shift their emotional dependence from the lost parent back to the self before attaching to someone else.

One of the participants in Edelman's study of daughters whose mothers have died reflects on her experience as a three-year-old and the time of her mother's death:

> I remember when my dad came in to tell us she had died ... I remember not even understanding what that meant, but seeing my dad cry. My sister immediately cried but I was kind of confused. A lot of my feelings from that time are confused and really fuzzy. (in Edelman 1998 p. 32)

She reflects on her early grief reaction:

> I remember feeling lost. My father told me once that the hardest part of those next few months for him was that I would wake up in the night screaming for her. Screaming and screaming. But I don't remember that. (Edelman 1998 p. 33)

Similar reactions were noted in a study of three- to five-year-olds in the United States (Christ 2000 p. 52), following the death of a parent from cancer. Despite preparation for the inevitable death, the death and permanence of that death was unreal and unexpected by the children. What is known from numerous studies is that young children cannot cognitively comprehend the permanence of death, believing instead that the person who has died will return (Grollman 1969). For example, Christ's study found that:

> No matter how carefully children were prepared for a parent's death or how often they had elaborated the theme of death and dying in their fantasies or play, they did not actually expect the parent to die, could not readily comprehend the permanence and irreversibility of death and the sadness associated with that eventuality. (Christ 2000 p. 52)

For children experiencing major loss at this young age, the key protective factors become the availability of a surviving parent and/or nurturing, consistent caregivers. As Christ (2000 p. 48) found, 'Most distressing to 3- to 5-year-olds was the change in the care-giving parent, that parent's pre-occupation, and frequent separations, not the illness' that preceded a death. During the terminal stage of the illness, children in this age group asked 'why?' far less frequently. Longitudinal studies and studies of mental health in later life show that a risk factor for mental health problems is the experience of early trauma and grief, and particularly through separation from a parent.

One of the commonly held beliefs about children's recovery from both trauma and/or loss is that they are more resilient than adults. Recent research has demonstrated that this is not necessarily the case, and may in fact be a harmful belief in that it enables adults to overlook the ongoing aspects of trauma for children as they age. Children are resilient in different ways from adults. Most children quickly re-engage with daily life following significant losses and traumas, and this re-establishment of routine and predictability is seen to be an important protective factor. Developmentally, however, many children need to revisit trauma and grief experiences later in life when they have the psychosocial skills to understand what occurred. In one study of children whose fathers died in the September 11 attacks on the World Trade Center, children who were aged five at the time of their father's death began asking questions about it some two years later, when mothers had often wanted to stop talking about the experience. This was consistent with Worden's study of children, finding that it was not the first year when children's difficulties with coping with the loss became apparent. For young girls in particular, it was about changes in academic performance two years after the death of their parent (Worden 2003).

Children's social, structural and cultural environments become key influences in a child's coping capacity in the aftermath of such adversity.

Promoting resilience

A multidimensional approach recognises the rapidly changing dimensions of inner and outer worlds and enables social workers to think about how young children's resilience can be promoted. As Garbarino (2008 p. 6) argues 'it depends on the unique combination of dimensions of a child's world—their gender, temperament, age, neighbourhood and culture'. To this list, we add other dimensions—their immediate family, their body and consistitutional health, and their structural context. The resourcing and support of families and the environments of young children remain the key factors in building children's protective and resilience resources.

Similarly, the absence of risk factors such as experiences characterised by anxiety and threat, significant separations from primary caregivers, mental health difficulties, poverty and family violence contributes to well-being for young children. A number of international and national studies demonstrate that financial stressors and a lack of educational opportunities already have an impact on well-being and development by the fifth year of life (Taylor & Macdonald 1998). Environments are major influences on children's experiences and critical sites for intervention. Thus, the structural dimensions of a child's context are central in shaping these environments. Policies relating to day care and early learning environments determine the quality and standards of experiences for children.

Perceptions differ across cultures as to how autonomous young children should be, varying in the extent to which children are seen as having unique rights or not, as being 'mini-adults' or people in their own stage of life. While cultures differ in the extent to which they focus on a rights perspective for children, increasingly the need for children to be treated with respect and dignity is being identified and upheld.

These key dimensions of a child's world can be summarised in terms of developmental assets. The Search Institute (2005) in the USA, for example, lists forty key developmental assets, adapted and summarised in Table 8.2.

Table 8.2: Forty developmental assets for children aged three to four years

Outer-world dimensions	Support	Family support Positive family communication Other adult relationships Caring neighbours Caring climate in child care and educational settings Parent involvement in child care and education
	Empowerment	Community cherishes and values young children Children seen as resources Service to others Safety
	Boundaries and expectations	Family boundaries Boundaries in child care and educational settings Neighbourhood boundaries Adult role models Positive peer relationships Positive expectations
	Constructive use of time	Play and creative activities Out-of-home and community programs Religious community Time at home
Inner-world dimensions	Commitment to learning	Motivation to mastery Engagement in learning experiences Home-program connection Bonding to programs Early literacy
	Positive values	Caring Equality and social justice Integrity Honesty Responsibility Self-regulation
	Social competencies	Planning and decision-making Interpersonal skills Cultural awareness and sensitivity Resistance skills Peaceful conflict resolution
	Positive identity	Personal power Self-esteem Sense of purpose Positive view of personal future

Source: Reproduced with permission from the Search Institute

By the end of early childhood, a child's well-being is optimally sustained through these assets being an integral part of their inner and outer worlds.

CHAPTER SUMMARY

In this chapter, we have looked at the key developmental tasks and transitions of early childhood, as well as some of the key threats to well-being. Rapid physical changes continue in early childhood, as children acquire new physical, psychological and relational skills. The regulation of emotional reactions is a critical milestone, enabling children to engage in mutual play and relationships with those around them. Early childhood is a time of moving out into the world in new social relationships and beginning to engage more independently of parents or primary caregivers in these relationships.

In the latter part of this chapter, we have explored how young children experience stress, trauma and loss and how these experiences have a unique impact given their developmental stage. While neurobiological research continues to fine-tune biological understandings of the impacts of stress, trauma and grief, socially supportive interventions continue to emerge as the key strategies to adopt so that children experiencing adversity can continue to engage in the social and learning environments around them.

APPLYING A MULTIDIMENSIONAL UNDERSTANDING

CASE STUDY

Damien: Physical violence at home

Damien is four years old and in kindergarten. His younger sister Emma is two years old. Damien is a thin and pale boy, smaller than many in his group. He is quiet, and reluctant to participate in many of the group activities. He has very few friends and prefers to play by himself during breaks. Damien arrives bruised at kindergarten one day. His teacher notices this and inquires about his safety. Child protection services are called in and, during an interview with two workers, Damien tells a little of what is going on in the home environment. Through an interview with Damien's mother, who is a single parent and currently unpartnered, it appears she regularly binge drinks and possibly becomes violent, both physically and verbally. Neighbours have previously made a notification but no further action was indicated at the time. The children's mother denies that there are any issues of physical violence in the home. The decision is made by protection services to remove both Damien and Emma and place them in temporary care.

Questions

1 What is your reaction to this scenario?
2 What are some of the ethical dilemmas this situation raises?
3 What are some of the structural and functional strengths and limitations in this family and social network?
4 What are the possibilities for intervention using a multidimensional approach?
5 What is the influence of culture in your understanding of this situation if Damien is of Middle Eastern, Indigenous or Anglo-Australian background?

KEY TERMS

affect regulation

aggression

authoritarian parenting style

authoritative parenting style

autonomy

early childhood

initiative

moral development

negativism

permissive parenting style

QUESTIONS AND DISCUSSION POINTS

1 What are some of the key biopsychosocial and spiritual developmental tasks of early childhood?
2 What are some of the different risk and protective factors across this early lifespan stages?
3 What are some of the dimensions of the structural and cultural context that influence this stage?
4 Reflecting on your experiences of early childhood, can you identify with the various transitions outlined in this chapter?
5 What social, structural and cultural changes have occurred that make your parents' experiences of these transitions different from your own?

FURTHER READING

Gibbs, J., Basinger, K., Grime, R. & Snarey, J. 2007, 'Moral judgment development across cultures: Revisiting Kohlberg's universality claims', *Developmental Review*, 27, pp. 443–500.

Harris, J. 1998, *The nurture assumption: Why children turn out the way they do*, Sydney: The Free Press.

Hemphill, S. & Sanson, A. 2001, 'Matching parenting temperament to child: Influences on early childhood behavioural problems', *Family Matters*, 59, pp. 42–7.

Jack, G. 2000, 'Ecological influences on parenting and child development', *British Journal of Social Work*, 30, pp. 703–20.

Shonkoff, J. & Phillips, D., eds. 2000, *From neurons to neighbourhoods: The science of early childhood development*, Washington: National Academy Press.

WEBSITES OF INTEREST

Association for Children's Spirituality: www.childrenspirituality.org
This organisation is located in the UK and their website includes a range of resources about children's worldviews and perceptions of spirituality. It also publishes the *International Journal of Children's Spirituality.*

The Australian Child & Adolescent Trauma, Loss & Grief: www.earlytraumagrief. anu.edu.au/resource_hubs/disasters_children/
The Australian National University's website provides a range of resources relating to responding to disasters.

Australian Indigenous HealthInfoNet: www.healthinfonet.ecu.edu.au
This site provides information and links relating to the health of Indigenous Australians.

Australian Institute of Family Studies (AIFS): www.aifs.org.au
The AIFS site provides extensive links to longitudinal studies of children within Australia, New Zealand, Europe and North America, including the Longitudinal Study of Australian Children.

Australian Research Alliance for Children and Youth (ARACY): www.aracy.org.au
This site provides information and links about ARACY, which is a national collaboration of researchers, policy makers and practitioners that focuses on children's and young people's well-being.

The Campbell Collaboration: www.campbellcollaboration.org
This site provides information about systematic reviews of social care.

Department of Education and Early Childhood Development, Best Start Strategy: www.beststart.vic.gov.au
This site reviews the demonstration projects associated with the Best Start strategy, as well as providing extensive links to international programs and research.

The Erikson Institute: www.erikson.edu
This applied research centre for child development, based in Chicago, USA, provides links to infant and child development research and training material on their website.

Life Chances Study, Brotherhood of St Laurence: www.bsl.org.au

> This website provides access to publications arising from the Life Chances Study, which is now tracking young Australians into their late adolescence.

National Association for Prevention of Child Abuse and Neglect (NAPCAN): www.napcan.org.au

> This site provides information and links relating to child abuse and neglect in Australia.

Child Welfare Information Gateway: www.childwelfare.gov

> This site is a US gateway for information relating to child abuse and neglect.

National Child Traumatic Stress Network (NCTSN): www.nctsnet.org

> The website of the NCTSN in the US has extensive resources for a wide range of childhood traumas.

Raising Children Network: http://raisingchildren.net.au

> This Australian site contains extensive developmental information for parents and those who work with children, from pregnancy through to school age.

Search Institute: www.search-institute.org

> The Search Institute's website includes a link to the list of forty developmental assets they advocate that children require, along with extensive child development data and literature.

CHAPTER 9

Middle Childhood

AIMS OF THIS CHAPTER

This chapter explores the developmental experiences of middle childhood. It considers the following questions:

» What are the biopsychosocial-spiritual developmental tasks and transitions of middle childhood?
» What are the experiences and impacts of stress, trauma and loss in middle childhood?
» How is resilience in middle childhood understood?

Middle childhood refers to the years from about age five or six through to around eleven or twelve. While earlier stages of the lifespan arguably hold more universal developmental tasks in terms of biological and psychosocial-spiritual development, this lifespan stage highlights the way in which social context shapes experience. Middle childhood is characterised by new social transitions, as children attend primary school and expand their own peer networks. Erikson noted that a capacity to be engaged with people and tasks, to be industrious, characterised the age. He stated:

> This is socially a most decisive stage: since industry involves doing things beside and with others, a first sense of a division of labor and of equality of opportunity develops at this time. (Erikson 1963 p. 260)

As social and cultural contexts and resources change, so too does the territory of middle childhood. Particularly for girls, middle childhood is characterised increasingly by the biological changes of puberty. With the earlier onset of puberty, many are coping at much younger ages with some of the tasks previously ascribed to adolescence, an issue we will focus on throughout the chapter. This chapter also explores the biopsychosocial-spiritual dimensions that characterise this socially 'most decisive stage'.

Key developmental tasks and transitions

Biological dimensions

Weight and height, and nutrition

Many Australian children maintain a healthy weight. However, in the past decade, the percentage of boys and girls who are either overweight or obese has become a major concern. The 2007 Australian National Children's Nutrition and Physical Activity Survey, a survey of 4,487 children, found that seventy-two per cent of these children were within normal weight limits, but seventeen per cent were overweight and six per cent were obese (Department of Health and Ageing 2008 p. 2). About five per cent of these children were underweight, typically children living in poverty.

The reasons for this increase in obesity are many. Studies show that children increasingly are not meeting daily fruit and vegetable requirements (AIHW 2009a) and instead are eating a diet of food and liquids that is high in sugar, salt and fats. In addition to a healthy diet with healthy serving sizes, recreation and exercise are protective factors against obesity. Increasingly, many Australian children are more sedentary than earlier generations, spending recreational time in front of computers or the television instead of engaging in sport or play outside.

Changes in the structural context and daily lives for children around nutrition and activity levels—such as what foods are available from school canteens and what sporting and recreational activities are available to them (Baur 2002)—are critical. However, a study in New Zealand, of 2000 children, showed that food intake was primarily sourced from home, not the school environment (Regan et al. 2008). Therefore, while many programs target children's awareness of healthy diet and exercise, some researchers argue that parent-led, rather than child-focused, interventions are more successful.

Sleep

Primary-school-aged children require nine hours of sleep, on average, per night for optimal functioning and growth. In one study in the USA of sleep patterns in 637 school-aged children, some of the key factors in attaining around nine hours sleep included a consistent sleep routine, having a parent present at the time of going to sleep, and having a parent read prior to sleeping (Mindell et al. 2009).

Televisions in bedrooms and sharing a room with a sibling or other people were factors that decreased sleeping hours. Importantly, the study found that a consistent sleep routine led to, on average, an extra hour of sleep per night compared with those who did not have a consistent sleep routine. Studies show that about ten per cent of children experience sleep problems. Some of these problems are associated with the factors discussed above, but sometimes sleep problems are indicative of stress and distress.

One of the changing sleep experiences throughout middle childhood is an increase in dreams and nightmares, peaking at around the ages of seven to nine years. One large-scale study found that scary dreams were reported by 80.5 per cent of the sample (Muris et al. 2000b). Importantly, in another study, seventy per cent of scary dreams related to information that had been gained by watching television. Dreams and nightmares seem linked with the developing cognitive capacities of middle childhood, an issue we return to later in this chapter.

Mobility and motor skills

Middle childhood is a time when there is growth in physical stature and musculature, and increased coordination (Germain 1991). In the box below, some key findings from the aforementioned Australian National Children's Nutrition and Physical Activity Survey (Department of Health and Ageing 2008) are presented in relation to the physical activity levels of children and their use of electronic media. While arguably increased electronic media use may enhance fine motor skills, it has had a negative impact on levels of physical activity. While the findings include adolescents, the trend is consistent across both middle childhood and adolescence—less physical activity than previous generations and increased media use. Girls were found to be less likely to use electronic media and to be have under two hours per day of screen time. Both school and home environments are key influences in these activity levels.

CHILDREN'S PHYSICAL AND RECREATIONAL ACTIVITY

» The majority of children aged 9–16 years met the guidelines for moderate to vigorous physical activity. On any given day, there was a 69% chance that any given child would get at least 60 minutes of moderate to vigorous physical activity.

» On average, children aged 5–16 years took approximately 11,800 steps per day.

» Few children aged 9–16 years met the guidelines for electronic media use. On any given day, there was only a 33% chance that any given child would not exceed 120 minutes of screen time.

Source: Department of Health and Ageing 2008 p. 2

Sexual development

Middle childhood is a time of learning about sex and reproduction, primarily through a growing sexual awareness and interest in the opposite sex, and through peer networks. With the changes in weight and height due to dietary and environmental changes, many girls now experience the onset of puberty in late middle childhood (Tremblay & Frigon 2005). What this can mean is that many young girls experience a mismatch in their psychological, social and sexual maturation experiences. Compounding this can be a lack of, or gaps in, sex education. Given the earlier onset of secondary sexual characteristics, and often sexual behaviour, and the subsequent risks of sexually transmitted infections and pregnancy, the Australian Medical Association has called for sex education to be provided for ten-year olds.

We look at the transitions of puberty in more detail in Chapter 10.

There are also biological risks associated with the early onset of puberty—or precocious puberty, as it is termed. According to one meta-analysis (Ahmed et al. 2009 p. 239), the risks of early onset puberty can include:

> increased adolescent risk-taking behaviour, shorter adult stature, increased adult BMI and subsequent adult-onset diabetes, increased cardiovascular disease risk markers, increased risk of premenopausal breast cancer and increased all-cause mortality.

The causes of this earlier onset are complex biopsychosocial factors. As such, some researchers argue for an adaptive, evolutionary focus to be kept on this phenomenon of earlier onset of puberty, rather than viewing it as a pathological occurence (Gluckman & Hanson 2006).

Physical appearance

Regardless of the level of familiarity within young children's friendships, it has been found that 'both children and adults judge and treat attractive children more positively than they do unattractive children' (Ramsey & Langlois 2002 p. 321). This is termed by some the 'beauty as good' stereotype. Given that stereotypes are cognitive structures or schemata that process information through these filters and exclude non-confirmatory evidence, the consequences are that for some children, their physical attractiveness means few negative traits or behaviours are ascribed to them, even in the face of contradictory evidence, and vice versa for children who are not physically attractive. This stereotyping has consequences, with physically attractive children receiving preferential attention in their families, peer groups and their school environments, at a time when developing self-esteem and confidence is critical.

Disability, injury and diseases

In middle childhood, the increased exposure to independent social activities, play and recreation, all of which are typically positive experiences, brings with it an increased likelihood of physical injuries. One study showed that 'one in four children (25%) had some kind of injury in the previous 4 weeks that required a "health action" (self-help or professional help)' (AIHW 2009a p. 276). For Australian children, 'injury is the leading cause of death and a major cause of disability among Australian children' and 'injury (including poisoning) was the second leading cause of hospitalisations for children overall, and the leading cause of hospitalisation for those aged 10–14 years'. Children were admitted to hospital with injuries related to 'falls (38% of all their injury hospitalisations), transport and pedestrian accidents (14%), and hitting something or being hit or crushed by something (8%)' (AIHW 2009a p. 276). Despite these higher levels of physical injury, fewer deaths occur during middle childhood than in most other lifespan stages, with the exception of early childhood. In 2007, for example, fifty-nine children aged five to nine and seventy-seven children aged ten to fourteen died (ABS 2008).

While transport accidents and drowning incidents for children have declined, they remain the most common causes of childhood death, followed by cancer and diseases of the nervous system (AIHW 2009a p. 278). About eight per cent of Australian children have a disability, and about half of these children have 'a severe or profound core activity limitation, indicating they sometimes or always needed assistance with activities of daily living, and 62% had schooling limitations' (AIHW 2009a p. 274). All of these experiences have a major impact on the child concerned, their family and their peers.

Psychosocial-spiritual dimensions

Cognitive development

From four to seven, children develop what is termed a more 'intuitive' cognitive style, which leads to a greater ability with language and reasoning. Thus, as Germain (1991 p. 240) states:

> The child now begins internally to build a story of what his or her life is like ... The connections to what actually happened may not be clear and may not even matter. The story is the way one's life is and feels, and it is a metaphor for actuality.

This story becomes possible because children have developed capacities around 'conservation, decentration and seriation' of concepts. That is, they 'can group objects and behaviors into categories' (Gollnick 2005 p. 68). Piaget termed the middle childhood changes from seven to eleven years as the 'concrete operations' phase of cognition. A child's way of thinking tends to be less egocentric, able to take into acount the ideas of others and be more logical in its overall structure. A narrative of competence, or not, forms along with concepts of fairness.

Vygotsky argued that these changes occur as a result of expectations of others around a child, rather than as an innate change in the child (Karpov 2006). Adults, therefore, are crucial agents in stimulating interest and motivating development and engagement. They are like the 'scaffolding' around learning and development.

Another feature of cognitive development throughout middle childhood is the emergence of fears and worries. They emerge in new ways for children as part of their increasing awareness of the worlds around them (Gilmore & Campbell 2007) and events occuring beyond their own worlds. Exposure to world events through television and internet can increase these fears and worries, particularly when major disasters occur and children are exposed to horrific and traumatic images.

In a study of 'fears, worries and scary dreams' (Muris et al. 2000b) researchers found that of the 190 four- to twelve-year olds, seventy-six per cent reported fears of some kind and sixty-seven per cent reported worries. They found that fears (and scary dreams, as mentioned earlier) peaked between seven and nine years, and that worries increased after the age of seven. In another study using open-ended questions, the most common things about which children reported being scared or worried were being in the dark, alone or lost, and animals such as spiders and snakes, followed by concerns about injury or death (Gilmore & Campbell 2007 p. 31). Other worries of children commonly recorded using standardised scales are outlined below.

WORRIES IN MIDDLE CHILDHOOD

Children's worries in middle childhood tend to be related to experiences such as:

- » being hit by a car or truck
- » not being able to breathe
- » fire, or getting burned
- » death or dead people
- » bombing attacks or being invaded
- » getting poor grades
- » having parents argue
- » being sent to the principal
- » a burglar breaking into their home
- » falling from a high place.

Other studies have shown that the worries frequently identified include the concern about parent and grandparent health, school issues, peer friendships, personal appearance, how babies are made and born, nuclear accidents or war, and the fear of being kidnapped, injured or killed (Germain 1991 p. 278). These worries seem connected with an emerging sense of self, independent from parents, and the developing realisation that parents, or adults per se, cannot always provide protection from the threats of the world. For some children though, these worries are connected with the very real stresses, traumas and losses they encounter in their daily lives, as we explore later in this chapter.

Language development

Language development is critical throughout this age. Primary school is a time of gaining writing and reading skills as well as verbal ones, and therefore it is about consolidating and expanding earlier language development, building on the 2000 words five-year-olds have typically acquired.

For many children, their home environments have already had a profound impact on their language and literacy skills. Poverty and migration, for example, influence many children's starting points in literacy. As Teese (2005 p. 241) notes:

> Only about one in two children in poor schools with high migrant density start their schooling with already established reading skills, compared to three in four children attending better-off schools with low migrant density.

School environments also have a profound impact, for example, as to whether they encourage bilingualism. This has been particularly important in relation to the preservation of Indigenous languages (Amery 2002). In many remote communities, as well as among migrant groups, children are often faced with speaking one language at home (Pitjantjara for example) and then studying all day at school with teachers who speak only English. This creates particular challenges for learning when teachers and students are not sharing the same verbal and cultural languages.

Personality and temperament

As with the earlier developmental stages looked at in Chapters 7 and 8, having an easy temperamental style continues to have the most positive outcomes, both in terms of self-esteem building for the child and in terms of the building of positive relationships with family, peers and others. The Australian Temperament Project (Prior et al. 2001; Smart & Sanson 2003) is closely examining how children develop these skills or qualities. A key finding to date, described by Smart and Sanson (2003 p. 4), is as follows:

temperament style, particularly low levels of 'negative reactivity' (volatility, intensity and moodiness) and high levels of 'persistence' (the ability to stay on task and see things through to completion), as well as high quality relationships with parents and peers, were powerful predictors of social competence in late childhood.

One of the other areas of research and practice interest has been the degree to which personality is linked with adaptive functioning, both in middle childhood and later in the lifespan, from adolescence onwards. In one ten-year study, primary school students showed evidence that continuity of mastery, agreeableness and engagement factors influenced both present and future competence (Shiner 2000 p. 323). This highlights the ways in which many factors, such as social environments and opportunities, have an impact on personality development, something we continue to look at throughout this chapter.

Emotional development

Early Freudian views of emotional development in middle childhood were that it was a time of latent or little development, following the rapid psychosexual development of the first three years of life and in anticipation of the sexual development of adolescence. The term 'middle childhood' reflects this notion of being 'in between'. As a consequence of this, little attention was paid to these years of development until relatively recently. Increasingly, the significance of this stage, particularly psychosocially, has been acknowledged. During these years, the child is able to move more autonomously into the world and direct their participation in it. The social networks of the child expand considerably over this time, as new relationships are formed with school, peers and neighbourhoods, and often with other groups such as sport, music or other extracurricular groups.

In relation to psychosocial development, Erikson proposed that children during these years were concerned with resolving the crisis of industry versus inferiority—'I am what I learn'. He stated that a child 'now learns to win recognition by producing things' (Erikson 1963 p. 259), and proposed that a sense of **industry** relates to a child's sense of being able to make things and make them well, a 'pleasure of work completion by steady attention and persevering diligence'. He proposed that failure to resolve this developmental crisis led to a sense of inadequacy and inferiority.

Thus, a key emotional task of the middle years is to develop a sense of self-competence, self-worth and mastery (Hutchison 2003), a task which some see as *the* key task of middle childhood, arising from the sense of successful engagement with the world around them. Influences in the development of **self-worth** and **competence** lie in the relational, social, structural and cultural dimensions of children's worlds. Research consistently highlights that these influences include a sense of belonging, particularly to a peer group; a supportive and reassuring home life; and positive school experiences, both social and educational.

Relational development

The protective factors that are commonly identified for children within their relational and social dimensions include a strong sense of continuity with their family; consistent values, norms and rules; a generally positive child–parent–family orientation; flexibility and responsiveness from adults within the child's world; and financial and social resources within these networks of relationships.

Parents

Parents continue to be important influences in children's lives. In Chapter 8, we looked at the three styles of parenting identified by Baumrind (1971; see also Aunola & Nurmi 2005): the authoritarian style with its low warmth and high rules; the authoritative style with high warmth and high rules; and the permissive style with high warmth and low rules. These qualities, rather than family structures, seem to have the greatest impact on children's experiences of well-being and secure attachment, continuing throughout middle childhood.

However, family structure does have an impact throughout middle childhood in the experiences of stress that some children experience. For many children, the financial impacts of growing up in a single-parent household, typically a female-headed household, can be profound, as we explore later in this chapter.

Family structure can have an impact in other ways too. For example, increasingly in Western societies, many children are growing up in gay- or lesbian-parented families. In a study of retrospective perceptions of being parented within gay or lesbian families, the overwhelming finding was that any problems that children experienced 'arose almost entirely from other people's negative views about lesbian and gay people' (Fairtlough 2008 p. 525). Stacey and Biblarz (2001), in their analysis of twenty-one studies of children living with gay or lesbian parents, found no differences on a range of outcomes such as depression, anxiety and self-esteem. They did find, however, that children living with gay or lesbian parents tended to have developed more skills in the areas of expressing feelings and greater empathy for diversity, as a result of facing the discrimination and homophobia within their school and social environments.

With increasing diversity of family forms in the Australian context, it seems that the protective factors for children continue to be secure attachments within these families and minimal discrimination and marginalisation within peer groups.

Siblings

There is an absence of extensive research about sibling relationships in middle childhood (Buhrmester & Furman 1990), in contrast to the focus on these relationships in infancy and adolescence. Throughout middle childhood, sibling relationships continue to be key influences in well-being and development.

From the available evidence, two key changes begin to occur throughout this period—sibling relationships in middle childhood tend to 'become more egalitarian and less assymmetrical with age' and they tend to 'become less intense with age' (Buhrmester & Furman 1990 p. 1387). This is quite a shift, as the sibling relationship is noted as being one in which there are, uniquely, 'inherited positions of authority and responsibility' (Buhrmester & Furman 1990 p. 1395).

The focus of understanding the sibling relationship has tended to be on the ways in which sibling relationships provide for the social and recreational needs of children, but as Gass, Jenkins and Dunn (2007 p. 168) ask, 'is it not possible for siblings also to be a source of support and comfort?'. In their study of 192 British families, they found that, independent of the mother–child relationship, where there was a positive sibling relationship and the experience of stressful life events, a positive sibling relationship significantly mediated the response, leading to less internalising of problems. Warm, supportive sibling relationships were found to be protective.

Three dominant typologies have been identified (Murphy 1993) as emergent in these childhood sibling relationships—the caretaker, buddy and casual types. The caretaker type refers to a sibling who assumes a parental and authoritative role with a sibling; the buddy type refers to siblings who relate as equals and as collaborators against parents, and the casual type refers to a sibling who assumes a relatively aloof and unfocused relationship with a younger sibling.

Some sibling relationships, however, are the source of significant conflict. Recently researchers have begun to examine the longer-term impacts of these relationships. In one study of 163 children, conflict in sibling relationships in middle childhood was found to be linked with increased anxiety, depression and delinquent behaviour in adolescence, independent of parental hostility and marital conflict (Stocker et al. 2002 p. 54).

Grandparents

Grandparents continue to play an important role in children's lives, not only in relation to care arrangements but also through the sharing of interests and activities. The relationship throughout these years often has the freedom of not being characterised by the rule-setting and limit-setting required of parental relationships. A study of younger children (four- to five-year-olds), the LSAC, found that 'the vast majority

In Chapter 13, we explore the experience of being a grandparent in more detail.

of grandparents reported having a good relationship with their grandchildren', relationships characterised by strong feelings of warmth (Gray et al. 2005 p. 16). These relationships were seen to be functionally important (for example, in the provision of care) but moreso to be symbolically important in both children's and grandparents' lives.

Peers

As children interact with schools and neighbourhoods, their peers become increasingly more significant influences in their lives. Throughout these years, more complex friendships form, and they become more psychologically based than behaviourally based. They are also increasingly characterised by a sense of belonging in relation to physical appearance, language, and culture (Peterson 1996). These relationships are primarily face to face, given that children have relatively limited access to communication technologies.

We look at bullying and cyber-bullying later in this chapter.

Research highlights that the friendships of middle childhood tend also to become more empathy-based and gender-based. In middle childhood, the capacity for empathy—that is, the ability to understand a situation from another's perspective and how they may be thinking or feeling—typically expands. Empathy towards others involves a sophisticated level of self-control and affect regulation and is essential for the development of positive, supportive relationships with others.

Teachers and other significant adults

In moving into the school environment, children move into new relationships with adults, primarily their class teacher. These relationships have been shown to be significant influences on children's lives, for good and bad. Not only does the school environment introduce new relationships, it often introduces new negotiations children have to undertake in managing either the consistencies or inconsistencies between their home and school environments, particularly in relation to degrees and styles of discipline and support. In Bronfenbrenner's terms, this leads to a new mesosystem between the home and the school, with which a child must now engage.

In Chapter 8, we looked at how Werner and Smith's study identified the availability of other adults as mentors and key factors in children's resilience. These adults are typically those involved in extracurricular activities such as sport, music or clubs, or could be neighbours or family friends. These adults provide a critical 'scaffolding' (Gilligan 2004) around children at risk, in particular.

Gender and sexual identity

In Chapter 8, we looked at the developing sense of gender identity, in relation to both self-identity and identifying the gender of others. During middle childhood, understandings and expressions of gender identity and roles shift again, with boys typically identifying more strongly with masculine role attributes but girls tending to identify less with feminine role attributes. That is, there tends to be a movement towards androgyny for girls. Some have argued that being androgynous—that is, demonstrating both feminine and masculine traits—enables resilience, as a child has a flexible repertoire of coping rather than a prescribed role of behaviour (Rouse 1998; Werner & Smith 1992).

The tendency for children from the age of five onwards to engage in play with same-sex peers and engage in sex-segregating behaviours has been well noted. Some argue that this segregation occurs because of cognitive development, and others because of socialisation influences. Others have argued that it is more to do with play style than gender compatability. For example, boys seem to like distress-inducing play, compared with girls preferring to engage in sympathy-inducing play, leading to rough-and-tumble play and relational play respectively. Thus, an awareness of gender may not be driving the behaviour as much as a preference for play styles (Aydt & Corsaro 2003 p. 1308). Others have found, though, that same-sex segregation is not as persistent as argued—and that children do engage in mixed-sex play more often than perceived.

While adolescence is typically seen as the time of forming sexual identities, sexual awareness does increase throughout later middle childhood. Some researchers have shown, for example, that the mean age of first experiences of sexual attraction is around ten years of age (McClintock & Herdt 1996). These experiences are strongly mediated by children's biological, social and cultural dimensions.

In Chapter 10, we explore issues of sexual identity formation.

Moral and/or spiritual development

In middle childhood, children begin to develop a stronger sense of conscience (Pearn 2003 p. 168) and a sense of what is right and wrong. They become social citizens in their many different worlds, and learn what it means to be part of a group. Children's moral codes tend to be derived throughout this stage from their parent's worldviews or those of significant adults around them. Thus, their sense of the world can be quite monocultural in many instances, framed only by their own experience and often without exposure to other cultures and religions. Both schools and families are influential in providing these opportunities for learning about other ways of living and other worldviews. Throughout their primary school years, children develop a greater capacity to seek out appropriate moral advisors based on whether they need to rely on moral or scientific knowledge (Danovitch & Keil 2007), whereas younger children cannot make this distinction.

In relation to theories of faith development, Fowler and Dell (2006) described the years of seven to eleven as the 'mythical literal' stage. This stage is linked with the 'concrete operational' phase of cognitive development, in which more 'stable forms of conscious interpretation' are possible (Fowler & Dell 2006 p. 38). Stories or narratives are constructed, relatively uncritically, whereby the child typically 'sees a sense of cosmic fairness at work: The child believes that goodness is rewarded and badness is punished' (Fowler & Dell 2006 p. 39). These narratives are typically reflected in children's movies, where good triumphs over evil and an overall and just order is upheld through parents or leaders.

Coping with risks and adversities

In Australia, most children lead a 'minority' childhood experience compared to international experiences of the 'majority' of children. 'Majority childhoods' are lived out in third-world countries, where children move rapidly from early childhood into working to support their family's livelihood (Punch 2003). Most Australian children are protected from adopting these roles, as middle childhood is seen as a time of primary school education and ongoing learning through play and extracurricular activities. Many in middle childhood begin to take on responsibilities in their homes, but this is typically in order to learn skills and participate in family life rather than to support livelihoods. Having said that, a significant number of Australian children, both Indigenous and non-Indigenous, live in poverty and are faced with many stressors and traumas, as this next section now explores.

Stress

In middle childhood, some of the stressful life events children experience are similar to those earlier in the lifespan—family poverty and violence; parental mental health and substance abuse issues; and daily stressors. Moving increasingly into school and neighbourhood environments, children also begin to rapidly expand their own networks of association, and with this expansion can come increased stressors. They also experience the onset of worries and fears, as part of their cognitive development, often compounded by difficulties experienced within their relationships and immediate contexts, and through television viewing. Some of these we consider now: the stressors within families, with poverty, bullying, and mental health and behavioural problems.

Many of these themes are echoed in the research that has been undertaken to examine what children themselves perceive to be stressful. Yamamoto, Davis, Dylak, Whittaker, Marsh and van der Westhuizen (1996) conducted a large study involving some 1,729 children who were second to ninth graders in South Africa, Poland, Australia, the UK and the USA. They asked children to rate twenty events in terms of how upsetting they were. Apart from Poland, the most stressful event across all the five other countries was the loss of a parent, and the least was a new baby sibling. In Poland, the birth of a new sibling was the most stressful event. Overall, the two types of events that caused most stress were threats to one's sense of security and those that led to personal denigration or embarrassment.

Family life

Throughout the primary school years, families often experience multiple and competing demands on their time and resources. It is seen as a particularly busy time within families, as people juggle the tasks of work and home life.

While parents, caregivers and families are typically thought of as being the source of support and nurturance, they are also the source of stress for some children. Within the Australian community, many parents have mental health difficulties, abuse drugs or alcohol, and/or engage in verbal and physical violence. For many children, during their primary school years they take on significant responsibilities within the home to support their parents and/or their siblings through these times. They can become 'parentified' into roles and responsibilities often well before others are expected to do so.

For other children, their family is making the major transition to life in Australia. Settler arrivals in 2007–08 (Department of Immigration and Citizenship 2009) included 12,354 in the five- to nine-year-old age range and 11,019 in the ten- to fourteen-year-old age range. For these 23,373 children, a period of enormous adjustment follows their arrival in Australia, with adaptations to a new home, school, neighbourhood and cultural context. For some children, this signifies the movement away from war-torn parts of the world. Irrespective of the circumstances, adjustment to a new homeland and culture is known to be a major family stressor.

One of the other key stressors that has been researched with children in this age range is divorce. Parental divorce occurred for 11.3 per 1,000 children aged zero to seventeen in 1999 (AIHW 2001 p. 142) although since then, the number of divorces involving children has decreased (ABS 2007). Parental divorce is more common during this phase, as parents have nurtured their children beyond the critical early years of development. Not only do families often experience divorce at this time, but some families re-form, presenting children not only with the task of dealing with the loss caused by their family of origin's separation, but also the task of adapting to new siblings and step-parents (Hughes 2000; Amato & Sobolewski 2001; Smyth et al. 2001). For some children, although a relatively small number, there are, therefore, multiple family separations and re-formations as their parents re-partner or remarry in the years following divorce (AIHW 2001).

Wallerstein and Kelly (1980), for example, conducted a ten-year longitudinal study of 131 middle-class children of divorce, who had been aged three to eighteen at the time of the divorce. They found that parents and children were suffering severe turmoil and stress at the end of the first post-divorce year. Of the children in the sample, five years after the divorce experience, only one-third of the children and adolescents were doing well. Thirty-four of the children who had been pre-schoolers (aged three to five) at the time of the divorce, at five years, were seemingly more disturbed. However, by the time of the ten-year follow-up, these children were actually managing better than the older children. One of the protective factors was that there were fewer memories of conflicts, and they were therefore more settled in their present circumstances.

In the case of divorce, the post-divorce environment and the comparisons with the pre-divorce environment are critical (Wallerstein & Blakeslee 1989; Lorenz et al. 1997; Amato & Sobolewski 2001). These critical factors include:

» the extent to which parents remain conflict-free and are in non-divisive contact with each other, without splitting the loyalties of the child
» the extent to which there is access to both parents, the consistency in custodial arrangements and the level of disruption this creates
» the socio-economic status and social supports of the custodial parents.

Not only does divorce bring with it a changed relationship with both parents, but it can also bring with it major changes in existing relationships with grandparents and peers, and new relationships with step- or half-siblings.

THEORY IN CONTEXT

BOYS UNDER PRESSURE

Some of the transitions discussed so far are highlighted in Karen's examples below, drawn from her research with boys aged nine to twelve whose families were clients of Anglicare.

In undertaking a research study with boys aged between nine and twelve, I noted a number of interesting adaptations to their circumstances. Two particular examples highlight the extreme differences of response.

Jimmy, aged twelve, was in his final year of primary school. His parents were cohabiting while his mother openly prepared for her marriage to another man, father of one of his best mates. He reported that his school attendance was poor and the limited contact I had with his parent to arrange an interview suggested a lack of structure, failure to set boundaries and unreliability. During his interview he appeared self-assured and confident, had clear ambitions and mentioned his heavy reliance on friendships maintained using MSN (messaging) for support. He spoke with disdain regarding his mother's planned marriage and an older sister whose behaviour was antisocial and self-harming. I understood that Jimmy was constantly derided for negative behaviour and lack of respect towards teachers, especially females.

Jimmy's self-sufficiency seemed linked to the lack of reliability of his parents, which led him to develop a strong support network outside the family.

Brian, also aged twelve, was a very friendly and helpful boy who was keen to engage in the interview process. He reported contact with friends and relatives and had plans for the future, including being a truck driver and living in the country with his family. In reporting missing his parent, he unexpectedly revealed his father's suicide some years earlier, which he associated with parental separation. His mother reported his response to this event as extreme anxiety which had developed into school refusal. His greatest support remained his mother. His contact with peers was rare and irregular.

For Brian, the betrayal of trust by one parent had led to extreme fears for the other, resulting in a complex dependency/fear, which was manifest in school refusal and not being able to separate from his mother.

Questions

1   What might be the possible factors influencing the boys' different responses to their family circumstances?
2   How might we understand these responses in the context of a multidimensional approach?
3   Ungar (2008a) suggests that 'problem' behaviour may be a child's hidden path to resilience. What are the positive elements in the coping or adaptive strategies employed by these boys?

As the statistics earlier in this chapter highlighted, many children and their families are coping with illness and disability as part of their daily life. For some children, these experiences were congenital and therefore part of a lifelong adaptation. For others, disability or illness is acquired, often creating major crises within families as they adapt to what has occurred. Early researchers talked about families living with a child with disability as experiencing chronic sorrow (Olshansky 1962) but this has shifted to recognise the extraordinary strengths within many families, the episodic nature of the stresses (Hewson 1997) they face and the significance of external resources and supports in determining adaptation or maladaptation.

See the conservation of resources theory in Chapter 4.

Poverty

Poverty continues to be a major risk factor for children, with a dramatic increase in recent years in the number of children living in poverty in Australia. Children who grow up in poverty are more likely to be born with low birthweight, to experience serious and chronic health problems and to receive poorer health care and nutrition

(AIHW 2001; 2008b. They are also likely to achieve lower levels of academic performance. These can profoundly influence social and educational development throughout the middle childhood years.

In the Brotherhood of St Laurence's Life Chances study, a study following children from birth through to early adulthood, the 'eleven plus' stage of the study highlighted some significant influences of poverty on the 142 children who were participating (Taylor & Fraser 2003). For example, they found that by the time the children in the study were eleven to twelve years of age:

» Only one-third of the families still lived in the same inner-city area.
» One-third had lived in a sole-parent family at some stage in their lives.
» Six per cent of children lived with fathers only.
» There was a slight decrease in families on low incomes.

Change was a key component of these children's lives—both in relation to some being able to move out of poverty, and also in relation to families physically relocating and restructuring throughout middle childhood.

The age at which these changes occur for children seems to have a profound impact on the outcomes, either positive or negative. This was highlighted in Glen Elder's (1974) classic study of the children of the Great Depression in the USA. The key findings of his study are presented below.

KEY FINDINGS FROM *CHILDREN OF THE GREAT DEPRESSION*

The *Children of the Great Depression* study looked longitudinally at children of the Great Depression of the 1930s in America, specifically, comparing families and children who had been affected by a greater than one-third drop in income or not. The Depression forced a greater participation in domestic roles for girls and outside jobs for boys. Elder found that the early experience in jobs appeared to have special impact on the motivation of boys from deprived families. Sons whose families were hardest hit by the Depression and had been eleven years old at the time had profited most by the experience some forty years later—in terms of vocational commitment and opportunity, stable career line, occupation of choice, and self-directedness. Adults whose families had escaped financial ruin were less successful educationally and vocationally. In contrast,among those who were born in 1928–29, whose earliest years were in the Great Depression, the opposite occurred for boys. Although the impact did not seem to emerge early in life—that is, they coped well during the Depression itself and their early years—in adolescence they were found to be less able to cope when demanding situations arose. A different repertoire of coping skills had been developed.

This study remains relevant today, in that it highlighted the different impact of responsibilities and roles as important mechanisms for self-esteem but showed that the outcomes were dependent upon the age at which they were experienced.

Bullying

Many children experience bullying throughout their primary school years. Bullying is the 'abusive treatment of a person by force or coercion' (Campbell 2005 p. 69) through unprovoked verbal, physical and social strategies. Its impact on children's mental, physical and social health is known to be serious and negative. Given that it often occurs at school, children are frequently exposed to bullying over a sustained period of time. However, bullying behaviour is complex and is best seen as encompassing a continuum of behaviours (Espelage & Swearer p. 371), with children often moving between roles of victims, bullies and bystanders, depending upon the circumstances. Importantly, it often occurs in a group context, yet tends to be considered as individual behaviour.

While bullying is well recognised as an enduring phenomenon and there are many proactive education programs and policies in place to try to prevent the harmful effects (Rigby & Thomas 2003), recent years have seen the development of cyber-bullying: the use of electronic media, particularly the internet, email and mobile phones, to engage in unprovoked, abusive treatment of others. Given that there is no face-to-face interaction and both the victim and the perpetrator of the bullying can remain hidden, the consequences are often unseen by others and yet tragic. As Campbell (2005) notes, the consequences of cyber-bullying have not yet been extensively researched. However, media reports of single incidents highlight that cyber-bullying is associated with several young people committing suicide. While children do use electronic media for social networking, parental and school monitoring and control of access to technology still tends to limit the extent of social networking throughout middle childhood, unlike adolescence.

Mental health

It is very difficult to get an accurate view of the prevalence of mental health difficulties for children. Only one major Australian study has been conducted, the 1997 National Survey of Mental Health and Wellbeing, that included data on children under the age of sixteen. From this study it was concluded that 393,000 four- to eleven-year olds in Australia have significant mental health problems (Sawyer 2000). Summarising the findings, the Australian Institute of Health and Welfare (2009b p. 276) reported that:

> ... it was estimated that around one in seven (14%) children aged 4–14 years had a mental health problem in 1998—13% of children aged 6–14 years had attention deficit hyperactivity disorder (ADHD), 3% had conduct disorder and 3% depressive disorder.

The survey has been criticised for drawing primarily on parental reports rather than formal diagnoses to establish these findings, and also for only focusing on three major types of mental health problems. Notwithstanding these criticisms, the findings highlight that a significant number of children and families report being affected by mental health problems.

Within this study, it has been possible to focus on different diagnostic groups. Three hundred and twenty four children were diagnosed with attention deficit hyperactivity disorder (ADHD), the most commonly reported disorder within the study. The key feature of ADHD is hyperactivity, which translates into a lack of attention and persistence, and an increase in impulsive and restless conduct (Bloch & Singh 1997 p. 209). In the Australian study, more than twice as many boys as girls were diagnosed with ADHD and they were found to be more likely to experience school performance difficulties (Graetz et al. 2005). One of the criticisms of the diagnosis of ADHD is that it is primarily an extreme expression of traits commonly found in boys, often exacerbated by the limitations and constraints of boys' lives, such as having to participate in the sedentary learning environments of classrooms. As Bloch and Singh note, the use of stimulant medication has been found, paradoxically, to focus attention, but its use is controversial (Bloch & Singh 1997 p. 210), in part because it is seen as a medicalised response to what is often a social, contextual problem.

Trauma

While many children experience trauma directly, there is a growing realisation that through media reports children can be indirectly traumatised by exposure to disasters and traumas around the world. This has been particularly noted in relation to the September 11 attacks in the USA in 2001 and the 2004 Indian Ocean tsunami. The management of these incidents at school, where information, and misinformation, is shared has become an important component of promoting children's well-being.

For many children, though, trauma is directly experienced. This discussion focuses on three different types of trauma children may experience—child abuse and neglect, natural disasters and war trauma.

Sexual abuse

Given that childhood sexual abuse is known to be under-reported, it is impossible to know how many children are sexually abused. Across all jurisdictions in Australia, girls are 'more likely to be the subject of a substantiation of sexual abuse than males' (AIHW 2009a p. 27). According to Putnam (2003 p. 270), the prevalence of sexual abuse increases with age throughout middle childhood, although this could be due to the increased capacity to verbally report incidents of abuse. He cites American statistics that show that:

Between ages 4 and 7 years, the percentage almost triples (28.4%). Ages 8 to 11 years account for a quarter (25.5%) of cases, with children 12 years and older accounting for the remaining third (35.9%) of cases (US Department of Health and Human Services, 1998).

The long-term effects of child sexual abuse are well documented (Mullen et al. 1996; Banyard et al. 2001; Scott & Swain 2002; Miller 2007), with studies showing an increased likelihood of re-victimisation in later life; mental health problems, such as depression, dissociation and anxiety; self-harm and suicidal behaviours; sexual difficulties; and interpersonal difficulties, particularly around intimacy and trust. For children experiencing sexual abuse it is typically within the context of family relationships, and in a context of secrecy and terror. Children's disclosures of abuse are sometimes negated by adults around them, met with disbelief and inaction, often compounding the sense of isolation and powerlessness.

PRACTICE IN CONTEXT

WORKING WITH CHILDREN AND TRAUMA

Julie reflects on running a group for girls who have experienced sexual abuse.

In establishing a group program for younger girls, aged eight to eleven years, who had been sexually abused, a unique set of developmental issues needed to be considered. Care needs to be exercised about making assumptions about their knowledge of, for example, names of body parts, and there needs to be awareness that some information may be more appropriately conveyed by a parent or carer and/or in culturally sensitive ways. Keeping parents informed is useful because it acknowledges the primacy of adult carers in the lives of children and avoids consternation when children test their new knowledge at home. While young people may appear 'pseudomature' (falsely mature) in relation to some social and sexual behaviour, or appear to know more than they do, they may also lack a significant amount of information about when and how to establish boundaries and when and how to respect the boundaries others may set.

There is a need for more concrete tasks and activities to illustrate concepts (for example, a personal space activity using hula hoops to define your own space and boundaries together) and for more time to explain and process activities (for example, making lists of who it would be okay to have in your personal space). The same activity with adolescents may be used to understand more complex concepts like how someone might use power to find ways to enter their personal space. Adolescents might be asked what they might say or do and how they might negotiate closeness with some people (for example, potential partners) and set firm boundaries when they choose to. The message for younger children may need to be less complex, more clear and concrete to avoid confusion and anxiety.

Questions

1 What do you think are the most important developmental considerations in working with this group of young girls?
2 How would you go about addressing these considerations?
3 What would you find most challenging?

For many children, the aftermath of abuse can compound further the effects of the primary trauma they have experienced. Investigations and court proceedings, and the care services that are available to children (Connolly & Cashmore 2009), along with family and school responses, are all part of the complex situation that can either inhibit or promote a child's well-being.

Natural disasters

Children are also affected by natural disasters such as floods and bushfires. These experiences often lead to ongoing dislocation throughout the recovery process, disrupting individual, family and community well-being. These situations are not single-incident traumas but often lead to ongoing chronic stress situations for children. Parents and other adults are often as adversely affected and disrupted by what has occurred. Consider the situation that arose with the Black Saturday bushfires in Victoria in 2009.

APPLY YOUR UNDERSTANDING: AFTER THE BUSHFIRES

In the Victorian fires of 2009, hundreds of young children, along with their families, were dislocated from their homes and schools that were destroyed in the fires of Black Saturday, that killed 173 people and destroyed some 3500 structures, including homes, shops, sheds and schools. Many witnessed horrific scenes as their homes blew up and people and animals died. This destruction to both human life and the community meant that children could not return to their schools and communities. Many of them subsequently lived with their families and others in temporary housing or caravans for at least eighteen months following the fires.

Questions

1 What strategies would you introduce to such trauma- and loss-affected communities for children, taking into account their developmental tasks and transitions?
2 What developmental issues would have an impact on children's capacity to understand the losses they have experienced?
3 What you think will be some of the longer term implications for children who were affected by the bushfires?

One of the most important strategies following the disruption of communities is the re-establishment of routines as quickly as possible. For children, this means being able to resume routines around sleeping and eating, be surrounded by any sources of familiarity (particularly familiar caregivers), and be able to engage in play and other familiar peer relationships (Belfer 2006). For most children, resuming school as soon as possible is identified as critical, as school provides the necessary daily structure of activity and, through that, provides some distraction from the traumatic events that have occurred. Another critical intervention involves managing media exposure, as repeated and unexpected exposure to traumatic images can compound worries and fears for children.

While this early resumption of routine is strongly advocated, alongside this there need to be strategies of support for children. For many, emotional responses and information processing about what has occurred occur later in time. One of the challenges with this is that such responses often emerge at a time when adults have dealt with many of the aspects of the trauma and may not be aware of these shifting needs of children.

War

In a peaceful country such as Australia, it may seem unusual to focus on war trauma in children. Yet Australia's history resonates with war and conflict—from the arrival of white settlers in the late 1700s and the massacres of Indigenous Australians, and through much of the subsequent migrant history of Australia. After the Second World War, many refugees came from war-torn Europe, some having experienced concentration camps and persecution. During and following the Vietnam War, in the late 1960s and 1970s, many people arrived by boat seeking refuge and a new life in Australia. More recently, refugees from Yugoslavian, Middle Eastern and African conflicts have arrived under the humanitarian resettlement programs. Many asylum seekers and refugees are fleeing war in their countries of origin, and it is vital that social workers and others are aware of the experiences many children have faced throughout their early years of life.

There is extensive literature on the biopsychosocial-spiritual effects of war and conflict on children (Fazel & Stein 2003; Williams 2007) and it is beyond the scope of this book to explore this in depth. In war zones, children may experience injury and disability, in addition to the loss of parents and others, their community, their education and any sense of safety. The experiences are often ones of social and physical dislocation, over many years. Others have experienced being trafficked or recruited as child soldiers. As Williams (2007 pp. 264–5) notes, they can be direct or indirect victims of violence and/or perpetrators of violence. Given the developmental stage at which these experiences occur, Pearn (2003 p. 168) notes that, in addition to the PTSD that is experienced by many and the overall dislocation of such experiences, one of the most devastating consequences is that 'if children are exposed to the maiming and killing of war, they carry into their adult lives a new datum reference point—that violence is the basic relationship that characterises humankind'.

This is being seen most vividly in the experience of former child soldiers. A relatively recent war strategy, particularly within Africa, this involves the often-brutal recruitment of children from the age of seven or eight to become child soldiers within guerrilla armies. This frequently involves the killing of their parents to force them to become dependent upon the military group. As one report notes (British Broadcasting Commission 2009), children so young are recruited for the following reasons:

> The development of lighter weapons—such as the AK47—means that boys as young as eight can be armed. The smallest boys are placed closest to the enemy. In war, they are said to be fearless. Children are often less demanding soldiers than adults. They are cheaper to keep as they eat less and are easier to manipulate. Both sides believe the unpredictability of small children makes them better fighters. Some are sent into battle high on drugs to give them courage.

These past experiences have a profound impact.

In Australia, the Refugee Minor Program works with children who are orphaned, dislocated and traumatised, and who have not participated in formal education either at all or irregularly.

Loss

As mentioned earlier in this chapter, approximately 120 children die in middle childhood each year in Australia. Each of these deaths has a profound impact on families and the peer group, and may be the first exposure to human death for their peers. For other children, the first exposure to death is through the death of a parent or grandparent.

Throughout middle childhood, the child's cognitive abilities are expanded to the point where the permanence of death and loss can be understood. However, death or loss is still likely to be understood through egocentric eyes, particularly in the earlier years of middle childhood. Children in this age group will typically see themselves as responsible in some way for the loss, although less so the older they are. For example, in situations of divorce, children may see themselves as having caused the arguments between their parents.

Children's grief is often complicated as a result of the factual information they receive about death and loss experiences. For example, they may hear some aspects of a situation but not have enough information to make sense of what is going on.

This often connects then with fears and worries that what has happened to others will happen to them.

Both families and cultures differ as to how they construct stories of dying and death—how much information is framed within religious concepts, for example, using the imagery of heaven and angels, or how much information is factual about death, and what happens to the body.

Acknowledgment of grief typically occurs at unexpected times in conversations, while simultaneously resuming life and activity, seemingly unaffected by the experience.

Promoting resilience

Middle childhood transitions primarily relate to a widening of the social networks on which children are dependent. Developmental, motivational and support needs can be increasingly met by other relationships in the social environment, although the family remains the primary site of nurture and resource. Friendships, neighbourhoods, affiliations with particular sport or music groups, along with the school, become key sources of identity affirmation and development (Erwin 1998).

Expanding on some of the protective factors that have been identified for children in this developmental stage (Hutchison 2003 p. 242), they include:

» Earlier developmental history. As explored in earlier chapters, a secure attachment history, minimal separations and the absence of traumatic life events (Rutter 1987) become important protective factors.
» An easy temperament (Chess & Thomas 1996). This enables positive relationships with others.
» Physical attractiveness. As explored in this chapter, studies affirm that physical attractiveness leads to higher social status, popularity and ultimately becomes a protective factor because of the links with self-esteem.
» Social competence. This underpins a capacity to be empathic, sociable and altruistic.
» Learning style. A match with school environments is critical to ensure positive learning experiences.
» Group membership. The degree to which children belong within the dominant or non-dominant culture becomes an important link with self-esteem and self-competence.

While these can be seen as relatively individual qualities, a multidimensional approach requires that they be seen as inextricably connected to the outer worlds in which children are living—that is, the relational, social, structural and cultural dimensions are all critical influences and in turn are influenced by these dimensions.

Family resources and values are core in influencing the day to day experiences of children, as we've explored earlier in this chapter. Similarly, schools and their resources and values are critical influences in relation to both the formal and informal relationships children build, and to the availability of educational and extracurricular activities such as sport and music (Gilligan 2000). Schools vary greatly in their resources, with Australia's system of both private and public schools influencing the extent of educational and other resources available to children. Many children have specific needs in the school environment—for example, those with disabilities may need integration aides—and some schools are able to meet these more fully than others.

Similarly, children need safe physical and emotional environments for optimal development. This includes stable housing arrangements, strong neighbourhoods (Nicotera 2005) and adequate recreational facilities such as play areas, yet there is often minimal discussion of the importance of place for children (Kemp 2008). Children also need access to affordable and quality health care. These are all critical elements of social inclusion.

One of the most important determinants of resilience in middle childhood, though, lies within the cultural dimensions of the childhood experience—the social construction of childhood. That is, how do we understand and interpret the experience of childhood, within families and within the broader social and cultural environment? Many would argue that our communities carry contradictory messages about what it means to be a child today—D'Cruz (2009), for example, writes about the ways in which childhood tends to be either idealised or demonised.

There are also contradictory messages about children and resilience. Many argue that children are inherently resilient and have a capacity to bounce back from adversity in different ways from adolescents or adults. While this may be the case in some respects, longitudinal studies of the impact of truama, for example, shows that children may be resilient in the present, but it all depends on the resources and supports around them as to whether they continue to be resilient. With that in mind, a summary of the key attributes of resilience in middle childhood, outlined by Masten and Powell (2003), is presented below.

ATTRIBUTES ASSOCIATED WITH RESILIENCE

Individual differences:

» cognitive abilities (IQ scores, attentional skills, etc.)
» self-perceptions of competence
» temperament and personality (adaptability, sociability, persistence)
» self-regulation skills (impulse control, affect and arousal regulation)
» positive outlook on life

Relationships:

» parenting quality

» close relationships with competent adults

» connections to pro-social and rule-abiding peers

Community resources and opportunities:

» good schools

» connections to pro-social organisations

» neighbourhood quality

» quality of social services and health care

CHAPTER SUMMARY

The early phases of the lifespan that we have looked at so far, from infancy through to middle childhood, are in many ways regarded as setting the stage for later life— the 'life chances' (Taylor & Macdonald 1998) that arise in all dimensions—both in our inner and outer worlds. This exploration of middle childhood transitions has emphasised the continuing importance of positive attachments with at least one parent or caregiver, positive relationships with peers, teachers and others in children's social networks, and the availability of key resources within a child's home, school and neighbourhood. Developing a sense of industry or self-worth and confidence is a key task in this developmental stage.

The protective factors we have considered have tended to come from theories of psychosocial development that focus on continuity across the lifespan and the successful attainment of certain capacities such as a sense of trust, autonomy, initiative and industry.

APPLYING A MULTIDIMENSIONAL UNDERSTANDING

Evie: Bullying

Evie spends every break in the school day in the library. She has found this is the only place where she can be by herself and avoid the teasing that she has been subjected to over the past two years of school. She is smaller than everyone in her class, as she had a brain tumour when she was three. She had the benign tumour removed but she still experiences difficulties, primarily because of the surgery and radiotherapy she had in order to ensure all the tumour had gone. She has learning difficulties and a slight paralysis of her left side. She has an integration aide with her for several hours a week. She finds this isolates her more in her Grade 1 classroom, as the other children

CASE STUDY

see her as different from them. She has become more withdrawn in recent weeks, as two other girls in particular have focused their bullying on her.

Justine: Family separation

Siblings Justine and Micky are in Grade 5 and Grade 3 respectively. They have both been experiencing difficulties at school this year, with noticeable drops in their grades and their concentration. Micky has been getting into fights during the breaks, and it seems he has been provoking these incidents with boys in Grade 1 and 2. Their parents have been called to the school but refuse to come to a meeting. They've been through an acrimonious divorce and haven't spoken in months. Through talking with the parents separately, and the children, it seems the children are having difficulty moving between two homes with their new parenting arrangements, particularly given their parents relate to them so differently.

Their father is very strict with them, and has become increasingly so since he re-partnered. He wants to keep things under control so that his new partner is not daunted by the parenting tasks she may be taking on. She has no children and didn't want to have any. Their mother is more relaxed about rules and believes that children should be left to play and to develop their own sense of control and what is right. She encourages them to talk through their feelings and negotiate different situations through compromise. She has the children most of the time.

Questions

1 What is your reaction to these scenarios?
2 What are some of the dilemmas these situations raise for you?
3 What are some possibilities for intervention using a multidimensional approach?
4 What cultural differences, if any, do you think emerge if these children are of Middle Eastern, Indigenous or Anglo-Australian background?

KEY TERMS

competence
industry
middle childhood
self-worth
poverty
siblings
worries

QUESTIONS AND DISCUSSION POINTS

1 What are some of the key biopsychosocial-spiritual developmental tasks of middle childhood?
2 What are some of the different risk and protective factors across this lifespan stage?
3 What are some of the structural and cultural dimensions that influence this stage?
4 Reflecting on your experiences of middle childhood, can you identify with the various transitions outlined in this chapter?
5 What social, structural and cultural changes have occurred that make your parents' experiences of these transitions different from your own?
6 Reflecting back on your childhood, do you recall the types of worries you experienced? What factors do you think have the greatest impact on the worries children experience?

FURTHER READING

Bowes, J. & Grace, R. eds, 2008, *Children, families and communities: Contexts and consequences*, 3rd edn. South Melbourne: Oxford University Press.

D'Cruz, H. 2009, 'Examining the meaning of childhood in critical social work practice' in J. Allan, L. Briskman & B. Pease, eds, *Critical social work: Theories and practices for a socially just world*, Crows Nest: Allen & Unwin, Chapter 10, pp. 132–44.

Gilligan, R. 2004, 'Promoting resilience in child and family social work: Issues for social work practice, education and policy', *Social Work Education*, 23(1), pp. 93–104.

Richardson, S. & Prior, M., eds, *No time to lose: The well-being of Australia's children*, Carlton: Melbourne University Press.

Siegal, M. 2008, *Marvelous minds: The discovery of what children know*, Oxford: Oxford University Press.

WEBSITES OF INTEREST

Australian Indigenous HealthInfoNet: www.healthinfonet.ecu.edu.au
This site provides information and links relating to the health of Indigenous Australians.

Australian Institute of Family Studies (AIFS): www.aifs.org.au
The AIFS site provides extensive links to longitudinal studies of children within Australia, New Zealand, Europe and North America, including the Longitudinal Study of Australian Children.

Australian Research Alliance for Children and Youth (ARACY): www.aracy.org.au/
This site provides information and links about ARACY, which is a national collaboration of researchers, policy makers and practitioners that focuses on children's and young people's well-being.

Footprints in Time: The Longitudinal Study of Indigenous Children (LSIC): www.fahcsia.gov.au/sa/indigenous/pubs/families/lsic
This site provides information about the 2,200 Indigenous Australian children participating in this longitudinal study.

Longitudinal Study of Australian Children (LSAC): www.aifs.gov.au/growingup/home.html
This site provides information about the longitudinal study of the development of Australian children undertaken by the Australian Institute of Family Studies.

National Association for Prevention of Child Abuse and Neglect (NAPCAN): www.napcan.org.au
This site provides information and links relating to child abuse and neglect in Australia.

Child Welfare Information Gateway: www.childwelfare.gov
This site is a US gateway for information relating to child abuse and neglect.

State Departments of Education
Each Australian state and territory has its own department of education. Visit your state or territory department for a range of educational resources.

Australian Capital Territory (Department of Education and Training): www.det.act.gov.au.

New South Wales (Department of Education and Training): www.det.nsw.edu.au

Northern Territory (Department of Education and Training): www.det.nt.gov.au

Queensland (Department of Education and Training): http://education.qld.gov.au

South Australia (Department of Education and Children's Services): www.decs.sa.gov.au

Tasmania (Department of Education): www.education.tas.gov.au

Victoria (Department of Education and Early Childhood Development): www.education.vic.gov.au

Western Australia (Department of Education): www.det.wa.edu.au/education

Telethon Institute for Child Health Research, Western Australia: www.ichr.uwa.edu.au
This site has information about the Western Australian Aboriginal Child Health Survey as well as a range of other health and mental health studies undertaken by the Institute.

CHAPTER **10**

Adolescence

AIMS OF THIS CHAPTER

This chapter explores the developmental transitions that occur in adolescence. It explores the following questions:

» What are the biopsychosocial-spiritual developmental tasks and transitions of adolescence?
» What are the experiences and impacts of stress, trauma and loss in adolescence?
» How is resilience in adolescence understood?

Adolescence has been a relatively recent addition to Western cultures' ways of thinking about the lifespan. In earlier generations, typically the distinction was between childhood and adulthood only, with children stepping directly into 'adult' roles. In this twenty-first century context, the parameters of adolescence are more complicated to define than the earlier life stages we have considered so far. In a Western context, it depends upon whether adolescence is viewed more as a biological or as a socio-cultural process.

As a biological experience, adolescence has been linked with the onset of puberty, and is thus strongly associated with the transition to sexual, along with emotional and cognitive, maturity. As this chapter explores, however, over recent decades, puberty has been occurring earlier, particularly for girls. Adolescence has also been defined in terms of chronological age as having an age between thirteen and nineteen. In this conceptualisation, adolescence is synonymous with being 'a teenager' and is often characterised more by the emotional and structural tasks and activities of adolescence.

Others have recognised the need to develop distinctive understandings of these different dimensions of adolescence, primarily due to the vastly different biopsychosocial-spiritual transitions for an early adolescent compared with a late adolescent. For example, a three-phase approach (McCarter 2003 p. 254) divides adolescence into the following stages:

1 early adolescence, from eleven to fourteen years
2 middle adolescence, from fifteen to seventeen years
3 late adolescence, from eighteen to twenty years.

Arguably, breaking down the broad adolescent years into these more discrete stages enables a closer understanding of the particular biopsychosocial-spiritual transitions of each. However, even this approach does not fit with how the Australian Bureau of Statistics refers to adolescence—as spanning the ages from fifteen to twenty-four, moving right into what others would consider to be a phase of early adulthood, or 'new adulthood' (Wyn 2009). These different conceptualisations highlight that, in many ways, adolescence is a social construction, requiring careful social, structural and cultural critique, particularly in relation to what constitutes risk throughout this lifespan stage.

In this chapter, we focus on adolescence through to the end of secondary schooling, and in Chapter 11, in focusing on early adulthood, we look at issues beyond this transition.

Key developmental tasks and transitions

Biological dimensions

Hormonal changes

Adolescence has most typically been seen as synonymous with the physical transitions of puberty and the associated psychosocial and sexual changes. **Puberty** is 'a stage of development that spans an extended period of time' and 'encompasses a large variety of morphological, physiological and behavioural changes' (Cameron 1990 p. 21 as cited in Tremblay & Frigon 2005 p. 74). It is a time of increased hormone production (testosterone and estrodial) for both girls and boys. These sex steroids promote the development of both primary and secondary sexual characteristics. Primary sexual characteristics include the capacity to produce eggs or sperm, and the development of the reproductive organs (Peterson 1996; Arnett 2007). For both sexes, secondary sexual characteristics include the development of pubic, underarm and facial hair, growth spurts, lowering of the voice, changes to skin (typically oilier, rougher and more prone to producing body odour) and other facial changes. Females typically reach puberty around two years earlier than males. For females, puberty also brings the onset of menstruation (menarche), breast development, weight changes and a broadening of the hip and pelvic areas. For males, puberty brings the capacity to produce sperm, increased muscle development, a broadening of the shoulders and chest areas, and the more extensive growth of hair across the body such as on the chest and back (see, for example, Arnett 2007 or Tanner 1962).

Researchers have noted that the onset of menstruation has shifted quite significantly, from an average of sixteen or seventeen years in the nineteenth century down to around thirteen years in the twentieth century (Ahmed et al. 2009) in developed countries.

In Chapter 9, we look at the impact of the early onset of puberty in middle childhood.

All of these changes are often quite rapid biological changes which bring with them both inner- and outer-world transformations and transitions. Young people are navigating their way through often very different experiences of both their own bodies and their sense of self, along with the changes that take place within friendships and the wider social context as a result. Increasingly, there can be a gap between sexual and psychosocial maturation.

Weight and height, and nutrition

The hormonal changes of puberty lead to weight and height changes for males and females—with males generally converting more fat to muscle and vice versa for females. Currently, there is widespread concern for weight changes in both directions for adolescencts—weight gain for some and weight loss for others. Australia's adolescents are, similar to younger children, experiencing significant changes in obesity rates. At the other end of the spectrum, adolescents, predominantly females, can develop eating disorders—about one per cent of the female population developing anorexia nervosa and four per cent bulimia. Anorexia is diagnosed when three key criteria are met: 'self-induced weight loss, intense fear of becoming fat and cessation of periods' (Bloch & Singh 1997 p. 127). Bulimia also involves hyper-consciousness about weight but binge eating rather than self-starvation.

Brain development

A much richer understanding is emerging of the transitions taking place within the human brain throughout adolescence. 'Distinct structural changes' occur as a result of the increase in the sex steroids of testosterone and estradiol (Peper et al. 2009). Within the brain, global grey matter decreases and the volume of white matter increases. The result of these changes is 'the refinement of neuronal connections which could be related to cognitive and emotional development' (Peper et al. 2009 p. 333). We look at these cognitive and emotional developments in the pages ahead.

What has been recognised recently is that adolescents' brains are still undergoing significant growth and change. They are particularly prone, therefore, to damage caused by drug and alcohol use, something harm minimisation strategies are directly targeting in current media campaigns.

Sleep

It has been long recognised that there are changes in the sleeping habits of adolescents compared with earlier patterns in childhood, and these are often seen as part of an antisocial attitude to conforming to the 'regular' hours of others. However, recent research has demonstrated that the more nocturnal hours and increased sleeping hours of adolescents may be a major part of brain development throughout this stage. Early in adolescence, young people typically require around nine hours of sleep, shifting to around seven hours during later adolescence. Many young people do not get this amount of sleep and coupled with a more nocturnal style of activity, some have suggested that adolescents are often existing in a state of chronic jet lag.

The other aspects of adolescent sleep recently recognised are the 'banking' and 'recovery' aspects of sleep, whereby long sleep-ins over the weekend, for example, can actually compensate for sleep deprivation at other times and enable adolescent bodies and minds to function more effectively. This is contrary to the earlier perception that occasional longer sleeps were detrimental (because they upset sleep routines) rather than restorative.

While the different sleep requirements of adolescents are increasingly better understood, these requirements are not well accommodated within school structures and work places, which continue to structure the day within the same hours as for younger children.

Disability, injury and diseases

As adolescents participate more fully and independently in the world around them, their exposure to the risk of injury and disease increases. Many adolescents experience chronic and acute illnesses, as well as disability and injury following risk-taking behaviours, particularly road trauma (Keating & Halpern-Felsher 2008. While younger children can survive a range of chronic illness experiences, during adolescence some diseases such as cystic fibrosis and muscular dystrophy reach their terminal phase. The box below highlights that young males are particularly vulnerable to death and injury occurring in adolescence. Each of these experiences can bring stress, trauma and/or grief into the lives of young people and those around them, something we explore later in this chapter.

We look at the impact of road trauma later in this chapter.

DISABILITY, DISEASE AND INJURY EXPERIENCES OF AUSTRALIAN YOUNG PEOPLE, 2005

» 1,309 deaths among young Australians—a rate of 46 deaths per 100,000 young people—with males accounting for 73% of these deaths.

» Injury (including poisoning) was the leading cause of death for young Australians ... 919 deaths, representing 70% of all deaths among this group.

» Motor vehicle traffic accidents and suicide were the main causes of these injury deaths (39% and 32% respectively).

» The overall decline in mortality among young people in the 20 years to 2005 can be attributed largely to a fall in the death rates from injury (including poisoning).

» Cancers were also a leading cause of death ... 114 deaths, accounting for 9% of all their deaths.

Source: AIHW 2008b p. 282, Reproduced with permission.

Throughout the 1980s, youth suicide was a major concern, as it increased in incidence at alarming rates, particularly for young men. Recent evidence suggests that a significant decrease has occurred in the number of young people who suicide (Morrell et al. 2007). However, many young people continue to engage in self-harming behaviours, from deliberate cutting behaviours through to excessive alcohol and drug use, something we look at in more detail later in this chapter.

Psychosocial-spiritual dimensions

Along with the physical changes that mark adolescence, a range of cognitive, psychological and social transitions has been identified as key processes throughout adolescence. These psychosocial-spiritual developmental tasks (Germain 1991 p. 354) include: identity formation; gaining independence; developing intimate relationships; developing sexual awareness and expressing this sexuality; pursuing vocational tasks; and developing values and a belief system or worldview. We look first at the cognitive changes associated with adolescence before considering these other major transitions.

Cognitive development

With the brain development that occurs as a result of hormonal changes in adolescence, significant cognitive transitions occur, enabling more complex cognitive processing of the world around us. Piaget identified the years from eleven onwards as the time when children entered what he termed a 'formal operations' stage of cognitive development, which 'permits a person to conceptualise about many simultaneously interacting variables. It allows for the creation of a system of laws or rules that can be used for problem solving' (Newman & Newman 2003 p. 72).

Thus, hypothetical and abstract thought becomes possible, opening up a range of new cognitive capacities. Formal-logical thinking, according to Vygotsky, opens up a 'whole world with its past and future, nature, history and human life' (Karpov 2006 p. 205), as it enables young people to engage in both self-reflective and self-conscious thought. As Lievegoed (2005 p. 102) notes, 'the distance between self and other that has been created brings awareness and set patterns of the adult world into sharp focus'. Peers and adults are critical in the development of these capacities, as young people begin to internalise a newly experienced self-consciousness.

According to McCarter (2003 p. 260), these cognitive changes enable the contemplation of the future, a comprehension of the nature of human relationships, consolidation of specific knowledge into a coherent system, an ability to demonstrate foresight, the capacity for abstract thought, a capacity for empathy, and a stronger sense of internal control. These capacities significantly influence an individual's emotional development and their interaction with the social world, as, in turn, they are influenced by the social world.

Personality development

Despite adolescence being associated with significant changes in all biopsychosocial-spiritual dimensions, research indicates that personality traits tend to remain relatively stable, with an increasing tendency towards the positive or **prosocial** elements of personality. As one study concluded, 'Most people become more dominant, agreeable, conscientious and emotionally stable over the course of their lives' (Caspi et al. 2005 p. 468), and for many this is the case from adolescence onwards.

Emotional development

If adolescence tends to characterised by one feature within mainstream Australian culture, it would be emotional turbulence. This belief has led to extensive research and come to be recognised as only partially true. Emotional turmoil is not necessarily the marker of the experience: 'Most teenagers are generally happy individuals, but, compared to earlier childhood, moodiness and periods of misery are more frequent' (Rutter 1987 p. 96). Bloch and Singh (1997 p. 200) suggest that thirty per cent of adolescents make a smooth transition to adulthood, fifty per cent have 'periods of purposeful activity alternating with withdrawal, a tendency to become angry easily and to blame others', and twenty per cent experience significant emotional turmoil.

However, it is critical to consider the context of these emotional changes. Is it that adolescents are cognitively capable of seeing the world in adult ways, yet have very few ways of expressing that adult self when families and systems often keep individuals within tightly bounded structures that do not recognise this capability? Formal-logical thought opens up different ways of seeing the world, enabling many of the discrepancies and injustices of the world to be seen for the first time. It also enables many adolescents, living in Western contexts in particular, to be aware of the multitude of choices they have in their world and be justifiably overwhelmed by them as they negotiate their way through educational, occupational, relational and other decisions.

In contrast to this perception of adolescence as an angst-ridden phase of development, child psychologist Ungar (2008b) has proposed that adolescents are not being exposed to enough risk and responsibility in the way that they need to, to develop the necessary emotional intelligence and coping skills. As the next few pages illustrate, his ideas may only relate to young people who are well-buffered socio-economically and psychosocially.

Erikson identified the central tasks for psychosocial development in adolescence as identity formation and, later in adolescence, the development of a capacity for intimacy with another. The first he identified as occurring between the ages of twelve and eighteen, where the young person comes to either successfully develop a sense of identity or, if not, develop a sense of role confusion. The ability to successfully develop a sense of identity then leads someone to experience a sense of fidelity. This sense of fidelity is described as being 'the ability to maintain loyalties freely chosen, despite the inevitable value conflicts involved in these choices' (Gollnick 2005 p. 96). In a post-structural context, identity as a concept has been widely critiqued, in recognition that there is no such thing as one identity that is fixed and specific; rather, people have fluid, contextually specific identities. A sense of coherence, as explored in Chapter 4, may perhaps be a more accurate way of holding together these notions of personal identity, in that it includes an understanding of 'who I am' and what matters.

Many cultures and religions have specific rituals to mark the transition into adolescence and early adulthood, providing a frame of reference for a personal sense of identity. For example, Australian Indigenous cultures mark the transition for boys to adolescence through 'Men's business' ceremonies and rites. Jewish cultures mark the transition for boys through the Bar Mitzvah and girls the Bat Mitzvah. Similarly for migrant and refugee young people, identity processes are affected by other dimensions of their experience, by a:

> sense of belonging in terms of nationality, cultural identity and family and by the response of the broader society to themselves and to their community. Multicultural young people may struggle to balance their parents/community's expectations with the expectations of their Australian peers and wider society. (Francis & Cornfoot 2007 p. 24)

Secular Australian culture has very little to mark the transition, and as a dominant culture it has a very ambivalent message for adolescents, which we explore later in this chapter.

In addition to the task of identity formation, the development of a capacity for **intimacy** is seen as a key part of adolescence, although typically in the later years. This is described as the capacity for a young person to merge psychologically and also sometimes sexually in relationship with another. Same-sex and opposite-sex friendships are expanded and maintained, and members of peer groups become a critical source of both identity formation and expression and intimate bonds. The outcome of the successful mastery of this stage is seen to be the capacity to love. The alternative is to experience isolation or solitude.

Relational development

Relational development takes on new dimensions in adolescence—including the formation of new, intimate relationships and relationships within wider social networks than the family.

Parents

Parents continue to be, for many adolescents, the secure base from which they can increasingly explore much wider relational and social worlds. Studies of attachment style during adolescence show that there is typically a continuing attachment style from earlier childhood. Within the context of parental relationships, young people become increasingly self-directive and gain independence from their parents, while maintaining mutually satisfying relationships with them—'at least up to age 16 years, most adolescents continue to trust and respect their parents, are upset by parental disapproval and on the whole follow parental guidance with respect to major issues' (Rutter 1987 pp. 97–8). This view has been confirmed in the Australian Temperament Project (ATP), in which young people at ages thirteen to fourteen and again at sixteen to seventeen completed surveys, along with their parents, about their perceptions of the relationship between them. The study found that:

> On seven of the eight items, the great majority of teenagers had positive perceptions of their relationship with their parents, with over 70% feeling their parents trusted their judgement, considered their point of view, sensed when they were upset, accepted them as a person, respected their feelings, understood them, and understood what they were going through. (Smart et al. 2008 p. 21)

The only negative perception was that they were less likely to confide in parents about problems they were experiencing, although given that intimacy needs are often met by peers, this may not need to be negatively interpreted but could be part of the move towards using other relationships for support and understanding.

Parents and young people tended to agree in these perceptions, and perceptions tended to be more positive at the later age of adolescence rather than at thirteen to fourteen years (Smart et al. 2008).

For many adolescents and their parents, though, negotiation and some conflict can occur in relation to boundaries and the expectations around them, particularly when they differ markedly from those of their peer group. Many young people also have to negotiate cultural expectations and boundaries, in navigating the different worlds in which they are living. By the later stages of adolescence, some young people begin the transition out of the home of their family of origin. For some, these moves are prompted by education and work transitions. For others, the transition is about leaving dysfunctional and abusive home environments.

In Chapter 11, we look at these transitions in more detail.

Siblings

Siblings have been identified as key influences throughout adolescence, as with earlier lifespan stages. The focus in research has been on the extent to which siblings influence risk-taking behaviours—particularly in relation to drug and alcohol use, and sexual behaviours—as well as providing support and friendship. In one study of drug use and its impact on siblings, for example, evidence was found for both increased drug use when older siblings used, and also for abstaining from drug use on the basis of seeing the impact on older siblings (Rose 2010). Thus, no predictable pathways of sibling influence have been established in relation to risk-taking behaviours.

However, sibling relationships often undergo changes in adolescence, with siblings seeking to de-identify with each other, rather than, as through middle childhood, identify strongly with each other. This process is thought to be 'a dynamic that is more common in adolescence when youth seek to establish a unique personal identity' (Feinberg et al. 2003 p. 1262).

See the discussion in Chapter 7 about attachment style.

Peers

Friendships with peers tend to be consistent with earlier attachment experiences, consistent with the notion that in infancy, internal working models are established as to how to relate to others and these are internalised as models to understand the world and relationships later in life. Throughout adolescence, however, the need to belong to a group of peers intensifies. Conformity to the peer group also intensifies significantly, often reflected in strict codes as to what can be worn, what music is in and what is acceptable behaviour, for example.

The key protective factor within adolescent relationships is seen to be intimacy—described as 'closeness to another person and as openness in describing and sharing thoughts and feelings' (Bauminger et al. 2008 p. 409). Intimate friendships have been found to provide emotional support and a safe environment for self-exploration.

Bauminger et al. (2008) found that self-disclosure was a key determinant of the extent to which there is intimacy within friendships.

For many young people, the peer group they belong to does offer intimacy and prosocial relationships—that is, relationships that foster and value self-esteem, competency and sociability. These peer relationships are also associated with less depression and anxiety in adolescence. For others, peer groups can lead to engagement in illegal and destructive behaviours.

As mentioned in Chapter 9, significant social networking now occurs via electronic media in adolescence—Facebook in particular. While these networking resources provide constant access to support and friendship, they do run the risk of taking the place of face-to-face and consequential dimensions out of the interaction. Many young people report cyber-bullying. As we explore later, cyber-bullying has been linked in several cases with suicidal behaviour, when young people have felt overwhelmed by the marginalisaton, abuse and stigma created in these peer interactions.

Teachers and other significant adults

As young people explore different ways of thinking and understanding the world, mentors become very influential in the formation of these ideas. Teachers and other significant adults can provide alternate viewpoints and ways of living.

Teachers are often key role models for young people. In recognition of this, models of school engagement have begun to incorporate understandings of effective parenting. Like authoritative parenting styles, teaching styles that provide positive, encouraging support and motivation to engage in tasks seem to motivate students optimally and lead to ongoing student engagement. School engagement is critical for young people—completing secondary school education is profoundly linked with employment opportunities, as we explore further in Chapter 10.

For some young people, other adults—such as counsellors, sports coaches and youth group leaders—also play significant roles. Engaging successfully with young people is about recognising them as individuals with their own views and rights.

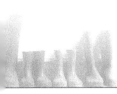

THEORY IN CONTEXT

WORKING WITH ADOLESCENTS

Anna describes how recognising young people as individuals was demonstrated in her social work placement.

It was only my third week of placement and I had started attending the initial meeting with the intake worker. Sally, who was about fifteen years old, came to the service with both her parents, Mary and Peter. Sally sat squashed between her parents on one of the couches in the intake room while I sat opposite. The intake worker sat between us in an arm chair. Sally seemed quite upset. She clenched a ball of damp tissues in her fist and her head hung low, her face obscured by her long fringe. The meeting started following the usual format: the intake worker asked the family why they had come today. Peter spoke, saying that Sally and Peter had both been struggling with depression and while Peter had been coping well and had recently stopped taking medication; Sally was not coping well and was refusing to go to school. Sally had been bullied throughout her schooling years, especially when she moved schools when she was about ten. The bullying continued throughout high school and most recently her group of friends turned on her at school. Mary described Sally's performance at school as 'average' and noted that Sally often got into trouble for speaking out of turn and 'being in the wrong place at the wrong time' but that otherwise she was 'a good kid'.

The intake worker addressed Sally, asking what had been going on for her in the last few weeks. Sally spoke into her lap with monosyllabic replies.

Sally: Nothing.
Worker: So, what are your favourite subjects?
S: Don't have one.
W: Do you like sport?
S: Nup.

This went on for a few minutes so the worker tried to engage Sally by asking her the 'easy' questions on the front page of the initial meeting form: date of birth, home address, siblings' names and ages, contact phone number, etc. Sally grunted her replies and turned to her mother several times, grumbling (I couldn't hear about what). The worker persisted, explaining privacy and confidentiality, then passing the forms for release of information to Sally and her parents.

Out of the blue, Sally lifted her head and addressed the intake worker: 'This is *$#@ing stupid! What are these? I'm not going to sign this $*#T!' A stunned silence ensued as Sally continued: 'Is THIS your job? … asking all these dumb questions about where I live and my brother's name … cos if it is, I think you should get a new one! This is a waste of time.'

The worker sat seemingly perplexed for a moment but gathered his wits and spoke: 'Well, thank you for your honesty Sally. Yes, this is my job, and I have been doing it for a long time. What you've pointed out to me is true, that this service probably isn't the best one for what you are looking for, but we wouldn't have worked that out had I not asked the questions.' The worker gestured behind him to the door: '… And you don't have to stay, this is a voluntary service …' Sally seemed shocked but stood up and left, slamming the door behind her. Her parents remained in the room and everyone breathed a little sigh of relief.

Although I was somewhat overwhelmed by the event, after some reflection and in discussion with the intake worker, I identified that the worker had taken the 'attack' and turned it into a strength for the young person. Strengths-based practice is at the core of all services here and this episode was no different. With a different approach, potentially this situation could have been exacerbated. The worker could have become defensive and accused the young person of being rude and disrespectful. Instead he was able to take the situation and flip it around so that it became positive. In this case the worker identified the 'attack' as a strength— honesty.

Young people are especially attuned to their weaknesses, especially those who come to use the services provided by us. When asked, most young people can reel off a list of things they cannot do or are 'bad' at. When it comes to strengths, most young people cannot identify any. Perhaps this is why Sally was so shocked at the worker's reply. Had the worker become angry and defensive, he would only have perpetuated Sally's past experiences of reactions to her behaviour. And while Sally chose to leave, I'm sure she was surprised at the worker's positive reaction. While I have found the strengths-based approach easy to comprehend and use in practice, in this situation it was difficult for me to immediately identify how this approach could be used. Had I been conducting the meeting I felt that I would have been stumped for a reply and most likely would have been compelled to respond in a negative way.

Questions

1   What is your reaction to this situation?
2   What developmental aspects do you think Anna is considering here?

Gender and sexual identity

Intimacy is an important aspect of the adolescent experience, particularly in the later years, and often finds its expression in sexual relationships. Sexual awareness is developed in late middle childhood, but in adolescence it is also expressed. Thus, both sexual awareness and experience emerges, with some research suggesting that one out of four to five Australian adolescents have had sex by the age of sixteen. Not all of these sexual encounters are positive experiences, many young women and men experiencing rape or sexual assault.

In Chapter 11, we look at the impact of sexual assault.

Adolescence is a time of exploring sexual identity and recognising sexual orientation. It is difficult to establish a relatively accurate picture of sexual identities for a range of reasons, including the fluidity of identities and sexual experiences. One study of 38,000 high-school students in the USA (Remafedi et al. 1992) found that eighty-eight per cent of students classified themselves as heterosexual, one per cent as gay, lesbian or bisexual and ten per cent classified themselves as uncertain about their orientation. Adolescence can be a very alienating time of struggling with issues of sexuality and sexual orientation, particularly if individuals find themselves in unsupportive and discriminatory environments. One Australian study of 390 people identified, for example, that:

> Sixty per cent of GLBT [gay, lesbian, bi-sexual, transgendered] young people aged 14 to 24 years hide their sexual orientation or gender identity from family and seventy per cent when attending an educational institution. (Leonard et al. 2008)

The impact on a young person's mental health of this silencing about who they are can be profound. Some Australian schools do not provide sex education classes at all, and therefore do not provide opportunities for sexuality to be discussed. For those that do, many do not provide education and support about gay, lesbian, bisexual and transgendered sexual experiences and identities.

All sexual relationships require communication and skills of emotional intelligence, so that roles, needs and rights within a sexual relationship can be negotiated. Relationships rely on communication skills and assertion skills. These skills are required not only in the context of the relationship itself, but sometimes with parents who may not support the adolescent's expression of their sexuality.

It is estimated that most sexually active adolescents are engaging in unsafe sexual practices, putting themselves at risk of sexually transmitted infections and pregnancy. Later in this chapter we look at risk-taking behaviour and some of the theories as to why adolescents are more likely to take risks than others. Sexual health is often compromised because of drug and alcohol issues, peer pressure and communication difficulties.

In relation to pregancy and adolescence, as the Australian Bureau of Statistics (ABS 2000) noted:

> The teenage fertility rate (the number of births in a given year per 1,000 females aged 15–19 years) has been declining since the 1970s, such that teenage girls are now less likely to be mothers than they were thirty years ago. The rate of childbearing among Australian teenage girls peaked at 55.5 births per 1,000 females in 1971, before falling to half its peak level (27.6) by 1980, and reaching its lowest ever rate of 18.1 births per 1,000 females in 1999.

By 2006, this teenage fertility rate had dropped as low as 15.3 babies per 1,000 women, and it rose only slightly in 2007 to 16.0 babies per 1,000 women (ABS 2007a p. 6). Indigenous women are more likely to have babies during their teenage years than non-Indigenous women.

While pregnancy rates have been declining, sexually transmitted infections (STIs) have been increasing among young people (Couch et al. 2006), with the AIHW noting that 'In 2006, there were 32,459 notifications for STIs among young

Australians (a rate of 1,135 notifications per 100,000 young people), representing 55% of all STI notifications that year' (AIHW 2008b p. 282). Significantly, in terms of health impacts and outcomes, notification rates of chlamydia have tripled and of gonococcal infections have doubled between 1996 and 2006. HIV notifications slightly decreased: 'In 2005, there were 88 HIV notifications for those aged 18–24 years (75 for males, 13 for females), a rate of four notifications per 100,000 in that age group' (AIHW 2008b p. 282). Arguably, though, these risk experiences are not specific to adolescence (or early adulthood), with many adults across the lifespan practising unsafe sex and using drugs and alcohol beyond recommended limits. However, the higher rates of sexual health problems among adolescents is a concern because of the consequences—such as an unwanted pregnancy, which might be able to be dealt with differently later in life, or the impact of drugs and alcohol on adolescent brain development.

One innovative study of teenagers' perceptions of sexual health (Kang et al. 2009) involved an audit of 1000 emails sent to *Dolly* magazine, a popular girl's magazine that has a circulation of around 400,000 per month. The letters outlined the concerns of adolescent girls, which fell into three broad categories: context of concern, health issue of concern (including body, sex, relationship, mind, and violence and/or safety) and advice sought for concern. GPs thought it was important to emphasise concerns such as 'health risk behaviours, mental health, pregnancy and sexually transmitted infections' (Kang et al. 2009 p. 1). What emerged from this study was that there was a mismatch of priorities and concerns between adolescent girls and GPs. This study, and other similar studies exploring adolescent concerns, highlight the issues young people have in accessing relevant health and mental health information.

The management of all of these aspects of sexuality is intimately connected with the social context—the extent to which there can be open discussion of such issues, and the extent to which there are adequate resources, both practical (such as access to condoms), educational and human. For example, some secondary schools, such as Plumpton High School in Sydney's western suburbs, provide programs to support young mothers complete their secondary education by offering child care and family-friendly school environments.

Vocational development

In Chapter 11 we look at the pathways out of school, particularly for early school leavers and the employment implications.

The majority of young people participate in secondary education throughout their adolescent years: 'Participation in education among young people aged 15–19 years has been consistently around 76%–77% since 1998' (AIHW 2007 p. 5). This statistic is influenced by employment levels also, but as the AIHW (2007 p. 5) report goes on to note, 'a considerable number of young people are neither studying nor working—8% of those aged 15–19 years in 2006'. For this group in adolescence, low educational levels and sometimes persistent unemployment can set up longstanding difficulties for life.

Vocational directions and decisions about school are profoundly influenced by the resources available to young people within their family context and the wider structural context. For many young people, educational and employment barriers have an effect on the types of opportunities that are open to them for the rest of their adult life. For example, for many Indigenous young people living in remote parts of Australia, secondary schooling may not be available within local communities, and therefore they must board in towns where it is available. Separation from family and culture can cause enormous distress and have an impact on academic success.

Many young people are simultaneously juggling school and casual work—about forty per cent of the casual workforce is aged fifteen to nineteen (ABS 2005a). Also, many young people are involved in volunteering in their community, learning critical skills and acquiring a sense of engagement and self-worth. Schools often provide an important structure around this type of involvement. Thus, their focus is not just on schoolwork but also on balancing other work and social demands.

Moral and/or spiritual development

The spiritual dimension is more consciously recognised at this stage of the lifespan, by both young people and researchers alike, than for earlier stages, as young people begin to question the meanings and purposes of their life and that of others. Participation in religious activities is seen to be a protective factor for some young people, minimising participation in various risk-taking behaviours (McCarter 2003).

From the ages of eleven to twelve, converging with the development of formal-operational cognitive capacities, Fowler proposes a stage of **synthetic-conventional faith**. Synthetic refers to the ways in which a person 'seeks to synthesize these disparate elements into a coherent identity, worldview and set of values', and conventional refers to the need 'to conform to expectations and judgements of others' (Gollnick 2005 p. 102). What this stage of faith development does not have is a third-person perspective that enables critical reflection or a viewpoint outside oneself. As Fowler and Dell (2006 pp. 40) note, there can be an 'overdependence on the mirroring and evaluation of influential significant others' rather than a critical self-evaluation about meaning and spirituality.

One concern about this lack of a critical reflective capacity is that young people are particularly vulnerable to the often strong influence of religious and/or spiritual groups. Young vulnerable people can be recruited into cults or terrorist cells, as they search for a sense of meaning and belonging. Cults can offer certainty, at times when complexity and uncertainty are overwhelming in a young person's life, along with acceptance and a strong sense of belonging (Calles et al. 2005).

However, for most young people in religious and/or spiritual communities, these communities offer significant positive peer and adult networks during adolescence. The resilience resources provided by participation in these communities have been identified as including: attachment relationships (with the divine, family and/or prosocial peers and mentors); social support; guidelines for conduct and moral values; and personal growth and development, and transformational opportunities (Crawford et al. 2006 p. 358).

Risk-taking behaviours are more commonly engaged in during adolescence than in earlier lifespan stages. Central to a lot of the research and discussion about these behaviours is the question of adolescent moral reasoning. In Chapter 8, the various stages proposed in relation to moral development were presented. In adolescence, many young people move from pre-conventional to conventional moral reasoning, as described earlier. Thus, they rely not only on what parents might think, but a vastly broader range of options and consequences. Moral reasoning becomes influenced by notions of reciprocity and an ability to think through more abstract and global consequences. This development is important given that it encourages more prosocial and self-protective behaviour. Young people engaged in pre-conventional moral reasoning, by contrast, have been found to be more likely to engage in high-risk activities more frequently than those who demonstrated low levels of preconventional moral reasoning (Kuther & Higgins-D'Alessandro 2000).

Coping with risks and adversities

Stress

Many of the stressors outlined in Chapter 9—family difficulties, poverty, bullying and mental health issues—continue to have an impact on the daily lives of adolescents. In addition to these experiences, a number of key stressors are reported by young people and reflected in the research data and in service use data across Australia. A survey of Year 11 students in Melbourne identified many of these common negative and stressful aspects of growing up in Australia:

> racism, family crisis and conflict, and crime/violence/drugs/alcohol (predominantly from the area of lower socioeconomic status). Less commonly reported negative aspects included exams/school pressure, war and terrorism, and limitations because of age, for example, having no voting or driving rights. (Prior 2005 p. 301)

The following discussion highlights some of these concerns in exploring mixed messages about adult states, school stress, peer pressure and risk-taking behaviour, mental health and substance use issues. Of course, many of these stressors occur simultaneously rather than occur as isolated issues.

Mixed messages

One stressor for many young people is the conflicting messages they receive about their status—alternating between adult and child. The ambivalent message about what it is to be an adolescent is described by Wyn and White (2000 p. 166) as the 'paradox of youth'—that young people are characterised as 'active agents who consciously shape and choose their own destinies' and as a 'relatively homogenous and powerless' group, 'objects of universal stages and institutional processes' such as secondary schooling. On the one hand, adolescence is seen as the prime time of life, yet on the other it arguably carries with it some of the most complex biopsychosocial-spiritual transitions and developments of the lifespan.

Some of the contradictions of the positioning of adolescence and the transition to adulthood within Australian culture include the various ages at which someone can obtain a drivers licence (eighteen years), legally drink alcohol (eighteen years), leave school (fourteen years), seek medical care autonomously (fifteen years), and obtain an independent Austudy allowance from Centrelink (sixteen years).

School and study

With most young people spending their day at school, it can be a major stressor in their lives. This can be because of both relational and educational issues. As discussed in Chapter 9, bullying can be a stressor for many young people, and in secondary school, it has found a new forum through the use of the internet and texting.

The educational experience also carries with it pressure and performance anxiety. Each state and territory has its own leaving examinations, which can be seen as determining lifelong pathways to work or university. Not only do students experience the stress of these processes, but their parents are also often heavily invested and involved, and thus stress is experienced at a family level as well as an individual one.

Peer pressure

One of the ironies of adolescence is that while conforming to parental and other norms is often rejected, conformity within peer groups is at its peak. Peer relationships can become very intense, and the importance of reputation and belonging sometimes overrides other bases of good decisions. For those involved in prosocial groups, the effects of belonging can be very positive, but for some young people, peer pressure can lead to engaging in antisocial behaviour, often with significant consequences such as involvement with the police and the legal system. As with other stages of the lifespan, the goodness of fit between friendships and family can make an important difference in the amount of conflict experienced between home and social networks. Where there is not a goodness of fit between peer groups and family, peer pressure can lead to greater conflict for some with their family of origin.

Risk taking

In Western cultures, in particular, adolescence has long been regarded as a time when young people challenge those in authority as they assert their own authority and seek to establish their own identity. Along with this has been an awareness that young people take risks and experiment in a wide range of behaviours—such as drug and alcohol use, driving at excessive speeds (often while under the influence of substances) or engaging in risky sexual behaviours such as unprotected sex.

Researchers and practitioners alike have attempted to identify why it is that adolescence is synonymous with risk-taking behaviours, often with fatal consequences, and whether risk-taking behaviour is, cross-culturally, a universal adolescent developmental task. Evidence for the universality of risk-taking at this time in the lifespan is emerging, along with the recognition that both the nature and consequences of these risk-taking behaviours does vary by context. Clearly culture and family culture, though, do play significant roles. For example, risk for adolescents in a Western context differs significantly from risk in the context of other cultural contexts (Kloep et al. 2009); for example, Kloep et al. (2009) raise issues such as the access many Western adolescents have to cars and alcohol, which predisposes them to certain risk situations. In contrast, risk situations for those in Eastern cultures may relate to 'reading certain magazines, working in risky, unregulated conditions, drinking contaminated water … or refusing to agree to arranged marriage' (Kloep et al. 2009 p. 136). In part then, risk is connected with resources and norms in the immediate environments in which young people are living.

Another way of studying risk-taking behaviour is to look more closely at the adolescent brain and understand what regulates emotion and behaviour. The assumption with risk-taking behaviour is that a choice is being made and that the choice to engage in risk-taking behaviour is an irrational one. That is, it is a failure to add up the benefits and costs. Harm minimisation strategies aim to provide young people with more information and education about the risks of various behaviours, assuming that information is the mediator of behaviour and that better information will lead to more rational decision-making processes. Recent research into the brain's pathways of decision making has highlighted that decisions are made more on the basis of emotional rather than factual information (Rivers et al. 2008). This means that in the moments preceding risk-taking behaviour, emotion rather than rational thinking is likely to drive the decision to continue or to discontinue a risky behaviour—for example, the emotional intensity of a sexual encounter is more likely to override cognitive awareness of the need to engage in safe-sex behaviours. So introducing more safe-sex programs may not result in better outcomes. Programs may need to ensure there is a rehearsal of dealing with emotional responses rather than informational or intellectual decisions.

For some young people, the consequence of some risk-taking behaviour is that they end up in contact with the police and the youth justice system. A recent Juvenile Justice report found, for example, 'on an average day in 2007–08, 4,708 young people were under supervision in all states and territories except New South Wales, for which data were not available', with about 630 of these young people being held in detention (AIHW 2009b p. 1). Almost forty per cent of young people under supervision were Indigenous, a trend that continues. Most of these young people are males and aged around sixteen to seventeen years of age.

Extreme risk-taking behaviour become a complex web of increased drug and alcohol use, exposure to violence and homelessness.

Mental health

Throughout adolescence, mental health issues can threaten well-being. Most mental illnesses and threats, such as depression, substance use, anxiety disorders and psychosis, have their peak period of incidence during adolescence, particularly late adolescence (Commonwealth Department of Health and Aged Care 2000). It has been proposed that about twenty per cent of young people in Australia suffer from depressed mood. At the more severe end of the spectrum, five per cent of young people suffer from a depressive disorder and the prevalence of major depressive disorder was found to be 2.7 per cent (Commonwealth Department of Health and Aged Care and AIHW 1999 p. 47). The Victorian Adolescent Health and Wellbeing Survey (Hibbert et al. 1996; Coffey et al. 2004) found that 4.3 per cent of Year 11 boys and 6.4 per cent of Year 11 girls had mild depression.

The causes of **depression** are multiple and complex (Burns et al. 2002 pp. S93–S94), with some of the key risk factors being identified as:

» poor interpersonal skills
» cumulative adverse life events, including 'exposure to family or community violence, chronic poverty, child physical and sexual abuse, bereavement or parental divorce or separation' (Burns et al. 2002 p. S93)
» life events involving loss
» cognitive style
» parental depression

» low self-esteem, particularly attributed to beliefs developed throughout middle childhood.

We look at suicidal behaviour later in this chapter.

In any one year, between five and ten per cent of young people from their young teens to their mid-twenties report making a suicide attempt.

Some young people are also at risk of developing eating disorders, which are strongly related to both age and gender, with young women typically being most affected. Around one per cent of Australian adolescent girls experience eating disorders (Patton et al. 1999). An increase in boys being affected has also been noted, raising interesting questions as to the cause of the disorder. Wyn notes (2009 p. 69) 'Young people who do not conform to standards of bodily perfection are marginalised until they learn how to produce the right kind of body'.

Overall, mental health issues form about fifty per cent of the disease burden in young people aged fifteen to twenty-four years (Mathers et al. 1999; AIHW 2008b p. 281). A related concern is that only a very small proportion of adolescents experiencing mental health difficulties seek help from professional services (Raphael 2000). In the Western Australian Child Health Survey, for example, across both childhood and adolescence only two per cent of four- to sixteen-year-olds with mental health problems had been in contact with mental health services in a six-month period (Sawyer et al. 2000). A reluctance to seek out help during this age period is well recognised as an inherent attribute of this age. However, youth-specific services are frequently limited and inaccessible to many already isolated young people. Young people's perceptions as to what social workers and other counsellors can offer also seem to stand in the way of help-seeking behaviour (Jorm 2007). Concerns about confidentiality also influence the decision as to whether or not to seek support.

Substance use and abuse

Substance misuse disorders also emerge in adolescence, peaking in late adolescence and early adulthood, before gradually declining throughout adulthood (Andrews et al. 1999). Most people throughout adolescence are experimenting with alcohol and cigarettes, and many also experiment with illicit drugs such as marijuana and ecstasy, or with harder illicit drugs. Given this, distinguishing between experimentation and the development of a drug or alcohol problem is important. Patterns of behaviour have been defined which identify the spectrum of alcohol and drug use—experimental, social and recreational, circumstantial (where, for example, a high degree of concentration is required in a short period of time), intensive or compulsive. Each of these patterns of substance use have very different motivations and impacts on daily life, and require different interventions, from none to intensive withdrawal and rehabilitation support.

PRACTICE IN CONTEXT

SIBLING RELATIONSHIPS

David presents the following situation from his practice, in which he highlights the compounding of many issues in one family situation.

Kate is a twenty-year-old student currently studying in her second year at university. She lives at home with her parents and her eighteen-year old brother, Lachlan. He frequently uses marijuana and amphetamines and regularly reports feeling depressed. He left school about two years ago when his drug use escalated and he is not currently working. Lachlan has threatened family members in the past when he needs money to purchase drugs, and there has been conflict in the family about how to best deal with his drug issues.

Kate has called a telephone counselling service as she is worried about her brother but also angry at him for the problems it is causing in the family. She still cares for her brother greatly, but feels that perhaps it would be better to move out of home and get away from the situation so she can concentrate on her studies and her own life.

Questions

1 While Kate and Lachlan have only two years in age between them, would you consider there to be different developmental tasks with which they're dealing?

2 How typical of sibling relationships do you think this situation is?

While there is concern about substance use and abuse among adolescents, it is important to note the following finding from the Australian Secondary Students' Alcohol and Drug Survey (AIHW 2008b p. 284):

> smoking prevalence among secondary students aged 12–17 years declined between 1999 and 2005 (AIHW 2007c) ... the use of illicit substances also declined or remained stable, with steady decreases in the proportion of students ever using marijuana/cannabis, inhalants, tranquilisers, amphetamine, hallucinogens and opiates.

While recent media campaigns have targeted alcohol use among young Australians, it is also important to note that:

> Results from the 1999, 2000 and 2005 surveys showed a significant decrease in the proportion of 12–17 year olds who had consumed alcohol (ever, in the last month or in the last week).

Rather than seeing substance abuse as an increasing social problem across the board within the Australian community, it is important to identify who uses substances at high-risk levels and why. For example, those young people who do drink tend to binge drink and consume dangerously high levels of alcohol. Targeted interventions may then be much more effective in reaching those most at risk in their substance use.

Homelessness

Some young people leave home throughout this stage of life because of intolerable circumstances within their family of origin—typically breakdown of family relationships, abuse and poverty. Many of these young people become homeless, an experience that places them at risk of mental and physical health problems. More than one third of the total 89,400 Australians who accessed the Supported Accommodation Assistance Program (SAAP), thirty-seven per cent, were aged twenty-four years and under, with thirteen per cent of this total group being under the age of eighteen (AIHW 2001). Table 10.1 shows the type of agency young homeless people approach for housing assistance. A key finding in these statistics is the high percentage of young women accessing domestic violence services for assistance with housing issues.

TABLE **10.1** Agencies approached by young homeless Australians, 2005–06

Client group (years)	Services for young people (%)	Services for single men only (%)	Services for single women only (%)	Services for families (%)	Services for women escaping domestic violence (%)	Cross-target, multiple/general services (%)	Total number
Male alone, under 25	59.6	13.5	—	1.1	0.5	25.3	19,700 (11% of total homeless population)
Female alone, under 25	59.5	0.2	3.8	1.7	14.0	20.8	22,400 (13% of total homeless population)

Source: AIHW 2007 p. 266

In the following example, Menka talks about her work within an intensive family preservation program, where homelessness may well become part of the eldest daughter's response to her family circumstances:

PRACTICE IN CONTEXT

WORKING WITH ADOLESCENTS AND THEIR FAMILIES

I was employed in an intensive family preservation program to provide aftercare services to a blended family comprising a biological mother, her three daughters and a stepfather. All three daughters, aged seven, nine and fifteen years, had been removed from their mother's care on numerous occasions due to chronic environmental neglect. The most recent notification concerned sexual abuse of the eldest daughter by a man who frequented the home as an acquaintance of the stepfather.

The mother was a gentle and friendly woman who spoke warmly to her children but was unable to discipline them and had lost parental authority. The stepfather appeared distracted by personal concerns, generally focused on financial difficulties and family-of-origin issues.

The family home had deteriorated to the extent that the two younger girls were unable to enter their bedroom due to debris and slept on mattresses on the parents' bedroom floor. They had drawn a large arrow on the wall at the entrance to the bedroom with the words 'sex in here' scrawled underneath. The kitchen and bathroom were extremely unhygienic; neighbours regularly complained about the accumulation of waste outside the house. The eldest girl assumed responsibility for her sisters' safety by insisting they remain within her bedroom until male guests left the home.

Questions:
1 What is your personal reaction to this situation?
2 What do you think are the particular developmental issues for the fifteen-year old girl? And the younger sisters?
3 What would you see as the important priorities for intervention in this situation?
4 What cultural dimensions do you think could be relevant?

Trauma

In Chapter 9, the traumatic impacts of sexual assault, natural disasters and war were examined, and they remain relevant issues to many adolescents' experiences also. The focus in this discussion is on physical trauma and injury, and suicidal behaviours. While not comprehensively addressing trauma in adolescence, these two experiences increase in prevalence throughout adolescence and are associated with lifelong outcomes. Sexual assaults continue throughout adolescence, but given their peak in early adulthood, the prevalence and impacts are considered in Chapter 11.

Trauma and risk

As highlighted earlier in this chapter, young men die at nearly double the rate of young women during this stage of life. A significant number of these deaths are through road trauma, with young males over-represented in the road trauma statistics. In many instances, younger drivers have a number of other occupants in the car, so the consequences affect many lives. Younger drivers are at increased risk of being involved in a car accident than older ones, due to less driver experience often coupled with higher risk-taking behaviour such as speeding (Catchpole et al. 1994). Street violence is also an ongoing issue, particularly for males. Road trauma and violence not only lead to death in many instances, but also to injury or lifelong disability. For some young males, this includes serious brain injury, leading to major physical, cognitive, social and relational losses.

These experiences can lead to grief reactions and trauma reactions. Studies tracking the impact of trauma on adolescents highlight that many of the factors that cause post-traumatic stress disorder responses in adults are similar for adolescents—in particular, the perceived threat to life and a sense of control over both the traumatic events themselves and/or their aftermath (Holbrook et al. 2005). However, adolescent trauma experiences are often the first occurrence in many young people's lives of such life-changing experiences—having a peer killed or injured in road trauma or violence can profoundly change risk-taking behaviour in the future. These traumas also significantly change family experiences and roles, at a time when young people are beginning to individuate from their family of origin. For young people who acquire severe disabilities, for example, it can mean that a renewed dependence on parents, often mothers, is created.

See Chapter 5 for an overview of trauma reactions.

Suicidal behaviour

Suicide is at one of its highest levels in early adulthood, although recent reports indicate that the previously high levels of youth suicide during the 1990s are reducing. While suicide may not be a common experience, when it does occur, its impact is profound—not only is a young person's life lost, but family and friends are affected for life. In the National Survey of Young Australians 2008, for example, 24 per cent of the sample of 45,558 young Australians (open to those aged eleven to twenty-four years) indicated that suicide was something that was of concern to them.

Many young people engage in suicidal and self-harming behaviours. In 2005, of the 1,309 deaths of young people in Australia, 32 per cent were from suicide (AIHW 2009b p. 282). For every completed suicide, there are an estimated three attempts for males and seventeen for females coming to the attention of hospital staff (Graham et al. 2000). This, of course, is likely to be a gross underestimation of the problem, as not everyone seeks medical attention. Males are more likely than females to commit suicide—partly to do with the means of suicide. Males tend to choose more violent and immediate means; females tend to use means that delay the effects and seek help in the meantime.

Some of the commonly identified risk factors throughout adolescence for suicidal behaviour are outlined below.

RISK FACTORS FOR ADOLESCENT SUICIDE

1 Living in a rural or remote area: The easier access to firearms; the socio-economic stressors of high unemployment and restricted choice of employment; and issues of sexual identity and limited social acceptance in small communities have been identified as risk factors.

2 Being unemployed: Morrell et al. (1993) found a correlation between the general suicide rates for men and periods of economic downturn—1912, 1930, 1962–67 and 1987.

3 Having a mental illness: Kosky and Goldney (1994) found that ninety per cent of those who had committed suicide had mental health issues.

4 Being Indigenous: The significant social obstacles faced by Indigenous young people lead to issues of opportunity, of discrimination and of reduced self-esteem.

5 Lacking a trusted adult: Particularly someone who is a role model, mentor or confidant.

6 Struggling with sexual identity: Some twenty-five per cent of suicides involve young males who were grappling with issues of homosexuality.

7 Suffering a recent loss: Inability to manage the extreme emotion of a relationship breakdown or a loss of an ideal can lead to suicide.

8 Previously attempting suicide: Those who have previously attempted suicide are estimated to be forty times more likely to suicide.

9 Being depressed: One key question is whether someone has to be depressed to be suicidal. Some people can be quite elated in the days before the suicide, having made the decision.

10 Being a survivor of physical or sexual abuse: Martin (1996) showed a clear association between history of childhood sexual abuse and increased likelihood of attempted suicides or repeated attempts.

11 Having low self-esteem.

In outlining these risk factors it is important to note that in many instances it is not possible to predict or identify suicidal behaviour. For some young people, suicide results from an impulsive action following overwhelming emotion—sometimes after receiving lower grades in an exam than expected, or the breakup of a relationship—

and there is no history of mental health difficulties. What constitutes significant loss for young people needs to be understood in developmental context.

Loss

Many young people are confronted with loss in their secondary school years—losses related to deaths of peers, family or others, and a wide range of other losses, including loss of a role, place or relationship. Adolescence is often when people first experience significant relationship loss (Toth et al. 2000), yet within peer networks, recognition is often not given to the intensity of grief experiences for young people. A breakup of a significant relationship, for example, can devastate the world of a young person, yet advice from peers and others is often to move on and focus on finding someone else. In addition, while social withdrawal is commonly identified as a reaction to loss, social participation expectations are high throughout adolescence. Young people can feel even more marginalised by the gap that can emerge between the expectations of their peers and others, and their own inner worlds.

Loss during adolescence co-occurs with the developmental tasks of searching for meaning and belonging in the world. With the expanded cognitive capacity for hypothetical and abstract thought, young people are often already exploring major existential issues. For some young people it can be very hard to cope with bringing a meaningful framework or narrative to what has occurred.

Promoting resilience

Adolescence is associated with the social, structural and cultural processes of individuation, identity formation and the transition to adult roles and responsibilities. However, these processes are complex, with some inherently contradictory messages arising within the structural and cultural dimensions. For this reason, researchers such as Wyn and Woodman propose that a generational perspective must be adopted to understand adolescent issues rather than what can become decontextualised developmental theories. They argue that notions such as Generation X and Generation Y 'disrupt the prevailing "youth as transition to adulthood" approach by asserting the nature of distinctive, defining experiences of successive generations of young people' (Wyn & Woodman 2006 p. 496). The structural and cultural contexts of adolescent experience are critical determinants of human experience, as they are for other lifespan stages.

Despite the many risk factors identified as part of the adolescent experience, it is a lifespan stage full of diverse experiences. Many protective factors have been identified as buffering the negative impact of these risks.

PROTECTIVE FACTORS THROUGHOUT ADOLESCENCE

» A positive self-concept

» An internal locus of control

» A more nurturant, responsible, achievement-oriented attitude towards life

» No prolonged separations during the first year of life (highlighting the importance of the early attachment period)

» A close bond with at least one caregiver from whom they received positive attention when they were infants

» Emotional support outside the family

» At least one, and usually several, close friends

» Participation in extracurricular activities: especially activities that were cooperative enterprises

» Constitutional factors (health and temperament characteristics): these were most important in infancy and early childhood but set the scene for later coping.

Source: Werner and Smith 1992

These protective factors arise within the context of supportive relationships, a sense of connectedness and prosocial experiences. They are also dependent upon structural resources—for example, easy access to health and mental health information and resources; and the availability of resources outside the home, such as in schools or in the casual and part-time workforce. Policies and laws—for instance, relating to drug and alcohol use, and driving—also shape the lives of young people. The adolescent experience is much more readily understood in the context of policy—education in particular, but also workforce, health and youth services policies. In Chapter 11, we will see that the pathways through these experiences continue to be influenced by the structural and cultural dimensions.

CHAPTER SUMMARY

In this chapter, we have looked at some of the key biopsychosocial-spiritual transitions associated with adolescence. While some of these transitions relate to biological processes associated with the onset of puberty, other transitions are related to the institutional and structural processes associated with the broader social and cultural context.

This discussion of adolescence highlights the effects of shifts taking place in other dimensions of experience. Many primary school children are engaging in tasks that were previously considered more the tasks of early adolescence, while simultaneously, adolescence seems to be extending further into stages of the lifespan that were previously considered adult phases, such as the twenties. This shortening of childhood and extending of the periods of adolescence and early adulthood reflect not only some of the significant changes in the biological dimension, but also changes within the structural and cultural dimensions.

APPLYING A MULTIDIMENSIONAL APPROACH

CASE STUDY

Hamed: Refugee student

Hamed Bah's story was published in *The Age* newspaper in December 2008. At the age of eighteen, he was living independently in Dandenong, studying for his Victorian Certificate of Education in 2009 and hoping to go to university to study accounting or business. He escaped from Sierra Leone at the age of six, after his parents and, some time later, his sister Mariam, were killed by rebels. He and his brother's girlfriend fled to Guinea on foot and on being joined by his brother, Ibrahim, lived in a 'one room shack in the ghetto' for nine years. In 2005 he arrived in Australia with his brother and his wife as refugees and without any English language skills. Other siblings survived the rebel attack but remain in Guinea. He supports them financially with his income from a fruit stall at Dandenong Market, where he works outside of school hours. As Johnston (2008 p. 3) reports, 'The new year, for Hamed Bah, is all about hope. Real hope. Sometimes lately he has even dared to think that the world is his, that he belongs in it. "I have a future" he says. "I can really say that now"'.

Li: Distress or despair?

Li has been starting to experiment with recreational drugs on the weekends. She spends hours on Facebook. She was incredibly humiliated recently when friends put up a photo of her when she was unconscious at a party. Everyone has been teasing her as a result, both online and in person at school. She is in Year 9. Her small group of friends have fluctuated between feeling guilty for setting her up like this and yet also pleased that she has seen how out of control she is when using. Luci is terrified her parents will find out about what has happened. She knows she will be grounded for weeks if they do. Her Chinese parents are already finding life in Australia hard and think that Luci's generation is just out of control compared to their adolescence back home.

Dave: Disability following injury

Dave was in Year 7, playing football during a lunch break with his friends at school. He went for a mark near the goal posts. He was accidently slammed into one of the posts as he fell backwards from his unsuccessful mark. He was knocked out and sustained a serious spinal injury. Three years later, he still experiences mild cognitive difficulties and behavioural problems as a result of the brain injury, but his spinal injury means he will never walk again. He still goes to the same school, with an integration aide. While all his friends surrounded him at the start of his rehabilitation, as time has gone on, they're finding the friendship hard to sustain. They feel their lives have moved in different directions. Dave is frustrated and lonely, and often expresses this through being verbally and physically aggressive. He wishes he had died in the accident.

Questions

1 What is your personal reaction to each of these situations?
2 What are key developmental risk and protective factors in each of the situations?
3 What are some possibilities for intervention using a multidimensional approach?

KEY TERMS

adolescence
depression
intimacy
prosocial
puberty
synthetic conventional faith

QUESTIONS AND DISCUSSION POINTS

1 What are some of the key biopsychosocial and spiritual developmental tasks of adolescence?
2 What are some of the different risk and protective factors across this lifespan stage?
3 What are some of the structural and cultural dimensions that influence this stage?
4 Reflecting on your experiences of adolescence, can you identify with the various transitions outlined in this chapter?
5 What social, structural and cultural changes have occurred that make your parents' experiences of these transitions different from your own?

FURTHER READING

Arnett, J. 2007, *Adolescence and emerging adulthood: A cultural approach*, Upper Saddle River: Pearson Education.
Prior, M., Sanson, A., Smart, D. & Oberklaid, F. 2001, *Pathways from infancy to adolescence: Australian Temperament Project 1983–2000*, Melbourne: Australian

Institute of Family Studies.

White, R. & Wyn, J. 2004, *Youth and society: Exploring the social dynamics of youth experience*, Melbourne: Oxford University Press.

Wyn, J. & Woodman, D. 2006, 'Generation, youth and social change in Australia', *Journal of Youth Studies*, 9(5), 495–514.

WEBSITES OF INTEREST

Australian Institute of Family Studies (AIFS): www.aifs.org.au
>The AIFS site provides extensive links to longitudinal studies of children within Australia, New Zealand, Europe and North America, including the Longitudinal Study of Australian Children.

Australian Research Alliance for Children and Youth (ARACY): www.aracy.org.au
>This site provides information and links about ARACY, which is a national collaboration of researchers, policy makers and practitioners that focuses on children's and young people's well-being.

Australian Research Centre in Sex, Health and Society: www.latrobe.edu.au/arcshs/
>This research centre's website has information relating to a wide range of Australian studies of sexuality and health.

Centre for Adolescent Health, Royal Children's Hospital, Melbourne: www.rch.org.au/cah/
>This Centre aims to improve the health and well-being of ten- to twenty-four-year olds. Both program and research links are accessible.

Early Psychosis Prevention and Intervention Centre (EPPIC): www.eppic.org.au
>This website has information about early psychosis, and the services available and research being conducted at EPPIC.

HealthInsite: www.healthinsite.gov.au
>This website is an Australian government initiative, enabling Australians to access current health information.

Jesuit Social Services, Strong Bonds: www.strongbonds.jss.org.au
>This site provides information about adolescence and related developmental issues.

Michael Ungar's website: http://michaelungar.ca
>Michael Ungar is Professor of Social Work at the School of Social Work, at Dalhousie University in Halifax, Canada. This website provides links to his resilience research and books on adolescent development.

Seattle Social Development Project: http://depts.washington.edu/ssdp/
> This site, from the University of Washington's School of Social Work, provides information about a long-term study of adolescent development and behaviour, focusing on both risk and resilience experiences.

Youth Beyond Blue: www.youthbeyondblue.com
> Youth Beyond Blue is a branch of Beyond Blue dedicated to depression and mental health issues for young people.

Youth Research Centre, University of Melbourne: www.edfac.unimelb.edu.au/yrc/
> Details of projects and publications, including by Wyn and White, are available on this site.

Early Adulthood

AIMS OF THIS CHAPTER

This chapter explores the developmental experiences of early adulthood. It considers the following questions.

» What are the biopsychosocial-spiritual developmental tasks and transitions of early adulthood?

» What are the experiences and impacts of stress, trauma and loss in early adulthood?

» How is resilience in early adulthood understood?

As with adolescence, the tasks and transitions of early and middle adulthood experiences have shifted in recent years in Western cultures. Some have proposed three different stages of adulthood in an attempt to focus on more unique specific developmental tasks. Hutchison (1999 p. 230), for example, proposes that 'provisional' adulthood occurs between eighteen and thirty, first adulthood between thirty and forty-five and second adulthood between forty-five and eighty-five. The term **early adulthood** is often seen as referring to people aged eighteen (post-secondary school) to thirty, or twenty to thirty, or even in some instances from twenty to forty. It depends on what criteria are used to assess development and change throughout this lifespan stage.

Another way of referring to early adulthood is as a stage of 'emergent adulthood' (Arnett 2000). This alludes to young people's transitions both practically and psychosocially. However, the terms 'provisional' or 'emergent' will not be used in this chapter as they imply that people within this significant age range—typically from eighteen or twenty through to the mid-thirties—are in waiting for 'proper' adulthood. This lifespan stage is only provisional or emergent in comparison with transitions that occurred during it in preceding generations. As Dwyer et al. (2003 p. 23) note:

> There is a reluctance to let go of established assumptions about what 'ought to be', and a failure to give due credit to a generation that knows it has grown up in a new kind of social environment and is making the necessary choices of coming to terms with it.

As this chapter outlines, today's transitions, tasks and challenges of early adulthood are unique in themselves and should not be seen, necessarily, as a preface to some later, fuller stage of adulthood. Given the pattern of increasing longevity in developed countries, and the range of other shifts (such as reproduction no longer governing sexuality, or employment opportunities not being mutually exclusive of pursuing higher education) the tasks, transitions and demands of this phase of life have shifted dramatically and will continue to do so. In one review of the changes in individual and family transitions, particularly as they affect early adulthood, McDonald and Evans (2003 p. 2) propose that another key reason why shifts have occurred in the timing of various tasks and transitions is 'the perception that young people must invest in human capital formation to a much greater degree than was the case in the past' (McDonald & Evans 2003 p. 2). That is, individual young people must resource themselves in new and extended ways. This chapter explores these transitions along with the biopsychosocial-spiritual developmental tasks now viewed as core to the early adulthood experience. It regards early adulthood as the years after secondary school through to the thirties, although as with the chapter on adolescence, some themes will be cross-cutting with both adolescence and middle adulthood.

Key developmental tasks and transitions

Biological dimensions

Weight and height, and nutrition

Consistent with other lifespan stages, an increasing number of young adults are overweight or obese in Australia. As the AIHW reports (2008b p. 284):

> Based on self-reported height and weight, 29% of young people aged 18–24 years were considered overweight or obese in 2004–05 (22% overweight, 7% obese). This is an increase from 1995, when 17% were considered overweight and 5% obese.

Another report noted that from 1995 to 2005, the prevalence of being obese or overweight has increased particularly for those in early adulthood, with the most marked increases being in those aged twenty-five to forty-four years and those aged seventy-five years and over (AIHW 2009a p. 160).

In part, this is due to many of the dietary issues outlined in earlier chapters. It is also due to the fact that many young people are leading sedentary lives, particularly those who are occupied in jobs or study that require long hours of sitting at a desk. The opportunities that were provided to them at school through sport programs are no longer available and physical activity and fitness needs to be sought out independently of formal structures of support.

Brain development

Our brains continue to develop in early adulthood. White matter continues to increase, and the volume of grey matter, after peak growth in adolescence, decreases (Bennett & Baird 2006). In an innovative study of young people transitioning from home to university environments, where major adaptations were required in all aspects of daily life, neuro-imaging studies found that the brain structures of young people continue to change. They concluded the changes in neural development 'may represent dynamic changes related to new environmental challenges' (Bennett & Baird 2006 p. 767). Rather than seeing the eighteen-year-old brain as the adult brain, Bennet and Baird propose that structural developments continue to occur into early adulthood and in the twenties in particular.

Sleep

Very little is known about sleep patterns throughout early adulthood, particularly when compared to earlier stages in the lifespan. Most adults require on average seven to nine hours sleep. Sleep patterns can change throughout early adulthood, as work, study and family commitments shift.

A major disruption to sleep in early adulthood is as a result of the birth of a baby. The first week following the birth of a baby is consistently found to be the most disrupted time for maternal sleeping. In a review of maternal sleep research from 1969 to 2008, Hunter, Rychnovsky and Yount (2009) confirmed that, for both mothers and fathers, sleep disruption can continue throughout the first six months post-birth, primarily due to the feeding and sleeping patterns of the baby. In some instances, maternal sleep disruption can be due to hormonal changes. While sleeping patterns usually balance out in the first year of life, some babies can remain unsettled well beyond this time due to health or mental health issues, requiring parents to attend to them several times throughout the night. Studies have shown that lack of sleep and the subsequent fatigue can then be linked to experiences of depression.

Sleep difficulties, as with earlier stages of the lifespan, are estimated to affect about ten per cent of the adult population. What shifts in adulthood are some of the strategies to deal with them. For example, one major study in the USA found that twenty-six per cent of their sample of 2181 eighteen to forty-five-year-olds used alcohol or medication to help them sleep. While the majority of those who used alcohol or medication did so for less than a week, six and nine per cent used alcohol or medication respectively for more than six months (Johnson et al. 1998).

Reproduction

While in adolescence males and females develop their reproductive capacity, it is typically in early adulthood that young women experience pregnancy and giving birth. Many women and men experience the role of parenting for the first time in this period. For some women, pregnancy and childbirth occur earlier, but we look at them in this chapter because the majority of Australian women give birth in early adulthood.

The average age of all women who gave birth rose from 27.9 years in 1991 to 29.8 years in 2005 (AIHW 2008b p. 266). Similarly, the average age of first-time mothers has risen, from 25.8 years in 1991 to 28. Most notably, 'the number of women over the age of thirty-five giving birth continues to increase' (AIHW 2008b p. 266). Not only has the average age increased, but the number of births has too. As reported by the ABS (2007a), the number of births registered in Australia in 2007 was the highest ever recorded. This has been attributed in part to the availability of the 'baby bonus'—the federal government scheme of a payment on the birth of a baby, which has been found to increase fertility rates (Drago et al. 2009).

BIRTHS IN AUSTRALIA, 2008

The Australian Bureau of Statistics noted the following fertility and birth trends:

» Australia's total fertility rate (TFR) in 2008 was 1.97 babies per woman, up from 1.92 babies per woman in 2007 and the highest since 1977 (2.01).
» The increase in the TFR between 2007 and 2008 was largely due to births to women aged 30 to 39 years, who accounted for 55% of the increase.
» At the national level, the teenage fertility rate in 2008 was 17.3 babies per 1,000 women aged 15-19 years, slightly higher than in 2007 (16.0 babies per 1,000 women).

Source: ABS 2009b

Many women, typically in couple relationships, have children by means of natural conception. Others seek increasingly accessible alternate ways of becoming a parent, such as IVF programs, now available not only to couples experiencing fertility problems but also to lesbian and/or single women, something that was previously legislated against. As noted in Chapter 7, adoptions no longer occur as frequently as they did in the past.

For those who have children, the task of adapting to parenthood is a major one, with many adaptations demanded of both the inner and outer worlds of parents.

Injury and disease

Late adolescence into early adulthood is often considered to be a peak physical period of the lifespan. Yet, as Eckersley, Wierenga and Wyn (2006 p. 7) note:

> Perceptions of young people's health and well-being vary greatly ... Young people are seen to be resilient, adaptable and doing well, and at the same time, experiencing increased rates of some important mental and physical health problems.

As with other age groups, the death rate among Australians decreased between 1997 and 2007. This still meant, though, that in 2007 some 2669 young men and 1187 women aged between twenty and thirty-nine died (ABS 2008). While a decrease overall occurred, young men continue to be more likely to die during early adulthood than young women, a phenomenon largely due to continued engagement in risk-taking behaviours, particularly on the roads. Intentional self-harm also remains a major concern throughout early adulthood.

The four most common causes of death for males and females are outlined in Table 11.1.

TABLE **11.1** Causes of death, 2007

	Cause of death	% of overall causes of death for the sex and age group
Males aged 25–34 years	Intentional self-harm	24.9
	Land transport accidents	17.9
	Accidental poisoning	11.1
	Coronary heart disease	2.9
Females aged 25–34 years	Intentional self-harm	14.4
	Land transport accidents	11.2
	Accidental poisoning	7.7
	Breast cancer	5.5

Source: AIHW 2009a p. 291

Overall, the majority of young people assess their health status as being good or excellent, according to national health surveys (AIHW 2009a p. 286). For twenty-five- to thirty-four-year-olds, the most commonly reported long-term health conditions experienced are short-sightedness (22.3 per cent), hayfever (22 per cent), back pain or disc problems (15.3 per cent), asthma (10.7 per cent) and migraine (10.4 per cent). Throughout early adulthood, the onset of some physical difficulties and diseases can occur although often no change in function is experienced.

One of the significant health threats experienced is the abuse of alcohol and drugs, with alcohol and drug use disorders reaching their peak in this age group. Later in this chapter we explore some of the implications for social and physical well-being.

Psychosocial-spiritual dimensions

Major transitions in early adulthood relate to psychosocial-spiritual developments: transitions through work and education, negotiating continuing relationships with one's family of origin and friends, and building new relationships and partnerships. By the end of early adulthood, many people have entered into parenting relationships themselves, by having children of their own. In this section, we explore these transitions in terms of cognitive, personality and emotional development.

Cognitive development

Throughout early adulthood, most people continue to develop their cognitive skills, in relation to verbal meaning, spatial orientation, inductive reasons, number and word fluency. These capacities enable more complexity of understanding and tasking, so that people are able to multitask—maintaining a home, relationships, jobs and increased responsibility from adolescence. Studies have shown that there are cognitive gains until the late thirties or early forties in all of these cognitive processes (Demetriou & Bakracevic 2009 p. 182).

Personality development

Many researchers have advocated for a relatively fixed experience of personality traits by the age of thirty years (McCrae et al. 2000). Within the five-factor model, declines are typically reported in relation to neuroticism, extraversion and openness to experience, and increases in agreeableness and conscientiousness. Positive personality traits continue to have a positive impact on development in early adulthood. This interconnectedness of psychosocial dimensions is reflected in the following statement from the Australian Temperament Study:

> The young person who is developing well is taking on norms of trust and tolerance at both an individual level and in relation to institutions, is to a lesser extent

engaged and active in civic and social groups, is attaining social competence, and is experiencing satisfaction with life. (Hawkins et al. 2009 p. 97)

In international studies, tolerance, or high self-control, seems similarly to be a key protective factor, enabling the reciprocal use of social resources and networks (Pulkkinen et al. 2005).

Emotional development

As discussed in Chapter 10, Erikson identified the development of a capacity for intimacy as the psychosocial task of late adolescence and early adulthood. Vaillant (2003 p. 1378) describes the successful achievement of this task of **intimacy** as permitting an individual 'to become reciprocally, and not narcissistically, involved with a partner'. Described this way, the capacity for intimacy underpins many of the transitions of young adults, as they negotiate new social roles within families, their studies and/or workplaces, and their relationships with colleagues, peers and those with whom they share deeply intimate and personal relationships.

Underpinning this emotional development is the continuing process of identity formation. Much of the focus on understanding early adulthood has been on the development of a sense of identity as an adult. This is because in previous generations, an adult identity was seen to be synonymous with four key role transitions—finishing education, entering the workforce, marriage and parenthood (Arnett 1997).

Identity formation is explored in Chapter 10.

This idea was challenged by a relatively small study conducted by Arnett in the USA, with the findings replicated in Australian studies (Wyn & White 1997). Arnett surveyed 346 college students aged eighteen to twenty-one, and 140 people aged twenty-one to twenty-eight years. It found that the key criteria indicating the successful transition to adulthood related to 'generally intangible, gradual, psychological and individualistic' (Arnett 1997) criteria, rather than the four key role transitions mentioned above. The following three criteria were identified instead:

» 'accept responsibility for your own actions'
'» decide on own beliefs and values independently of parents or other influences'
» and 'establish a relationship with parents as an equal adult'.

Thus, the most commonly endorsed criteria for being an adult focused on aspects of individualism (Noller et al. 2001 p. 81). Some propose that this focus has emerged because young people now 'have an extended period of time to explore and try on various possible selves' (Nelson & Barry 2005 p. 246). The focus on these more intangible, gradual, psychological and individualistic aspects of emotional development is seen to be related to the shift in what young people are doing in their working, studying and partnering.

This immediately raises questions as to how these criteria may be culturally specific. Aboriginal author Clark (2000), for example, has noted that Indigenous identity formation follows different steps from identity formation by non-Aboriginal people, given what is often a personal history of colonisation, separation and trauma.

For many, a sense of generativity (the sense of investing in future generations) also begins to emerge, particularly through the transition to parenting that many experience later in early adulthood.

We explore generativity in Chapter 12.

Relational development

For young adults, significant relationships continue with members of their family of origin and their peers. New relationships are formed with partners and, for many, with their own children. Workplaces also become major social contexts.

Parents

One of the demographic shifts that has occurred in the past twenty years is the increase in the number of young adults who continue to live with their parents in the family home. A recent report by the Australian Bureau of Statistics (2009a p. 24) noted that 'In 2006, almost one in four (23%) people aged 20–34 years were living at home with their parents compared with 19% in 1986'. This demographic shift means that families are staying together in close proximity for longer periods of time than in previous generations.

As within many cultures, the family of origin therefore continues to be core to young people's lives, as an emotional and financial base. With adolescence seen as the time of individuating from parents, early adulthood is typically seen as a time when adult children enter into more equal relationships with their parents. While this is assumed to be the transition, Australian research about the shifts that typically occur within these relationships is scarce. One recent study to shed some light on what is occurring is the Australian Temperament Project (ATP), in which 1000 young people aged twenty-three to twenty-four years of age and 968 parents reported on their perceptions of interdependence during this stage of life (Vassallo et al. 2009). The study highlighted some important issues. For example, adult children were more likely to see themselves as relying on their parents for emotional support (88 per cent) than parents were (70 per cent). Nearly two-thirds of parents (63 per cent) continued to provide financial or material support to their adult children (Vassallo et al. 2009 p. 11). Financial and material support tended to be provided more commonly when adult children were still living at home with their parents.

The lengthening of time that young people are living with their parents is due to a number of different factors, including major shifts in the age at which many people get married, the way in which people engage in tertiary study, and rental and financial difficulties. Moving in and out of the family of origin's home is also a common pattern. These transitions occur because of financial crises and the need to rely back on parents for financial support; housing crises due to fluctuations in student housing and a tight rental market; and relationship crises (Kilmartin 2000). Ethnicity also plays a part in these transitions, as the study found that Vietnamese young adults were significantly more likely to remain living with parents for longer periods of time. Another factor may well be relational, in that young men were more likely to live with their parents. Table 11.2 shows some of these transitions in and out of the family home between 2006 and 2007 across the age range of early adulthood.

TABLE **11.2** Transitions in and out of the family home, 2006–07

	Age group (years)			
	20–24 %	25–29 %	30–34 %	20–34 %
Has never left home	34.9	7.8	3.0	15.6
Left home and has returned	12.3	9.0	5.2	8.9
Total lives with parents	47.2	16.8	8.2	24.5
Left home and has not returned	37.2	49.5	55.4	47.2
Left home and returned at least once	12.4	26.5	27.3	21.9
Has never left home, but lives separately from parents	3.2	7.3	9.1	6.5
Total does not live with parents	52.8	83.3	91.8	75.6
	'000	'000	'000	'000
Total persons	1,495.3	1,389.6	1,433.5	4,318.5

Source: ABS 2009a p. 25

Late adolescence or early adulthood is often a time when parents divorce. This has been associated with pathways of financial hardship for the divorcing parents, particularly given that most children continue to live with their mother. Some research has highlighted that young people often stay home to support this situation, particularly to support the mother who typically has lower earning capacity and lower labour force participation than the father (Kilmartin 2000).

Siblings

Within the family of origin are also the continuing sibling relationships, although as young people move out into independent living situations, there is often not as much connection as in previous or in future years. Siblings can draw on the support of parents without having to have contact with siblings necessarily.

Typologies of sibling relationships across the lifespan typically distinguish the relative qualities of warmth, conflict and rivalry. In one study of sibling relationships in early adulthood (Stewart et al. 1998), evidence was found of the three dominant typologies described by Murphy (1993) as typical of childhood—the caretaker, buddy and casual types. As described in Chapter 9, the caretaker type refers to a sibling who assumes a parental and authoritative role with a sibling; the buddy type refers to siblings who relate as equals and as collaborators against parents, and the casual type refers to a sibling who assumes a relatively aloof and unfocused relationship with a younger sibling. These relationships were found in a sample of eighteen to fifty-five year olds, a diverse group, and thus reflecting the diversity of relationship types. A fourth type was also identified, described as loyal, where a sibling relationship is seen as part of a broader kinship commitment rather than as anything particularly warm or close within the two-person relationship. In this study, the participants who identified as having loyal sibling relationships tended to describe them in fairly 'tepid' terms (Stewart et al. 1998 p. 73).

Peers

With young people transitioning out of the family home often into shared households or residential colleges, rather than into marriages, as occurred in previous generations, one of the shifts is an increased connection with and reliance on peer networks throughout early adulthood. Peers in workplaces, or universities, become key emotional and practical supports. Watters (2003) wrote about this as the phenomenon of young people living in 'urban tribes'. Reflecting on his own experience, he states:

> Like myself, my friends were all leading busy and upbeat postcollege/prefamily lives. They lived alone or with roommates and worked along in their careers. In their love lives, they suffered through two-year cycles that went from singleness to crush to relationship to heartbreak and back to singleness. We absolved ourselves from these failures by believing that we just hadn't met the right person. (Watters 2003 p. 18)

His summary raises critical questions about the quest for happiness and fulfilment in early adulthood, the managing of multiple transitions over many years and the increased reliance on peer networks as the stable base for relationships.

Rather than see 'failures' in these shifts, the trend of the current generation is to engage differently with friends, housemates, work peers and community groups as the focus of social activities, rather than necessarily a reliance on partnership as the core of this social interaction. Online social networks, of course, have widened the opportunity for these peer networks to be maintained, over and above geographical location.

Partners

Throughout adolescence and early adulthood, young people typically experience multiple close, typically sexual, relationships. What is very difficult to establish is a clear understanding of the patterns and nature of these relationships, whether heterosexual or homosexual.

While marriage is not off the agenda for many young people in Australia, studies conducted by the Australian Institute of Family Studies, for example, show that it is no longer a transition that takes place in the early twenties for many of them. For example, Kilmartin (2000 p. 36) found, in the Young Adult's Aspirations Study conducted by the Australian Institute of Family Studies in 1998 with 580 adults aged twenty to twenty-nine, that sixty per cent were married by their late twenties and a further twenty per cent thought they 'were likely to marry in the next two years'. For those who do marry, living circumstances prior to marriage have also changed. Seventy-three per cent of couples are now choosing to live together before marriage compared with thirty per cent some twenty years ago.

According to the ABS (2009d), 'In 2008, the median age for first-time marriage was 29.6 years for men and 27.7 years for women, compared to 26.3 years and 24.2 years respectively in 1989'. With over 118,000 marriages and 47,000 divorces registered in 2008, there is a trend overall for an increase in marriage from 2007, and a decrease in the divorce rate. Just under two-thirds (sixty-two per cent) of women were under the age of forty-five at the time of divorce, whereas only fifty-two per cent of men were under this age (ABS 2009d). Thus, marriage and divorce under the age of forty-five happen more commonly for women than for men, making divorce a transition that occurs in early to middle adulthood for women, compared to men experiencing this more commonly in mid-life. Just under half of these divorces involved children under the age of eighteen.

Each of these partnership beginnings and endings involves the formation of new, and often multiple, relationships with other people—the family of origin and friends of each partner. Partnering is influenced by cultural, religious and familial expectations and norms. Within some cultural groups in Australia, pressure is exerted on young people to establish same-cultural partnerships and marriages such as within orthodox Jewish, Christian and Muslim communities. Other cultural groups are undergoing significant changes, as intercultural marriages extend into multicultural partnerships and families. For example, more marriages occur now between Indigenous and non-Indigenous adults than between Indigenous adults (Heard et al. 2009).

Parenting

Throughout the early 2000s, concern was expressed about the declining and low fertility rates, with the population reaching zero growth through births. The prevailing view was that this generation of young adults was not as interested in having children. Research shows, however, that aspirations towards parenting are strong. As Table 11.3 highlights, these aspirations shift according to age, and no doubt, relational and environmental circumstances. What is interesting to note is the consistently higher percentage of males who wish to have children than females.

TABLE **11.3** Men's and women's aspirations to have children

	Planning to have children?	20–24 years (%)	25–29 years (%)	30–34 years (%)	Total (%)
Females	Definitely not	2.5	2.1	10.0	6.6
	Probably not	5.1	2.1	8.0	5.3
	Ambivalent	11.9	11.3	8.0	11.4
	Probably want	23.7	22.0	22.0	22.2
	Very much want	56.8	62.4	52.0	54.5
Males	Definitely not	3.4	4.3	9.0	6.8
	Probably not	4.2	3.5	4.0	5.1
	Ambivalent	11.0	6.4	18.0	11.4
	Probably want	15.3	16.3	11.0	14.1
	Very much want	66.1	69.5	58.0	62.6

Source: HILDA (2001, cited in de Vaus 2004 p. 19)

In 2007, the most births ever in Australian history were recorded. This shift has highlighted that fertility rates change according to specific relational, social, structural and cultural contexts. People make the decision to have a baby for many different reasons. For many, having children is part of a plan within the context of their relationship with another person. Another factor is clearly the financial one, as the federal government's baby bonus payment was found to have a positive impact on fertility rates (Drago et al. 2009). For other people, pregnancies may not be planned at all, and the decision whether to continue with the pregnancy or not is influenced by many relational, social and cultural dimensions.

As noted earlier in this chapter, significant shifts have taken place in patterns of having children. As de Vaus (2004 p. 197) notes, in 1986, forty per cent of women aged twenty-four to twenty-nine had not had a child, but by 2001, fifty-six per cent of women in this age group had not had a child. About one in every four of Australia's women is making a choice not to have children, and the number is increasing. The reasons for not having children are complex, raising important questions about choice and circumstances for both women and men in relation to reproduction. For some women, it has been related to waiting for the right partner and not finding them, and thus losing the option of becoming a parent, or about career expectations, both leading to 'circumstantial childlessness' (Cannold 2000, 2005). For some couples, infertility or pregnancy loss prevent them from being parents. Later in this chapter we explore the experience of grief for some women and men who are unable to have children. For other women, though, it has been about not wanting to have children and being able to exercise that wish both through contraception and through increasing social recognition that not every woman wishes to have a baby.

Attachment theory is described in Chapter 7.

The experience of becoming a parent is profoundly influenced by many factors, both past and present. Attachment theory studies have shown a remarkably high correlation between the attachment style of the mother pre-birth, and both the anticipated and actual attachment style with their baby (Fonagy et al. 1991). The birth itself has been found to have an impact on the bonding that occurs between mothers and their babies, with some women experiencing post-traumatic stress disorder as a result of their birthing experience and subsequent difficulties in bonding with their infant. Up to fifteen per cent of women experience post-natal depression (NHMRC 2006). Some mothers are able to breastfeed easily, with this experience often building a strong sense of intimacy, leading to both physical and emotional well-being. For other mothers, the experience is stressful and painful, and coloured by the strong social expectations that women should breastfeed. Underpinning all these direct relationships, too, is the quality of the relationship between the parents, along with the availability of resources within the wider environment.

In Chapter 7, Melissa, a social worker in her thirties, introduced her daughter, Isabel. In the following scenario, she reflects on her own transition to motherhood and some of the key factors that influenced her adaptation throughout this time.

PRACTICE IN CONTEXT

REFLECTING ON MATERNAL SUPPORTS

Melissa reflects on her transitions.

During the first two years you, the mother, and your baby have pretty regular contact with a Maternal and Child Health Centre nurse close to your home. For me this was Faye, who visited us at home when Isabel was two weeks old, and whom I then visited at the centre with Isabel for her check-ups at four weeks, eight weeks, three months, four months, six months, eight months and ten months.

There was a different nurse at the centre for Isabel's check-ups at twelve months, fifteen months and eighteen months. Even though I was a well-read and confident parent overall, I felt an acute sense of loss and a moderate sense of panic at the departure of Faye: she had known us all along and was knowledgeable about child development, pragmatic, and perceptive in her questioning. She was reassuring when I worried about Isabel, at six months, falling from the fiftieth percentile to the twentieth in length and from the fifteenth percentile to the fifth in weight (it was months and months later that I learnt these charts are based on formula-fed American infants from the 1970s). She knew about and shared my pride in Isabel's rapid development in areas other than size: her early gross motor development, vision and fine motor skills, language and speech, and social behaviour and play.

While many people keep in active contact with members from their Mothers' Support Group after the six weeks of information-based sessions are over I did not. I found the constant comparisons made between the babies somewhat competitive and a wearying experience. However, the loss of a single, reliable support outside my household, someone who was professional and therefore more objective, was indeed missed.

Questions

1 What is your personal reaction to this situation Melissa describes?
2 How typical do you think Melissa's experiences are of the transition to motherhood?
3 What is your experience and knowledge of these transitions?

Gender and sexual identity

As noted by Montgomery (2005 p. 348), 'One of the most striking differences between young adolescents and emerging adults is in the place of romantic relationships in their lives'. In her study of adolescents and 'emerging adults', she found that as people moved into their twenties, they were less likely to idealise romantic relationships than younger adolescents, and more likely to be seeking commitment within these relationships. Given the lack of accessible research populations, apart from through research with university students, it is very difficult to understand the diversity of intimate relationship experiences of young adults.

For many young people, sexual identities continue to shift in response to relationships, opportunities and the broader social and cultural dimensions that permit or inhibit sexual experiences. In one longitudinal New Zealand study, participants at age twenty-one and twenty-six years were asked about their sexual attractions and experiences (Dickson et al. 2003). Some key findings were that the majority of participants, both male and female, 'had only ever been sexually attracted to the opposite sex' (Dickson et al. 2003 p. 1609). However, women were more likely than men to have been same-sex attracted (24.5 per cent compared with 10.7 per cent) at some point in time in their lives, and were more likely to be at the age of twenty-six (16.4 per cent compared with 5.6 per cent). That is, as women age, they are more likely than men to be same-sex attracted.

Moral and/or spiritual development

While Australia's young adults are identified as among the least religious of young people in the Western world, census data have highlighted that twenty-three of women and sixteen per cent of young men aged eighteen to twenty-four years had participated in church or religious activities (ABS 2006b. According to Fowler and Dell's faith development framework, young people can engage in three different stages of adult faith experience. Table 11.4 provides an overview of the key indicators of each of these stages.

TABLE **11.4** Faith development in adulthood

	Key indicators of each of the 'stages' of faith development
Individuative-reflective faith	An ability to reflect critically on previously held values, beliefs and commitments A development of 'self-identity and self-worth capable of independent judgment'
Conjunctive faith	An ability to recognise that 'truths of all kinds can be approached from multiple perspectives' An interest in deepening understanding of other faith traditions in order to enhance their own
Universalising faith	A concern about 'creation and being as a whole'

Source: Fowler and Dell 2006 p. 41

Occupational identity

From the Life Patterns Study, a longitudinal study of some two thousand young people who left school in 1991, only a third of participants could be said to have taken a 'linear' pathway through education and training and into work (Dwyer & Wyn 2001).

For most Australians, non-linear pathways between education and work occur. In the current structural and cultural context, completing secondary school, and usually tertiary educational pathways, is essential to economic security. However, schools themselves are linked with and arguably determinative of these pathways, creating structural inequalities within education and within the broader social context in which young people are living (Teese & Polesel 2003). The push for higher completion rates of secondary school education is primarily related to an economic agenda, as stated in the federal government's *Education Revolution* policy:

School attainment is positively linked to higher levels of employment and labour force participation; lower unemployment; labour force re-entry; higher wages; and higher levels of productivity. (Department of Education, Employment and Workplace Relations 2008 p. 6)

The report cites Access Economics research that directly links completion of Year 12 with employment rates. Tertiary education is similarly linked with employment options, reflected in the 2.9 and 1.3 percentage point difference in employment rates for men and women with no post-school qualification. Secondary school completion is linked not only with an economic objective, but also with a social one:

Societies with a strong commitment to education enjoy higher levels of civic participation, greater social cohesion, lower levels of crime and disadvantage, and a more trusting, equitable and just society. (Department of Education, Employment and Workplace Relations 2009 p. 2)

Students in remote Australia experience educational lags of up to one-and-a-half years compared to their urban peers, thus Indigenous educational experiences are particularly identified as needing attention and redress. Many young people who disengage with secondary school do so because of poverty, family violence and lack of engagement within a relevant curriculum.

Post-secondary school, more young Australians are continuing to study until well into their twenties, with a recent study finding that only sixty-six per cent of twenty-five-year-olds were working in full-time employment. At this age of twenty-five, many were in casual employment, unrelated to their career of choice, in the retail, food and service sectors (Wyn & White 1997). While many young people undertake tertiary study in their late teens and early twenties, 'by the time people reach their late twenties and early thirties, those working full-time were even less likely to be studying (89% of full-time employed 25–34 year olds were not studying' (ABS 2005a).

Young people today face the challenges of a casualised workplace and increasing pressure to have tertiary qualifications in order to be employed in many positions that previously would not have required such qualifications. For many young people, this suits the Generation Y tendencies to live more in the 'here and now' and move from opportunity to opportunity on their own terms. For others, this creates instability and exploitation in a constantly fragile, shifting market. Table 11.5 highlights some of the shifts that have occurred in recent decades in relation to workforce participation for those aged twenty to twenty-four years.

TABLE **11.5** Australian social trends

	1983	2003
	20–24 years (%)	20–24 years (%)
Labour force participation	80.2	79.1
Unemployment	14.7	8.7
Employed full time	89	66.9
Employed part time	11	33.1

Source: ABS 2005a

Employment provides financial security and independence. In many instances, but by no means all, it also provides a social network, a sense of identity and a source of self-esteem.

Coping with risks and adversities

According to the Australian Temperament Study, 'over 80 per cent of young people were satisfied with their lives, including lifestyle, work or study, relationships with parents and friends, accomplishments and self-perceptions' (Eckersley et al. 2006 p. 14). While this indicates that for many young people, early adulthood is a positive, rewarding time, it is not without its own unique pressures. Thus, Eckersley et al. also found that '50 per cent were experiencing one or more problems associated with depression, anxiety, antisocial behaviour and alcohol use' (2006 p. 14). In the following pages, we explore some of the unique stressors, traumas and griefs experienced during this lifespan stage.

Stress

Coping with choice

After secondary school, many young people experience the freedom to travel, work and relate relatively free of other commitments. For many, but certainly not all, in early adulthood in Western cultures, stress experiences arise as a result of having so many choices and having to negotiate a sense that there is a right way to do things, in terms of education, employment and family, in particular. Given that there are multiple pathways through education, employment and partnering, it is up to the individual to navigate their own pathway and thus when things do not work out, such as in relationship, housing or employment arrangements, there may be fewer safety nets and more room for a domino effect of stressors to emerge. For example, while the casualisation of the workforce brings flexibility of hours, it also comes without provision for sick and annual leave. Illness experiences can lead to loss of employment, whereas this typically does not occur in a more protected employment context. Problems can tend to be seen as individual problems rather than as systemic, structural problems

Parenting

The birth of a child, especially the first, is a powerful turning point in adult identity, although often a high stress period in relationships. It involves multiple adaptations within a family, and the establishment of a relationship with a new baby. It involves managing shifting relationships with other extended family members such as grandparents, aunts, uncles and cousins. It typically involves a shift in peer relationships, particularly when peers may not have children themselves. While the initial adaptation typically occurs after the first few months (Schmidt Neven 1990), many people report that parenting involves constant adaptation, both to the child or children and between parents. Relationships change fundamentally as a result of having children, and as explored in Chapters 7 and 8, are also affected by the goodness of fit between parents and child.

For parents with a child with an illness or disability, the difference between the fantasy of parenting and the reality can be stark. The emotional, social, financial and practical implications of caring for a child with a disability or a chronic illness present unique and often exhausting challenges.

Many parents report that one of the complexities of becoming a parent is managing the strong social and cultural expectations. New parents frequently cite one of the major stressors as managing the advice they receive from everyone around them as to how to parent properly. The parental 'blame game' can exert enormous influence on parents' self-esteem and sense of competence as parents (Chodorow 1999).

Later in this chapter we explore some of the impacts of the death of a child on parents.

PRACTICE IN CONTEXT

BECOMING A PARENT

Menka describes the situation of a mother with whom she worked who is making the transition again to being a parent.

A referral from a specialist alcohol and other drug service was received by the agency for a thirty-year-old mother with a significant history of poly-drug use, incarceration and homelessness, who had recently delivered a premature infant. Completion of a genogram with the mother revealed intergenerational substance-abuse, loss of children to parental care, family violence and incarceration. Constant friction between family members occasionally escalated into violence with little resolution of problems. The family was close in terms of proximity and emotional connection and largely isolated from the wider community. All were unemployed and the generations socialised together with a small number of neighbours.

Questions

1 What is your personal reaction to this situation?
2 What do you see as the key issues for this mother in her transition to parenting?
3 What do you see as the risk and protective factors, using a multidimensional approach?

Mental health problems

As noted earlier, Australia's young people report high levels of mental health difficulty. In part this is due to the fact that many adult mental health disorders have their onset, and also their peak, in late adolescence and early adulthood. According to Slade et al. (2009 p. 599), 'The prevalence of 12 month mental disorders was highest in young adults aged 16–24 and declined with age'.

According to the 2007 *National Survey of Mental Health and Well-being* (Slade et al. 2009), the most recent survey of some 8,841 Australians, one in every sixteen people in Australia, about six per cent of the population, will have experienced an affective disorder, either clinical depression or bipolar mood disorder in the past twelve months. The DSM-IV diagnostic criteria (*The Diagnostic and Statistical Manual of Mental Disorders IV-TR*, American Psychiatric Association 2000) for a major depressive episode are that a person must experience five or more symptoms (including number 1 or 2) within a two-week period, 'causing clinically significant distress or impairment in social, occupational or other important areas of functioning' (APA 2000 p. 356). Young Australian women were more likely to experience affective disorders than men. The symptoms are outlined below.

DIAGNOSTIC SYMPTOMS OF MAJOR DEPRESSIVE EPISODES

1 Depressed mood most of the day, nearly every day
2 Markedly diminished interest in pleasure in all, or almost all, most of the day nearly every day
3 Significant weight loss when not dieting, or weight gain
4 Insomnia or hypersomnia (excessive sleeping) nearly every day
5 Psychomotor retardation (physical slowing) or agitation nearly every day
6 Fatigue or loss of energy every day

7   Feelings of worthlessness or excessive or inappropriate guilt

8   Diminished ability to think or concentrate, or indecisiveness, nearly every day

9   Recurrent thoughts of death (not just fear of dying), recurrent suicidal ideation without a specific plan, or a suicide attempt or a specific plan for committing suicide.

Source: APA 2000 p. 356

According to the 2007 *National Survey of Mental Health and Well-being* (Slade et al. 2009 p. 599), one in seven people, or fourteen per cent of the Australian population, will have experienced an anxiety disorder in the past twelve months. Anxiety manifests itself in a range of physical, cognitive, emotional, behavioural and social symptoms, such as insomnia, lack of energy, difficulties breathing, difficulties correctly interpreting situations and solving problems, excessive worry, feelings of helplessness, and hypervigilance, often resulting in isolation and poverty. The DSM-IV identifies many different forms of anxiety, including:

» generalised anxiety disorder—'characterised by at least 6 months of persistent and excessive anxiety and worry' (APA 2000 p. 429).

» agoraphobia

» panic disorder (with or without agoraphobia)

» specific phobia

» social anxiety disorder (or social phobia)

» obsessive compulsive disorder.

In Chapter 5, we explore post-traumatic stress disorder and acute stress disorder.

The risk factors for anxiety are a complex interaction of genetic and environmental risk factors, including disturbances of brain chemistry, personality traits, learnt behaviours, early life adversity and stressful events. Females are more likely to report a higher prevalence of anxiety orders, particularly in relation to social phobia, generalised anxiety disorder and post-traumatic stress disorder.

While the spotlight around binge drinking and recreational drug use has been on adolescents, research suggests that the group most at risk of substance use disorders is sixteen- to twenty-four-year-old males. Men overall have a higher prevalence rate than women. Five per cent of the population is estimated to have had a substance use disorder in the past twelve months, and 24.7 per cent are estimated to experience it at some point in their lifetime.

The *2007 National Survey of Mental Health and Well-being* (Slade et al. 2009 p. 601) also found that younger people, particularly young men aged sixteen to twenty-four years were very unlikely to seek help (13.2 per cent) from a mental health service or health professional. Yet these young men were experiencing a relatively high prevalence of mental disorders (22.8 per cent in this age group).

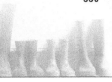

PRACTICE IN CONTEXT

WORKING WITH EARLY ADULTHOOD ISSUES

Lenice, a social worker within a mental health service, describes the situation of Andrew, a young man with whom she worked who is perhaps typical of this trend.

Andrew, a twenty-three-year-old man, lives at home with his parents and elder sister in an Australian city. On referral to a mental health service, he reported symptoms of anxiety and depression co-morbid with an opiate dependence. Andrew started using heroin when he was thirteen years old, with his sister and a group of peers at school. Andrew used over a ten-year period and gradually withdrew from school and jobs to become involved in crime. The lifestyle Andrew led had an impact on his ability to undertake and sustain protective developmental tasks during adolescence in areas of education, work and relationships. Andrew reported constant worry and self-criticism, often leading him to feel overwhelmed and out of control. Andrew has memories of early sensitivity to loss, uncertainty and abandonment from as early as four years. Andrew recalled the death of his grandfather as a significant loss in his late childhood. He reported dreaming about his grandfather and experiencing unresolved grief in times of stress. Family members have a history of mental illness, indicating a genetic predisposition. Both parents are second-generation European migrants to Australia. Andrew characterised his family relationships as protective, but at times critical.

Questions

1 What is your personal reaction to this situation?
2 What do you think are key developmental risk and protective factors?
3 What do you think are the possibilities for intervention, using a multidimensional approach?

Stress characterises all these mental health issues, both in the lived experience of them but also in the often devastating impact they have on young people's lives. Depression and anxiety can prevent people from engaging in social relationships, intimate relationships and employment. Accessing support, psychosocial and medical interventions can greatly minimise the negative impacts of these experiences.

Trauma

Some of the traumas most commonly experienced throughout early adulthood continue to be the ones experienced in adolescence—suicidal behaviour and road trauma, for example. Early adulthood brings some other traumas, and we consider here the traumas of interpersonal violence, specifically sexual assault, and traumatic births.

According to the Personal Safety Survey (ABS 2006a):

> just under one-third (31%) of those who experienced sexual assault were aged between 25–34 years old. The most likely perpetrators of sexual assault were family members or friends (39% for women and 44% for men).

The impact of sexual assault is profound—with many survivors experiencing traumatic stress and other mental health issues. While the experience can be understood broadly using a gendered analysis of power and violence, for individuals affected by such traumas, the experience is deeply personal and often violates a sense of safety and control. Suicidal behaviours and eating disorders are often reported as longer-term impacts of sexual violence experienced by both young men and women in adolescence and early adulthood (Ackard & Neumark-Sztainer 2002).

While violence is recognised as having negative mental health impacts, particularly traumatic ones, birth experiences are typically constructed as positive experiences. In many cases, this is true. However, studies of birth experiences have highlighted that for two per cent of women giving birth is a highly traumatic experience, leading to post-traumatic stress disorder. A British qualitative study of twenty-five women who developed post-traumatic stress disorder during or after the traumatic birth (matched with twenty-five women who did not have traumatic births), found that women with more trauma symptoms 'reported more panic, anger, thoughts of death, mental defeat, and dissociation during birth' (Ayers 2007 p. 253). As Ayers, Harris, Sawyer, Parfitt and Ford (2009) note, while birth experiences are different from many other traumas in that they are typically voluntary experiences with a positive outcome, aspects of the birth experience overwhelm a woman's control over her own body and what is done to it during the birthing process, leading to a loss of control and a sense of a threat to life, two factors often associated with the onset of post-traumatic stress disorder.

Loss

Loss experiences during early adulthood relate to many of the social roles and relationships discussed throughout this chapter—the loss of significant relationships and the loss through death of parents, partners, friends, colleagues or their own children. In this chapter, we focus on the grief associated with relationship loss and with a child's death. While many in early adulthood experience the death of parents and friends, this is more typically a mid-life experience, and so we explore these losses in Chapter 12.

Throughout early adulthood, young people often experience multiple, significant intimate relationships. Some of these relationships bring significant and sudden losses when they end. Some have suggested that young adults' grief experiences tend to be minimised or disenfranchised (Harvey & Miller 2000). It is interesting to reflect on why this phenomenon occurs; it may be shaped by strong cultural expectations of 'getting over' grief and moving on at this point in the lifespan.

There are also a range of losses, stresses and traumas associated with pregnancy, for both women and men—for example, through the experience of terminations (due to medical or social reasons), miscarriage or stillbirth. Also, as noted in earlier chapters, many children die each year from a range of chronic and acute illnesses or accidents. The death of a child is often regarded as the most profound grief a person can experience (Peskin 2000). While it is in some respects impossible and undesirable to measure the relativities of grief experiences, studies do tend to confirm the view that parental grief is a more complicated, intense grief experience, with more enduring negative impacts (Burnett et al. 1997). One of the key reasons why parental bereavement is thought to be so profound in its impact is that it disrupts the normal expectation that parents should pre-decease their own children.

Parental loss experiences have profound impacts in other ways. There are often siblings, who experience both the death of their sibling and often the unavailability of their parents through their grief. Alongside the emotional distress and strain of the death of a child, parental loss often has a profound financial impact, too, a fact that is often minimised or ignored but that has a major impact on lifestyle and stress. For example, in one study of the financial costs for parents whose child had experienced illness and died, the cost was found to be between $16,000 and $60,000 by the time lost work hours and the cost of care and funeral needs were factored in (Stebbins & Batrouney 2007).

In studies of the grief experiences of parents, the dual process model has been usefully applied to show that parents often cope in vastly different ways at different times. Some studies have shown, for example, that mothers tend to have a loss orientation in their grief and men a restoration one, leading to very different emotional reactions and priorities, and therefore often to misunderstanding and unavailability for each other (Dyregrov & Matthiesen 1981; Schut 2008).

In Chapter 6, we explored the dual process model.

Promoting resilience

Resilience in early adulthood arises in response to many of the foundational individual factors we have explored in earlier chapters, such as a positive self-concept, an internal locus of control, a more nurturant, responsible, achievement-oriented attitude towards life, no prolonged separations during the first year of life, a close bond with at least one caregiver, access to emotional support outside of the family, at least one, and usually several, close friends, participation in extracurricular activities, and constitutional factors (Werner & Smith 1992).

Shaping many of these inner-world experiences, though, are the relational, social, structural and cultural dimensions of resilience. For young people moving from secondary school into tertiary education, employment and adult relationships, a whole range of social and educational policies, for example, become critical. Commonwealth supported places within universities enable students to study and defer fees for this study until they can pay fees through income; first home buyers grants enable people to move from an unstable and limited rental market into their own housing; family-friendly workplace policies enable women and men to move in and out of the workforce as they have their families and support their development. Each of these policy areas is contentious and complex, but these examples highlight that educational, employment and family opportunities can be well supported through both individual factors and the broader social and structural context that values these experiences.

Similarly, the cultural attitudes and expectations of young people can enhance or inhibit well-being. This chapter has explored some of the impacts on the transition to parenting, for example, and touched briefly on the ways in which stressors can be created or relieved through broader social expectations. Generation Y adults continue to be assessed according to the generations that have preceded them. The tendency to see the tasks and transitions of the current generation moving through early adulthood as somehow problematic is to ignore the profound impact that structural and cultural experience has in shaping and changing the daily lives of young people.

CHAPTER SUMMARY

In this chapter, we have explored some of the major transitions and experiences of early adulthood, a relatively new lifespan stage that has emerged as people live longer lives and have the means to manage reproduction, work and educational pathways in very different ways than earlier generations. This creates many opportunities for young adults, but at the same time brings stressors and risks, as uncertainty, freedom and inequalities may characterise their experiences.

Transitions occur from secondary schooling into a range of educational and work-based opportunities and pathways. Transitions also occur within families and across new peer and partner networks. Stress, loss and trauma experiences unique to this developmental stage highlight that a sense of identity is often threatened through these experiences, but that social support and social validation continue to be critical protective factors in the aftermath of these experiences.

APPLYING A MULTIDIMENSIONAL UNDERSTANDING

Debbie: Under pressure

Debbie lives in a share household with four other people in their mid- to late twenties. She is studying part-time at university, working part-time and occasionally goes out with friends. The other people in the house are working full-time, and have a lot more money and social activities. Debbie's boss has mentioned that her casual work may not be available after the next month or so. Debbie has very little contact with her parents. She feels they don't understand where she's coming from and she thinks they see her as stressed out all the time. More and more often, Debbie is finding that no one understands the pressures she faces. They keep telling her 'this is the time of your life'. She is staying in her room a lot more and sleeping long hours. In the past few weeks she's declined offers to go out to clubs because she just can't be bothered.

Jimmy: Staying out of trouble

Jimmy has just left prison, after serving a three-year term for violent assaults and selling drugs. He's had a very difficult childhood, moving in and out of protective care and home. At twenty-three, he's just beginning a supported apprenticeship, and is living in transitional housing until he can secure a rental property. He is trying hard to stay away from his old networks, but last weekend, he went binge drinking with his mates and used again, and he feels he is getting back into his old lifestyle.

Questions

1 What is your personal reaction to each of these situations?
2 What developmental factors would you take into account?
3 What do you think are the key relational, social, structural and cultural dimensions that are influencing these situations?
4 What are some possibilities for intervention using a multidimensional approach?

KEY TERMS

early adulthood
intimacy
parenting
pregnancy
sexual identities

QUESTIONS AND DISCUSSION POINTS

1 What are some of the key biopsychosocial and spiritual developmental tasks of early adulthood?

2 What are some of the different risk and protective factors across this lifespan stage?

3 In what ways are the transitions of early adulthood supported by the wider structural context in which young people are living? For example, consider influences within the labour market, education systems, housing policies, and Medicare.

4 In what ways are the transitions of early adulthood acknowledged by wider community and cultural contexts?

5 What would you identify as the messages conveyed within your family about experiences of early adulthood?

6 How do you see gender and culture being experienced in early adulthood?

7 What would you identify as the markers of adulthood?

8 What cultural dimensions are informing this understanding of adulthood for you?

FURTHER READING

Arnett, J. 1997, 'Young peoples' conceptions of the transition to adulthood', *Youth and Society*, 29(1), pp. 3–24.

Arnett, J. 2007, *Adolescence and emerging adulthood: A cultural approach*, Upper Saddle River: Pearson Education.

Smart, D. & Sanson, A. 2003, 'Social competence in young adulthood, its nature and antecedents', *Family Matters*, 64, pp. 4–9.

WEBSITES OF INTEREST

Clinical Research Unit for Anxiety and Depression: www.crufad.org

This site provides online information about health and well-being.

Australian Research Centre in Sex, Health and Society, La Trobe University: www.latrobe.edu.au/arcshs/

This research centre's website provides teaching materials, research and information relating to sexual health issues.

Beyond Blue: www.beyondblue.org.au

This site is the home of the national depression initiative and has extensive information about depression and other mental health issues.

Centre for Mental Health Research, Australian National University: http://cmhr.anu.edu.au/

This site has information about longitudinal and mental health studies.

Department of Education, Employment and Workplace Relations, Australian Government: www.deewr.gov.au

This site has statistics, reports and information about programs for secondary and tertiary education, along with employment-related policies and programs.

Negotiating the Life Course, Australian National University: http://lifecourse.anu.edu.au

This ANU site provides information about and publications from Negotiating the Life Course, a national study of 'the changing life courses and decision-making processes of Australian men and women as the family and society move from male breadwinner orientation in the direction of higher levels of gender equity'.

Urban Tribes the Blog: http://urbantribes.typepad.com/

This site provides direct source material relating to Ethan Watter's notion of 'urban tribes', the way young people form strong peer networks of support outside of their family of origin.

CHAPTER 12

Middle Adulthood

AIMS OF THIS CHAPTER

This chapter explores the developmental experiences of middle adulthood. It considers the following questions.

» What are the biopsychosocial-spiritual developmental tasks and transitions of middle adulthood?

» What are the experiences and impacts of stress, trauma and loss in middle adulthood?

» How is resilience in middle adulthood understood?

The parameters of what is considered to be **middle adulthood** have shifted considerably, with increasing recognition of an extended early adulthood at one end and increased longevity at the other. Perceptions of middle adulthood reflect these shifts, both in the research literature and in everyday life. As Lachman and James (1997 p. 3) note:

there is evidence that what defines midlife depends on whom you ask ... Younger adults in their 20s typically reported that middle age begins at around 30 and ends at 55. Older adults, in their 60s and 70s, perceived middle age as starting around 40 and extending into the 70s.

Within the research and practice contexts, middle adulthood is most typically regarded as referring to the years from around forty and ending around sixty to sixty-five years. Understandings of middle adulthood are highly variable and range from the notion that this phase in the lifespan is one of great stability through to the notion that it is a phase of crisis and change. There are some parallels with middle childhood, with it having been previously considered to be a relatively stable phase, 'in between' the turbulence of adolescence and the decline of late adulthood.

Many different expressions have been used to characterise mid-life: for example, in the 1990s, those in later mid-life were termed 'empty nesters' (Bovey 1995), because young children had grown up and left home. Many still see middle adulthood as a 'sandwiched' generation (Kingsmill 1998), caring and responsible for the generations on either side. Some regard mid-life as a time 'of reduced biological capacities but also a period when many people are energized by satisfying intimate relationships and gratifying contributions at work and in the community' (Hutchison 1999 p. 230). Mid-life carries many possibilities, based on the view that: 'A person in the middle feels safe. Middle age is sometimes described as a time of feeling settled and secure. Or perhaps bored and in a rut. There are no major adjustments to make' (Helson 1997 p. 21). The 'mid-life crisis' is seen as emerging when the yearning for major change overwhelms the sense of stability that mid-life can bring. More commonly perhaps, mid-life is seen as a time of 'balancing the competing and often overwhelming demands of paid work and family commitment' (Milkie & Peltola 1999 p. 476). The diversity of terms associated with mid-life illustrate the fact that many different tasks and transitions can take place in this phase of life.

Increasingly, research has focused on middle adulthood both for interest in the phase in and of itself, and for its links with functioning in later life. However, many of the transitions and qualities of middle age identified are typically referring to a Western, middle-class experience, as the next section highlights. We will now consider some of these key transitions, recognising the complexity of doing so given the multiple and unpredictable effects of environment, and the importance of the subjective perceptions of these changes.

Key developmental tasks and transitions

Biological dimensions

Weight and height, and nutrition

Consistent with each of the earlier lifespan stages, weight and nutrition factors are regarded as major risk factors, threatening health and longevity. In middle adulthood, obesity and being overweight, sedentary lifestyles and poor nutritional intake have been identified as problems. Some of the findings from the National Health Survey highlighting these issues are shown in Table 12.1.

While this table demonstrates health risk and protective factors for those aged twenty-five through to sixty-four years, the risk factors tend to increase at the latter end of this age group.

TABLE **12.1** Risk and protective factors for people aged 25–64

Risk or protective factor	Males (%)	Females (%)	Total (%)
Risky or high-risk alcohol consumption	16.8	12.5	14.7
Sedentary exercise	33.6	31.5	32.5
Overweight or obese	64.2	42.2	53.1
Usually eats less than recommended daily fruit intake	53.6	40.4	47.0
Usually eats less than recommended daily vegetable intake	88.0	82.9	85.4

Source: AIHW 2008b p. 292

Brain development

One of the challenges in identifying the normal ageing processes of the brain is the lack of research on brain changes in healthy adults. Most of the research has focused on those with brain injuries or brain diseases such as dementia. What is known, though, is that brain volume decreases with age, particularly over the age of fifty (Willis & Schaie 2005 p. 264) and that some parts of the brain are more susceptible to age-related changes than others—the prefrontal cortex, in particular. These changes begin to affect speed of processing information, for example.

Sleep

Sleep disturbance or insomnia can be associated with psychological factors such as worry. Other causes of sleep disturbance for both men and women are related to breathing difficulties (commonly arising from the risk factors of snoring, obesity, and high blood pressure) and alcohol use and dietary factors. For women, insomnia associated with menopause is often an increasing problem throughout middle adulthood, with studies noting a particular connection between hot flushes and sleeplessness (Shaver & Zenk 2000). The consequences of insomnia can be profound, with increased irritability, loss of concentration and, for some, depression. This in turn can affect every aspect of physical, relational and social functioning.

Hormonal changes

For women, the middle adulthood years are strongly associated with the biological process of menopause, or the 'change of life' as it is commonly referred to, perhaps depicting the deep social and individual symbolism of such a phase. Menopause is 'the permanent cessation of menstruation', a gradual process that occurs over many years (Hutchison 2003 pp. 356–7). Technically, menopause is the last menstrual period, an event that marks the end of a woman's fertility, just as menarche defined its commencement. However, it is regarded not so much as a single event but as a process that usually spans two to six years. For most women, it occurs between forty-five and fifty-five years of age. The symptoms of menopause associated with the decreased production of oestrogens, such as irregular periods, hot flushes and sweats, palpitations, decreases in vaginal lubrication and depressed mood, are not consistently reported cross-culturally, leading many researchers to conclude that the process of menopause is strongly influenced by subjective, social and cultural views.

Many Western, middle-class women use hormone replacement therapy (HRT), although in recent years it has become the subject of considerable controversy, with research connecting HRT to increased risks of breast cancer and other health difficulties (Hutchison 2003). Some are critical that the use of HRT highlights the way in which this life transition, a normal process, has become increasingly medicalised and pathologised (Greer 1999). There is evidence to suggest that Chinese women in the USA, for example, are not taking up HRT to the same extent, indicating that its use is related to social and cultural context. Others comment about the way that a whole range of experiences for women are written off by the label 'menopause' rather than, for example, viewing them as a reactive depression to a particular environmental circumstance or as the effects of ageing. For example, Melbourne's Midlife Health Project found that the 'well-being of urban Australian-born, mid-aged women was related to current health status, psychosocial and lifestyle variables rather than to endocrine changes of the menopause' (Dennerstein et al. 1994). Although some have tried to argue that there is an equivalent male menopause, this has not been evident in research in recent years.

How the individual and society define, understand, value or devalue these changes will largely determine an individual's self-concept and how others behave towards them. For example, in societies where older adults are regarded as the 'keepers of meaning' (Vaillant 2002; see discussion below) and held in high esteem, it is unlikely that ageing is viewed as a loss experience. However, Western society tends to be obsessed with youth and beauty, rather than the ageing body (Wolf 1991; Greer 1999). The ageing body is portrayed as something to prevent, evident in any of the television and media print advertisements for the endless cures for baldness or impotence, or for plastic and laser surgeries that will minimise the visible signs of ageing. This societal message can have a strong impact on individuals' self-concepts.

Disability, injury and diseases

Throughout middle adulthood, significant biological changes occur, including changes in physical appearance (weight, skin and hair changes), in mobility, in the reproductive system and sexuality (discussed below) and in health status (Hutchison 2003 pp. 354–63). While neither life-threatening nor necessarily limiting of day-to-day functioning, chronic health problems—such as respiratory and cardiac diseases, and arthritis (Deeg 2005 p. 216; AIHW 2009a p. 286–7)—increase.

From self-assessments of health, more than half of the men (57.5 per cent) in the National Health Survey and two-thirds of women (66.1 per cent) in the thirty-five to forty-four year age group described their health as excellent or very good, with those aged forty-five to fifty-four still likely to report this (53.2 per cent of men and 56.1 per cent of women). By fifty-five to sixty-four, the latter years of middle adulthood, less than half the males and females (46.8 per cent and 47.6 per cent respectively) were reporting excellent or very good health (AIHW 2008b p. 286).

From the age of forty-five onwards, the number of deaths increases, as shown in Table 12.2.

TABLE **12.2** Deaths in Australia

	1997	2007
Males		
40–44 years	1,321	1,065
45–49 years	1,688	1,706
50–54 years	2,384	2,295
55–59 years	3,027	3,226
60–64 years	4,532	4,321
Females		
40–44 years	737	669
45–49 years	1,068	1,037
50–54 years	1,438	1,431
55–59 years	1,788	1,906
60–64 years	2,473	2,628

Source: ABS 2008

However, given health and social inequalities, Indigenous Australians have a significantly shorter lifespan. Cotter et al. (2007), in their discussion of Indigenous ageing, highlight that while it is difficult to get precise data for Indigenous longevity, it seems that 'about 20 per cent of the total Australian population are over 60 (about

4 million people), but less than 5 per cent of Indigenous people (25,000 people) are above that age' (Cotter et al. 2007 p. 67). Thus, for many Indigenous Australians, middle adulthood, in health terms, reflects more of the tasks of late adulthood for non-Indigenous Australians.

Psychosocial-spiritual dimensions

Some key psychosocial-spiritual dimensions are identified as significant in the mid-life period, including psychological and psychosexual changes; relationships with partners, parents, children and peers; and the search for meaning and purpose (Lachman & James 1997). We explore some of these key themes now.

Cognitive development

Cognitive development during mid-life is not as well understood as it is earlier and later in the lifespan, in that mid-life has been seen as a relatively stable period compared to the rapid cognitive developmental growth of earlier stages and often the cognitive decline of later adulthood. Increasingly, though, attention is being paid to what occurs from the late thirties through to the early sixties, both because of its potential link with later life patterns of decline or retention and because of the ways in which people are often functioning at a peak cognitive developmental stage of performance during middle adulthood.

Middle adulthood is seen as a time of very different tasks and demands compared with childhood and later adulthood, in that people are typically engaged in 'work and family environments requiring the particular skills of organizing, planning, problem solving and multitasking' (Willis & Schaie 2005 p. 180). Consistent with this is the finding that:

> for inductive reasoning, vocabulary, verbal memory, and spatial orientation, the average performance peaks occur in the ages from the early 40s to 60s. (Willis & Martin 2005 p. 182)

A key study in establishing these understandings is the Seattle Longitudinal Study. It has been tracking cohorts of people since 1956 and adding new cohorts up until 1984, so as to incorporate both longitudinal and cross-sectional analyses of intelligence and cognitive change. The multiple cohorts are followed up at seven-year intervals; one group has been followed up for forty-two years. Some of the key findings are that 'there is no uniform pattern of age-related changes across all intellectual abilities' (Schaie 2005 p. 15), although there is 'a decline in numeracy skills and overall perceptual speed' (Wills & Schaie 2005). These researchers have concluded that consistent, age-related decline in cognitive functioning does not occur prior to the age of sixty years (Schaie 2005 p. 15).

Emotional development

In relation to emotional development in mid-life, Erikson identified the seventh crisis as the crisis of generativity versus stagnation (Erikson 1959). According to this theory, this could occur at any point within a time period of some thirty years, from twenty to fifty years. Developing a capacity for **generativity** essentially means someone is able to focus on, invest in and care for others. This task of generativity versus stagnation involves 'productivity and creativity' (Erikson 1963 p. 267), but it extends beyond simply referring to the reproductive task of having children. It is about a widening social radius and concern beyond the individual and his or her family, the 'demonstration of a clear capacity to unselfishly care for and guide the next generation' (Vaillant 2003 pp. 1378–9). This is echoed in Crawford and Walker's (2005 p. 93) observation that 'this stage of life presents the challenge of contributing to society ... Thus this stage is linked with parenting, employment and occupation'.

According to Erikson, an adult is ideally the individual who has been able to arrive at adulthood with ego strengths derived from the earlier challenges of building a capacity for trust, autonomy, initiative, industry, identity and intimacy. This experience was well-documented in Werner and Smith's study of the mid-life participants in their resilience study, where they found that:

> 'Being forty' turned out to be a milestone that brought satisfaction to the overwhelming majority of the members of this cohort. They told us of significant improvements in their accomplishments at work, in their interpersonal relationships, their contributions to their community, and their satisfaction with life. (Werner & Smith 2001 p. 166)

Vaillant (2002) continued the work of Erikson, with the same sample of participants, as well as other samples, and added two other dimensions (career consolidation and keeper of the meaning) to Erikson's adult stages of psychosocial development, as follows (Peterson et al. 1988; Vaillant & Mukamal 2001; Vaillant 2002):

1 identity
2 intimacy
3 career consolidation
4 generativity
5 keeper of the meaning
6 integrity.

Vaillant argued that being a **keeper of the meaning** involved 'passing the traditions of the past to the future', and that the 'the focus of a keeper of the meaning is with conservation and preservation of the collective products of mankind (*sic*)—the culture in which one lives and its institutions—rather than with just the development of its children' (Vaillant 2003 p. 1379). In Chapter 13, we look at the development of ego integrity, the final task of Erikson's theory and one of late mid-life and early late adulthood (Sneed et al. 2006).

Preceding the Eriksonian notions of emotional development in mid-life were those of Jung, a Swiss psychoanalyst. He also proposed that there was a mid-life transition or crisis, but was referring to a different inner-world crisis than that of Erikson. Jung's notions continue to be popularised in Western culture. Jung wrote extensively about mid-life experience as a time of individuation, when the development of an androgynous, adult identity took place. He proposed that men come to accept and understand their feminine side, and women come to accept their masculine side, as well as other aspects of the shadow side, as he termed it. This crisis often brings with it major changes in relationships, careers and sense of meaning.

Changes in fertility and family formation patterns mean that much of the literature from the 1970s and 1980s about the mid-life crisis is now redundant. Many of the issues that were seen to be part of the mid-life crisis are now being addressed in different ways much earlier in the lifespan: for example, with many Australians delaying making decisions about relationship commitments, having a family and pursuing a single career. Some researchers have supported the concept of a mid-life crisis (O'Connor 1981; Kalish 1989) and others have rejected it. A key question is whether change at mid-life is really about mid-life opportunity (when individuals discover a new economic and psychological freedom) or is part of a distinctive inner-world transformation.

Whether or not it is about resolving psychological and gender identities or developing a capacity for generativity, for many people mid-life brings a sense of stability. Another influential study on understanding mid-life was conducted by Neugarten and Birren from 1962 to 1965. They interviewed 100 highly successful men and women selected from *Who's Who* and the USA equivalent. They concluded that: 'Midlife is a time when individuals seem to come into their own', and termed mid-life 'the executive years'. They found that, regardless of socio-economic success, the middle years represented a period when an individual's ability to handle problems is at a peak in relation to their earning capacity, their generally good health, and their greater experience of self and society that compensates for any social or physical losses.

Relational development

Throughout mid-life, shifts typically occur in relationships with and expectations about family. As Kohli and Kunemund (2005 p. 35) note:

> For some it is the life course window for childbearing that closes; for others, it is the realization of what is possible and legitimate to expect from one's growing children or the extent of autonomy vis-a-vis one's aging parents.

Parents and siblings

For many, the mid-life becomes a time of caring for elderly parents. This is primarily a family role taken on by women rather than men. This highlights the gendered inequalities of care as many women take on part-time work or withdraw from the workforce in order to provide care for family members. This can lead to financial and psychological burdens for women at critical points in their careers and build inequalities in later life as a result. On the other hand, care roles can be greatly rewarding as well, enabling a sense of generativity and integrity to be developed.

We explore the death of parents later in this chapter.

While some have argued that there is a life-cycle effect on relationships between parents and adult children as these roles shift, evidence seems thin (de Vaus 1995). That is, children do not inevitably 'swap' roles and become parents to their own parents. Rather, he argues that caring within families takes place within the context of the long-standing family relationships. This is perhaps the clearest way to understand the complexity and diversity of family of origin relationships in middle adulthood—as a continuation of pre-existing relationships, in the context of changes that are both opportunities and challenges. Thus, sibling relationships tend to continue on these pathways of earlier trajectories, although with ageing parents, there can be more contact around family matters. This can lead to either enhanced relationships or increased conflict in dealing with financial issues and decisions with ageing parents.

Parenting

Mid-life has previously been seen as the time of parenting adolescent children. However, with the transition to parenting now occurring later in life, for many, mid-life is about parenting younger children. This trend is occurring not only because parenting is being delayed into the thirties, but also because many divorced men are beginning second families through remarriage with younger women, creating the possibility of two childbearing periods. Family reformation also occurs in this stage, through parents repartnering and the addition of step-children into these new families.

Some of the dimensions frequently examined within family units include the nature and focus of exchanges (the giving and receiving of emotional, instrumental and practical support).

These social support dimensions are explored in Chapter 2.

For thousands of Australians, one of the two national apologies made by the federal government has provided recognition of their lifelong impact of separations from their family of origin during childhood. In 2008, the apology to the Stolen Generations was made, and in 2009, to the Forgotten Australians. Later in this chapter we explore the impact of these experiences of forced separation from families, and some of the devastating consequences in adulthood.

Partners

Partnerships or intimate relationships continue to be of major significance in health and well-being throughout middle adulthood. It is a relatively stable time of partnering, with marriages tending to hold together having survived the typically more turbulent earlier years. For the marriages that do not end in divorce, the mid-life phase is associated with a heightened level of marital satisfaction.

Where marital separation and divorce occurs, women are more likely to initiate this change, although they typically come out of divorce with increased stress in two domains—economically and with the care of children. Studies of patterns of repartnering after divorce show that men are more likely to repartner, but 'women and men with few resources are less likely than other men and women to repartner by marriage or de facto relationship' (Hughes 2000 p. 21). While it is more typical for children to live with their mother post-divorce, many fathers report wanting more contact than they maintain (Smyth et al. 2001).

In a study of seventeen countries where data were available, the issue of the links between marital status and happiness was able to be more fully examined. Marriage was found to protect well-being for men and women equally, but importantly, 'marriage was not the most important correlate of happiness. Reported health and financial satisfaction were the two principal predictors of happiness' (Stack & Eshleman 1998 p. 535). Cohabitation was also correlated to happiness but to a lesser degree than marriage.

Wallerstein and Blakeslee (1995) in a study of fifty couples in the USA found that the characteristics of happy marriages were 'respect, integrity, friendship, trust and feeling cherished; a view of their spouse as special in some important way and someone whose company they still enjoy; and the sense that creating their marriage and family has been their major commitment and their greatest achievement' (cited in Parker 2000 pp. 74–5). These findings were replicated in a small Australian pilot study, with an added dimension, namely the importance of the symbolism and social celebration of the marriage relationship.

For those who are not married or in long-term partnerships, middle adulthood may be a time of continuing casual, short-term relationships or of seeking to establish longer-term partnerships. For others, it can be a time of forming gay or lesbian relationships, given freedom from parental disapproval and the increased social acceptability of such relationships in Western cultures (Isay 1998 p. 426).

Peers

While much research explores the nature of family relationships, for the provision of both support and recreational needs, friends and acquaintances outside the family form the majority of contacts adults have on a daily basis. As Liebler and Sandefur (2002 p. 2) note:

for many individuals in our society, a friend, neighbor, or coworker is likely to be especially accessible in a time of need, and their needs are also likely to be more readily apparent than are the needs of family members.

In their study of mid-life friendships, they found that more than half the women in their sample (of 6,705 white Americans in their early fifties) were more likely to be 'emotional support exchangers' across their social- and work-based relationships, and that more than half the men in their sample were considered to be 'low exchangers'. These patterns have been seen in many studies internationally, reinforcing the finding that women tend to form more emotional, supportive social networks, and men tend to form more task-focused networks with those around them.

Friendships are essential for a sense of well-being and for mental health generally. For example, Westermeyer (1998) found in a thirty-two-year study of eighty-seven young men that the successful predictors of mid-life mental health included satisfactory peer social adjustment, little or no angry behaviour, and a mentor relationship in young adulthood. The overall finding was that mental health was associated with developing social relationships, a theme consistent with resilience in earlier phases of the lifespan.

Gender and sexual identity

Perhaps more visibly than at other times in the lifespan, gender plays a profound role in the daily experiences of adults. For example, gender influences career trajectory, remuneration levels, care roles and responsibilities. Research has emphasised that 'caregiving responsibilities lead to increased sex-role-typical employment behavior in late midlife' (Dentinger & Clarkberg 2002 p. 857). These examples highlight the impact of the structural and cultural dimensions in reinforcing these roles, through policies that do or do not support different health, family and care-related transitions. A feminist analysis enables an important analysis of power, resources and gender to occur. This facilitates looking at these interactions between individual experience and broader social, structural and cultural dimensions and understanding (and changing) the ways in which women and men are shaped and constrained by gender-role expectations (see, for example, Fox & Murry 2000).

In relation to sexual identity and sexuality, very little relative emphasis is placed on these experiences in mid-life and later adulthood when compared to adolescence and early adulthood. Yet, given that sexual identity is recognised as a fluid construct, influenced by many inner- and outer-world dimensions, it is likely that many in adulthood continue to encounter similar questions of sexual identity, sexual attraction and sexual expression.

Moral and/or spiritual development

Running as a constant theme right throughout all these issues of health, family formation and partnering and the world of work are issues of meaning and purpose; this is often a time of searching for a philosophy or a religion that accommodates the different concerns of mid-life. Mid-life is seen to be a time of rejecting old frameworks or worldviews that no longer fit or work, and a time of reviewing or strengthening the spiritual dimensions of the inner world (Macnab 1992). This process of life review has become synonymous with two new noted phenomena for Australians in middle and early late adulthood: the 'tree change' or 'sea change', denoting the experience of those who leave urban life to go and live and work either in the bush or by the sea, both connected strongly with the idea of a new search for meaning and purpose.

In Chapter 11 we explore the adult phases of Fowler and Dell's understandings of faith development.

Occupational transitions and experiences

Employment or the world of work (whether paid or unpaid) is considered to be another critical dimension in the mid-life. Capacity to fulfil this task is often used as the measure of adult maturity (Hutchison 2003 pp. 381-383). A sense of usefulness is often found in our working lives. In meaningful activity, we are able to derive a sense of competence and purpose. Equally, if not more important, is the fact that from this involvement in the paid workforce, people are able to acquire the financial resources necessary to sustain their daily lives. The economic reality of mid-life is that for many people options have not been available to them previously. The economic stability that many people reach at mid-life opens up some of these options for the first time in their lifespan—for example, the possibility of divorce, travel or a change of living environment.

On the other hand, those who have not been able to find employment or who become unemployed at mid-life through retrenchment face long-term financial difficulty, particularly given the current government emphasis on self-funding of retirement. As Carson and Kerr (2001 p. 4) note:

> The current employment profile of people aged over 45 years is therefore increasingly tenuous, with casual, under- and un-employment being prevalent amongst this group, many of whom become discouraged and give up in their attempts to find work once they do indeed become unemployed.

The HILDA study is described in Chapter 3.

At the end of mid-life, many people are considering retirement options. The HILDA study has provided insights into retirement expectations of men aged forty-five to fifty-five years and women aged fifty to fifty-five years (Cobb-Clark & Stillman 2006). Below are some of the findings about what influences these decisions.

» Approximately two-thirds of men and more than half of women appear to be making standard retirement plans.

» More than one in five middle-aged individuals seem to have delayed their retirement planning.

» Approximately one in ten either do not know when they expect to retire or expect to never retire.

» Formulating expectations about the age at which one will retire appears to be easier for workers in jobs with well-defined pension benefits and standard retirement ages.

» Those who anticipate working forever appear to do so out of concerns about the adequacy of their retirement incomes rather than out of increased job satisfaction or a heightened desire to remain employed.

» Gender also plays a part in retirement decisions, with men more likely to make retirement plans based on the current economic environment and women on the basis of the health statuses of themselves and/or their partner.

Source: Cobb-Clark and Stillman 2006; reproduced with permission.

Coping with risks and adversities

Stress

As this chapter has described, middle adulthood tends to bring with it peak demands in relation to family, work and personal life. Therefore, it is typically about juggling multiple roles, frequently while meeting the demands of the generations on either side. In this chapter we look at two particular stress experiences in middle adulthood: managing illness and disability as a carer and managing financial stress. Later in this chapter, we explore health crises as traumatic events.

In Chapter 4, we explore the nature of stress and, in particular, the notion of daily hassles.

The picture of coping with stress in middle adulthood is a curious one. While middle adulthood tends to bring more complexity of demands, many studies highlight that the daily hassles aspect or the stressfulness of these demands seems to diminish with ageing. Aldwin and Levenson (2001 p. 206), in their study of mid-life, propose the following reason:

We hypothesize that individuals in mid-life have developed better management or anticipatory coping strategies which decrease the probability of experiencing those types of daily stressors that can be avoided with a little forethought.

This is reflected in some of the findings from research into the impact of health crises. For example, Cagnetta and Cicognani (1999), in their study of road trauma survivors, commented on the fact that older participants were generally much more actively engaged with a recovery process, noting that, 'they often succeed in finding by themselves good opportunities to be optimistic about their evolution; they examine their conscience and perhaps decide to change their "reckless" or "risky" behaviours' (Cagnetta & Cicognani 1999 p. 559).

While many experience their own health crises, others find that middle adulthood brings with it increased responsibility towards others, particularly ageing parents but also partners, with the onset of chronic or acute illnesses and/or children with disabilities, acquired or congenital. Middle adulthood brings with it caring roles, primarily for women. About twenty per cent (20.1%) of 13,869 women aged between forty-five and fifty identified themselves as carers in the Australian Longitudinal Survey on Women's Health (Lee & Powers 2002). One of the key protective factors in these roles seems to be the centrality, or personal importance, of these roles (Martire et al. 2000 p. 153): 'greater centrality of the parent care, mother, wife, and employee roles was associated with better psychological well-being'.

> This finding highlights the link between appraisal and coping, explored in Chapter 4.

Financial stress

Some interesting shifts occur across the lifespan in relation to financial risk and employment opportunities. Werner and Smith's (2001) study, for example, found that those who had been experiencing financial hardship and had been 'troubled teenagers' were employed by middle adulthood and were in stable, supportive relationships. For many, poverty and unemployment are stressors they are able to leave behind. In part, this is due to opportunities that emerge, particularly educational and vocational.

For many others, though, financial stress is part of daily life. The Australian dream of home ownership, the tight rental market and the realities of supporting dependent family members come to the fore in middle adulthood. For some, it is about competing for economic success. These pressures are explored by Hamilton and Denniss (2005 p. 3) in their book, *Affluenza*, which they define as the following condition:

> Af-flu-en-za (n). 1. The bloated, sluggish and unfulfilled feeling that results from efforts to keep up with the Joneses. 2. An epidemic of stress, overwork, waste and indebtedness caused by dogged pursuit of the Australian dream. 3. An unsustainable addiction to economic growth.

For others, however, it is about staying financially afloat during very difficult times of unemployment and the global financial crisis. Recent figures show that, while the rate of jobless families over all is decreasing, 'in 2007–08, there were 266,000 families with at least one child aged less than 15 years with no employed parent' (ABS 2009c). In addition, the structure of families where there is an unemployed parent has changed:

> In 1997–98 one-parent families made up three-fifths (61%) of all families without an employed parent, but by 2007–08 this had increased to around three-quarters (76%). Most jobless one-parent families were headed by mothers (93%). (ABS 2009c)

This leaves many women in early and middle adulthood in financially stressful circumstances, with little opportunity to move out of this entrenched family poverty.

The other factor many families face in relation to financial stress is the experience of gambling and its often devastating impact on relationships and finances. From a Victorian study of the prevalence of problem gambling (Department of Justice 2009), men aged twenty-five through to thirty-four years had the highest prevalence of problem gambling (1.42 per cent), that is, in late, early adulthood. However, at the other end of the middle adulthood spectrum, the fifty to sixty-four-year-old age group had the second highest prevalence (1.07 per cent). For women, both the twenty-five to thirty-four-year-old age group and the thirty-five to forty-nine-year-old age groups had the highest prevalence of problem gambling (0.56 per cent each). Problem gambling has major impacts on the individual gambler, their family and the wider community, both in relation to the financial resources that are typically lost and in terms of the time spent away from others in isolation.

Trauma

In previous chapters, we have explored many traumatic life events that are relevant to those in middle adulthood also. Here we focus on two trauma experiences that are either currently having an impact on those in mid-life in Australia (the impact of early traumatic separations in out-of-home care) or become more prevalent in middle adulthood (the traumas of life-threatening illnesses).

Adult impact of early traumatic separations

The *Bringing them home* report (1997) first documented many of the horrific experiences of forced separation of Aboriginal children from their families and communities, the Stolen Generations as they are now known. It is impossible to know how many children were removed under these government policies, given the difficulties with historical records (or lack thereof) and due to the fact that some children were not aware that they were Aboriginal following their placement with white families. However, the consequences for thousands of Aboriginal children, now forty and older, have been profound both for them as individuals, and for their families and culture.

Similarly, a Senate enquiry was held, documenting the experiences of adults who were placed in out-of-home care in Australia, particularly between the 1930s and 1970s. This resulted in the report, *Forgotten Australians: A report on Australians who experienced institutional or out-of-home care as children* (The Senate 2004). It is estimated that more than 500,000 children were in some form of institutional care. About 7,000 of these children were British child migrants (Humphreys 1994), brought out under a scheme to relocate England's poor from orphanages and resettle them in Australia.

Many people in their forties and beyond have been advocating strongly for many years to have these experiences publicly acknowledged, and the two national apologies form significant starting points in that process. The impact of the experiences of traumatic separation, often followed by neglect and abuse, has been profound for both groups of survivors. For instance, many of the care leavers continue to experience:

> low self-esteem, lack of confidence, depression, fear and distrust, anger, shame, guilt, obsessiveness, social anxieties, phobias, and recurring nightmares. Many care leavers have tried to block the pain of their past by resorting to substance abuse through lifelong alcohol and drug addictions. Many turned to illegal practices such as prostitution, or more serious law-breaking offences which have resulted in a large percentage of the prison population being care leavers. (The Senate 2004 p. xvi)

These descriptions of effects are consistent with post-traumatic stress symptoms, and are commonly experienced by Stolen Generations survivors. For those who were part of the Stolen Generations, the early separations also led to cultural loss and deprivation. These groups of survivors have highlighted the importance of public recognition and acknowledgment as part of the process of healing and restoration, at individual and community levels. They have also highlighted the lifelong consequences of early separations from parents or caregivers, from family and community and from cultural connectedness. For both groups, betrayal trauma theory (Freyd et al. 2007) provides a way of understanding the violations that occurred at both individual and collective levels of experience.

See Chapter 5 for more on betrayal trauma theory.

Health

While health crises can be conceptualised as stressors, for many people they are more typically experienced as traumatic stress, as they often present a direct threat to life and undermine any sense of personal control.

Diagnosis of a life-threatening illness such as cancer or heart disease is more common in middle adulthood than in earlier stages. One study identified that eight per cent of men being treated for prostate cancer were experiencing post-traumatic stress disorder (PTSD) (Mehnert et al. 2009), with the younger men in the sample (in middle adulthood) more likely to develop PTSD and other negative psychological impacts than those over sixty-five years. Some studies of women diagnosed with breast cancer have highlighted lower rates of PTSD—for example, one study found that while 'a substantial minority (41%) reported responding to cancer with intense fear, helplessness, or horror' cancer-related PTSD was only identifiable in four per cent of the sample and was thus uncommon. (Palmer et al. 2004). In a study of the partners of women with breast cancer, though, more than one-third of the sample had clinically significant PTSD scores, and the predictor variable for both pre- and post-partner death trauma symptoms was the anticipated impact of the loss (Butler et al. 2005, p. 498). That is, PTSD emerged for those who had anticipated the loss more than others.

However, as with other trauma experiences, survivors have typically reported post-traumatic growth experiences, alongside their post-traumatic stress ones. For example, in a study of married couples facing the trauma of breast cancer, post-traumatic growth was reported by both partners, with 'general social support, positive qualities of the marital relationship and the level of wife's PTG' being associated with husbands' reported levels of growth (Weiss 2004 p. 265). These findings highlight that the contexts, particularly relational, of the experience of cancer, particularly the immediate relational ones, make a major difference in the coping trajectory.

In the following box is an example of how these issues may emerge in practice.

PRACTICE IN CONTEXT

FACING STRESS IN MIDLIFE

Lee, a social worker, describes her assessment of a woman facing multiple stressors and traumas in middle adulthood.

Rosa, a Polish migrant, has a mild bipolar disorder. Despite her illness, she has been leading a rich life, raising her two sons (aged seven and nine), helping her husband with a family business and practising various art forms. However, five years ago the family lost the business. Since then Rosa's husband has been drinking and verbally abusing her, sometimes in front of their children. The sons have behavioural problems, with the young boy talking occasionally about killing himself. Recently Rosa, who always took pride in her appearance, was diagnosed with breast cancer. Her left breast was removed.

Currently Rosa receives family and individual counselling in community mental health services, and also uses art to cope. She documents her struggles with family problems and a mental illness, and her grief about her changed appearance through painting, photography and writing. Her long-term goal is to produce an illustrated book about her experiences.

Questions

1 What is your personal reaction to Rosa's situation?

2 What would you identify as the risk and protective factors in Rosa's situation?

3 What do you see are developmental tasks and transitions associated with middle adulthood?

4 What do you think is the impact of Rosa's cultural identity?

Loss

Throughout adulthood, exposure to multiple losses occurs through the death or loss of children, partners, peers, colleagues and parents. Loss can also occur through the realisation that some things are not going to happen, because of lost opportunities or of the consequences of particular pathways being taken. As Neugarten noted in her study of mid-life, the focus changes for many people so that it is on the time left to live rather than the time since birth. There can be a heightened consciousnessness of mortality, and in part this is compounded by the experience of a parent's death.

Despite the commonality of the experience, very little research is available in relation to the experience of mid-life parental death. The limited research available has highlighted that there typically is an impact of the death of a parent on their adult children—for many adults, the death of a parent can be overwhelmingly distressing, but for others, a time of release and relief. In a very small, qualitative study, some relevant themes were identified by adults whose parents had both died while they were in mid-life (Pope 2005). In particular, changes in family relations (realisation of an increased dependence on their own children rather than their parents for a sense of family), change in a sense of maturity, and a realisation that elder status was now transferred to them were noted.

The negative impacts that have been noted include reports of increased stress, increased alcohol consumption, and increased health problems (Umberson & Chen 1994). The factors that mediated these impacts were the age and marital status of the adult; their gender and the gender of the deceased parent; the quality of the relationship, with greater ambivalence about the relationship leading to poorer health outcomes; and childhood memories of the deceased parent.

Promoting resilience

This chapter has emphasised the significant roles of relationships, family and work in middle adulthood. Each of these experiences is shaped by the environments in which people live, as well as by the accumulation of risk and protective factors in earlier developmental stages.

People's employment experiences are influenced by global and local financial markets, which in turn influence the availability of casual, part-time or full-time work. Taxation and superannuation policies influence people's immediate and long-term financial security. Within workplaces, policies relating to leave and family-friendly practices continue to be important influences on daily life. These pressures within workplaces, or the pressure of unemployment, in turn, have an impact on relationships with partners and within families.

People in middle adulthood experience diverse relational and social networks. For those who experience demands from generations on both sides, structural factors such as carer leave and respite care, along with school policies, all influence daily stressors and demands. Relationships are also influenced by laws around marriage, separation and divorce. Cultural factors such as familial expectations and obligations also play a major part in determining priorities and pressures for people. Gender has been identified as a key risk or protective factor in middle adulthood, creating different expectations and obligations for men and women and leading to some significant risk factors, particularly for women around financial problems in later life. Cultural factors also determine how ageing throughout this lifespan stage is understood—whether it is a time of increased autonomy and independence or a time of beginning decline and lost opportunity.

CHAPTER **SUMMARY**

In this chapter, we have focused on the biopsychosocial-spiritual transitions of middle adulthood. For many adults it is a time of consolidation and yet simultaneously a time of juggling multiple demands. From a developmental perspective, it is often seen as an optimal time in the lifespan, where health and capacities reach their peak. Seeking satisfaction in family, social and work domains is seen as a key developmental task. Stress in middle adulthood arises in the main because of the multiplicity of demands in all of these domains, and we have looked at carer and financial demands in particular. We have explored some of the trauma experiences unique to the current generation in middle adulthood in Australia—the experience of surviving as one of the Stolen Generations or Forgotten Australians, as well as the health traumas that are more generally experienced in middle adulthood. We concluded with an exploration of an experience that becomes more common as we age, the death of parents, and the impact of this loss.

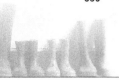

APPLYING A MULTIDIMENSIONAL UNDERSTANDING

Jim: Early retrenchment

At the age of fifty-one, Jim is devastated to hear that he has been retrenched. As a middle manager in a large manufacturing company over the past twenty years, he had always been aware of the possibility but had thought it would never happen to him. His partner, Sue, works part-time as a sales assistant. Three years ago, she had been forced to go part-time in her work, to care for her elderly mother the rest of the time. While Sue and Jim both have siblings, they are not involved on a day-to-day basis with the care of Sue's mother. She changed her employment status, rather than have her mother go into a nursing home. Their eldest child, Kelly, is at university and lives out of home in a student house. However, she experiences episodes of severe depression and often moves back home during these times. Their youngest child, Peter, still lives at home and is in his final year of high school. Sue's mother, Irene, is ninety and lives in the next street. Physically, she is very frail but she is adamant that she will live at home until she dies.

Questions

1 What are the key stressors facing this family?
2 What are some of the developmental risk and protective factors for each individual in this situation?
3 What are the possibilities for intervention using a multidimensional approach?
4 What difference does it make to your understanding of this family's situation if their ethnic identity is identified as being Indigenous Australian, Greek, Anglo-Australian or Vietnamese?

KEY TERMS

employment
generativity
keeper of the meaning
middle adulthood

QUESTIONS AND DISCUSSION POINTS

1 What are some of the key biopsychosocial and spiritual developmental tasks of middle adulthood?
2 What are some of the risk and protective factors across this stage?

3 What are some of the dimensions of the structural and cultural context that influence this stage?

4 What would you identify as the messages conveyed within your family about experiences of mid-life?

5 What messages about ageing do you see the mass media convey?

6 How do you see gender being constructed in middle adulthood?

FURTHER READING

Kalish, R. ed. 1989, *Midlife loss: Coping strategies*, New York: SAGE Publications.

Lachman, M. 2004, 'Development in midlife', *Annual Review of Psychology*, 55, 305–31.

Pope, A. 2005, 'Personal transformation in midlife orphanhood: An empirical phenomenological study', *Omega*, 51(2), pp. 107–23.

Willis, S. & Martin, M. eds, 2005, *Middle adulthood: A lifespan perspective*, Thousand Oaks: SAGE Publications, Chapter 7, pp. 209–41.

WEBSITES OF INTEREST

Centre for Ageing Studies, Flinders University: http://flinders.edu.au/sabs/fcas/
This site includes details of the Australian Longitudinal Study of Ageing (ALSA).

Conducting a National Survey of Midlife Development in the United States:
http://midmac.med.harvard.edu/research.html
This site provides provides information about a major midlife project by Lachman and others at Harvard University.

Forgotten Australians: www.forgottenaustralians.org.au
This site has been formed by advocates for Australians who were institutionalised or in out-of-home care as children.

Life Course Project, Australian National University: http://lifecourse.anu.edu.au
This ANU site provides information about and publications from 'The Negotiating the Life Course Project', a national study of 'the changing life courses and decision-making processes of Australian men and women as the family and society move from male breadwinner orientation in the direction of higher levels of gender equity'.

Pathways Victoria: www.pathwaysvictoria.info/
This site provides information for those who have experienced out-of-home care, including records of orphanages and institutes, staff and children. It was

developed in response to lack of information for the Forgotten Australians and Stolen Generations.

Stolen Generations Alliance: www.sgalliance.org.au/

The Stolen Generations Alliance is committed to bringing about healing, truth and reconciliation for Indigenous Australians and between both Indigenous and non-Indigenous Australians.

University of Melbourne, Melbourne Women's Midlife Health Project: www.psychiatry.unimelb.edu.au/midlife

This site is the homepage of the Melbourne Women's Midlife Health Project, a study of women's health at mid-life and through menopause.

Up Series: www.pbs.org/pov/fortynineup/

This site has information about the British documentary *Up*, following the lives of fourteen adults since they were aged seven. They are now in mid-life.

CHAPTER 13

Late Adulthood

AIMS OF THIS CHAPTER

This chapter explores the lifespan stage of late adulthood, beginning at the age of sixty-five years. It considers the following questions:

» What are the biopsychosocial-spiritual developmental tasks and transitions in late adulthood?
» What are the experiences and impacts of stress, trauma and loss in late adulthood?
» How is resilience in late adulthood understood?

Late adulthood is viewed typically as the time period from sixty-five years onwards. Given that people in developed countries are living longer than previous generations, this means that late adulthood can refer to people who are sixty-five years through to those living to well over one hundred years of age. It is a vast age range to be capturing through the one developmental category and stands in stark contrast to the two- to three-year age ranges of the earliest lifespan stages: infancy and early childhood. It also means that two generations of a family may coexist in this lifespan stage, and thus raises the question as to whether the age range is too large to be useful in practice and policy considerations.

The age range of later adulthood is often divided, therefore, into more discrete age ranges, to enable differentiation of the tasks and transitions facing sixty-five year olds from centenarians, for example. One way of thinking about these different groups is to identify the young-old as ranging in age from sixty-five to seventy-four; the middle-old as aged seventy-five to eighty-four; and the oldest-old as aged eighty-five or over

(Hutchison 2003). A further distinction is sometimes made within the oldest old age group, by referring to them as the elite elderly, including those in their nineties and beyond, and centenarians, those who are aged one hundred years and beyond.

The resilience or successful ageing of many elite elderly people, in particular, and a generational shift towards an increasingly **ageing** population, have brought about new challenges to the public perceptions of late adulthood. Old age has often been regarded as a state of, as Macnab (1992 p. 58) highlights:

> failing health, disease, confusion and ineptitude; a mindless state—creativity and problem-solving decline and senility and dependence are inevitable; a sexless state; a state of disengagement from activity, social interaction and intimate companionship; and a decline in intelligence and a regression in mental age.

While these perceptions continue to be held by some younger people, they are now widely challenged. Generational differences in the ways in which ageing is perceived are also evident, with the current sixty-plus age group being 'much less accepting of being seen and described as older than the generation before it' (Tongue & Ballenden 1999 p. 6). As Edgar (2002 p. 17), former and foundation director of the Australian Institute of Family Studies, comments:

> Our new aged are the healthiest, wealthiest and most active cohort of old people in history. They will drive major social and cultural changes to ensure better quality of life … It is time to stop the scare tactics and think clearly about what ageing might mean for a good society and how our social institutions might react to get the most out of the maturing of its citizens.

This chapter explores the transitions and developmental tasks, as well as the risk and protective factors for people currently ageing in the Australian context.

Key developmental tasks and transitions

Biological dimensions

In exploring the biological dimensions of late adulthood, an important distinction needs to be made from the outset between the three broad categories of the late adulthood lifespan stage. Biological changes in early late adulthood are vastly different from the biological changes confronting the centenarian or those demonstrating 'exceptional longevity' (Perls & Terry 2003). While the physical changes and transitions of older age tend to be characterised by the experience of physical health decline and loss of function, this does not accurately reflect the entire experience for people throughout these thirty-five plus years of life.

For social workers, it is particularly important to refrain from 'medicalising' the experience—that is, seeing the experience of ageing only through a biological or medical lens. As Vincent (2003 p. 138) notes:

> contemporary west think[s] about old age predominantly in terms of sickness and disability. The dominance of western scientific medicine has transformed old age from a natural event to a disease.

To do so is to overlook the importance of successful ageing, and the significance of strong and sustaining interactions with environments, people and places as we go through the various transitions of the ageing experience.

Longevity

Globally, populations are ageing, particularly within developed countries where access to good nutrition, housing and health resources has been achieved. Whereas some other countries (such as Japan and Italy) have had aged populations for many years, Australia is moving towards a rapid increase in the ageing of its population in the next ten years. This aged population stands in stark contrast to the situation just over one hundred years ago, when, at the time of Federation (1901), only one per cent of the population was over the age of sixty-five. By 1976, this had increased to nine per cent and in 1998, an estimated twelve per cent of the population was over the age of sixty-five years. The dramatic shift will occur in the next forty or so years, with estimates for 2051 forecasting that there will be six million Australians over the age of sixty-five, twenty-four per cent of the population (ABS 2004). The increase in longevity has been referred to as the 'greying of Australia' (Kendig & McCallum 1988).

In each of the earlier lifespan stages we have explored, there have been more males than females. Once people reach late adulthood, for the only time across the lifespan, there are more females than males. The ageing Australian population will become predominantly a female population, with women typically living longer than men, and thus reflecting a higher number of 'the very old (68% of people aged 85 years or over)' (AIHW 2007 p. 82). Table 13.1 provides the breakdown on the basis of sex of those in late adulthood in Australia in 2007.

Since the 1970s in Australia there has been a steady increase in those living to, and beyond, one hundred years of age. In 1996, 2,744 Australians were aged ninety-nine or older, with at least 1,726 known to be centenarians (McCormack 2000). Currently, just over three thousand Australians are aged one hundred years and more. Centenarian males have been found to be generally healthier than centenarian females (Perls & Terry 2003). The number of centenerians is also expected to increase over the next two decades.

TABLE **13.1** Distribution of the older Australian population

Age range	Non-Indigenous males (number)	Indigenous males (number)	Non-Indigenous females (number)	Indigenous females (number)	Total
65–69 years	383,234	2,901	391,708	3,576	774,942
70–74 years	301,705	1,861	324,834	2,430	626,539
75–79 years	251,619	1,059	298,296	3,173	549,915
80–84 years	165,650	523	238,704	1,575	404,354
85 and over	103,983	392	217,011	871	320,994

Source: ABS 2010a & 2010b

The projected increase in longevity in Australia will see the transition of those born in the 'baby boom' generation after the Second World War into their later years of life. They are supported by a health system that is superior to other historical periods, have benefited from advances in medical technology and knowledge that contribute to living longer and healthier lives, and have had access to good nutrition.

Significant health inequalities in late adulthood are evident, though, particularly for Indigenous Australians. The life expectancy for non-Indigenous females born in 2000 is eighty-two years, and for non-Indigenous males, seventy-seven years (ABS 2004)—one of the highest in the world. However, life expectancy for Indigenous females and males born between 1996 and 2000 is sixty-five and fifty-nine years respectively (AIHW 2008b p. 68). While the Indigenous population is ageing too, it is not to the same extent as the non-Indigenous population. This highlights the interconnectedness of biopsychosocial-spiritual dimensions and the structural and cultural contexts in which people are living, and the impact of continuing health and social inequalities for Indigenous Australians.

In view of the increasing number of people living into late late-adulthood, several studies have focused on identifying the pathways to successful ageing. The Study of Human Development (Vaillant & Mukamal 2001) explored the significance of uncontrollable variables (parental social class, family cohesion, major depression, ancestral longevity, childhood temperament and physical health at fifty) and variables reflecting arguably more personal control (alcohol use, smoking, marital stability, exercise, body mass index, coping mechanisms and education). Following a cohort for sixty years, they found at age eighty there were several factors that seemed critical for longevity (Vaillant 2002 p. 13). They are outlined on page 387 in this chapter.

In addition to these psychosocial factors in ageing successfully, others are exploring the genetic determinants of longevity. Extreme longevity seems possible when people have 'genetic variations that affect the basic mechanisms of ageing and that result in a uniform decreased susceptability to age-associated diseases' (Perls & Terry 2003 p. 445). The genetic basis of this longevity is supported by studies that have shown that children of centenarians had reduced risk of heart disease, hypertension and diabetes (Perls & Terry 2003 p. 448).

Weight and height, and nutrition

As with other stages in the lifespan, obesity has increasingly become a common health problem in late adulthood, with the often-associated problems of diabetes and high cholesterol levels not only linked with physical health problems but also cognitive decline and therefore all aspects of a person's health.

More typically, though, older people tend to lose weight, with possible reasons including the protective function of a lower body weight and the link therefore with survival, or eating less generally, a greater consciousness of eating less or a current cohort phenomenon (that is, just affecting this current group of older people at this point in time) (Berger 2008 p. 541). While late-life weight loss can also be associated with the onset of serious illness, some studies have found increased weight (by measuring body mass index, BMI) to be a protective factor, particularly of some illnesses. For example, Fitzpatrick, et al. (2009 p. 341) 'found that whereas higher BMI at mid-life may increase the risk of dementia, when measured after age 65 years, increased BMI may actually be a marker for decreased dementia risk'. Nutrition for older people can be a major problem, both in terms of reduced mobility to access healthy fresh food and in terms of reduced motivation to prepare diverse, healthy meals. Being able to maintain a healthy diet is a key protective factor.

Brain development

The focus in brain development in ageing is on the well-documented memory changes and cognitive losses associated with ageing, particularly in relation to short-term memory capacities. While significant changes in the brain's structure continue to occur as a person ages, this tends to be attributed to sudden changes as people reach their sixties, when in fact many of these changes have begun from a person's twenties or early adulthood. Changes in brain structure have been noted in relation to a number of areas, including regional brain volume, cortical thickness, and serotonin receptor binding (Salthouse 2009 p. 507). These declines have an impact on cognitive functioning in various ways, which we will explore in the following pages. Of particular interest to researchers have been changes in the brain that lead to dementia, and particularly Alzheimer's disease. Studies suggest that the older a person is, the more likely they are to develop dementia.

Sleep

Adults tend to experience changes in sleep patterns and requirements in late adulthood, in particular, reductions in both REM sleep and deep sleep (Klerman & Dijk 2008) as well as increases in wakefulness, restlessness and difficulties falling asleep (Berger 2008 p. 623). Others have found an increase in daytime napping. These changes are thought to be related to both lifestyle factors, such as less physical mobility during the day, and neurological changes associated with ageing. This can be a source of considerable anxiety for people as they experience changes in sleep patterns and requirements. For those less physically active, this makes sense—less energy is being used and thus less needs to be restored. However, some studies have shown that older adults, similar to adolescents and younger adults, have sleep 'debts' too (Klerman & Dijk 2008).

Loss of sleep can have an impact on cognitive performance, with poor sleep habits being shown in one study to have a negative impact on 'working memory, attentional set shifting, and abstract problem solving but not on processing speed, inhibitory function, or episodic memory' (Nebes et al. 2009 p. 180). Concern about changes in sleep patterns can also lead to different interventions—both informal and formal—that have other consequences. Some older adults increase their alcohol intake to facilitate sleep, for example, or take prescription medication. Both of these interventions can have other significant, negative impacts on overall health and functioning.

Sexuality

Sexuality is a neglected aspect of many older people's lives. As many authors note, sexuality is culturally seen to be the domain of youth and young adulthood, and is of diminishing interest for older adults and researchers alike. Many lifespan texts will not even include discussion of sexuality in late adulthood despite having examined it at every other stage.

Sexual function does change across the lifespan, with peak sexual functioning during adolescence and early adulthood. From a reproductive perspective, this makes sense. Sexuality is more than reproduction though; it is an important way of experiencing and expressing intimacy and sexual desire. Thus, the changes in sexuality that are often reported need to be understood as multidimensional.

Some of the reasons for the changes experienced in later adulthood include a slowing of sexual responses, a loss of libido and a loss of sexual function (erectile dysfunction for men and decreased vaginal lubrication for women). However, other changes in sexuality occur for environmental reasons: the loss of a partner, stress, illness and disability, and social prohibitions. In part, the social prohibition of older people expressing their sexuality is reflected in the lack of knowledge about people's sexual behaviours and experiences in later adulthood. Sexuality in older people is silenced in many ways.

In one study by Ginsberg, Pomerantz and Kramer-Feeley (2005), 166 Australians (66 per cent female, from lower income areas and predominantly white) reported on their experiences and wishes in relation to sexual behaviours. The study found that:

> overall, the majority reported to have had physical and sexual experiences in the past year such as touching/holding hands (60.5%), embracing/hugging (61.7%) and kissing (57%) daily to at least once a month; mutual stroking, masturbation and intercourse were experienced 'not at all' by 82% or more. (Ginsberg et al. 2005 p. 475)

Importantly, the study found that these participants wished for greater sexual contact but were unable to attain it.

Physical and motor skills

As discussed further in this chapter, 'Over half of all people aged 65 years or over experience some type of disability that restricts everyday activities' (AIHW 2008b p. 85). For many people, this is linked with reduced physical mobility—through loss of eyesight, physical mobility or pain. Key protective factors with mobility issues include not only individual motivational issues but structural factors such as the nature of the built environment in which older people are living—whether public transport, disabled parking or reduced taxi fares are accessible and available, for example.

Maintaining mobility is key to maintaining optimal health—minimising the risk of falls through maintaining muscle strength for example, and maximising social engagement as well. Many older people are encouraged to participate in walking groups or other forms of physical exercise. This is in response to the finding that older Australians tend to not exercise at all or have low levels of physical activity (National Ageing Research Institute 2003). Motor skills in late adulthood can be affected as a result of illness (strokes, for example, causing paralysis) and/or pain, for example through the limitations caused by arthritis. These changes often lead to a sense of frustration and loss, as independence, self-care and leisure activities can be affected.

APPLY YOUR UNDERSTANDING: NEVER TOO OLD?

Consider the following scenarios and the different perceptions of late adulthood that they create or challenge:

» In 1983, a sixty-one-year-old potato farmer, Cliff Young, rose to fame as he won the Melbourne to Sydney road race of 875 kilometres.
» A woman in India gives birth at the age of seventy years.
» An eighty-year-old woman goes parachuting for the first time.
» A person completes their Doctor of Philosophy degree in their eighties.

Sensory changes

For many older people, a daily frustration and loss is the experience of deteriorating sensory capacity—particularly the experiences of diminishing visual and hearing abilities. These changes can have an impact on every aspect of a person's life—for example, their capacity to read and watch television, engage in conversations and social relationships, be independently mobile and be independent in self-care and self-responsibility. Other changes noted in sensory capacities include loss of a sense of smell and/or taste and changes to experiences of heat and cold, as circulation changes.

Disability, injury and diseases

While many of the physical changes have begun years earlier in the lifespan, increasingly some are experienced as problematic in late adulthood. Changes in the cardiovascular, respiratory and skeletal systems lead to increasing problems in daily functioning. There is the onset of cardiovascular conditions such as stroke, chronic conditions such as diabetes and arthritis, and psychogeriatric conditions such as dementia, which particularly affects women as a result of their increased longevity. The incidence of cancers also increases. As noted earlier, 'Over half of all people aged 65 years or over experience some type of disability that restricts everyday activities' (AIHW 2008b p. 85). This can increase care needs and brings people into contact with a range of health care providers. A review of hospital data shows that 'older people are still much higher users of hospitals than their younger counterparts, making up 53% (29,000) of people in hospital' (AIHW 2008b p. 294) in a census in 2004. This review also found that older men are more likely to be hospitalised than older women.

Another factor that can increase biological risks throughout late adulthood is that of both prescribed and illicit drug use. Given the complexities of drug interactions, multiple use and sometimes abuse of drugs (both knowingly and unknowingly) can place older people at risk (Patterson & Jeste 1999).

As the final stage of the lifespan, late adulthood brings with it the inevitability of death, both a biological transition as well as a psychosocial one. The causes of death have shifted over the last three decades, particularly as medical advances have changed the nature of cardiovascular diseases, through reducing the mortality rate. While some diseases may have become less likely to cause death, they remain strongly linked with disability and impairment, thus affecting the daily lives of older people. It is important to note also that 'The most economically and socially deprived sections of society have higher mortality rates, experience more ill health and use fewer preventive services' (Greig et al. 2003 p. 51). Table 13.2 shows the causes of death among Australians aged sixty-five years and over by sex in 2005.

Later in this chapter we look at the psychosocial aspects of dying and death.

TABLE **13.2** Leading causes of death among Australians aged 65 and over, by sex, 2005

Males—causes	Deaths	Per cent of total	Females—causes	Deaths	Per cent of total
Coronary heart disease	10,016	20.1	Coronary heart disease	10,565	19.7
Cerebrovascular disease	4,226	8.5	Cerebrovascular disease	6,527	12.2
Lung cancer	3,542	7.1	Other heart diseases	4,050	7.6
Prostate cancer	2,752	5.5	Dementia and related disorders	3,234	6.0
Other heart diseases	2,625	5.3	Lung cancer	1,990	3.7
Chronic obstructive pulmonary disease	2,589	5.2	Chronic obstructive pulmonary disease	1,839	3.4
Colorectal cancer	1,687	3.4	Influenza and pneumonia	1,615	3.0
Diabetes	1,462	2.9	Diabetes	1,594	3.0
Dementia and related disorders	1,445	2.9	Breast cancer	1,450	2.7
Cancers (unknown primary site)	1,353	2.5	Colorectal cancer	1,448	2.7
Influenza and pneumonia	1,227	2.6	Cancers (unknown primary site)	1,294	2.4
Diseases of arteries etc	1,090	2.2	Diseases of arteries etc	1,110	2.1
Total (12 leading causes)	34,014	68.2	Total (12 leading causes)	36,716	68.5
Total (all deaths 65+)	49,920	100.0	Total (all deaths 65+)	53,566	100.0

Source: AIHW 2008b p. 295

One of the key factors in successful ageing is the subjective experience of ageing and we explore how this influences overall well-being later in the chapter. An evaluation of subjective perceptions of ageing is regularly undertaken and highlights some important trends in current perceptions of Australia's older people in relation to their health and well-being: 'Overall, 33.8% of over sixty-five-year-olds self-assessed their health as excellent or very good, 34.2% as good and 32% as fair/poor' (AIHW 2008b p. 294). Older Indigenous Australians, however, when asked about their health and well-being, reported markedly lower perceptions of their own health status.

Psychosocial-spiritual dimensions

Some of the challenges in understanding the experiences of older adults include the enormous diversity of experience across years of life, across cultures and contexts, the variability in health and wealth statuses, and the challenge of universalising developmental experiences given these diversities. While arguably these diversities are inherently present earlier in the lifespan, more credibility to the challenges these issues present seems to be given in considering later life.

Where older people live and spend their time will influence their life chances and health opportunities. In rural and remote locations, accessing health care and assistance in activities of daily living in late adulthood can be extremely difficult. The vast majority of older Australians continue to live at home, with ninety-four per cent 'living in private dwellings' (AIHW 2008b p. 144). That is, 'only around 5% of older people live in cared accommodation but this is the situation for 31% of those aged 85 years or over' (AIHW 2008b p. 144). Currently twenty-nine per cent of those over sixty-five years who are not in care accommodation live alone and this percentage is expected to increase. Interestingly, McCormack (2001 p. 5), in his study of centenarians, found that thirty-nine per cent of them were living in private dwellings, challenging the notion of late late-adulthood necessitating formal care. He states:

> The fact that almost four in ten (39%) live in the community with nearly two in ten living alone (17%), hardly depicts these very old people as all being totally frail and dependent. (McCormack 2001 p. 5)

Living alone may be more of a psychosocial protective factor than a risk factor, enabling people to maintain control over their lives. This reflects Martin's (1997) argument that the predictability and controllability of events determine whether they are stressful or not.

Another significant factor within ageing in the Australian context is the diversification of ethnicity. Australia's migrant population across the mid- to late twentieth century was comprised typically of people in their early to middle adulthood years. Migrants who are in or beginning to move into late adulthood at this time are those who arrived in Australia from Europe after the Second World War and from Vietnam following the Vietnam War, in particular. This is reflected in the statistics relating to the current non-English speaking countries of origin that are represented by more than 20,000 people over the age of sixty-five in Australia:

> The largest groups were from Italy, Poland, Germany, the former Yugoslavia, Greece, the Netherlands and China. By 2026, population projections indicate that there will be 16 such groups, six of which will be from Asian countries (Vietnam, China, Philippines, India, Malaysia and Sri Lanka). (Rowland 2007 p. 118)

It is estimated that 22.5 per cent of the total older population will have been born overseas and therefore the older population will be culturally and linguistically diverse (ABS 2005b). This will shift again in decades to come as migrants and refugees from war-torn African and Middle-Eastern countries continue to settle in Australia, and live through into late adulthood beyond the 2020s and 2030s. For each of these migrant populations, specific opportunities, stressors and losses can occur in late adulthood, and we will explore some of these later in the chapter.

There are vast social policy implications for all of these shifts in the ageing population—particularly in relation to the overall rapid increase in this age group but also in relation to the gender, ethnicity and health issues associated with this increase. Concern has been raised as to the implications for the 'dependency ratio' and how it will change; that is, the shift in the number of people in paid employment, housing arrangements, aged care facilities, care arrangements, Medicare and superannuation. While concerns are expressed about the shift, there are also benefits, which some suggest get overlooked because of Australia's long history of ageism. For example, Edgar (2002 p. 17) notes:

> There is no careful noting of the fact that dependency ratios (the number of productive workers relative to dependent others) are also affected by reduced costs for dependent children, longer and more productive working lives, more effective approaches to care of the aged.

Changes in the structural dimensions of Australian ways of living will be critical to ensure that adequate and appropriate access to transport, health care and community engagement is available, supporting the ongoing development of optimal lifestyles and coping capacities of older people. What emerges consistently from studies of ageing is the continuing, profound interaction between people and their environments in relation to risk and resilience in this stage of the lifespan, as with other stages. Thus, as we have explored in other chapters, 'ageing may be a universal phenomenon but its impact and meaning are mediated by economic, structural and cultural factors' (Hendricks & Achenbaum 1999 p. 22).

Table 13.3 highlights some of domain-specific theories typically used to understand the transitions of ageing.

Key psychosocial theories

The psychosocial dimensions of ageing are considered from a number of different theoretical perspectives, each of which emphasises particular dimensions. Table 13.3 provides a summary of Bengston, Burgess and Parrott's (1997) meta-analysis of the theoretical underpinnings of published research that they reviewed throughout the early 1990s and termed 'third generation' theories of social gerontology.

TABLE **13.3** Ways of theorising the psychosocial aspects of ageing

Theory	Level or focus of theory	Key tenets
Social constructionist theory	Micro-level or individual level	Individuals are connected with their social-structural contexts • Social meanings of ageing are negotiated discourses • Meanings shift over time
Social exchange theory	Micro-level or individual level	Exchange behaviours shift as people age • What is received and given in exchanges can be analysed • Resources and exchanges will be different and often unequal and 'governed by norms of reciprocity' (Bengston et al. 1997 p. S78)
Life course and age stratification theories	Micro-macro level or person:environment level	Ageing is a dynamic, contextual process • Transitions are age-related • Ageing is influenced by social, structural and cultural dimensions • Time dimensions influence ageing, particularly cohort experiences
Feminist theories	Micro-macro level or person:environment level	Gender is a major organising factor in social life • Gender influences the equality experiences and resources of ageing
Political economy of ageing theories	Macro-level or structural/cultural level	'socio-economic and political constraints shape the experience of ageing' (Bengston et al. 1997 p. S82)
Critical gerontology	Macro-level or structural/cultural level	Ageing needs to be theorised critically, and subjectively • Positive, heterogeneous understandings of ageing should be developed

Source: Adapted from Bengston et al. 1997

Previous generations of ageing theory focused on disengagement and activity theories—notions of a gradual and necessary disengagement from relationships and of a 'use it or lose it' notion of capacities. While elements of these theories linger, third generation theories have become increasingly multidimensional (taking into account structural and cultural dimensions as well as individual and relational) in their focus, and strengths bases.

As we consider each of biopsychosocial-spiritual dimensions of late adulthood, reflect on the way in which each of the broader theoretical lenses outlined below influence (both explicitly and implicitly) and privilege certain understandings of these key transitions and tasks of ageing.

Cognitive development

Studies of cognitive changes in late adulthood have found that factors influencing these changes were related to health risk factors such as hypertension and diabetes, and with more environmentally determined protective factors such as education, environmental complexity, cognitive engagement, and exercise:

> We conclude then that many of the phenomena of cognitive ageing, at least in those individuals who will eventually become cognitively impaired or those who represent the sparse group of the unusually well-functioning 'super-aged' can be traced back to physiological and behaviour changes that begin in midlife (or even earlier). (Willis & Schaie 2005 p. 266)

While cognitive changes, such as changes in short-term memory, are identifiable in a functional way in late adulthood, they are strongly connected with earlier developmental tasks and experiences.

Many people report changes in memory capacity, such as word-finding difficulties or 'seniors moments' when known information is temporarily irretrievable. Studies highlight that the information is still stored in people's memories, it just takes a longer time to process and access certain information.

For many older people of non-English speaking backgrounds, a return to a first language and attrition in the skills of a second or additional language has been noted with increased ageing (Goral 2004). This too has been associated with changes in information retrieval capacities. This has implications for aged care facilities or caregivers who may not share the language of the older person, and communication difficulties can arise.

Others have noted new cognitive developments in late adulthood, particularly in relating to the complex skills of insight and wisdom. As Berger (2008 p. 676) notes: 'Many people become more responsive to nature, more interested in creative endeavours, and more philosophical as they grow older'. This highlights the bringing together of learnings from earlier experiences, observations of the complexity of human experience and a vocabulary with which to pass on these observations to others.

Reminiscence therefore plays an important part in late adulthood, defined as 'the volitional or nonvolitional act or process of recollecting memories of one's self in the past' (Cappeliez et al. 2008 p. 266). Through interviews with eighty older people, one study found that 'narrative reminiscence very frequently sets up or amplifies positive emotions' and thus has a strong positive impact on well-being (Cappeliez et al. 2008 p. 270). Reflecting back on what was, rather than focusing in the present on what may no longer be, serves a positive, protective function for many people. Validation therapy (Day 1997) was developed as a way of affirming the cognitive capacities and strengths of older people. Questions focus on exploring an individual's reality rather than orienting them to a factual focus, and questions support the emotional and subjective reality they are describing.

Emotional development

Emotional development in later life is described in relation to 'accepting oneself and seeing one's life as meaningful' (Hutchison 2003 p. 426). Erikson described this lifespan stage as leading to an emergent wisdom, as developing a capacity to maintain a sense of ego-integrity rather than despair: 'the task of achieving some sense of peace and unity with respect to one's life' (Vaillant 2003 p. 1379). Erikson (1968 p. 141) saw this 'final' stage of psychosocial development as relating to a sense of 'I am what survives of me'. He saw integrity as a new form of ego strength:

> Strength here takes the form of that detached yet active concern with life bounded by death, which we call wisdom in its many connotations from ripened 'wits' to accumulated knowledge, mature judgment and inclusive understanding. (Erikson 1968 p. 140)

Kalish (1989 p. 48) summarises **ego-integrity** as follows: 'The older person must maintain the wholeness, the adequacy, the meaning of self, in the face of stresses and losses that can readily bring about despair'. Studies of emotional expression in late adulthood tend to show an effective regulation of emotions overall (Labouvie-Vief et al. 1989 p. 262), but curiously do not support the popularly held view that wisdom is a feature of ageing (Labouvie-Vief 1999).

Temperament and personality development

Personality traits tend to be relatively stable across the lifespan, particularly in relation to temperament and to the big five personality factors (McCrae & John 1992): openness, conscientiousness, extroversion, agreeableness and neuroticism. Personality seems to be 'less affected by age-related decline than is true for intellectual functioning' (Smith & Baltes 1999 p. 165). However, studies have highlighted the increasing importance of a sense of optimism and humour in coping with the adversities and challenges of ageing (Vaillant 2002). Optimism continues to be strongly linked with both a healthier inner-world experience and relational and social connections, through eliciting positive reactions from others (Seligman 1992).

Remember the discussion of the protective role of optimism in Chapter 4.

Relational development

The risk and protective factors evident in relationships earlier in the lifespan continue to emerge in relationships in later adulthood. Positive psychosocial engagement and attachments remain key to all of the biopsychosocial-spiritual dimensions of health and well-being. A significant risk factor in later adulthood relationships, though, and particularly in late late adulthood, that is arguably more unique to this stage in the lifespan is the experience of loss within these relationships.

Research into the relationship patterns of later adulthood highlights that for many people there is a contraction of social networks down to closer ties with family members and a smaller group of friends. The shrinkage in opportunities for socialising is related both to mobility and access issues, and through the reduction of friendship networks as other people become ill or disabled, or die. These changes were evident as people aged, for example, in the General Social Survey conducted by the Australian Bureau of Statistics in 2003, where seventy-two per cent of fifty-five- to sixty-four-year-olds, compared with only forty-one percent of people over eighty-five, reported going out with or meeting a group of friends in outdoor activities. Only slightly more, forty-eight per cent, reported meeting friends for indoor activities in the last three months (AIHW 2008b p. 144).

While much of the emphasis in the ageing literature is on the loss of relationships later in the lifespan, in this section we look also at the research that highlights the ongoing significance of good, secure relationships right throughout life. We look at some of what is known about relationships with partners, with children, with grandchildren, with siblings and with friends/peers. Later in this chapter we look at the stress, trauma and loss aspects of relationships. Part of the challenge in understanding relational development in late adulthood is the diversity of experience and the absence of extensive research.

Partners

Partnerships continue to be an important source of emotional, economic and practical support throughout late adulthood, although many partnerships undergo significant transitions as people retire, become grandparents, and experience their own transitions in health and well-being. Census data suggests that many people over the age of sixty-five continue to live together in marriage, with a smaller number of people cohabiting (ABS 2006b) until the death of one partner. For the current generational cohort, marital satisfaction tends to be high for couples who have stayed together over many decades (Parker 2002). The resilience factors within these enduring relationships seem to include separating from the family of origin, building togetherness and creating autonomy, becoming parents, coping with crises, making a safe place for conflict, exploring sexual love and intimacy, sharing laughter and keeping interests alive, providing emotional nurturance, and preserving a double vision—that is, keeping in mind 'images from the past and of the realities of the present' (Parker 2002 pp. 19–22). Women, given their longevity, are more likely to be widowed than men (AIHW 2002).

A small increase in the numbers of divorces in later life is being seen, although most divorces occur earlier in the life of a relationship. The concern for this group is that they 'may find themselves without the family support they need in older age' (Millward 1997 p. 30). This is particularly the case with divorced fathers who may have weak ties with adult children, particularly if they have remarried. The Later Life Families Study has shown that marital history, rather than whether people are living alone or not, is the determinant of the perceived and received support between the generations (Millward 1997 p. 31), as is the frequency of contact. For men, later life divorce has been found to lead to increased social isolation and distance from family contact, compared with women experiencing the opposite (Schapiro 2003). However, men who are widowed in later adulthood are more likely to repartner in late adulthood.

For older gay and lesbian couples, while less is known about relationship patterns across the lifespan, many of the issues of late adulthood relationships are similar (Hughes 2009). Discrimination and homophobia can continue to play a part in a gay and lesbian couple's experiences, particularly in relation to partners having to move into health care settings.

Many partnerships undergo significant changes when one partner's health declines; there is a transition for one partner to a carer role and all of its responsibilities (Ozanne 2007) and for the other to being dependent and having to be cared for.

Families

The emphasis within much of the research on families and ageing is on the shifting dependence from one generation to the next. The 'Families, household and care data' (ABS 1999) from the 1996 census, for example, revealed that:

» most older people live with other family members
» fifteen per cent of those aged between sixty-five and seventy-four years live alone, compared to thirty-five per cent of those aged between seventy-five and eighty-four
» four per cent of those aged between sixty-five and eighty-four live in aged care accommodation, compared with thirty-four per cent over the age of eight-five years (predominantly female)

» twenty-one per cent of sixty-five to seventy-four-year-olds are caring for someone else, compared with eighteen per cent of those aged seventy-five to eighty-four.

Rather than the 'role reversal' that is often talked about between the generations, what occurs is some role change or even task reversal, signifying that although the subjective or qualitative aspects of the relationship do not change, there is a shift in some of the 'doing' or practicalities of that relationship (de Vaus 1995). The reciprocal nature of relationships is sustained throughout social and family networks, as described in Chapter 2, into late adulthood. Many Australians in early late adulthood find themselves 'in the middle' still in terms of family roles and responsibilities, juggling the needs of three other generations around them—their ageing parents, their adult children and their grandchildren. Families are not static entities and many people in later adulthood continue to experience shifts in families, through divorce or separation in their adult children's partnerships. This often requires the management of multiple roles between multiple family members, as the relationships of the younger generations shift (Millward 1997).

Grandparenting

Another relationship transition that occurs typically in late adulthood, if not in middle adulthood, is the transition to a grandparent role. This transition, like many others, varies enormously depending on a range of issues. Geographical distance, the health of the grandparents, and the pre-existing relationship with children, for example, influence the extent of interaction. For many grandparents, this role is a source of a sense of generativity and a sense of purpose, engaging in these relationships in different ways and with different responsibilities from their earlier roles with their own children. For this reason, when families divorce or separate, the loss of contact between grandparents and grandchildren can be a major source of loss and grief, often unrecognised by others (Ferguson 2004).

Australia is witnessing an increase in the number of grandparent-headed families, often when parents are unable to be care providers for their own children as a result of mental health and/or substance abuse issues. In Australia in 2003, 22,500 families were grandparent families providing support and care for 31,100 children under the age of seventeen years. Of these families, 3,300 were raising 6,800 children aged zero to four years. Nearly half (forty-seven per cent) of these families were headed by one grandparent only, and in sixty-one per cent of these grandparent-headed families, the youngest grandparent was over the age of fifty-five years (AIHW 2007 p. 23).

Grandparents are contributing significantly to family life also through the provision of day care. It is estimated that grandparents provide informal care to twenty per cent of all children aged zero to seventeen (AIHW 2007 p.24). This highlights the strength of intergenerational relationships within many families.

Siblings

Another way in which family relationships remain strong is in the connections between siblings. Carrying a shared history over so many years and being able to reminisce together about an earlier history is part of this significant connection. Some studies suggest that elderly female siblings are more likely to keep connected with each other, and female siblings are more emotionally supportive to both female and male siblings (Cicirelli 1989). Attachments to siblings are important across the lifespan and tend to have been minimised as important psychological, if not instrumental, sources of support in late adulthood.

Remember the discussion of learning to manage aggression in early childhood through sibling rather than peer relationships because siblings had more knowledge of each other.

Peers

Relationships with friends of all ages are important continuing protective factors. Age, class, ethnicity and gender factors are all significant influences in these networks of support. One Dutch study of 4,494 people showed that only fifteen per cent of those aged eighty or more had contact with people under the age of sixty-five years, highlighting that older people's networks become increasingly age-segregated (Uhlenberg & De Jong Gierveld 2004). Gender differences, too, continue to be apparent in people's social networks, with men's relationships particularly influenced by the opportunities available (Perren et al. 2003). Men's relationships historically have relied on workplace connections and on their partner as confidante. For men who are retired, single and/or widowed, the formal and informal opportunities in communities to form new and ongoing connections become critical. One such initiative in the Australian context is the Men's Shed program, which recognises the space a man's shed can provide to potter about in, as well as build and repair things, Men's Sheds create these spaces communally now in neighbourhoods around Australia.

Refer to Chapter 2 for the discussion of the importance of social networks.

Remember the story of Elsie Brown in Chapter 2, who died alone and was undiscovered for years given she lived alone and disconnected from her local community.

Local neighbourhoods can become particularly important sources of networks. People can become increasingly isolated if they are unable to access friendships and networks on a regular basis.

Gender and cultural identity

Gender identities are profoundly influenced by the ageing experience. Late adulthood is the only lifespan stage where women outnumber men. This has implications for relationships, well-being and care. Much has been written about the need for a feminist analysis of the gendered nature of ageing, particularly in relation to poverty and health. For many ageing women of the current cohort, who have not had the same level of economic independence as young women currently do throughout their lives, the same capacity to develop financial management skills and reserves has not been possible, leading to concern for older women, in particular, who have never married.

Russell (2007 p. 110) argues that gendered identities are 'alive and well at older ages', particularly relating to preferred lifestyles after retirement and privatised experiences such as the meanings and connections with 'home' (Russell 2007 p. 111). As we look at later in this chapter, there is a tendency to homogenise the ageing experience—overlooking the significance of differences in gender, class, ethnicity and culture, and sexuality for older people.

Moral and/or spiritual development

Wisdom is often cited as an emergent quality of later adulthood (Le 2008), connected with the ego-integrity tasks of facing death, reviewing life and finding meaning and coherence. Wisdom is often connected with a strong sense of morality and/or spirituality—a sense of knowing about the ultimate and important things in life (Erikson 1959). Fowler and Dell's faith development model supports this view, in proposing that many adults go on to develop a universalised faith focus.

> The faith development model is discussed in Chapter 11.

Spirituality is seen by many to have a more important role in well-being in later life. Two of the major areas of investigation around the protective value of religion and/or spirituality include understanding their role in promoting well-being and understanding their role in facing the inevitability of death and therefore mediating death anxiety (Morris & McAdie 2009).

For those in later adulthood at present, formal religious practice has been a major part of many of their lives, throughout their childhood and, for many, continuing throughout their adulthood. Australian data show that, 'In 2001, 82% of persons aged 65 years and over identified themselves as Christian, compared with 60% of 18–24 year olds' (ABS 2006b). It is hard to determine whether these affiliations reflect strong spiritual connections or the more practical connections that church environments offer, such as regular contact, social support and, in many instances, social activities and meals.

> We explored the significance of practical or instrumental support in Chapter 2.

Extensive research looked at spiritual development and experience in late adulthood particularly in relation to coping with dying and death. Many people report that religion and/or spirituality provides an important framework for maintaining hope and meaning in the face of inevitable death, particularly given that most religious traditions involve some belief in an afterlife (Morris & McAdie 2009).

Vocational identity

Like other phases in adulthood, work is seen as a core domain of well-being. The focus within the work dimension is largely on retirement, the transition out of the workplace. Recent statistics show that the majority of people retire between the ages of sixty and sixty-nine years.

TABLE **13.4** Retirement patterns and intentions

Males:	60–64 years	65–69 years	70+ years
Retirement status:			
Retired	35.9	67.7	90.8
Not retired	64.1	32.3	9.2
Employed			
Intends to retire	81.8	76.2	56.0
Never intends to retire	18.2	23.8	44.0
Females:	60–64 years	65–69 years	70+ years
Retirement status:			
Retired	56.5	84.4	97.1
Not retired	43.5	15.6	2.9
Employed			
Intends to retire	86.9	77.7	72.3
Never intends to retire	13.1	22.3	27.7*

* Estimate has a standard error of twenty-five to fifty per cent and should be used with caution.

Source: ABS 2009c p. 25

The transition of retirement is a subjective one, dependent upon many factors. Weiss (1997) compares research to show that it can be a 'burden' or 'boon' experience, with every study showing that there are substantial proportions of samples that are dissatisfied and substantial proportions that are satisfied. Some of the determinants in the retirement experience relate to what the person is retiring from and to, with the main cited reason for retirement being the person's health (AIHW 2009a). In studies of men's experiences of retirement, professional men experience fewer reported difficulties compared with those in managerial or administrative roles, with the argument being that there is frequently an opportunity to continue skills as a retired professional than if retired from management positions. Australia is slowly seeing a resurgence of demand for older workers, following a devastating decade of redundancies and early retirement packages during the late 1980s and the early 1990s. There is increasing recognition of the expertise and wisdom of experienced workers, the longer retirement periods that individuals are facing, and the political clout of the baby boom generation who are creating a shift of influence in policy development. In addition, with the global financial crisis of 2009, and the subsequent loss of up to thirty per cent of superannuation and life savings, many older Australians now face a less financially secure future and may postpone retirement until later again in their life.

Women's retirement patterns are less well known than those of men, with the generation of the baby boomers being the first cohort of women to remain in the paid workforce in Australia throughout their lives. For many women in late adulthood, family life has been the vocational task and orientation of their lives, and continues to be so through their retirement.

How and where older people spend their day can have a profound impact on health and well-being, as daily occupations shape a sense of identity and self-worth and provide important relationships and connections. For many older people, volunteering and participating in the community and unpaid workforce is a part of daily life. In addition to the Men's Shed project mentioned earlier, many organisations provide opportunities for older people to meet together and meet new people, such as the University of the Third Age, Probus, Legacy, Rotary, and neighbourhood house, public library or community health centre programs.

RESEARCH IN CONTEXT

'MAKING THE MOST OF IT': LIVING TO AGE 100 YEARS OR MORE IN AUSTRALIA

John McCormack, from La Trobe University has been researching the experiences of Australian centenarians.

The first part of the title of this heading is a quote from a lady named Eileen, aged 101 years, in response to one question from the author's Australian Centenarian Study which asks 'Is it good to live to 100 years or more?' The meaning of her response, that she was 'making the most of it', however was not so much about squeezing every last drop of life from an already long existence, but more a common reflection expressed in this study among our oldest old of an adaptive attitude to life and longevity. It is an approach to life that is positive and accepting without being unrealistic. At very old age no-one escapes some serious aches and pains, arthritis being a common disease, or indeed something even more life-threatening such as some degree of cardiovascular disease, which nevertheless might be controlled with medication and lifestyle changes (Andersen-Ranberg, Schroll & Jeune 2001). However, in the main, the centenarian respondents in the survey illustrate a fairly stoic optimism, gratitude and enjoyment towards the life they have experienced and continue to live. They illustrate resilience and a successful adaptation to a very long life, which is at odds with a common misconception that anyone who lives this long must be frail and decrepit.

These insights into the lives and heterogeneity of the very old are important because although awareness and even knowledge of 'the aged', i.e. those aged 65 years or more, is now reasonably widespread, research findings are often presented at such a highly aggregated age level that it can be difficult to detect differences within the older group. In fact centenarians may well have adult children alive who would also fit the 'aged' category because they are in their in the sixties, seventies or even eighties, yet we know little about these inter-generational relations. Also, despite our rapidly increasing knowledge of ageing, we still see very little written about the self-assessed quality of life and coping skills at old age let alone very old age. There may be valuable health and social lessons we can learn from people who have survived to great ages, not so much about preventing death as about promoting health, and this knowledge may be useful for the large numbers of baby-boomers coming through behind the current cohort of very old people. This is about the 'Longevity Revolution'—that we are living longer (and healthier?).

Questions

1   What are the multidimensional determinants of this longevity phenomenon?
2   Are there really 'secrets' to living to 100 years?
3   If you do get to this age, do you think life will still be worth living? What is the quality of life at this very old age?
4   Do you have a great-grandparent alive?
5   How many of your grandparents are still alive?

Coping with risks and adversities

Stress

As much of the discussion throughout this chapter has highlighted, ageing can bring with it many unique stressors. Changes can occur very rapidly or gradually and incrementally, causing stress and fear for older people. Many of these stressors are well managed, but social workers should be aware of the multiplicity of changes with which older people are typically coping. Think about the scenarios presented in the following box and the ways in which risk and stress in later adulthood could be understood differently for people in each of these situations:

APPLY YOUR UNDERSTANDING: THINKING ABOUT STRESS AND AGEING

» Ending up in hospital after a fall can mean the person never returns to live at home independently again.

» Gradually experiencing visual and memory problems, making it very difficult to negotiate daily life.

» Relying on the Centrelink age pension of $569.80 per fortnight to support all the financial needs of a single person—including housing, food and medical supplies.

Questions

1 What impact do you think being over eighty-five at the time of experiencing these stressors would have?

2 What difference would gender make in each of these scenarios?

3 What difference could ethnicity make in each of these scenarios?

In this section, we explore briefly some of the key stress experiences for older people, including poverty, health, mental health, caregiving, retirement, loneliness and isolation, and ageism.

Poverty continues to be a major stressor for many people in late adulthood. The socio-economic resources of an individual not only determine their immediate material circumstances and the resources available to them by way of housing, access to care, and financial security, it also, as many studies have shown, determines longevity and health status. To reiterate from an earlier in this chapter: 'The most economically and socially deprived sections of society have higher mortality rates, experience more ill health and use fewer preventive services' (Greig et al. 2003 p. 51).

Ethnicity also influences the experience of ageing, shaping expectations within ethnic groups and families about roles and hierarchies within family, familial care obligations, and understandings of ageing and death. Many assumptions surround families of particular ethnicities in relation to the value and care they express for their extended family networks, with some ethnic groups assumed to be providing more extensive vertical care than others. In the multicultural context of Australian life, what seems to be the conclusion about this is that 'when younger members of an ethnic group value their ethnic identity, the position of older members as symbols and or specialists is likely to be strengthened' (Germain 1991 p. 42).

Throughout earlier sections of this chapter, we looked at the biological changes of ageing. Many people experience frustration and stress at the changes in health status, often engaging in self-blame when they are unable to prevent some of the illnesses and frailties of ageing—such as preventing falls or the onset of cancer.

Fears of hospitalisation and/or uncertainties about having to move from home are frequently reported concerns of older people.

In relation to mental health, many of the illnesses and difficulties of earlier adult life continue, with anxiety, depression and suicidal behaviour still prevalent (Bloch & Singh 1997). Substance abuse, which is associated with some of these mental health difficulties, particularly depression, continues in late adulthood. Men over the age of seventy-five are one of the highest risk age groups for suicide (Graham et al. 2000 p. 4). The risk factors for suicide among older men include financial stress, managing family discord and severe physical illness (Duberstein et al. 2004). The reasons proposed for suicidal behaviour in older men include the loss of spouse, the loss of status and organisational affiliation, depression, financial problems, chronic or life-threatening illness, a fear of placement in residential care, hopelessness and alcoholism (Germain 1991 p. 428). Many of these factors are consistent with Durkheim's (2002 [1897]) theory of suicide, in which he proposed that suicide was strongly correlated with the degree of connectedness or belonging within a particular group.

The 'burden' of care giving and its role changes and responsibilities (Ozanne 2007) can be very stressful for people, typically women, and often brings about sleep deprivation, frustration and despair. Some of the other aspects of the 'burden' of ageing for both the carer and the person being cared for are related to the loss of independence, of identity, control, spontaneity and the right to take risks (Thompson 2001 p. 167).

The major burden of retirement is the financial burden, particularly with the expected increase in longevity and the current global financial crisis. Many studies overlook this important issue in considering the adaptation to retirement, focusing instead on identity and quality of life issues. There are serious implications for retirement at sixty-five if an individual is going to live well into their nineties. Poverty for older Australians, and the financial burden that this could create for younger Australians, will be a critical issue for the future, as will the gendered nature of this situation (de Vaus & Qu 1998). Women who are currently in the over sixty-five year age group have not historically been fully employed within the work force, and did not have the same superannuation and equal pay rights as younger generations. Retirement can bring with it significant financial loss, a loss of structure and routine, a loss of sources of self-esteem, a loss of role, a loss of support and contact through the networks established in the workplace, and significant changes in relationships with a partner. On the other hand, it can bring a new liberation, and a new phase of growth and development of interests, far more satisfying than paid employment.

Perhaps the underlying stressor throughout many of these changes described in this chapter is the increased experience for many older people of isolation and loneliness. The high stress often experienced in earlier stages of the lifespan changes to being low or hypostress, along with reduced formal contact with a wide range of people. Stress management strategies for older people often place the rebuilding of social networks at their centre.

In addition to this isolation and loneliness, many people can also experience overt and covert ageism. The International Year of Older Persons was declared in 1999 to challenge the negative assumptions and the ageism that is rife in not only our community but also the international community. The United Nations principles for the year focused on 'the circumstances and contributions of older people', including 'independence, participation, care, self-fulfilment and dignity' (United Nations 1999). This was to challenge some of the long-held and often incorrect assumptions about ageing. Some of the ways in which older people can experience ageism from those around them are outlined in Table 13.1, based on Thompson's identified common categories of discrimination.

See Chapter 4 for a discussion of the different ways in which stress can be experienced, both through too little demand and too much demand.

TABLE **13.5** Processes of discrimination

Form	Description
Stereotyping	Filtering and simplifying complex information about people into fixed 'typifications' so that they are not seen as unique individuals in unique circumstances Example: Making a generalisation that all older people no longer continue to experience intimacy in relationships
Marginalisation	Pushing people 'to the margins of society' through various behaviours, attitudes and social structures Example: Assuming all older people are in nursing homes and not active citizens in the community
Invisibilisation	Rendering minority groups invisible 'in language and imagery' in the dominant discourse Example: Labelling
Infantilisation	Ascribing a childlike status to an adult Example: Speaking slowly and loudly to older adults and calling them 'darling' or 'love'
Welfarism	Regarding 'certain groups as necessarily in need of welfare services by virtue of their membership of such groups' Example: Assuming all older people are pensioners
Medicalisation	Ascribing 'the status of "ill" to someone' Example: Assuming all older people are frail and unwell
Dehumanisation	Using language to treat people as things Example: Calling them 'pet'
Trivialisation	Ascribing a trivial status or no status to issues of inequality Example: Assuming all older people are accustomed to death and dying and therefore the death of another friend should have little or no impact

Source: based on Thompson 2003, pp. 82–92

Trauma

For many older people, traumas are an inescapable part of life. Furthermore, given the accumulation of experiences over a lifespan, it is possible that some past traumas are exacerbated, have a late onset or re-emerge in later adulthood (Graziano 2003 p. 4). Older adults 'at risk of the reemergence of symptoms of traumatic stress' identified by Graziano (2003 p. 14) include victims of interpersonal violence, veterans of war and immigrants from war-torn or traumatised countries. Many older people have to deal with current traumas such as natural disasters. In this section we look at each of these, but begin with a focus on older people and natural disasters.

For people in late adulthood, natural disasters can bring unique challenges— both in terms of immediate survival and in terms of longer term adaptation to them. Studies highlight that older age can be associated with poorer outcomes, as in the case of recovery from the Newcastle earthquake. Older women, in particular, who participated in a study of earthquake survivors, had greater difficulty adjusting in the aftermath of the earthquake, as they were physically relocated and lost their sense of community and belonging (Carr et al. 1995). It makes sense that the loss of place, social connections and history may have more impact on well-being for older people, given that there is not necessarily a sense or a reality that in time these can be recreated or reestablished.

In other studies, old age has been found to be more protective, as in the case of breast cancer studies, whereby older women were more accepting of their diagnosis and prognosis (Northouse 1994). These findings highlight the complexities within both the nature of the traumatic events and in the responses people have, highlighting the importance of careful assessment in each trauma context.

Many older people experience interpersonal violence and trauma, either in the privacy of their own homes and families, in institutional care or in public places, a fact that has only recently been acknowledged. Elder abuse, through physical, emotional, sexual or financial abuse and neglect, has been estimated to affect in the realm of 80,000 people per year in Australia, with some suggesting a figure five times this is more realistic (Elder Abuse Prevention Association 2009). Given that there is no public system for reporting elder abuse, this trauma often remains silenced within the community, rendering many older people powerless.

Other older people are coming to terms with intergenerational traumas—such as those experienced through being part of Australia's Stolen Generations (Atkinson 2003), or through parents who survived the Holocaust and other attrocities of war (Valent 2002). In this sense, trauma is alive in people's memories both in the past and the present. An awareness of people's trauma histories can make a critical difference, such as understanding the implications of institutional care on survivors of concentration camp experiences. The distance of time and the psychosocial tasks of ageing can sometimes give some opportunity to address these experiences and begin to make some sense of them. Traumas that were previously silenced or unmentionable can be talked about, both collectively and individually, sometimes for the first time in people's lives. Some veterans of the Vietnam War, many of whom are now in their sixties and seventies, are experiencing group therapy as a useful way of talking through their experiences, and learning to manage their post-traumatic stress symptoms (Creamer & Singh 2003). These traumas come to life in late adulthood, sometimes as people are more actively engaged in reminiscing about their lives and are arguably in a safer place in their lives. For some it is about ensuring history is not forgotten and politicising their trauma experiences (Tummala-Nara 2007).

It is important to remember that communities now engage in responding to traumas in very different ways than even a couple of decades ago. In much of the twentieth century, people were expected to cope by repressing what had happened and moving on with things. This less expressive way of coping with a whole range of traumas and losses was encouraged. It is unknown whether older people may be liberated or further traumatised by the more open emotional and verbal expression that is promoted today in Australia.

Refer to Chapter 5 for current understandings of trauma reactions.

Loss

Old age, particularly late old age, inevitably brings with it an increase in exposure to loss experiences. Increases in longevity mean that there are more years for strong relationships to form, not only with family members, but also within informal friendship networks. As Walter argues, 'bereavement becomes less a loss of status or of income, more the loss of a deeply personal attachment' (Walter 1999 p. xvi). Old age also brings with it losses in function, often with decreasing physical and mental capacity, and often losses of place, with the need to move on the basis of health issues to live with family or in a form of institutional care. For example, as women reach ninety years and more, in particular, the majority (eighty-two per cent) will be in aged care (AIHW 2008b p. 99). Within Western cultures, a loss of social status is often experienced with all of these changes.

A major area of change is in relation to the death of contemporaries, both partners and friends. As we examined in earlier chapters, having at least one friend as a confidante is stress buffering. Many relationships for older people have been maintained over many decades. Research shows that these friendships tend to follow the patterns established in earlier years. Their loss is often the loss of the only people who have known them and their personal history, and a continuity of meaning and identity can be eroded. Grief in late adulthood is often minimised and disenfranchised, as people are expected to accept these losses as part of growing old.

A more specific area of focus has been on the transition to widowhood with the death of a partner. For most people, this constitutes a major loss, which requires significant readjustment in every dimension of experience. Parkes's early studies of grief in England highlighted that the first year following the death of a spouse, the widowed partner was at increased risk of mortality and serious illness (Parkes 1972), a phenomenon that continues today (Stroebe 2006).

While death can occur at any point in the lifespan, it is inevitable in late adulthood. The experience of **death anxiety** among older adults has been the focus of a great deal of research (Langs 1997). An essential factor in alleviating some of the stress, trauma or loss of these experiences is often associated with the extent of control people will have over decisions regarding end-of-life care, and the ways in which dignity and a pain-free death can be managed.

Terror management theory (Greenberg, Solomon & Pyszynski 1997) outlines a way of understanding the strategies of emotion regulation in the face of this reality of death. This theory proposes that human beings have developed cultural worldviews, and religion in particular, as a way of defending against the anxiety and reality of our own mortality. Seeing our lives in a bigger context, of history and culture, enables us to place our lives in a meaningful context beyond the level of individual experience (Benton et al. 2007), enabling the terror of non-existence to become a relatively manageable anxiety.

Chapter 6 examined ways in which moving towards our own deaths might be conceptualised.

Remember the discussion of the protective factors in the cultural dimensions shaping our experience, discussed in Chapter 3.

Promoting resilience

Resilience in later adulthood is characterised by many of the resilience resources in earlier life—the availability of strong social and financial supports and the inner-world strengths of optimism and a sense of coherence. Many people have shown resilience in ageing, described as **successful ageing**. The determinants of successful ageing have been looked at in a number of studies, the most well known being that of Vaillant (2002), mentioned earlier. Vaillant has been following a sample of men from Harvard University into late adulthood. At the age of seventy-five, the mortality rate of the Harvard sample is only half that expected of them as white males when compared with their birth cohort. Sixty per cent of men have survived or will survive past their eightieth birthday, compared with only thirty per cent of white American males born in the 1920s cohort. They are seen as people who are ageing well. The conclusions Vaillant has drawn to date about the protective factors for this sample are summarised in the box below. Late adulthood, therefore, brings with it continuing opportunities for growth and change, although the balance tends to tip towards increasing experiences of adversity.

VAILLANT'S CONCLUSIONS FOR AGEING WELL

» It is not the bad things that happen to us that doom us; it is the good people who happen to us at any age that facilitate enjoyable old age.

» Healing relationships are facilitated by a capacity for gratitude, for forgiveness and for taking people inside.

» A good marriage at fifty predicted positive ageing at eighty, but surprisingly, low cholesterol levels at age fifty did not.

» Alcohol abuse—unrelated to unhappy childhood—consistently predicted unsuccessful ageing, in part because alcoholism damaged future social supports.

» Learning to play and create after retirement and learning to gain younger friends as we lose older ones add more to life's enjoyment than retirement income.

» Objective physical health was less important to successful ageing than subjective health.

Source: Vaillant 2002 p.13

CHAPTER SUMMARY

The Australian population is a rapidly ageing population, bringing new challenges and opportunities to all dimensions of individual and social life. Some of the challenges and opportunities of this changing demographic can be already anticipated, but others will be surprises. If it was a seemingly impossible task to generalise the developmental tasks of earlier developmental phases, it is more difficult to generalise the developmental tasks and experiences of adulthood, spanning some sixty or so years beyond adolescence. As people live longer lives, with changing relationship and family patterns, the diversity of experience, particularly in middle adulthood, makes it profoundly complicated to generalise in any way.

Despite these difficulties in generalising, there are some recurrent themes relating to significant influences across these lifespan stages. For adults of all ages, the protective value of relationships, family, work and health seem to be recurrent themes in well-being, along with a search for a sense of purpose and meaning. The factors connected with resilience continue to reflect the themes of resilience from earlier in the lifespan—positive attachments and social connectedness, and social competence in particular. The risk factors from earlier in life continue to echo throughout adult life —poor health and mental health outcomes continue to be related to the absence of supportive relationships, and certainly the absence of strong structural supports—income security, nutrition and health, employment and housing.

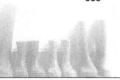

APPLYING A MULTIDIMENSIONAL UNDERSTANDING

CASE STUDY

Max and Helen: Looking after a parent

Max and Helen are in their mid to late sixties. Helen is a first generation Australian, whose parents were both in concentration camps in the Second World War in Poland. Helen's mother survived the camps, pregnant with Helen at the time, and she migrated to Australia, where she remarried and had two other sons. Max was born in Poland and migrated with his parents as a young child, just escaping ghetto and concentration camp experiences. Both his parents died when he was in his late forties.

Helen's mother, Rachel, is now in her nineties and is widowed for a second time. She wants to continue to live independently but she is increasingly physically frail and showing short-term memory loss. Helen's stepbrothers and their families are keen for Rachel to go into an aged care facility and Helen realises this may be necessary but is very ambivalent about it all. Helen is caring for her own grandchildren, who are two and four, two days a week, so that her daughter can return to work part-time.

Questions

1 What are the key stressors facing this family?
2 What else would you need to know about this situation in forming your psychosocial assessment?
3 What are some of the developmental risk and protective factors for each person in this situation?
4 What are some of the key structural and cultural dimensions that could have an impact on this family's situation?
5 What are the possibilities for:
    * practice interventions?
    * program interventions?
    * policy interventions?

KEY TERMS

ageing
death anxiety
ego-integrity
successful ageing
terror management theory

QUESTIONS AND DISCUSSION POINTS

1   What are some of the key biopsychosocial and spiritual developmental tasks of late adulthood?
2   What are some of the different risk and protective factors across this lifespan stage?
3   What are some of the structural and cultural dimensions that influence this stage?
4   What would you identify as the messages conveyed within your family about experiences of ageing?
5   What messages about ageing do you see in the wider community?
6   What expectations of the family are both explicit and implicit in the current structural context of aged care?
7   How do you see gender being constructed in late adulthood?
8   Imagine you are moving into an aged care facility—what are the most important qualities of that facility in your opinion?
9   In what ways do you see processes of discrimination occurring for older people? In what ways can these processes be challenged?

FURTHER READING

Birren, J. and Schaie, K. eds, 2006, *Handbook on the Psychology of Aging*, 6th edn, San Diego: Elsevier.
Borowski, A., Encel, S. & Ozanne, E. 2007, *Longevity and social change in Australia*, Sydney: University of NSW Press.
Day, C. 1997, 'Validation therapy: A review of the literature', *Journal of Gerontological Nursing*, April, 23(4), pp. 29–34.
Vaillant, G. 1993, *The wisdom of the ego*, Cambridge, MA: Harvard University Press.
Vaillant, G. 2002, *Ageing well: Surprising guideposts to a happier life from the landmark Harvard study of adult development*, Melbourne: Scribe Publications.

WEBSITES OF INTEREST

Alzheimers Australia: www.alzheimers.org.au
Alzheimers Australia is a peak body providing support and advocacy to Australians living with dementia and their carers. There are useful links to services, information and research on their website.

Australian Research Centre in Sex, Health and Society, La Trobe University: www.latrobe.edu.au/arcshs/
This research centre's website provides teaching materials, research and information relating to sexual health issues.

Centre for Speech, Language and the Brain, Cambridge University: http://csl.psychol.cam.ac.uk/research/ageing.html

This site provides information about the resilience of the ageing brain and the research centre's particular focus on language and ageing.

Cornell Institute for Translational Research on Aging (CITRA): www.citra.org/wordpress/

CITRA, associated with the Bronfenbrenner Life Course Center, has a particular emphasis on practitioner-researcher engagement. Its website provides information about the Institute's research on ageing.

Council on the Ageing (COTA): www.cota.org.au

COTA is Australia's leading seniors' organisation. This site provides information about the work of the Council, as well as useful policy, publication and advocacy information.

Department of Health and Ageing, Australian government: www.health.gov.au

The Australian government's Department of Health and Ageing website has extensive information on policies, programs and publications related to health and ageing.

Flinders Centre for Ageing Studies: http://flinders.edu.au/sabs/fcas/

This site includes details of the Australian Longitudinal Study of Ageing (ALSA).

Gay and Lesbian Ageing Issues in Australia: http://members.ozemail.com.au/~jamms/

This site focuses on ageing issues for gays and lesbians, and provides extensive links to other sites addressing sexuality.

Harvard Medical School: www.hms.harvard.edu

The Department of Social Medicine, in particular, has research material and links relating to the biopsychosocial dimensions of health. George Vaillant is Professor of Psychiatry at this institution.

Negotiating the Life Course, Australian National University: http://lifecourse.anu.edu.au

This ANU site provides information about and publications from Negotiating the Life Course, a national study of 'the changing life courses and decision-making processes of Australian men and women as the family and society move from male breadwinner orientation in the direction of higher levels of gender equity'.

Max Planck Institute for Demographic Research, Germany: www.demogr.mpg.de

This site provides international demographic data and research relating to ageing.

National Ageing Research Institute (NARI): www.nari.unimelb.edu.au

NARI, located at the University of Melbourne, has research projects associated with all aspects of ageing, with a focus on ageing well. Their website contains useful national and international links relating to ageing.

Seattle Longitudinal Study: http://geron.psu.edu/sls/publications/Schaie/

This site presents the extensive work of Schaie and Willis in relation to ageing, with a particular focus on cognitive changes and ageing.

PART **5**

Drawing the Themes Together

CHAPTER **14**

Reviewing a Multidimensional Approach

AIMS OF THIS CHAPTER

This chapter draws together the major themes of a multidimensional approach. It considers the following questions:

» What are the ongoing challenges in thinking about development and adaptation as multidimensional?
» What are the ongoing challenges in thinking about development and adaptation as influenced by both normative and non-normative factors?
» What are the implications of a multidimensional approach for theory and practice in social work and the human services?

Throughout the previous thirteen chapters, a multidimensional approach has been presented as one way in which we can begin to understand human development and adaptation. We began by examining our critical inner-world dimensions—the biological, psychological and spiritual dimensions. We then examined the critical outer-world dimensions—our relational, social, structural and cultural dimensions, all influenced by the dimension of time. In all of these levels of analysis, we examined the interdependence of these various dimensions, and the notions of risk and protective factors, and resilience within them.

In the second part of the book, we looked at issues of adaptation and coping following the specific life events and experiences of stress, trauma and grief, and seeing the extent to which this way of regarding human development differed from or expanded the more normative understandings of development. In the third part of the book, we examined coping and adaptation across the lifespan—the ways in which coping and adaptation are intimately connected with where an individual is at, according to the identified stages of the life course. While these discussions have been necessarily summary in their approach, many of the major issues for consideration for practice within social work have been raised.

To conclude the discussion, some of the ongoing issues related to the seven themes of a multidimensional approach that were proposed in Chapter 1 are now revisited and critiqued.

Critical dimensions

» An individual's inner world is multidimensional.

» The outer world, or context, in which individuals live is multidimensional.

» Time is multidimensional.

A multidimensional approach places an emphasis on the constant interaction of the biological, psychological and spiritual dimensions of our inner worlds with the relational, social, structural and cultural dimensions of our outer worlds. Influencing all of these is the dimension of time, which is in itself a multidimensional factor. The previous chapters have highlighted the very complex and reciprocal nature of the interactions between these dimensions, leading to different outcomes for our health and well-being.

A summary of the key developmental tasks, as discussed in this book, is given in Table 14.1. What these notions of stages attempt to capture is something of individual maturation processes and universal developmental stages. Throughout human experience, there are some biological givens—the transitions of birth, puberty, ageing and death, for example. Developmental stages and transitions, therefore, can be identified according to these predictable changes and the associated cognitive and emotional changes in capacities and skills across the lifespan. However, each of these stages and transitions is intimately linked with outer-world experiences and environments—aspects of our relational, social, structural and cultural dimensions.

In exploring specific stages of the lifespan, inevitably criticisms and questions emerge about such an approach. Questions arise as to the evidence-base for some of the theories, as they are sometimes derived from small samples or ones that are culturally, racially or gender biased. Questions arise, also, in relation to the cultural assumptions implicit in many of the perceived 'tasks' of development. For example, within Western cultures, individuation and gaining autonomy are seen as key developmental tasks from childhood to adulthood, whereas within collectively oriented cultures, including Australia's Indigenous communities, these are not culturally valued qualities or skills. How strongly, therefore, should they be promoted as developmental tasks for all children or adults? Is it possible or desirable to think about universal notions of development given the diversity of individuals, families, groups and communities and the uniqueness of environmental and cultural influences on individual experiences? Or is this a dangerously essentialist task in which to engage? Many major developmental studies now attempt to accommodate the relevant and unique social, structural and cultural dimensions in specific contexts that influence expectations about coping at each of these specific lifespan stages, thus building a richer, multidimensional approach to lifespan development and adaptation. As D'Cruz (2009 p. 133) highlights, as social workers, we should be 'simultaneously open to critique our own normative assumptions about what we are doing, why we are doing it and the consequences, including for the clients we aim to help'.

Notwithstanding these significant criticisms and challenges, a lifespan focus enables social workers to understand risk, resilience and adaptation, particularly because of the emphasis on the potential burden of adversities at particular ages, and the accumulative effects of these risk factors. It provides a framework for interventions in age-appropriate ways and contexts.

One of the challenges for understanding individual development in this way relates to the need for an awareness and conceptualisation of so many distinctive dimensions of experience. We have to be critically aware of which dimensions we attend to within research and practice agendas. For example, the spiritual dimension has only recently re-emerged in the resilience literature, yet it is still to be put into operation and integrated fully into programs and practices. The sexual dimension, experienced within both our inner and outer worlds, is also a critical developmental dimension, yet how frequently is this dimension acknowledged? The physical dimensions of the built and natural environments around us are crucial, yet they are only alluded to briefly in many discussions. Some dimensions, particularly the biological and psychological, continue to be privileged over and above other dimensions.

Some dimensions continue to be focused on more at particular stages in the lifespan than at others. The social needs of children, for example, have been well researched, but the social needs of middle and older Australians are less well documented. The spiritual dimension in infants and children is little understood, because of its interconnectedness with the cognitive dimension of abstract and hypothetical thought that emerges typically during adolescence. The emotional dimension in older people tends to be overlooked as the physical or biological dimensions become increasingly significant in care contexts. The structural and cultural dimensions in which we live privilege certain dimensions at different times and within the context of different experiences. This was evident in the discussion of trauma experiences, and the tendency to 'psychiatrise' trauma responses.

TABLE **14.1** Developmental tasks across the lifespan

Stage	Developmental tasks
Infancy	Maturation of sensory, perceptual and motor functions Attachment Sensori-motor and early causal schemes Understanding the nature of objects and creating categories Emotional development
Early childhood	Development of locomotion Language development Fantasy play and later peer play Self-control Gender identification Early moral development Self-theory
Middle childhood	Friendship Concrete operations Skill learning Self-evaluation Team play
Early adolescence	Physical maturation Formal operations
Late adolescence	Emotional development Membership in the peer group Sexual relationships Autonomy from parents Gender identity Internalised morality Career choice
Early adulthood	Exploring intimate relationships Childbearing Work Lifestyle
Middle adulthood	Managing a career Nurturing an intimate relationship Expanding caring relationships Managing the household

Stage	Developmental tasks
Late adulthood	Accepting one's life
	Redirecting energy towards new roles and activities
	Promoting intellectual vigour
	Developing a point of view about death
	Coping with physical changes in ageing
	Developing a biographical perspective
	Travelling through uncharted terrain

Source: Adapted from Newman & Newman 2003

The distinction between inner and outer worlds remains a somewhat problematic and artificial one. The question as to whether it is a useful distinction is an important one. At one level we are talking about or describing human experience in its totality, which should implicitly incorporate all of these dimensions. To separate them into two separate 'worlds' might seem unnecessary. Yet we know that different dimensions do tend to get privileged or emphasised over and above others— some human service professionals privilege the inner-world dimensions as both the causation of difficulties and the key resources for recovery. Others privilege the outer-world dimensions, viewing the structural and cultural dimensions as the cause of all adversities and difficulties, neglecting the inner-world dimensions. The important point is the constant attention to both worlds within human services delivery, so that everything is not seen as either an inner-world issue or an outer-world issue. A difficulty remains in how to visually represent this adequately, with Figure 1.8 (page 18) limited in its capacity to really emphasise the ways in which the many dimensions of human experience are so fundamentally and more fluidly interconnected.

Human development and adaptation

» Human experience is multidimensional.
» Adaptation is multidimensional.

Optimal development has been conceptualised as a two-fold process. First, we have examined development from the point of view of the adaptations we make to the various tasks, demands and opportunities of each developmental stage of the lifespan. Second, we examined development from the point of view of the adaptations to unique life events or adversities that each one of us may encounter, often profoundly influencing our sense of identity and belonging. Such a conceptualisation involves holding in mind our understandings of the developmental trajectories or pathways we are on and simultaneously understanding the impact of unexpected or unpredictable life events that occur, often profoundly influencing our sense of identity and belonging. Development, adaptation, coping and recovery are therefore all continual and complex processes right across the lifespan.

One of the ongoing challenges with this broad understanding of human development and adaptation is the degree to which we think of human experience as occurring along 'stability' or orderly models of change and development, or more random change models. As the discussions have highlighted, to what extent do we acquire skills over time that are fixed? The stability and orderly change models of human development propose that we carry and build a biography and a memory, but to what degree is there continuity as to who we are? The developmental chapters highlighted that we do seem to acquire a biography, or an inner map of ourselves, and our roles, in the various worlds in which we function. However, these normative views of development run the risk of being very prescriptive. They tend to assert that certain things should be happening at particular times. To some extent, this is true of human experience, in that there are realities in the biological processes that influence our experiences. Similarly, much of our lives is organised through the social structures of school and work life, and of family routines, that also give rise to specific and contextual expectations and demands. Thus, there is some predictability to be found within the dimensions of family, work and health right across the lifespan. So a tension exists between not wanting to universalise or normalise human experience on the one hand, and saying that there is a connection between being part of a cohort and particular experiences on the other.

In recent decades, the understanding of predictability in human experience has shifted. It is no longer so rigidly defined. This can be seen, for example, with some of the shifts in understanding adolescence and early adulthood, or notions of the mid-life crisis, of family formation and of ageing. Chapters 10 and 11 highlighted the shifting boundaries around some of the psychosocial tasks, with what were considered to be the tasks of adolescence being now often delayed into early adulthood. Within the Australian context, in some experiences, there is a far greater diversity of role expectations and demands. A multidimensional approach encourages the anticipation of these shifts, as a continual reflection of the changes occurring within the broader social, structural and cultural dimensions.

The research that has been considered throughout this book has examined risk and protective factors from the points of view of both developmental trajectories and adversity experiences. The key risk experiences continue to be poverty, war, trauma, family conflict and divorce, separations, disability and illness, and losses early in the lifespan, parents with substance abuse or mental health difficulties, chronic stress situations, abuse and neglect experiences. Other risk factors that influence these experiences include the unique age, sex, personality, social support, structural and cultural dimensions of each individual. These risk factors are all part of the trauma, grief and stress experiences that test and reshape the biographies and meanings we build, and the developmental pathways we are on.

What continues to be a challenge is the identification of new risk factors, and the impact of the accumulation of them. Adversities and challenges shift continually and often rapidly. For example, in recent years, the prevalence of substance abuse issues among parents who abuse or neglect their children has increased rapidly, requiring very different assessment procedures and understandings of the impact of substance abuse on the well-being of both parents and their children. Another example is that in recent decades, many people who have illnesses formerly considered terminal, such as AIDS and cancer, are now able to live with these illnesses for extended periods of time, presenting a range of very different challenges for them and those around them. Terrorism has meant that many Australians are alert to international threats and influences, which, prior to September 11, remained more localised in specific parts of the world. Any understandings of risk and protective factors must carry a strong sociocultural lens, so that they can shift and be specific to the particular context in which the risk factors are emerging.

Ultimately, social workers aim to minimise risk and maximise opportunity and possibility in order to promote positive adaptations across the lifespan. This involves an emphasis on the protective, or salutogenic, factors (Antonovsky 1979; 1987) that promote health and well-being, rather than only factors that protect against adversity and risk.

It would be naïve to suggest that risk can be prevented altogether, as loss, trauma and grief are part of the human experience. And outer-world dimensions, whether the cause or not, do influence all experiences of risk in terms of the aftermath experience. Hence, the task of the human services is to minimise risk and to create, at minimum, safety nets around these experiences of risk and vulnerability. That is why the emphasis on protective factors and resilience is such an important part of this understanding.

The key protective factors identified within both the developmental and the adversity understandings of experience, include dimensions of the inner world such as good intellectual skills, a positive temperamental style and positive views of the self, as well as a sense of coherence and meaning. Key protective qualities of the relational and social dimensions include high warmth, cohesion, expectations and involvement, as well as a diversity of resources available from different supportive networks of people outside of immediate family relationships (Garmezy 1985).

Throughout this book, an emphasis on resilience has highlighted the extraordinary adaptability of individuals under conditions of, at times extreme, adversity:

> The conclusion that resilience arises from *ordinary magic* (Masten 2001) refers to the idea that human individuals are capable of astonishing resistance, coping, recovery and success in the face of adversity, equipped only with the usual human adaptational capabilities and resources, functioning normally. (Masten & Powell 2003 p. 15)

This adaptability involves the capacity to bounce back and continue to develop optimally, in spite of the presence of risk factors. The resilience attributes of individuals and their relational, social, structural and cultural dimensions across the life course that have been explored throughout this book are summarised below.

THE ATTRIBUTES OF RESILIENCE

Individual dimensions of resilience:
» Developed cognitive capacities
» Self-perceptions of competence, worth and confidence
» Adaptable and sociable temperament and personality
» Emotional regulation skills
» Positive appraisal (optimism, hopefulness)
» A sense of coherence or meaning

Relational dimensions of resilience:
» Secure attachment with at least one other adult
» Relational quality—high warmth, low ambivalence
» Close relationships with competent others—availability of role models and mentors

Social dimensions of resilience:
» Safe neighbourhoods
» Perceived and received social support, via both formal and informal networks

Structural dimensions of resilience:
» Community resources and facilities
» High-quality human services—including social and health services
» Adequate policies and resources for educational, nutritional, housing, financial and employment needs

Cultural dimensions of resilience:
» Non-stigmatising, anti-discriminatory attitudes towards individual experience
» Traditions and worldviews that give a sense of coherence and meaning to life
» Participation in rituals and rites of passage

Without neglecting other important resilience attributes, one crucial attribute that has continually emerged throughout this book is having at least one significant and supportive relationship. This highlights the importance of attachment relationships right across the life course. A sense of belonging and mattering, whether at age three months, three years, or ninety-three years, seems to profoundly contribute to our sense of well-being. Many of the adversities of life that lead to human service involvement are related to the loss or threat of loss within these significant relationships.

Relative to our understandings of the role of risk factors, we continue to know little about the specific mechanisms that activate resilience. We know significantly more about the nature of various risk factors, and the protective factors that ought to mobilise resilience, but the process of mobilising these resources is only emerging as an area of understanding (Masten & Powell 2003). In trying to bring the notion of resilience into operation, the fact that we need to know a great deal more about the interconnectedness between our inner and outer worlds is highlighted. The recurrence of human relationships as a resilience factor reinforces this—experiences in the outer world of good relationships lead to integrated and strengthened experiences in the inner world of self-esteem and self-worth. Thus, it is a dynamic not a static process.

It is important that resilience does not become the expectation of individuals without acknowledging the interactive nature of inner- and outer-world dimensions. Ideally, resilience will be regarded as an attribute of communities—that is, as a resource that is part of the wider social capital available to individuals. To promote resilience, clearly resources are required in all dimensions—both within inner and outer worlds. Promoting resilience for individuals and families within communities involves innovative service development and adequate funding in areas of prevention.

This leads us to think about what the implications of a multidimensional approach are for theory and practice within the human services.

Implications for theory and practice

» Attempts to theorise human development and adaptation should be multi-dimensional.
» Human service responses must be multidimensional.

If we draw all these themes together—the themes of understanding individuals in their particular contexts, and of understanding development from both a normative and a non-normative perspective—we have a sound map for considering what resources might be necessary to facilitate optimal development for individuals, families and communities.

A multidimensional approach enables understanding of the critical dimensions that influence adaptation, and the different specific ways in which they can be theorised. Chapters 4 to 6 highlighted the ways in which our responses to a range of stress, trauma and grief experiences can be understood using very different theoretical perspectives—from cognitive and psychodynamic understandings to socio-cultural understandings of grief, for example. Chapters 7 to 13 highlighted the understandings of human development when chronological age, and its associated inner- and outer-world dimensions, is used as the key dimension of influence. The strength of a multidimensional approach is that it emphasises that there are many ways of understanding human experience. This then challenges us to discern how we come to reach certain understandings and to work towards the best fit between the identified issues and the possible human service responses.

One of the ongoing challenges relates to the theoretical tensions that emerge. With a multidimensional approach to human experience, tensions clearly arise as a result of the range of theoretical understandings that can be used to analyse and intervene within specific situations. Social workers are faced with, for example, tensions between social constructionist and chaos approaches, both current and theoretical approaches which recognise the importance of the subjective experience, and positivist trends focusing on evidence-based research and practice. Theoretical positions such as these are based on opposing fundamental values and assumptions about the nature of human experience and the nature of any intervention. Similarly, tension exists in the application of systems theories, because chaos theories have demonstrated that causation factors are often far more random and unpredictable than proponents of earlier systems theories would have us believe. For practitioners, this presents interesting challenges and opportunities to apply theory in critical, unique and sensitive ways, rather than assuming there is predictability in the way people respond to change, stress, loss and/or trauma.

Another core challenge relates to understanding and respecting **diversity** and difference. In the discussions of the themes relating to multidimensionality, the emphasis throughout has been on uniqueness—particularly the uniqueness of an individual's inner and outer worlds. No two people, irrespective of the degree of similarity in circumstances, react to life's experiences and adversities identically. This raises the critical issues of difference and diversity. It also highlights the importance of listening to the subjective experiences of people and incorporating a **consumer perspective** into all practice. In developing human services, a need exists to universalise issues, yet at the same time, this process of identifying particular risk factors has the potential to create stigma and marginalisation. For example, as Chapter 3 highlighted, many people experience disempowerment and oppression as a result of persistent circumstances of poverty, substance use and/ or violence. How do we intervene sensitively, without adding to the experiences of stigma and marginalisation that occur for many people as a result of adversity? The term 'diversity' assumes that there is a baseline experience somewhere, so the use of the term leads us to the question: diversity from what? Within the pluralism of the Australian context, where diverse cultural dimensions are present, multicultural theorising is critical. Yet the baseline still tends to be that of a Western experience, with many understandings of adaptation and development still a long way from being culturally inclusive.

The discussions in previous chapters raise complex questions specifically in relation to the translation of these concepts into good practice. How can interventions be flexible enough to respond to the uniqueness of each human situation respecting diversity, yet at the same time be adequately recognised and funded by the relevant government or non-government agencies? Because human services, as a result of funding limitations, are so frequently working in a crisis-driven, reactive way, a radical refocusing is required if they are to work in proactive, preventive ways. Bringing the knowledge we have of risk and resilience into operation in programs and practices is one of the greatest challenges faced in the design, practice and function of human services.

These challenges continue to be met in new ways. For example, within the broader context, increasingly, the human services now recognise the need for **cross-sectoral practice**. This is consistent with a multidimensional approach in that it recognises the need to work across fields and sectors within human services, such as child and family welfare and drug and alcohol services, leading to more informed practices around families at risk. For optimal work with an extremely vulnerable population within the Australian community, multidisciplinary teams are required, emphasising the importance of bringing together specialist knowledge bases relating to the various dimensions of human experience. A strong tension exists between the degree to which every social worker focuses generically on all of the dimensions or to which they develop specialist knowledges of particular dimensions.

Within the more specific context of the individual practitioner level, all of the above factors give rise to continual uncertainty, complexity and challenge in practice. Given the nature of human services work, **reflective practice** is a critical aspect in all service delivery, which:

> … involves the ability to locate oneself in a situation through the recognition of how actions and interpretations, social and cultural background and personal history, emotional aspects of experience, and personally held assumptions and values influence the situation. (Fook 1999 p. 199)

As discussed in Chapter 1, the ongoing review of our own value stance is vital, occurring through such reflective practice, typically through regular, formal supervision. Supervision ideally addresses three core aspects of practice—our professional accountability requirements, our educational needs, and our emotional support needs. A continuing review of practice enables some analysis of the inner- and outer-world dimensions that influence both the human service worker and the client, ideally leading to optimal adaptations for both.

CHAPTER **SUMMARY**

In this final chapter, some of the ongoing challenges in adopting a multidimensional approach have been explored—the challenges of understanding all the essential dimensions of individuals and their contexts, of understanding the experiences arising as a result of both developmental trajectories and specific adversities, and of understanding the implications of all of these issues for theory and practice within the human services.

Understandings of human development and adaptation will necessarily continue to change over time. A multidimensional approach offers one way of understanding the risk factors in inner-world experiences, outer-world contexts, and the events of life, and the critical protective factors and resilience attributes within all these dimensions. While it will not lead to the immediate development of interventions, it will provide a useful map of what should be considered in a broad framework for understanding human development across the life course. The value of a multidimensional approach is that it promotes the continual recognition of the many diverse risk experiences. It also promotes the continual recognition of the protective and resilience attributes that lead to growth, health and satisfaction, and therefore to optimal human development.

APPLYING A MULTIDIMENSIONAL UNDERSTANDING

CASE STUDY

Ed: Mental health and homelessness

Ed is a thirty-nine-year-old man, who has been living on and off the streets for the past twenty years. He was diagnosed at the age of nineteen as having schizophrenia. He takes his medication for short periods of time, usually after a crisis admission to hospital, or during one of several brief episodes in prison. When he is on his medication, he feels fine—the voices stop, he feels less anxious and angry about the world. But this is when he decides he does not need the medication, and so stops it again, and after a few weeks, the symptoms of his illness are back out of control.

Ed's sister has been desperately trying to get him into some stable housing. The waiting lists are long, and Ed prefers to have the freedom of living where he likes. He keeps in irregular contact with a worker through the Salvation Army emergency service. However, when he saw the worker yesterday, he physically assaulted her. She is uncertain as to whether she will report the incident to the police.

Questions

1 Which dimensions of Ed's experiences do you see as either risk and/or protective factors?
2 What could prevent this situation, in terms of intervention at a:
   • direct practice level?
   • program level?
   • policy level?
3 If you were the case worker in this situation, how do you imagine you would be feeling? What do you imagine you would do?
4 What would you want your supervisor to assist you with?

KEY TERMS

consumer perspective
cross-sectoral practice
diversity
reflective practice

QUESTIONS AND DISCUSSION POINTS

1 What are some of the ongoing challenges for working within social work or more broadly within human services?
2 What are some of the key attributes of resilience across the various individual, relational, social, structural and cultural dimensions?
3 What specific challenges do you anticipate in your practice within social work or the human services?
4 What understandings of human development have changed for you as a result of reading this book?

FURTHER READING

Connolly, M. & Harms, L. eds, 2009, *Social work: Context and practices*, 2nd edn, South Melbourne: Oxford University Press.

McDonald, C. 2006, *Challenging social work: The institutional context of practice*, Basingstoke: Palgrave.

WEBSITES OF INTEREST

Australian Association of Social Workers (AASW): www.aasw.asn.au

The AASW's site includes ethics and practice guidelines for social workers, giving an insight into the expectations for one group of professional human service workers.

The Cochrane Collaboration: www.cochrane.org

This site provides a database of systematic reviews related to social care for children and adolescences.

Australian Health Promotion Association: www.healthpromotion.org.au/

This site is a national site for health promotion practice and research. It also hosts the *Health Promotion Journal of Australia* (HPJA). It is a professional association specifically for people interested or involved in the practice, research and study of health promotion.

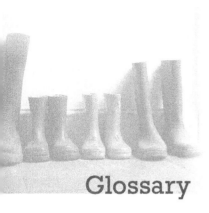

Glossary

acute stress disorder (ASD)
an anxiety disorder in the first month after exposure to a traumatic stress experience. It includes symptoms of avoidance, intrusion (uncontrollable thoughts and feelings) and hyperarousal (a heightened awareness and readiness to respond).

adaptation
the way in which people (and environments) change and accommodate experiences. Adaptation can be rapid or gradual, positive or negative.

adolescence
the process and lifespan stage of transitioning from childhood to adulthood.

adversity
the condition of hardship, difficulty, stress or trauma. It refers most commonly to outer-world events and circumstances.

affect regulation
the capacity to control or regulate emotions, for example being able to control anger or express empathy towards someone else.

ageing
processes of maturation and living longer.

aggression
verbal and physical behaviour that harms another person or object. It is often unprovoked and is intended to cause hurt or damage.

anticipatory grief
grief experiences where the loss is known about before it occurs, such as someone dying from a terminal illness. It is presumed that people have some time to adapt to the reality of an inevitable death or loss and to begin aspects of grieving before the loss occurs.

appraisal
the process by which we cognitively review or assess situations. It refers to both immediate assessments and longer-term reflections. It is key to determining our behaviour.

approach coping
strategies that are used to 'move towards' a problem and to actively resolve it. It is used in constrast to **avoidant coping**.

assets
the inner-world or outer-world resources that an individual, family or community is able to access. They are seen as protective factors that provide people with the means and ways of coping effectively with adversity and change.

attachment theory
proposes that all human beings require social bonds, particularly with a primary caregiver, from birth, and that attachment styles are co-created by the infant and the caregver. A secure attachment in infancy is linked with effective coping later in

life, on the basis that a secure attachment leads to positive inner working models that enable a sense of trust, competence and confidence.

authoritarian parenting style
a parenting style in which parents are strict in their discipline and use of rules and typically show lower warmth in their relationship style.

authoritative parenting style
a parenting style in which parents have clear rules and boundaries and demonstrate high warmth and negotation in the maintenance of them.

autonomy
acting with or expressing self-determination and independence, and exercising free will.

avoidant coping
coping strategies that avoid or fail to address a problem: for example, procrastinating, refusing to acknowledge there is a problem, or staying away from people. It is only problematic if the situation requires **approach coping** to resolve it.

basic trust
an inner sense of security and confidence that translates into trusting relationships with others, arising from a secure relationship with a primary caregiver in infancy and early childhood.

bereavement
the experience of having lost something of significance. Most typically, it refers to the state of having lost a significant relationship with a person through death.

betrayal trauma theory
proposes that two processes affect the individual in trauma experiences— the extent to which a social betrayal occurs in relation to the traumatic experience and its aftermath, and the extent to which the trauma is terror- or fear-inducing.

biographical time
our individual sense and experience of time, a perception of our own history or biography.

biological dimensions
all aspects of our biological and physical states of being: our height, weight, health and age, also taking into account the impact of the physical environment, social interactions and stress on our well-being.

biological time
our age and stage from birth through to our death, with each age and stage having an impact on our experiences and our resources to cope with them.

biopsychosocial-spiritual dimensions
the individual (biological, psychological and spiritual) and environmental (social, including structural and cultural) dimensions that an individual occupies simultaneously.

chronic sorrow
a term that was used to describe the experience of people living with constant loss and grief, for example the experience of parents with a child who has a disability or life-threatening illness. The concept has been challenged from a resilience perspective, as studies have demonstrated that individuals and families cope positively with many adversities and are more likely to experience episodic grief and stress rather than any prolonged state of distress.

chronosystem
Bronfenbrenner's term for the time dimensions of our experiences.

cohort
a group of people sharing a particular quality, most typically that of being born in a similar era or age group.

competence

a capacity to successfully fulfil a task or demonstrate a skill.

complementarity

a relationship in which the behaviour of each participant differs from, but complements, that of the other.

complicated grief

less common patterns of observed grief; grief that is intractable, intense and creates distress and dysfunction in ways that are beyond the common experience.

conservation of resources (COR) theory

proposes that people have four major types of resources (object, condition, personal and energy) and that stress experiences both draw on available resources and lead to further resource loss or gain.

consumer perspective

the perspective of the consumer (individual or group) in human services work. Originating from mental health experiences, in which (particularly involuntary) clients felt their rights and voice were not considered and set about establishing their rights and voice, consumer perspectives often differ from worker perspectives in valuing and prioritising different aspects of interventions.

content

the subjective experience of a social network, the perception and meaning a person has of their various relationships.

continuing bonds

the continuing relationship (primarily through memory) someone has with a person who has died or something that has been lost. Even though the person, object or experience may be inaccessible, aspects of them may be and should not be denied. This idea counteracts earlier

theories that emphasised 'breaking the bond'.

coping

the process of using thoughts, feelings or behaviours to adapt to a situation or condition.

coping strategies

the biopsychosocial-spiritual efforts taken to adapt to a situation. They can be **approach** or **avoidant strategies.**

coping style

the tendency a person has to cope in a particular way, using a particular repertoire of thoughts and/or strategy.

crisis

a sudden turning point or decision that places demands on people and their resources.

critical incident stress management (CISM)

the range of interventions that are used in response to crisis events. Interventions may be preparatory or focused on actions to be taken during and after a critical incident.

cross-sectoral practice

practice that extends beyond the boundaries of a specific field of practice. For example, an agency may address mental health, drug and alcohol and child protection issues with a family, rather than refer them to three distinct agencies to deal with each of these issues separately.

cultural dimensions

the many aspects of culture that inform and influence our daily lives.

cultural responsiveness

the way in which people's cultural diversity is respected, heard and integrated into appropriate interventions.

cultural safety

the extent to which people feel safe to express who they are and have that cultural expression acknowledged, respected and supported. It shifts the emphasis to considering the environments and interactions in which people are functioning rather than the individual and their particular cultural background.

culture

ways of living and understanding the world that are shared among a particular group of people.

cyclical time

a sense of recurring time and events, such as anniversaries or seasons.

daily hassles

the minor frustrations or stressors that accumulate throughout the day. Their impact is often underestimated; they create significant stress and tension for people.

death anxiety

the anxiety provoked by the recognition of the inevitability of our own death.

defence mechanisms

unconscious responses we develop from infancy to manage anxiety. For example, denial and repression are common mechanisms that enable us to overlook issues that might otherwise cause us unwanted emotions.

depression

a commonly used word to describe a low mood state. As a clinical diagnosis, it refers to the persistent experience of a sense of hopelessness, low self-esteem and a sense of having no future.

developmental tasks

tasks seen as universal to all human experience, typically related to physical, psychological and social development across the lifespan.

direct practice

social work practice methods that engage directly with clients to effect change, such as through counselling, casework, groupwork or family work.

disenfranchised grief

grief experiences that are not acknowledged by others because they are not presumed to be significant: for example, the death of a lesbian or gay partner in a relationship that was not publicly acknowledged. The person grieving is denied the usual recognition and support for their loss.

distress

arises when stress has a harmful effect on us.

diversity

differences of experience, specifically of biopsychosocial-spiritual experiences.

dual process model

a model developed by Stroebe and Schut to reflect both the loss and restoration orientations that people experience in grief. Adaptation over time involves moving between both loss and restoration issues, and people move across these issues in different ways and at different times.

durability

the extent to which relationships last over time,

early adulthood

the years after secondary school through to the thirties.

early childhood

the pre-school years, typically from the age of two to around four to five years.

ecomap

a clinically useful visual tool that maps out the relationships a person has or would like to have. It encourages discussion: for example, people can talk about risk and protective factors within these relationships and/or talk about the gaps in their social worlds.

ego-integrity
a person's sense of identity that is self-aware, coherent and stable.

emotional support
the resources we receive when we are seeking validation, opportunities for ventilation, advice, consolation, comfort or a listening ear.

ethnicity
the cultural or national identity of a person; a group with a common heritage or ancestry. It is a contested term as people often hold multiple identities, and their self-ascribed ethnicity may differ from others' views.

exosystem
Bronfenbrenner's term for the networks and organisations that influence a person's experience but over which the person does not have direct influence: for example, transport, education and health organisations.

exploitation
a form of oppression, whereby the results of the labor of one social group benefit another.

family
a complex term, referring conservatively to only blood or marriage relationships (such as children, parents, siblings), and liberally to groups of people who identify each other as key relationships. Definitions of family profoundly influence eligibility for services and supports within the community.

fight-or-flight response
recognised by Selye as the key stress response in humans, whereby when under threat people respond automatically in ways that prepare them to physically and/or mentally fight the stressor or flee from it.

freeze response
a stress response that occurs when stress is so overwhelming a person's coping capacity shuts down.

frequency
the number of contacts that occur between the individual and the people within the social network.

future time
a sense of time ahead in which to do things, strongly associated with **optimism**.

gender
classification as masculine, feminine or androgynous. These classifications are not necessarily directly associated with a person's physical status as male or female, they are primarily psychological and emerge from both innate characteristics and the social environment.

generativity
a sense of investing in future generations. It is often associated with parenting, as well as passing on traditions, knowledge and wisdom to others.

genogram
a diagram that documents family relationships, typically showing at least three generations. A clinically useful tool for opening up discussion about patterns of behaviour and expectations that may be strongly influenced by family experiences.

geographic dispersion
the physical distance between people, which often influences the nature of interactions and relationships within friendship and family networks.

grief
the emotional response to loss.

grief reaction
the biopsychosocial-spiritual reactions to loss.

hardy personality
defined by Kobasa as evident when a person experiences stress as a challenge and has both a sense of commitment to coping well and a sense of control in spite of what is occurring.

health
an experience of biopsychosocial-spiritual well-being. The World Health Organization importantly distinguishes that health is not just the absence of disease. It is a broader sense of well-being.

heterogeneous network
a particular network with a great degree of diversity among its members.

homogeneous network
a particular network with a great degree of similarity among its members.

historical/social time
particular years, eras or events that happen that then define people's inner and outer worlds: for example, specific wars or conflicts, specific political eras or natural disasters.

hope
an expectation or anticipation of something positive in the future; an important protective factor in health and well-being.

indirect practice
social work interventions that influence people's lives in less visible and indirect ways, such as through policy or research.

industry
Erikson's notion of the focus in middle childhood; a sense of engagement and competence in undertaking tasks.

infancy
the first year or two years of life following birth.

initiative
Erikson's notion of the focus in early childhood: a capacity to engage in tasks and relationships independently.

inner world
the unique biological, psychological and spiritual sense of self that is unique to each one of us.

insecure and ambivalent attachments
parenting style is marked by uncertainty, inconsistency, misinterpretation of signs, frequent separations and rejections, and the children are anxious prior to separation and want close bodily contact on return.

insecure and avoidant attachments
parenting involves excessive early deprivation or absences, and the children display little or no distress in the separation episodes and avoided contact in the reunion episodes.

insecure and disorganised attachments
parenting involves excessive early deprivation or absences.

instrumental support
practical assistance, such as help negotiating legal or health systems, with transport arrangements or with child-care arrangements.

intervention strategies
a range of direct and indirect methods used by social workers and others to bring about change: for example, counselling, advocacy, group work, policy or practical resources.

intimacy
Erikson's notion of the focus in adolescence: a capacity to share in sustained, deep relationships with others, both psychologically and sexually.

keeper of the meaning
someone who passes traditions of the past and present to the future, concerned with the preservation of culture.

lagged reciprocity
the alternate exchange of similar behaviour in a relationship, with a long span of time intervening.

learned helplessness
a psychological state whereby someone has learnt to not even attempt tasks or relationships because of earlier defeating experiences.

life course approach
an adversity-focused approach to understanding human devleopment.

lifespan approach
an understanding of human development.

locus of control
the appraisal of one's capacity to deal with events. An **internal** locus of control exists when a person believes they have the capacity to change events and circumstances around them. An **external** locus of control exists when a person believes they cannot control circumstances but others around them will and can.

loss orientation
in the dual process model of grief, a focus on the gaps and losses created by a person's death (or by another loss) and experiences of primarily negative emotions.

maladaptation
negative adaptation following an event.

macrosystem
Bronfenbrenner's term for the cultural dimensions of our experiences.

main effect model
Hutchinson's argument that social networks and connections provide us with positive experiences, stable expectations about behaviour, and thus with a sense of self worth and of situations as non-threatening.

marginalisation
the experience of being on the outer of society, not included in the life of a community. It is a form of oppression as it typically leads to lacking a voice, recognition and resources.

material support
the tangible resources that are exchanged in a relationship.

memory
the capacity to retain information and recall past experiences, both in the short term and the longer term.

mesosystem
Bronfenbrenner's term for our social networks or webs of influence. We are not directly a part of these relationships necessarily but their influence on us is profound, particularly in relation to accessing resources.

microsystem
Bronfenbrenner's term for our direct system of relationships: our families, friends, workplace and neighbourhood. We interact regularly with some and irregularly with others, but all these relationships are important risk and protective factors.

middle adulthood
the mid-life period of the lifespan, typically from forty through to sixty-five.

middle childhood
the primary school years, from around age five to twelve.

moral development
the development of a sense of what is right and wrong, and of appropriate individual and social responses.

mourning
an individual's and community's rituals and social processes following loss experiences.

multidimensional approach
an approach to understanding human development that acknowledges that people occupy, influence and are influenced by multiple dimensions simultaneously.

negativism
developed in early childhood, the capacity to refuse to do things, to say 'no' and to refuse adults, through both verbal and physical tantrums.

network composition
the characteristics of network members: who is in the network.

non-attachment
a fourth form of attachment, where parent and child fail to form a successful attachment bond.

non-finite grief
ongoing and recurrent grief that occurs in response to anniversaries or particular milestones that would have been reached had the loss not occurred.

normative
concerned with establishing a norm or pattern.

oppression
a state of powerlessness, typically inflicted by dominant groups; the unjust use of authority.

optimism
generalised expectancy for positive outcomes.

optimistic style
a positive orientation towards the self and the world, in the past, present and future.

othering
seeing other people as non-human, or as part of one indistinct group, and therefore as not worthy of respect or understanding.

outer world
the external environments, both social and physical, in which individuals live and by which they are influenced.

perinatal
of or relating to the period closest to the time of birth.

permissive parenting style
parenting style characterised by high warmth in relationships and a low level of rules and discipline.

person:environment configuration
a term for the relationship between person and environment, which highlights that all human behaviour emerges as a result of an inextricable link between people and their environments.

pessimistic style
a negative orientation in life, drawing negative conclusions about past and present circumstances and anticipating poor outcomes in the future.

post-traumatic growth
the positive aftermath of traumatic events for individuals, involving, for example, an enhanced sense of self, enhanced relationships with others or a stronger philosophy or personal belief system.

post-traumatic stress disorder (PTSD)
a stress disorder resulting from trauma, with symptoms including intrusive and avoidant symptoms and hyperarousal. To be diagnosed the disturbance must occur for at least a month and impair normal functioning.

postvention strategies
strategies that are used after traumatic or stressful events have occured, to provide

support and to minimise the negative impacts.

potentially traumatising events (PTEs)
a categorisation of events that recognises that events experienced as traumatic by one person may not be experienced that way by another.

prevalence
how many cases or how widespread a phenomenon is in a community or a defined group of people. It is not always possible to know the prevalence of a phenomenon (for example, sexual assault) as the number of reported instances may be under-reported.

prevention strategies
strategies that are used before a phenomenon occurs, to minimise both the occurrence and/or the effects it has on people or environments.

prolonged grief disorder
a new term to identify **complicated grief** reactions.

prosocial
qualities or behaviours that positively promote and enhance social connections, as distinct from anti-social qualities and behaviours (which are negative social interactions).

protective factors
factors in our inner and outer worlds that promote optimal well-being and resilience.

psychological dimensions
aspects of our psychological world (thoughts, memories, emotions) that influence our functioning and well-being.

psychological first aid
the provision in the aftermath of trauma of immediate psychological and emotional support and coping strategies for those affected.

psychosocial stages
stages identified across the lifespan that individuals go through to acquire particular psychological and social skills and outcomes.

puberty
the time of increased hormone production (testosterone and estrodial) for both girls and boys, promoting the development of primary and secondary sexual characteristics.

reachability
how readily an individual can reach information or support via others in the network, or by a process of referral.

reciprocity
an exchange of similar behaviour, either simultaneously or alternately, in a relationship.

reflective practice
practice that includes reflecting on our own position and assumptions, and becomes reflexive practice when we use these insights to enhance outcomes for clients.

relational dimensions
our immediate and direct connections and interactions with other people.

religion
beliefs and practices associated with the formal structures and doctrines of a faith tradition, such as Christianity, Buddhism, Islam or Judaism.

resilience
the human capacity to 'bounce back' from adversity and to continue to live and develop in positive ways.

restoration orientation
in the dual process model of grief, a focus on the new demands and realities created by the loss situation. It therefore has a task and future focus.

risk factors
factors in our inner and outer worlds that may lead to poor outcomes or compromise well-being.

secure attachments
relationships between an infant and their primary caregiver which are characterised by a sense of basic trust. That is, the infant trusts that its needs will be met. This trust and security enables the infant to explore the world around them but also ensures that when the infant feels threatened, they will seek the proximity and protection of their caregiver.

segmentalisation
the extent to which different groups of people are compartmentalised within a person's network.

self-efficacy
a sense of self-worth and competence.

self-worth
a sense of personal value and mattering.

sense of coherence
a person's sense that their world and their behaviour within it is predictable, manageable and controllable.

sensori-motor phase
the first stage of Piaget's four-stage model of cognitive development, occurs from birth until around eighteen months, during which time the infant develops sensory and motor schemes.

shattered assumptions
the experience following trauma of having one's previously held beliefs in onself and in the world or others as being good shattered.

social capital
the resource base that people have within their relational and social context. Greater social capital enables access to higher levels of social support and resources.

social dimensions
the social network each one of us has around us, including both our direct relationships and the ways and extent to which these relationships are interconnected.

social network
the families, relationships, groups and communities in which a person lives, and the links between them.

social support
the resources available to us through our relationships and social connectedness, often referred to as being emotional, practical or instrumental in the resources it provides.

social time
see historical/social time.

spiritual dimensions
the different aspects and expressions of our sense of **spirituality**, such as prayer, meditation or a commitment to social justice or religious activity.

spirituality
our sense of connectedness with meaning and purpose in life. It often involves belief in a higher or transcendent being.

strength of weak ties
our capacity to draw resources from within our social networks, even when connections might be quite loose and distant.

stress
demands placed on a person that cause them to use resources to respond in some way.

stress buffering model
a model of resources that provide support and response to stress demands.

stressful life events
specific events, positive or negative, that

create stress for a person by increasing the demands they usually experience.

stressor
a particular demand on a person, such as an event or an expectation held by others.

stress reactions
behaviours and responses to stress in the physical, psychological, social and/or spiritual dimensions.

stress response
the non-specific physiological response that people have to stress. They are typically more instantaneous and unconscious than **stress reactions**, preparing the person for the fight-or-flight response.

structural dimensions
the organisational, legislative and policy context in which a person lives, and which profoundly influences resources and experiences.

subjective experience
the unique, inner-world experience of an individual.

successful ageing
the capacity to maintain positive development and health throughout later life, associated with increased longevity.

synthetic-conventional faith
a stage of faith development, in addolescence, where there is no third-person perspective allowing critical reflection or a viewpoint outside oneself.

temperament
a person's visible behavioural and relational styles that are evident from early childhood.

terror management theory
proposes that human beings have developed cultural worldviews, and religion in particular, as a way of defending against the anxiety and reality of our own mortality

theory of mind
the capacity of a child to recognise that other people are separate from them and have minds and emotions of their own.

thriving
the capacity to not only bounce back from a traumatic event, but also to grow from the experience in positive ways, finding new strengths, meaning and relationships.

toddlerhood
the period between two and three years of age.

trauma
the major psychosocial impact of events that overwhelm our coping capacity.

traumatic bereavement
the experience of the death of someone through traumatic circumstances, resulting in both grief and trauma reactions and responses.

Bibliography

ABS *see* Australian Bureau of Statistics

Ackard, D. & Neumark-Sztainer, D. 2002, 'Date violence and date rape among adolescents: associations with disordered eating behaviors and psychological health', *Child Abuse and Neglect*, 26(5), pp. 455–73.

Adam, B. & Van Loon, J. 2000, 'Introduction: Repositioning of risk; the challenge for social theory' in B. Adam & J. Van Loon, *The risk society and beyond: Critical issues for social theory*, London: SAGE Publications, pp. 1–31.

Adams, S., Jones, D., Esmail, A. & Mitchell, E. 2004, 'What affects the age of first sleeping through the night?', *Journal of Paediatrics and Child Health*, 40(3), pp. 96–101.

Affleck, G., Tennen, H., Croog, S. & Levine, S. 1987, 'Causal attribution, perceived benefits and morbidity after heart attack: An 8 year study', *Journal of Consulting and Clinical Psychology*, 55, pp. 29–35.

Ahmed, M., Ong, K. & Dunger, D. 2009, 'Childhood obesity and the timing of puberty', *Trends in Endocrinology and Metabolism*, 20(5), pp. 237–42.

Ahmed, S., Morrison, S. & Hughes, I. 2004, 'Intersex and gender assignment: The third way?', *Archives of Disease in Childhood*, 89, pp. 847–50.

AIHW *see* Australian Institute of Health and Welfare

Ainsworth, M. S. 1985, 'Attachment: Retrospect and prospect' in M. Lamb, ed. *Infant–mother attachment: the origins and developmental significance of individual differences in strange situation behavior*, Hillsdale: Lawrence Erlbaum Associates, Chapter 1, pp. 3–27.

Aldwin, C. 1993, 'Coping with traumatic stress', *PTSD Research Quarterly*, 4(3), pp. 1–3.

Aldwin, C. 1994, *Stress, coping and development: An integrative perspective*, New York: The Guilford Press.

Aldwin, C. & Levenson, M. 2001, 'Stress, coping, and health at mid-life: A developmental perspective' in Lachman, M. ed. *The handbook of midlife development*, New York: Wiley. Chapter 6, pp. 188–216.

Alford, B. & Beck, A. 1997, *The integrative power of cognitive therapy*, New York: The Guilford Press.

Allan, J. 2009, 'Loss and grief: Weaving together the personal and the political' in J. Allan, B. Pease & L. Briskman, eds, *Critical social work: Theories and practices for a socially just world*, Crows Nest, NSW: Allen & Unwin, Chapter 16, pp. 214–27.

Allan, J., Pease, B. & Briskman, L. eds, 2009, *Critical social work: Theories and practices for a socially just world*, Crows Nest, NSW: Allen & Unwin.

Allen, J. 2003, 'Childhood attachment trauma and adulthood psychopathology', *The Menninger Clinic Lecture Series*, Melbourne: The Cairnmillar Institute.

Amato, P. & Sobolewski, J. 2001, 'The effects of divorce and marital discord on adult children's psychological well-being', *American Sociological Review*, 66 (December), pp. 900–21.

American Institute of Stress 2006, 'Why is there more stress today?' viewed at www.stress.org/americas.htm, August 2009.

American Psychiatric Association 2000, *Diagnostic and statistical manual of mental disorders IV-TR*, Washington: American Psychiatric Association.

Amery, R. 2002, *Indigenous language programs in South Australian schools: Issues, dilemmas and solutions*, Adelaide: Office of the Board of Studies.

Andersen-Ranberg, K., Schroll, M. & Jeune, B. 2001, 'Healthy centenarians do not exist, but autonomous centenarians do: A population-based study of morbidity among Danish centenarians', *Journal of the American Geriatrics Society*, 49(7), pp. 900–8.

Anderson, I., Crengle, S., Leialoha Kamaka, M., Chen, T., Palafox, N. & Jackson-Pulver L. 2006, 'Indigenous health in Australia, New Zealand, and the Pacific', *The Lancet*, 367(9524), pp. 1775–85.

Andrews, G., Hall, W., Teesson, M. & Henderson, S. 1999, 'The mental health of Australians', *National survey of mental health and wellbeing report 2*, Canberra: Commonwealth Department of Health and Aged Care.

Ansbacher, H. & Ansbacher, R. eds, 1970, *Superiority and social interest: A collection of later writings*, Evanston: Northwestern University Press.

Antonovsky, A. 1979, *Health, stress and coping*, San Francisco: Jossey-Bass.

Antonovsky, A. 1987, *Unraveling the mystery of health: How people manage stress and stay well*, San Francisco: Jossey-Bass.

Argyle, M. 1987, *The psychology of happiness*, London: Methuen.

Armstrong, K., Van Haeringen, A., Dadds, M. & Cash, R. 1998, 'Sleep deprivation or postnatal depression in later infancy: Separating the chicken from the egg', *Journal of Paediatrics and Child Care*, 34(3), pp. 260–2.

Arnett, J. 1997, 'Young peoples' conceptions of the transition to adulthood', *Youth and Society*, 29(1), pp. 3–24.

Arnett, J. 2000, 'Emerging adulthood: A theory of development from the late teens through the twenties', *American Psychologist*, 55(5), pp. 469–80.

Arnett, J. 2007, *Adolescence and emerging adulthood: A cultural approach*, Upper Saddle River: Pearson Education.

Atkinson, J. 2003, *Trauma trails, recreating song lines: The transgenerational effects of trauma in Indigenous Australia*, North Melbourne: Spinifex Press.

Atwater, E. 1990, *Psychology of adjustment*, Englewood Cliffs: Prentice Hall.

Aunola, K. & Nurmi, J. 2005. 'The role of parenting styles in children's problem behavior', *Child Development*, 76(6), pp. 1144–59.

Australian Academy of Science 2004, *The human genome project: Discovering the human blueprint*, Canberra: Australian Academy of Science.

Australian Bureau of Statistics 1996, *Women's Safety Survey*, Canberra: ABS.

Australian Bureau of Statistics 1999, *Australian social trends, Population, population projections: Our ageing population*, Canberra: ABS.

Australian Bureau of Statistics 2000, *Australia now: A statistical profile*, Canberra: ABS.

Australian Bureau of Statistics 2004, *Australian social trends 2004: Population—Population Projections: Projections of the aged population*, Canberra: ABS.

Australian Bureau of Statistics 2005a, *Education and work: Young people at risk in the transition from education to work*, Canberra: ABS.

Australian Bureau of Statistics 2005b, *Year Book Australia: 2005*, cat. no. 1301.0, Canberra: ABS.

Australian Bureau of Statistics 2006a, *Personal safety, Australia, 2005 (Reissue)*, Canberra: ABS, viewed at www.abs.gov.au/ausstats/abs@.nsf/mf/4906.0, February 2010.

Australian Bureau of Statistics 2006b, *Year Book Australia: 2006*, cat. no. 1301.0, Canberra: ABS.

Australian Bureau of Statistics 2007a, *Births*, Canberra: ABS.

Australian Bureau of Statistics 2007b, *Patterns of internet access in Australia*, 2006, cat. no. 8146.0.55.001, Canberra: ABS, viewed at www.abs.gov.au/AUSSTATS/abs@.nsf/Lookup/8146.0.55.001Main+Features12006?OpenDocument, February 2010.

Australian Bureau of Statistics 2007c, *Divorces Australia, 2007*, Canberra: ABS, viewed at http://www.abs.gov.au/AUSSTATS/abs@.nsf/mf/3307.0.55.001, April 2010

Australian Bureau of Statistics 2008, *Deaths: Australia 2007*, Canberra: ABS.

Australian Bureau of Statistics 2009a, *Australian social trends*, cat. no. 4102.0, Canberra: ABS.

Australian Bureau of Statistics 2009b, *Births: Australia 2008*, cat. no. 3301.0, Canberra: ABS.

Australian Bureau of Statistics 2009c, *Jobless families*, Canberra: ABS, viewed at www.ausstats.abs.gov.au/ausstats/subscriber.nsf/LookupAttach/4102.0Publication10.12.092/$File/41020_Joblessfamilies.pdf, November 2009.

Australian Bureau of Statistics 2009d, *More marriages and less divorces in 2008*, media release, 31 August, Canberra: ABS.

Australian Bureau of Statistics 2010a, *Australian Demographic Statistics, Sep 2009: Estimated resident Australian non-Indigenous population, Age groups* (31010DO001_200909), Canberra: ABS, accessed at www.abs.gov.au, May 2010.

Australian Bureau of Statistics 2010b, *Australian Demographic Statistics, Sep 2009: Estimated resident Australian Indigenous population, Age groups* (31010DO001_200909), Canberra: ABS, accessed at www.abs.gov.au, May 2010.

Australian Centre for Posttraumatic Mental Health.2007, *Australian guidelines for the treatment of adults with acute stress disorder and posttraumatic stress disorder*, Melbourne: ACPMH.

Australian Institute of Health and Welfare 2001, *Australia's welfare 2001*, Canberra: AIHW.

Australian Institute of Health and Welfare 2002, *Australia's health 2002: The eighth biennial health report of the Australian Institute of Health and Welfare*, Canberra: AIHW.

Australian Institute of Health and Welfare 2004, *Children with disabilities in Australia*, AIHW cat. no. DIS 38. Canberra: AIHW.

Australian Institute of Health and Welfare 2007, *Australia's welfare 2007*, Canberra: AIHW.

Australian Institute of Health and Welfare 2008a, *Adoptions Australia 2006–07*, Child welfare series no. 44. cat. no. CWS 32. Canberra: AIHW.

Australian Institute of Health and Welfare 2008b, *Australia's health*, Canberra: AIHW.

Australian Institute of Health and Welfare 2009a, *Australia's health*, Canberra: AIHW.

Australian Institute of Health and Welfare 2009b, *Juvenile justice in Australia 2007–08*, Juvenile justice series no. 5. Cat. no. JUV 5. Canberra: AIHW.

Australian Institute of Health and Welfare 2010, *Child protection Australia 2008–09*, Canberra: AIHW.

Averill, J., Catlin, G. & Chon, K. 1990, *Rules of hope*, New York: Springer-Verlag.

Aydt, H. & Corsaro, W. 2003, 'Differences in children's construction of gender across culture: An interpretive approach', *American Behavioral Scientist*, 45, pp. 1306–25.

Ayers, S. 2007, 'Thoughts and emotions during traumatic birth: A qualitative study', *Birth*, 34(3), pp. 253–63.

Ayers, S., Harris, R., Sawyer, A., Parfitt, Y. & Ford, E. 2009, 'Posttraumatic stress disorder after childbirth: Analysis of symptom presentation and sampling', *Journal of Affective Disorders*, 119(1), pp. 200–4.

Azar, A., Mast, B. & Murrell, S. 2003, 'Effect of health locus of control on depression, anxiety, and health status in a community sample of older adults', *Gerontologist*, 43(1), pp. 326–36.

Baird, J. & Sokol, B. eds, 2004, *Connections between theory of mind and sociomoral development*, San Francisco: Jossey-Bass.

Bandura, A., Caprara, G., Barbaranelli, C., Gerbino, M. & Pastorelli, C. 2003, 'Role of affective self-regulatory efficacy in diverse spheres of psychosocial functioning', *Child Development*, 74(3), pp. 769–82.

Banyard, V., Williams, L. & Siegel, J. 2001, 'The long-term mental health consequences of child sexual abuse: An exploratory study of the impact of multiple traumas in a sample of women', *Journal of Traumatic Stress*, 14(4), pp. 697–715.

Barnes, C., Mercer, G. & Shakespeare, T. 1999, *Exploring disability: A sociological introduction*, Cambridge: Polity Press.

Barnes, S. 2003, 'Determinants of individual neighbourhood ties and social resources in poor urban neighbourhoods', *Sociological Spectrum*, 23(4), pp. 463–97.

Bauminger, N., Finzi-Dottan, R., Chason, S. & Har-Even, D. 2008, 'Intimacy in adolescent friendship: The roles of attachment, coherence and self-disclosure', *Journal of Social and Personal Relationships*, 25(3), pp. 409–28.

Baumrind, D. 1971, 'Current patterns of parental authority', *Developmental Psychology*, 4(1), pp. 1–103.

Baumrind, D. 1995, *Child maltreatment and optimal caregiving in social contexts*, New York: Garland Publishers.

Baur, L. 2002, 'Child and adolescent obesity in the 21st century: An Australian perspective', *Asia Pacific Journal of Clinical Nutrition*, 11(Supp), pp. S524–8.

Beekman, A., de Beurs, E., van Balkom, A., Deeg, D., van Dyck, R. & van Tilburg, W. 2000, 'Anxiety and depression in later life: Co-occurrence and communality of risk factors', *American Journal of Psychiatry*, 157(1), pp. 89–95.

Belfer, M. 2006, 'Caring for children and adolescents in the aftermath of natural disasters', *International Review of Psychiatry*, 18(6), pp. 523–8.

Bell, R. 1981, *Worlds of friendship*, London: SAGE Publications.

Bengston, V., Burgess, E. & Parrott, T. 1997, 'Theory, explanation and a third generation of theoretical development in social gerontology', *Journal of Gerontology: Social Sciences*, 52B(2), pp. S72–88.

Bennett, C. & Baird, A. 2006, 'Anatomical changes in the emerging adult brain: A voxel-based morphometry study', *Human Brain Mapping*, 27, pp. 766–77.

Benton, J., Christopher, A. & Walter, M. 2007, 'Death anxiety as a function of aging anxiety', *Death Studies*, 31, pp. 337–50.

Berger, K. 2008, *The developing person: Through the life span*, 7th edn, New York: Worth Publishers.

Berger, P. & Luckman, T. 1966, *The social construction of reality: A treatise in the sociology of knowledge*, London: Allen Lane.

Bessarab, D. 2000, 'Working with Aboriginal families: A cultural approach' in W. Weeks & M. Quinn, *Issues facing Australian families: Human services respond*, Frenchs Forest: Longman, Chapter 7, pp. 79–90.

Bettelheim, B. 1991, *The informed heart*, Ringwood: Penguin Books.

Biernat, M. & Herkov, M. 1994, 'Reactions to violence: A campus copes with serial murder', *Journal of Social and Clinical Psychology*, 13(3), pp. 309–34.

Birren, J. & Schaie, K. eds. 2006, *Handbook of the psychology of aging*, 6th edn, San Diego: Elsevier.

Blanchard, E. & Hickling, E. 1998, *After the crash: Assessment and treatment of motor vehicle accident survivors*, Washington: American Psychological Association.

Blanchard, E., Hickling, E., Taylor, A., Buckley, T., Loos, W. & Walsh, J. 1998, 'Effects of litigation settlements on posttraumatic stress symptoms in motor vehicle accident victims', *Journal of Traumatic Stress*, 11(2), pp. 337–54.

Blankenship, K. 1998, 'A race, class and gender analysis of thriving', *Journal of Social Issues*, 54(2), pp. 393–404.

Bloch, S. & Singh, B. 1997, *Understanding troubled minds*, Melbourne: Melbourne University Press.

Bluebond-Langner, M. 1978, *The private worlds of dying children*, Princeton: Princeton University Press.

Bonanno, G. 2001, 'Introduction: New directions in bereavement research and theory', *American Behavioral Scientist*, 44(5), pp. 718–25.

Bonanno, G. & Kaltman, S. 2001, 'The varieties of grief experience', *Clinical Psychology Review*, 21(5), pp. 705–34.

Bonanno, G. & Keltner 1997, 'Facial expressions of emotion and the course of conjugal bereavement', *Journal of Abnormal Psychology*, 106, pp. 126–37

Bornstein, M., Davidson, L., Keyes, C. & Moore, K. eds, 2003, *Well-being: Positive development across the life course*, Mahwah, NJ: Lawrence Erlbaum Associates.

Borowski, A., Encel, S. & Ozanne, E. 2007, *Longevity and social change in Australia*, Sydney: University of NSW Press.

Boscarino, J. 1995, 'Post-traumatic stress and associated disorders among Vietnam veterans: The significance of combat exposure and social support', *Journal of Traumatic Stress*, 8(2), pp. 317–36.

Bourke, E. & Bourke, C. 1995, 'Aboriginal families in Australia' in R. Hartley, ed., *Families and cultural diversity in Australia*, St Leonards: Allen & Unwin, Chapter 3, pp. 48–69.

Bovey, S. 1995, *The empty nest: When children leave home*, New York: New York University Press.

Bowes, J. & Grace, R. eds, 2008, *Children, families and communities: Contexts and consequences*, 3rd edn, South Melbourne: Oxford University Press.

Bowlby, J. 1980, *Loss: Sadness and depression*, Ringwood: Penguin.

Bowlby, J. 1984, *Attachment*, London: Penguin.

Bowling, A. 1997, *Measuring health: A review of quality of life measurement scales*, Buckingham: Open University Press.

Bowman, M. 1997, *Individual differences in posttraumatic response: Problems with the adversity-distress connection*, Mahwah, NJ: Lawrence Erlbaum Associates.

Brackney, B. & Westman, A. 1992, 'Relationships among hope, psychosocial development and locus of control', *Psychological Reports*, 70, pp. 864–6.

Brazelton, T. 2009, *The Neonatal Behavioral Assessment Scale: What Is It?: Understanding the baby's language*, viewed at www.brazelton-institute.com, November 2009.

Brazelton, T. & Greenspan, S. 2000, *The irreducible needs of children: What every child must have to grow, learn and flourish*, Reading: Perseus.

Brehmer, Y., Li, S., Muller, V., von Oertzen, T. & Lindenberger, U. 2007, 'Memory plasticity across the lifespan: Uncovering children's latent potential', *Developmental Psychology*, 43, pp. 465–78.

Bremner, G. & Slater, A. eds, 2004, *Theories of infant development*, Carlton: Blackwell Publishing.

Bremner, J. 1994, *Infancy*, 2nd edn, Oxford: Blackwell.

Breslau, N., Davis, G., Andreski, P., & Peterson, E. 1991, 'Traumatic events and posttraumatic stress disorder in an urban population of young adults', *Archives of General Psychiatry*, 48, pp. 216–22.

Briere, J. & Scott, C. 2006, *Principles of trauma therapy: A guide to symptoms, evaluation and treatment*, London: SAGE Publications.

British Broadcasting Commission 2009, *Children of conflict: Child soldiers*, viewed at www.bbc.co.uk/worldservice/people/features/childrensrights/childrenofconflict/soldier.shtml, August 2009.

Briton, C. & Jackson, A. 1996, *The place of hope in adjusting to living with HIV/AIDS: A conceptual review*, Living, Surviving and Caring Issues in HIV and AIDS Research Program: Working Paper no. 6, Melbourne: School of Social Work, University of Melbourne.

Brody, L. 1999, 'The socialization of gender differences in emotional expression: Display rules, infant temperament and differentiation' in Fischer, A. ed. *Gender and emotion: Social psychological perspectives*, New York: Cambridge University Press, Chapter 2, pp. 24–47.

Bronfenbrenner, U. 1979, *The ecology of human development: Experiments by nature and design*, Cambridge, MA: Harvard University Press.

Brown, L., Callahan, M., Strega, S., Walmsley, C. & Dominelli, L. 2009, 'Manufacturing ghost fathers: The paradox of father presence and absence in child welfare', *Child and Family Social Work*, 14, pp. 25–34.

Brown, L., ed., 1993, *The new shorter Oxford English dictionary*, Oxford: Clarendon Press.

Bruce, E. & Schultz, C. 2001, *Nonfinite loss and grief: A psychoeducational approach*, Eastgardens: MacLennan & Petty.

Buhrmester, D. & Furman, W. 1990, 'Perceptions of sibling relationships during middle childhood and adolescence', *Child Development*, 61, pp. 1387–98.

Bulman, R. & Wortman, C. 1977, 'Attributions of blame and coping in the "real world": Severe accident victims react to their lot', *Journal of Personality and Social Psychology*, 35, pp. 351–63.

Burnett, P., Middleton, W., Raphael, B. & Martinek, N. 1997, 'Measuring core bereavement phenomena', *Psychological Medicine*, 27(1). pp. 49–57.

Burns, J., Andrews, G. & Szabo, M. 2002, 'Depression in young people: what causes it and can we prevent it?' *Medical Journal of Australia*, 177, 7 October, pp. S93–6.

Butler, L., Field, N., Busch, A., Seplaki, J., Hastings, A. & Spiegel, D. 2005, 'Anticipating loss and other temporal stressors predict traumatic stress symptoms among partners of metastatic/recurrent breast cancer patients', *Psycho-Oncology*, 14, pp. 492–502.

Cagnetta, E. & Cicognani, E. 1999, 'Surviving a serious traffic accident: Adaptation processes and quality of life', *Journal of Health Psychology*, 4(4), pp. 551–64.

Calhoun, L. & Tedeschi, R. 1998, 'Beyond recovery from trauma: Implications for clinical practice and research', *Journal of Social Issues*, 54(2), pp. 357–71.

Calles, J., Lagos, M., Kharit, T., Nazeer, A., Reed, J. and Sheikh, S. 2005, 'Religious cults' in Gullotta, T., Adams, G. & Ramos, J. eds, *Handbook of adolescent behavioral problems: Evidence-based approaches to prevention and treatment*, New York: Springer Science. Chapter 28, pp. 611–30.

Callister, L., Semenic, S. & Foster, J. 1999, 'Cultural and spiritual meanings of childbirth', *Journal of Holistic Nursing*, 17(3), pp. 280–95.

Cameron, N. & McDermott, F. 2007, *Social work and the body*, Melbourne: Palgrave Macmillan.

Campbell, D., Moore, G. & Small, D. 2000, 'Death and Australian cultural diversity' in A. Kellehear, *Death and dying in Australia*, South Melbourne: Oxford University Press, Chapter 5, pp. 68–79.

Campbell, M. A 2005, 'Cyber bullying: An old problem in a new guise?', *Australian Journal of Guidance and Counselling*, 15(1) pp. 68–76.

Cannold, L. 2000, *The abortion myth: Feminism, morality and the hard choices women make*, London: University Press of New England.

Cannold, L. 2005, *What, no baby?: Why women are losing the freedom to mother, and how they can get it back*, Freemantle: Fremantle Arts Centre Press.

Capitulo, K. 2004, 'Perinatal grief online', *The American Journal of Maternal Child Nursing*. 29(5), pp. 305–11.

Caplan, G. 1974, *Support systems and community mental health: Lectures on concept development*, New York: Behavioral Publications.

Cappeliez, P., Guindon, M. & Robitaille, A. 2008, 'Functions of reminiscence and emotional regulation among older adults', *Journal of Aging Studies*, 22(3), pp. 266–72.

Carlson, E. 1996, *Trauma research methodology*, Lutherville: The Sidran Press.

Carr, V., Lewin, T., Webster, R., Hazell, P., Kenardy, J. & Carter, G. 1995, 'Psychosocial sequelae of the 1989 Newcastle earthquake: I. Community disaster experiences and psychological morbidity 6 months post-disaster', *Psychological Medicine*, 25(3), pp. 539–55.

Carson, E. & Kerr, L. 2001, 'Bust for the "baby-boomers": The real mid-life crisis', *Journal of Economic and Social Policy*, 6(1), pp. 1–17.

Carter, E. & McGoldrick, M. 1999, *The expanded family life cycle: Individual, family and social perspectives*, Boston: Allyn and Bacon.

Caruth, C. 1995, *Trauma: Explorations in memory*, Baltimore: The Johns Hopkins University Press.

Carver, C. 1998, 'Resilience and thriving: Issues, models and linkages', *Journal of Social Issues*, 54(2), pp. 245–66.

Caspi, A., Roberts, B. & Shiner, R. 2005, 'Personality development: Stability and change', *Annual Review of Psychology*, 56, pp. 453–84.

Catchpole, J., Macdonald, W. & Bowland, L. 1994, *Young driver research program: The influence of age-related and experience-related factors on reported driving behaviour and crashes*, Clayton: Monash University Accident Research Centre.

Cattell, V. 2001, 'Poor people, poor places and poor health: The mediating role of social networks and social capital', *Social Science and Medicine*, 52, pp. 1501–16.

Chess, S. & Thomas, A. 1996, *Temperament: Theory and practice*, New York: Brunner/Mazel.

Child and Youth Health 2009, *Developmental milestones: 2 to 3 years*, viewed at www.australianbabyguide.com.au/practical-information/childrens-health-and-safety/developmental-milestones:-2-to-3-years/, February 2010.

Child Development Insitute 2009, *Language development in children*, viewed at www.childdevelopmentinfo.com/development/language_development.shtml, November 2009.

Chodorow, N. 1999, *The reproduction of mothering*, 2nd edn, Berkeley: University of California Press.

Christ, G. 2000, *Healing children's grief: Surviving a parent's death from cancer*, New York: Oxford University Press.

Christakis, N. & Iwashyna, T. 2003, 'The health impact of health care on families: A matched cohort study of hospice use by decedents and mortality outcomes in surviving, widowed spouses', *Social Science and Medicine*, 57, pp. 465–75.

Cicirelli, V. 1989, 'Feelings of attachment to siblings and well-being in later life'. *Psychology and Aging*, 4(2), pp. 211–16.

Cicirelli, V. 1995, *Sibling relationships across the life span*, New York: Plenum Press.

Clark, Y. 2000, 'The construction of Aboriginal identity in people separated from their families, community, and culture: Pieces of a jigsaw', *Australian Psychologist*, 35(2), pp. 150–7.

Cobb-Clark, D. & Stillman, S. 2006, 'The retirement expectations of middle aged Australians', *Discussion Paper No. 2449*, Bonn: Institute for the Study of Labor, viewed at http://doku.iab.de/externe/2006/k061127p02.pdf, May 2009.

Coffey, C., Ashton-Smith, C. & Patton, G. 2004, *Victorian adolescent health cohort study report: 1992–1998*, Melbourne: Centre for Adolescent Health, Royal Children's Hospital.

Cohen, J., Mannarino, A., Greenberg, T., Padlo, S. & Shipley, C. 2002, 'Childhood traumatic grief: Concepts and controversies', *Trauma Violence Abuse*, 3, pp. 307–27.

Collins, N., Dunkel-Schetter, C., Lobel, M. & Scrimshaw, S. 1993, 'Social support in pregnancy: Psychosocial correlates of birth outcomes and postpartum depression', *Journal of Personality and Social Psychology*, 65, pp. 1243–58.

Commonwealth Department of Health and Aged Care 2000, *Promotion, prevention and early intervention for mental health: A monograph*, Canberra: Mental Health and Special Programs Branch, Commonwealth Department of Health and Aged Care.

Commonwealth Department of Health and Aged Care and Australian Institute of Health and Welfare 1999, *National health priority areas report: Mental health 1998*, AIHW cat.no. PHE 13, Commonwealth Department of Health and Aged Care and AIHW, Canberra.

Commonwealth of Australia, 2007, *Life in Australia*, Canberra: Commonwealth of Australia.

Commonwealth Office of the Status of Women 2004, *Partnerships against domestic violence*, Canberra, Commonwealth of Australia, viewed at www.padv.dpmc.gov.au, December 2007.

Connolly, M. & Cashmore, J. 2009, 'Child welfare practice' in M. Connolly & L. Harms, eds, *Social work: Contexts and practice*, 2nd edn, South Melbourne: Oxford University Press, Chapter 20, pp. 275–90.

Connor, S. & McIntyre, L. 2002, 'The effects of smoking and drinking during pregnancy' in J. Willms, ed. *Vulnerable children: Findings from Canada's National Longitudinal Survey of Children and Youth*, Edmonton: The University of Alberta Press, pp. 131–48.

Cordova, M., Cunningham, L., Carlson, C. & Andrykowski, M. 2001, 'Posttraumatic growth following breast cancer: A controlled comparison study', *Health Psychology*, 20(3), pp. 176–85.

Cotter, P., Anderson, I. & Smith, L. 2007, 'Indigenous Australians: Ageing without longevity' in A. Borowski, S. Encel & E. Ozanne 2007, *Longevity and social change in Australia*, Sydney: University of NSW Press, Chapter 3, pp. 65–98.

Couch, M., Dowsett, G., Dutertre, S., Keys, D. & Pitts, M. 2006, *Looking for more: A review of social and contextual factors affecting young people's sexual health*, Melbourne: The Australian Research Centre in Sex, Health and Society, La Trobe University.

Coyne, J., Aldwin, C. & Lazarus, R. 1981, 'Depression and coping in stressful episodes', *Journal of Abnormal Psychology*, 90(5), pp. 439–47.

Crawford, E., Wright, M. & Masten, A. 2006, 'Resilience and spirituality in youth' in E. Roehlkepartain, P. King, L. Wagener & P. Benson, eds, *The handbook of spiritual development in childhood and adolescence*, Thousand Oaks: SAGE Publications, Chapter 25 pp. 355–70.

Crawford, K. & Walker, J. 2003, *Social work and human development*, Exeter: Learning Matters.

Creamer, M. & Singh, B. 2003, 'An integrated approach to veteran and military mental health: an overview of Australian Centre for Posttraumatic Mental Health', *Australasian Psychiatry*, 11, pp. 225–7.

Currer, C. 2001, *Responding to grief: Dying, bereavement and social care*, New York: Palgrave.

Currier, J.; Holland, J. & Neimeyer, R. 2006, 'Sense-making, grief, and the experience of violent loss: Toward a mediational model', *Death Studies*, 30(5), pp. 403–28.

D'Abbs, P. 1982, *Social support networks: A critical review of models and findings*, Melbourne: Institute of Family Studies.

Danovitch, J. & Keil, F. 2007, 'Choosing between hearts and minds: Children's understanding of moral advisors', *Cognitive Development*, 22, pp. 110–23.

Darlington, Y. & Bland, R. 1999, 'Strategies for encouraging and maintaining hope among people living with serious mental illness', *Australian Social Work*, 52(3), pp. 17–23.

Davidson, K., Daly, T. & Arbor, S. 2003, 'Exploring the social worlds of older men' in S. Arber, K. Davidson & J. Ginn, *Gender and ageing: Changing roles and relationships*, Maidenhead: Open University Press, Chapter 11, pp. 168–85.

Davis, C. & Nolen-Hoeksema, S. 2001, 'Loss and meaning: How do people make sense of loss?', *American Behavioral Scientist*, 44(5), pp. 726–41.

Davis, H. 1999, 'The psychiatrization of post-traumatic distress: Issues for social workers', *British Journal of Social Work*, 29, pp. 755–77.

Day, C. 1997, 'Validation therapy: A review of the literature', *Journal of Gerontological Nursing*, April, 23(4), pp. 29–34.

D'Cruz, H. 2009, 'Examining the meaning of childhood in critical social work practice' in J. Allan, L. Briskman & B. Pease, eds, *Critical social work: Theories and practices for a socially just world*, Crows Nest: Allen & Unwin. Chapter 10, pp. 132–44.

Deeg, D. 2005, 'The development of physical and mental health from late midlife to early old age' in S. Willis, S. & M. Martin eds, *Middle adulthood: A lifespan perspective*, Thousand Oaks: SAGE Publications, Chapter 7, pp. 209–41.

Delahanty, D., Herberman, H., Craig, H., Hayward, M., Fullerton, C., Ursano R. & Baum, A. 1997, 'Acute and chronic distress and posttraumatic stress disorder as a function of responsibility for serious motor vehicle accidents', *Journal of Consulting and Clinical Psychology*, 65(4), pp. 560–7.

Demetriou, A. & Bakracevic, K. 2009, 'Reasoning and self-awareness from adolescence to middle age: Organization and development as a function of education', *Learning and Individual Differences*, 19, pp. 181–94.

Dennerstein, L., Smith, A. & Morse, C. 1994, 'Psychological well-being, mid-life and the menopause', *Maturitas*, 20, pp. 1–11.

Dentinger, E. & Clarkberg, M. 2002, 'Informal caregiving and retirement timing among men and women: Gender and caregiving relationships in late midlife', *Journal of Family Issues*, 23(7), pp. 857–79.

Department of Education, Employment and Workplace Relations 2008, *Quality education: The case for an education revolution in our schools*, Canberra: DEEWR.

Department of Health and Ageing 2008, *2007 Australian National Children's Nutrition and Physical Activity Survey—Main Findings*, Canberra: Department of Health and Ageing.

Department of Immigration and Citizenship 2009, 'Settler arrival data: Selected countries of birth by migration stream for the financial year 2007–08', *Settler Arrival Data*, Canberra: Department of Immigration and Citizenship, viewed at www.immi. gov.au/media/publications/statistics, November 2009.

Department of Immigration and Citizenship 2010, *Fact Sheet 60: Australia's refugee and humanitarian program*, Canberra: Department of Immigration and Citizenship, viewed at www.immi.gov.au/media/fact-sheets/60refugee.htm, February 2010.

Department of Justice 2009, *A study of gambling in Victoria: Problem gambling from a public health perspective*, Melbourne: Department of Justice.

Dettling, A., Gunnar, M. & Donzella, B. 1999, 'Cortisol levels of young children in full-day childcare centers', *Psychoneuroendocrinology*, 24, pp. 519–36.

De Vaus, D. 1995, 'Adult-parent relationships: Do life cycle transitions make a difference?', *Family Matters*, 41, pp. 22–9.

De Vaus, D. 2002, 'Marriage and mental health' *Family Matters*, 62, pp. 26–32.

De Vaus, D. 2004, *Diversity and change in Australian families: Statistical profiles*, Melbourne: Australian Institute of Family Studies.

De Vaus, D. & Qu, L. 1998, 'Intergenerational family transfers: Dimensions of inequality', *Family Matters*, 50, pp. 27–30.

Deveson, A. 2003, **Resilience**, Crows Nest: Allen & Unwin.

Dickson, N., Paul, C. & Herbison, P., 2003, 'Same-sex attraction in a birth cohort: Prevalence and persistence in early adulthood', *Social Science and Medicine*, 56(8), pp. 1607–15.

Dohrenwend, B. 1998, *Adversity, stress and psychopathology*, New York: Oxford University Press.

Doka, K. 1989, *Disenfranchised grief: Recognizing hidden sorrow*, New York: Lexington Books.

Drago, R., Sawyer, K., Sheffler, K., Warren, D. and Wooden, M. 2009, *Did Australia's baby bonus increase the fertility rate?*, Melbourne Institute of Applied Economic and Social Research Working Paper Series No. 1/09.

Draper, M. 2000, 'In sickness and health' in W. Weeks & M. Quinn, eds, *Issues facing Australian families: Human services respond*, Frenchs Forest: Longman, Chapter 27, pp. 331–42.

Duberstein, P., Conwell, Y., Connor, K., Eberly, S. & Caine, E. 2004, 'Suicide at 50 years of age and older: Perceived physical illness, family discord and financial strain', *Psychological Medicine*, 34(1), pp. 137–46.

Durham, C. 1997 [1897], *Doing up buttons: A deeply personal yet practical account of understanding head injury*, Ringwood: Penguin Books.

Durkheim, E. 2002, *Suicide: A study in sociology*, London: Routledge.

Dwyer, P., Smith, G., Tyler, D. & Wyn, J. 2003, *Life-patterns, career outcomes and adult choices*, Youth Research Centre Research Report 23, Carlton: The University of Melbourne.

Dwyer, P. & Wyn, J. 2001, *Youth education and risk: Facing the future*, Melbourne: Routledge/Farmer.

Dyregrov, A. & Matthiesen, S. 1981, 'Similarities and differences in mothers' and fathers' grief following the death of an infant', *Scandinavian Journal of Psychology*, 28, pp. 1–15.

Eckenrode, J. & Gore, S. 1981, 'Stressful events and social supports: The significance of context' in B. Gottlieb ed. *Social networks and social support*, Beverley Hills: Sage, pp. 43–68.

Eckersley, R., Wierenga, A. & Wyn, J. 2006, *Flashpoints and signposts: Pathways to success and wellbeing for Australia's young people*, Melbourne: Australian Youth Research Centre.

Edelman, H. 1998, *Motherless daughters: The legacy of loss*, Sydney: Hodder.

Edgar, D. 2000, 'Families and the social reconstruction of marriage and parenthood in Australia' in W. Weeks & M. Quinn eds, *Issues facing Australian families: Human services respond*, Melbourne: Longman Australia, Chapter 2, pp. 19–31.

Edgar, D. 2002, 'Costello's scariest budget', *The Age*, Melbourne, 16 May, p. 17.

Eisendrath, P. 1997, *The resilient spirit: Transforming suffering into insight, compassion and renewal*, St Leonards: Allen & Unwin.

Eitinger, L. 1961, 'Pathology of the concentration camp syndrome', *Archives of General Psychiatry*, pp. 371–9.

Elder, G. 1974, *Children of the Great Depression: Social change in life experience*, Chicago: University of Chicago Press.

Elder, G. 1994, 'Time, human agency and social change: Perspectives on the life course', *Social Psychology Quarterly*, 57(1), pp. 4–15.

Elder Abuse Prevention Association 2009, *Elder abuse: A hidden crime*, viewed at www.eapa.asn.au, February 2010.

Ellard, J. 1997, 'The epidemic of post-traumatic stress disorder: A passing phase?', *Medical Journal of Australia*, 166(20), pp. 84–7.

Elliott, T., Witty, T., Herrick, S. & Hoffman, J. 1991, 'Negotiating reality after physical loss: Hope, depression and disability', *Journal of Personality and Social Psychology*, 61(4), pp. 608–13.

Ellis, A. 1995, *Better, deeper, and more enduring brief therapy: The rational emotive behavior therapy approach*, Bristol, PA: Brunner/Mazel.

Ellison, C. & Levin, J. 1998, 'The religion-health connection: Evidence, theory and future directions', *Health Education and Behavior*, 25(6), pp. 700–20.

Erikson, E. 1959, 'Identity and the life cycle', *Psychological Issues*, Monograph 1, 1(1), pp. 1–171.

Erikson, E. 1963, *Childhood and society*, New York: W. W. Norton & Co.

Erikson, E. 1978, 'Reflections on Dr Borg's life cycle' in E. Erikson ed. *Adulthood*, New York: W. W. Norton and Company..

Erwin, P. 1998, *Friendship in childhood and adolescence*, London: Routledge.

Espelage, D. & Swearer, S. 2003, 'Research on school bullying and victimization: What have we learned and where do we go from here?' *School Psychology Review*, 32(3), pp. 365–73.

Evanoo, G. 2007, 'Infant crying: A clinical conundrum', *Journal of Pediatric Health Care*, 21 (5), pp. 333–8.

Fairtlough, A. 2008, 'Growing up with a lesbian or gay parent: Young people's perspectives', *Health and Social Care in the Community*, 16(5), pp. 521–8.

Family Planning Queensland 2007, Fact sheet: Sexual development in early childhood, Brisbane: Family Planning Queensland.

Fazel, M. & Stein, A. 2003, 'Mental health of refugees: Comparative study', *British Medical Journal*, 327(7407), p. 134.

Feinberg, M., McHale, S., Crouter, A. & Cumsille, P. 2003, 'Sibling differentiation: Sibling and parent relationship trajectories in adolescence', *Child Development*, 74(5), pp. 1261–74.

Ferguson, N. 2004, 'Children's contact with grandparents after divorce', *Family Matters*, 67, Autumn, pp. 36–41.

Field, T. 2007, *The amazing infant*, Carlton: Blackwell Publishing.

Fitzpatrick, A., Kuller, L., Lopez, O., Diehr, P., O'Meara. E., Longstreth, W. & Luchsinger, J. 2009, 'Midlife and late-life obesity and the risk of dementia: Cardiovascular health study', *Archives of Neurology*, 66(3), pp. 336–42.

Folkman, S. & Lazarus, R. 1980, 'An analysis of coping in a middle-aged community sample', *Journal of Health and Social Behaviour*, 21, pp. 219–39.

Fonagy, P. 2001, *Attachment theory and psychoanalysis*, New York: Other Press.

Fonagy, P., Steele, H. & Steele, M. 1991, 'Maternal representations of attachment during pregnancy predict the organization of infant-mother attachment at one year of age', *Child Development*, 62, pp. 891–905.

Fonagy, P., Steele, M., Steele, H., Higgitt A., & Mayer, L. 1994, 'The Emanuel Miller Lecture 1992: The theory and practice of resilience', *Journal of Child Psychology and Psychiatry*, 35(2), pp. 231–58.

Fontana, A. & Rosenheck, R. 1998, 'Effects of compensation-seeking on treatment outcomes among Veterans with post-traumatic stress disorder', *The Journal of Nervous and Mental Disease*, 186(4), pp. 223–30.

Fook, J. 1999, 'Critical reflectivity in education and practice', in B. Pease & J. Fook, eds, *Transforming social work practice: Postmodern critical perspectives*, St Leonards: Allen and Unwin, Chapter 13, pp. 195–208.

Fook, J. 2000, *Social work: Critical theory and practice*, London: SAGE Publications.

Fowler, J. & Dell, M. 2006, 'Stages of faith from infancy through adolescence: Reflections on three decades of faith development theory' in E. Roehlkepartain, P. King, L. Wagener & P. Benson, eds, *The handbook of spiritual development in childhood and adolescence*, Thousand Oaks: SAGE Publications, Chapter 3, pp. 34–45.

Fox, G. & Murry, V. 2000, 'Gender and families: Feminist perspectives and family research', *Journal of Marriage and the Family*, 62(November), pp. 1160–72.

Francis, S. & Cornfoot, S. 2007, *Multicultural youth in Australia: Settlement and transition*, Canberra: Australian Research Alliance for Children and Youth.

Frankl, V. 1984, *Man's search for meaning*, New York: Washington Square Press.

Fraser, M., Richman, J. & Galinsky, M. 1999, 'Risk, protection and resilience: Toward a conceptual framework for social work practice', *Social Work Research*, 23(3), pp. 131–43.

Frazier, P. & Schauben, L. 1994, 'Causal attributions and recovery from rape and other stressful life events', *Journal of Social and Clinical Psychology*, 13(1), pp. 1–14.

Frazier, P., Tix, A., Klein, C. & Arikian, N. 2000, 'Testing theoretical models of the relations between social support, coping and adjustment to stressful life events', *Journal of Social and Clinical Psychology*, 19(3), pp. 314–35.

Fredrickson, B. 2000a, *Cultivating positive emotions to optimize health and well-being*, American Psychological Association, viewed at http://journals.apa.org/prevention/volume3, September 2007.

Fredrickson, B. 2000b, *Cultivating research on positive emotions*, American Psychological Association.

Freud, A. 1937, *The ego and the mechanisms of defence*, London: Hogarth Press.

Freud, S. 1982, 'Introductory lectures on psychoanalysis' in J. Strachey & A. Richards, *The Pelican Freud library*, Ringwood: Penguin Books.

Freud, S. 1984, 'Mourning and melancholia' in J. Strachey & A. Richards, *The Pelican Freud library, On metapsychology: The theory of psychoanalysis*, Ringwood: Penguin Books, vol. 11, pp. 251–68.

Freyd, J., Deprince, A. & Gleaves, D. 2007, 'The state of betrayal trauma theory: Reply to McNally—Conceptual issues, and future directions', *Memory*, 15(3), pp. 295–311.

Gallagher, H. & Murdoch, S. 2003, 'Shut away and forgotten, Elsie Brown died alone', *Age*, Melbourne, 17 March, p. 3.

Garbarino, J. ed. 1992, *Children and families in the social environment*, New York: Aldine de Gruyter.

Garbarino, J. 2008, *Children and the dark side of human experience: Confronting global realities and rethinking child development*, New York: Springer

Garbarino, J. & Abramowitz, R. 1992a, 'The ecology of human development', in J. Garbarino ed. *Children and families in the social environment*, New York: Aldine de Gruyter, pp. 11–34.

Garbarino, J. & Abramowitz, R. 1992b, 'Sociocultural risk and opportunity', in J. Garbarino, ed., *Children and families in the social environment*, New York: Aldine de Gruyter, pp. 35–70.

Gardner, H. 2004, *Frames of mind: The theory of multiple intelligences*, New York: Basic Books.

Garmezy, N. & Rutter, M. eds, 1988, *Stress, coping and development in children*, Baltimore: The Johns Hopkins University Press.

Gass, K., Jenkins, J. & Dunn, J. 2007, 'Are sibling relationships protective? A longitudinal study', *Journal of Child Psychology and Psychiatry*, 48(2), pp. 167–75.

Gay, P. 1988, *Freud: A life for our time*, London: Macmillan.

George, L., Larson, D., Koenig, H. & McCulloch, M. 2000, 'Spirituality and health: What we know, what we need to know', *Journal of Social and Clinical Psychology*, 19(1), pp. 102–16.

Germain, C. 1991, *Human behavior in the social environment: An ecological view*, New York: Columbia University Press.

Germain, C. & Bloom, M. 1999, *Human behavior in the social environment: An ecological view*, 2nd edn, New York: Columbia University Press.

Germain, C. & Gitterman, A. 1995, *The life model of social work practice: Advances in theory and practice*, New York: Columbia University Press.

Gibbs, J., Basinger, K., Grime, R. & Snarey, J. 2007, 'Moral judgment development across cultures: Revisiting Kohlberg's universality claims', *Developmental Review*, 27, pp. 443–500.

Giddens, A. 2002, *Runaway world: How globalisation is reshaping our lives*, London: Profile Books.

Gilbert, S. 2006, *Death's door: Modern dying and the ways we grieve*, New York: W. W. Norton and Co.

Gilbert, S. 2009, 'Aboriginal issues in context' in M. Connolly & L. Harms eds, *Social work: Contexts and practice*, 2nd edn, South Melbourne: Oxford University Press, Chapter 7, pp. 94–106.

Gilding, M. 1997, *Australian families: A comparative perspective*, Melbourne: Addison Wesley Longman.

Gilding, M. 2001, 'Changing families in Australia: 1901–2001', *Family Matters*, 60, pp. 6–11.

Gilding, M. 2002, 'Families of the new millenium: Designer babies, cyber sex and virtual communities', *Family Matters*, 62, pp. 4–10.

Gilligan, C. 1993, *In a different voice: Psychological theory and women's development*, Cambridge, MA: Harvard University Press.

Gilligan, R. 2000, 'Adversity, resilience and young people: The protective value of positive school and spare time experiences', *Children and Society*, 14, pp. 37–47.

Gilligan, R. 2004, 'Promoting resilience in child and family social work: Issues for social work practice, education and policy', *Social Work Education*, 23(1), pp. 93–104.

Gilmore, L. & Campbell, M. 2007. 'Spiders, bullies, monsters or terrorists', *Children Australia*, 32(3), pp. 29–33.

Ginsberg, T., Pomerantz, S. & Kramer-Feeley, V. 2005, 'Sexuality in older adults: Behaviours and preferences', *Age and Ageing*, 34(5), pp. 475–80.

Ginzburg, K., Solomon, Z. & Bleich, A. 2002, 'Repressive coping style, acute stress disorder, and posttraumatic stress disorder after myocardial infarction', *Psychosomatic Medicine*, 64(5), pp. 748–57.

Gist, R. & Lubin, B. eds, 1999, 'Response to disaster: Psychosocial, community and ecological approaches', *The Series in Clinical and Community Psychology*, Philadelphia: Brunner/Mazel.

Gluckman, P. & Hanson, M. 2006, 'Evolution, development and timing of puberty', *Trends in Endocrinology and Metabolism*, 17(1), pp. 7–12.

Godfrey, J. 1987, *A philosophy of human hope*, Lancaster: Martinus Nijhoff Publishers.

Goldstein, E. 1995, *Ego psychology and social work practice*, New York: The Free Press.

Gollnick, J. 2005, *Religion and spirituality in the life cycle*, New York: Peter Lang Publishing.

Goodin, R. 2005, 'Responsibilities for children's well-being' in S. Richardson & M. Prior, eds, *No time to lose: The wellbeing of Australia's children*, Carlton: Melbourne University Press, Chapter 3, pp. 60–88.

Goral, M. 2004, 'First language decline in healthy aging: Implications for attrition in bilingualism', *Journal of Neurolinguistics*, 17(1), pp. 31–52.

Gottlieb, B. ed. 1981, *Social networks and social support*, SAGE studies in community mental health, Beverly Hills: SAGE Publications.

Gottlieb, B. ed. 1997, *Coping with chronic stress*, The Plenum Series on Stress and Coping, New York: Plenum.

Graetz, B., Sawyer, M. & Baghurst, P. 2005, 'Gender differences among children with DSM-IV ADHD in Australia', *Journal of the American Academy of Child and Adolescent Psychiatry*, 44(2), pp. 159–68.

Graham, A., Reser, J., Scuderi, C., Zubrick, S., Smith, M. & Turley, B. 2000, 'Suicide: An Australian Psychological Society discussion paper', *Australian Psychologist*, 35(1), pp. 1–28.

Granot, H. 1996, 'The impact of disaster on mental health', *Counselling*, May, pp. 140–3.

Granovetter, M. 1982, 'The strength of weak ties: A network theory revisited' in P. Marsden & N. Lin, *Social structure and network analysis*, London: SAGE Publications, pp. 105–30.

Gray, M., Misson, S. & Hayes, A. 2005, 'Young children and their grandparents', *Family Matters*, 72, Summer, pp. 10–17.

Graziano, R. 2003, 'Trauma and aging', *Journal of Gerontological Social Work*, 40(4), pp. 3–21.

Green, M., McFarlane, A., Hunter, C. & Griggs, W. 1993, 'Undiagnosed post-traumatic stress disorder following motor vehicle accidents', *Medical Journal of Australia*, 159, pp. 529–34.

Greenberg, J., Solomon, S. & Pyszczynski, T. 1997, 'Terror management theory of self-esteem and cultural worldviews: Empirical assessments and conceptual refinements', *Advances in Experimental Social Psychology*, 29, pp. 61–139.

Greene, R. & Ephross, P. 1991, *Human behavior theory and social work practice*, New York: Aldine de Gruyter.

Greer, G. 1999, *The whole woman*, Sydney: Doubleday.

Greig, A., Lewins, F. & White, K. 2003, *Inequality in Australia*, Port Melbourne: Cambridge University Press.

Grollman, E. ed. 1969, *Explaining death to children*, Boston: Beacon Press.

Gunnar, M., Bruce, J. & Grotevant, H. 2000, 'International adoption of institutionally reared children: Research and policy', *Development and Psychopathology*, 12, pp. 677–93.

Habibis, D. & Walter, M. 2009, *Social inequality in Australia: Discourses, realities and futures*, South Melbourne: Oxford University Press.

Haggerty, R., Sherrod, L., Garmezy, N. & Rutter, M. eds, 1996, *Stress, risk and resilience in children and adolescents: Processes, mechanisms and interventions*, Cambridge: Cambridge University Press.

Hamilton, C. 2000, 'Continuity and discontinuity of attachment from infancy through adolescence', *Child Development*, 71(3), pp. 690–4.

Hamilton, C. & Denniss, R. 2005, *Affluenza: When too much is never enough*, Sydney: Allen & Unwin.

Harari, E. & Meares, R. 2001, 'Personality disorders' in S. Bloch & B. Singh, *Foundations of clinical psychiatry*, Melbourne: Melbourne University Press, Chapter 14, pp. 246–68.

Harms, L. 2002, *An analysis of experiences of psychosocial recovery from road trauma*, unpublished doctoral thesis, Melbourne: School of Social Work, University of Melbourne.

Harms, L. & McDermott, F. 2003, 'Trauma: A concept and a practice across borders', *Psychotherapy in Australia*, 10(1), pp. 32–7.

Harris, J. 1995, 'Where is the child's environment—a group socialization theory of development', *Psychological Review*, 102(3), pp. 458–89.

Harris, J. 1998, *The nurture assumption: Why children turn out the way they do*, Sydney: The Free Press.

Harris, J. 2000, 'Socialization, personality development and the child's environments: Comment on Vandell (2000)', *Developmental Psychology*, 36(6), pp. 711–23.

Harrison, D., Boyce, S., Loughnan, P., Dargaville, P., Storm, H. & Johnston. L. 2006, 'Skin conductance as a measure of pain and stress in hospitalised infants', *Early Human Development*, 82(9), pp. 603–8.

Hartman, A. & Laird, J. 1983, *Family centred social work practice*, New York: The Free Press.

Harvey, J. 2001, 'The psychology of loss as a lens to a positive psychology', *American Behavioral Scientist*, 44(5), pp. 838–53.

Harvey, J. & Miller, E. eds, 2000, *Loss and trauma: General and close relationship perspectives*, Philadelphia: Brunner-Routledge.

Harvey, M. 1996, 'An ecological view of psychological trauma and trauma recovery', *Journal of Traumatic Stress*, 9(1), pp. 3–23.

Haslam, N. 2007, *Introduction to personality and intelligence*. London: SAGE Publications.

Hawkins, M., Letcher, P., Sanson, A., Smart, D. & Toumbourou, J. 2009, 'Positive development in emerging adulthood', *Australian Journal of Psychology*, 61(2), pp. 89–99.

Heard, G. Birrell, B. & Khoo, S. 2009, 'Intermarriage by Indigenous and non-Indigenous Australians', *People and Place*, 17(1), pp. 1–14.

Helson, R. 1997, 'The self in middle adulthood' in M. Lachman & J. James, *Multiple paths of midlife development*, Chicago: University of Chicago Press: Chapter 2, pp. 21–43.

Hemphill, S. & Sanson, A. 2001, 'Matching parenting temperament to child: Influences on early childhood behavioural problems', *Family Matters*, 59, pp. 42–7.

Hendricks, J. & Achenbaum, A. 1999, 'Historical development of theories of aging' in V. Bengston & K. Schaie eds, 1999, *Handbook of theories of aging*, New York: Springer Publishing Company, Chapter 2, pp. 21–39.

Hepworth, D., Rooney, R. & Larsen, J. A. 2002, *Direct social work practice: Theory and skills*, Pacific Grove: Brooks/Cole.

Herman, J. 1992, *Trauma and recovery*, New York: Basic Books.

Hewson, D. 1997, 'Coping with loss of ability: "Good grief" or episodic stress responses?', *Social Science and Medicine*, 44(8), pp. 1129–39.

Hibbert, M., Caust, J., Sloman, F., Patton, G. & Bowes, G. 1996, 'Computerised Administration of a Survey of Health in Adolescence', *Journal of Paediatrics and Child Health*, 32, pp. 372–7.

Hickling, E., Blanchard, E., Buckley, T. & Taylor, A. 1999, 'Effects of attribution of responsibility for motor vehicle accidents on severity of PTSD: Ways of coping and recovery over six months', *Journal of Traumatic Stress*, 12(2), pp. 345–53.

Hinde, R. 1979, *Towards understanding relationships*, Sydney: Academic Press Inc.

Hirsch, B. 1981, 'Social networks and the coping process: Creating personal communities' in B. Gottlieb, *Social networks and social support*, Beverley Hills: SAGE Publications, pp. 149–70.

Hiscock, H., Canterford, L., Ukoumunne, O. & Wake, M. 2007, 'Adverse associations of sleep problems in Australian preschoolers: National Population Study', *Pediatrics*, 119(1), pp. 86–93.

Hobbs, M., Mayou, R., Harrison, B. & Worlock, P. 1996, 'A randomised controlled trial of psychological debriefing for victims of road traffic accidents', *British Medical Journal*, 313(70), pp. 1438–9.

Hobfoll, S. 2001, 'The influence of culture, community, and the nested-self in the stress process: Advancing conservation of resources theory', *Applied Psychology: An International Review*, 50(3), pp. 337–421.

Hobfoll, S. ed. 1986, *Stress, social support, and women*, Washington: Hemisphere Pub. Corp.

Hobfoll, S., Ennis, N. & Kay, J. 2000, 'Loss, resources and resiliency in close interpersonal relationships' in J. Harvey & E. Miller, eds, *Loss and trauma: General and close relationship perspectives*, Philadelphia: Brunner-Routledge, Chapter 17, pp. 267–85.

Hobfoll, S., Watson, P., Bell, C., Bryant, R., Brymer, M., Friedman, M., Friedman, M., Gersons, B., de Jong, J., Layne, C., Maguen, S., Neria, Y., Norwood, A., Pynoos, R., Reissman, D., Ruzek, J., & Shalev, A., Solomon, Z., Steinberg, A. & Ursano, R. 2007, 'Five Essential Elements of Immediate and Mid–Term Mass Trauma Intervention: Empirical Evidence', *Psychiatry*, 70(4), pp. 283–315.

Holbrook, T., Hoyt, D., Coimbra, R., Potenza, B., Sise, M. & Anderson, J. 2005, 'Long-term posttraumatic stress disorder persists after major trauma in adolescents: New data on risk factors and functional outcome', *The Journal of Trauma: Injury, Infection, and Critical Care*, 58 (4), pp. 764–71.

Holman, E. & Silver, R. 1996, 'Is it the abuse or the aftermath? A stress and coping approach to understanding responses to incest', *Journal of Social and Clinical Psychology*, 15(3), pp. 318–39.

Holmes, T. & Rahe, R. 1967, 'Social Readjustment Rating Scale', *Journal of Psychosomatic Research*, 11(2), p. 213.

Holtz, T. 1998, 'Refugee trauma versus torture trauma: A retrospective controlled cohort study of Tibetan refugees', *The Journal of Nervous and Mental Disease*, 186(1), pp. 24–34

Holub, S., Tisak, M. & Mullins, D. 2008, 'Gender differences in children's hero attributions: Personal hero choices and evaluations of typical male and female heroes', *Sex Roles*, 58, pp. 567–78.

Horowitz, M. 1992, *Stress response syndromes*, Northvale: Jason Aronson Inc.

Horowitz, M., Wilner, N. & Alvarez, W. 1979, 'Impact of Event Scale: A measure of subjective stress', *Psychosomatic Medicine*, 41(3), pp. 209–18.

Howe, D. 1995, *Attachment theory for social work practice*, London: Macmillan Press.

Hudson, C. 2000, 'At the edge of chaos: A new paradigm for social work?' *Journal of Social Work Education*, 36(2), pp. 215–30.

Hughes, J. 2000, 'Repartnering after divorce: Marginal mates and unwedded women', *Family Matters*, 55, pp. 16–21.

Hughes, M. 2009, 'Lesbian and gay people's concerns about ageing and accessing services', *Australian Social Work*, 62(2), pp. 186–201.

Humphreys, M. 1994, *Empty cradles*, Sydney: Doubeday.

Hunter, L., Rychnovsky, J. & Yount, S. 2009, 'A selective review of maternal sleep characteristics in the postpartum period', *Journal of Obstetric, Gynecologic, and Neonatal Nursing*, 38(1), pp. 60–8.

Hutchinson, J. & Smith, A. eds, 1996, *Ethnicity*, Oxford: Oxford University Press.

Hutchison, E. 1999, *Dimensions of human behavior: The changing life course*, Thousand Oaks: SAGE Publications.

Hutchison, E. 2003, *Dimensions of human behavior: The changing life course*, 2nd edn, Thousand Oaks: SAGE Publications.

Hyer, L., McCranie, E., Boudewyns, P. & Sperr, E. 1996, 'Modes of long-term coping with trauma memories: Relative use and associations with personality among Vietnam veterans with chronic PTSD', *Journal of Traumatic Stress*, 9(2), pp. 299–316.

Isay, R. 1998, 'Heterosexually married homosexual men: Clinical and developmental issues', *American Journal of Orthopsychiatry*, 68(3), pp. 424–32.

Jack, G. 2000, 'Ecological influences on parenting and child development', *British Journal of Social Work*, 30, pp. 703–20.

Janoff-Bulman, R. 1979, 'Characterological versus behavioural self-blame: Inquiries into depression and rape', *Journal of Personality and Social Psychology*, 37, pp. 1798–809.

Janoff-Bulman, R. 1992, *Shattered assumptions: Towards a new psychology of trauma*, New York: The Free Press.

Jansen, J., de Weerth, C., & Riksen-Walraven, J. 2008, 'Breastfeeding and the mother-infant relationship: A review', *Developmental Review*, 28, pp. 503–21.

Japel, C., Normand, C., Tremblay, R. & Willms, J. 2002, 'Identifying vulnerable children at an early age' in J. Willms ed. *Vulnerable children: Findings from Canada's National Longitudinal Survey of Children and Youth*, Edmonton: University of Alberta Press, Chapter 5, pp. 105–20.

Jeavons, S., Greenwood, K. & Horne, D. 1996, 'Reported consequences following road accidents', *Australian Journal of Primary Health—Interchange*, 2(2), pp. 29–35.

Johnson, E., Roehrs, T., Roth, T. & Breslau, N. 1998, 'Epidemiology of alcohol and medication as aids to sleep in early adulthood', *Sleep*, 21(2), pp. 178–86.

Johnston, C. 2008, 'For the boy who lost it all, hope is the greatest gift', *The Age*, 26–27 December, p. 3.

Jordan, B., Heine, R., Meehan, M., Catto-Smith, A. & Lubitz, L. 2006, 'Effect of antireflux medication, placebo and infant mental health intervention on persistent crying: a randomized clinical trial', *Journal of Paediatric Child Health*, 42, pp.49–58.

Jorm, A. 2007, 'Mental health literacy: Public knowledge and beliefs about mental disorders', *The British Journal of Psychiatry*, 177, pp.396–401.

Joyce, A. 2005, 'The first six months: The baby getting started' in E. Rayner ed. *Human development: An introduction to the psychodynamics of growth, maturity and ageing*, 4th edn, New York: Routledge, Chapter 3, pp. 23–46.

Kahana, E., Kahana, B., Harel, Z. & Rosner, T. 1995, 'Coping with extreme trauma' in J. Wilson, Z. Harel & B. Kahana, eds, *Human adaptation to extreme stress: From Holocaust to Vietnam*, New York: Planum Press, Chapter 3, pp. 55–79.

Kalish, R. ed. 1989, *Midlife loss: Coping strategies*, New York: SAGE Publications.

Kang, M., Cannon, B., Remond, L. & Quine, S. 2009, '"Is it normal to feel these questions ...?": A content analysis of the health concerns of adolescent girls writing to a magazine', *Family Practice*, Advanced Access, pp. 1–8.

Kaplan, T., Black, D., Hyman, P. & Knox, J. 2001, 'Outcome of children seen after one parent killed the other', *Clinical Child Psychology and Psychiatry*, 6(1), pp. 9–22.

Karpov, Y. 2006, *The neo-Vygotskian approach to child development*, Melbourne: Cambridge University Press.

Katz, P. & Kofkin, J. 1997, 'Race, gender and young children' in P. Katz & J. Kofkin, *Developmental psychopathology: Perspectives on adjustment, risk and disorder*, Cambridge: Cambridge University Press, Chapter 3, pp. 51–74.

Keane, T. & Wolfe, J. 1990, 'Comorbidity in post-traumatic stress disorder: An analysis of community and clinical studies', *Journal of Applied Social Psychology*, 20(21), pp. 1776–88.

Keating, D. & Halpern-Felsher, B. 2008, 'Adolescent Drivers: A developmental perspective on risk, proficiency, and safety', *American Journal of Preventive Medicine*, 35(3), pp. S272–7.

Kellehear, A. ed. 2000, *Death and dying in Australia: Interdisciplinary perspectives*, Melbourne: Oxford University Press.

Kelly, G. 1955, *The psychology of personal constructs*, New York: W. W. Norton.

Kemp, S. 2008, 'Practicing place: Everday contexts in child and family welfare', *Social Work Now*, April, pp. 29–37.

Kenardy, J. 1996, 'Psychological (stress) debriefing: Is it effective?', *Psychotherapy in Australia*, 3(1), pp. 64–5.

Kenardy, J., Webster, R., Lewin, T., Carr, V., Hazell, P. & Carter, G. 1996, 'Stress debriefing and patterns of recovery following a natural disaster', *Journal of Traumatic Stress*, 9(1), pp. 37–49.

Kendig, H. & McCallum, J. 1988, *Greying Australia: Future impacts of population ageing*, Canberra: AGPS.

Kilmartin, C. 2000, 'Young adult moves: Leaving home, returning home, relationships', *Family Matters*, 55, pp. 34–40.

Kingsmill, S. 1998, *The family squeeze: Surviving the sandwich generation*, Toronto: University of Toronto Press.

Kinnear, P. 2002, *New families for changing times*, Canberra: The Australia Institute.

Kissane, D. 2000, 'Death and the Australian family' in A. Kellehear, ed. *Death and dying in Australia: Interdisciplinary perspectives*, Melbourne: Oxford University Press, Chapter 4, pp. 52–67.

Klass, D. 2001, 'Continuing bonds in the resolution of grief in Japan and North America', *American Behavioral Scientist*, 44(5), pp. 742–63.

Klass, D., Silverman, P. & Nickman, S. 1996, *Continuing bonds: New understandings of grief*, Washington: Taylor & Francis.

Kleber, R., Figley, C. & Gersons, B. eds, 1995, *Beyond trauma: Cultural and societal dynamics*, New York: Plenum Press.

Kleinman, A., Eisenberg, L. & Good, B. 2006, 'Culture, illness and care: Clinical lessons from anthropologic and cross-cultural research', *Focus*, 4, pp. 140–9.

Klerman, E. & Dijk, D. 2008, 'Age-related reduction in the maximal capacity for sleep: Implications for insomnia', *Current Biology*, 18(15), pp. 1118–23.

Kloep, M., Guney, N., Cok, F. & Simsek, O. 2009, 'Motives for risk-taking in adolescence: A cross-cultural study', *Journal of Adolescence*, 32(1), pp. 135–51.

Kobasa, S. 1979, 'Stressful life events and health: An inquiry into hardiness', *Journal of Personality and Social Psychology*, 37, pp. 1–11.

Kochanska, G., Friesenborg, A., Lange, L. & Martel, M. 2004, 'Parents' personality and infants' temperament as contributors to their emerging relationship', *Journal of Personality and Social Psychology*, 86(5), pp. 744–59.

Kohli, M. & Kunemund, H. 2005, 'The midlife generation in the family: Patterns of exchange and support' in S. Willis & M. Martin eds, *Middle adulthood: A lifespan perspective*, Thousand Oaks: Sage, Chapter 2. pp. 35–62.

Kondrat, M. E. 2002, 'Actor-centered social work: Re-visioning "person-in-environment" through a critical theory lens', *Social Work*, 47(4), 435–48.

Koopman, C., Classen, C. & Spiegel, D. 1996, 'Dissociative responses in the immediate aftermath of the Oakland/Berkeley firestorm', *Journal of Traumatic Stress*, 9(3), pp. 521–40.

Kosky, R. & Goldney, R. 1994, 'Youth suicide: A public health problem?', *Australian and New Zealand Journal of Psychiatry*, 28(2), pp. 186–7.

Kubler-Ross, E. 1970, *On death and dying*, Sydney: Tavistock Publications.

Kuther, T. & Higgins-D'Alessandro, A. 2000, 'Bridging the gap between moral reasoning and adolescent engagement in risky behavior', *Journal of Adolescence*, 23(4), pp. 409–22.

LaBar, K. 2007, 'Beyond fear: Emotional memory mechanisms in the human brain', *Current directions in psychological science*, 16(4), 173–7.

Labouvie-Vief, G., DeVoe, M. & Bulka, D. 1989, 'Speaking about feelings: conceptions of emotion across the life span', *Psychology and Aging*, 4(4), pp. 425–37.

Lachman, M. 2004, 'Development in midlife', *Annual Review of Psychology*, 55, 305–31.

Lachman, M. & James, J. 1997, *Multiple paths of midlife development*, Chicago: University of Chicago Press.

Langs, R. 1997, *Death anxiety and clinical practice*, London: Karnac Books.

Lapsley, D. 2006, 'Moral stage theory' in Killen, M. & Smetana, J. eds, *Handbook of moral development*, Mahwah: Lawrence Erlbaum Associates, Chapter 2, pp. 37–66.

Laub, D. 1995, 'Truth and testimony: the process and the struggle' in C. Caruth 1995, *Trauma: Explorations in memory*, Baltimore: The Johns Hopkins University Press, pp. 61–75.

Laub, D. & Auerhahn, N. 1993, 'Knowing and not knowing massive psychic trauma: Forms of traumatic memory', *International Journal of Psychoanalysis*, 74, pp. 287–302.

Laws, P. & Hilder, L. 2008, *Australia's mothers and babies 2006*, Perinatal statistics series no. 22, cat. no. PER 46, Sydney: AIHW National Perinatal Statistics Unit.

Lazarus, R. 1998, *Fifty years of the research and theory of R. S. Lazarus: An analysis of historical and perennial issues*, Mahwah, NJ: Lawrence Erlbaum Associates.

Lazarus, R. & Folkman, S. 1984, *Stress, appraisal, and coping*, New York: Springer Publishing Company.

Le, T. 2008, 'Age differences in spirituality, mystical experiences and wisdom', *Ageing and Society*, 28, pp. 383–411.

Lee, C. & Powers, J. 2002, 'Number of social roles, health, and well-being in three generations of Australian women', *International Journal of Behavioral Medicine*, 9(3), pp. 195–215.

Lehman, D., Davis, C., Delongis, A., Wortman, C., Bluck, S., Mandel, D. & Ellard, J. 1993, 'Positive and negative life changes following bereavement and their relations to adjustment', *Journal of Social and Clinical Psychology*, 12, pp. 90–112.

Lehman, D., Wortman, C. & Williams, A. 1987, 'Long-term effects of losing a spouse or child in a motor vehicle crash', *Journal of Personality and Social Psychology*, 52(1), pp. 218–31.

Leick, N. & Davidsen-Nielsen, M. 1991, *Healing pain: Attachment, loss and grief therapy*, London: Tavistock/Routledge.

Lein, L. & Sussman, M. eds, 1983, *The ties that bind: Men's and women's social networks, Marriage and family review*, New York: Haworth Press.

Leonard, W., Mitchell, A., Patel, S. & Fox, C. 2008, *Coming forward: The underreporting of heterosexist violence and same sex partner abuse in Victoria*, Melbourne: The Australian Research Centre in Sex, Health & Society, La Trobe University.

Leys, R. 2000, *Trauma: A genealogy*, Chicago: University of Chicago Press.

Lieberman, A. & Knorr, K. 2007, 'The impact of trauma: A developmental framework for infancy and early childhood', *Pediatric Annals*, 36(4), pp. 209–15.

Liebler, C. & Sandefur, G. 2002, 'Gender differences in the exchange of social support with friends, neighbors, and co-workers at midlife', *Social Science Research*, 31, pp. 364–91.

Lievegoed, B. 2005, *Phases of childhood: Growing in body, soul and spirit*, Glasgow: Bell and Bain.

Lifton, R. 1988, 'Understanding the traumatized self: Imagery, symbolization and transformation' in J. Wilson, Z. Harel & B. Kahana, eds, 1988, *Human adaptation to extreme stress: From the Holocaust to Vietnam*, New York: Plenum Press, pp. 7–31.

Lifton, R. 1993, *The protean self: Human resilience in an age of fragmentation*, Chicago: University of Chicago Press.

Liiceanu, A. 2000, 'Parallel selves as the end of grief work' in J. Harvey & E. Miller, eds, *Loss and trauma: General and close relationship perspectives*, Philadelphia: Brunner-Routledge, Chapter 7, pp. 112–20.

Lindemann, E. 1944, 'Symptomatology and management of acute grief', *American Journal of Psychiatry*, 101, pp. 141–9.

Lindsay, R. 2002, *Recognizing spirituality: The interface between faith and social work*, Crawley: University of Western Australia Press.

Little, G. 1999, *The public emotions: From mourning to hope*, Sydney: ABC Books.

Litz, B. 2008, 'Early intervention for trauma: Where are we and where do we need to go? A commentary', *Journal of Traumatic Stress*, 21(6), pp. 503–6.

Lobo, M. 1990, 'Stress in infancy', in L. Arnold, *Childhood stress*, New York: John Wiley & Sons, Chapter 6, pp. 173–93.

Loewenthal, K. 2000, *The psychology of religion: A short introduction*, Oxford: Oneworld Publications.

Lorenz, F., Simons, R. Conger, R., Elder, G., Johnson, C. & Chao, W. 1997, 'Married and recently divorced mothers' stressful events and distress: Tracing change across time', *Journal of Marriage and the Family*, 59(1), pp. 219–32.

Luthar, S., Cicchetti, D. & Becker, B. 2000, 'The construct of resilience: A critical evaluation and guidelines for future work', *Child Development*, 71(3), pp. 543–62.

Lyubomirsky, S. 2000, *On studying positive emotions, prevention and treatment*, Washington: American Psychological Association. viewed at http://journals.apa.org/prevention/volume3, September 2007.

Maclean, K. 2003, 'The impact of institutionalization on child development', *Development and Psychopathology*, 15, pp. 853–84.

Macnab, F. 1989, *Life after loss: Getting over grief, getting on with life*, Newton: Millennium Books.

Macnab, F. 1992, *The thirty vital years*, Melbourne: Hill of Content.

Macnab, F. 2000, *Traumas of life and their treatment: An application of contextual modular therapy*, Melbourne: SAGE Publications.

Mafile'o, T. 2009, 'Pasifika social work' in M. Connolly & L. Harms, eds, *Social work: Contexts and practice*, South Melbourne: Oxford University Press, pp. 121–34.

Marris, P. 1986, *Loss and change*, London: Routledge.

Marris, P. 1993, 'The social construction of uncertainty' in C. Parkes, J. Stevenson-Hinde & P. Marris, *Attachment across the lifecycle*, London: Tavistock/Routledge, Chapter 5, pp. 77–90.

Marris, P. 1996, *The politics of uncertainty: Attachment in private and public life*, London: Routledge.

Martin, P. 1997, *The sickening mind: Brain, behaviour, immunity and disease*, London: HarperCollins.

Martin, C., Ruble, D. & Szkrybalo, 2002, 'Cognitive theories of early gender development', *Psychological Bulletin*, 128(6), pp. 903–33.

Martire, L., Parris, M. & Townsend, A. 2000, 'Centrality of women's multiple roles: Beneficial and detrimental consequences for psychological well-being', *Psychology and Aging*, 15(1), pp. 148–56.

Maslow, A. 1968, *Toward a psychology of being*, New York: D. Van Nostrand Co.

Maslow, A. 1996, *Future visions: The unpublished papers of Abraham Maslow*, Thousand Oaks: SAGE Publications.

Masten, A. 2001, 'Ordinary magic: Resilience processes in development', *American Psychologist*, 56(3), pp. 227–38.

Masten, A. & Powell, J. 2003, 'A resilience framework for research, policy and practice' in S. Luthar, ed. *Resilience and vulnerability: Adaptation in the context of childhood adversities*, Cambridge: Cambridge University Press, Chapter 1, p. 25.

Mathers, C., Vos, T. & Stevenson, C. 1999, *The burden of disease and injury in Australia*, AIHW cat. no. PHE17, Canberra: AIHW.

Mattaini, M., Lowery, C. & Meyer, C. eds, 1998, *The foundations of social work practice: A graduate text*, Washington: NASW Press.

Mayou, R., Bryant. B. & Duthie, R. 1993, 'Psychiatric consequences of road traffic accidents', *British Medical Journal*, 307, pp. 647–51.

McCalman, J. 2005, 'The past that haunts us: The historical basis of well-being in Australian children' in S. Richardson & M. Prior, eds, *No time to lose: The wellbeing of Australia's children*, Carlton: Melbourne University Press, Chapter 2, pp. 36–59.

McCarter, S. 2003, 'Adolescence' in E. Hutchison, ed. *Dimensions of human behavior: The changing life course*, Thousand Oaks: SAGE Publications, 2nd edn, Chapter 6, pp. 249–304.

McClintock, M. & Herdt, G. 1996, 'Rethinking puberty: The development of sexual attraction', *Current Directions in Psychological Science*, 5(6), pp. 178–83.

McColl, M., Bickenbach, J., Johnston, J., Nishihama, S., Schumaker, M., Smith, K., Smith M. & Yealland, B. 2000, 'Spiritual issues associated with traumatic-onset disability', *Disability and Rehabilitation*, 22(12), pp. 555–64.

McCormack, J. 2000, 'The same but different: Social work with centenarians', *Australian Social Work*, 53(4), pp. 27–32.

McCormack, J. 2001, 'Exploring quality of life with centenarians and supercentenarians', *Proceedings of 3rd Australian Conference on Quality of Life*, Deakin University, 16 November.

McCrae, R. 1984, 'Situational determinants of coping responses: Loss, threat and challenge', *Journal of Personality and Social Psychology*, 46, pp. 919–28.

McCrae, R. & Allik, J. 2002, *The five-factor model of personality across cultures*, New York: Kluwer Academic/Plenum Publishers.

McCrae, R., Costa, P., Ostendorf, F., Angleitner, A., Hrebickova, M., Avia, M., Sanz, J., Sanchez-Bernardos, M., Kusdil, M., Woodfield, R. & Saunders, P. 2000, 'Nature over nurture: Temperament, personality, and life span development', *Journal of Personality and Social Psychology*, 78(1), pp. 173–86.

McCrae, R. & John, O. 1992, 'An introduction to the five factor model and its applications', *Journal of Personality*, 60, pp. 175–215.

McDermott, F. 2002, *Inside group work*, Crows Nest: Allen & Unwin.

McDonald, P. 1995, *Families in Australia: A socio-demographic perspective*, Melbourne: Australian Institute of Family Studies.

McDonald, P. & Evans, A. 2003, 'Negotiating the Life Course: Changes in individual and family transitions', *Negotiating the Life Course Discussion Paper Series Discussion Paper DP–013*, Canberra: ACSPRI Centre for Social Research, Australian National University.

McFarlane, A. 1992, 'Avoidance and intrusion in posttraumatic stress disorder', *The Journal of Nervous and Mental Disease*, 180(7), pp. 439–45.

McFarlane, A. 1995, 'PTSD in the medico-legal setting: Current status and ongoing controversies', *Psychiatry, Psychology and Law*, 2(1), pp. 25–35.

McFarlane A.C. 1995a, 'The Severity of the Trauma: Issues about its Role in Post Traumatic Stress Disorder' in R. J. Kleber, C. R. Figley & B. P. R. Gersons, *Beyond trauma: Cultural and societal dynamics*. New York: Plenum Press, 1995, pp. 31–54.

McIntosh, I. & Punch, S. 2009, '"Barters", "deals", "bribes" and "threats": Exploring sibling interactions', *Childhood*, 16(1), pp. 49–65.

McMillen, J. C. & Fisher, R. 1998, 'The perceived benefit scale: Measuring positive life changes after negative events', *Social Work Research*, 22(3), pp. 173–87.

McMillen, J. C., Smith, E. & Fisher, R. 1997, 'Perceived benefit and mental health after three types of disaster', *Journal of Consulting and Clinical Psychology*, 65(5), pp. 733–9.

McMillen, J., Zuravin, S. & Rideout, G. 1995, 'Perceived benefit from child abuse', *Journal of Consulting and Clinical Psychology*, 63, pp. 1037–43.

McNair, R., Brown, R., Perlesz, A., Lindsay, J., De Vaus, D. & Pitts, M. 2008, 'Lesbian parents negotiating the health care system in Australia', *Health Care for Women International*, 29(2), pp. 91–114.

McNair, R., Dempsey, D., Wise, S. & Perlesz, A. 2002, 'Lesbian parenting: Issues, strengths and challenges', *Family Matters*, 63, Spring/Summer, pp. 40–9.

McSherry, W. & Smith, J. 2007, 'How do children express their spiritual needs?', *Paediatric Nursing*, 19(3), pp. 17–20.

McVeigh, M. J. 2003, '"But she didn't say no": An exploration of sibling sexual abuse' *Australian Social Work*, 56(2), pp. 116–26.

Meadows, S. 1993, *The child as thinker: The development and acquisition of cognition in childhood*, London: Routledge.

Mehnert, A., Lehmann, C., Graefen, M. Huland, H. & Koch, U. 2009, 'Depression, anxiety, post-traumatic stress disorder and health-related quality', *European Journal of Cancer Care*, Online advance viewed at www3.interscience.wiley.com/journal/122649900/abstract?CRETRY=1&SRETRY=0, December 2009.

Mikulincer, M. 2008, 'An attachment perspective on resilient and complicated grief reactions', Fifth International Conference on Grief and Bereavement in Contemporary Society, Melbourne, July.

Mikulincer, M. & Shaver, P. 2008, 'An attachment perspective on bereavement' in M. Stroebe, R. O. Hansson, H. A. W. Schut & W. Stroebe, eds, *Handbook of bereavement research and practice: 21st century perspectives*, Washington, DC: American Psychological Association. pp. 87–112.

Milkie, M. & Peltola, P. 1999, 'Playing all the roles: Gender and the work–family balancing act', *Journal of Marriage and the Family*, 61, pp. 476–90.

Miller, R. 2007, *Cumulative harm: A conceptual overview*, Melbourne: Victorian Government Department of Human Services.

Millward, C. 1997, 'Divorce and family relations in later life', *Family Matters*, 48, pp. 30–3.

Minas, I. & Klimidis, S. 1994, 'Cultural issues in posttraumatic stress disorder' in R. Watts & D. Horne eds, *Coping with trauma: The victim and the helper*, Brisbane: Australian Academic Press, Chapter 9, pp. 137–54.

Mindell, J., Meltzer, L., Carskadon, M. & Chervin, R. 2009, 'Developmental aspects of sleep hygiene: Findings from the 2004 National Sleep Foundation "Sleep in America" Poll', *Sleep Medicine*, 10, pp. 771–9.

Mitchell, J. 2003, *Siblings: Sex and violence*, Cambridge: Polity Press.

Montgomery, M. 2005, 'Psychosocial intimacy and identity: From early adolescence to emerging adulthood', *Journal of Adolescent Research*, 20(3), pp. 346–74.

Moore, T. 1991, *Cry of the damaged man: A personal journey of recovery*, Sydney: Picador.

Moos, H. & Schaefer, J. eds, 1986, *Coping with life crises: An integrated approach*, New York: Plenum Press.

Morrell, S., Page, A. & Taylor, R. 2007, 'The decline in Australian young male suicide', *Social Science & Medicine*, 64, pp. 747–54.

Morphy, F. 2006, 'Lost in translation: Remote Indigenous households and definitions of the family' *Family Matters* 73, pp. 23–31.

Morrell, S. 1993, 'Suicide and unemployment in Australia 1907–1990', *Social Science and Medicine*, 36(6), pp. 749–56.

Morris, G. & McAdie, T. 2009, 'Are personality, well-being and death anxiety related to religious affiliation?', *Mental Health, Religion and Culture*, 12(2), pp. 115–20.

Mullaly, B. 2002, *Challenging oppression: A critical social work approach*, Ontario: Oxford University Press.

Mullen, P., Martin, J., Anderson, T., Romans, S. & Herbison, G. 1996, 'The long-term impact of the physical, emotional and sexual abuse of children: A community study', *Child Abuse and Neglect*, 20(1), pp. 7–21.

Muris, P., Meesters, C., Merckelbach, H. & Hulsenbeck, P. 2000a. 'Worry in children is related to perceived parental rearing and attachment', *Behavior Research and Therapy*, 38, pp. 487–97.

Muris, P., Merckelbach, H., Gadet, B. & Moulaert, V. 2000b. 'Fears, worries and scary dreams in 4- to 12-year-old children: Their content, developmental pattern and origins', *Journal of Clinical Child Psychology*, 29(1), pp. 43–52.

Murphy, J. 2002, 'Breadwinning: Accounts of work and family life in the 1950s' *Labour and Industry*, 12(3), pp. 59–75.

Murphy, S. 1993, *The family context and the transition to siblinghood: Strategies parents use to influence sibling-infant relationships*, paper presented at the biennial meeting of the Society for Research in Child Development, New Orleans, LA.

Nancarrow, K. 2004, 'It's a small world, *The Age*, 14 March, pp. 4–5.

Narayan, D. 1999, *Bonds and bridges: Social capital and poverty*, Washington: World Bank.

National Ageing Research Institute 2003, *Participation in physical activity amongst older people*, Melbourne: NARI.

National Association of Social Workers 2007, *Indicators for the achievement of the NASW standards for cultural competence in social work practice*, Washington, DC: NASW.

National Economic and Social Forum 2003, *The policy implications of social capital*, Dublin: National Economic and Social Forum, p. 6.

National Health and Medical Research Council 2006, *Postnatal depression*, Canberra: NHMRC, viewed at www.nhmrc.gov.au/publications/synopses/wh29syn.htm, August 2009.

National Inquiry into the Separation of Aboriginal and Torres Strait Islander Children from their Families (Australia) 1997, *Bringing them home: Report of the National Inquiry into the Separation of Aboriginal and Torres Strait Islander Children from their Families*, Sydney: Human Rights and Equal Opportunity Commission.

National Institute of Child Health and Human Development 2006, *The NICHD study of early child care and youth development: Findings for children up to age 4½ years*, US Department of Health and Human Services.

National Institute of Child Health and Human Development Early Child Care Research Network 2001, 'Nonmaternal care and family factors in early development: An overview of the NICHD study of early child care', *Applied Developmental Psychology*, 22, pp. 457–92.

National Institute of Child Health and Human Development Early Child Care Research Network 2003, 'Does amount of time spent in child care predict socioemotional adjustment during the transition to kindergarten?' *Child Development*, 74(4), pp. 976–1005.

Nebes, R., Buysse, D., Halligan, E., Houck, P. & Monk, T. 2009, 'Self-reported sleep quality predicts poor cognitive performance in healthy older adults', *The Journals of Gerontology: Series B Psychological Sciences and Social Sciences*, 64(2), pp. 180–7.

Neimeyer, R. & Stewart, A. 1996, 'Trauma, healing and the narrative emplotment of loss', *Families in Society: The Journal of Contemporary Human Services*, pp. 360–75.

Nelson, D. & Burke, R. 2002, *Gender, work stress, and health*, Washington: American Psychological Association.

Nelson, L. & Barry, C. 2005, 'Distinguishing features of emerging adulthood: The role of self-classification as an adult', *Journal of Adolescent Research*, 20, pp. 242–62.

Nelson-Feaver, P. & Warren, I. 1994, 'Taking care of the deceased' in R. Watts & D. Horne, *Coping with trauma: The victim and the helper*, Brisbane: Australian Academic Press, pp. 155–8.

Neugarten, D. ed. 1996, *The meanings of age: Selected papers of Bernice L. Neugarten*, Chicago: University of Chicago Press.

Newman, B. & Newman, P. 2003, *Development through life: A psychosocial approach*, South Melbourne: Thomson.

Nicotera, N. 2005, 'The child's view of neighborhood: Assessing a neglected element in direct social work practice', *Journal of Human Behavior in the Social Environment*, 11(3/4), pp. 105–33.

Noller, P., Feeney, J. & Peterson, C. 2001, *Personal relationships across the lifespan*, Hove: Psychology Press.

Norris, F. 1992, 'Epidemiology of trauma: Frequency and impact of different potentially traumatic events on different demographic groups', *Journal of Consulting and Clinical Psychology*, 60(3), pp. 409–18.

North C., Tivis, L., McMillen, J., Pfefferbaum, B., Cox, J., Spitznagel, E., Bunch, K., Schorr, J. & Smith, E. 2002, 'Coping, functioning, and adjustment of rescue workers after the Oklahoma City bombing', *Journal of Traumatic Stress*, 15(3), pp. 171–5.

Northouse, L. 1994, 'Breast cancer in younger women: Effects on interpersonal and family relations', *Journal of the National Cancer Institute Monographs*, 16, pp. 183–90.

O'Brien, M. 2009, 'Social work, poverty and disadvantage' in M. Connolly & L. Harms, eds, *Social work: Contexts and practice*, South Melbourne: Oxford University Press, pp. 68–80.

O'Connor, P. 1981, *Understanding the mid-life crisis*, South Melbourne: Sun Books.

O'Hagan, K. 2001, *Cultural competence in the caring professions*, London: Jessica Kingsley Publishers.

O'Leary, V. & Ickovics, J. 1995, 'Resilience and thriving in response to challenge: An opportunity for a paradigm shift in women's health', *Women's Health: Research on gender, behavior and policy*, 1, pp. 121–42.

Olshansky, S. 1962, 'Chronic sorrow: A response to having a mentally defective child', *Social Casework: The Journal of Contemporary Social Work*, 43, pp. 190–3.

Omi, M. & Winant, H. 2001, 'Racial formation' in S. Seidman & J. Alexander, eds, *The new social theory reader*, New York: Routledge, Chapter 36, pp. 371–83.

Ornish, D. 1998, *Love and survival: The scientific basis for the healing power of intimacy*, Sydney: Random House.

Ozanne, E. 2007, 'Family and intergenerational relationships in the long-lived society' in A. Borowski, S. Encel & E. Ozanne eds, *Longevity and social change in Australia*, Sydney: University of NSW Press, Chapter 14, pp. 334–62.

Palmer, S., Kagee, A., Coyne, J. & DeMichele, A. 2004, 'Experience of trauma, distress, and posttraumatic stress disorder among breast cancer patients', *Psychosomatic Medicine*, 66, pp. 258–64.

Park, C., Cohen L. & Murch, R. 1996, 'Assessment and prediction of stress-related growth', *Journal of Personality*, 64(1), pp. 71–105.

Parker, R. 2000, 'How partners in long-term relationships view marriage', *Family Matters*, 55, pp. 74–81.

Parker, R. 2002, *Why marriages last: A discussion of the literature*, report no. 28, Melbourne: Australian Institute of Family Studies, July, pp. 1–26.

Parkes, C. 1972, *Bereavement: Studies of grief in adult life*, New York: International Universities Press.

Parkes, C., Stevenson-Hinde, J. & Marris, P. 1993, *Attachment across the life cycle*, London: Tavistock/Routledge.

Patterson, R. & Jeste, D. 1999, 'The potential impact of the baby-boom generation on substance abuse among elderly persons', *Psychiatric Services*, 50, pp. 1184–8.

Patton, G. C., Selzer, R., Coffey, C., Carlin, J. B. & Wolfe, R. 1999, 'The onset of adolescent eating disorders: A population based cohort study over three years', *British Medical Journal*, 318, pp. 765–8.

Pearn, J. 2003, 'Children and war', *Journal of Paediatric and Child Health*, 39, pp. 166–72.

Peper, J., Brouwer, R., Schnack, H., van Baal, G., van Leeuwen, M., van den Berg, S., Delemarre-Van de Waal, H., Boomsma, D., Kahn, R. & Hulshoff Pol, H. 2009, 'Sex steroids and brain structure in pubertal boys and girls', *Psychoneuroendocrinology*, 34, pp. 332–42.

Perls, T. & Terry, D. 2003, 'Understanding the determinants of exceptional longevity', *Annals of Internal Medicine*, 139(5), pp. 445–9.

Perren, K., Arber, S. & Davidson, K. 2003, 'Men's organisational affiliations in later life: The influence of social class and marital status on informal group membership', *Ageing and Society*, 23, pp. 69–82.

Perry, S., Difede, J., Musngi, G., Frances, A. J. & Jacobsberg, L. 1992, 'Predictors of posttraumatic-stress disorder after burn injury', *American Journal of Psychiatry*, 149(7), pp. 931–5.

Peskin, H. 2000, 'The ranking of personal grief: Death and comparative loss' in J. Harvey & E. Miller, eds, *Loss and trauma: General and close relationship perspectives*, Philadelphia: Brunner-Routledge, Chapter 6, pp. 102–11.

Peterson, C. 1996, *Looking forward through the lifespan: Developmental psychology*, Sydney: Prentice Hall.

Peterson, C. & Bossio, L. 1991, *Health and optimism: New research on the relationship between positive thinking and physical well-being*, New York: The Free Press.

Peterson, C., Maier, S. & Seligman, M. 1993, *Learned helplessness: A theory for the age of personal control*, Oxford: Oxford University Press.

Peterson, C. & Seligman, M. 1983, 'Learned helplessness and victimization', *Journal of Social Issues*, 2, pp. 103–16.

Peterson, C., Seligman, M. & Vaillant, G. 1988, 'Pessimistic explanatory style is a risk factor for physical illness: A thirty-five year longitudinal study', *Journal of Personality and Social Psychology*, 55, pp. 23–7.

Phillips, R. 1988, *Putting asunder: A history of divorce in Western society*, Cambridge: Cambridge University Press.

Piaget, J. 1995, *The essential Piaget*, Northvale, NJ: J. Aronson.

Pine, K. & Nash, A. 2003, 'Barbie or Betty? Preschool children's preference for branded products and evidence for gender-linked differences', *Journal of Developmental and Behavioral Pediatrics*, 24(4), pp. 219–24.

Pinker, S. 2003, *The blank slate: The modern denial of human nature*, London: Penguin.

Polatinsky, S. & Esprey, Y. 2000, 'An assessment of gender differences in the perception of benefit resulting from the loss of a child', *Journal of Traumatic Stress*, 13(4), pp. 709–18.

Pope, A. 2005, 'Personal transformation in midlife orphanhood: An empirical phenomenological study', *Omega*, 51(2), pp. 107–23.

Prigerson, H. & Maciejewski, P. 2005, 'A call for sound empirical testing and evaluation of criteria for complicated grief proposed for DSM-V', *Omega*, 52(1), pp. 9–19.

Prior, M. 2005, 'The views of young people' in S. Richardson & M. Prior, eds, *No time to lose: The wellbeing of Australia's children*, Carlton: Melbourne University Press, Chapter 12, pp. 298–307.

Prior, M., Sanson, A., Smart, D. & Oberklaid, F. 2001, *Pathways from infancy to adolescence: Australian Temperament Project 1983–2000*, Melbourne: Australian Institute of Family Studies.

Prior, P. 1999, *Gender and mental health*, New York: New York University Press.

Pulkinnen, L., Feldt, T. & Kokko, K. 2005, 'Personality in young adulthood and functioning in middle age' in S. Willis & M. Martin eds, *Middle adulthood: A lifespan perspective*, Thousand Oaks: SAGE Publications. Chapter 4, pp. 99–142.

Punch, S. 2003. 'Childhoods in the majority world: Miniature adults or tribal children?' *Sociology*, 27, pp. 277–95.

Putnam, F. 2003, 'Ten-year research update review: Child sexual abuse', *Journal of the American Academy of Child & Adolescent Psychiatry*, 42(3), pp. 269–78.

Putnam, R. 1995, 'Bowling alone: America's declining social capital', *Journal of Democracy*, 6(1), pp. 65–78.

Pyszczynski, T., Greenberg, J. & Solomon, S. 1999, 'A dual-process model of defense against conscious and unconscious death-related thoughts: An extension of terror management theory', *Psychological Review*, 106(4), pp. 835–45.

Queralt, M. 1996, *The social environment and human behavior: A diversity perspective*, Needham Heights: Simon and Schuster.

Quinn, M. 2000, '"Being there together": The Broadmeadows poverty action group' in W. Weeks & M. Quinn, eds, *Issues facing Australian families: Human services respond*, Frenchs Forest: Longman, Chapter 12, pp. 154–64.

Ramsden, I. & O'Brien, L. 2000, 'Defining cultural safety and transcultural nursing', letter to the editor, *Kai Tiaki: Nursing New Zealand*, 6(8) p. 4.

Ramsey, J. & Langlois, J. 2002. 'Effects of the "beauty is good" stereotype on children's information processing', *Journal of Experimental Child Psychology*, 81(3) pp. 320–40.

Rando, T., ed. 1986, *Loss and anticipatory grief*, Toronto: Lexington Books.

Raphael, B. 1984, *The anatomy of bereavement*, London: Hutchinson.

Raphael, B. 2000, *Promoting the mental health and wellbeing of children and young people: Discussion paper—key principles and directions*, Canberra: National Mental Health Working Group, Department of Health and Aged Care.

Raphael, B. & Meldrum, L. 1994, 'Helping people cope with trauma' in R. Watts & D. Horne, *Coping with trauma: The victim and the helper*, Brisbane: Australian Academic Press, pp. 1–19.

Raphael, B. & Swan, P. 1997, 'The mental health of Aboriginal and Torres Strait Islander people', *International Journal of Mental Health*, 26(3), pp. 9–22.

Rapp, C. 1998, *The strengths model: Case management with people suffering from severe and persistent mental illness*, Oxford: Oxford University Press.

Rawsthorne, M. 2009, 'Just like other families? Supporting lesbian-supported families', *Australian Social Work*, 62(1), pp. 45–60.

Ray, V. & Gregory, R. 2001, 'School experiences of the children of lesbian and gay parents', *Family Matters*, 59, pp. 28–34.

Read, P. 1996, *Returning to nothing: The meaning of lost places*, Melbourne: Cambridge University Press.

Regan, A., Parnell, W., Gray, A. & Wilson, N. 2008, 'New Zealand's dietary intake during school hours', *Nutrition and Dietetics*, 65, pp. 205–20.

Reiter, A. 2000, *Narrating the Holocaust*, London: Continuum.

Remafedi, G., Resnick, M., Blum, R. & Harris, L. 1992, 'Demography of sexual orientation in adolescents', *Pediatrics*, 89(4), pp. 714–21.

Resick, P. 2001, *Stress and trauma*, Philadelphia: Taylor and Francis Inc.

Rey, J., Hazell, P. & Walker, G. 2007, 'Clinical and adolescent psychiatry' in S. Bloch & B. Singh eds, *Foundations of Clinical Psychiatry*, 3rd edn, Carlton: Melbourne University Press. Chapter 18, pp. 387–419.

Reynolds, H. 1998, *This whispering in our hearts*, St Leonards: Allen & Unwin.

Rice, S. 2002, 'Magic happens: Revisiting the spirituality and social work debate', *Australian Social Work*, 55(4), pp. 303–12.

Richardson, S., & Prior, M. eds, 2005, *No time to lose: The wellbeing of Australia's children*, Carlton: Melbourne University Press.

Richmond, M. 1945, *Social diagnosis*, New York: Russell Sage Foundation.

Richmond, T. & Kauder, D. 2000, 'Predictors of psychological distress following serious injury', *Journal of Traumatic Stress*, 13(4), pp. 681–92.

Rigby, K. & Thomas, E. 2003, *How schools counter bullying: policies and procedures in selected Australian schools*, Point Lonsdale: Professional Reading Guide for Educational Administrators.

Rivers, S., Reyna, V. & Mills, B. 2008, 'Risk taking under the influence: A fuzzy-trace theory of emotion in adolescence', *Developmental Review*, 28, pp. 107–44.

Robinson, R. & Mitchell, J. 1993, 'Evaluations of psychological debriefings', *Journal of Traumatic Stress*, 6(3), pp. 367–82.

Robinson, R. & Mitchell, J. 1995, 'Getting some balance back into the debriefing debate', *The Bulletin of the Australian Psychological Society*, October, pp. 5–10.

Rose, D. 2010, *Living with drugs in the family: The needs and experiences of siblings*, unpublished PhD thesis, The University of Melbourne.

Roth-Hanania, R., Busch-Rossnagel, N. & Higgins-D'Alessandro, A. 2000, 'Development of self and empathy in early infancy: Implications for atypical development', *Infants and Young Children*, 13(1), pp. 1–14.

Rothbart, M. & Bates, J. 1998, 'Temperament' in W. Damon, series ed., & E. Eisenberg, volume ed., *Handbook of child psychology: Social, emotional and personality development*, 5th edn, vol. 3, New York: Wiley.

Rotter, J. 1966, 'Generalised expectancies for internal versus external control of reinforcement', *Psychological Monographs*, 80, pp. 1–28.

Rouse, K. 1998, 'Infant and toddler resilience', *Early Childhood Education Journal*, 26(1) pp.47–52.

Rowland, D. 2007, 'Ethnicity and ageing' in A. Borowski, S. Encel & E. Ozanne 2007, *Longevity and social change in Australia*, Sydney: University of NSW Press.Chapter 5, pp. 117–41.

Rowlands, A. 1999, *"Can't buy me love": The impact of circles of support for adults with acquired brain injury*, Newcastle: University of Newcastle.

Russell, C. 2007, 'Gender and ageing' in A. Borowski, S. Encel & E. Ozanne, eds, *Longevity and social change in Australia*, Sydney: University of NSW Press. Chapter 4, pp. 99–116.

Rutter, M. 1985, 'Resilience in the face of adversity', *British Journal of Psychiatry*, 147, pp. 598–611.

Rutter, M. 1987, *Helping troubled children*, Ringwood: Penguin.

Rutter, M. & English and Romanian Adoptees study team 1998, 'Developmental catch-up, and deficit, following adoption after severe global early privation', *Journal of Child Psychology and Psychiatry*, 39(4), pp. 465–76.

Rutter, M. & Tienda, M. eds, 2005, *Ethnicity and causal mechanisms*, Melbourne: Cambridge University Press.

Saade, R. & Winkelman, C. 2002, 'Short- and long-term homelessness and adolescents' self-esteem, depression, locus of control and social supports', *Australian Journal of Social Issues*, 37(4), pp. 431–45.

Saleebey, D. 1997, *The strengths perspective in social work practice*, New York: Longman.

Salmon, K., & Bryant, R. 2002, 'Posttraumatic stress disorder in children: The influence of developmental factor'. *Clinical Psychology Review*, 22, 163–88.

Salthouse, T. 2009, 'When does age-related cognitive decline begin?', *Neurobiology of Aging*, 30, pp. 507–14.

Sandler, J. & Freud, A. 1985, *The analysis of defense: The ego and the mechanisms of defense revisited*, New York: International Universities Press.

Sawyer, M. 2000, *Child and adolescent component of the National Survey of Mental Health and Wellbeing*, Canberra: Department of Health and Aged Care, Mental Health and Special Programs Branch.

Sawyer, M., Kosky, R., Graetz, B., Arney, F., Zubrich, S. & Boghurst, P. 2000, 'The National Survey of Mental Health and Wellbeing: the child and adolescent component', *Australian and New Zealand Journal of Psychiatry*, 34(2), pp. 214–20.

Schacter, D. 1996, *Searching for memory: The brain, the mind and the past*, New York: Basic Books.

Schaefer, J. & Moos, R. 1992, 'Life crises and personal growth' in B. Carpenter, ed. *Personal coping: Theory, research and application*, Westport: Praeger, pp. 149–70.

Schaefer, J. & Moos, R. 1998, 'The context for Posttraumatic Growth: Life crises, individual and social resources, and coping' in R. Tedeschi, C. Park & L. Calhoun 1998, *Posttraumatic growth: Positive changes in the aftermath of crisis*, London: Lawrence Erlbaum Associates, Chapter 5, pp. 99–126.

Schaie, K. 2005, *Developmental influences on adult intelligence: The Seattle Longitudinal Study*, New York: Oxford University Press.

Schapiro, A. 2003, 'Later-Life Divorce and Parent-Adult Child Contact and Proximity', *Journal of Family Issues*, 24(2), pp. 264–85.

Scheier, M., Carver, C. & Bridges, M. 1994, 'Distinguishing optimism from neuroticism (and trait anxiety, self-mastery and self-esteem): A re-evaluation of the Life Orientation Test', *Journal of Personality and Social Psychology*, 67, pp. 1063–78.

Scheier, M., Weintraum, J. & Carver, C. 1986, 'Coping with stress: Divergent strategies of optimists and pessimists', *Journal of Personality and Social Psychology*, 51(6), pp. 1257–64.

Schmidt Neven, R. 1990, *The new explorers: A psychodynamic approach to parenting in a changing society*, Melbourne: Full Circle Publications Cooperative.

Schore, A. 2002, 'Dysregulation of the right brain: a fundamental mechanism of traumatic attachment and the psychopathogenesis of posttraumatic stress disorder', *Australian and New Zealand Journal of Psychiatry*, 36, pp. 9–30.

Schut, H. 2008, 7th International Conference on Grief and Bereavement in Contemporary Society, Melbourne, July.

Scott, D. 1992, 'The ecology of the family and family functions', in A. Clements, *Infant and family health in Australia: A textbook for community health workers*, London: Churchill Livingstone, pp. 203–17.

Scott, D. & Swain, S. 2002, *Confronting cruelty: Historical perspectives on child abuse*, Carlton: Melbourne University Press.

Search Institute 2005, '40 Developmental Assets for Early Childhood (ages 3 to 5)' viewed at www.search-institute.org/40-developmental-assets-early-childhood-ages-3-5, August 2007.

Seligman, M. 1992, *Learned optimism*, Milsons Point: Random House.

Selye, H. 1987, *Stress without distress*, London: Corgi.

Sénéchal, M. & LeFevre, J. 2002, 'Parental Involvement in the Development of Children's Reading Skill: A Five-Year Longitudinal Study', *Child Development*, 73(2), pp. 445–60.

Serbin, L. & Karp, J. 2004, 'The intergenerational transfer of psychosocial risk: Mediators of vulnerability and resilience' *Annual Review of Psychology*, 55, pp. 333–63.

Serbin, L., Poulin-Dubois, D., Colbourne, K., Sen, M. & Eichstedt, J. 2001, 'Gender stereotyping in infancy: Visual preferences for and knowledge of gender-stereotyped toys in the second year', *International Journal of Behavioral Development*, 25(1), pp. 7–15.

Shapiro, E. 1994, *Grief as a family process: A developmental approach to clinical practice*, New York: The Guilford Press.

Shaver, J. & Zenk, S. 2000, 'Review: Sleep disturbance in menopause', *Journal of Women's Health & Gender-Based Medicine*, 9(2), pp. 109–18.

Shiner, R. 2000, 'Linking childhood personality with adaptation: Evidence for continuity and change across time into late adolescence', *Journal of Personality and Social Psychology*, 78(2), pp. 310–25.

Shonkoff, J. & Phillips, D., eds, 2000, *From neurons to neighbourhoods: The science of early childhood development*, Washington: National Academy Press.

Siegal, M. 2008, *Marvelous minds: The discovery of what children know*, Oxford: Oxford University Press.

Siegrista, J., Petera, R., Jungea, A., Cremerb, P. & Seidel, D. 1990, 'Low status control, high effort at work and ischemic heart disease: Prospective evidence from blue-collar men', *Social Science and Medicine*, 31(10), pp. 1127–34.

Silove, D. 2007, 'Increased prevalence of post-traumatic stress disorder, anxiety, and depression in displaced tsunami survivors from southern Thailand', *Evidence-based Mental Health*, 10(1), p. 31.

Silva, E. & Smart, C. eds, 1999, *The new family?*, London: SAGE Publications.

Silver, R., Boon, C. & Stones, M. 1983, 'Searching for meaning in misfortune: Making sense of incest', *Journal of Social Issues*, 39(2), pp. 81–102.

Silverstein, M., Conroy, S., Wang, H., Giarrusso, R. & Bengston, V. 2002, 'Reciprocity in parent-child relations over the adult life course', *Journal of Gerontology*, 57B(1), pp. S3–13.

Slade, T., Johnston, A., Oakley Browne, M., Andrews, G. & Whiteford, H. 2009, '2007 National Survey of Mental Health and Wellbeing: Methods and key findings', *Australian and New Zealand Journal of Psychiatry*, 43(7), pp. 594–605.

Smart, D., Sanson, A. & Toumbourou, J. 2008, 'How do parents and teenagers get along together?: Views of young people and their parents', *Family Matters*, 78, pp. 18–27.

Smart, D. 2007, 'Tailoring parenting to fit the child', AFRC Briefing, viewed at www.aifs. gov.au/afrc/pubs/briefing/briefing4.html, February 2010.

Smart, D. & Sanson, A. 2003, 'Social competence in young adulthood, its nature and antecedents', *Family Matters*, 64, pp. 4–9.

Smart, D. & Sanson, A. 2008, 'Do Australian children have more problems today than twenty years ago?', *Family Matters*, 79, pp. 50–7.

Smith, J. & Baltes, P. 1999, 'Trends and profiles of psychological functioning in very old age', in P. Baltes & K. Mayer, eds, *The Berlin Aging Study: Aging from 70 to 100* Cambridge: Cambridge University Press, pp. 197–226.

Smyth, B., Sheehan, G., & Fehlberg, B. 2001, 'Post-divorce parenting patterns', *Family Matters*, 59, pp. 61–3.

Sneed, J., Whitbourne, S. & Culang, M. 2006, 'Trust, identity and ego integrity: Modeling Erikson's core stages over 34 years', *Journal of Adult Development*, 13, pp. 148–57.

Snyder, C. 2000, 'The past and possible futures of hope', *Journal of Social and Clinical Psychology*, 19(1), pp. 11–28.

Snyder, C., Harris, C., Anderson, J., Holleran, S., Irving, L., Sigmon, S., Yoshinobu, L., Gibb, J., Langelle, C. & Harney, P. 1991, 'The will and the ways: Development and validation of an individual-differences measure of hope', *Journal of Personality and Social Psychology*, 60(4), pp. 570–85.

Sorkhabi, N. 2005, 'Applicability of Baumrind's parent typology to collective cultures: Analysis of cultural explanations of parent socialization effects', *International Journal of Behavioral Development*, 29(6), pp. 552–63.

Spiegel, D., Bloom, J., Kraemer, H. & Gottheil, E. 1989, 'Efforts of psychosocial treatment on survival of patients with metastatic breast cancer', *The Lancet*, 2, pp. 888–91.

Spitz, R. 1965, *The first year of life: A psychoanalytic study of normal and deviant development of object relations*, New York: International Universities Press.

St James-Roberts, I. 2007, 'Infant crying and sleeping: Helping parents to prevent and manage problems', *Sleep Medicine Clinics*, 2(3), pp. 363–75

Stacey, J. & Biblarz, T. 2001, '(How) does the sexual orientation of parents matter?' *American Sociological Review*, 66(April), pp. 159–83.

Stack, S. & Eshleman, J. 1998, 'Marital status and happiness: A 17-nation study', *Journal of Marriage and the Family*, 60, pp. 527–36.

Stauffacher, K. & DeHart, G. 2006, 'Crossing social contexts: Relational aggression between siblings and friends during early and middle childhood', *Applied Developmental Psychology*, 27, pp. 228–40.

Stebbins, J. and Batrouney, T. 2007, *Beyond the death of a child: Social impacts and economic costs of the death of a child*, Canterbury: The Compassionate Friends.

Stewart, R., Verbrugge, K. & Beilfuss, M. 1998, 'Sibling relationships in early adulthood: A typology', *Personal Relationships*, 5, pp. 59–74.

Stocker, C.; Burwell, R. & Briggs, M. 2002, 'Sibling conflict in middle childhood predicts children's adjustment in early adolescence', *Journal of Family Psychology*, 16(1), pp. 50–7.

Stone, W. 2001, *Measuring social capital: Towards a theoretically informed measurement framework for researching social capital in family and community life*, Melbourne: Australian Institute of Family Studies.

Stoppard, J. 2000, *Understanding depression: Feminist social constructionist approaches*, London: Routledge.

Stotland, E. 1969, *The psychology of hope*, San Francisco: Jossey-Bass Inc. Publishers.

Strathearn, L., Gray, P., O'Callaghan, M. & Wood, D. 2001, 'Childhood neglect and cognitive development in extremely low birth weight infants: A prospective study', *Pediatrics*, 108(1), pp. 142–51.

Strathearn, L., Li, J., Fonagy, P. & Montague, P. 2008, 'What's in a smile? Maternal brain responses to infant facial cues', *Pediatrics*, 122(1), 40–51.

Strathearn, L. Mamun, A. Najman, J. & O'Callaghan, M. 2009, 'Does breastfeeding protect against substantiated child abuse and neglect? A 15-year cohort study', *Pediatrics*, 123(2), pp. 483–93.

Stroebe, M. 2006, 'The broken heart phenomenon: An examination of the mortality of bereavement', *Journal of Applied and Community Social Psychology*, 4(1), pp. 47–61.

Stroebe, M. & Schut, H. 1999, 'The dual process model of coping with bereavement: Rationale and description', *Death Studies*, 23(3), pp. 197–224.

Stroebe, M., Stroebe, W. & Schut, H. 2003, 'Bereavement research: Methodological issues and ethical concerns', *Palliative Medicine*, 17, pp. 235–40.

Stroebe, M., van Son, M., Stroebe, W., Kleber, R., Schut, H. & van den Bout, J. 2000, 'On the classification and diagnosis of pathological grief', *Clinical Psychological Review*, 20(1), pp. 57–75.

Stroebe W., Stroebe M., Abakoumkin, G. & Schut, H. 1996, 'The role of loneliness and social support in adjustment to loss: A test of attachment versus stress theory', *Journal of Personality and Social Psychology*, 70(6), pp. 1241–9.

Sue, D. 2004, 'Whiteness and ethnocentric monoculturalism: Making the "invisible" visible', *American Psychologist*, 59(8), pp. 761–9.

Sun, M. & Rugolotto, S. 2004, 'Assisted infant toilet training in a Western family setting', *Journal of Developmental and Behavioral Pediatrics*, 25(2), pp. 99–101.

Tacey, D. 1995, *Edge of the sacred: Transformation in Australia*, Blackburn North: HarperCollins.

Tacey, D. 2003, *The spirituality revolution: The emergence of contemporary spirituality*, Pymble: HarperCollins.

Tannen, D. 1996, *Gender and discourse*, Oxford: Oxford University Press.

Tanner, J. 1962, *Growth at adolescence*, Oxford: Blackwell Scientific.

Taylor, J. & Fraser, A. 2003, *Eleven plus: Life chances and family income*, Melbourne: Brotherhood of St Laurence.

Taylor, J. & Macdonald, F. 1998, *Life at six: Life chances and beginning school*, Melbourne: Brotherhood of St Laurence.

Taylor, S. 1983, 'Adjustment to threatening events: A theory of cognitive adaptation', *American Psychologist*, 38, pp. 1161–73.

Taylor, S. 1989, *Positive illusions: Creative self-deception and the healthy mind*, New York: Basic Books.

Taylor, S. & Armor, D. 1996, 'Positive illusions and coping with adversity', *Journal of Personality*, 64(4), pp. 873–98.

Taylor, S. & Brown, J. 1988, 'Illusion and well-being: a social psychological perspective on mental health', *Psychological Bulletin*, 103(2), pp. 193–210.

Taylor, S., Lichtman, R. & Wood, J. 1984, 'Attributions, beliefs in control and adjustment to breast cancer', *Journal of Personality and Social Psychology*, 46, pp. 489–502.

Tedeschi, R. & Calhoun, L. 1995, *Trauma and transformation: Growing in the aftermath of suffering*, London: SAGE Publications.

Tedeschi, R. & Calhoun, L. 1996, 'The Posttraumatic Growth Inventory: Measuring the positive legacy of trauma', *Journal of Traumatic Stress*, 9(3), pp. 455–71.

Tedeschi, R., Park, C. & Calhoun, L. 1998, *Posttraumatic growth: Positive changes in the aftermath of crisis*, London: Lawrence Erlbaum Associates.

Teese, R. 2005. *'For which young people do schools work well and why?'* in S. Richardson & M. Prior eds, *No time to lose: The wellbeing of Australia's children*, Carlton: Melbourne University Press, Chapter 9, pp. 240–54.

Teese, R. & Polesel, J. 2003, *Undemocratic schooling: Equality and quality in mass secondary education in Australia*, Carlton: Melbourne University Press.

Tennen, H., Affleck, G., Urrows, S., Higgins, P. & Mandola, R. 1992, 'Perceiving control, construing benefits, and daily processes in rheumatoid arthritis', *Canadian Journal of Behavioral Science*, 24, pp. 186–203.

The Senate 2004, *Forgotten Australians: A report on Australians who experienced institutional or out-of-home care as children*, Canberra: Commonwealth Government.

Thoits, P. 1991, 'On merging identity theory and stress research', *Social Psychology Quarterly*, 54(2), June, pp. 101–12.

Thompson, N. 2001, *Anti-discriminatory practice*, 3rd edn, Basingstoke: Palgrave.

Thompson N. 2003, *Promoting equality: Challenging discrimination and oppression*, 2nd edn, London: Palgrave Macmillan.

Thompson, N. 2006, *Anti-discriminatory practice*, 4th edn, Basingstoke: Pagrave Macmillan.

Tongue, A. & Ballenden, N. 1999, 'Families and ageing in the 21st century', *Family Matters*, 52, pp. 4–8.

Toth, P., Stockton, R. & Browne, F. 2000, 'College student grief and loss' in J. Harvey & E. Miller eds, *Loss and trauma: General and close relationship perspectives*, Philadelphia: Brunner-Routledge, Chapter 15, pp. 237–48.

Trainor, B. 2002, 'Postmodernism, truth and social work', *Australian Social Work*, 55(3), pp. 204–13.

Traynor, P. 1997, *Roads to recovery: Inspiring stories from survivors of illness, accident and loss*, St Leonards: Allen & Unwin.

Tremblay, L. & Frigon, J. 2005, 'Precocious puberty in adolescent girls: A biomarker of later psychosocial adjustment problems', *Child Psychiatry and Human Development*, 36(1), pp. 73–94.

Tummala-Narra, P. 2007, 'Conceptualizing trauma and resilience across diverse cultures: A multicultural perspective' in M. Harvey & P. Tummala-Narra eds, *Sources and expressions of resiliency in trauma survivors: Ecological theory, multicultural practice*, New York: The Haworth Press. Chapter 3, pp. 33–54.

Uhlenberg, P. & De Jong Gierveld, J. 2004, 'Age-segregation in later life: An examination of personal networks', *Ageing and Society*, 24(1), pp. 5–28.

Umberson, D. & Chen, M. 1994, 'Effects of a parent's death on adult children: Relationship salience and reaction to loss', *American Sociological Review*, 59(1), pp. 152–68.

Ungar, M. 2008a, 'Resilience across cultures', *British Journal of Social Work*, 38, pp. 218–35.

Ungar, M. 2008b, *Too safe for their own good*, St Leonards: Allen and Unwin.

United Nations 1999, *International year of older persons*, viewed at www.un.org/esa/socdev/iyop, June 2004.

Updegraff, J. & Taylor, S. 2000, 'From vulnerability to growth: Positive and negative effects of stressful life events' in J. Harvey & E. Miller eds, *Loss and trauma: General and close relationship perspectives*, Philadelphia: Brunner-Routledge, pp. 3–28.

Upper Hunter Community 2009, *Working with Aboriginal and Torres Strait Islander Communities*, viewed at www.workingwithatsi.info/content/PI_family.htm, October 2009.

US Department of Health and Human Services 1998, *Child Maltreatment 1996: Reports from the States to the National Child Abuse and Neglect Data System*, Washington, DC: US Government Printing Office.

Vaillant, G. 1993, *The wisdom of the ego*, Cambridge, MA: Harvard University Press.

Vaillant, G. 2002, *Ageing well: Surprising guideposts to a happier life from the landmark Harvard study of adult development*, Melbourne: Scribe Publications.

Vaillant, G. 2003, 'Mental health', *American Journal of Psychiatry*, 160(8), pp. 1373–84.

Vaillant, G. & Mukamal, K. 2001, 'Successful aging', *American Journal of Psychiatry*, 158(6), pp. 839–47.

Valent, P. 2002. *Child survivors of the Holocaust*, New York: Routledge.

van der Kolk, B. 1994, 'The body keeps the score: Memory and the evolving psychobiology of PTSD', Harvard Review of Psychiatry, 1, pp. 253–65.

van der Kolk, B., McFarlane, A. & Weisaerth, L. eds, 1996, *Traumatic stress: The effects of overwhelming experience on mind, body and society*, New York: The Guilford Press.

van Griensven, F., Chakkraband, M., Thienkrua, W., Pengjuntr, W., Cardozo, B., Tantipiwatanaskul, P., Mock, P., Ekassawin, S., Varangrat, A., Gotway, C., Sabin, M., & Tappero, J. 2006, 'Mental health problems among adults in tsunami-affected areas in southern Thailand', *Journal of Australian Medical Association*, 296, pp. 537–48.

Vassallo, S., Smart, D. & Price-Robertson, R. 2009, 'The roles that parents play in the lives of their young adult children', *Family Matters*, 82, pp. 8–14.

Vincent, J. 2003, *Old age*, New York: Routledge.

Vygotsky, L. 1998, *The collected works of L. S. Vygotskii*, New York: Plenum Press.

Wake, M., Sanson, A., Berthelsen, D., Hardy, P., Misson, S., Smith, K., et al. 2008, *How well are Australian infants and children aged 4 to 5 years doing? Findings from the Longitudinal Study of Australian Children Wave 1*, Canberra: Department of Families, Housing, Community Services and Indigenous Affairs.

Wakefield, J. 1996, 'Does social work need the eco-systems perspective? Part 1: Is the perspective clinically useful?', *Social Service Review*, March, pp. 1–32.

Walker, S., Berthelsen, D. & Irving, K. 2001, 'Temperament and peer acceptance in early childhood: Sex and social status differences', *Child Study Journal*, 31(3), pp. 177–92.

Wallerstein, J. & Blakeslee, S. 1989, *Second chances: Men, women and children a decade after divorce*, New York: Ticknor & Fields.

Wallerstein, J. & Blakeslee, S. 1995, *The good marriage*, New York: Warner Books.

Wallerstein, J. & Kelly, J. 1980, *Surviving the breakup: How children and parents cope with divorce*, New York: Basic Books.

Walter, T. 1999, *On bereavement: The culture of grief*, Buckingham: Open University Press.

Waters, E., Hamilton, C. & Weinfield, N. 2000, 'The stability of attachment security from infancy to adolescence and early adulthood: General instruction', *Child Development*, 71(3), pp. 678–83.

Watters, E. 2003, *Urban tribes: A generation defines friendship, family, and commitment*, New York: Bloomsbury.

Watts, R. 1994, 'Follow-up to survivors of large-scale road accidents', in R. Watts & D. Horne, eds, *Coping with trauma: The victim and the helper*, Brisbane: Australian Academic Press, Chapter 2, pp. 21–36.

Weinberg, M. & Tronick, E. 1996, 'Infant Affective Reactions to the Resumption of Maternal Interaction after the Still-Face', *Child Development*, 96, pp. 905–14.

Weiss, R. 1973, *Loneliness: The experience of emotional and social isolation*, Cambridge, MA: MIT Press.

Weiss, R. 1988, 'Loss and recovery', *Journal of Social Issues*, 44(3), Blackwell Publishing, pp. 37–52.

Weiss, R. 1997, 'Adaptation to retirement', in I. Gotlib & B. Wheaton, eds, *Stress and adversity over the life course: Trajectories and turning points*, Cambridge, UK: Cambridge University Press, Chapter 12, pp. 232–45.

Weiss, T. 2001, *Posttraumatic growth in women with breast cancer and their husbands: An intersubjective validation study*, unpublished doctoral thesis, New York: Adelphi University, School of Social Work.

Weiss, T. 2004, 'Correlates of posttraumatic growth in husbands of breast cancer survivors', *Psycho-Oncology*, 13, pp. 260–8.

Werner, E. 1995, 'Resilience in development', *Current Directions in Psychological Science*, 4(3), pp. 81–5.

Werner, E. & Smith, R. 1992, *Overcoming the odds: High risk children from birth to adulthood*, Ithaca: Cornell University Press.

Werner, E. & Smith, R. 2001, *Journeys from childhood to midlife: Risk, resilience and recovery*, Ithaca: Cornell University Press.

Westermeyer, J. 1998, 'Predictors and characteristics of mental health among men at midlife: A 32-year longitudinal study', *American Journal of Orthopsychiatry*, 68(2), pp. 265–73.

Wheat, K. & Napier, M. 1997, 'Claiming damages for psychiatric injury following a road accident' in M. Mitchell, *The aftermath of road accidents: Psychological, social and legal consequences*, London: Routledge. pp. 123–134.

Wheaton, B. 1997, *Coping with chronic stress*, New York: Plenum Press.

White, R. & Wyn, J. 2004, *Youth and society: Exploring the social dynamics of youth experience*, Melbourne: Oxford University Press.

Wilkins, R. Warren, D. & Hahn, M. 2009, *Families, Incomes and Jobs, Volume 4: A Statistical Report on Waves 1 to 6 of the HILDA Survey*, The University of Melbourne: Melbourne Institute of Applied Economic and Social Research.

Williams, R. 2007, 'The psychosocial consequences for children of mass violence, terrorism and disasters', *International Review of Psychiatry*, 19(3), 263–77.

Willis, S. & Martin, M. eds, 2005, *Middle adulthood: A lifespan perspective*, Thousand Oaks: SAGE Publications.

Willis, S. & Schaie, K. 2005, 'Cognitive trajectories in midlife and cognitive functioning' in S. Willis & M. Martin eds, *Middle adulthood: A lifespan perspective*. Thousand Oaks: SAGE Publications, Chapter 6.

Wilson, J. 1995, 'The historical evolution of PTSD diagnostic criteria: From Freud to DSMIV' in G. Everly & J. Lating eds, *Psychotraumatology: Key papers and core concepts in post-traumatic stress*, New York: Plenum Press, pp. 9–26.

Winnicott, D. 1968, *The family and individual development*, London: Tavistock.

Wolcott, I. 1997, 'The influence of family relationships on later life', *Family Matters*, 48, pp. 20–6.

Wolf, N. 1991, *The beauty myth*, London: Vintage.

Woody, D. 2003a, 'Early childhood' in E. Hutchison, ed. *Dimensions of human behavior: The changing life course*, Thousand Oaks: SAGE Publications, Chapter 4, pp. 159–98.

Woody, D. 2003b, 'Infancy and toddlerhood' in E. Hutchison, ed. *Dimensions of human behavior: The changing life course*, Thousand Oaks: SAGE Publications, Chapter 3, pp. 113–58.

Worden, J. W. 2003, *Grief counselling and grief therapy: A handbook for the mental health practitioner*, Hove, East Sussex: Brunner-Routledge.

World Health Organization 2003, *Constitution of the World Health Organization*, Geneva: United Nations.

World Health Organization 2009, *WHO Child growth standards*, Geneva: United Nation, viewed at www.who.int/childgrowth/en/, November 2009.

Wyn, J. 2009, *Youth health and welfare*, South Melbourne: Oxford University Press.

Wyn, J. & White, R. 1997, *Rethinking youth*, Crows Nest: Allen & Unwin.

Wyn, J. & White, R. 2000, 'Negotiating social change: The paradox of youth', *Youth and Society*, 32(2), pp. 165–83.

Wyn, J. & Woodman, D. 2006, 'Generation, youth and social change in Australia', *Journal of Youth Studies*, 9(5), 495–514.

Yalom, I. 1985, *The theory and practice of group psychotherapy*, New York: HarperCollins Publishers.

Yalom, I. & Lieberman, M. 1991, 'Bereavement and heightened existential awareness', *Psychiatry*, 54, pp. 334–45.

Yamamoto, K., Davis, O., Dylak, S., Whittaker, J., Marsh, C. & van der Westhuizen, P. 1996, 'Across six nations: Stressful events in the lives of children', *Child Psychiatry and Human Development*, 26(3), pp. 139–50.

Yehuda, R. & McFarlane, A. 1995, 'Conflict between current knowledge about posttraumatic stress disorder and its original conceptual basis', *American Journal of Psychiatry*, 152(12), pp. 1705–13.

Young, A. 1995, *The harmony of illusions: Inventing posttraumatic stress disorder*, Princeton: Princeton University Press.

Young, I. 1990, *Justice and the politics of difference*, Princeton: Princeton University Press.

Zigler, E. & Finn-Stevenson, M. 1995, 'The child care crisis: Implications for the growth and development of the Nation's children', *Journal of Social Issues*, 51(3), pp. 215–31.

Zisook, S. & Lyons, L. 1988, 'Grief and relationship to the deceased', *International Journal of Family Psychiatry*, 9(2), pp. 135–46.

Index

Printed in Australia
21 Apr 2016
467723

9 780195 551556